Bob Withers
Oct. 26, 1996

The President Travels by Train

~ Politics and Pullmans ~

Bob Withers

1996
TLC Publishing Inc.
Route 4, Box 154
Lynchburg, Va. 24503-9711

Front Cover Illustration: Franklin D. Roosevelt shakes hands with Baltimore & Ohio engineer J.W. Walmsley on Aug. 10, 1934, just after the president returned to Washington (D.C.) Union Station from a Hawaiian vacation and a tour of the drought-stricken Pacific Northwest. Waiting their turns for a presidential greeting are conductor R.C. Chittendon, foreground, and brakeman G.W. Wayne. (Wide World)

Back Cover Illustrations: Top: George and Barbara Bush wave to supporters from the rear platform of CSX Transportation private car *Baltimore* on Sept. 26, 1992, during a day of whistlestopping in northeastern Ohio. (Susan Biddle/The White House) **Bottom:** Harry Truman whistlestops at Ashland, Ky., on Oct. 1, 1948. (George Wolford/*The* Ashland, Ky., *Daily Independent*)

Front End Sheet: Theodore Roosevelt campaigns on the Chicago, Milwaukee & St. Paul Railway in Wisconsin. (Arthur Dubin collection)

Back End Sheet: A famous scene from a different angle: President Harry S. Truman holds aloft a copy of the early edition of *The Chicago Tribune* for Nov. 3, 1948, in which the editors mistakenly told the world "DEWEY DEFEATS TRUMAN." Truman is on his special train in St. Louis Union Station the next day on his way back to Washington, D.C., from his home in Independence, Mo., two days after his upset election victory over New York Gov. Thomas E. Dewey. Bernard F. Dickmann, St. Louis postmaster and former mayor, shares the president's jubilation on the rear platform of the *Ferdinand Magellan*. (National Archives)

© Copyright 1996
TLC Publishing Inc.

Library of Congress Catalogue Card Number 95-61264
ISBN 1-883089-17-4

Layout and Design by Kenneth L. Miller
Miller Design & Photography, Salem, Va.

Printed by
Walsworth Publishing Co.
Marceline, Mo. 64658

Table of Contents

Foreword v

Author's Foreword vii

Introduction ix

Chapter 1

Presidential Pioneers 1

Chapter 2

Abraham Lincoln and the Civil War 9

Chapter 3

The Reconstruction Era 31

Chapter 4

Twentieth-Century Travels 63

Chapter 5

The Golden Era is Born: The Franklin Roosevelt Years 131

Chapter 6

The Golden Era Matures: Truman's Whistlestopping 179

Chapter 7

The Golden Era's Sunset Years: The Eisenhower Presidency 237

Chapter 8

Modern Times 281

Chapter 9

The Last Miles 325

Chapter 10

The Cars They Rode 375

Appendix

Sample Train Consists 393

Acknowledgments and Bibliography 399

Index 408

PULLMAN COLLECTION/SMITHSONIAN INSTITUTION

This book is dedicated to the author's lovely wife,
Sue Ann,
and their three charming daughters,
Elizabeth, Julie and Leah,
whose love for their husband and father is matched only by
their tolerance of an exasperated writer.

Foreword

As a White House staff member, I enjoyed the thrill of riding with President Harry S. Truman on many of his campaign trips. I confess I had a deep crush on his daughter, Margaret, who with her mother accompanied the president on several of his trips. Margaret was a real trouper, who collected applause, whistles, flowers and many other gifts from the local citizenry as she smiled and waved her way along the rail routes. Local responses to President Truman were overwhelmingly favorable, but during the 1952 campaign, there were one or two crowds that offered a few razzes. After one of these, Margaret put her arms around her father's shoulders and drew a big laugh when she exclaimed, "Dad, did you know that ours is the only campaign train which carries its own 'hechler' right on board?"

Bob Withers was born in my home city of Huntington, W.Va., which was established by and named for that great railroad mogul, Collis P. Huntington. I have known Bob for more than 30 years, since he was a student at Huntington East High School. Even in those days, everybody who knew Bob realized that the railroad bug had bit him permanently.

But Bob is more than a "railroad buff" who just glories in riding the rails and spinning stories about the industry's golden era. As an employee of *The Herald-Dispatch* in Huntington, he has honed his talent to become an excellent writer. Not only has he composed many articles and columns on railroad subjects, but he also has authored some interesting contributions to trade magazines such as *Trains*. When Bob writes, you can smell the smoke belching from the old steam engines, taste the gourmet delicacies prepared by expert chefs of the past and feel the gentle sway of the Pullmans as you fall asleep in your berth.

There is another side of Bob that

By Ken Hechler

(Ken Hechler served as special assistant to President Truman from 1949 to 1953. A West Virginia congressman from 1959 to 1977, in 1993 he began his third term as West Virginia's secretary of state.)

I didn't fully appreciate until he told me about his plans for this book.

He not only is a journalist; he is a true historian, with the ability to dig into records, conduct personal interviews, travel to far-flung locales in search of materials, weighing objectively what he turns up, and then present his findings in sequential yet dramatic fashion. I had some doubts that a subject as big and broad as the coverage of the railroad travel of all presidents could ever be compressed into one book. But like the engineer who masters the challenge of pulling a 200-car freight train, Bob has ably kept many details in perspective and holds the reader's interest through more than 150 years of railroading.

The author's enthusiasm shines in these pages. From John Quincy Adams to Bill Clinton, there is never a dull moment as we experience the vicarious feeling that we are actually aboard with every chief executive in more than a century and a half. This book is a masterpiece of sound research, the end result of delving into obscure records and long-forgotten articles, news accounts and data not ordinarily available to those without a burning desire to soak up every possible fact and run down every possible lead.

When it comes to discovering new, primary materials to flesh out his story, Bob has set some kind of a record. For example, when the Baltimore & Ohio Railroad closed its Huntington passenger station on June 30, 1965, he was on the scene to collect not only some furniture but also a literal roomful of old records, including a detailed file of Dwight D. Eisenhower's 1952 campaign visit. Bob was also at Huntington's Chesapeake & Ohio station in 1969 when the Eisenhower funeral train stopped there in the predawn chill as hundreds waited to pay their last respects. This produced not only personal observations, but also a thick file of railroad documents, wire dispatches, photos, clippings and souvenirs.

In 1987, Bob decided to write two articles on Ike's campaign and funeral trains, which caught the attention of *Trains* magazine's editor, David P. Morgan. Unwilling to settle for the material he already had, Bob, who also serves as a part-time Baptist minister, combined a trip to a Billy Graham crusade in Denver with a search for more data. So he visited the Eisenhower Library in Abilene, Kan. That wasn't enough, so he made a side trip to Colorado Springs, Colo., where he met with David A. Watts Jr., formerly of C&O/B&O but then an employee of the Association of American Railroads, who gave Bob—guess what?—another thick file on the Eisenhower funeral train.

I vividly recall the excitement that Bob expressed to me when he told me in the spring of 1990 that he was planning a full-length book on every president who has ridden a train. At that point, I cautioned Bob that he was biting off more than he could chew. He quickly realized that he could not spend his life compiling an encyclopedia, but here was where his experience as a journalist came in handy. He knew that, in writing and editing for a newspaper, there comes a point when your deadline is upon you and you just have to cut off further research, limit your objective and package what information you have into a finished product.

But the difference between Bob and most journalists is that he did not want to produce a quick "potboiler." He was determined to track down, travel, interview and take advantage of as many available sources as he could uncover. The publication of the articles in *Trains* magazine in February and March 1990 sparked a nationwide interest in what the author was trying to compile. Soon he was the beneficiary of many volunteers who came out of the woodwork to furnish valuable documentary materials.

During the summer and fall of 1990, Bob's publisher, appropriately named TLC Publishing Inc. of Lynchburg, Va., financed two research trips for the author. In August, Bob and his wife, Sue Ann, traveled to Washington, Baltimore and New York, collecting additional data from the U.S. Department of Transportation Library, the Library of Congress, the National Archives, the libraries of *The New York Times* and the Engineering Society, as well as the Baltimore & Ohio Railroad Historical Society. On that trip, they tracked down railfan author and publisher Robert Wayner, who made available extensive archives of the Pullman Company. Then in October, Bob and Sue Ann went out to Kansas, Missouri, Iowa and Illinois. They rode the steampowered Union Pacific train celebrating the centennial of Eisenhower's birth, interviewed Ike's granddaughter, Susan Eisenhower Atwater, visited the Eisenhower, Truman and Hoover presidential libraries and even

took time to stop and view the various Lincoln shrines in Springfield, Ill.

In addition to the standard reference books, Bob made full use of interlibrary loans in assembling every scrap of research data. One little gold mine was an obscure volume titled *Lincoln and the Railroads*, of which only 227 copies were printed.

Then, on Sept. 26-27, 1992, Bob wangled a ride on President Bush's campaign train as it wound its way through a series of whistlestops in Ohio and Michigan. He struck up a conversation with one of the functionaries carrying a wire and earpiece, checking all personnel on the train to make sure they were rightfully aboard.

"Are you Secret Service?" Bob asked.

"No, I'm with the White House Travel Office," answered Gary Wright, its assistant director. Both Wright and his aide, John Dreylinger, were very helpful as Bob sought more data.

The on-board conversation gave Bob a chance to pose a question that had been on his mind ever since he had unearthed an article about Dewey Long, director of the travel office for several chief executives.

The article, appearing in a 1951 issue of *The Saturday Evening Post*, mentioned the existence of a ledger started by Long's predecessor, E.W. "Doc" Smithers, that chronicled every presidential trip since William McKinley's term began in 1897. Bob lamented that he had not been able to find the ledger anywhere.

"Have you checked with my boss, Billy Dale?" Wright asked Bob.

Armed with this information, in February 1993 Bob and Sue Ann paid a visit to the White House Travel Office on the ground floor of the Old Executive Office Building next door to the White House. That visit was before the big blowup during the Clinton administration's investigation of the office that resulted in Dale's and Wright's retirements, dismissals of five other employees and the big brouhaha over how the whole matter was handled.

Bob was there when the atmos-

phere was friendly and helpful, resulting in the opportunity to see and copy many train trip records.

There was only one disappointment in his visit, the main purpose of which was to locate the old log that had been started in McKinley's day. "Well, the pages in that ledger were getting kind of brittle, so we just pitched it out about five years ago," they told Bob to his horror. But he was able to copy a large number of more recent documents maintained by the White House.

The February trip to Washington carried several unexpected dividends. At the B&O Historical Society, Bob was able to copy a 1946-47 file on Truman's travels that was discovered among the B&O operating vice president's records. A side visit to the Woodrow Wilson House in Washington enabled the author to pick up some relevant photos of Wilson's journeys, as well as an itinerary of his ill-fated 1919 League of Nations tour—which would have gone through Bob's own Huntington, W.Va., if the president had not gotten sick enroute.

It is possible that additional documentation will turn up to add to or alter Bob's story. But few writers will have the advantage of the richly personal narratives he has included by many of those who worked on the trains involved. These interviews take us behind the scenes and give us all the kind of background that will be lost when these old railroaders and politicians die off. Thus Bob has preserved a slice of Americana that will never return.

As one who has participated actively in presidential campaigns, I am amazed at the rich insight the author has shown, not only of the strategy and tactics of campaigning, but also of the elaborate arrangements with which only railroaders are familiar. I can think of no other individual who could have put this all together with the professionalism of a true expert and the drama of an excellent writer.

Author's Foreword

(Bob Withers is a veteran copy editor for The Herald-Dispatch, *the daily newspaper in Huntington, W.Va. He is also a part-time Baptist minister who is a lifelong railroad enthusiast.)*

Fascination with two subjects dear to my heart—railroading and the U.S. presidency with its images of patriotism and history—prompted me to write this book.

I feel as if I have traveled along with these men, watching history unfold as specially chosen coaches creaked and groaned away the miles. I enjoyed seeing Abraham Lincoln, sitting on the floor of a boxcar while he waited for his train during a rain shower, characteristically weighing the impossibility of a "sucker" like him becoming president. Or frugal Calvin Coolidge, as he tried traveling in an ordinary Pullman, only to have a parade of curious passengers stare through the open compartment door at him. Or Woodrow Wilson, when he offered two hobos a ride—and they turned him down! Or Franklin Roosevelt, when he stopped a super-secret wartime inspection train because someone had forgotten to pack horse meat for his cousin's Irish setter. Or Harry Truman, the night he and his aides taught Winston Churchill how to play poker. Or, of course, with Rutherford B. Hayes, Teddy Roosevelt, Warren Harding, Truman, and young Robert Todd Lincoln as they sweet-talked their way into locomotive cabs. And, finally, the chance to generate some memories of my own when I rode—for real—with George Bush in Ohio and Michigan.

The author stands at President George Bush's podium on CSXT office car Baltimore *minutes after the president disembarked from his first 1992 whistlestopper at Grand Blanc, Mich., Sept. 27.*

This volume by no means exhausts the references in existence on the subject of presidents and passenger trains. I was able to spend just enough time on this project to know that it would take several lifetimes to put together a definitive work. It is such a wide open field—virtually no books have been produced on it, despite the fact that periodical indices, card catalogs and library computers are filled with thousands of references to whistlestop or POTUS funeral trains calling on small-town America. Bound by the awesome restrictions of space and time, I have selected especially interesting or historically significant trips by each chief executive rather than try to catalog them all. In the first place, it would have been impossible to find them all.

Secondly, there just isn't sufficient room in a single book to chronicle such a topic over more than a century and a half. But therein lies the key to this book's value—it calls attention to a field with wide appeal that is seriously lacking in documentation. If I can whet someone's appetite to further the research, as mine was when I did a package of articles in 1990 for *Trains* magazine on Dwight Eisenhower's travels, then I have fulfilled my purpose. If it will inspire people to dig long-forgotten clippings or photos or souvenirs out of their attic trunks or scrapbooks that I didn't find, then my book—while not definitive—will have served as a launching pad for such a work someday. I've brought the train to the first division point; now it's time for a crew change.

New York Central Hudson 5244 eases up to the rear of Franklin D. Roosevelt's funeral train at Hyde Park, N.Y., on April 15, 1945, ready to pull it back to Poughkeepsie for servicing and turning during the 32nd president's burial service.

Introduction

Washington, D.C.
April 12, 1945.

Shock streaked across Dan Moorman's ashen face as he hung up his telephone.

The Baltimore & Ohio Railroad's general passenger agent for the nation's capital stared in dull disbelief at the secret schedule he had just completed for President Franklin D. Roosevelt's rail trip to San Francisco for the World Security Conference.

The dismal truth began to sink in. The president wouldn't need Moorman's itinerary. Roosevelt, resting at his Warm Springs, Ga., hideaway, had just died of a massive cerebral hemorrhage.

Instantly, hundreds of railroaders throughout the South and Northeast sprang into action and hastily executed a plan to do what railroads had done for decades with an enviable efficiency—transport the president of the United States.

Ferman White, a young general roundhouse foreman at the Southern Railway's North Avenue Yard in Atlanta, was on his way home from work that afternoon when he heard the grim tidings at a grocery store.

He knew that the 10-car special train in storage near his roundhouse that had brought the president south on March 28-29 would be needed at any moment. He called Charles Craft, the foreman on duty.

"We will need two light Pacifics," White ordered after telling Craft what happened. "What do you have in sight?"

"The 1262 and 1337 are on the cinder pit," Craft replied.

"Well, get 'em going," White directed.

Returning to work, White stayed with the Pacific-type passenger locomotives from the time their inspection began until they were ready to leave the roundhouse. Then he rode them to Terminal Station, listening and watching for anything that may have been overlooked. He stayed with them several more hours at the station, checking them again and again and sharing memories of their fallen leader with the crew that had been called for 6 p.m. only to wait for instructions.

Roosevelt's train, with an 11th car added, was hastily iced and serviced and also taken to Terminal Station, where it was backed into track 10 at about 7 p.m. Only after engineers H.E. Allgood and O.B. Wolford and firemen H.L. Decker and A.A. Washington pulled their train southward for Warm Springs at 9:53 p.m., did White return to the roundhouse to prepare heavy Pacifics 1409 and 1394 for the second lap of the journey back to Washington.

Once the special reached Williamson, 53.3 miles south of Atlanta, the locomotives were turned so they would be headed north the next day. Then they backed the train the remaining 30.7 miles to Warm Springs, arriving at 2 a.m. for the somber job of loading the president's automobiles and other personal belongings. The Pullman Company's 7-compartment sleeper-lounge *Conneaut* was switched to the rear of the train, behind FDR's car, the armor-plated *Ferdinand Magellan*, because it had a window in its lounge that could be removed for the loading of Roosevelt's coffin.

Once dawn broke, railroaders up and down the line—from Warm Springs back to Atlanta, and on to Washington and Hyde Park, N.Y.—would be called on to perform their jobs with utmost precision, caution, security and sympathy—something they did well because the industry had refined its procedures for years.[262]

From the days when the stagecoach and steamboat gave way to steel rails and flanged wheels until air travel came into its own in the 1950s, the chief executive of the United States depended on the railroads to get where he was going.

At first, he was just another passenger, riding just another train. But presidential moves became increasingly complicated as the power of the office increased. Staffs grew and security became more complex. Eventually the president rode in a private car coupled to regular trains, then graduated to special trains of four or five cars in length.

Finally, with Franklin Roosevelt's era came the age of modern communications and a persistent press that reported his every move. FDR's trains graduated into full-blown events of 16 to 18 cars that drew extensive coverage and massive crowds wherever they went—a tradition perfected by Harry Truman's "whistlestop" campaign trains—only to fall into decline in the Eisenhower years.

After jet travel became commonplace, presidential trains became fewer in number and retrenched to one- or two-day photo opportunities, operated as if to resurrect memories of an era that would never return—when the president, or aspiring president, or remains of a president, reached into the small towns and stations and sidings that were people's lives.

Those holding the presidency seemed to realize the railroads' potential only gradually. The first five presidents—Washington, Adams, Jefferson, Madison and Monroe—never rode a train, having lived out their days before the advent of the industry.

To celebrate the opening of the then longest rail line in America, the Erie Railroad arranged a now famous junket for May 14, 1851. Included among the guests who made the 427-mile trip were President Millard Fillmore, several members of his cabinet and Daniel Webster, who is pictured here as he elected to travel.

SAMPLE OF THE NEW AND BETTER

In his hair was the snow of 69 active years—but in the heart and mind of Daniel Webster was ever-youthful eagerness to sample new and better things.

So when the Erie Railroad celebrated the opening of the first "long" rail line, he prescribed his own accommodations. Other distinguished guests could ride in coaches if they preferred—Mr. Webster would take a rocking chair on an open flatcar, so as not to miss anything new and exciting.

Were he with us today, Daniel would still find new and better things along the lines of the Erie. Heavy grades that "bottlenecked" freight movements for a long time, have bowed down before General Motors Diesel locomotives—and long strings of freight cars now move with dependable on-time regularity without split-up between Chicago and Jersey City.

Here, as in the service of 83 other major lines and heavy industries, this modern motive power is dramatically heralding new and better things to come.

For their great power, their speed, their unmatched smoothness make one thing clear: *When whole lines become completely GM Dieselized, schedules can be clipped, costs still more reduced — and all your travels blessed with fresh new comfort and ease.*

This General Motors ad heralding diesel locomotives includes a drawing purporting to show President Millard Fillmore's train traveling from Piermont to Dunkirk, N.Y., to celebrate the completion of the New York & Erie Railroad May 14-15, 1851. The presence of Secretary of State Daniel Webster in a rocking chair on the flatcar, however, reveals that this is the second of two trains; Fillmore was on the first.

Presidential Pioneers

John Quincy Adams

It was Federalist John Quincy Adams of Massachusetts who was the first chief executive to record a train ride, although after he left office. In the fall of 1830, he was elected to represent his home district in Massachusetts in the U.S. House of Representatives, and even though the 22nd Congress was not scheduled to convene for a year, Adams returned to Washington to have a ringside seat on political developments. His wife, Louisa, didn't like steamboats, so she set out on the 500-mile trip via an overland route. Adams had no such trepidation, so his route included steamboats, canal boats and "the new and frightening horse-drawn railway cars"[346] of the fledgling Baltimore & Ohio Railroad from Baltimore to Relay House, Md.

The Dec. 17, 1830, journey was significant in another way. The former president's party made the seven-mile trip in a horse-drawn carriage that had been loaded onto a long, open railroad freight car that was itself pulled by horses—perhaps the nation's first piggyback operation. At Relay House the front end of the car was dropped down—as the opposite end had been to permit loading—to allow Adams' horses, carriage and party to be unloaded and continue the journey to Washington by highway.[437]

Louisa's trip had taken 14 days; Adams left four days behind her and arrived in Washington just an hour after his wife—no doubt in part because of the contribution of the breathtaking new rail technology.

Adams was nearly killed in the first major railroad accident in the United States. On Friday, Nov. 8, 1833, he was riding across New Jersey toward Washington about halfway between Spotswood and Highstown on the Camden & Amboy Rail Road and Transportation Co.—at an unheard of speed of more than 25 miles an hour—when an overheated journal bearing caused an axle on his coach to break. The cars careened down an embankment; Adams' coach remained upright and no one in it was hurt. But the one behind his, with 24 passengers aboard, overturned. Two men were killed instantly, 15 were injured and a woman and her child were "mutilated beyond expectation of recovery."[346]

Industrialist Cornelius Vanderbilt, on a business trip, was in this car and was nearly fatally injured. The burning axle had not been detected by the agent who constantly surveyed the train in these pioneer days, because he was putting out a burning cotton bale at the time. Such bales were hauled on flatcars between the locomotive and its coaches as a buffer to protect the latter and their passengers from sparks.

For more than 100 feet, the ground was covered with "mangled and bleeding" men, women and children, and "limbs in frightful varieties of distortion."[346] Adams continued to the capital by rail, leaving Philadelphia at 7:30 a.m. the next day, laying over in Baltimore from 2:30 to 5 p.m. and arriving at his destination at 9 p.m.

Adams recorded that even though he liked the precision of the new transportation mode, 11 hours of rail riding was "very tedious"[346] and he liked neither the speed nor the sparks.

Andrew Jackson

Democrat Andrew Jackson of Tennessee, the seventh president, was the first to ride a train while in office. He traveled on the B&O from Ellicotts Mills, Md., to Baltimore on Thursday, June 6, 1833.

Jackson had embarked on an ambitious tour of the Northeast to unify the nation after a divisive conflict over nullification, a doctrine that encouraged states to declare unconstitutional any federal law they didn't like. He and his party traveled by carriage to the point where the Washington Turnpike intercepted the infant B&O's track. There he met a delegation of 200 Maryland politicians that had ridden out from Baltimore's Three Tuns Inn at Pratt and Paca streets in a train of "steam carrs"(sic),[318] as Jackson called them. The carriages had departed at 12:30 p.m. and had been pulled separately by horses to Baltimore's "outer depot,"[251] thence together behind the steam engine *Atlantic*—which recently had been improved and was now "most efficient."[251]

At Ellicotts Mills, the train was "arranged for the return just before the president arrived, and as he was being greeted, it was "thrown back" so the center car was "brought in front of the place where he stood" and he boarded for the return trip into town at 2 p.m.[251]

"We arrived here half after 2 o'clock

This engine is B&O's Atlantic, *which is said to have pulled President Andrew Jackson's train from Ellicotts Mills to Baltimore on June 6, 1833—the first rail trip by a sitting president. This locomotive, however, originally was the* Andrew Jackson, *built three years after that trip. It was later renamed and altered to resemble the original, of which no photograph is known to exist.*

p.m. without fatigue or injury," Jackson wrote to his son Andrew Jr. "[We were] met by a number of the citizens with the steam carrs 12 miles in advance of the city which took us into Baltimore in a few minutes, where we were met by a numerous crowd." [201]

The throng cheered as Jackson arrived, perhaps more smitten by the new transportation marvel than by their president. The "carrs" were so efficient that they arrived an hour earlier than expected, disappointing many who had wanted to see the chief executive.

Martin Van Buren

Thanks to its geography, the B&O played host to many presidents. Democrat Martin Van Buren stayed in the governor's man-

sion in Albany, N.Y., during his campaign except for a few brief excursions around his state. But the B&O did help handle crowds for the inauguration.

Once Van Buren left office, he called on his successor, Virginia-born Whig William Henry Harrison, on Thursday, March 11, 1841, to wish him well, then two days later boarded "the cars" [281] for Baltimore on his way home. He stayed there until the following 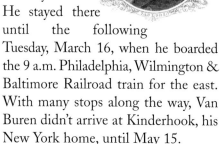 Tuesday, March 16, when he boarded the 9 a.m. Philadelphia, Wilmington & Baltimore Railroad train for the east. With many stops along the way, Van Buren didn't arrive at Kinderhook, his New York home, until May 15.

William Henry Harrison

William Henry Harrison, who settled in Ohio, is said to have been the first presidential candidate to campaign by rail, even though in that day campaigning was considered a violation of political proprieties. He rode from Wilmington, Del., to Trenton, N.J., in September 1836 during his first—and unsuccessful—race via the PW&B and Philadelphia & Trenton lines. In 1840, he was victorious and became the first president-elect to travel by train to his inauguration. Journeying from Cincinnati by boat and stagecoach, he was greeted by cheering crowds at every stop and arrived in Frederick, Md., on the evening of Feb. 5, 1841. After a reception at Dorsey's City Hotel, the next day he boarded a B&O train for Baltimore, having been provided a "distinct car" [436] by company management. Leaving there on Feb. 9, his 68th birthday, he continued to Washington via B&O and registered at Gadsby's Hotel.

John Tyler

After Harrison's inauguration, Vice President John Tyler, another Virginia Whig, returned home to Williamsburg, expecting four years of peace and quiet. His government involvement would include only intermittent visits to Washington to preside over the Senate.

Imagine his surprise, then, when at dawn on Monday, April 5, 1841, Fletcher Webster, Daniel's son and chief clerk of the State Department, and Robert Beall, the Senate's assistant doorkeeper, knocked loudly on his front door. Tyler was informed that

This Camden & Amboy train of around 1840 was the usual mode of travel in the days of Presidents William Henry Harrison and John Tyler.

Harrison had died at 12:30 a.m. on Sunday the 4th, being in office only a month. Wading through a horribly long inaugural speech in dismal weather, he had caught cold and contracted a fatal case of pneumonia. 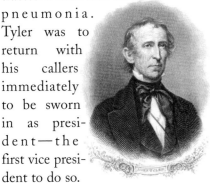 Tyler was to return with his callers immediately to be sworn in as president—the first vice president to do so.

Tyler made hasty preparations for the trip, and with his two sons he boarded Webster and Beall's chartered boat at about 8 a.m. for Richmond. By 5:30 p.m., the party was ready to board a special train for the quick trip to the capital. Using a riverboat connection from the end of the Richmond, Fredericksburg & Potomac's track at Aquia Creek, Va., the travelers reached Washington at 5 a.m. Tuesday. The new president had covered the 230 miles in 21 hours—a remarkable record for that day.

Only once during his term did Tyler make a trip of any length. He had been battered in papers controlled by the Whigs because he dared exercise all the powers of the presidency, and finally had been thrown out of the party. Despised by political foes and the public alike, he surmised that contact with the people might restore his fortunes. So he boarded a special train in Washington at noon on Thursday, June 8, 1843, enroute to Charlestown, Mass., to dedicate the Bunker Hill Monument. The president received a big sendoff, with a procession by foot and carriage led by a band from the Executive Mansion to the B&O station.

The party stopped in Baltimore for a day and a night, with a banquet and public reception at Barnum's City Hotel and a theater party. The next morning, Tyler left on a PW&B train for Wilmington, where a Philadelphia delegation escorted him to their city on a steamboat. Another reception ensued, from which the Whigs were conspicuously absent, for another day and night. Continuing via the Camden & Amboy, Tyler spent all day

Raleigh & Gaston locomotive Romulus Saunders *was no doubt on hand somewhere on the line when President James K. Polk made his trip south in 1847.*

Sunday in Princeton, N.J., then continued to New York, where 60,000 people met his ferry at Castle Garden. After three days, he continued to Providence, R.I., and on to Boston by rail, arriving on Friday, June 16, the day before the big celebration.

The tour was cut short by the sudden death of one of Tyler's traveling companions, Attorney General Hugh S. Legare. The chief executive had intended to return leisurely by detouring through the Midwest, but after attending Legare's funeral, he returned quickly to Washington.

At one point during his term, Tyler planned a trip and sent his son Bob to order a special train. The B&O superintendent, a devout Whig, told Bob he didn't run special trains for presidents. "What?" cried Bob. "Didn't you furnish a special train for the funeral of Gen. Harrison?" "Yes," admitted the superintendent. "And if you will bring your father here in that shape, you shall have the best train on the road!"[43]

James K. Polk

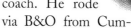

Democrat James K. Polk traveled by rail from Cumberland, Md., to Washington on Feb. 13, 1845, for his inauguration, having come from his Tennessee home by riverboat and stagecoach. He rode via B&O from Cumberland to Relay, where a Baltimore delegation offered an artillery salute and continued with him over the Washington Branch. George M. Dallas, the vice president-elect, rode down from Baltimore and joined Polk's party at Relay.

In one of the original first-person narratives of a presidential rail trip, Polk described in his diary a journey he made two years later to visit his alma mater, the University of North Carolina. On Friday, May 28, 1847,

the Polks and six others rode a boat a few miles down the Potomac River to Aquia Creek, connecting with the RF&P's railroad cars. When the party arrived in Richmond at 5 p.m. after an 8 ½-hour journey, they were met by local dignitaries, military companies and crowds. "I was placed in an open carriage and conducted by the mayor and committee to the Capitol," Polk wrote, "where many thousand persons, ladies and gentlemen, were assembled. I exchanged salutations and shook hands with many hundreds of them." The artillery company fired a salute. Mrs. Polk was received by the ladies of the city at the executive chamber in the Capitol. "... The demonstration of respect at Richmond was without distinction of party and was highly gratifying to me," Polk wrote.

After an hour and a half of pageantry, the Polks were taken to the Richmond & Petersburg depot, where they boarded a train for Petersburg, Va., arriving shortly after dark. There was another welcoming committee, a brilliantly lighted hotel, and another crowd. The rail journey continued via the Petersburg Railway to Gaston, N.C., which was reached at 4 a.m.

"I retired to a room in the hotel, shaved and dressed," Polk wrote. "About sunrise, on entering the parlour below stairs, I was received by a committee of citizens ... who welcomed me to my native state."

After breakfast, the journey continued on the Raleigh & Gaston line. "At intervals of every few miles, and especially at all the railroad depots, many persons, male and female, were assembled to see me," the president recalled. "At most of these places I descended from the cars and shook hands with as many of them as my time would permit."

Near Warrenton, Polk noted an assemblage of 40 or 50 carriages "in which the ladies had come to greet me." During a 90-minute stop at

Henderson, where he dined, were several thousand persons, and crowds engulfed the track at Franklinton and Raleigh, which was reached at 5:30 p.m. Saturday, for more salutes, fireworks and greetings that were fatiguing but gratifying. The party continued to Chapel Hill the following Monday by carriage.

Polk must have been weary after his visit, because his entry for the return trip, after a commencement in which 37 young gentlemen were graduated, is considerably shorter:

"We arrived at Petersburg shortly after day light this morning [Saturday, June 5, 1847], and after being detained a short time at the hotel proceeded to Richmond, where we took breakfast. Proceeding on our journey we arrived at Washington about five o'clock p.m. and thus ended my excursion. ... It was an exceedingly agreeable one. No incident of an unpleasant character occurred. My reception at the University, and the attentions paid me on the route going and returning, was all I could have desired it to be."[278]

Zachary Taylor

Gen. Zachary Taylor began his journey to the Executive Mansion from his sugar plantation in Baton Rouge, La., on Jan. 24, 1849. He sailed on the Mississippi and Ohio rivers to Wheeling, Va., took a stagecoach to Uniontown, Pa., and rode 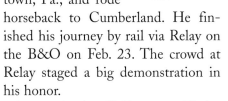 horseback to Cumberland. He finished his journey by rail via Relay on the B&O on Feb. 23. The crowd at Relay staged a big demonstration in his honor.

During his brief Whig term, Taylor made a three-mile trip somewhere over the Pennsylvania Railroad during a test of a new 23.5-ton passenger locomotive traveling at 60 miles an hour. It is said the company was trying to establish a speed record for the transportation of presidents. Other than this one venture, Taylor rarely rode the rails while in office.

Millard Fillmore

Whig Millard Fillmore of New York and his entire Cabinet accepted invitations to ride the inaugural trip over the entire 446-mile length of the New York & Erie Railroad upon its  completion from Piermont, N.Y., just up the Hudson from New York City, to Dunkirk, on Lake Erie, on May 14-15, 1851. It was at the time the longest railway in the world and the first to reach what was considered the American West.

With the nation already torn apart over slavery and states' rights, Fillmore used every opportunity on the two-day trip to encourage gala peace demonstrations.

The junket had actually started two days before with a special train from Washington operated on the B&O and Camden & Amboy. After a six-hour breakfast at Baltimore's Barnum Hotel and a night of revelry in Philadelphia, the party arrived in Manhattan a little frayed around the edges. They had been met at South Amboy by Erie President Benjamin Loder, a detail of 9,000 militia in dress uniform, five platoons of police, six bands and 40 barkeeps. Another night of partying at the Astor House

and Irving hotels precluded any sleep for the travelers, so—as the story goes—they wouldn't miss the 6 a.m. steamer connection from Battery Park to Piermont.

The steamer *Erie*, docking at railside at 7:30, was met by Dodsworth's Band, a salvo of artillery and champagne for everyone as a prelude to a breakfast of beefsteak, roast fowl, spiced eels, broiled shad, sausages and johnnycake served right on the pier.

Wearing well-brushed beaver hats, frock coats, ascot ties and smiling over their best gold-headed walking canes, the special party boarded two excursion trains—the president on the first—decorated with flags and bunting.

Like picnickers stiffened by their formal clothing, the excursionists braced for one final salvo of cannon fire and the trains pulled out. The locomotive's exhaust drifted through open windows in the coaches, keeping celebrants busy dodging hot ashes. Secretary of State Daniel Webster, on the second train, must not have minded the grit. Equipped with a steamer rug and knitted scarf to secure his top hat, he rode in a platform rocker fastened to a flatcar so that he might have a better view.

The locomotive on Fillmore's train developed trouble somewhere short of Goshen, N.Y. At Middletown, Erie Supt. Charles Minot met the emergency by using the company's new telegraph line to wire instructions—some of the world's first train orders—21 miles ahead to the Erie roundhouse at Port Jervis to have another locomotive ready.

There were stops all along the way for the president's rear-platform speeches. His Cabinet would gather behind him, listening attentively as Fillmore addressed the crowds. Hundreds heard him at Goshen and Middletown and the trains paused for lunch at a private home in

Narrowsburg. Further oratory ensued at Cochecton, Callicoon and Deposit while notables admired the "combined handiwork of God and man"[36] at Cascade Bridge and Starrucca Viaduct. At Susquehanna, the artillery salute was augmented by the whistles of 16 locomotives lined in military array at the roundhouse, and at Binghamton, Fillmore addressed 4,000 listeners, quoting poetry and Scripture.

The party paused overnight in Elmira, where amid the speeches at Brainard's Hotel, everyone enjoyed a seven-hour, 24-course banquet. "It was an extraordinary occasion," historian Edward H. Mott noted. "Great liberty and license were permitted everyone. Everybody was celebrating and making merry. Men who were known as staid and strict men were more than unbent and dallied, perhaps overmuch with the help of the good cheer which prevailed everywhere without money and without price."[36]

Groggy but game, the party was off the next morning with stops at Corning, Hornellsville and Allegheny. An enthusiastic citizen at Dayton overcharged a gun left over from the War of 1812 and blew both his arms off as the trains roared past. A collection was hastily lifted for his reassembly.

A triumphal floral arch greeted the specials at Dunkirk—coupled together to run into town as a doubleheader—and the *U.S.S. Michigan* fired her cannon joyously in the harbor. The 65th Regiment's mounted artillery and every church steeple in town added to the cacophony as the trains came into sight. A banquet for the dignitaries followed at the new Loder House—named for the Erie Railroad chief—and plainer folk repaired to an immense pavilion where a 300-foot-long table offered chowder, 10 oxen roasted whole, beef a la mode, corned beef, buffalo tongues, bologna sausage, beef tongues both smoked and spiced, roasted fowls, coffee and "etceteras"[36] —the latter mostly in square-faced bottles.

The shanty where the oxen were being roasted caught fire and burned to the ground amid great municipal enthusiasm; the crowds cheered firemen on their way to the blaze. The oxen turned out a little overdone but were pronounced delicious. Bread appeared in loaves 2 feet square and 10 feet long and some unidentified scoundrel slipped a quantity of high-proof French cognac into the coffee urn, causing some to note that certain churchmen were behaving peculiarly.

Franklin Pierce

Tragedy struck New Hampshire Democrat Franklin Pierce shortly before he took office in 1853. Pierce, his wife, Jane, and their 12-year-old son, Benjamin, were returning to their home in Concord, N.H., from a visit with friends in Andover, Mass., on the Boston & Maine on Jan. 6. One mile north of Andover, the only coach in the train overturned and "fell among the rocks, down a precipice 20 feet and was turned so as to change ends."[389a] The only other car, a baggage car, and the locomotive remained upright, but the passenger coach was broken in two. The Pierces were sitting four or five seats from the front, and when the car overturned, Bennie was struck by a piece of the car's wooden frame that pinned him down and crushed his head. Pierce, only shaken and bruised, rescued Jane from the wreckage and set out to find his son. He soon found Bennie, but the boy was beyond help. The accident cast a pall on his entire term.

James Buchanan

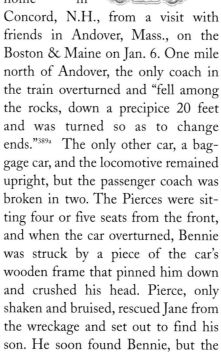

Pennsylvania Democrat James Buchanan was the first of several presidents with railroad experience— in the 1830s, he was president of the Portsmouth & Lancaster Railroad in his home state. Later, Abraham Lincoln and Grover Cleveland did legal work for several carriers— Lincoln for the Illinois Central and the Chicago & Rock Island, and Cleveland for the Buffalo, Rochester & Pittsburgh and the Lehigh Valley—and Harry Truman served as timekeeper for an Atchison, Topeka & Santa Fe contractor. (Lincoln and Cleveland each were offered positions as legal counsel for the New York Central, but each refused. How different history would have been had either accepted—and turned away from a life of politics!)

The fact that Buchanan had been in Europe as the campaign of 1856 neared enabled him to avoid the period's national political strife and made him an ideal compromise candidate. When his vessel docked at New York that April 24, he remained aloof and increased his chances. His arrival without notice and refusal of ceremony alienated no one and brought out all the scrapping factions to see him. He put the psychological triumph to good use on the train trip home to Lancaster.

He stopped over for a short speech at Philadelphia's Merchants Exchange and a reception, fireworks, parade and band serenade at the Merchants Hotel. The next morning, Buchanan

James Buchanan says goodbye to well-wishers at Lancaster, Pa., on March 2, 1857, enroute to his inauguration in Washington, D.C.

was provided a special train by the Pennsylvania Railroad for the last lap home.

The locomotive, *Young America*, had been draped with bunting and signs reading "Welcome Home, Pennsylvania's Favorite Son."[220] Buchanan stood on the back platform and waved his hat at all the stops. A short stop was made at Gap, Pa., home of PRR Supt. Joseph B. Baker, where the engine took on water and the official party champagne. Lancaster celebrated his return for two days and Buchanan knew he was on his way.

Nearly a year later, on a snowy March 2, 1857, the president-elect departed for Washington. Lancaster's church bells pealed at 6 a.m. to inform the townsfolk it was time for the march to the railroad station. A band tried to play, but it was too cold and the musicians clambered aboard a wagon to shiver and wait. Finally the marchers walked to Wheatland, Buchanan's mansion, and waited until his carriage appeared. Then, with the Lancaster Fencibles leading, the happy but chilled procession got under way.

Baker had provided a special four-car train, the sides of which were adorned with patriotic symbols and Wheatland scenes. Enroute on the Northern Central, a message was delivered to the train that about a thousand Know-Nothings, anti-Buchanan demonstrators, were gathered around NC's Calvert Street Station in Baltimore and were looking for trouble. The special party therefore detrained early at Bolton Station, where several companies of cavalry, with sabers drawn, waited to accompany the president-elect to Barnum's City Hotel for a huge midday banquet. Buchanan was ill, however, and napped in his room until 3 p.m., when he boarded a B&O train at Camden Station for the trip to Washington.

Hanover Jct., Pa.., is a busy place on Nov. 18, 1863, as Abraham Lincoln travels to Gettysburg, Pa. Sharp eyes will notice a man in a stovepipe hat on the station platform who may be Lincoln himself.

Abraham Lincoln and the Civil War

2

Abraham Lincoln

By the mid-19th century, it was dawning on presidential candidates that railroads could help their campaigns.

Democrat Stephen Douglas may be said to have started the wheel rolling during the Illinois senatorial campaign of 1858. Running against the nominee of the brand new Republican Party, Abraham Lincoln, Douglas mounted a cannon on a flatcar attached to his special—and shot it off at way stations and whistlestops to announce his arrival.

From one town to another in Illinois, Lincoln and Douglas journeyed, mostly on the Illinois Central. Honest Abe, the rail-splitter lawyer, got the cold shoulder from the IC, even though he often represented the railroad in court, because its vice president, George B. McClellan, was a personal friend of Douglas.

Lincoln was no stranger to rail travel, having ridden often in connection with his work. Before starting a trip, he would walk the length of the train to the cab and shake hands with the engine crew. He wanted to meet, he explained, the men who were running the thing before he took the ride.

He must have smiled when he said it. In his time, the coaches were rough and sleeping cars merely rebuilt coaches with hard immovable seats. At night, light was provided by candles. There were berths and mattresses of a kind but no sheets or blankets.

"At all points on the road where meetings between the two great politicians were held," wrote Lincoln's friend Ward Hill Lamon, "either a special train or a special car was furnished to Judge Douglas; but Mr. Lincoln, when he failed to get transportation on the regular trains in time to meet his appointments, was reduced to the necessity of going as freight. There being orders from headquarters to permit no passenger to travel on freight trains, Mr. Lincoln's persuasive powers were often brought into requisition. The favor was granted or refused according to the politics of the conductor.

"On one occasion, in going to meet an appointment in the southern part of the state—that section of Illinois called Egypt—Mr. Lincoln and I, with other friends were traveling in the caboose of a freight train, when we were switched off the main track to allow a special train to pass in which Mr. Lincoln's more aristocratic rival was being conveyed. The passing train was decorated with banners and flags, and carried a band of music which was playing 'Hail to the Chief.' As the train whistled past, Mr. Lincoln broke out in a fit of laughter and said: 'Boys, the gentleman in that car evidently smelt no royalty in our carriage!' "[364]

Some sources say Lincoln was irked—the sidetracking made him arrive late for the debate. It is said he didn't like the cannon either.

Carl Shurtz, a fellow passenger on a train bound for the sixth debate at Quincy, penned a great description of Lincoln as a passenger.

"The car in which I traveled," wrote Shurtz, "was full of men who discussed the absorbing question [of slavery] with great animation. A member of the Republican State Committee accompanied me and sat by my side.

"All at once, after the train had left a way-station, I observed a great commotion among my fellow-passengers, many of whom jumped from their seats and pressed eagerly around a tall man who had just entered the car. They addressed him in the most familiar style: 'Hello, Abe! How are you?' and so on. And he responded in the same manner: 'Good evening, Ben! How are you, Joe? Glad to see you, Dick!' and there was much laughter at some things he said, which, in the confusion of voices, I could not understand.

" 'Why,' exclaimed my companion, the committeeman, 'there's Lincoln himself!' He pressed through the crowd and introduced me to Abraham Lincoln, whom I then saw for the first time.

"I must confess that I was somewhat startled by his appearance. There he stood, overtopping by several inches all those surrounding him. Although measuring something over 6 feet myself, I had, when standing quite near to him, to throw my head backward in order to look into his eyes. That swarthy face, with its strong features, its deep furrows, and its benignant, melancholy eyes, is now familiar to every American. ... At that time it was clean-shaven and looked even more haggard and careworn than later, when it was framed in whiskers.

"On his head he wore a somewhat battered 'stovepipe' hat. His neck emerged, long and sinewy, from a white collar turned down over a thin black necktie. His lank, ungainly body was clad in a rusty black frock coat with sleeves that should have been longer; but his arms appeared so long that the sleeves of a 'store' coat could hardly have been expected to cover them all the way down to the wrists. His black trousers, too, permitted a very full view of his large feet. On his left arm he carried a gray woolen shawl, which evidently served him for an overcoat in chilly weather. His left hand held a cotton umbrella of the bulging kind, and also a black satchel that bore the marks of long and hard usage. His right he had kept free for hand-shaking, of which there was no end until everybody in the car seemed to be satisfied. I had seen in Washington and the West, several public men of rough appearance, but none whose looks seemed quite so uncouth, not to say grotesque, as Lincoln's.

"He received me with an off-hand cordiality, like an old acquaintance, having been informed of what I was doing in the campaign; and we sat down together. In a somewhat high-pitched but pleasant voice, he began to talk to me, telling me much about the points he and Douglas had made in the debates at different places, and about those he intended to make at Quincy. ... When, in a tone of perfect ingenuousness, he asked me—a young beginner in politics—what I thought about this and that. I should have felt myself very much honored by his confidence, had he permitted me to regard him as a great man. But he talked in so simple and familiar a strain, and his manner and homely phrases were so absolutely free from any semblance of self-consciousness or pretension of superiority, that I soon felt as if I had known him all my life, and we had very long been close friends. He interspersed our conversations with all sorts of quaint stories, each of which had a witty point applicable to the subject in hand, and not seldom concluded an argument in such a manner that nothing more was to be said. He seemed to enjoy his own jests in a childlike way. His usually sad-looking eyes would kindle with a merry twinkle, and he himself led in the laughter; and his laugh was so genuine, hearty and contagious that nobody could fail to join in it. [364]

Chicago Press and Tribune reporter Horace White once was afforded a little extra rail travel because of Lincoln. After the Freeport debate, Lincoln's party went to Carlinville, where Lincoln and John M. Palmer spoke on behalf of the Republican cause. Then they departed for Clinton by way of Springfield and Decatur.

"During this journey," White wrote, "an incident occurred which gave unbounded mirth to Mr. Lincoln at my expense. We left Springfield about nine o'clock in the evening for Decatur, where we were to change cars and take the north-bound train on the Illinois Central Railroad. I was very tired and curled myself up as best I could on the seat to take a nap, asking Mr. Lincoln to wake me up at Decatur, which he promised to do.

"I went to sleep, and when I did awake I had the sensation of having been asleep a long time. It was daylight and I knew we should have reached Decatur before midnight. Mr. Lincoln's seat was vacant. While I was pulling myself together, the conductor opened the door of the car and shouted, 'State Line.' This was the name of a shabby little town on the border of Indiana. There was nothing to do but to get out and wait for the next train going back to Decatur. About six o'clock in the evening I found my way to Clinton. The meeting was over, of course, and the Chicago Tribune had lost its expected report, and I was out of pocket for railroad fares.

"I wended my way to the house of Mr. C.H. Moore, where Lincoln was staying and where I too had been an expected guest. When Mr. Lincoln saw me coming up the garden path, his lungs began to crow like a chanticleer, and I thought he would laugh, sans intermission, an hour by his dial. He paused long enough to say that he also had fallen asleep and did not wake up till the train was starting FROM Decatur. He had very nearly been carried past the station himself, and, in his haste to get out, had forgotten all about his promise to waken me. Then he began to laugh again."[364]

IC brakeman B.F. Smith saw a great deal of contrast in Lincoln and Douglas. "Sen. Douglas rode with me in the brakeman's seat from Odin to Champaign one trip in 1859," Smith said. "He offered me a cigar, which I refused, saying that I had never learned to smoke. At Champaign he took a seat in the second-class car, next to the baggage car. Here he emptied a small bottle of liquor into his stomach, or nearly all of it. When I went through the car at Chicago, he roused up before his friends came to meet him and offered me a drink from his bottle, which I refused. It seemed strange to him for a railway brakeman to refuse to smoke or drink with him.

"The other distinguished man who rode with me about that time was Abraham Lincoln. He sat in my seat on the run from Champaign to Tolono. It was about sunrise. There was only one farm then between those two stations, in 1859, all green prairie. A beautiful sun rising attracted Mr. Lincoln. He called my attention to it, the sun just rising over those beautiful, undulating hills. He wanted me to share with him his admiration of the scene. I admitted that it was lovely. I had been seeing the sun rise every morning between those two stations, as we left Chicago at 9 p.m., and hadn't thought much about the beauty of it. Mr. Lincoln had been asleep until we reached Champaign.

"Well, the moral of this is the contrast of the two great men. One of them tempted me by offering a cigar at the beginning of the journey and at the end of it desired me to help him empty a bottle of whiskey. The other called my attention to that beautiful sunrise over the virgin prairies of Illinois and invited me to share with him the impression of it." [364]

A Chicago & Alton conductor was accustomed to having many of the Illinois politicians on his trains.

"Lincoln was the most folksy of any of them," he said. "He put on no airs. He did not hold himself distant from any man. But there was something about him which we plain people couldn't explain that made us stand a little in awe of him. ... You could get near him in a sort of neighborly way, as though you had always known him, but there was something tremendous between you and him all the time.

"I have eaten with him many

times at the railroad eating houses, and you get very neighborly if you eat together in a railroad restaurant. ... Everybody tried to get as near Lincoln as possible when he was eating, because he was such good company, but we always looked at him with a kind of wonder. We couldn't exactly make him out.

"Sometimes I would see what looked like dreadful loneliness in his look, and I used to wonder what he was thinking about. Whatever it was, he was thinking all alone. It wasn't a solemn look, like Stephen A. Douglas sometimes had. Douglas sometimes

B&O locomotive 17, at Harpers Ferry, Va., in 1860, is typical of rail travel during the Lincoln era.

made me think of an owl. He used to stare at you with his great dark eyes in a way that almost frightened you. Lincoln never frightened anybody. No one was afraid of him, but there was something about him that made plain folks feel toward him a good deal as a child feels toward his father, because you know every child looks upon his father as a wonderful man."[364]

Although Lincoln lost the 1858 Senatorial race, the real verdict would develop two years later with his ascension to the presidency. A rail trip east in the spring of 1860 guaranteed him the Republican nomination.

Lincoln undertook the journey ostensibly to check out his son, Robert, who had flunked out at Harvard the year before and was now attending Phillips Exeter Academy at Exeter, N.H. He wanted to know if his son had now buckled down and was serious about successfully completing his studies. But Lincoln also scheduled several speaking engagements—adding several more enroute — that resulted in the East becoming well-acquainted with his brilliant logic and down-to-earth humility. Years later, Robert Lincoln commented ruefully that his "abysmal flunk"[289] had made his father a president.

Lincoln secured the Republican nomination in Chicago, and once again, Douglas and Lincoln sparred. Douglas operated his campaign train with a vengeance, traveling on all the leading rail routes in the Middle West and South. This "steam engine in britches"[44] offended many people because it was still considered outlandish for presidential candidates to electioneer. Newspapers ridiculed Douglas; crowds jeered at him. He tried to defuse the critics during one trip in the East by saying he was going to visit his mother. But the trip took a month, with many stopovers and speeches, and the critics hounded him with monickers such as "Boy Lost" and "Wandering Son."[44]

Lincoln didn't lower himself to Douglas' level and actively campaign; he let the delegations come to him. The Great Western Railroad ticket office in Springfield did a land-office business in the summer and fall of 1860. Office-hunters, favor-seekers and would-be political advisers kept up the momentum well into winter.

After winning the nation's highest office, Lincoln planned a leisurely, roundabout inaugural rail trip that would allow the president-elect to tour the nation "to see and be seen."[205]

One item of unfinished business, however, had to be taken care of first. The president-elect determined to visit his stepmother, Sarah Bush Lincoln, one more time before leaving the Illinois prairies. She lived with a daughter at Farmington in Coles County, with Charleston being the closest rail approach.

The devoted stepson departed Springfield on the morning of Jan. 30, 1861, taking with him Henry C. Whitney, an old circuit-riding friend and law associate who had come to his home to talk over a business matter. Since Lincoln's time was short, Whitney got roped into the train ride so the two could talk. The itinerary would include the Great Western to Tolono, the Illinois Central to Mattoon, and the Terre Haute & Alton to Charleston. Let Whitney describe his fellow passenger:

"The nation at large would have been extremely surprised to behold their president-elect at this time. He had on a faded hat, innocent of a nap; and his coat was extremely short, more like a sailor's pea-jacket than any other describable garment. ... A well-

---

Henry Villard, writing for the *New York Staats-Zeitung*, once told about a conversation he had with Abraham Lincoln in a boxcar.

"He and I met accidentally," narrated Villard, "about nine o'clock on a hot, sultry evening, at a flag railroad station about 20 miles west of Springfield. ... He had been driven to the station in a buggy and left there alone. I was already there.

"The train that we intended to take for Springfield was about due. After waiting vainly for half an hour for its arrival, a thunderstorm compelled us to take refuge in an empty freight car standing on a side track, there being no buildings of any sort at the station.

"We squatted down on the floor of the car and fell to talking on all sorts of subjects. It was then and there he told me that, when he was clerking in a country store, his highest political ambition was to be a member of the State Legislature.

" 'Since then, of course,' he said laughingly, 'I have grown some, but my friends got me into THIS business. I did not consider myself qualified for the United States Senate, and it took a long time to persuade myself that I was. Now, to be sure,' he continued, with another of his peculiar laughs, 'I am convinced that I am good enough for it; but in spite of it all, I am saying to myself every day: "It is too big a thing for you; you will never get it." Mary [his wife] insists, however, that I am going to be senator and president of the United States, too.'

"These last words he followed with a roar of laughter, with his arms around his knees, and shaking all over with mirth at his wife's ambition. 'Just think,' he exclaimed, 'of such a sucker as me for president!'

"Our talk continued till half-past ten, when the belated train arrived," Villard concluded his story. "My companion of that night has become one of the greatest figures in history."[364]

worn carpet-bag, quite collapsed, comprised his baggage. After we had started for the depot, across lots, his servant came running after us and took the carpet-bag, but he was soon sent back after some forgotten thing, and we trudged on alone."[364]

The pair engaged in small talk, ranging from politics to what Lincoln should do with his home while in Washington. As they neared the station, Lincoln remarked that since his "hat" wasn't "chalked" on this particular road anymore (a euphemism for passengers allowed to ride free), he "reckoned" he would have to purchase a ticket. Whitney went to work.

"I ridiculed him," he said, "and handing him the attenuated carpet-bag, I went into Mr. Bowen's office, who was superintendent of the road, and asked for a pass for Mr. Lincoln. Mr. Bowen was entirely alone—not even a clerk being present, it being breakfast time for them—and, as he commenced to write a pass, he suggested that I invite Lincoln in there to wait, the train not yet having come in from the west. Repairing to the waiting room, I found the president-elect surrounded by the few persons who were also waiting for the train, tying the handles of his carpet-bag with a string."

Lincoln accompanied Whitney to the superintendent's office.

"Bowen," he asked when comfortably seated, "how is business on your road now?"

"Pretty good, just now," replied the superintendent.

"You are a heap better off," Lincoln went on, "running a good road, than I am playing president. When I first knew Whitney, I was getting on well—I was clean out of politics and continued to stay so; I had a good business, and my children were coming up, and were interesting to me, but now, here I am—"[364]

The *Morning Express* pulled in and Lincoln and Whitney boarded. Joining them were Judge John Pettit, a former U.S. senator from Indiana seeking a federal appointment, and Thomas Marshall, a state senator from Coles County. They were due to depart Springfield about 9:45, so Lincoln had time to share a story or two with the passengers who had gathered around to gawk at him.

With the train under way, Whitney was eager to take care of his business, but was delayed once again when "Lincoln took pains, though not with ostentation, to secure an humble old lady whom he knew a double seat." Finally the important matter was discussed and Whitney detrained at Tolono, 75 miles away, at 1:30 to catch the first westbound back to Springfield.

Lincoln successfully made his connection to the IC at Tolono for a two-hour, 35-mile ride south to Mattoon.

At Tuscola, lawyer Joseph G. Cannon boarded for Mattoon to try a suit there. He saw Lincoln seated with Marshall, and the latter beckoned to the new passenger, who was a constituent of his.

"Mr. Lincoln," Marshall said, not knowing the two had met before. "I want to introduce you to a young lawyer in this country."

After some conversation, Cannon had to step back because of other people crowding close for introductions of their own, now that it had been announced who he was.

"He was," said Cannon, "of course the most distinguished man on the train, and he was constantly surrounded by the other passengers. But he was just one of the passengers in the day coach, in all his bearings."

Lincoln didn't do much of the talking, but in response to a query from a man named Morgan he did say, "I am going down to spend a day

visiting (my mother) before I go to Washington to take the oath of office."[364]

The IC train missed its Terre Haute & Alton connection at Mattoon, meaning the last 10 miles of the journey would have to be covered in the caboose of an eastbound evening freight.

Others besides Lincoln and his fellow travelers were disappointed. Attorney James A. Connolly and other Charlestonians had gone to their station to see the newly elected president arrive on the passenger train. Now they had to wait several more hours.

"When the (freight) train finally drew in and stopped," Connolly recalled years later, "the locomotive was about opposite the station, and the caboose ... was some distance down the track.

"Presently, looking in that direction, we saw a tall man wearing a coat or shawl descend from the steps of the car and patiently make his way through the long expanse of slush and ice beside the track as far as the station platform. I think he wore a plug hat. I remember I was surprised that a railroad company, with so distinguished a passenger aboard its train ... did not manifest interest enough in his dignity and comfort to deliver him at the station instead of dropping him off in the mud several hundred feet down the track.

"Quite a crowd of natives were gathered on the platform to see him," Connolly continued. "I confess I was not favorably impressed. His awkward, if not ungainly figure, and his appearance generally failed to attract me, but this was doubtless due to the fact that I was a great admirer of Douglas. ... There were no formalities. Mr. Lincoln shook hands with a number of persons, whom he recognized or who greeted him, and in a few min-

Tears fill Abraham Lincoln's eyes as he bids farewell to the homefolks at Springfield, Ill., Feb. 11, 1861, just before he starts for Washington and his inauguration.

utes left for the residence of a friend, where, it was understood, he was to spend the night."[364]

Lincoln was entertained in Charleston in the home of Col. A.H. Chapman, who had married a daughter of Dennis Hanks, Lincoln's cousin and boyhood playmate. Several people called at the home that evening, and the next morning Lincoln and Chapman made for Farmington.

After his last visit with his beloved stepmother, during which he visited his father's grave and saw other relatives, Mrs. Lincoln accompanied her son back to Charleston on the afternoon of the 31st, where an impromptu reception was scheduled that night.

On the morning of Feb. 1, as his mother embraced Lincoln, she must have had a premonition that this was farewell. She said, in a quavering voice, "God bless you and keep you, my good son."[364] His own eyes were wet as he boarded the train for home.

It was a bittersweet triumph when he bid his townsfolk in Springfield farewell from the rear platform of his special train as he set out from the Great Western's little brick depot at 8 a.m., Feb. 11, 1861, bound for Washington and his inauguration.

The elaborate preparations for this trip—superintended by W.S. Wood of New York on the recommendation of Lincoln's secretary of state-designate, William H. Seward—called for Lincoln to follow a 12-day roundabout itinerary on 23 railroads, with a separate pilot train preceding most of the way. The train would travel only by daylight for safety, Lincoln's desire to meet the crowds, and the lack of good sleeping-car accommodations.

He would make several speeches designed to convince the American people to stifle their growing sectional animosities lest they erupt in a shooting war. Already such rumblings were in the air and a large part of the nation refused to recognize him as the president-elect. Lincoln had been advised by some of his friends against such an endeavor, but he was adamant.

No retinue of servants were aboard to answer Lincoln's beck and call on that Monday morning. He roped up his own trunks at the Chenery House hotel —he had rented out his home a few days before. He personally wrote on the back of some hotel cards, "A. Lincoln, Executive Mansion, Washington, D.C.," and attached them to his trunks. The landlord's daughter watched, asking for and receiving Lincoln's autograph on another card. Eldest son Robert— home from college—was to ride with his father, as were a host of business and political associates, personal secretaries, reporters, railroad officials, Lincoln's physician and an Army guard of four soldiers. Some would travel part way, others all the way. J.J.S. Wilson, superintendent of the Caton Telegraph Co., carried a portable instrument that could be attached to the telegraph wires at any point enroute in case of emergency. Lincoln's wife, Mary, and their other two sons, Tad and Willie, were to travel eastward later on a more direct path.

Some sources say Mary Lincoln didn't leave with her husband because she was having one of her "spells." Henry Villard, planning to ride the special for the *New York Herald*, said he was told by the man who went to the hotel looking for the tardy presidential family that he found Mrs. Lincoln on the floor and refusing to budge until her husband promised that a certain man would be appointed to a federal post. Finally, Lincoln and son Robert left without her and the two youngest boys. [144]

The train included a baggage car and coach pulled by the engine *L.M.*

Wiley, a Hinkley Locomotive Works American type, meaning it had four small leading wheels, four giant driving wheels and no trailing wheels (or 4-4-0). Its brasswork glistened and flags decorated the cowcatcher, although they were sodden and limp because of a gloomy rain. The cars' exterior wooden panels had been painted bright orange, splashed with flourishes of black and varnished to a high gleam. The coach's interior walls had been decorated with crimson plush; red, white and blue festoons hung from its molding. Between the windows was heavy blue silk studded with 34 silver stars, one for each state. The furniture was dark mahogany, contrasting with the light-colored tapestry carpet. At either end, two American flags were crossed above the doorways.

The crew included conductor Walter C. Whitney, engineer E.H. Fralick, baggagemaster Platt Williamson and brakeman Thomas Ross. Everyone on board and at stations enroute had copies of the train's schedule and special instructions to ensure its safety.

The hotel's horse-drawn omnibus halted at the depot and Wood, the trip planner, was among the well-wishers who pressed the tearful president-elect to wish him a fond farewell. He had asked for no celebration and planned no speech; the rain and semi-darkness seemed to match his mood. Perhaps some of his sadness could be traced to the turmoil he had just left at the hotel.

At 7:55 a.m., Wood and Lincoln boarded the rear car, and just as the conductor reached for the bell rope to signal the engineer to start, Lincoln changed his mind and decided to speak to the crowd.

"My friends," he said, "no one, not in my situation, can appreciate my feelings of sadness at this parting. To

this place, the kindness of these people, I owe everything. Here I have lived a quarter of a century, and have passed from a young to an old man. Here my children have been born, and one [Edward] is buried. I now leave, not knowing when or whether ever I may return, with a task before me greater than that which rested upon Washington. Without the assistance of that Divine Being who ever attended him, I cannot succeed. With that assistance, I cannot fail. Trusting in Him, who can go with me, and remain with you, and be everywhere for good, let us confidently hope that all will yet be well. To His care commending you, as I hope in your prayers you will commend me, I bid you an affectionate farewell." [364]

As he stopped speaking, the train eased away and Lincoln, standing in the doorway of the coach, took his last look at Springfield as a private citizen and, as it turned out, in his lifetime.

Newspaper correspondents on board flocked to Lincoln for copies of his little speech, and the president elect obligingly asked his secretary John G. Nicolay for paper and pencil to record the impromptu remarks.

Because the trip was well-publicized, crowds gathered along the track everywhere, waving flags and shouting as the train passed at 30 miles an hour. It paused at Decatur at 9:24. Lincoln tried to speak, but was drowned out by the noise, so he got off and started shaking hands. As the train lurched into motion, he clambered aboard and waved "lustily."

Brakeman Ross recalled later his special passenger's journey across his home state.

"The enthusiasm all along the line was intense. As we whirled through the country villages, we caught a cheer from the people and a glimpse of waving handkerchiefs and of hats tossed high into the air. Wherever we stopped there was a great rush to shake hands with Mr. Lincoln, though of course only a few could reach him. The crowds looked as if they included the whole population. There were women and children, there were young men, and there were old men with gray beards. It was soul-stirring to see these white-whiskered old fellows, many of whom had known Lincoln in his humbler days, join in the cheering, and hear them shout after him, 'Goodbye, Abe. Stick to the Constitution, and we will stick to you!' "[364]

The special stopped a few miles beyond Decatur, where pranksters had blocked the track with a stake-and-rider rail fence. As the crew removed the obstruction, its creators cheered as Lincoln came out and waved to them. Near Bement, the special negotiated a high trestle. A uniformed soldier, placed there with rifle in hand to guard the fixture, presented arms as the train passed.

Tolono was reached at 10:50, and while the crew loaded cordwood and water for the locomotive, Lincoln mounted a bench to speak to a crowd gathered in a grove of trees.

"At Danville," Ross continued, "I well remember seeing him thrust his long arm over several heads to shake hands with George Lawrence," a man he did not further identify.

State Line, where the train transferred to the Toledo & Wabash, was reached at 12:38, eight minutes late. While the locomotive was replaced, the official party went to the State Line Hotel for lunch.

"There was such a crowd," Ross said, "that Lincoln could scarcely reach the dining room. 'Gentlemen,' said he, 'if you will make me a little path, so that I can get through and get something to eat, I will make you a speech when I get back.' "[364]

The earlier stages of the journey were easily accomplished. Glimpses have been preserved in the notebook of Capt. George W. Hazzard, who was detailed to accompany the family.

"Mr. Lincoln is by no means ugly; he is one of the most excessively pleasant men I ever saw. ... Don't get disheartened about secessioners; Mr. Lincoln is just the man for the emergency. ... I believe that we shall get to Washington without any trouble, but all preparations to avoid difficulty will be made."[197]

Col. Edwin V. Sumner, however, joined the train at State Line with disturbing rumors of a plot against the president-elect. As the train steamed northeasterly toward Lafayette, Ind., a melancholy Lincoln rode the back platform to get a last look at his beloved Illinois prairies. Re-entering the coach, he heard his friend Col. Ward Lamon strumming his banjo and singing "The Lament of the Irish Emigrant"; Sumner brushed his uniform; Col. Elmer Ellsworth was studying a military tactics manual and portly Judge David Davis snoozed after the hearty meal. Shaking off his despondency, Lincoln engaged some recently boarded Indiana politicians in a stimulating discussion.

At Lafayette, shortly before 2:30, there was another crowd, another speech and cannon fire. Then, on the Lafayette & Indianapolis line, a stop for wood at Thorntown.

A crowd called for "Speech, speech!" Lincoln went to the rear platform and said if he talked at every stop he'd never get to Washington. However, he would tell a story "if you promise not to let it out."

"No, no, we'll never tell!"

"There was once a man who was to be nominated at a political convention," Lincoln started, "and he hired a horse to journey there. The horse was so confoundedly slow, however ..."

The tardy train pulled away, inter-rupting the story in midsentence. The crowd shouted, "We'll never let THAT story out," and Lincoln joined in the merriment as the train disappeared around a bend.

At Lebanon, people were seen running down the track toward the train. "There comes the folks from Thorntown," someone said to Lincoln, "to hear the rest of your story."

The jovial president-elect related what happened at Thorntown and finished his story: The candidate, he said, arrived so late that he found his opponent nominated and the convention adjourned. He returned the horse, advising the stableman never to sell him to an undertaker.

"Why not?" the owner inquired.

Because, said the candidate, if the horse were hitched to a hearse, Resurrection Day would come before he reached the cemetery. "And so," Lincoln concluded, "if my journey goes on at this slow rate, it will be Resurrection Day before I reach the capital."[291]

Lincoln and his party reached Indianapolis on time at 5 p.m. and detrained at West Washington Street rather than Union Station so the parade would have a longer route. Conductor Whitney, who stayed on the train beyond State Line, later told brakeman Ross that after Lincoln got into a carriage, men got hold of the hubs and carried the vehicle for a whole block. The march ended at the Bates House, where the party spent the night amid much hoopla.

The president-elect's good friend Orville H. Browning joined the party here. The former state senator had planned to ride all the way, but had written earlier that day in his diary that "the trip to Indianapolis has been very pleasant, but is just about as much of that sort of thing as I want."[291] He planned to return home to Quincy the next day and wanted a

This New Jersey Railroad & Transportation Company train, posing at Point of Rocks, N.J., is similar to the special that forwarded Abraham Lincoln on that line toward his 1861 inauguration in Washington, D.C.

moment alone with Lincoln.

The traveler asked him to go over his inaugural address, which, along with several speeches organized in envelopes for towns along the way, was tucked away in Lincoln's black oilcloth gripsack that he had entrusted to Robert's care without telling him what was in it.

But the gripsack was not to be found. And neither was Robert. Lincoln was told his son was "off with the boys," [291] to which he ordered in reply to find him at once lest all those speeches fall into the hands of the press and the president-elect get scooped.

One tense hour later, Robert reported to his father and confessed that since no room had been provided for him, he had left the gripsack behind the hotel clerk's counter with the other luggage.

Horrified, Lincoln threw open his room door and elbowed his way through the crowd to the desk. A single stride carried him over the desk and he began frantically searching through the bags. The clerk was terrified; the crowd was wide-eyed. Lincoln put his key in the first gripsack that resembled his own, and out fell a deck of cards, a dirty shirt and some paper collars. The unexpected find was too much for Lincoln's dignity; he joined in the crowd's laughter.

Within moments he located his bag, and returned to his room informing Robert that from now on the gripsack would stay in his own possession.

Lincoln greeted the crowd at the hotel the next morning, breakfasted at the governor's mansion and addressed the Indiana Legislature before going to the station. It was Tuesday, Feb. 12.

The Indianapolis & Cincinnati Railroad had added three freshly varnished wooden coaches to the special; the entire train was now decorated with tri-color bunting and American flags. The new locomotive, the *Samuel Wiggins,* was covered with portraits of Lincoln and past presidents, and the sides were draped with flags and evergreen branches. Local delegations were directed to the first two coaches, members of the presidential party to the third, and the Lincoln family to the fourth.

Departure was at 11 a.m. The train crept along a drab industrial area and into the suburbs, with armed sentinels stationed every half-mile to ensure safety. Only after Lincoln finally entered his car did he find that Mary, Tad and Willie had joined him. They had been rushed to Indianapolis on an overnight run on the grounds that anyone would think twice about harming Lincoln with his family present. With moist eyes, he hugged the boys and kissed Mary, who wished

him a happy 52nd birthday—he had forgotten in the rush of things.

All day long, Lincoln greeted crowds at every stop and scanned newspapers placed on board to see how his trip was being covered. The reviews were good, except in Southern papers.

The I&C train entered Ohio & Mississippi trackage at Lawrenceburg on a trackage rights agreement and proceeded toward Cincinnati. At North Bend, Ohio, the president-elect went to the back platform, took off his stovepipe hat and bowed his head in respect as the train passed the grave of William Henry Harrison.

A few minutes after the scheduled time of 3 p.m., the train halted at the Ohio & Mississippi's station at the foot of 5th Street in Cincinnati. Another parade, more crowds, military escorts and band music ensued as the party made its way to the Burnet House at 3rd and Vine for a speech, dinner and overnight stay. After an evening of gaiety, Lincoln returned to his suite and became a family man again. As usual, Tad was dozing in a chair waiting for his daddy to put him in bed. The president-elect carried his little boy into the bedroom, receiving a half-awake smile as he undressed him, pulled the nightshirt over his head and tucked him in next to a sleeping Willie.

The next morning, Wednesday,

Feb. 13, Lincoln was full of foreboding. There were rumors of Southern plots to take over the capital, and besides, electoral votes were not to be counted until noon today and word had it that Lincoln's foes would seize the U.S. Capitol at that precise moment and keep him from being elected. Unknown to Lincoln, friends traveling with him were receiving messages about a plot on his life in the Baltimore area. Something would have to be done to protect him.

The Little Miami Railroad had provided a train of three coaches: for the press and railroad personnel, local committees and staff members, and the Lincoln family. Anson Stager, a Western Union superintendent, carried the all-important portable telegraph instrument. Rumors abounded. An effort had been made near State Line to derail the train and someone said a grenade was found in one of the coaches. Only newspaper talk, Lamon chided. The train left at 9 a.m.; Lincoln chatted with members of the press with a voice hoarse from speechmaking.

Xenia, Ohio, would be the dinner stop shortly before 1 p.m., but the party found that the prepared meal had been consumed by the crowd awaiting Lincoln. The passengers departed on the Columbus & Xenia line with empty stomachs.

At London, Lincoln spied some uniformed musicians and told them, "I perceive a band of music present, and while the iron horse stops to water himself, I would prefer they should discourse in their more eloquent music than I am capable of."[291] The people laughed, the band played and the train pulled out.

As the train approached Columbus just before 2 p.m., state Sen. James Monroe explained to Lincoln as he stood up that he was to take him by the arm and escort him to his carriage.

Seeing Lincoln's 6-foot-4 frame stretch itself, the senator added, "Although it is etiquette you should take 'my' arm, your stature makes that awkward, so we had better reverse the order."

Lincoln chuckled and agreed. "As for etiquette, I was never overburdened with it."[291]

The president-elect addressed the Ohio Legislature and spoke to several crowds. In the private office of Gov. William Dennison, he was handed a telegram that said, "The votes were counted peaceably. You are elected."

Looking up, Lincoln saw everyone watching him. Turning to Dennison, he said, "What a beautiful building you have here!" Everyone knew there had been no crisis in Washington.[291]

Thursday, Feb. 14, was rainy, but the mood of the official party and the spectators was buoyant as the trek continued. The Steubenville & Indiana's presidential special consisted of the locomotive *Washington City*, the baggage car and two coaches; officials having found that the more cars on the train, the more people wanted to ride. As the train proceeded via trackage rights on the Central Ohio to Newark, Lamon favored some younger riders with "Sparkin' on a Sunday" and "Dixey's Land" on his banjo. The rain failed to dampen anybody's enthusiasm at Newark, Frazeyburg, Dresden, Cochocton, Newcomerstown or Uhrichsville.

At Cadiz Junction, the entire party was treated to a dinner prepared by Mrs. T.L. Jewett, wife of the S&I's president, at the nearby Parks House. Afterward, Lincoln told a crowd from the back platform that he could not make a speech because he was "too full of utterance."[291] Leaving town, the president-elect scanned more newspapers.

The sun broke out just before the Steubenville stop, and at half-past two the train started northward on the Cleveland & Pittsburgh line along the Ohio River.

"God bless ye, Mister Lincoln," greeted an old man who pushed his way to the edge of the platform in Wellsville. "I didn't vote for ye, but I sure would like to shake yer paw."

Lincoln smiled and asked who received the gentleman's vote.

"Mister Dooglas," came the reply, to hearty laughter from the crowd.

"Well, my friend," Lincoln answered, "if you and the other friends of Mr. Douglas will help me keep the ship of state afloat for the next four years, then Mr. Douglas will have another chance. But if we allow it to go to pieces, Mr. Douglas will never get to be president."[291] Wild applause split the air as the train eased away.

The train was now venturing around a narrow finger of Virginia (which would be West Virginia's Northern Panhandle two years later) that separated Ohio from Pennsylvania. Faces on the train grew somber as they realized that slaveholding territory was just across the river, but if the president had any misgivings about being that close to southern soil, he didn't let on.

Tensions on the train dissipated as it crossed into Pennsylvania and approached Rochester. Though his hoarseness was worsening, he spoke to the crowd, saying that once he arrived in Washington, he would speak to all who would listen. A heckler piped up, "What will you do with the secessionists, then?" Sadness appeared in Lincoln's eyes as he turned toward the voice and responded: "My friend, that is a matter which I have under very grave consideration."[291]

Now on the Ohio & Pennsylvania line, the train made an unscheduled stop near Freedom, Pa., and passengers were told a freight derailment had blocked the track up ahead. Word quickly spread, and the whole town turned out to see the presidential party.

"Abe, you say you're the tallest man in the United States," a coal miner yelled. "But I don't believe you're any taller than I am.

Lincoln laughed heartily. "Come up here and let's measure," he challenged.

The miner, in dusty workclothes, climbed over the back railing and stood back-to-back with Lincoln. Col. Ellsworth, a stubby little man, climbed on the railing to referee, ran his hand over the two heads and announced that they were the same height. The contenders grinned and shook hands.[291]

The young agent/operator at Alleghany City was among the privileged few allowed on board Lincoln's car. "I shall never forget the deep impression which his towering form and his already-sad and always-kindly face made on me as he took my hand," the agent said.[364]

Arrival in Pittsburgh was at 7 p.m., two hours late. The rain had become a torrent, and a parade was canceled. Lincoln and his party ducked into a carriage to be taken to the Monongahela House. A frightened horse reared, its front hoofs coming perilously close to Lincoln's carriage, but he took no notice.

Friday, Feb. 15, was still rainy, but the crowd around the hotel that morning was Pittsburgh's largest ever. The O&P train hadn't arrived at the depot by the time its passengers did, and the crowd followed Lincoln inside the station. There was a lot of shoving, which amused more than annoyed the president-elect. A man passed his son over the heads of the people into Lincoln's arms, and the boy received a hearty kiss on the cheek. Three young women secured the same response, but repelled efforts of the younger members of the party to return the same favor. Lincoln laughed with everyone else.

The special—with baggage car and two coaches—was in place now and everyone took their places on board. For Lincoln's son Robert, that meant a thrilling ride in the cab of the locomotive *Comet,* where, under the direction of engineer Williamson, he would help manage the controls!

The train retraced its path to Rochester and, on the C&P again, to Wellsville, Ohio. At the latter stop, a division point, an old man pushed forward and handed Lincoln a highly polished red apple while the *Comet* was being replaced.

"Say, Mr. Lincoln," shouted a small boy at the edge of the crowd. "That man is running for postmaster!" The president-elect was amused.[291]

At Salineville and Bayard, Ohio, Lincoln just waved from the platform. His voice was so weak he felt he had to save it for the major stops. Conversation on board was held to a minimum; Lincoln made a few penciled notes, but was more interested in the game Willie and Tad were playing on the coach's floor.

During the dinner stop at Sourbeck's Hotel in Alliance—hosted by the C&P president, John McCullough—an artillery salute was fired too close to the building and Mrs. Lincoln was sprayed with flying glass from broken windows. No one was hurt.

Stops at Hudson and Ravenna preceded the arrival in Cleveland. The railroad had run excursions from Akron and Cuyahoga Falls to see Lincoln, and a throng of 6,000 elicited a raspy response from him.

It was almost dark when the special—drawn by the locomotive *Sam Hill*—slowed for Cleveland's Euclid Street depot, two miles from the center of town. Robert climbed down from the locomotive cab and rejoined his family, and the hoopla started all over again as the party made its way to Weddell House.

On Saturday morning, Feb. 16, the party departed at 9 a.m. from the Cleveland, Painesville & Ashtabula station.

"Ladies and gentlemen," Lincoln addressed the crowd at Painesville, "I have stepped upon this platform that I may see you and that you may see me, and in the arrangement I have the best of the bargain." Hilarious applause followed.[291]

Lincoln was barely audible at Ashtabula. "I can only say how do you do, and farewell," he croaked, "as my voice, you perceive, will warrant nothing more. I am happy to see so many pleasant faces around me and to be able to greet you as friends."[291]

As he turned to enter the coach, a woman asked for the first lady. "I should hardly hope to induce her to appear," he answered, smiling, "as I have always found it difficult to make her do what she did not want to."

At Conneaut, Lincoln whispered that his intentions were good and thanked the people for coming.

There was at least one occasion where trains failed to figure in Abraham Lincoln's life, through no fault of his own. When he was 8, the story goes, an 11-year-old friend named Austin Gollaher rescued young Abe from the flood-swollen Knob Creek near where they lived in what is now LaRue County, Ky. During his White House years, Lincoln invited his old friend up for a visit, but Gollaher declined because he was afraid to ride trains![452]

Abraham Lincoln arrives at Frederick, Md., in October 1862 to inspect Union troops and confer with his military staff.

Someone shouted, "Don't give up the ship!" And he responded, "With your aid, I never will as long as life lasts."[291]

Horace Greeley, the noted "go West, young man" newspaper editor and a political ally of Lincoln's at the time, unexpectedly boarded at Girard, Pa., and left the train at Erie while the Erie & North East engine was being coupled on, to deliver a lecture. Dinner was served upstairs in the station.

The train followed the E&NE to the New York line, then the Buffalo & State Line Railroad. As he made his way to Buffalo, Lincoln's mind surely must have been on a very special letter he had received the previous October. Little Grace Bedell of Westfield, N.Y., had written to Lincoln that he would look better if he grew whiskers. Thinking he wouldn't have time to reply, Grace had said a letter from

Lincoln's daughter would suffice. Lincoln himself had responded on Oct. 19, telling her he had no daughter. "As to the whiskers," he continued, "having never worn any, do you not think people would call it a piece of silly affectation if I should begin it now?"[44]

When the train stopped in Westfield, at Lincoln's prompting an aide called out to see if the little girl was in the crowd. She was, and the crowd parted to allow her to timidly approach the president-elect, who told her that he had grown whiskers at her request. Then he reached out his long arms, bent down and kissed her.

From Buffalo, Capt. Hazzard wrote his wife:

"Horace Greeley came with us yesterday from Conneaut to Erie. He talks very much like a Quaker. ... We came into Cleveland through Euclid Street, and the scene was gorgeous. ... Do you recall the finest house in that street, in fact the finest in Ohio? A brownstone Gothic, with observatory and spires on the roof? It is on the side of the street near the lake, and is the residence of Mr. Stone, president of the Lake Shore [CP&A] Railroad. Col. Sumner, Judge Davis, Mr. Lamon and myself dined there on Friday evening. ... There was a terrible jam at the depot yesterday. Mr. Hunter came very near having his arm broken. ...

"Every village sends a reception committee of twenty or thirty and some of them bring their wives, so that not only are all the seats in the car taken, but the passageway is filled with people standing. Neither the president nor his wife has one moment's respite and they are evidently tired of it. ... It is probable that we will be in Baltimore on Saturday, the 22nd. ..."[197]

Former President Millard Fillmore greeted Lincoln upon his arrival at Buffalo's Exchange Street Station. The crowd was dense; a military guard dislocated a shoulder while shielding the white-haired former chief executive and his lanky new boss. Lincoln spoke to a crowd at the American House, despite the noise from a man, who, in losing an election bet, had to saw up a half cord of wood in front of the hotel and give it to the poorest family in the city.

Travel was suspended over the Lord's Day, being considered inappropriate at the time. Fillmore took the Lincolns to church, then home for dinner. Most of the president-elect's day was spent in relaxation, including a round of presidential leapfrog with the boys at the hotel.

On a snowy Monday, Feb. 18, everyone stirred before daylight to make a 5:45 a.m. departure on the New York Central. Once again, Robert was invited into the locomotive cab.

Lincoln continued showing his down-home friendliness across New York State. At Rochester, he admonished a small boy who climbed up on the rear platform just as the train started to be careful jumping off while it was moving. At Syracuse, he declined to mount a substantial platform from which to speak, saying it was too much for his few words, joking that "though I am unwilling to go upon this platform, you are not at liberty to draw any inferences concerning any other platform with which my name has been or is connected."[291]

Heavy snow fell as a picnic lunch was brought aboard for the presidential party to consume enroute, very likely the first meal eaten by a president-elect on a train. He addressed the crowd at Utica from a flatcar.

Once out of town, Mrs. Lincoln summoned from the baggage car a new broadcloth overcoat and hat she had bought for her husband, saying he could throw away the worn overcoat and weather-beaten stovepipe hat he had been wearing. Lincoln obeyed, and shortly *The New York Times* said he looked 50 percent better and commended him for following his wife's counsel.

At Schenectady, a celebrating cannon misfired, hitting the train and breaking out windows and a door. Lincoln was nonplussed. Albany was attained at 2:20, and the crowd was so rowdy Lincoln had to wait for military reinforcements so he could leave the train. His parade to the Capitol passed a theater where actor John Wilkes Booth was starring in *The Apostate*, and after dinner at the executive mansion, Lincoln returned to the Delavan House for two receptions and a night's rest. Lincoln's mind probably wasn't in Albany, however; he had been advised that in Montgomery, Ala., that afternoon, Jefferson Davis had been inaugurated as president of the newly formed Confederate States of America. The nation was now formally divided. Was civil war inevitable?

Departure from Albany on Tuesday, Feb. 19, involved a detour. A sudden thaw had sent ice floes down the Hudson, rendering the ferry to the east bank inoperable. The train, departing at about 8 behind the locomotive *L.H. Tupper,* traveled north on the Albany & Vermont line, being operated by the Rensselaer & Saratoga Railroad Company, to Waterford Jct., thence via the R&S proper to Green Island, crossing the Troy Union Railroad Company bridge, the only railroad span across the Hudson, into Troy.

At that point, the passengers transferred to a new train provided by the Hudson River line. The rear car had been built especially for Lincoln, with lounges and armchairs designed for his comfort. It had heaters, ventilators and four wax-candle chandeliers with cut-glass globes provided illumination.

The train left East Albany pulled by the locomotive *Union* to Poughkeepsie and the *Constitution* to New York, both 4-4-0's. Stops were made enroute at Hudson, Rhinebeck, Poughkeepsie, Fishkill and Peekskill, where Lincoln made short speeches. Extra employees guarded the track all along the way. Aboard in addition to

HR President Samuel Sloan was William Creamer, who had invented a safety brake with which the cars were equipped.

At Poughkeepsie, the crowd spotted Mary, who opened her coach window and returned the salutation. Then they wanted to see the boys. Robert and Willie dutifully walked to the window, but Tad fell on the floor and refused to budge. Mary apologized that the "pet of the family" didn't want to be put on exhibition.[291]

The train arrived at 3 p.m. on the 19th at the Thirtieth Street Station in New York City, which was opened for business several weeks early for the occasion. Lincoln's two-day stay was at the Astor House and he was given elaborate police protection. During a parade, Lincoln gratefully noticed a banner across 8th Avenue reading "Fear not, Abraham, I am thy shield and thy exceeding great strength," a paraphrase of Genesis 15:1.

On Wednesday evening, Vice President-elect Hannibal Hamlin and his wife joined the official party, and a quiet dinner was arranged so that the Lincolns and the Hamlins might become better acquainted.

The atmosphere was a little stilted until a plate of oysters on the half shell was placed before each guest. Looking quizzically at the oysters, the homespun Lincoln remarked, "Well, I don't know that I can manage these things, but I guess I can learn."[291] That put everyone at ease and the dinner party was pleasant. That night the Lincolns attended an opera.

At 8 a.m. on Thursday, Feb. 21, an hour early in only a partly successful ploy to avoid the crowd, the Lincolns departed New York via the Cortlandt Street ferry, using a new, handsomely decorated boat named the *John P. Jackson*. The locomotive *William Pennington* of the New Jersey Railroad & Transportation Company hauled the special from Jersey City to New Brunswick, where the Camden & Amboy took charge to Trenton. Snow changed to sunshine there at 11:50 a.m., where a buffet lunch was enjoyed at the Trenton House. Arriving at the Philadelphia & Trenton's Kensington depot in Philadelphia at 4 p.m., the party spent the night at the Continental Hotel.

Lincoln's party grew increasingly restless as southern soil drew closer, with good reason. Plans had called for the train to proceed via the Pennsylvania Railroad to Harrisburg, Northern Central to Baltimore, and B&O to Washington. But the ill feeling was growing toward Lincoln even then and rumors of plots against him grew more persistent.

One, a plan to wreck the train, was whispered to his men as he addressed members of the Pennsylvania Legislature. The hushed disclosure claimed that the Northern Central's line had been mined and its bridges weakened, and that armed men lay in the bushes waiting for the train to derail so they could rush in and either kill the passengers or take them prisoner.

Another conspiracy uncovered by railroad detective Allan Pinkerton, whose minions had infiltrated a bunch of militant Southerners in Baltimore, had Lincoln being gunned down during the transfer from NC's Calvert Street Station to B&O's Camden Station in that city.

Pinkerton, who had arrived from Baltimore after discovering the plot, and Norman Judd, Lincoln's friend who had ridden from Illinois with him and who had been in quiet contact with Pinkerton by telegraph, confronted Lincoln in Judd's hotel room and advised him to enter Washington by another route secretly.

At first Lincoln scoffed.

"What would the nation think of its president stealing into the capital like a thief in the night?" he asked.[197]

Lincoln finally capitulated, but only if his friends delayed the plan until his visit in Harrisburg, which would fulfill all his speaking obligations. The alternate plan was perfected; the next morning Lincoln spoke at Independence Hall as scheduled and the train left for Harrisburg.

That night, after an afternoon address to the legislature and during a dinner at the Jones House, a "message" was brought to Lincoln and he quickly left. The crowd was told Lincoln had been suddenly taken ill, but at that moment—with only Lamon and Pinkerton—he was sneaking out of the hotel in his old overcoat, a green shawl over his arm and a soft wool hat given to him in New York City instead of the familiar stovepipe model.

The trio rode a swift PRR one-car special back to West Philadelphia, where the three transferred to the Philadelphia, Wilmington & Baltimore station at Broad and Prime streets to board the PW&B's 11 p.m. express to Baltimore. The detour had been personally arranged by presidents Thomas A. Scott of the PRR and Samuel M. Felton of the PW&B, after which all telegraph lines were cut by the railroads to maintain secrecy.

Felton told H.P. Kenney, PW&B's general superintendent, that a "valuable package"[68] was to go through on the night train of Feb. 22. Conductor Litsenburg was informed that, under no circumstances, was he to start his train until the package had been delivered personally into his hands. Felton was to be advised of the delivery of the package at the Willard Hotel in Washington the following morning.

The package, consisting of nothing more than a packet of old railroad reports, was handed to Litsenburg as

B&O locomotive 42 rests at Mount Clare in Baltimore in 1863, the year Abraham Lincoln took a train to Gettysburg, Pa.

his train stood in the station. Just before that moment, a tall man wrapped in an overcoat and green shawl, drooping as if ill, had alighted from a carriage and entered the train's sleeper. As he handed Litsenburg the tickets that provided for the transport of himself, his two companions and a woman working with them, the conductor lightly remarked, "Well, old man, it's lucky for you that we've got to wait for some dispatches; we're half an hour late now." The tall man—Lincoln—smiled.[197]

The president-elect was well guarded in that sleeper—not only by Pinkerton and Lamon, but also by one unknown to them, George Stearns of the railroad's own forces. As the train departed, the conductor drew Stearns aside and said to him: "George, I thought we were old friends. Why didn't you tell me we had Old Abe aboard?" Stearns, thinking the secret had been leaked, acknowledged the special passenger and asked Litsenburg to share his responsibility. "Yes," replied the conductor, "I will, if it costs me my life." So the two watched through the night, one at each door of the car.[197]

It turned out afterward that Litsenburg had mistaken his man. A person strongly resembling Lincoln had boarded the train a half-hour before it started; and this man the conductor had mistaken for the president-elect.

There were two likely danger spots—at Havre de Grace, Md., where the cars had to be taken across the Susquehanna River individually by ferry, and Baltimore, where they would be transferred, again individually, by horsepower from PW&B's President Street Station to B&O's Camden Station, a mile away.

Pinkerton anxiously surveyed the darkness at Havre de Grace from the sleeper's platform, but a prearranged lantern signal from one of his agents on the ground told him everything was all right and the transfer was accomplished without incident. A little after 3 a.m. on Saturday, Feb. 23, the express's cars were transferred along Baltimore's Pratt Street. There were still people in the streets when Lincoln passed through, but the city was loaded with Southern sympathizers and any crowds could have been unfriendly. So no one locally—not

even railroad employees— knew of the famous passenger as his train made its nightly meander down the street. Lincoln was unable to sleep in the short berth, but stayed behind the curtain and remained quiet. The only exception to ordinary practice were orders that the train not miss the connection from Philadelphia, which it apparently sometimes did.

There was one anxious moment. The reassembled train did not start out as it should have, and the men could hear people outside milling about and singing. Were the conspirators out there, waiting for a signal to rush the sleeper?

Finally, the conductor informed them they were waiting on passengers riding a train from the West; it was late and no one knew when it would arrive. After an hour, the delayed passengers burst into the car and, in a day before reserved space, looked for empty berths. Pinkerton fretted; he feared that one of those passengers might be an assassin.

This train was pulled by B&O 25, the American type 4-4-0 later known as the *William Mason*, an 1856 locomotive still preserved in the

B&O Railroad Museum in Baltimore. This trip wasn't the *Mason's* only claim to fame—93 years later, in one of those ironies of history, it played the part of the Civil War locomotive *General* in Walt Disney's *The Great Locomotive Chase.*

Elihu B. Washburne, in whom William Seward had confided plans for the secret detour, recalled the arrival in Washington about daylight that Saturday morning: "I planted myself behind one of the great pillars in the old Washington and Baltimore depot [the B&O station at New Jersey Avenue and C Street] where I could see and not be observed. Presently the train came rambling in. ... I could not mistake the long, lank form of Mr. Lincoln, and my heart bounded with joy and gratitude. ... When [Lincoln, Lamon and Pinkerton] were fairly on the platform, a short distance from the car, I stepped forward and accosted the president: 'How are you, Mr. Lincoln?' At this unexpected and somewhat familiar salutation, the gentlemen were apparently somewhat startled, [Lamon reached for his pistol and Pinkerton raised his fist] but Mr. Lincoln, who recognized me, relieved them at once by remarking in his peculiar voice, 'This is only Washburne.'

Then we all exchanged congratulations and walked out to the front of the depot, where I had a carriage in waiting. Entering the carriage, we drove rapidly to Willard's Hotel, entered on 14th Street, before it was fairly daylight.[197]

Railroad President Felton hadn't slept that night. The telegraph wires between Philadelphia and Baltimore were rejoined at 8 a.m., after which the first words they bore from Washington were: "Your package has arrived safely and has been delivered."[197]

Mrs. Lincoln and the boys followed the itinerary as laid down for the presidential party. A telegram, "plums delivered nuts safely"—of which the code translation was "Lincoln's in Washington"—reached her Saturday morning at the breakfast table in her hotel in Harrisburg to her great relief.[197] The coming day dispelled the rumors of danger, and the special came through quickly and easily. The connection between the NC and B&O was handled in similar fashion to that with the PW&B; i.e., horses pulling the cars singly on a track along Howard Street from the NC's Bolton Station to B&O's Camden. Baltimore was disappointed not to have seen Lincoln, and rowdies angry at being fooled gave Mrs. Lincoln and the boys a scare as they shouted expletives and tried to pry open coach windows. Washington was reached without further incident.

Most of Lincoln's travels during his term of office centered around the Civil War and the need for inspections of Union troops and military installations. Many of these trips were made by horse, carriage or boat. A few included rail travel.

On Sept. 30, 1862, shortly after the Battle of Antietam, Lincoln left Washington for Gen. George B. McClellan's headquarters via B&O to find out why the sluggish general had not pressed his advantage against the enemy. The Army of the Potomac was now quartered along the Potomac River and Lincoln arrived at Harpers Ferry, Va., on Oct. 1. On the 4th, he left for Frederick, Md., stopping at several encampments on the way.

Gen. O.O. Howard recalled a bit of humor during the Harpers Ferry review. "As the generals and handsome staff officers escorted the president near to my front, I joined the reviewing party. Mr. Lincoln rode along in silence, returning the salutes. ... Suddenly we saw a little engine named *The Flying Dutchman* fly past us on a railroad track. Mr. Lincoln seeing it and hearing a shrill, wild scream from its saluting whistle, laughed aloud. He doubtless was

---

Gen. W.W. Blair, in command of Baltimore's defenses, was unable to join the military brass presenting themselves to Abraham Lincoln on his way to Gettysburg because he was suffering from boils. The report gave rise to a conversation between Lincoln and Francis Blair, his postmaster general

"Blair," the president said in a mischievous tone, "did you ever know that fright has sometimes proved a sure cure for boils?"

"No, Mr. President," Blair answered. "How is that?"

"I'll tell you. Not long ago, when Col. _____, with his cavalry, was at the front, and the 'rebs' were making things rather lively for us, the colonel was ordered out on a reconnaissance. He was troubled at the time with a big boil where it made horseback riding decidedly uncomfortable. He hadn't gone more than two or three miles when he declared he couldn't stand it any longer, and dismounted and ordered his troops forward without him. He had just settled down to enjoy his relief from change of position when he was startled by the rapid reports of pistols and the helter-skelter approach of his troops in full retreat before a yelling rebel force. He forgot everything but the yells, sprang into his saddle, and made capital time over fences and ditches till safe within the lines. The pain from his boil was gone, and the boil, too, and the colonel swore that there was no cure for boils so sure as fright from rebel yells, and that the secession had rendered to loyalty one valuable service at any rate."[364]

thinking of John Brown's terrorism of a few years before, for we were near the famous engine-house where John Brown was finally penned up and made prisoner; for, referring to the locomotive, Mr. Lincoln said: 'They ought to call that thing *The Skeared Virginian.'* " [364]

Lincoln's most noted wartime trip was to Gettysburg, Pa., for consecration of the National Soldiers' Cemetery after one of the conflict's most decisive battles had been fought there.

In the five months after the engagement, the battlefield had been cleaned up, the bodies assembled, identified when possible and decently buried. A prompt dedication was felt prudent and Lincoln was invited even though the chief oration of the day was to be delivered by former Sen. Edward Everett of Massachusetts.

William Prescott Smith, master of transportation for B&O, wrote to J.N. DuBarry, superintendent of the Northern Central, on Nov. 8, saying:

"Mr. Lincoln and a portion of the Cabinet expect to go to the Gettysburg Consecration, and have sent to me making inquiries as to the route and facilities.

"Will you take them up in our private cars, through from Washington, if we will deliver them to you at Bolton? How near to Gettysburg can you take them by rail? Which is the best route—by Hanover or Westminster? Please answer promptly. I will confer with you further about details, after the route is determined."

DuBarry replied at once by telegraph: "Message received. Will be most happy to take your cars with party mentioned. Route, Baltimore to Hanover Jct. by NC Railway, thence to the town of Gettysburg by Hanover Branch Road. Westminster is not on the route. Advise me fully of time, etc., as early as possible to make all necessary arrangements." [197]

B&O President John W. Garrett added his own warning to Smith on Nov. 18, 1863, the day of departure:

"Supt. DuBarry's telegram of 17th inst. indicates a design to attend thoroughly to the president and suite. You will of course see fully to having Howard Street clear, and that all arrangements upon our line are as perfect as possible for the comfort, safety and rapidity of movement of the party. Be very vigilant regarding an understanding for their return. Have this point understood as early as practicable, and be specially careful to have the street track clear for them, and your arrangements made so that there will be no cause for complaint." [197]

At 12:10 p.m. that day, Lincoln left Washington "a day early instead of on the morning of the dedication, an idea that Lincoln had dismissed as "a mere breathless running of the gauntlet." [364]

As it turned out, Lincoln was late arriving at the station. Provost Marshall Gen. James B. Fry came as a War Department escort to the Executive Mansion but the president was slow about getting into the carriage. They had no time to lose, Fry remarked. Lincoln said he felt like an Illinois man who was going to be hanged. As the man passed along the road on the way to the gallows, the crowds kept pushing into the way and blocking passage. The condemned man at last called out, "Boys, you needn't be in such a hurry to get ahead; there won't be any fun 'til I get there!" [364]

Flags and red-white-and-blue bunting decorated the four-car special. Joining Lincoln were Seward, his secretary of state; John P. Usher, secretary of the interior; Postmaster General Francis P. Blair Jr.; the French and Italian ministers and their attaches; members of Congress; Capt. Henry A. Wise and his wife, who was Everett's daughter; Lincoln's secretaries John G. Nicolay and John Hay; newspapermen; and the redoubtable Col. Lamon, who always made it his business to protect the president's life with his own.

The rear third of the last coach—a directors' car—had a drawing room with seats around the walls, where from time to time the president talked with nearly everyone on board as they came and went. Marine Lt. Henry Clay Cochrane noted:

"I happened to have a *New York Herald* and offered it to Mr. Lincoln. He took it and thanked me, saying, 'I like to see what they say about us.' The news was about Gens. A.E. Burnside at Knoxville, Ulysses S. Grant and William T. Sherman at Chattanooga and George G. Meade on the Rapidan, all expecting trouble. He read for a little while and then began to laugh at some wild guesses in the paper about troop movements. It was pleasant to see his sad face lighted up. He was looking sallow, sunken-eyed, thin, care-worn and very quiet. He returned the paper, remarking among other things that when he had first passed over the B&O road on his way to Congress in 1847, he noticed square-rigged vessels up the Patapsco River as far as the Relay House and now there seemed to be only small craft.

"...Secretary Seward began to get uneasy as we approached Baltimore. Upon reaching the [Camden] Station [at 1:20 p.m.], all was quiet, less than 200 people assembled, among them women with children in arms. They called for the president. He took two or three of the babies up and kissed them, which greatly pleased the mothers." [334]

Here the train was met by Garrett, Smith and NC's president,

This U.S. Military Railroad locomotive was in service during the days that Abraham Lincoln visited Gen. Ulysses S. Grant's headquarters at City Point, Va., in the spring of 1865.

J.D. Cameron. The Marine Band piled off and played a selection while the locomotive was being replaced by the horses that would transfer the cars.

All the way up Howard Street, the sidewalks were thronged with orderly but enthusiastic crowds. Lincoln came to the platform repeatedly and acknowledged the cheers. The pleasure of that hour showed on his face. At the Bolton depot, there was more cheering and as the train, together again behind a locomotive, moved off about 2 p.m., Lincoln came to the door a final time, lifted his great hat to the populace and kissed two or three of the children. That was to be his last—almost his only—public

appearance in Baltimore.

At Baltimore a baggage car had been added to the train, in which a luncheon had been prepared. Upon departure, everyone was invited in to dine.

The train was passing through a cut as Lincoln sat at the head of a table, making the car darker and noisier than usual.

"This situation," he said, "reminds me of a friend of mine in southern Illinois, who, riding over a corduroy road where the logs were not sufficiently close together, was frightened by a thunderstorm. In the glimpse of light afforded by the lightning, his horse would endeavor to reach another log, but too frequently missed it, and fell with his rider. As a result of

several such mishaps, the traveler, although not accustomed to prayer, thought that the time had come to address his Maker, and said, 'Oh, Lord, if it would suit you equally well, it would suit me better if I had a little more light and a little less noise.' "[364]

Lt. Cochrane continued: "Gen. [Robert C.] Schenck [commander of federal forces in Baltimore] and staff joined us, and soon after the president went forward in the car and seated himself with a party of choice spirits. ... They told stories for an hour or so, Mr. Lincoln taking his turn and enjoying it. Approaching Hanover Jct., he arose and said, 'Gentlemen, this is all very pleasant, but the people will expect me to say something to them

This view of the Union troops' storehouse and construction camp at City Point, Va., shows the coach Lincoln used to visit that city in the spring of 1865.

tomorrow, and I must give the matter some thought.' He then returned to the rear room of the car."[334]

The story goes that he wrote his speech aboard the train, but the fact is he began his first draft several days before the trip. The first page was on Executive Mansion stationery. But he probably polished the remarks both on the train and after arriving in Gettysburg. One account says a rough piece of foolscap—large, course paper—was handed to him on the train and he retired to a seat by himself in the private compartment to write "or polish" the speech. Lt. Col. Scully later said Lincoln held the same sheet as he delivered the address.

An elderly gentleman got on the train and, shaking hands, told the president he had lost a son at Little Round Top at Gettysburg. The president answered that he feared a visit to that spot would open fresh wounds, and yet if the end of sacrifice had been reached, "we could give thanks even amidst our tears."[334]

The encounter put Lincoln in a morose mood. "When I think of the sacrifices of life yet to be offered, and the hearts and homes yet to be made desolate before this dreadful war is over, my heart is like lead within me, and I feel at times like hiding in deep darkness," he lamented.[334]

At one stop, a little girl who was lifted to an open window thrust a bunch of rosebuds into the car.

"Flowerth for the prethident," she said. Lincoln stepped over, bent down and kissed her face. "You are a little rosebud yourself," he smiled.[334]

At Hanover Jct., 46 miles north of Baltimore, Lincoln's train was supposed to meet a special due out of Harrisburg at 1:30 p.m., but an accident had delayed it. The president's train was then to proceed alone, but military movements—which were always given the right of way—delayed it again at that station, for eight minutes, and at several others.

Upon arriving in Gettysburg at 6:30 p.m., Lincoln spoke modestly and informally to the crowds for a few moments, then yielded to Everett, whose presence had been much heralded. Excursion trains brought folks in from many miles around. Hotels and private homes were filled to overflowing, and finally churches were opened up so men and women could sleep in their pews.

The president spent the night with David Wills, where he revised and rewrote the first draft, then wrote out a third draft the following morning which he read at the dedication—an address that has come to be regarded as one of history's briefest and greatest.

After Everett's long oration and Lincoln's following remarks, which the press mostly ignored, the crowds left for home. But no trains were allowed to leave before Lincoln's did at 7 p.m. Lincoln waved from the back platform until the town was out of sight.

Bolton was reached at 11, but the trip through Baltimore was quiet and unheralded. The weary president was plagued with a headache. He stayed in his car, stretching out on one of the side seats in his drawing room and had a wet towel laid across his eyes and forehead. The special left Camden Station at 11:30 and arrived at Washington a little after 1 a.m. All the president's men breathed easier. Secretary of the Navy Gideon Welles said the president returned from his trip ill, with a "light form" of "the varioloid," that "held on longer than was expected."[364]

The Lincolns were away from Washington for an extended period during the spring of 1865, visiting Gen. Ulysses S. Grant's headquarters at City Point, Va., on the James River. Much of the time, they traveled on water, but there were some rail journeys.

On March 24, news arrived at the headquarters of an engagement in which Union forces were successful and Lincoln determined to visit the scene.

"A special train was made up about noontime" the next day, recalled Naval Capt. [John S.] Barnes. "With a large party, we slowly proceeded over the Military Railroad, roughly constructed between City Point and the front, to Gen. Meade's headquarters. On our arrival there, and indeed before we reached the scene, while we were passing through a portion of the field of battle, the very serious nature of the conflict of that morning became apparent.

"The Confederates under Gen. [John B.] Gordon, at early daylight, had made a swift and sudden assault upon our lines of investment at Petersburg, had captured Fort Stedman and several other batteries, with many persons, including a general officer, and driven our men back close to and over the railroad embankment upon which our train was then halted. The ground immediately about us was still strewn with dead and wounded men, Federal and Confederate. The whole army was under arms and moving to the left, where the fight was still going on, and a desultory firing of both musketry and artillery was seen and heard."[364]

Lincoln and Meade toured the carnage by horseback, hearing the cries and groans of the wounded and dying.

"Once again on the train," Barnes continued, "to which cars filled with our wounded men had been attached, Mr. Lincoln looked worn and haggard. He remarked that he had seen enough of the horrors of war, that he hoped this was the beginning of the end, and that there would be no more bloodshed or ruin of homes."[364]

The train returned to City Point, and Lincoln, declining an invitation to take supper with Grant, repaired to his vessel.

On April 2, after Grant had moved his headquarters to Petersburg, nine miles away, the general sent a telegram to Lincoln informing him that the city was secure and inviting him to come see for himself.

The president departed from City Point on a special train consisting only of an engine and car on Monday, April 3. One of the party, a French marquis, has left behind his recollections.

"Our car was an ordinary American car, and we took seats in its center, grouping ourselves around Mr. Lincoln. In spite of the car's being devoted to Mr. Lincoln's special use, several officers also took their places in it without attracting any remark. Curiosity, it seems, also had induced the Negro waiters of the *River Queen* [Lincoln's boat] to accompany us. The president, who was blinded by no prejudices against race or color, and who had not what can be termed false dignity, allowed them to sit quietly with us.

"For several miles, the train followed the outer line of federal fortifications which extended at our left; we were a half hour without noticing them; at the end of that time we reached a place known as Fort Stedman; there a battle had been fought less than a fortnight before. ... Since then, however, both armies had buried their dead and carried away their wounded. The ground, foot-trodden and here and there broken up by the wheels of artillery wagons, had retained no other traces of a past so recent and so terrible.

"Farther on, we crossed the Confederate lines of defense that had protected Petersburg. Soon Petersburg loomed up in the distance. Mr. Lincoln gazed awhile on its first houses, which had been partly destroyed by Federal bullets. When we had passed these, the train slackened its speed; it had been hardly possible to open us a path through the mass of ruins; at our left the depot buildings were torn down, on the right the railroad bridge had been wrenched by the explosion of a mine."[364]

A correspondent covered Lincoln's arrival at Patrick Station, about a mile from town. "I heard the whistle of the locomotive on the military railroad," he wrote, "and saw the train which brought President Lincoln to the scene. The soldiers saw him, swung their hats and gave a yell of delight. He lifted his hat and bowed. Perhaps I was mistaken, but the lines upon his face seemed far deeper than I had ever seen them before. There was no sign of exultation in his demeanor."[364]

As occupied as he was, Lincoln still had time for a little boy—the son of a slave. The ragged urchin was among those who pressed against the cars to see the president. He ventured into the coach, and in replying to several questions, used the word "tote."

"Tote?" Lincoln remarked. "What do you mean by 'tote'?"

"Why, massa," the child answered, "to tote 'um on your back."

"Very definite, my son," the president said. "I presume when you tote a thing, you carry it. By the way, Sumner," he continued, turning to Gen. Edwin V. Sumner, "what is the origin of 'tote'?" Thereupon, the two engaged in a lighthearted but thorough analysis of its usage.[214]

After a conference with Grant, Lincoln returned to City Point on his train. At one point when it was moving slowly, the president spied a terrapin basking in the warm sunshine near the right of way. He had the conductor stop the train and send a brakeman to bring the terrapin to Tad. Its movements seemed to delight both father and son, who amused themselves with it until the train reached the presidential steamer docked on the James River.[214]

From City Point, he sailed to Richmond, where he sat for a while in an office chair occupied until recently by Confederate President Jefferson Davis. Then he returned to City Point briefly before boarding another special train for Petersburg. He traveled from there to Washington by steamer, arriving home on the 10th.

Four days later, John Wilkes Booth's bullet had done its fatal work.

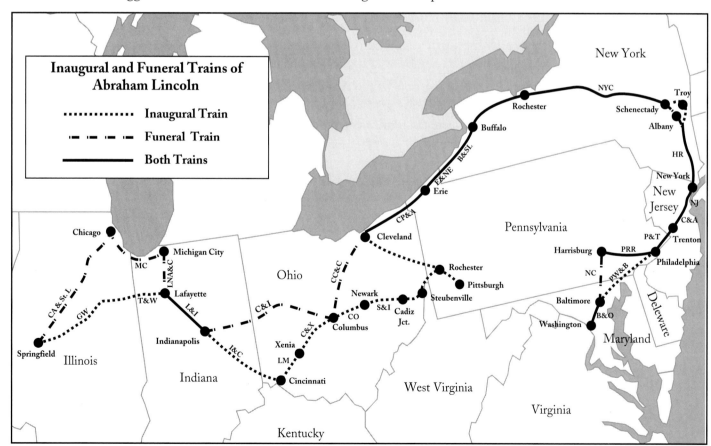

Map shows the routes Abraham Lincoln took to his inauguration and, four years later, back to Springfield, Ill., for his burial.

President Rutherford B. Hayes travels on the PRR March 1, 1877, from Columbus, Ohio, to his inauguration. Here, at Newark, Ohio, he reads a telegram apprising him of the progress of the electoral vote count, which was in doubt until 4 a.m. the next day as his train neared Harrisburg, Pa.

The Reconstruction Era

3

Andrew Johnson

Because Andrew Johnson of Tennessee was Lincoln's second vice president, the events of April 14, 1865, changed the course of his life, too, propelling him unelected into the Executive Mansion. Johnson was the first chief executive to cast aside pre-cedent and take to the campaign trail

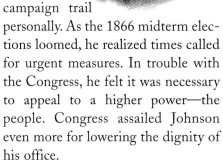

personally. As the 1866 midterm elections loomed, he realized times called for urgent measures. In trouble with the Congress, he felt it was necessary to appeal to a higher power—the people. Congress assailed Johnson even more for lowering the dignity of his office.

On Aug. 28, 1866, he boarded a special train in Washington to begin a 19-day, 10-state "swing around the circle." The gamble didn't pay off; Wall Street lawyer George Templeton Strong—more in sorrow than sarcasm—labeled the misadventure "Andrew Johnson's Adventures in Blunderland."[339]

The stated reason for Johnson's journey was not political; he was invited to dedicate a monument to Stephen A. Douglas in Chicago. Prominent Wall Street businessmen followed up with an invitation for Johnson to accept the tribute of a civic banquet in New York City on his way west. Other doors opened that generated a grueling schedule for the best of men.

Reaction to the plan was a mix of curiosity and censure. The president was known not to have an overabundance of tact, and his easy excitability before a crowd prompted fears of a loss of dignity and twisted press reports. "You are followed by the reporters of a hundred presses who do nothing but misrepresent you," advised Sen. James R. Doolittle of Wisconsin. "I would say nothing which has not been most carefully prepared, beyond a simple acknowledgement for their cordial reception. Our enemies, your enemies, have never been able to get any advantage from anything you ever wrote. But what you have said extemporaneously, in answer to some question or interruption, has given them a handle to use against you."[399]

The president ignored this rebuff and others. What could be more undignified, he thought, than giving place to a slanderer without a word in reply? That's not the way things were done in his native Tennessee.

William H. Seward, whom Johnson retained as secretary of state, was sure Johnson would do well, and Secretary of the Navy Gideon Welles was equally sure radicals would try to blow up the train. He insisted Seward go along, which the latter planned to do until at the last minute his wife was taken ill.

The party included Gen. Ulysses S. Grant and Admiral David G. Farragut, seven other generals including George Custer, another admiral, two surgeons, the secretaries of state and Navy and, part of the way, Johnson's new postmaster general, Alexander Randall. Martha Patterson accompanied her presidential father, as did her senator-husband, David T.

Patterson of Tennessee. Mexico's minister to the United States was aboard, as were several wives of the distinguished guests, two presidential secretaries and a brigade of newspaper correspondents.

The B&O train departed at 7:30 a.m., with the president—looking trim in a well-fitting black broadcloth coat—in good spirits. His special carried a baggage car and three coaches, and the run to Baltimore was made in 90 minutes. Perhaps 100,000 people greeted the arrival, prompting even an opposition paper to term the crowd "simply enormous." Johnson tried to speak, but was drowned out by cheers.

Philadelphia, reached via the PW&B shortly before 3 p.m., had refused to plan a civic reception and the mayor saw to it he was away on vacation, but a massive welcome was generated privately. Gen. George G. Meade and a military delegation took Johnson to the Continental Hotel for a speech on national unity and an overnight stay. The streets were garnished with flags and streamers.

The next day, Johnson's Camden & Amboy special was met by enthusi-

THOMAS W. DIXON JR. COLLECTION

This Pullman palace car catered to the sleepy traveler about the time that President Andrew Johnson made his "swing around the circle" in 1866.

astic crowds at every stop across New Jersey. Shortly after noon, prominent New Yorkers took him across the Hudson to Manhattan on a chartered ferry for a mayoral greeting in Battery Park. There were parades, military reviews, speeches. Johnson eloquently badgered Congress for wanting to punish the South by withholding representation in that body.

"The Son of God," he intoned to uninterrupted applause, "when he descended and found men condemned under the law, instead of executing the law, put himself in their stead and died for them. If I have erred in pardoning (the South), I trust God I have erred on the right side."[399]

On Aug. 30, the presidential party steamed up the Hudson to Albany on the yacht *River Queen,* stopping to review cadets of the U.S. Military Academy at West Point. By the time Johnson faced another friendly crowd at the state capital, the press began to notice a device that would give campaigners cause for concern in the following century. The president was making the same speech over and over, with slight variations. He had done this in rural Tennessee when papers were fewer and more narrowly circulated. But now his words were being read by millions every day, and some of the stereotyped phrases were taking on a ludicrous tone.

Nonetheless, the president was succeeding, and that rankled the anti-Union radicals. They moved in with a vengeance. The papers they controlled started mimicking Johnson as he struck out on the New York Central across the state to Buffalo. Large crowds along the way were attributed to curiosity, and the president was belittled for his "egotistic and self-glorifying harangues," because of his frequent references to "my policy," his repeated use of the personal pronoun "I" and his cataloging of offices he had moved

through before attaining the presidency. They jumped on his grammatical slips, concluding that "the president continues to make himself ridiculous and to disgust sensible people."[399]

There were other problems, too. As the train neared Buffalo, Grant was tipping the bottle a bit much, and Mrs. Farragut complained that he was becoming "stupidly communicative." Gen. John A. Rawlins, Grant's confidential aide during the war, quietly put Grant aboard a steamer for Detroit, and the scandal was kept private.

After leaving Buffalo at 1 p.m. Monday, Sept. 3, Johnson headed into northern Ohio, a center of militant abolitionism, via the Buffalo & State Line and the Cleveland, Painesville & Ashtabula. The entrenched radicals, surprised and worried about the president's popularity, formulated a counteroffensive baited with hecklers. The president walked into the trap.

The heckling started at Westfield, N.Y., when Johnson made his usual fictitious remark about not intending to make a speech.

"Don't," a heckler shouted.

"Keep quiet until I have concluded," Johnson retorted. "Just such fellows as you have kicked up all the rows of the last five years."[399]

The crowd at Ashtabula laughed, chatted and cheered, but didn't let the president speak. The throng at Cleveland that night was large and friendly, but kicked up a ruckus when it found out Grant wasn't aboard. The president was to stay at the Kennard Hotel, and, against better advice, went out on a balcony and consented to talk. By now everybody was familiar with his speech beginning with his preference not to speak, and it brought rude laughter. Knowing he had enemies in the crowd, the president grew defensive.

Suddenly a man cried, "What about Moses?", alluding to Johnson's

1864 Moses speech in Nashville where he had promised to lead Negroes in the South to freedom.

"Let your own Negroes vote before you talk about Negroes voting in Louisiana," the president advised. "Cast the beam out of your own eye before you see the mote in your neighbor's."

Boos and catcalls ensued, because Johnson had struck a nerve. Ohio didn't let its Negroes vote.

"What about New Orleans?" came a shout. The president tried to show that the riot there was radical-inspired, but groans and laughter drowned him out. More taunts ensued, and the aroused Johnson tried to counter that Lincoln, had he lived, would have met the same hatred that was spoiling this party, but a roar of protests cut him off.

"I love my country," he continued when he could be heard. "I defy any man to put his finger on anything to the contrary. Then what is my offending?"

"You ain't a radical!" came the rejoinder.

"Veto!"

"Traitor!"

"I wish I could see that man," Johnson called angrily, looking in the direction of the last insult. "Show yourself. Come out here where I can see you. If ever you shoot a man, you will do it in the dark."

The disturbance showed signs of being organized, but Johnson didn't back down.

"With all the pains this Congress has taken to poison the minds of their constituents against me, what has this Congress done?" he yelled. "Have they done anything to restore the Union of these states? No, on the contrary, they have done everything to prevent it; and because I now stand where I did when the rebellion commenced, I have been denounced as a traitor! ... There is no power that can control me save you ... and the God that spoke me into existence!"

The disorder had become general now, and amid shouts of "It's a lie!", the president turned and went back into the hotel.

With this the radical press had a field day, writing that the president was a crude, coarse, vulgar Southerner who traded insults with a mob. Some said he was intoxicated, and an Iowa paper charged that the trip was "a big drunk ... When we reflect on the solemn object of the journey, we just blush crimson at this monstrous impropriety, this cold-blooded impiety ... A president of the United States reeling to Chicago."[399]

Onward from Cleveland via the Cleveland & Toledo, the Michigan Southern & Northern Indiana and the Michigan Central, the mood continued to grow dark. A house on the hillside overlooking the station at Elyria, Ohio, displayed a large black flag. Toledo and Detroit produced friendly crowds, but those at Ypsilanti and Ann Arbor, Mich., repeatedly cheered Grant—who had rejoined the trip—in the middle of Johnson's speech. The Battle Creek crowd cheered Congress and booed Johnson. At Michigan City, the president was answered with three rousing cheers for the Congress he blasted. Official receptions vanished, and governors and mayors along the route disappeared.

The Douglas ceremony on Sept. 6 in Chicago was muted. Pickets with anti-Johnson placards hissed the president, and the Tribune picked up the drunkenness theme: "A. Johnson, the 'humble individual,' after one or two ineffectual attempts to land in the gutter, was handed, or rather lifted, into the buggy awaiting his august presence."[399]

The party traveled to Springfield, Ill., on Sept. 7 via the Chicago & Alton for a rainy visit to Lincoln's

More often than not, Andrew Johnson struck back when hecklers disrupted his speeches during the embattled president's 1866 midterm election politicking.

tomb. No state or city official was around, and the streets were empty.

The next day, Saturday, the party boarded 36 steamboats (one for each state) for the trip to St. Louis. The president's was named *Andy Johnson*, and another paper took a swipe at him by noting that the boat carried "a very good bar," so the president hasn't "suffered ... for want of a brandy-and-water."

The crowd at St. Louis was better behaved. Bargeloads of folks met the armada as it neared the city that afternoon, and streets around the Southern Hotel, where the president would stay until Monday, were filled. Johnson greeted the throng, then spoke at a banquet given in his honor. The street crowd clamored for another talk, and although Johnson was tired, he consented.

The people were noisy from the start, and got worse. Johnson kept his cool until someone shouted "Judas, Judas!" That did it.

"There was a Judas," he yelled,

"and he was one of the 12 apostles. ... The 12 apostles had a Christ. ... If I have played the Judas, who has been my Christ that I have played the Judas with? Was it Thad Stevens? Was it Wendell Phillips? Was it Charles Sumner?" He referred to "radical" Republicans who—unlike Johnson— favored a harsh, unforgiving Reconstruction policy toward the South.

The groans and whistles continued, but so did Johnson. "These are the men who compare themselves with the Savior! And anybody who differs with them is denounced as a Judas!"

"Why don't they impeach him?" a heckler cried, and the roar became deafening.

"Yes, they are ready to impeach!" another shouted.

"Let them try it," a voice answered.

"And if they were satisfied that they had the next Congress by as a decided majority as this ...upon some pretext or another ...they would vacate the executive department of the government," Johnson exclaimed.

"Too bad they don't," came the reply.

"But as we are talking about this Congress," the president bravely continued, "let me call the soldiers' attention to this immaculate Congress. Let me call your attention ... Oh, yes, this Congress that could make war upon the executive ... because he stands for the Constitution and vindicates the rights of the people ... exercising the veto power in their behalf ... because he dared to do this ... they clamor and talk about impeachment. ... So far as offenses are concerned ... upon this question of offenses ... let me ask you what offenses I have committed."

"Plenty, here, tonight," the response flew.

Standing in the torchlight, Johnson seemed so enraged that he lost touch with reality. He babbled, he shot back insults, he lost control. The press had another field day.[399]

Grant again took leave of the party at St. Louis, saying he wanted to visit his father and promising to catch up with the president at Cincinnati. But privately he told insiders he didn't want to travel with a man who was "digging his own grave,"[399] and implied that he came along anyway only in obedience to an order from the commander in chief.

Johnson headed eastward from St. Louis via the St. Louis, Alton & Terre Haute, the Terre Haute & Indianapolis and the Jeffersonville, Madison & Indianapolis. The 7:30 a.m. Monday departure was dampened by a driving rainstorm, but the carnival was repeated at most stops nevertheless. The Indianapolis crowd wanted Grant and told their president to "shut up! ... We don't want to hear from you."[399] During a second try at a speech that evening, a riot broke out in which one was killed and several injured. The president was blamed.

From Louisville on Tuesday night, Johnson's party booked overnight passage on the steamer *United States* up the Ohio River to Cincinnati, then continued its rail journey via the Little Miami, the Pittsburgh, Columbus & Cincinnati, and the Pennsylvania Central. Louisville received Johnson well, but the Cincinnati and Columbus crowds on Wednesday were rowdy. At New Market, on Thursday, crowds raised a cheer for Thad Stevens, and Custer dressed them down. The general had been born two and a half miles from there, he said, and he was ashamed of them. At Steubenville, Ohio, the president was not permitted to speak. Johnson enjoyed a bright moment at Mansfield, Pa., eight miles west of Pittsburgh. An elderly admirer by the name of J.E. McCann approached him and said: "I ought not to be afraid to shake hands with you, for I have shaken hands with President Washington. His principles I love, and I love you because you advocate high principles."[389b]

The disturbances started at once in Pittsburgh. A radical parade, with drums, a band and placards marched at the edge of a throng waiting to hear Johnson speak from his hotel balcony. He tried to speak, but the crowd only greeted Grant and Farragut. Finally Johnson conceded. "I bid you good night," he snapped, and retreated inside. The mayor left town to "preserve ... self-respect" and a private banquet crowd heard Johnson respectfully.[399]

The disaster climaxed at Johnstown, Pa., on Friday. A covering of planks over an old canal hastily installed near the tracks collapsed, dropping 500 spectators 20 feet. Eight died instantly, more later, and at least a hundred were injured. The opposition charged that the president callously continued eastward without a word of sympathy, although Johnson left behind a military aide to render assistance and started a relief fund with a $500 donation. Still there was awe and adoration on the part of the crowd and a man gave Grant a Conemaugh cigar "to match the one in his mouth."[389c]

The stop in Altoona, at 12:45 p.m. Friday, was another exception to the rule. The town extended its arms in welcome, cheering the president and serenading him with band music

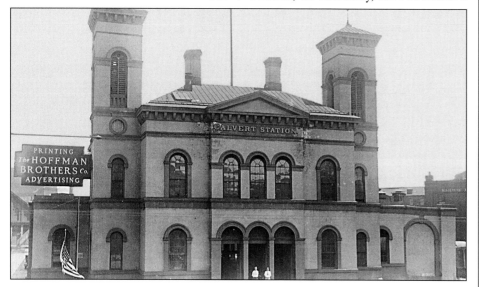

THOMAS W. DIXON JR. COLLECTION

The Northern Central's Calvert Street Station in Baltimore was the last intermediate stop of President Andrew Johnson's troubled trip around the Northeast and Midwest in 1866.

as he made his way to Logan House for a "most sumptuous repast."[9a] A welcoming committee had even boarded his train at Gallitzin. When the train moved off, Johnson, Grant and Farragut appeared on the rear platform to acknowledge the salutes.

Johnson reached Harrisburg at 6:30 p.m., where Grant left the party again to take an earlier train to Washington. The president paid him little mind; he had a very important call to make. Seward, who had caught up with the party at Louisville, shortly afterward had come down with cholera. His condition grew steadily worse, and at Pittsburgh he had started back to Washington in a private car ahead of the president's train. Seward's attacks of diarrhea had grown worse, and the car was switched to a siding at Harrisburg to await his death.

When the chief executive hurried to his side, Seward was incredibly weak. Speaking in a whisper, he assured Johnson that his "mind is clear, and I wish to say that your course is right, and that I have felt it my duty to sustain you in it; and if my life is spared I shall continue to do so. Pursue it for the sake of the country. It is correct."[399] Seward recovered, living six more years.

On Saturday, Sept. 15, the swing around the circle was completed with Johnson's arrival in Washington via the Northern Central and the B&O. The train was late, but the crowd waited until it pulled in at 7 p.m., four and a half hours behind Seward's and two hours behind Grant's. There were parades, speeches and crowded sidewalks all along the way back to the Executive Mansion, and Johnson stood up in his carriage and waved his hat in response to cheers. But the extent of the debacle he had suffered wasn't appreciated at once. It could have hardly been more complete, helping lead to an impeachment vote that

missed conviction by only one vote.

Ulysses S. Grant

Republican Ulysses S. Grant modestly remained at his post as commanding general of the United States Army until July 1868, when he and wife, Julia, started for home in Galena, Ill. They traveled in a fancy wooden sleeper equipped with black walnut woodwork with much inlay and many mirrors. The car was crudely illuminated with candles, but had plush French upholstery. Julia had prepared for the trip by buying a short suit (one that cleared the ground) of handsome black silk, which she wore with an ash-colored bonnet.

A persistent tradition says Grant loved his special car so much that he didn't want to leave it. So, the story goes, he requested—in a heavyhanded way—that a narrow-gauge line between Chicago and Galena be widened so he wouldn't have to change trains. Grudgingly this was done, it is said. But documentation for such an event is lacking, and it is probably apocryphal.

The Grants headed for St. Louis via Cincinnati, where they spent a few days on their farm. Then Julia went home to Galena and her husband continued westward on the Pacific Railway of Missouri and the Kansas Pacific for a tour of the Indian War country. He took along Lt. Gen. William T. Sherman and, from Leavenworth, Kan., Major Gen. Phillip H. Sheridan, gaining their political endorsement without a word from them. They were simply three soldiers, doing their duty, inspecting the keeping of the Great Plains peace.

Of course, that came close to being a campaign tour, but Grant refused to make any speeches.

Publicly, there was to be no involvement in politics, but aboard the train Grant's private secretary, Orville Babcock, took an informal poll among the passengers and found that his boss was expected to win the presidency, among the ladies of the party 11 to 4, and among the gentlemen 44 to 13.

Grant wrote to Julia from Leavenworth on July 17 and revealed that the trip wasn't without its problems. "We arrived here last evening, seven hours behind time, and after all sorts of delays. Owing to a strike among the engineers on the [PR&M] road we were detained at Webster station [Mo.], awaiting the train, until between 9 and 10 o'clock at night. The country ... is beautiful, and this is one of the most beautiful military posts in the United States. We leave it in the morning for the far West. ... Instead of returning from the end of the [KP] road, as I had intended, we will cross over to the other road [Union Pacific] and return by that. This arrangement will extend my trip about four days beyond what it would have been had I returned from the end of the road. This will probably be the last chance I will ever have to visit the plains, and the rapid settlement is changing the character of them so rapidly, that I thought I would avail myself of the opportunity to see them. It will be something for Buck [the Grants' middle son, Ulysses S. Grant Jr.] too, in after life, to know that he had traveled on the plains whilst still occupied by the Buffalo and the Indian, both rapidly disappearing now. He is delighted with the prospect. Sherman, Sheridan, Fred [brother-in-law Frederick Tracy Dent], Buck and myself each carry with us a Spencer Carbine and hope to shoot a Buffalo and Elk before we

Southern Pacific 4-4-0 No. 115 and its crew— three with handlebar mustaches and a conductor with none—stand ready to start former President Ulysses S. Grant across the country after his two-year around-the-world tour. Grant's portrait adorns the tender.

return. There are military stations all the way across only 10 miles apart. The time taken in travel is three days to the other road. About Tuesday week is the time you may look for me back. —Love and kisses to Nellie [daughter Ellen Grant] Jess [youngest son Jesse Root Grant] & yourself. Ulys."[156]

Across the Kansas plains they continued; Grant spent much of the time in silence, making notes on a large map. A passenger noted that the candidate never smoked (which was out of character for him), didn't drink, didn't swear and didn't talk. Sherman, on the other hand, never stopped talking. At Grantville, the candidate was told the town was named for him.

Grant wrote to Julia again from Denver on the 21st: "We have just arrived in this city of the Mountains, all well, enjoying the trip by stage, across the plains, very much. I would not have missed it for a great deal, and Buck has enjoyed it hugely. Yesterday we rode One hundred & twenty miles in stage, over the plains, between 6:30 a.m. and 10 p.m. firing from the stage frequently at Antelope. We killed two, one of which was shot either by Buck or Gn. Sheridan, we could not tell which. Buck will have a great deal to tell when he gets home, which will be about the 30th of this month. We will be detained here two days longer than I would have staid [sic] on account of our baggage. From Leavenworth our baggage was all checked through, but when we got to the end of the railroad we found that Fred's & my trunks were not along. By telegraphing back we found that in changing cars at Lawrence, Kansas, the baggage man had left our trunks on the platform. Next day being Sunday no train was coming up, consequently it put the baggage back two days. I do not regret it now however because I shall spend the two days in the gold mines in the mountains which probably I would never see but for this accident.

"Buck has enjoyed his trip beyond any he has ever yet taken. He has seen wild horses, Buffalo, wolf & Antelope and had frequent shots at the two latter. I have regreted [sic] so much not bringing Jesse with me. He would have enjoyed the trip and this high mountain air would have made him strong and well, given him an appetite for anything. We have felt no oppression from heat for three days.

"Love and kisses to you, Nellie & Jesse. Yours affectionately, ULYS.

"[P.S.:] The towns we visit are Golden City, Central City, Black Hawk & Georgetown, the latter 60 miles from here. We go to-morrow and return next day."[156]

The party caught the Union Pacific to Laramie, Wyo., then returned eastward. They continued on UP to Omaha, the St. Joseph & Council Bluffs to St. Joseph, Mo., and the Hannibal & St. Joseph and North Missouri railroads to St. Louis.

In St. Joseph, the military inspection trip began looking like a whistlestop campaign. Bonfires illuminated the streets and when Grant and the other generals were summoned to the hotel, he got away with saying only "I return my sincere thanks. I am fatigued, weary, dusty and unable to address you."[249]

Sheridan was more open, but as he began a speech someone shouted "Seymour," (a reference to the opposition candidate, Democrat Horatio Seymour), and disclaiming advocacy of violence Sheridan retorted that if he were a resident of the town, he "would duck that fellow in the Missouri River." Sherman characteristically spoiled the fun by growing testy, warning that no one would speak until the crowd "learned to behave."[249] They never hushed, so Sherman finally gave up: "Well, I'll eat my supper and go to bed; you can do what you please."[389e]

Back in St. Louis, Grant spent a few more days at his farm, then proceeded to Chicago on the Chicago & Alton. As he made his way through Illinois, he was accompanied by the uneasy accusation that he was courting the black vote. When the candidate opened a window to shake hands with the platform crowd at Carlinville, he was struck in the face by a hat. Feeling the sting, he pulled back as his friends kicked the assailant, Bill O'Brien, and pushed him away. The train departed without any handshaking. At his brother Orville's house in Chicago, he received a delegation of 5,000 tanners but made no speech. He went home to Galena to quietly await a call to duty, riding on the Chicago & North Western general superintendent's private car and arriving home at last at 6:30 p.m. on Aug. 7.

The year the new president took office, he made a mad dash via the Rensselaer & Saratoga, United

During Ulysses Grant's 1868 western trip, the special party crossed the rugged gap from the end of the Kansas Pacific's track to Denver by stagecoach. They met the southbound stage at a remote spot, and its passengers were quite surprised to find that Grant was aboard the northbound stage. Everyone on the other stage disembarked for a better look—all but one man, that is, who kept his seat and shouted, "Hooray for Seymour!" a reference to the Democratic opposition candidate, Horatio Seymour. That brought an angry reaction from Grant's driver: "Moze," he snapped, "I be blessed if I'd drive that cuss to the station for the coach and the horses to boot!"[389d]

Companies of New Jersey, Philadelphia, Wilmington & Baltimore and the Baltimore & Ohio on Sunday and Monday, Sept. 5-6, 1869, from the fashionable resort area of Saratoga Springs, N.Y., to Washington to rush to the bedside of his dying friend from the war days, Gen. John A. Rawlins. The secretary of war had consumption (tuberculosis) and was fading fast. Grant had been sent a telegram saying Rawlins was not expected to survive the day.

Sherman was at Rawlins' bedside in Washington.

"What time is it?" Rawlins asked him, following with another query: "When will he get here?" Sherman gently lied: "in about 10 minutes."[249]

Grant hadn't left Saratoga, not wanting to interrupt Julia's plans and not wanting to be dramatic enough to order a special train on a Sunday. But a second telegram came at 4:45 saying Rawlins was asking for his buddy and Grant made plans to leave at once.

The president set out without his wife on the 5:50 p.m. train. A private area had been screened off for Grant in the dining car, but he had to endure the company of New York politicians

Roscoe Conkling and Judge Ward Hunt, who had come to escort him on an aborted side trip to Utica. When he got off the train, Conkling told reporters that Grant was "melancholy" and "talked of little else but the close relationship that had long been held between himself and Gen. Rawlins."[249]

Reaching Albany at 7 p.m., Grant found the New York Central & Hudson River's special train he had ordered was not there. The next regular train from Chicago wasn't due until 2 a.m., so he took the night boat down the Hudson, spending much of his time sitting alone on the deck, talking to no one. Arriving in New York City after daylight Monday, he had breakfast with wealthy railroad financier Jay Gould and caught a taxi and ferry for Jersey City. To his consternation, another promised special to be provided by the United Companies of New Jersey also hadn't shown up.

At Wilmington, on a regular train, Grant got a message that Rawlins was sinking, and at Baltimore a special B&O locomotive and car at last appeared and sped him to Washington. Sherman and Secretary of the Interior Jacob D. Cox were on the platform and, filled with sorrow, "the president almost buried himself in the carriage"[249] on the drive from the station. He entered Rawlins' room at 5:15 p.m.; his friend had succumbed at 4:12.

Grant rode the rails so often he was taken to task by Congress. The question even came up as to whether executive acts performed outside the White House were legal. Grant, who spent the torrid Washington summers at Long Branch, N.J., was ordered by a House resolution to account for actions taken away from the capital. The angered president cited chapter and verse to prove that he was not constitutionally bound to exercise his duties of office at the seat of govern-

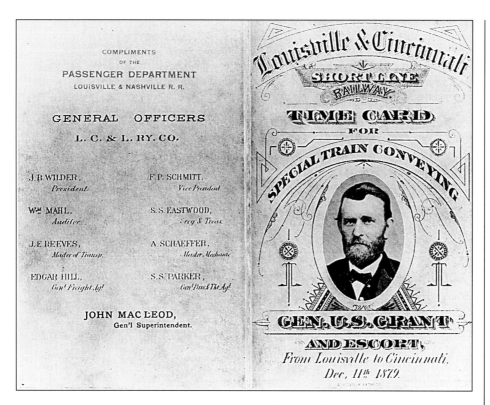

This Louisville & Cincinnati timetable shows arrangements for Ulysses S. Grant's passage between that line's namesake cities on Dec. 11, 1879.

ment. He supplied statistics to show how much time his predecessors spent out of town and listed the acts they performed while they were away. The Democratic Congress' curiosity seemed satisfied when Grant pointed out that the president who spent the most time away from Washington was Jefferson, the party father.

Grant's travels may have been frequent, but in his day they were still simple and uncomplicated, usually with small parties going along. Often the president traveled with only a secretary or aide to handle formalities.

One hot night in 1870, a sleeping car passenger on a Washington-New York run went back to the washroom for a before-bed scrubbing. In the next car, a noisy excursion crowd was whooping it up with yowling abandon.

While the traveler was slopping water over the light veneer of soot that identified most travelers of the day, a quiet man slipped into the washroom, sat down on the long seat and lighted a cigar.

The traveler, a Virginian named John S. Wise, mopped the water from his face and said casually to his new companion, "My, what a noisy crowd—if they keep that up we'll not get much sleep."

The man with the cigar puffed reflectively. "They are not going far, I think," he said. "It is an excursion from Wilmington, I believe. I like to see them happy."

Wise turned and looked again. The man with the cigar was President Grant. Flustered, he babbled an apology for having spoken so familiarly with the chief executive. Grant chuckled and told him to spare his explanation.

"I like a cigar before retiring and slipped in here to have a smoke," he said.[358]

Leaving office on March 4, 1877, the Grants and daughter Nellie moved in with former Secretary of State Hamilton Fish until Nellie's baby was born on March 17. Then the Grants set out for Ohio.

They were escorted to the train by outgoing Secretary of the Interior Zachariah Chandler, who thanked Julia for the "propriety and dignity" with which she had "presided over the Executive Mansion during these eight years past." Ulysses and Julia waved to the crowd on the platform as their train pulled out, and then Julia went to her compartment and wept. The general heard her crying and went in, asking what the trouble was. "Oh, Ulys," she sobbed. "I feel like a waif." "Is that all?" he replied. "I thought something had happened. You must not forget that I too am a waif."[157]

The Grants were hardly waifs. Once the general was out of office, they traveled extensively, including a two-year around-the-world tour that ended with a meandering cross-country train trip from the West Coast.

The ex-president was involved in a derailment on the New York & Long Branch on June 29, 1882. Central of New Jersey's northbound train 7, the *Brokers' Train*, consisting of engine 163, a baggage car, Pullman drawing room car, smoker and four coaches, split a switch at the south end of the Parker's Creek bridge between Little Silver and Oceanport, N.J. The locomotive and first five cars were thrown off the bridge and into the 4-foot-deep creek. The switch had been installed to allow additional rail traffic to use the spur into the Monmouth Park racetrack.[455]

Grant was pulled from the wreckage through a window by fireman Foster. He had scratched his knee and lost his hat, but his cigar was still lighted. Once safe, the former chief executive helped rescue others. With characteristic coolness, he directed the railroad hands how to do their work.

Grant was to make one more historic rail journey. Noticing a persistent sore throat during the summer of 1884, the general was diagnosed as suffering from terminal throat cancer. Living in New York City and striving to finish his memoirs in time, Grant became the subject of intense exploitation by those outside his family as his death approached.

The summer of 1885—Grant's last—was nigh, and businessmen tried to manipulate him so he would spend it where it would do them the most good. As one put it, "I thought if we could get him to come to Mount McGregor, and if he should die there, it might make the place a national shrine—and incidentally a success."[249] The real-estate promoter was talking about a cottage on the grounds of his resort hotel, Balmoral, a few miles north of Saratoga Springs, N.Y., in the foothills of the Adirondacks.

The would-be exploiter was W.J. Arkell, a successful upstate New York butcher who had branched out into politics, newspaper publishing and real estate. In 1882, he had built a 12-mile narrow gauge line—the Saratoga, Mount McGregor & Lake George Railroad Co.—from Saratoga Springs to Mount McGregor and then up a spectacularly steep grade to the summit. There he had constructed the Hotel Balmoral and opened it for the 1884 season.

The rail line was built under the supervision of John McGee, who had experience building railroads in the Andes. From the northern edge of Saratoga Springs, the route shot fairly northward, following the foot of the mountains briefly then ascending the steep slope on a series of sharp curves.

Even though the line was narrow gauge, its ties were standard-gauge and were spaced only 20 inches apart. The ruling grade was 4.1 percent.

The resort was modeled after the successful and beautiful Mohonk Mountain House farther down the Hudson; rustic gazebos were placed along gently sloping paths where slow-paced, overdressed walkers could pause and admire lovely vistas. There were lakes below, with the Saratoga battlefield and the Adirondack peaks to the north and west. In June 1885, ads appeared for "Hotel Balmoral, 1,200 feet above the sea, on Mount McGregor … No Dew, No Malaria, No Mosquitoes, Certain Relief from Hay Fever."[249]

Another clever tycoon, Joseph W. Drexel of New York City, the younger brother of the head of the banking firm that had long curried Grant's favor, bought a cottage that had been moved to make room for the hotel. Drexel had it in mind for a summer home, but Arkell convinced him to persuade his ex-presidential friend that the mountain air might relieve his suffering—and, he kept to himself, also line both men's pockets!

The Grants had sold their lovely cottage at Long Branch, N.J., and so had nowhere else to go. In late April, the bargaining had been completed and Arkell announced that he had convinced the family to take the general to Mount McGregor. By mid-June the hot weather was bothering Grant. The cancer had become rooted in deeper tissue, his neck was swollen, and he found it painful and difficult to speak.

On June 16, William H. Vanderbilt of the NYC&HR lent Grant his private car and the general and his party disembarked. The locomotive pulled Vanderbilt's coach and one other car.

"The car in which Gen. Grant will travel," wrote the *New York World*, "is fitted up most luxuriously and every detail which can be added to his ease and comfort during the journey has been attended to."[296]

When the carriage that had brought him from his home pulled up at Grand Central Station that morning, the general got out and walked to the train on his son Fred's arm. He was emaciated, pale, and so weak he looked as if he would fall at every step. Railroad officials met him at the train. Some of them offered a military salute, which he returned waveringly. Before he entered his car, he turned around and took a long last look at the New York skyline.

Grant was asleep as his train proceeded up the east bank of the Hudson until it neared West Point. Then he aroused himself and asked to be placed at the window so he could see the gray stone buildings of the military academy across the river. There they stood, just as they had 46 years before when he had seen them for the first time. His mind was filled with memories of those days, and he whispered an anecdote of cadet life. Smiling, he beckoned to Dr. John Hancock Douglas and motioned toward the academy, where the cadets stood at present arms as the train passed. He gaze was fixed on West Point until it was out of sight.

The Grants' summer trips to Long Branch, N.J., were major undertakings.

Says one account: "The president and his family arrived here by special train at fifteen minutes past five in the afternoon in a Pullman palace car. The president's baggage had been arriving all day. … Eight furniture wagons had been driven down Ocean Avenue to the president's cottage containing the federal baggage.

Four carriages and a buggy had been towed in the train of furniture wagons, comprising a seaside phaeton for Miss Nelly, a two-seat buggy for the president and a friend, and the huge, high-backed English carriage for the united family, a dog cart for the boys, a modest rockaway for Mrs. Grant's accommodation. …"[144]

All along the way, crowds gathered at the stations to watch the great general go by in his splendid car. The attention stimulated him.

The train crossed the river below Albany and reached Saratoga Springs at 1:55 p.m., where Grant was met by a line of Grand Army of the Republic veterans in uniform. He was cheered when, before anyone could help him, he got off Vanderbilt's car, stepped over to the narrow gauge car that would take him to Mount McGregor and climbed up alone. In a few minutes he stepped out again, exasperated by the bumbling efforts of his aides to transfer the huge upholstered easy chair, in which he had been sleeping since his choking attacks in the spring, and the chair upon which he propped his feet. Son Fred and his helpers were having trouble getting the chairs through the door of the little car, and Grant came back out to supervise. The furniture finally in place, they were on the move once more. Drexel was aboard, as were several reporters, and Arkell "was thoughtfully attentive to all on the train over which he exercised supervision."[249] It was proposed to have Grant stop at Drexel's house in Saratoga, but "the heat there, however, was hardly less trying than at Albany, and the general wanted the trip over."[296]

The journey was uneventful except for Grant's irritation with the smoke that drifted into the car from the little engine struggling up the mountain. The coach lurched on uneven rails around the sharp curves "like a boat in stormy sea."[296] With great relief he disembarked at Mount McGregor at 2:40 p.m., ignored a hospital litter, and started walking up the hill. He tottered after a few steps, though, and let himself be carried in a rattan chair the rest of the way to the ample cottage. It had a reception room and three bedrooms on the first floor, six more upstairs rooms and a wide porch on three sides. It's still open to tourists.

Rutherford B. Hayes

By the time Republican Rutherford B. Hayes of Ohio took office as the nation's 19th president, railroad travel had become routine. Hayes traveled by rail often, in office and out. He and his opponent, Democrat Samuel J. Tilden, rolled around the rail circuit in 1876 in 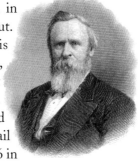 coaches now equipped with oil lamps—and air brakes, allowing greater speed and safety.

When Hayes, his wife, Lucy, and their party departed from Columbus, Ohio, for Washington, the outcome of the election wasn't clear. Hayes believed he had lost to Tilden, who had received a clear popular majority, but a few Southern states had submitted two sets of electoral vote totals, throwing the decision to Congress. The conflict dragged on for months because the Constitution was not specific on how to solve it. Finally, an electoral commission appointed by Congress spent months haggling with various political factions and awarded all disputed votes to the Republican. He became president by one electoral vote.

All this was uncertain on Thursday, March 1, 1877, when Hayes and his party boarded two special cars Pennsylvania Railroad President Thomas A. Scott's private car, No. 120, and one other—on the end of a regular PRR train. His use of Scott's cars was ironic. The PRR chief executive was also president of the Texas & Pacific; as a part of the negotiations that propelled Hayes to the presidency, the Republicans had promised federal aid to extend the T&P to the Pacific coast.

Not wanting to look like he was seizing control of the country by claiming his office before the commission announced its decision, Hayes had waited as long as he could, until Feb. 28, to resign as the governor of Ohio. When his train pulled out the next day, he still didn't know if he had a job.

He left for the station shortly after noon.

"A large crowd followed us to the depot," Hayes wrote. "We were escorted by the college cadets."[443]

The farewell was reminiscent of Lincoln's from Springfield, Ill., 16 years before. In a short speech, Hayes recalled from the back platform how he had marched off to war then to help save the Union. Now he was leaving again, not to save the Union by force of arms but to seek a union of people's hearts by works of love and peace, something Lincoln died trying to achieve. Acknowledging that his election was still in doubt, he told the crowd that "public affairs in Washington were uncertain,"[273] and that the next week he might be back in the governor's office instead of the White House.

When the train pulled out at 1 p.m., Hayes advised the crowd to disperse to avoid accident by the movement of the cars.

"Crowds met us at Newark, Dennison, Steubenville and other points," Hayes wrote in his diary. "The enthusiasm was greater than I have seen in Ohio before."[443]

About dawn on Friday, March 2, Hayes was awakened near Harrisburg and told of a telegram received on the train that a joint session of Congress had finally declared him president-elect at 4 a.m. Word of the messenger's boarding spread quickly and the private car resounded with cheers.

"Boys, boys," the happy Hayes

admonished. "You'll awaken the passengers."[43]

Northern Central engine 91 hauled his train from Harrisburg to Baltimore in two hours and 26 minutes, then Baltimore & Potomac engine 12 took over at Baltimore's Union Station. With completion of the Wilson Street Tunnel in 1873, it was now possible for both locomotive and train to run through the city. Two thousand people met his train in Washington despite a "fearful rainstorm."[106]

The Hayeses used railroads frequently once in office, making many trips back to Ohio—the president's family lived in Fremont and Lucy's in Chillicothe—and to a cottage they owned at Deer Park, Md. He was especially fond of baked apples as prepared on the B&O's dining cars by Chef Joseph Brown.

A typical jaunt home began on Friday night, July 19, 1878, when they left Washington "after a fine thunder shower"[443] aboard the *Maryland*, B&O President John W. Garrett's private car. Hayes made a few notes:

"A pretty comfortable night. Saturday very hot. The motion of the cars in the Mts mad[e] Mrs. [Harriet Little Platt] S[ollace] & Gen [E.B.] Tyler seasick! Met by crowds at Zanesville & Newark. Got quietly and almost unobserved into Columbus. Found all well at [niece] Laura[Platt Mitchell]'s, and [had] a delightful time. Sunday, a North wind brought relief. ... Monday, Newark. Weather good and demonstration successful. Stand too weak, as usual. [J. Warren] Keifer's speech good and delivered admirably. I got off a few words satisfactorily. Found all well on our return. Absence, four days."[443]

During the annual congressional hiatus in Washington during the summer of 1879, Hayes planned a tour of Midwestern states for the fall. He decided to remind them that his pre-

diction of a year ago about good times returning had come true. The trick now, he would say, is to make the good times stay by keeping out of debt. He also would condemn the denial of rights to Negroes in the South.

Hayes himself entered into the planning process. "I am not well informed as to routes," he wrote in a private note to William H. Smith, general agent of the Western Associated Press and a close Hayes adviser. "I understand you to recommend Fremont to Neosho [Falls, Kan.] via Chicago, St. Louis, Kansas City, Topeka. I see no objection to it. I must leave F.[remont] Monday [Sept.] 22d A.M.—Will this get me to Neosho by noon 25th? I shall have a B&O car during the trip."[169]

To Ohio Gov. Richard M. Bishop, who had invited him to stop over in Columbus, Hayes responded on Sept. 4 to "accept my thanks for your polite offer but I regret that arrangements have been made to reach Cincinnati Tuesday afternoon about half after six by the Baltimore & Ohio Railroad." The same day he wrote to Isador H. Burgoon, general superintendent of the Lake Erie & Western: "I may want to go from Cinci to Fremont via [Cincinnati] Ham[ilton] & Day[ton] RR to Lima and thence by your line to F. so as to reach F. Saturday morning the 13th inst. Please write me at Grand Hotel, Cincinnati, if you can take my car through—a B&O car about that time."[169]

Also on the 4th to Cincinnatian George W. Jones, an old friend from college days, he advised, "I expect to reach Cincinnati via B&O and Chillicothe [Ohio] Tuesday afternoon." The next day he wrote to Jones that "I go by Baltimore & Ohio to Parkersburg [W.Va.] and Chillicothe. I leave Chillicothe for Cincinnati about two PM tuesday[sic] next."[169]

A note on Sept. 7 from R.P. Hamm at Neosho Falls asked Hayes to designate his route. "If you have no choice we prefer that you enter the State at Fort Scott, via Mo. Kan. and Texas R.R., Answer." To which Hayes did: "No arrangement yet made, will follow your preference. Can come from Fremont either via Wabash Railway, or Chicago."[169]

Finally, a note to Jones, indicating the president wasn't the best speller: "We expect to leave here Monday morning via B&O and to reach Chillicothe Tuesday 2 ½ a.m. & remain over one train, reaching Cinti about 6 ½ p.m. Tuesday evening. Gen. [William T.] Sherman, & his aids[sic] Col [John E.] Tourtlelotte [Tourtellotte] and Col [John Mosby] Bacon and Gen. [Charles] Devens Atty. Gen 1, Birchard two servants and two children form the Party. It is probable that my family only, will stop over one train at Chillicothe, and that Gen [William T.] Sherman, Devens, aids[sic] Cols Bacon and Tourtlelotte will arrive Tuesday morning in C.

"Gov [John Lee] Carrol [Carroll] of Md is a gentleman with whom we have a very agreeable acquaintance, and if he is on the same train we shall ask him into our car, but as you can see by my list, we are not in a condition for more in the party at night.

"We ought not to stay away from the Hotel at night—otherwise your plan is good. ..."[169]

The special party left Washington Monday, Sept. 8, via B&O. Wrote Hayes: "We go this morning. The thunder storm last night cooled the air and laid the dust. The morning is beautiful. All are well and in good spirits."[443] They stopped over in Chillicothe to see Lucy's Uncle Matthew Scott Cook and several of her other relatives, then spent three days in Cincinnati, in part for the Cincinnati Exposition. As planned, they continued to Fremont via the CH&D and LE&W for a much-needed rest, interrupted by side trips to Youngstown (via the Atlantic & Great Western) and Detroit (via Lake Shore & Michigan Southern).

The western trip officially started on Monday morning, the 22nd, via Chicago and Hannibal, Mo., on the LS&MS, Chicago Burlington & Quincy and MK&T. The president jotted down this note in his diary at Hannibal: "We were late. … It had rained—the night was dark and threatening, and a few youngsters were persistent in calling 'Hayes,' 'Hayes,' 'President Hayes' &c &c. I finally stepped out and talked a few minutes—was treated with respect but the papers got it that the crowd was insolent and violent. Nothing of it in fact."[443] The travelers stopped overnight in Sedalia before continuing to the Neosho Falls fair.

After the visit to Neosho, the party continued to Dodge City via MK&T, Emporia and the Atchison, Topeka & Santa Fe. Starting east on the 26th, the travelers visited a county fair at Larned and stopped over at Fort Leavenworth for the Sabbath. More diary notes: "The Arkansas [River] nearly dry. At Larned, a fair and great spirit. Evening with noise, fireworks and welcoming shouts at Topeka. … Receptions at Topeka [and] Lawrence. … At night, a most uproarious welcome at Leavenworth—especially by the colored people. … Church in the excellent military prison, A.M., and at the Episcopal army chaplain's services in the evening."[443]

Sailing up the Missouri River on Monday, they boarded a special train and took the Hannibal & St. Joseph, CB&Q and Chicago & Alton to a daylight Tuesday arrival in Springfield, Ill., via a Mississippi River crossing at Louisiana, Mo. Recalled Hayes: "The tomb of Lincoln, and its

monument, &c &c with the associations are most impressive. His old home is neglected—It may as well be taken down as left so."[443] [The home still stands.]

Hayes made appearances at the Illinois statehouse, executive mansion and a fair, then caught the Indianapolis, Decatur & Springfield for Indianapolis. He continued to Fremont possibly via the Indianapolis, Peru & Chicago to Tipton, Ind., and the LE&W, arriving at Fremont at 8 a.m. Friday, Oct. 3.

A number of fairs and receptions in Ohio followed, and the chief executive and first lady finally left Columbus via the B&O on the 20th, arriving in Washington the next morning at 8. The tour was successful; they had been well-received everywhere.

Hayes departed from the usual policy of using a private accommodation for a visit to Philadelphia to spend the 1879 Thanksgiving holiday with the family of Methodist Bishop Matthew Simpson. Accompanied by his valet, Isaiah Lancaster, he bought two tickets for "the common car"[443] on the 5:30 p.m. Baltimore & Potomac train. Hayes liked to appear incognito so he could find out what people thought of him without inhibiting them by his high office. He discovered that his trick didn't work so well now that he was president.

"I preferred to go without fuss," he wrote in his diary. "I had a ticket to Baltimore. But paid 40 cents apparently for Isaiah, but I didn't understand it. A family ticket which I had, included I suppose servants. I was as polite as the conductor, and made no remark. Fare was paid from Baltimore to Phila. for both of us—I think $3 each. On my return I paid $15 for fare on the B&O and for sleeping births [sic]—two sections, leaving Phila. at 11:30 p.m. Soon after lying down the conductor told me he had orders to

return my fare. I took it without counting. This morning at 7 p.m. [sic] before leaving the car, the conductor told me he had orders to return me the fare paid on the 26th and gave me $3. This was for fare I suppose leaving me to pay for my own sleeping birth [sic]. All of this pleasantly done, but I suspect I make less trouble if I ask for a special car. On the way up a Mr. Sutton of the Eastern Shore—clerk in the great whole sale store of Jacob _____ & Co., Phila., took a seat by my side. I got much interesting information about his business and the trade generally. … The bishop and his son Barney met me at Broad St. depot at midnight, or near it."[443]

Hayes had decided right off he would be a one-term president, so the Republican nomination in 1880 went to James A. Garfield. Hayes did not actively campaign for him, but he helped the Republican cause by making a transcontinental tour—the first by a U.S. president while in office, as well as the longest journey by a chief executive to that time—and talking everywhere to enthusiastic throngs.

Accompanying the chief executive were Lucy; two of their sons, Birchard and Rutherford; Gen. William T. Sherman; Secretary of War Alexander Ramsey; family members; staff; and friends.

Generally, the railroads provided a director's car for the president's comfort. The travelers stopped at military posts enroute and used hotels sparingly, receiving their accommodations and hospitality as a courtesy of army generals, well-known businessmen and public officials. Hayes kept in constant touch with Washington by telegraph in case some emergency required his speedy return to the capital. None did, and he kept to the schedule worked out by Sherman.

The party's size fluctuated throughout the trip, but usually averaged about 19. A limiting factor, especially for the women, was the need to use army field ambulances to cover more than 500 miles of rough roads and desert country between railheads.

The travelers left Washington late Friday night, Aug. 27, journeying to Fremont via B&P and PRR lines to Cleveland, then on LS&MS.

"We reached F[remont] last night at 8 p.m.," Hayes wrote on Aug. 28, "twenty-two and one-half hours from Washington—in the new car of Mr. [Charles Edmund] Pugh, superintendent of inspection of (the) Pennsylvania Railroad. We brought my old friend [Rowland E.] Trowbridge sick [sciatica or Bright's disease], Comm[issioner] of Indian Affairs, and Mr. [Col. John] Jamison, of railway mail service, with [children] Fan[ny and] Scott, and the colored servants, [nurse] Winnie [Monroe] and Scott. At several points in Ohio, although all my movements were kept private, we were met by good crowds who cheered us heartily. I was pleased when cheers were heartily given on a call of 'Three cheers for the model

president.' We got home after dark. Rud had the house in as good case as could be in view of the improvements [a large addition was under construction]. They strike us both well, particularly the external appearance, the porch, and the rooms in the bay-window addition on the south side. Lucy is 49 today. I never loved her so much as now."[441]

The Hayeses backtracked to Canton on Tuesday, Aug. 31, via the LS&MS to Cleveland and the Valley Railway to attend the next day's Grand Soldiers and Sailors Reunion of 1880, which included the 23rd regiment, Ohio Volunteer Infantry, of which the president was a past commander. They rode in PRR chief Tom Scott's car, welcoming aboard at Cleveland two future presidents and their wives—Garfield, whose home was in Mentor, and William McKinley, who lived in Canton.

The presidential car and another carrying veterans of the 155th OVI were coupled to the Valley's regular 4:15 p.m. train for the departure from

Cleveland. The 2 ½-hour trip was uneventful, but it had its pleasant moments:

• At Akron, an old man, who said he was 80 and had never voted for a president, told Garfield he had been a sailor—as he had been—and would cast his first ballot for him. The platform crowd cheered.

• At Middlebury, a man named Townsend without further remark introduced Hayes, who also without remark introduced Garfield. By the time the cheering stopped, the train was moving again. "This is the way Mr. Townsend took to get out of [speaking]," Garfield quipped, "and the way President Hayes took to get out of it, and this is the way I take to get out of it." The crowd roared.[70]

• At Uniontown, a drummer boy with the 132nd Pennsylvania Volunteers shook hands with Garfield and said, "If I were as sure of getting to heaven as you are of being the next president, I would be satisfied."[70]

A presidential picnic party arrives at the Dalrymple Farms in South Dakota on Sept. 6, 1878. The man with the dark beard and top hat in his hand near the corner of the platform and the woman with a shawl alongside him are President and Mrs. Rutherford B. Hayes.

Northern Central 4-4-0 No. 100, seen here at Altoona, Pa., was in service during the Hayes administration.

- At Greentown, Garfield asked the crowd how far it was to Canton and hoped that veterans in the area would be "coming down tomorrow."[70]
- Between Greentown and Canton, a newspaper correspondent watched as Hayes and Garfield sat in a corner of the car and discussed politics. "The differences in their modes of talking were noticeable," he wrote. "Hayes moved only his head when conversing, but Garfield's hands were constantly going, now clinched and now open, and all his sentences were elucidated, German-like, by expressive gestures."[70]

The party arrived at Canton at 6:45 p.m., a little more than two hours ahead of a special carrying 800 veterans to the reunion. The engineer apparently stopped where he always did, but the longer-than-usual train left the presidential car a good distance from the station. When an overly enthusiastic crowd tried to board it, he pulled past the crossing with the PRR's Pittsburgh, Fort Wayne & Chicago line so Hayes' car would be positioned next to the platform.

Newspapers noted that pickpockets were in abundance. Twenty-five pocketbooks were found on the floor of the PFtW&C's Fort Wayne depot after the party ended, and a Brimfield, Ohio, man reported that he was relieved of $72 at the Valley station. "The [pocket] book, empty, stale, flat and unprofitable, was found near the depot," the article said.[70]

The Hayeses launched their western tour from Canton, leaving there at 11 that night via the fast express on the PFtW&C. It arrived at Chicago an hour late, at 9:50 a.m. on Thursday the 2nd, amid a torrential morning downpour that had diminished the crowd. When the locomotive's whistle was finally heard, the *Chicago Evening Journal* said, "the waiting expectants brushed the mud off their pants, and adjusted their neckties and got themselves ready."[80] Everyone went to the front end of the last car—the president's—only to find he had gone out the back door. Sherman, now with the party, emerged first—in a linen duster that about hid him from view—and then the president and Mrs. Hayes.

Hayes "was dressed in a very presidential black suit, white necktie and black silk hat," the article explained. "Mrs. Hayes was also dressed in black and looked remarkably pleasant. She is a very handsome lady, anyway, with unusually expressive dark brown eyes and dark hair." The party went to the Grand Pacific Hotel, during an hour's layover for breakfast. Sherman had remarked that he was "very hungry," so no time was lost.[80]

The party arrived at the Chicago, Burlington & Quincy depot a few minutes after 11, shook a few hands and boarded a five-car train hurriedly. There were no on-board decorations except for a few flowers and some fruit, but the cars were "furnished in their usual elegant manner."[80]

The first stop was at Naperville, where the president addressed a reunion of the 105th Illinois volunteers. But Sherman stole the show during the three-minute stop when he found out that some of the veterans had marched with him from Atlanta to the sea.

"Boys," he said, "that tells the whole story. You have earned a right to meet anywhere you please and as often as you like. There is no use of further talk. You wanted to see how Old Uncle Billy looked (cheers and laughter) and I wanted to look into your faces and see that you are happy. God bless you all. Be good citizens as you were good soldiers."[80]

Stops were made at Aurora, Galva, Princeton —where demands to see the president interrupted his dinner—Galesburg and Burlington. People clambered over the rear platform in their enthusiasm to shake Hayes' hand and catch a glimpse of his wife. A special train from Burlington met the travelers at Monmouth and escorted them back to their city.

A pattern developed during the first few days. Local Republican politicos would board the president's train to greet him and often ride to the next stop. Wherever the train stopped, Hayes spoke a few words extemporaneously, with Sherman and Ramsey following. Then Mrs. Hayes and the other ladies were presented to the crowd. Cannon, rifle or whistle salutes, martial music or a band playing "Hail to the Chief" or "Marching Through Georgia" followed.

The president avoided speechmaking on Sundays as much as possible. To pass time on long idle stretches between stops, the group played guessing games or sang patriotic and popular songs.

Lt. Charles Rutherford Noyes, son of the president's cousin, Horatio Noyes, who was stationed near Cheyenne, Wyoming Territory, joined the train—now on the Union Pacific—at that point and rode to Salt Lake City.

Shortly after the train entered Utah Territory, it stopped at Emory Station. Noyes and four others—the president and Mrs. Hayes, Dr. D.H. Huntington and Mrs. John Herron—were invited to ride in the locomotive and on its cowcatcher for an exciting ride through Echo Canyon. After 25 miles, they returned to the coaches, well pleased.

The Hayes brothers and Noyes took a brief excursion at Salt Lake City to Black Rock for a swim in the famous salt water and then rejoined the party for a tour of the city. When the party proceeded west on Sept. 6 after a delightful weekend, Noyes found time to win a rubber of cribbage with Rachel Sherman, the general's daughter, and then returned to his Army post.

"Upon arriving (back) at Ogden," Noyes wrote, "the party changed cars to Central Pacific sleeping cars, and the director's car of the Central Pacific was in readiness for the president. This was the finest car which I think I ever saw, its upholstery was of the richest, and all its appointments complete."[106]

At Virginia City, Nev., Hayes toured the Comstock Lode's Big Bonanza at the 2,300-foot level. He took to a stage, then rode the steamer *Meteor* on Lake Tahoe and then rolled from Truckee, Calif., over the Sierra Nevada's Donner Summit via CP and Western Pacific to Benicia, where he took ferries to Oakland and San Francisco, arriving Sept. 9. Here he was given an opulent welcome at the Grand Palace Hotel and recuperated from his travels during 12 days of local sightseeing.

While in California, the first family made a side trip to Monterey via Southern Pacific, continuing to Menlo Park by stage. During a stop at San Jose, the Women's Christian Temperance Union presented Lucy with an impressive silk banner in honor of her prohibition of alcoholic beverages in the White House. It was inscribed with her name and the line from the Bible, "She hath done what she could" (Mark 14:8). Setting out again from San Francisco (by ferry) and Benicia (via WP), they paused in Sacramento, where they were greeted by Gov. George C. Perkins. Then it was northward on CP's Oregon Division via Chico and Cherokee, where the president visited the world's largest hydraulic gold mine.

Because the railroad had not been completed from Redding, Calif., for 275 miles to Roseburg, Ore., Hayes once again resorted to stagecoach, traveling for six days only by daylight to see the scenery and visit a government fish hatchery and several old mining camps.

At Roseburg, the *Portland Special* of the Oregon & California took the party to its namesake city. After a side trip to Forest Grove via the Western Oregon line, he took a succession of steamers from Portland to Walla Walla, Washington Territory, arriving on Monday, Oct. 4 (Hayes' 58th birthday), at which point Sherman bragged on Mount Hood and Mount St. Helens. After another foray from Portland into Washington state, with stops at Kalama, Olympia and Tacoma via a combination of steamers and the Northern Pacific Railway, everybody took an ocean steamer back to San Francisco.

Hayes and his party took a train to Madera, where they embarked on a side trip by stage to Yosemite National Park. Then it was back to Madera and a Southern Pacific train to Los Angeles.

After quick looks at the orange groves, an agricultural fair, the new University of Southern California campus and Pasadena's vineyards, the party proceeded to Mission San Gabriel, where it boarded an SP train for Arizona and New Mexico territories.

As Hayes and his party traveled east toward Tucson, a delegation from that city struck out on a special train at 6 a.m. on Sunday, Oct. 24, to meet the president at Casa Grande, where they asked him to stop over for a celebration. The next day's *Daily Arizona*

Lucy Hayes tried to avoid the autograph hunters on the Hayeses' 1880 West Coast tour. At one town, she kept out of sight until time for the train to depart, then sat down by a window. When the people outside saw her, they began handing autograph books, cards and newspapers through the window for her to sign. Soon she was exhausted from signing so many items. Once the party was under way, the Hayes' mischievous son Rutherford came running into the presidential car waving an album he had been passing through the window to her. She had signed it 56 times.[45]

Citizen listed locomotive 39—over which Engineer Ingles presided—at the point of Hayes' five-car Southern Pacific special when it arrived at Casa Grande. It had made the distance from Yuma, 249 miles west, in seven hours and 10 minutes. That averaged a little more than 35 miles an hour, a fast trip for the time.

The coach from Tucson was added to the presidential train for the continued trip east, and several of its occupants "were invited into the president's car and were made to feel thoroughly at home by the affable and kindly manner of the entire party." The visitors were especially impressed with Mrs. Hayes, with "her beautifully kindly face and simple manners winning the hearts of all present."[95]

"The entire presidential party seemed more like a picnic excursion than like a congregation of the chief people of our nation," one article declared. "All were dressed in traveling attire, and nothing could exceed the pleasant cordiality with which they received their visitors."[95]

Hayes turned the tables and interviewed the reporter, asking all sorts of questions about Tucson's people, mines, churches and schools; so thoroughly, in fact, that the humble writer had to defer to other members of his party for some of the answers.

Once leaving Casa Grande, Sherman repaired to the citizens' car and made the acquaintance of several gentlemen there. One of them remarked that the general was the "best single-handed talker in the United States," and he lived up to his reputation. In answer to a comment to the effect that the Indian Victorio would not likely bother them during their trip, the general winked and replied, "Oh, Victorio wouldn't bother me; if there's any scalping to be done, I generally do it myself!" Then he added seriously that completion of the rail line to the east should solve the Indian problem.[95]

The new friends discussed camels that had been imported years before for transportation across the desert and their descendants still in the Gila Valley, then moved on to a discussion of Jefferson Davis and how he never wanted secession.

"He always opposed secession," Sherman explained. "He is of a most despotic nature, and he wanted to rule the whole country. ... He didn't want secession—he wanted empire."[95]

As the passengers neared Tucson, they saw an immense dust cloud in the vicinity of the depot, where thousands were gathering to see Hayes. Once he had consented to stop, the citizens' party had telegraphed the news back home from Casa Grande. That didn't give much time to organize a celebration, but the city did the best it could.

Someone on the train remarked that the assemblage was "just like that in an Eastern town," expressing surprise at the preponderance of well-dressed people. Twelve carriages, with an escort of cavalry, were drawn up to take the party into town, to the residence of Messrs. Lord & Williams, for a public reception and lunch. Although the last-minute word precluded any decorations around town, the Sixth Cavalry Band was present to play "Hail to the Chief." The procession was followed by many citizens on foot and Indians on horseback. The crowd lining the streets made way for the entire student bodies from a public school and a parochial one to see—and shake hands with —the Hayeses. After greeting thousands at the home, the president and his party were served lunch, the "members of the pulpit" among those in the city invited to stay. Soft band music provided a backdrop for the diners.[95]

The travelers returned to their train at 4 p.m., a half-hour before departure, and the crowd clamored to hear Hayes. The president, who avoided Sunday speeches, stood on the back platform of his car good-naturedly and said he would not make a speech, but he would talk to the people for a little while. Ramsey and Sherman used the same line, and all three of them bragged on Tucson until near departure time.

"In a few minutes ... the signal 'all aboard' was heard and the train moved off," the paper said. "The last thing seen being Mrs. Hayes' good face beaming a smile in response to the genuine Godspeed waved from hundreds of hands."[95]

The train proceeded another 182 miles to the end of the Southern Pacific's track at Shakespeare Ranch, New Mexico Territory. There the Army prudently posted pickets and stationed several fresh relays of horses for the hazardous two-day journey by field ambulances across the desert and hostile Apache country. An Atchison, Topeka & Santa Fe special picked up the party at the railhead at San Marscal, N.M.T., and took them the 200 overnight miles to Santa Fe, arriving on Thursday morning, Oct. 28. The party enjoyed a concert and fiesta, and the president bought some Indian artifacts.

From Santa Fe the special headed northeast, reaching Kansas early on Saturday, Oct. 30. At Dodge City, Hayes wired Garfield in Mentor, Ohio: "We have had a most delightful and instructive trip."[106] Then it was on to Topeka, Kan., on Santa Fe, thence via the Kansas City, Topeka & Western to Kansas City, Mo., and the Wabash, St. Louis & Pacific to Toledo.

Sherman and his daughter left the party in Kansas City and caught a limited for their home in St. Louis. Ramsey made a connection for St. Paul. Hayes and his wife took a Wabash express for Toledo via Hannibal, Mo. In the wee hours of

Monday, Nov. 1, a carriage bearing the weary presidential family pulled up at Spiegal Grove, their home in Fremont, arriving just in time to cast their absentee ballots for Garfield on Nov. 2. They had skipped a stop in Denver to be home on time.

"We left Washington on the Pacific tour Thursday evening, Aug. 26, and returned Saturday morning, Nov. 6, after an absence of 71 days," Hayes wrote after returning to the capital. "Our trip was most fortunate in all of its circumstances. Superb weather, good health, and no accidents. A most gratifying reception greeted us everywhere from the people and from noted and interesting individuals. I must not forget to make acknowledgements. ..."443

After Garfield was sworn in as president on Friday, March 4, 1881,

members of the Cleveland City Troop came to Washington to escort Hayes to Fremont the next afternoon. But the trip home was not without incident. Hayes and his family boarded a special train headed by locomotive 283 at the Baltimore & Potomac depot in Washington. On the same train were, in addition to the presidential escort, a group of inaugural visitors returning to Shamokin, Pa. Extra passenger trains were running on the B&P that day in an effort to get all the inaugural revelers home, and freight runs had been canceled.

As the president's train started toward Baltimore at about 1 p.m., B&P locomotive No. 1—with Northern Central engine 147 in tow—was preparing to head south from Baltimore. The two locomotives—running light and running

extra—were to pick up two more trains of inaugural participants in Washington. In their cabs were conductors and a baggagemaster as well as the engineers and firemen.

Engineer Henry Freeburn, running the 1-spot, had received orders to take siding at Severn, Md., 15 miles south of Baltimore, for the presidential special. At Odenton, the Hayeses' train got its order to wait at Severn for the light engines.

A mile north of Severn, as Hayes was finishing his lunch aboard the private car on his northbound train, southbound engineer Jacob Rider shut off the throttle of the 147 because Freeburn was going too fast. Conductor John Roy, in the cab of No. 1, reminded Freeburn about the meet and told him to stop so he could throw the switch to the siding, but

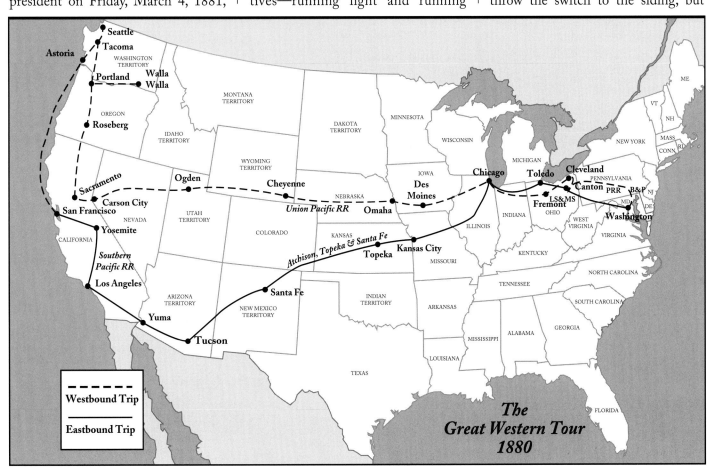

KENNETH L. MILLER

Map shows President Rutherford B. Hayes' itinerary on his 1880 cross-country trip.

Freeburn barreled on. Once they were in a curve beyond the siding, Freeburn saw the 283, piloted by engineer John Unglaub. Both engineers reversed their engines, but at speeds of 25 miles an hour or more it was too late. Roy; Robert Everhart, the 147's fireman; and Bernard McKeever, the 283's fireman, jumped onto the snow-covered right of way. Other crew members and the passengers were trapped as the locomotives pounded each other into "an almost indescribable mass of ruins," according to one newspaper.[438]

Locomotive 1 twisted on its side and plowed the bank of a slight cut. Another locomotive also lay sidelong, the third partially overturned. A fog of liberated steam engulfed them and water gushed beneath. Fragments of the wooden coaches flew like chips of kindling as the train shuddered and compressed. In the last car, the Cleveland Troop's horses were thrown about like bowling pins. In the Hayeses' car, fifth from the front, Hayes' chair flew forward with him in it. Mrs. Hayes and several friends were thrown to the floor.

"Children," the president asked, "are any of you hurt?" None was, aside from bruises.[438]

Uninjured railroad employees and male passengers, including Hayes and his sons, braved the bitter cold to reach those injured or trapped. Engineer Rider managed to walk away from the wreckage and sent fireman Everhart up the track to flag following trains. While Rider and others extinguished the fires in the locomotives' fireboxes, fireman McKeever made sure the cars' heating stoves wouldn't set them ablaze.

The second, third and fourth cars, sleeping cars *Brockton*, *Arcola*, and an unidentified car, had partially overturned, throwing the Cleveland soldiers out of their seats. Escaping from the cars, they grabbed axes and helped extricate other passengers. Some, finding doors blocked, jumped or pulled each other through windows, slashing heads and hands in their panic.

The first car, sleeper *Syria*, was damaged the worst when it telescoped onto engine 283 and its tender; the second car partially telescoped onto the *Syria*. The oak platforms of both cars were "crushed into threads," one newspaper wrote, "like the coarse brooms used by street sweepers."[438] Men tore away the *Syria's* side and found some severely injured passengers among the Pennsylvania group. Their leader, J. Weimar Young, a Shamokin merchant who had chartered the car for the trip, lay dead. Men wrapped his body in some of the car's blankets and laid it in the snow.

Unglaub, badly cut and bruised, crawled out of the debris and fell unconscious. Freeburn was wedged in the cab of the No. 1. He had suffered burns, a fractured skull, and a crushed foot, and cascading coal had bruised his legs. John Oliver, the baggagemaster riding in No. 1, lay crushed and scalded beneath one of the locomotive's cylinders. Raising the cylinder with levers, railroad men freed him, but he died moments later.

Some of the injured were placed in the horse car, which had been pressed into service as a field hospital, and were administered to by the Cleveland Troop's surgeon. Unglaub and Freeburn were laid beside the track and later carried to the Severn depot. Tragically, local folks, who were still full of Southern prejudice against Northern uniforms, would not allow the injured Cleveland soldiers to be placed in their beds.

At the depot, Hayes expressed his sympathy and offered assistance. Mrs. Hayes and several of the other ladies tore up their clothing to make bandages, and the president's wife lulled to sleep Young's 12-year-old son.

Word was sent to Baltimore Union Depot of the tragedy, and a special B&P train was dispatched to the scene carrying extra coaches, a wreck crew and three company physicians. While the passengers who could continue were transferred to the new train, a wire was sent ordering rails and ties for a shoofly around the collision site. Another doctor met the rescue train at Baltimore and redressed wounds attended to hurriedly earlier.

The Hayeses spent the evening at the home of Samuel Shoemaker, a close friend and manager of the Adams Express Company, until about midnight, when they, most of the other passengers and Young's coffin departed for Pennsylvania on another special train. "We [rode] then in a new car, a Pullman,"[443] Hayes wrote. They would go home via PRR-Cleveland-LS&MS.

Crowds came out on Sunday to watch the Severn cleanup. Freeburn stayed in the depot until Sunday afternoon, and then was returned to his home in Washington, where he died the following day. A coroner's inquest blamed the accident on his and Roy's carelessness. The wreck did have one grim benefit—it convinced the B&P to double-track its Baltimore-Washington line.

"We ... expect to reach the home at Fremont Tuesday," Hayes wrote to William Chase on Sunday, March 6, during a layover at Altoona. "The only untoward event connected with our leaving Washington was the accident at Severn by which a number of lives, perhaps four, were unfortunately lost. This caused a delay of several hours. ..."[441]

"Our engineer, John M. Unglaub, behaved in the most devoted and brave way," Hayes wrote in his diary. "He staid [sic] by the engine, at his post, doing all he could to save us. Happily he will recover."[443]

The Hayeses did not forget the experience or its victims. They financed extensive medical treatment for Unglaub, who recovered in a few months. And on New Year's Day, 1882, the couple presented him with an engraved gold watch.

Hayes made at least one other rail trip—one that he barely finished.

On Thursday, Jan. 12, 1893, he recorded a trip from Fremont to Cleveland on the LS&MS to call on Western Reserve University the next day. On Saturday at the Cleveland station about to board a train for home, the ex-president was hit with an attack of angina pectoris. His son, Webb, wanted to take him back to the home of Linus Austin, where he had stayed, but Hayes declined. "I would rather die at Spiegel Grove than to live anywhere else."[31]

His son administered a shot of brandy that relieved the pain and allowed him to make the trip home with no additional suffering.

Once there, he was put to bed, where he died the following Tuesday night at the age of 70.

James A. Garfield

Republican James A. Garfield's most famous rail trip in office was one he never made. The president had taken his wife, Lucretia, to their cottage at Elberon, near Long Branch, N.J., to recover from a bout with malaria, and had returned to Washington to clear up some business before going to Williamstown, Mass., to give the commencement address at Williams College, his alma mater. Then he would rejoin his wife, whom he called "Crete."

July 2, 1881, dawned as a hot Saturday in Washington. Garfield was still at the breakfast table when his secretary of state, James G. Blaine, pulled up in a State Department carriage to accompany him to the B&P depot at B Street (now Constitution Avenue) and 6th, where the National Gallery now stands. After finishing breakfast, Garfield went upstairs to get $500 out of the safe, then talked with Blaine for several minutes in the Cabinet room before going to aide Joe Brown's office to say goodbye. Years later, Brown remembered the

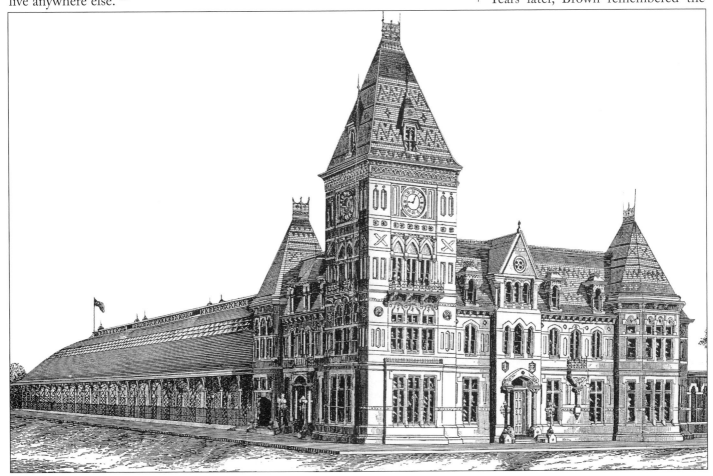

THOMAS W. DIXON JR. COLLECTION

The Baltimore & Potomac station at 6th and B streets N.W. in Washington, D.C., became a landmark when President James A. Garfield was mortally wounded there on July 2, 1881.

familiar way that the president put his hand on the young man's shoulder and how Garfield and Blaine looked "their very best"[229] in their new spring suits and boutonnieres.

As the president went outside, a baggage cart was just starting for the depot and a White House carriage pulled up for sons Hal and Jim and presidential aide Ollie Judd. Farewells to the staff were made, then Garfield and Blaine climbed into the State Department's small coupe, which had facing seats, and were off shortly after 9. The White House carriage followed.

Already at the depot was a short, slightly built 39-year-old man with a small mustache and thin dark beard named Charles Guiteau. He had gotten up at 5 a.m. at the Riggs House, at 15th and I streets, had walked for a while and sat in Lafayette Park across from the White House reading a newspaper, relaxing and enjoying "the beautiful morning air." He returned to the hotel for breakfast and to retrieve

a loaded revolver from his room that he had purchased three weeks earlier. After spending another half-hour in the park, he boarded a horse car for the B&P depot shortly before 9, aware that the president's train was scheduled to leave at 9:30. Dressed in a dark business suit and wearing a slouch hat that was pulled down over his forehead only a little more than usual, he was not likely to attract much attention.

Guiteau was, in a word, a failure. He often ran out on his debts, couldn't keep his marriage going and made a shambles of attempted careers in law and theology. He was interested in politics and fancied himself a presidential speechwriter—even having some of them printed and handed out at conventions and rallies. But no one took him seriously, and he was never successful in giving his scripts to their intended deliverers.

The election of 1880 having been won by Republicans, Guiteau came to

believe he deserved an appointment. He wrote to Garfield twice, once before the election and once afterward, desiring the Austro-Hungarian mission. Arriving in Washington two days after Garfield's inauguration, he often sought the attention of the president and the secretary of state, and once even barged into a White House room where the chief executive was conferring with several other men, but he never was able to talk to Garfield.

Guiteau became disenchanted as a split developed between the president and two New York senators, Roscoe Conkling and Thomas Platt. He sent several notes to Garfield offering to act as peacemaker, which were ignored. By now he was considered a pest around the White House and State Department, and instructions had been quietly issued to keep him away. He came to believe Garfield's policies were leading to the ruin of the party and were a danger to the nation. Guiteau bought a British

Drawing shows the scene as James A. Garfield sustains a mortal wound from the pistol of Charles Guiteau as the president walked across the ladies' waiting room of the Baltimore & Potomac station in Washington with Secretary of State James G. Blaine on July 2, 1881.

Bull Dog .44-calibre five-shooter from John O'Meara's sporting goods store at 15th and F streets—across from the Treasury Department—and stalked Garfield for weeks. He nearly shot him several times, but postponed the deed for various reasons.

So when Garfield arrived at the depot, Guiteau was there. He spoke to a cabman about driving him in the direction of the Congressional Cemetery—near the District jail—had his boots blacked and entered the station. He went into the water closet to inspect his revolver, then left several of his papers at the newsstand. He went outside, walked around a few minutes, noted that it was 9:20 a.m. and entered the ladies' room—a special waiting room meant to protect the weaker sex from choking cigar smoke and unsightly cuspidors.

The White House carriage arrived first, since the president and Blaine had stopped to pick up Dr. William H. Hawkes, the Garfield children's tutor, at his rooming house. The driver went to the baggage stand; the boys stayed outside; Cabinet officers and other members of the party had boarded the train or milled around on the platform. Garfield's carriage arrived at the B Street entrance, and he asked police officer Patrick Kearney how much time they had: about 10 minutes. The men in the carriage continued conversing for a moment, then disembarked. Garfield took Blaine's arm and started up the steps, but Blaine stepped ahead when Garfield paused to return Kearney's salute with a smile and a lifted hat. Then he, too, went into the station through the ladies' room.

The president and secretary moved across the room toward the door of the main waiting room. They had gone about two-thirds of the way when there was a loud report a few feet behind them, quickly followed by another. Blaine touched Garfield as if

to hurry him away from trouble that didn't relate to them. Almost at the same time, the president threw up his arms, crying "My God! What is that?"[229] Guiteau, pistol in hand, passed Blaine on the right and made for the B Street exit. Blaine started to follow him, then turned back to see that the president had sunk to the floor. Kearney apprehended Guiteau before he even reached the door as pandemonium broke out in the station. Sarah White, matron of the ladies' waiting room, cradled the president's head in her lap. Jim was crying; Hal was trying to be helpful. Doctors were summoned; Garfield began to vomit. A mattress was brought from a sleeping car and the wounded president was carried up a winding staircase to an empty room.

As Kearney wrestled his suspect toward the 6th Street door, the ticket agent grabbed Guiteau's neck and knocked his hat off. Another officer assisted Kearney in getting the subject outside. Guiteau exclaimed: "I did it. And I will go to jail for it. Arthur is president and I am a Stalwart."[229] The officers took Guiteau to police headquarters, where their report that he had shot the president was met with derision until Kearney produced the weapon and a letter in Guiteau's possession that explained—in his twisted mind—his justification for the deed.

Dr. Smith Townshend, District health officer, was the first medical man on the scene. The president's coat and waistcoat were removed, stimulants administered and the patient examined. Dr. D. Willard Bliss, whom Garfield had known in rural Ohio, arrived within 15 or 20 minutes and took charge. The first bullet had grazed the president's right arm, and the second had entered his body 3 ½ inches to the right of the spinal column between the 10th and 11th ribs. Bliss probed for the bullet, but it was never found until the

autopsy.

During all this, the president himself made two suggestions.

Beckoning to Col. Almon F. "Jarvis" Rockwell, who had driven his carriage, he asked that word be sent to his wife in Long Branch: "Jarvis, I think you had better telegraph to Crete." He then dictated a "very pathetic dispatch" that Rockwell signed and sent. Later, Garfield said, "I think you had better get me to the White House as soon as you can." A police ambulance was already on its way.[229]

Down the winding stairs and past the very spot where he had fallen, the president was carried to the ambulance. Rockwell sat beside him in the vehicle, taking his hand and supporting his head. The ambulance clattered over rough cobblestones near the depot, then reached the asphalt pavement of Pennsylvania Avenue. An excited crowd followed the galloping horses all the way to the White House. His wife arrived from Long Branch that evening by special train. Garfield, who had inquired about her frequently, asked that they be left alone for their meeting.

The president lived for 80 days. Doctors hovered over him continually, Bliss complaining later that it ruined his practice. Folks tried to devise ways to keep the patient cool during the hot Washington summer; Alexander Graham Bell was called in to probe for the bullet with electrical devices. An Irish White House servant tried her own cure by sprinkling holy water in the president's milk. Meanwhile, Garfield slowly wasted away, never raising his head from his pillow, never smiling, seldom talking.

After two months, doctors decided to grant Garfield's request to move him to the New Jersey shore, away from the sultry capital, in the hope that the fresh saline breezes and sea vistas might help him. On Sept. 5, 2,000 men working for the Central

Railroad of New Jersey started at 3:30 p.m. and worked through the night to lay five-eighths of a mile of track from CNJ's New York & Long Branch line at Elberon to the front door of the president's cottage.

"To see that they had food," said E.T.M. Carr, Long Branch's general agent, "bakeries remained open all night and a tally-ho carried bread, etc., to where the track was being built. The temperature during the entire night did not go below 110 degrees."[262]

The work was finished at daybreak. Meanwhile, at 6 a.m. in Washington, the president was carried to an express wagon that took him to a three-car special train at the B&P depot. Even at that hour, crowds were out all along the route. The president's bed was put on heavy springs in a car cooled by iceboxes, and once under way, the train sometimes raced at 80 miles an hour. Too fast, Garfield was asked? "Oh no, let her go," he answered.[324] During the seven-hour trip of more than 200 miles, people waited at all the villages enroute, silent, hats off, heads bowed, weeping.

The train arrived via the Pennsylvania Railroad and Monmouth Jct., N.J., continuing to Jamesburg, Freehold and Sea Girt, and north up the NY&LB to Elberon behind PRR class D-4 4-4-0 type locomotive No. 658. CNJ operating people decided the engine was far too heavy for the temporary spur and brought in a light CNJ 4-4-0 type to inch Garfield's car toward his cottage. The move was entrusted to two top CNJ men: engineer Dan Mansfield and fireman Martin Maloney.

For a few days, Garfield seemed to be doing well. But on the 16th, he took a turn for the worse. On the 19th, as he talked with two aides, he screamed out as a painful hemorrhage occurred and lost consciousness. Mrs. Garfield and others were summoned; death came in a few minutes—at 10:35 p.m.

Chester A. Arthur

Chester Arthur's 1883 Florida fishing vacation began on Thursday, April 5, at Washington's B&P station—where his running mate had met his doom. The trek was designed as much to provide some much-needed rest and forestall serious illness as to gauge the nation's political pulse. The president was accompanied by Secretary of the Navy William E. Chandler, close New York friend Charles E. Miller, his private secretary, his valet, White House Chef M. Cuppinger and four reporters.

The journey was hot and dusty and marked by many discomforts. The first problem reared its head even before the regular RF&P train's scheduled 11 a.m. departure. Cuppinger, the chef labeled by one paper as "a gentleman with a well-developed waist,"[389f] developed a dreadful anxiety over a hamper of provisions sent to the White House instead of Arthur's car by mistake. The error was corrected without caus-

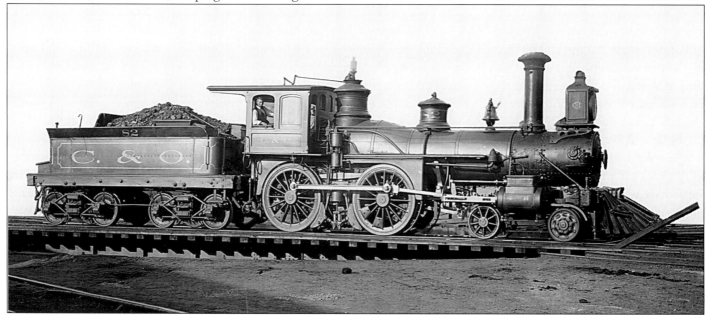

C&O 4-4-0 No. 82 plied its company's rails during the Arthur administration. Perhaps locomotives similar to this one pulled Arthur's special from Washington to White Sulphur Springs, W.Va., and Louisville.

ing serious delay.

Once the train had crossed the Long Bridge over the Potomac and was threading past the switches of Alexandria, Va., Arthur considered himself officially on vacation. He traded his high silk hat for a broad-brimmed, light-colored felt one, and rarely came outside to speak to anyone. His car was switched to another train at Richmond shortly after 3 p.m., and continued south via the Richmond & Petersburg, Petersburg, and Wilmington & Weldon lines.

An overzealous and "old, gray-headed and gray-bearded"[389f] conductor counted 18 seats in Arthur's car and demanded immediate payment of $47.50 in fares from the special party, but got his comeuppance in a company dispatch handed to him at Belfield, Va.

Arthur ignored a crowd at Goldsboro, N.C., because he was having dinner. He came out at Wilmington at 11 p.m. only because it was sultry inside. Wilmington & Manchester workers equipped with turpentine torches took an hour to exchange the standard-gauge trucks on his car to the W&M's 5-foot set. The president sat on a camp stool and smoked a cigar, not realizing several local folks were staring at him as a locomotive headlight illuminated the back platform. He went inside and went to bed before the train proceeded south after midnight on April 6.

Then at 2:30 a.m., about 60 miles south of Wilmington, a coupler broke on Arthur's car and left it stranded in the woods while its train continued about two miles down the track. No one was hurt, and no one knows if Arthur even knew of the incident. The party continued south via the W&M, North Eastern, Charleston & Savannah and Savannah, Florida & Western without further incident.

At Savannah on the afternoon of the 6th, Arthur's car was switched to a siding for a stopover. Some of his rel-

atives boarded, finding his parlor door open because of the heat and everything inside coated with dust and exuding the odor of wood smoke from the locomotive. Arthur switched his plans and decided to rush southward, but his kinfolks were given a ride to the next station.

That evening, when a reception committee boarded at Callahan Station, 21 miles north of Jacksonville, its members found the president's white suit travel-stained and Arthur himself quite weary. Noticing Jacksonville's 90-degree heat, Arthur immediately transferred to his fishing vessel and started up the St. Johns River instead of staying on the car overnight as planned.

A hotel at Sanford was so pleasant he didn't want to leave, and so was irritable and sullen when boarding his South Florida train for Kissimmee City in accordance with his original plans. Near Maitland, the party stopped to visit some orange groves, and after all other means of getting ripe fruit had failed, Chandler blithely climbed a tree to pick some; but nothing could restore the spirits of the president. He refused to go through with a school picnic and reception program at Orlando and sat indignantly inside his stuffy, hot railroad car while the train stopped, contrary to his wishes, beside the picnic grounds.

The vacationing chief executive had planned to return by sea to Fortress Monroe, Va., stopping again in Savannah to see his relatives. But on Thursday the 19th he developed a fever, chill and "bad bellyache"[389h] after having shrimp salad for lunch in Savannah and spending the rest of the day in the hot sun. After a bad night, he decided to return to Washington quickly—by rail—and he departed on his special car at 4:15 p.m. Saturday at the rear of the C&S's fast mail train. Irritated that news of his illness leaked out, the brooding president spent

most of his return trip in bed or sipping a few spoonfuls of chicken broth. When he disembarked in Washington at 9:30 p.m. Sunday, weak but under his own power, it was the first time he had been out of his car since boarding in Savannah. He had wished for no public demonstrations during his trip, and papers of the day indicated the sometimes-surly politician got his wish. It was "doubtful," one said, "if any president traveled with so little annoyance from demonstrative crowds."[389i]

As spring proceeded toward summer, many of Arthur's old acquaintances observed changes in his appearance, his loss of buoyancy, failing ruddiness and increasing gray in his carefully groomed hair and whiskers. They didn't know it at the time, but the president was coming down with Bright's disease, a kidney disorder, which would eventually take his life. A lightened workload didn't seem to help, so his aides organized another rail vacation—a month-long stay in the 11-year-old Yellowstone National Park in Wyoming Territory.

Arthur and several of his Cabinet officers departed for the West on July 30, swinging by Louisville so the president could open the Southern Exposition. Their Chesapeake & Ohio special, consisting of a baggage car and two palace coaches, one of which was outfitted as a diner, was spotted at the B&P station in Washington on Sunday night the 29th. Since Arthur didn't want to commence his trip on a Sunday, everybody boarded the cars and went to bed and the train rolled westward at 4 a.m. Monday. The party stopped over at The Greenbrier resort at White Sulphur Springs, W.Va., from Monday afternoon to 2 a.m. Tuesday, then proceeded to Louisville.

Arthur's address at noon Wednesday was short. When he had spoken from a platform at the fair for less than five minutes, saying nothing in the process, he turned to pull the silken cord dangling above the stand, "thereby …putting in operation all the engines in the machinery department."[188] Kentucky Gov. Luke P. Blackburn, whose seat was under the cord, thought that Arthur's hand was held out to him, and reached to clasp it. With swift tact, Arthur gave that hand to him and, at the same time, with the other, pulled the cord. Simultaneously, the machinery, a set of chimes, an organ, a band and a chorus of 500 voices started up, the latter singing the well-known air, "America."

The president continued northward and westward on the PRR to Chicago, Chicago & North Western to Omaha and Union Pacific to Green River, Wyoming Territory. The departure from Chicago was at noon Friday, Aug. 3, on the private car of Sidney Dillon, UP's president.

The hardy vacationers proceeded from Green River by spring wagon to Fort Washakie on the Shoshone Reservation, where they were entertained by Shoshone and Arapahoe Indians and by the garrison's cavalry. The trip did Arthur more good than the fishing venture in Florida. There, he had curtly turned down the well-intended gift of a large young eagle; at Fort Washakie he gratefully accepted the gift of an Indian pony for his daughter Nell.

The presidential party traveled through Yellowstone National Park on horseback—some 300 miles of fishing, hunting, camping and sightseeing. They returned to railroad travel at the end of track at Cinnebar, Montana Territory, just outside the park and 51 miles south of Livingston, at 6 a.m. Friday, Aug 31, on a Northern Pacific train that had waited for them for several days. The eastward trip was speedy, via the NP, Chicago, Milwaukee & St. Paul and PRR, with arrival in Washington at 10 a.m. Friday, Sept. 7. Arthur's appearance if not his health had improved. During a St. Paul stopover, he had addressed a banquet attended by four trainloads of revelers—including former President Grant—headed for Gold Creek, Montana territory, to celebrate the completion of Henry Villard's NP.

Grover R. Cleveland

One of the most popular train trips during the tenure of New York Democrat Grover Cleveland, the only president to have two non-consecutive terms, was a private journey during his first one—his honeymoon.

The noted bachelor's engagement to the beautiful and highly educated Frances Folsum, a recent graduate of Wells College, was announced on May 28, 1886. The nation was stunned; but the announcement merely confirmed plans known within the family for a year. On Decoration Day, Cleveland traveled to New York City to review parades there and in Brooklyn. He called on his fiancée at the Gilsey House, where Miss Folsum and her mother had gone following travels in Europe. The press jumped on this one; reporters dogged the president's every move from then until the wedding—and then some. Cleveland would be one of three presidents to wed while in office (besides John Tyler and Woodrow Wilson), and the only one to say his vows in the Executive Mansion.

The wedding was set for June 2. Cleveland, 57 at the time, had known this young woman of 22 since the day she was born. They were married in the Executive Mansion's Blue Room and immediately after an informal reception and supper in the State Dining Room, the couple slipped out under cover of darkness to a two-car B&O special train—including B&O private car *Maryland*, which had been used by the late B&O President John W. Garrett and would be by several U.S. presidents. The train was lurking in the yard, not the B&O station, and

Engineer Pat Dailey is at the throttle of St. Louis, Vandalia & Terre Haute engine 142, ready to pull President Grover Cleveland's honeymoon train over the Terre Haute and Indianapolis line out of the latter city in June 1886.

was waiting to take them on their secret honeymoon. At least for this occasion, Cleveland didn't want great crowds and publicity, so no reports were released concerning destinations.

They departed soon after 9 p.m. for Deer Park in Western Maryland. Arrival was achieved before sunrise the next morning in a drizzling rain. Cleveland had rented a cheerful little cottage surrounded by trees and commanding a view of the Blue Ridge.

There were well-stocked trout streams, the president having remarked that "if I am going to keep my reputation as a fisherman, I must go where there are plenty of trout."[277] There were lovely drives with long views across the misty Blue Ridge. There were historical associations, for near Deer Park ran the old road over which George Washington had led part of Braddock's army, and nearby John Brown had prepared for his raid at Harpers Ferry. Henry Gassaway Davis of West Virginia, now retired from the Senate, had developed much of the land as a summer resort and was staying there. At one of the cottages, occupied by future West Virginia Sen. Stephen B. Elkins, many Republican leaders—Grant, Sherman, Garfield, Blaine—had once been entertained.

The serpents in this Eden were a pack of nosy reporters. A carload of them followed the honeymooners on an express train, and arriving shortly after they did, roused a telegraph operator to file their stories, and took up a position in a pavilion several hundred yards from Cleveland's cottage. The irate owner of the house stationed pickets around it, but in vain. On the first day, long dispatches were sent to Eastern newspapers describing the appearance of the couple on the piazza at 10 a.m.: Cleveland's black frock coat, Mrs. Cleveland's blue tulle, their breakfast, their afternoon drive, their seven-course dinner and their evening stroll. Some reporters lifted the covers of the dishes sent from the hotel to inspect their contents; others counted the president's letters. The idea that the metropolitan papers should hire a pack of writers to infest the shrubbery and use spyglasses to watch every movement of the bridal pair struck most Americans as

Philadelphia, Wilmington & Baltimore engine No. 98 rests in Philadelphia during the Grover Cleveland era.

A crowd waits for President Grover Cleveland to alight from his Richmond & Danville coach in Atlanta on Oct. 18, 1887, enroute to visit the Piedmont Exposition during a tour of the West and South.

detestable.

One thing was certain—the honeymoon was no longer a secret. The train came to be officially called *The Grover Cleveland Wedding Train.* It continued westward following the Deer Park visit and ended up on the PRR and its predecessors bound for St. Louis, on a daylight schedule west of Indianapolis.

Engineer Pat Dailey handled the special from Indianapolis Union Station to Terre Haute, Ind., at the controls of 4-4-0 type locomotive No. 142, a product of the Baldwin Locomotive Works. The engine was owned by the Terre Haute & Indianapolis, although its tender was still lettered for predecessor St. Louis, Vandalia & Terre Haute. A great amount of time had been spent decorating the engine so the flags and bunting would stay in place. Some of the bright colors were actually painted onto the locomotive itself. Crews checked the decorations all along the route. They did their jobs well; the picture of Cleveland on the smokebox door and most of the bunting stayed on all the way to East St. Louis.

An immense crowd met the special at the Terre Haute Union Station, as at most of the others, and the president made some perfunctory remarks during the five-minute stop. Engine 142 was oiled and inspected and engineer "Baldie" Idler pulled the train from Terre Haute to Effingham, Ill. Idler had a good bit of difficulty threading the train cars through the crowd at Terre Haute, but once the crowd was out of sight, good time was made into Effingham. There the crowd was even larger; many had come on Illinois Central specials from both north and south. But it was probably the luncheon that was waiting for the special party at the Pacific House—which was just about 50 feet from the front of the train —that put the president in such a jovial, festive mood.

At 142's throttle on the last leg of the trip was "Dutch" Andy Ospring. Everyone who lived along the right of way knew Dutch Andy, and no one was surprised when he made an extra stop at Vandalia to sort of show off his famous passenger by taking on a little water that wasn't really needed.

The Clevelands made an extensive western and southern tour beginning Sept. 30, 1887, that took them as far west as St. Paul and Omaha. They were received everywhere with interest and enthusiasm.

Conductor W.W. Berry remembered well his part in forwarding Cleveland's special from LaCrosse, Wis., to Minneapolis on the River Division of the Chicago, Milwaukee & St. Paul line.

The special would pass through on Monday, Oct. 10. The week before, Berry and another conductor, Jerry Coughlin, were called to Chief Dispatcher E.W. Batchelder's office in Minneapolis for final instructions.

"Jerry was to be the conductor of the presidential special and, because I was a telegrapher in addition to being a freight conductor on the division, I was selected to pilot the envoy engine which was to precede the special by 10 minutes. A lineman was assigned to the envoy engine, fitted out with the necessary equipment to tap the train wire, together with a box relay for my use in case of necessity.

"Two standard McQueen engines, the 224 and 225, had been dolled up for the service and were to be piloted from Minneapolis to LaCrosse by Jerry and me on Sunday, Oct. 9. Mr. Batchelder suggested that we leave South Minneapolis at 10 Sunday morning, but to this Jerry protested, saying that he would be at Mass at that hour and the time was set at 2 p.m. instead. Of course, the earlier hour would have been much better, because of less traffic interference down the line. John Johnson was engineer of the 224 assigned to handle the special, while I had Josh Lantry with the 225. There were eight regular passenger trains and 12 regular freight trains on the division and as the wheat rush was on, many extras, or 'wild trains' as they were called then, were operated.

"At Hastings we received the following order: 'Two light engines east, Berry and Coughlin conductors, will meet two wild trains west, Flynn and Laughlin conductors, at Etter, and train 11, Langan conductor, at Red Wing.' As Jerry signed this order, he declared that we must be in Ireland.

"Lantry and I made a few close meets and left Jerry and Johnson far behind. When they began meeting the fleet of westbound freights, they were badly stuck and did not reach North LaCrosse until the small hours of Oct. 10."[41]

Cleveland's special—gaily decorated—was lined up at the Vine Street Depot when the Minneapolis crews reported back to work at 10 a.m. Monday. Superintendent W.J. Underwood arranged for his crews to meet the Clevelands on their private car. Berry recalled that except for two members of the crews, no one said anything at the meeting at first. "Jerry and I were, of course, the other two Democrats in Minnesota at the time, and were very proud indeed."[41]

After greeting the workmen, the president turned toward his wife and said, "Gentlemen, Mrs. Cleveland."

As the beautiful young lady arose to greet the men in coveralls and uniforms, a handkerchief fell from her lap."

With a quick stride of his long legs, Jerry had the kerchief in hand," Berry recalled. "Dropping it upon the table, he extended his hand and in the richest of Irish, said: 'How do you do; my great pleasure in meeting the first lady of the land.' All present joined Mrs. Cleveland in her hearty laugh."[41]

Berry recalled that the envoy engine was instructed to pass stations where crowds were expected at a slow walk and notify the agents there would be no stops. But Coughlin disobeyed those orders and decided to make short stops at Winona, Lake City, Red Wing and Hastings, where the president received the crowd's accolades on the rear platform.

Cleveland took to the rails in 1888 in an unsuccessful attempt to prevent Republican Benjamin Harrison of Indiana from taking his job. His sleeper, with high windows, high-backed seats, mahogany finish and rich carpets, was in the full glory of the late Victorian period. The cars also had another new development—closed vestibules between them.

Benjamin Harrison

Benjamin Harrison—William Henry Harrison's grandson—mostly allowed the 1888 campaign to come to him. During that summer, Indianapolis became a second home for the press and numerous business and political leaders as thousands ventured across the 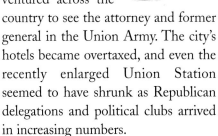 country to see the attorney and former general in the Union Army. The city's hotels became overtaxed, and even the recently enlarged Union Station seemed to have shrunk as Republican delegations and political clubs arrived in increasing numbers.

By the time Harrison moved into the Executive Mansion, presidential specials had become quite ornate. It was an event of nationwide impor-

Norfolk & Western No. 29, an 1887 Baldwin product, was in service when President Benjamin Harrison rode the N&W enroute to the West Coast in 1891.

tance when the Pennsylvania Railroad supplied a train for Harrison's journey.

When the day of departure dawned, the Harrisons had breakfast, the devout Presbyterian president-elect read aloud a chapter from the Bible, and then he held the usual morning prayer service in his library. After that, it was time for his wife, Carrie, and him and other family members to leave. The general's private secretary, Elijah W. Halford, recorded that Harrison appeared "badly broken up. He was alone in his library for a time and full of tears when the time came to take his leave."[348]

Escorting the Harrisons to the station were Indiana Gov. Alvin P. Hovey, Mayor Caleb S. Denny, Gen. Lew Wallace, columns of GAR veterans and several thousand excited Indianapolis citizens. Thirty-two of the more prominent ones walked in a hollow-square formation, surrounding the president-elect's carriage with a guard of honor. As the procession moved slowly along Pennsylvania Street, members of the Indiana Legislature saluted and joined the cortege. The 15 blocks to the depot, lined solidly with cheering admirers,

took almost an hour to traverse.

The four-car special departed from Indianapolis at 3:15 p.m. Monday, Feb. 25, 1889. It was operated as the second section of PRR No. 20, the *Atlantic Express,* but the usual presidential precautions were in effect. Orders were labeled "POTUS," the acronym for "President of the United States"; track walkers were told to be doubly vigilant, with a man stationed along every mile of track; watchmen were assigned to every switch; and wreck trains placed on duty to remove on a moment's notice any obstacle that should foul the line.

Among towns that registered disappointment at the presidential passage was Altoona. "The presidential train passed Altoona at 7 a.m. today [Tuesday] on schedule time to the notch but no one saw the distinguished occupant," fumed the *Altoona Mirror.* "Every soul on board was fast asleep."[8a]

A thousand people had swamped the depot to cheer Harrison, but were thwarted when an engine trade was made down the track at 24th Street— probably with the railroad's intention of protecting its patron's slumber.

Gen. Harrison never found out

that busy, booming Altoona, the home of many protected and unprotected workingmen and mechanics, was on his route to Washington, and those who turned out to shower their respect and benediction witnessed the train shoot like a red streak down the yard at a 35-mile-an-hour rate, followed by an extra engine in case of emergency.

"The presidential train reached Pittsburg[h] at 3:55 this morning, 40 minutes behind schedule time," the *Mirror* said. "Like at Altoona, the blinds were drawn and the occupants were wrapped in slumber. The reporters listened intently to hear Ben snore or to catch a possible wail from [Harrison's grandson] Kid McKee, but both man and baby slept soundly."[8a]

Only the best engineers, of course, were used on this trip. From Dennison, Ohio, Barney Bannon was engineer, operating locomotive No. 58. Alexander Pitcairn held the throttle on the Pittsburg[h] Division to Altoona, and Jack Pitcairn served as conductor. An unusual arrangement called for Alexander Pitcairn to operate the train all the way to Washington, but apparently the idea fell through. The crew from Altoona included engineer Jones, fireman Drake, conductor Long and brakemen Walzer and Kinter.

The paper kept up with the train even after it left town, noting that breakfast was served just as the presidential party entered the Lewistown Narrows.

Harrison's rail travel continued while he was in office. The president crowed about "the handsomest train I ever saw"[262] when he, his family, his Cabinet, the Supreme Court justices and several reporters boarded a nine-car special at Washington's B&P station April 29, 1889, enroute to New York for the centennial fete celebrating George Washington's inauguration.

President Benjamin Harrison greets a crowd on the rear platform of his private car.

"The train included four vestibuled drawing-room sleeping cars, a composite car, a vestibule buffet combination car, and [PRR First] Vice President [Frank] Thompson's private car, No. 60," wrote the *Philadelphia Railway World*. The private car was "specially fitted up for President Harrison and his family in a unique manner that attracted universal admiration. It was placed at the rear of the train, and the novel idea was successfully carried out of decorating its interior with a wealth of floral beauty. ... A table on the left-hand side of the room was covered with flowers, the gift of Pennsylvania Railroad officials. ..."[262] It also boasted an "elaborate wood-burning fireplace in the main lounge, framed by a mantle that reached to the top of the car. The mantle was bracketed by large bookcases and cabinets ... for display of bric-a-brac."[358]

"The cars," exulted the *Pittsburgh Post*, "are lighted with electricity and heated by steam. They are fitted up with every appliance luxury could desire. A well-stocked library is in one car, and a complete barber's outfit in another. Bathrooms are at every hand, and by a new invention, an electric light furnishes illumination."[262]

Harrison and his staff toured several Midwestern states during the midterm campaign of 1890, riding in the Pullman private car *Haslemere*. On one crisp October day, he rode in a Chicago, Burlington & Quincy locomotive between Peoria and Galesburg, Ill., with engineer Frank Hilton, with whom he had served in the Army during the Civil War. Harrison blew the whistle at all crossings and stations, while Secretary of the Navy Benjamin F. Tracy handled the bell rope.

A more extensive journey followed a year later when Harrison made a trip to the West Coast. Departing Washington Monday

Swords mounted on the pilot are among the decorations on Southern Pacific engine 214 as it waits to pull Benjamin Harrison's special out of Los Angeles on April 24, 1891.

evening, April 13, 1891, he proceeded on the Richmond & Danville to Lynchburg, Va.; the Norfolk & Western to Roanoke and Bristol; the East Tennessee, Virginia & Georgia to Knoxville and Chattanooga; and the Nashville, Chattanooga & St. Louis to Atlanta. The train was an elegant five-car affair, with *The Presidential Special* inscribed in large gilt letters on the forward panels of the smoker.

Atlanta's presidential welcome was noisy—and dangerous. As the special entered town, a locomotive ran ahead of it pulling a flatcar upon which was mounted a heavy gun of the Atlanta Artillery. Soldiers fired it all along the right of way. Closer in, another cannon on a stationary flat car was fired just as the special passed, breaking out three plate-glass windows in the dining car *Coronado* and

knocking down a waiter standing in the aisle. Harrison was at the rear of the train and didn't know about the incident until told about it. From Atlanta, the party moved westward on R&D's Georgia Pacific Division to Birmingham and the Kansas City, Memphis & Birmingham to Memphis. By the time the train stopped at Jasper, Ala., at 11 p.m. on Thursday the 16th, the president had retired to his car, the *New Zealand.* But visitors were allowed to board observation car *Vacuna* briefly and listen to talks by presidential son Russell B. Harrison.

In the tremendous late-night crowd in Memphis was Esther Mosby, a former slave once owned by Harrison's maternal grandfather, John E. Page. She and the president had been playmates as children at Page's estate in Page Brook, Va., and she

wanted to see him. Police kept her back but a reporter discovered who she was and got her on the train. From window to window, they searched for Harrison until they spotted him, boarded, and she clasped his hand. Reporters said it was hard to tell which one enjoyed the reunion more. After she left, Harrison was handed a letter she had written to him in case she couldn't see him, stirring up more precious memories.

After the train crossed the Mississippi on a Little Rock & Memphis ferry, it continued on that line to Little Rock.

It was somewhere on that stretch of LR&M trackage that George Frederick Ege stood in for Harrison. Ege was in charge of the cross-country movement. He was known as the "Chesterfield of Pullman conductors," a reference to Britain's Lord

Chesterfield, a statesman and author noted for his debonair and urbane dress. The train halted for a few moments in a section of Arkansas woods and a crowd of hillbillies (as reported in the *Pullman News*) demanded a speech. The president having presumably retired, Ege was "taking the air" alone on the observation platform. He thanked his "fellow citizens of the great state of Arkansas" in a few words, and they, nothing wiser, applauded lustily. As the train moved ahead, a slight noise behind him caused the conductor to turn. To his embarrassment, he discovered Harrison in shirt sleeves and convulsed with laughter. Ege's apologies for his "lese majeste" were cut short by his excellency's assurance that "no president could have done better."[302]

Ege preserved an itinerary of the trip upon which he collected the signatures of President and Mrs. Harrison, son Russell, presidential daughter Mrs. Mary Scott Harrison McKee and her husband, J.R. McKee, Mrs. Mary Scott Dimmick—whom the president married after his wife died of cancer the following year—Postmaster General John Wanamaker, Secretary of Agriculture Jeremiah M. Rusk, newsman Richard V. Oulahan and others.

From Little Rock, Harrison rode the St. Louis, Iron Mountain & Southern to Texarkana, Texas; the Texas & Pacific to Galveston; and the Southern Pacific to California.

The president was a trouper without doubt. The train stopped briefly at a way station in Arizona, where a half-dozen ranchers drew close in the darkness. Harrison thought the crowd was "pathetic," but was moved when he noticed Grand Army of the Republic buttons on two or three lapels and heard one of the men shout, "There are but a few of us, but let's give a cheer for the old flag, boys."[96]

Harrison spent several days in California, visiting several cities near Los Angeles via the SP and the Atchison, Topeka & Santa Fe. Then he took the SP to Oakland for a lengthy stay at San Francisco's Palace Hotel and side trips to Palo Alto, Del Monte and Sacramento. As the president made his way through the state, news reports surfaced that Oregon Gov. Sylvester Pennoyer, a states' rights advocate, would not greet him on his arrival in Portland. It was a matter of protocol to Pennoyer, not politics. "If the governor of Oregon went to Washington," he pontificated, "no one would expect the president to meet him. The president represents the dignity of the federal government; I represent the dignity of the government of Oregon. We are equal."[389h] But the next day, a follow-up story depicted a red-faced governor who claimed he had spoken those harsh remarks in confidence and had no idea they would be published. "It would make it appear I want him to hunt me up," he whined. "I will receive the president with all the courtesy due his exalted position."[389l]

On Sunday night, May 3, Harrison started toward Oregon on the SP. The train reached Tehama, Calif., early Monday morning to meet a hardy, early rising crowd that was being drenched by the first rain the presidential train had encountered. Their tenacity was rewarded; Harrison was the only one up, and he spoke to them.

From Portland, the president continued to Tacoma via Northern Pacific and (by boat) to Seattle, then back to Tacoma and eastward on the Union Pacific to Boise City and Pocatello, Idaho, and down to Salt Lake City. He continued to Glenwood Springs, Leadville, Colorado Springs and Denver, Colo., via the Denver & Rio Grande Railroad. In Denver, he was guest of honor at the opening of the

Hotel Metropole.

He headed home on the CB&Q to Omaha via Hastings and Lincoln, Neb. Between those two points, engine 203—covered with the customary flags and bunting—was on the point, operated by Robert Smith, the "B&M flying engineer" (the moniker referred to CB&Q predecessor Burlington & Missouri River). In Omaha, Adjutant General Albert Cole was the first to make an appearance from the train, decked out in full dress uniform complete with gold cord, shining buttons, black plumes and three-cornered hat. A middle-aged lady in the crowd who apparently was expecting to see Harrison emerge in such garb, bellowed out: "Hey, there he is—there's the president—there on the steps—in his own togs! My, ain't he fine!"[96]

From Omaha the party traveled on the Wabash to Springfield and Decatur, Ill.; the Indianapolis, Decatur & Western to Indianapolis; and the PRR and B&P back to Washington. They arrived at 5:30 p.m. Friday, May 15. Nearly home, Harrison called all of his fellow passengers, including family, guests, politicians and even crew, and made speech No. 140 of the trip. He had ridden more than 10,000 miles, he said, having a delightful time throughout—and he was grateful. Then he shook hands with them all.

Theodore Roosevelt looks as if he may be trying to bum a cab ride from the crew of Colorado & Southern locomotive 110, which has stopped alongside his private car at Emery Gap, N.M.

Twentieth Century Travels

4

William McKinley

Democrat William Jennings Bryan, noted orator and three-time presidential candidate, first lost to Republican William McKinley in 1896. But it was Bryan who gave presidential rail campaigning its big break. During that race, he traveled 18,009 miles by train, making almost 3,000 speeches—including 569 major addresses—during the course of dozens of 18-hour days. 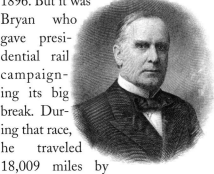 Sometimes taking side trips by buggy when the train stopped long enough, Bryan made 10 to 20 speeches a day. His record—24 talks in one day—still stands. In all, Bryan rode for three months in hot wooden coaches and even cabooses to speak to an estimated 5 million people in 27 states.

He was nominated at the Democratic convention in Chicago in June after a stirring appeal that addressed the gold/silver money standard crisis of that day: "You shall not press down upon the brow of labor this crown of thorns, you shall not crucify mankind upon a cross of gold."[44]

Bryan was offered the use of a private Pullman car for his trip home to Lincoln, Neb., but a friend dissuaded him. "Mr. Bryan," he said, "you should not accept this offer. You are the 'Great Commoner,' the people's candidate, and it would not do to accept favors from the great railroad corporations." Bryan agreed and rejected the offer.[44]

On Saturday, Aug. 8, Bryan and his wife, Mamie, left Lincoln on the Rock Island day train to Chicago. The candidate's initial rostrum was the rear car, or "platform coach,"[446] of the train, where he promised the crowd who came to see him off that "whether what I do meets with your approval or not, I shall do my duty as I see it and accept all consequences which may follow."

Thus launching a poor man's campaign for the poor man's vote, the Bryans traveled at first as everyday coach passengers, although later more luxurious accommodations were provided at the discretion of the Democratic National Committee.

From that very first morning in Nebraska, Bryan hurried to the rear to speak to whatever crowd showed up—and continued speaking until the train eased away. The train crews frequently trotted back to listen until it became necessary to return to their duties. Bryan was pleased by the size of the crowds who came to see and hear him.

Farmers drove horses and buggies up to 100 miles to hear the free-silver advocate. Their wives and daughters brought him home-baked apple pies and decorated his car with flowers.

The "Great Commoner"[44] convinced the American people he was one of them. During a brief stop in upstate New York, a sturdy farmer hitched his plow team to the fence post nearest the halted train, strolled into the observation car, and without introduction shook Bryan's hand. He explained, "I have always been a Republican, but I am for silver. We farmers know what is good for us."[446] With that, the typical American made a quick exit and went on with his plowing.

Forty or 50 pickpockets would board Bryan's train each morning, sit in the smoker and fan out among the crowd at each stop. Bryan would ask those who had gold in their pockets to raise their hands, then silver likewise, to point out that both metals were commonly accepted. The pickpockets quietly moved in. They made a killing for a while—until Bryan hired a Pinkerton detective to accompany him.[44]

Despite the fact that he was the "people's candidate," Bryan turned out to be the first presidential nominee to officially campaign from the back platform of a private car. Finally persuading him was a man whose middle initial and last name spelled "Bryan"—Charles B. Ryan, assistant general passenger agent of the Chesapeake & Ohio Railway.

Ryan suggested to company President M.E. Ingalls that the nominee be given the free use of a C&O business car, a private coach designed for use by railway officials when traveling over its lines. "It would be good publicity," he said.[20] Ingalls, a Democrat but not a free-silver man, agreed reluctantly.

As Bryan proceeded west on the C&O, Ryan met him in Huntington, W.Va.—where the candidate spoke at noon one day—and offered him the use of the private car as long as he traveled over C&O.

The Silver-Tongued Orator accepted graciously and the car was coupled onto his train. Suddenly, he seemed to revel in this distinction.

"Neither he nor I nor any of us realized at the time that this car was making political history (or) was rev-

Former President Benjamin Harrison campaigns for William McKinley on the C&O at Alderson, W.Va., in 1896.

olutionizing campaign methods," Ryan explained later. "It was, indeed, the first private car ever used by a presidential candidate; but since then, in presidential campaigns, rear-platform speeches on private cars have been counted upon heavily to reach the multitudes."[192]

For one thing, use of the car would give better play to Bryan's appetite. Even in scorching weather, he was a hearty trencherman. His typical breakfast included a steak or chops, baked potatoes, sliced tomatoes, buttered hot muffins and coffee, sweetened and creamed—but no liquor or tobacco. On a hot day, he would consume quarts of lemonade and cool himself with a big palm-leaf fan. A teetotaler, he often took off his clothes and rubbed himself with gin to remove the odor of perspiration, but that caused him to smell "like a wrecked distillery" and spawned nasty rumors.

Between Huntington and Cincinnati, huge crowds acclaimed him and the "Great Commoner" spent between one and five minutes at each stop to say a few words and shake hands.

But at Newport, Ky., the nominee had a stand-in. One of the politicians touring the Bluegrass State in Bryan's entourage was Newport-born Rep. Albert Berry, D-Ky. As the train neared its Newport stop and the customary cheering crowd, Berry learned that Bryan was not planning an appearance there. Further, Bryan had taken off his shirt and was planning to go over the speech he would deliver in Cincinnati that night. A clean shirt, collar, cuffs, and a black bow tie lay on the table beside his broad-brimmed black felt hat.

"Where is Mr. Bryan?" Berry asked as the lights of his hometown twinkled in the distance. "In his room," Ryan answered, "getting ready for his speech in Cincinnati."[192]

Berry was distressed. "Those people know I'm traveling with Mr. Bryan," he told Ryan, as reporters overheard. "If he fails to speak in my hometown for a minute or two, after having spoken everywhere else along the line all afternoon, it will ruin me for life."[192]

One reporter, whose name history has shrouded, had an idea. He was

One of William McKinley's trips west used B&O rails to Pittsburgh, according to P.H. Delaplaine, a railroad telegraph operator at Cumberland, Md., in 1901. Circumstances gave Delaplaine an experience he would never forget.

"An empty coal train was taking water at Patterson Creek,[W. Va.]" Delaplaine recalled. "Another train was waiting behind that one, when a third freight ran into the rear of the second and piled up loaded and empty cars for quite a distance, blocking both main line tracks. I was relieved by another operator, rode the wreck train to the scene, and used a box relay for connection with the dispatcher's office.

"I sat on a crosstie all morning while wreckage was cleared up. A crane picked up salvageable material and the rest of the rubble was rolled down a bank and set afire. Trees were cut down to cover the wreckage, so that all would be well when the presidential special arrived. The McKinley train passed through at 1 p.m. and all signs of the accident had been removed. I saw the president sitting in his private car as the train rolled past Patterson Creek Tower."[47]

William Jennings Bryan campaigns in West Virginia.

about Bryan's height, with a vague facial resemblance. He guessed that few—if any—of the Newport folks gathered in the semidarkness had actually seen Bryan or heard his voice but probably all were familiar with newspaper photos that showed him wearing that broad-brimmed Western hat. So he dashed into Bryan's room with a cryptic explanation and grabbed the hat.

As the train eased to a stop, Berry ceremoniously escorted the reporter to the rear platform and introduced him as "our next president, William Jennings Bryan!"[205] The crowd roared its approval. The reporter uttered a few Bryanesque platitudes and shook outstretched hands. "The Boy Orator from the Platte"[44] himself, who had been tipped off and had approved of the charade, remained out of sight in his room, silently shaking with laughter. The engine's whistle screamed and the train chugged away. And no one was the wiser.

The story was kept under wraps for 40 years. Not until Bryan and Berry were both dead did the aged Ryan reveal it.

As the campaign entered its last month, Bryan campaigned constantly, giving the lie to the name of his private car, the *Idler*. He traveled 12,837 miles through the Midwest and Upper Mississippi Valley. He had traveled more miles, and spoken to more people, than any other presidential candidate to date.

William McKinley of Canton, Ohio—an Army veteran who had fought under Rutherford B. Hayes and later became an attorney—let the voters come to him. His front-porch campaign was styled after Benjamin Harrison's and others', but he refined the procedure to a science.

Supporters started for McKinley's house literally at the moment his nomination was secured. In St. Louis, the Republicans began a roll call of the states at 5 p.m. on June 18, and it was his home state of Ohio that put him over the top. A private telegraph wire, installed in McKinley's home and running directly to convention hall, informed the major—a Civil War-earned title—of the results instantly, and he had time only to cross the hall into the parlor and kiss his wife and mother before neighbors began swarming in to offer congratulations. Within 45 minutes, a special train that had started from Alliance the minute Ohio's vote was announced brought 2,000 more supporters, and at 7:15, 19 more coaches arrived from Massillon—with passengers jammed in so tightly they were clinging to the sides and riding the tops of the cars. At 7:40, four trains of 10 cars each arrived with 4,000 people from Akron, and at 10 p.m. another delegation arrived from Niles, 60 miles away. Between 5 p.m. and midnight, at least 50,000 visitors listened to McKinley's speeches, and he greeted many of them personally.

Campaign Manager Mark Hanna arranged for thousands of "gold standard pilgrims"[205] to take the train to see him, sometimes to the tune of 15 to 30 trains a day. As the idea caught on, Republican managers were flooded with applications from delegations wanting to come. It required careful scheduling, in which the railroads cooperated and offered special low fares; careful timing so that one delegation could arrive as another departed; and a temporary expansion of Canton's facilities.

A holiday atmosphere greeted the delegations that unloaded at Canton's overtaxed depot. Enroute to the major's home, they marched past store windows overrun with bunting and pictures, under arches of "protected"[265] tin covered with McKinley's face, and by hot dog stands, cigar drummers, candy sellers, lemonade vendors and souvenir peddlers. The streets wore down under the tramp of marching feet, and lucky was he who could find a decent meal or a quiet moment between the dawn and midnight.

McKinley delivered short, carefully crafted compliments and received short, carefully crafted responses. It was all hard on the homestead, for between June 19 and Nov. 2, McKinley spoke to 750,000 people from 30 states in more than 300 delegations. The front lawn looked "as if a herd of buffalo had passed that way,"[265] and the pilgrims took so many souvenir pieces of wood from the porch that it threatened to fall on the candidate's head.

Hanna tried to get McKinley to go on the road against Bryan, but he flatly refused.

"I cannot take the stump against that man," he said. "If I took a whole train, Bryan would take a sleeper. If I took a chair car, he would ride a freight train. I might just as well put up a trapeze on my front lawn and compete with some professional athlete as go out speaking against Bryan. I have to THINK when I speak. I can't outdo him and I'm not going to try."[44]

But McKinley DID outdo Bryan and won the election. The triumphant president-elect left Canton for Washington on March 1, 1897, with some 50 relatives and friends—and six steamer trunks full of applications from eager job seekers. They boarded a

President and Mrs. William McKinley arrive at Camp Meade, Pa., on Aug. 12, 1898, where the president signed a peace protocol formally ending the Spanish-American War. Maj. Webb Hayes, a member of the First Ohio Cavalry and a son of former President Rutherford B. Hayes, walks on Mrs. McKinley's right.

luxurious train furnished by the Pennsylvania Railroad as Canton turned out with enthusiastic citizens, the usual bunting, flags and brass bands.

A stiff, formal reception committee greeted him the following morning in Washington. A large crowd of both curious and well-wishers saw the president-elect alight from his car and walk to the engine, where he shook hands with the grimy crew and gave each a carnation. Ida McKinley leaned on her husband's arm, but Mother McKinley, a spry 87, alighted gingerly from her car, carrying an armload of deep red roses she had thriftily gathered on the train, and faced cameramen with a smile and light wave. Not even her widely beloved son would receive as much praise and press adoration as did Nancy Allison McKinley. She filled many places in the nation's heart that her ailing daughter-in-law could not reach. But the photographers, the smiling crowds to whom she waved,

never turned her head. The spectacle and pageantry of power meant little to her. William was her dearest, but she cherished a hope that he would enter the ministry, a dream that would die hard. On inauguration eve, the president's brother Abner was overheard pleading with her, "But, Mother, this is better than a bishopric."[265]

McKinley toured the Midwest and West in October 1898 in an unprecedented presidential effort to support Republican congressional candidates in the off-year election. For two weeks, he spoke several times daily from his special train in most of the states between Ohio and the Dakotas. The chief event of the tour would be an appearance at the Trans-Mississippi Exposition at Omaha on Oct. 12.

The task of planning the president's itinerary fell to E.W. "Doc" Smithers, his transportation chief, who went to work in the White House Feb 15, 1898, and held the post until his death in 1939.

The presidential special was scheduled to leave Washington at 9 a.m. Monday, Oct. 10, but the week before, McKinley's wife's brother, George D. Sexton, was shot to death. The McKinleys and several relatives left Washington for the funeral at 7:20 p.m. Saturday the 8th on the private car *Campania*, which was attached to the rear of PRR's regular *Western Express*. Arrival in Canton was at 10:26 a.m. Sunday, and Sexton's funeral was conducted Monday afternoon. The presidential train, carrying a baggage car, a diner, five Pullmans and an observation car, left Washington as scheduled, and at 9 p.m. Monday McKinley's car was coupled on at Canton and the westward trek began.

A year later, the McKinleys went on a "stumping tour"[251] of Midwestern and Western states in the fall of 1899, starting on Wednesday, Oct. 4. Having vowed the previous summer not to campaign in 1900 should he receive another nomination for office, the president conveniently used this trip as his first and last great campaign effort as well as a test of public support for his policies. They took along all the Cabinet members except Treasury Secretary Lyman J. Gage, who was already in the West.

Meanwhile, Bryan kept at it, campaigning in earnest all during McKinley's first term. First came a stint in the Army during the Spanish-American War. Answering a call from the president for volunteers, Bryan was commissioned a colonel in the Third Nebraska Regiment—soon to be known as the Silver Regiment. On July 19, 1898, the unit boarded four trains totaling 18 coaches at Fort Omaha for Jacksonville, Fla., for final combat training. Bryan's train included a Pullman observation car for the colonel-who-would-be-president and his staff.

The regiment soon realized it was riding a campaign train. At almost every stop a crowd waited to cheer the

Nebraska heroes, and Bryan most of all. Again and again he addressed them, offering praise of his men, hopes for an early victory with a peace of freedom for Cuba and an escape from the "Poisoning Tentacles of Imperialism,"[446] more commonly known as expansionism. The train crews joined the crowd, and found each speech different from the one before. As the train moved into Illinois, crowds grew larger. Town bands played marches and at night depots became focal points for torchlight parades.

In Chicago, the convoy transferred from the Burlington to the Illinois Central and headed south. A press account chronicled the passage through Bloomington, Ill.:

"The first section of the train passed through this city at three o'clock and the train bearing Col. Bryan about a half-hour later. The excessive heat of the day prevented an elaborate celebration from being carried out, but the booming of a cannon still told of the coming of the great leader and his followers. ...

"Amid the booming of cannon and the cheering of several thousand people, the first section of six coaches loaded to the guards came in. The men looked both happy and hot. The train arrived at 3:22, and after stopping a few minutes for water, pulled out. Col. Bryan was on the second train in the last coach with his staff. When this announcement was made the excitement grew, the cannon became louder and everything in general became animated. ...

"As Bryan's train rolled in, a mighty cheer went up from the multitude. It was the event of the afternoon. Bryan himself, with his smiling yet commanding face, appeared at the rear platform, followed by his officers, all his regimental staff. The vociferous cheering continued and on the appearance of the great leader the enthusiasm broke all bounds. Hats went up in the air and everyone tried to outdo his fellow enthusiast in making a demonstration.

"The hands went up faster than Col. Bryan could grasp them. He had

a pleasant word for all and when quiet was restored he began speaking: 'Ladies and gentlemen: I had the pleasure of speaking here two years ago and I am glad to speak and meet you now. I am proud of my regiment of sturdy, healthy fellows, as only one of them out of the 1,300 was not well enough to leave Omaha. I am very glad to know that you take a great interest in them and me. I had a letter from an Illinois man who could not get here, asking to join my Nebraska regiment. In time of peace you can all help fight your country's battles.' "[57]

The article said applause was prolonged, and when Bryan finished, the handshaking began again. Women, boys and men fought for a chance to grasp the colonel's hand.

On July 21, an on-board reporter wrote that "the Third Regiment is having a very hard time of it running the doughnuts and cake and ice cream gauntlet that the people of the South seem to have thrown across its march. ..."[446]

At Nashville, the edible contributions included 1,342 pies and 300 quarts of coffee. A newspaper article there said the first section of the train would arrive via the Nashville, Chattanooga & St. Louis line at 11 a.m. and that a welcoming committee had made arrangements with the Tea Room to prepare a thousand box lunches and a thousand gallons of hot coffee—nearly a complete lunch and a gallon of coffee for each soldier. Each lunch contained two sandwiches, two hard-boiled eggs, two tomatoes, two beaten biscuits and a lemon.

"It is supposed that most of the boxes will contain about the same articles," a paper said, "though some enthusiastic ladies may have disobeyed the order with regard to cake and pickles."[57]

Jacksonville's citizens greeted the arriving regiment with 1,800 box lunches—a full one and part of anoth-

Riding on the rear of this six-car train are President and Mrs. William McKinley on a stumping tour of the Northwest with most of his Cabinet in October 1899. McKinley had vowed to refrain from campaigning should he be renominated in 1900; doubtless having second thoughts, he got around that pledge by doing so a year early. Ironically, the name of his private car was Campania.

B&O engine 851 prepares to take a train out of that company's station at New Jersey Avenue and C Street N.W. in Washington. This station and the Baltimore & Potomac depot a few blocks away, both of which saw many presidential arrivals and departures, were replaced by Washington Union Station in 1907.

William McKinley shakes some hands in Alliance, Ohio. With him are, from left, Secretary of Agriculture James Wilson, Secretary of the Interior Ethan A. Hitchcock and the president's personal secretary, George B. Cortelyou.

er for each soldier.

Following his seven-month military career was Bryan's association with Chautauqua, a traveling lecture program that had its origins in the 1870s as a summer assembly for religious revivals, Bible-study seminars and Sunday School teacher-training at Lake Chautauqua, N.Y. It had expanded its curriculum to include music, history, literature and the arts. Bryan saw Chautauqua as a way to earn money and try out his political tenets on live audiences. He made his first circuit in June 1899 and continued his lectures until 1912.

Chautauqua travel was strenuous, usually at night by railroad day coach, but often by buggy, wagon, horseback or foot. Bryan found it had much in common with campaigning—bad weather, bad food and accidents, but also warm, receptive audiences.

He offered a taste of Chautauqua life in a letter back home to Mamie: "What a night I had last night! I left Watertown on the 5 p.m. train for Sioux Falls, 103 miles away. When we got to Badger, about 30 miles out, we found a car off the track, and not knowing when the train could go on, we got out at 6:30 and started for Sioux Falls, wiring to Sioux Falls to send a fast car to meet us. We made pretty fair time for 42 miles. (We found the distance by wagon road some 85 or 90 miles.) Once we got off the road and lost half an hour and then [got] stuck in the mud. We waked up a farmer and were going to have him haul us out of the mud, but by the time he had dressed, the Sioux Falls car arrived and took us about 45 miles in two hours, i.e.: 10:30 to 12:30. But the Chautauqua audience was still there and shouting, and I spoke from 12:40 midnight to 2:08 a.m. That is my record for Chautauqua—it almost equals my political meetings. I am approaching my last town. Then I drive 15 miles and catch a train for Chicago."[57]

Thanks to his military travels and Chautauqua, Bryan's second campaign was already in high gear when it was officially declared. The crowds were there; the coverage was complete.

A typical trip took place across West Virginia on the Baltimore & Ohio, Ohio River, Kanawha & Michigan and Chesapeake & Ohio lines in 1899. Former West Virginia Gov. William Alexander MacCorkle met Bryan in Grafton to escort him through the state in his private car.

"I met Mr. Bryan at daylight and transferred him to my car," MacCorkle wrote in his memoirs. "He was then making a speech which continued 30 minutes. At its conclusion he took a cup of coffee, a roll and a small piece of steak for his breakfast. He arose with the cup of coffee in his hand to make another speech."[244]

MacCorkle recalled that the talks continued every 15 minutes until the candidate arrived in Parkersburg at noon, where he spoke to 30,000 people for an hour. The pace slackened only slightly until arrival in Wheeling that evening.

"He had been speaking continuously, with few exceptions, since daylight," MacCorkle wrote, "shaking hands, meeting people, talking, arguing, placating the disgruntled whom he met, in the midst of the greatest physical, as well as mental, strain. When he arrived in Wheeling, it was to meet a mass of people such as I never in my experience saw assembled in a political meeting. The car was besieged by thousands, there were whole squares of people. He made a speech at the car, another speech on his way to the place of meeting, where there were 70,000 people waiting for him. … There was no indication of physical weariness. … Every sentence was as clear and sparkling and bright as a summer's morn."[244]

Bryan made two more talks, the ex-governor said, as his phalanx of policemen escorted him back to the private car at midnight. Finally, he was out of reach of the people for the first time that day.

"Before he had gone to the meeting, I asked him if he wanted to eat anything when he came back. He said 'yes,' and I called in my cook, Deck Anderson, who was a Democratic Negro, a free-silver man and ardent admirer of Mr. Bryan. The latter told Deck what he wanted for his supper: … a large beef steak cooked in onions, a full pan of french-fried potatoes, a lot of hot biscuit, celery, and a large pot of the strongest coffee that Deck could make. I saw my friend after the tremendous efforts of that day, sit down with his wet shirt and wet clothes on, eat the steak and onions which I could not have eaten in four meals, clean up all the potatoes, eat all the celery, make away with the hot biscuit and drink a quart of coffee that would swim an iron wedge, yet talking all the time with half a dozen men who sat around him. And then, with a sigh of contentment, he lay down on the bed and in five minutes was sleeping the sleep of a child."[244]

At daylight the next day, following a southbound overnight run on the Ohio River Railroad, Bryan addressed a "great assembly"[244] at Point Pleasant, then, continuing up the Kanawha River on the Kanawha & Michigan, made two more talks on the way to Charleston. There he spoke to 20,000, then moved onto the C&O to a dense crowd of 40,000 at Huntington. He returned to the private car at midnight, at which time MacCorkle had to leave him.

Campaigning in the fall of 1900 at his usual hectic pace, Bryan covered more than 16,000 miles in six weeks, making 600 speeches, traveling mostly in coaches rather than private cars. The voters loved him—but didn't elect him.

McKinley repeated the pattern of his first campaign, never leaving Canton, Ohio; nevertheless, he won the election.

The McKinleys crossed the nation in the spring of 1901 aboard the private car *Olympia* in an effort to win support for trust-busting and for extending commercial reciprocity. It seemed fitting to inaugurate the second term with such a tour. He had not seen the Far West, and the trip—scheduled to last six weeks—would take him south, across the desert Southwest, and then up the coast to San Francisco, where he would launch the recently finished battleship *Ohio*. The return would be climaxed at the newly inaugurated Pan-American Exposition in Buffalo, N.Y., where he would make a major address in celebration of Presidents Day.

The route west and south from Washington included the Southern

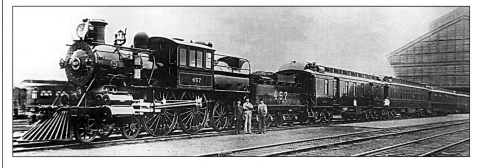

CHARLES B. CHANEY COLLECTION/SMITHSONIAN INSTITUTION
The train of Garret Augustus Hobart, William McKinley's vice president until Hobart's death in 1899, departs Jersey City, N.J., behind CNJ 4-4-2 Camelback locomotive No. 457.

The McKinleys' 1901 cross-country special pauses on the Southern Railway at Decatur, Ala., home of Spanish-American War hero Gen. Joseph "Fighting Joe" Wheeler.

The McKinleys' 1901 cross-country trek makes its first stop along the Mexican border at Del Rio, Texas.

The location of this town is unknown, but the blur indicates it lacked sufficient population to warrant a stop for William McKinley's 1901 cross-country train. Looks like the locals came out anyway, hoping to catch a presidential glimpse.

William McKinley seems impatient to depart this town, perhaps perturbed over the small turnout of supporters.

Railway to Lynchburg, Va.; Norfolk & Western to Bristol, Va./Tenn.; Southern again to Chattanooga, Huntsville, Ala., and Memphis; Illinois Central to New Orleans; and Southern Pacific to San Francisco.

The presidential train carried McKinley and his wife, Secretary of State John Hay, Postmaster General Charles Smith and their wives, and reporters—in all a party of 43. Of all his tours, this last one aroused more genuine interest throughout the country, yet it was politically less significant than any of the others. It was a continuous demonstration of the firm hold the president had on the affections of the people.

The tour was all that could be expected and more. Receptions in Memphis, New Orleans, Houston, San Antonio and El Paso were cordial. Every appearance signaled cheers and flowers. McKinley was ideal in the role of traveling statesman, always choosing the right word, the proper tone, the expected reference at every stop and for every delegation. At one stop, a welcoming party told him that his appearance had drawn the crowd away from a visiting circus. "Why, of course," he laughed, "you can't expect a 50-cent show to draw any people when there's a free show in town."[265]

The train paused briefly in the rugged beauty of the desert so that P.M. Rixey, a Navy doctor and the family's physician, could lance a painful felon on Mrs. McKinley's finger. The procedure was complicated by the fact that the president's wife was an epileptic, and she had collapsed because of that malady at El Paso. Still confident that Ida would withstand the trip without difficulty, the president got off the train while the minor operation was performed to admire the desert vistas.

Californians staged a marvelous floral display accompanied by generous hospitality. Fiesta celebrations covered Los Angeles during the second week of May, and McKinley's appearance in Los Angeles was an unqualified demonstration of popular affection. Rose petals poured down on his reviewing stand until they covered his shoe tops, and he stood smiling and waving his hat for what seemed like hours. With typical California zeal, the citizenry could not do him enough honor. Pickpockets circulated freely in the crowd, however, and a flustered Secretary of Agriculture, James Wilson, lost his wallet. One watcher refused to leave the line of march when told his house was on fire; the house was doomed anyway and he might never again get to see the president of the United States. The entourage left Los Angeles for Del Monte on Friday, May 10, intending to spend a quiet weekend before beginning a visit to San Francisco the following Tuesday.

The schedule was discarded midroute. Mrs. McKinley had grown worse as the trip continued. Seizures threatened, and a general weakness and fever brought on by the blood infection in her finger brought her to the edge of collapse. At Del Monte, the president was forced to give up all further plans and decided to take her directly to San Francisco.

A special train was made up from the presidential equipment for the run, consisting of a baggage car and the *Olympia*. It departed Del Monte at 12:30 p.m. Sunday, the small gathering of well-wishers indicative of the lack of publicity. The rest of the party remained in Del Monte for a time. The McKinleys left the train at the Valencia Street Station to avoid a bigger metropolitan crowd.

In San Francisco, Ida was treated by trained nurses at the home of Henry T. Scott. For two weeks she hovered between life and death, her husband remaining at her bedside and at one point even planning her funeral train for the trip home. All presidential engagements were canceled. At last the crisis passed, and Mrs. McKinley began to regain her strength. The president hurried to the docks to dedicate the battleship that Scott's firm had built, pausing to give public thanks for his wife's recovery. As soon as she was able to travel, all plans for a leisurely return to Washington were canceled. The train—with the McKinleys using a different private car—departed May 25 and sped across the continent via SP's Central Pacific line to Ogden, Utah; Union Pacific to Omaha; C&NW to Chicago; and PRR. Virtually all stops were made only for operating reasons; crews were changed a few miles from normal division points to throw off crowds. The original itinerary had called for the tour to end in Buffalo, N.Y., on June 12—after traveling 11,000 miles—but the change necessitated a postponement of that visit until September.

So the McKinleys spent the summer in Canton, then the president started an overnight trip to Buffalo at 10 p.m. Tuesday, Sept. 3, to pay his

Southern Pacific Company--Pacific System

COAST DIVISION

SPECIAL TIME TABLE

— FOR THE —

"PRESIDENT'S SPECIAL"

To take effect Friday, May 10, 1901, at 2 o'clock, P. M., and void after 10 P. M., Tuesday, May 14, 1901

The "President's Special" will leave Santa Barbara May 10, 1901, and run to San Francisco on the following time, and will have absolute right of track over all trains, which must clear its time thirty minutes:

Friday, May 10			
Leave Santa Barbara....	2.00 p. m.	Leave Hathaway Ave...	8.03 p. m.
" Irma	2.08 "	" Goldtree	8.11 "
" Goleta..........	2.16 "	" Serrano..........	8.24 "
" La Patera........	2.19 "	" Cuesta...........	8.36 "
" Coromar.........	2.23 "	" Santa Margarita..	8.45 "
" Elwood..........	2.26 "	" Havel	8.55 "
" Naples	2.36 "	" Atascadero	9.00 "
" Capitan	2.49 "	" Asuncion	9.07 "
" Orella	2.53 "	" Templeton	9.14 "
" Tajiguas	3.00 "	" Paso Robles	9.25 "
" Gaviota.........	3.16 "	" Wellsona	9.36 "
" Sacate	3.29 "	" San Miguel	9.44 "
" Santa Anita......	3.30 "	" Nacimiento	9.56 "
" San Augustin	3.38 "	" Bradley.........	10.07 "
" Gato	3.41 "	" Wunpost........	10.20 "
" Concepcion	3.53 "	" San Ardo	10.35 "
" Jalama	4.05 "	" Upland	10.45 "
" Leda	4.09 "	" San Lucas	10.56 "
" Sudden	4.14 "	" Welby..........	11.06 "
" Arguello.........	4.25 "	" Kings City	11.14 "
" Honda	4.38 "	" Coburn	11.24 "
" Surf	4.51 "	" Metz	11.37 "
" Tangair	5.06 "	" Riverbank	11.47 "
" Narlon	5.15 "	" Soledad	11.56 "
" Antonio	5.24 "	" Camphora.May 11.	12.01 a. m.
" Casmalia	5.30 "	" Gonzales.......	12.12 "
" Schumann	5.37 "	" Chualar	12.24 "
" Waldorf	5.47 "	" Spence	12.32 "
" Guadalupe	5.58 "	" Spreckels Junc...	12.40 "
" Bromela	6.08 "	" Salinas	12.45 "
" Callender	6.15 "	" Graves	12.49 "
" Oceano	6.25 "	" Cooper	12 52 "
" Grover	6.30 "	" Castroville	1.00 "
" Edna	6.45 "	" Morocojo	1.08 "
Arrive San Luis Obispo..	7.00 "	" Neponset	1.11 "
Leave San Luis Obispo..	8.00 "	" Bardin	1.20 "
" Ramona Hotel....	8.02 "	" Seaside	1.54 "
		Arrive Del Monte	2.00 "

(OVER)

(CONTINUED)

Monday, May 13			
Leave Del Monte	8.00 a. m.	Leave Edenvale	2.14 p. m.
" Seaside	8.04 "	" Hillsdale	2.17 "
" Bardin	8.19 "	" Valbrick	2.24 "
" Neponset	8.23 "	" 4th St., San Jose..	2.26 "
" Morocojo	8.26 "	Arrive San Jose	2.30 "
" Castroville	8.30 "	Leave San Jose, May 14.	9.00 a. m.
" Elkhorn	8.40 "	" College Park ...	9.02 "
Arrive Pajaro	8.50 "	" Santa Clara	9.04 "
Leave Pajaro	9.00 "	" Lawrence	9.10 "
" Watsonville.....	9.04 "	" Sunnyvale	9.13 "
" Laguna	9.08 "	" Mountain View..	9.18 "
" Ellicott........	9.15 "	" Castro	9.21 "
" Claus..........	9.26 "	" Mayfield	9.26 "
" Aptos	9.28 "	Arrive Palo Alto	9.30 "
" Capitola	9.35 "	Leave Palo Alto	12.40 p m.
Arrive Santa Cruz	9.45 "	" Menlo Park	12.42 "
Leave Santa Cruz ..	12.10 p. m.	" Fair Oaks	12.44 "
" Capitola	12.21 "	" Redwood	12.47 "
" Aptos	12.29 "	" San Carlos	12.50 "
" Claus.........	12.30 "	" Belmont	12.52 "
" Ellicott.......	12.42 "	" Pansy	12.54 "
" Laguna	12.49 "	" San Mateo	12.57 "
" Watsonville....	12.56 "	Arrive Burlingame	1.00 "
" Pajaro	1.00 "	Leave Burlingame	4.00 "
" Vega	1.06 "	" Millbrae	4.06 "
" Aromas.......	1.10 "	" San Bruno	4.10 "
" Logan	1.13 "	" Tanforan......	4.11 "
" Chittenden	1.15 "	" Baden	4.13 "
" Betabel	1.20 "	" Holy Cross....	4.15 "
" Sargent	1.24 "	" Emanuel......	4.16 "
" Miller.........	1.29 "	" Sholim	4.17 "
" Carnadero	1.31 "	" Colma	4.18 "
" Gilroy	1.35 "	" Union Park ...	4.19 "
" Rucker	1.41 "	" Spring Valley...	4.20 "
" San Martin	1.45 "	" Ocean View ...	4.22 "
" Tennant	1.49 "	" Bernal........	4.27 "
" Morganhill	1.51 "	" Valencia Street..	4.34 "
" Madrone	1.54 "	" Eighteenth Street	4.34 "
" Perry	1.59 "	" Channel Street..	4.38 "
" Coyote........	2.04 "	Arrive San Francisco ..	4.40 "

J. A. FILLMORE,
MANAGER.

*Gratefully yours
William M. Bailey
May 12 1901*

RAILROAD MAGAZINE/CARSTENS PUBLICATIONS

Special Southern Pacific timetable outlines President and Mrs. McKinley's scheduled journey from Santa Barbara to San Francisco, Calif., May 10-13, 1901. The schedule was discarded at Del Monte because of Mrs. McKinley's illness.

Two gaily decorated Ten-wheeler type locomotives wait at Sacramento, Calif., to pull President William McKinley's Southern Pacific special over the Sierra Nevada Mountains in 1901.

CALIFORNIA STATE RAILROAD MUSEUM

long-deferred visit to the Pan-American Exposition.

On Friday the 6th, after a morning rail excursion to Niagara Falls—where he ventured out exactly halfway across the Suspension Bridge that connected the United States and Canada lest a sitting president leave home soil—McKinley scheduled a 4 p.m. appearance at a reception at the Temple of Music.

George B. Cortelyou, his personal secretary, thought the president was needlessly exposing himself to danger and wanted to cancel the reception.

"Why should I?" asked McKinley. "No one would wish to hurt me." Cortelyou protested that since only a few people would get to shake his hand in the 10 minutes allocated for the reception, others might become offended. "Well," said the president, "they'll know I tried, anyhow." Cortelyou sighed, added another man to the Secret Service staff, and hoped for the best.

Just after the 10-minute period had expired and the doors closed, a professional anarchist named Leon Czolgosz—already inside—approached McKinley with a revolver concealed in his handkerchief and fired two shots even as the president extended his hand to him. Horrified, people nearby grabbed the assassin and wrestled him to the floor. McKinley, still standing, was helped to a chair. He looked up at the scuffle, and said, "Don't let them hurt him." Then he gasped, "My wife—be careful, Cortelyou, how you tell her—oh, be careful."[265]

The crowd's initial stupefaction gave way to panic that threatened to block all exits, but miraculously the ambulance arrived from the exposition's small emergency hospital. As he was being transported there, the president sighed, "It must have been some poor misguided fellow."[43]

By 4:18, the president was being undressed for an examination, in shock but conscious. One bullet rolled from his clothing, apparently deflected by a button, but the other had cut a path through his stomach, perhaps a kidney, losing itself somewhere in the muscles of the back. It was never found. Attending physicians advised an immediate operation to probe and clean the wound, lest gangrene interfere, and to survey the damage. At 5:20, as the ether was administered, the president spoke the Lord's Prayer.

The surgery was only a partial success. The bullet remained hidden and X-ray was never used, even though one of the new machines was on display at the exposition. In the failing afternoon light, Dr. Rixey focused the sun's rays on the surgeon's work with a mirror. The incision was closed without drainage, and an antiseptic bandage applied. Precautions against infection were few. Still under the effects of the ether, the president was taken back to the home of exposition President John G. Milburn, where he and Ida had been staying.

There followed a series of rallies and relapses, but in the end infection and gangrene took their toll. On Saturday the 14th, death came. Late Friday afternoon McKinley rallied from his comatose state and talked to his doctors. Life was prolonged by the use of oxygen and heart stimulants, but the president felt it was hopeless. "It is useless, gentlemen," he said. "I think we ought to have prayer."[265] As the day ended, he asked for his wife, and Cortelyou led her in. A small knot of relatives stood and sat around the bedside as she wanly bade him farewell. "Goodbye, goodbye all," he said weakly. "It is God's way. His will, not ours, be done."[265] He murmured as best he could his favorite hymn, "Nearer my God to Thee." They were his last words; he expired about 2:15

Saturday morning, Sept. 14, 1901.

McKinley became the third American president to die by an assassin's bullet. He had been shot 20 years to the day after James Garfield's special track had been built at Elberon, N.J.

Robert Todd Lincoln, Abraham's son, having been invited by McKinley to meet him at the exposition, arrived in time to see rescuers bent over his host just after the fatal shots were fired and thus became a witness to all three presidential assassinations. He was in Ford's Theater the night his father was shot; as Garfield's secretary of war he had gone to the B&P depot in 1881 to discuss business when he found his boss lying on the floor in a pool of blood. Now this.

The president's demise came despite a history-making run the day before by Engineer John Draney of the Delaware, Lackawanna & Western Railroad to rush New York City heart specialist Dr. E.J. Janeway and three assistants from Hoboken, N.J., to Buffalo.

Draney's special included engine 134, the line's presidential private car, two sleepers and a smoker. The train's rear car was weighted down with pig-iron as a safety measure, and it covered the 395 miles in 405 minutes—a record that still stands—but its passengers arrived too late to save their dying patient.

Bryan skipped the 1904 race but tried again in 1908. That year, he wound up his campaign on the steps of New York City Hall, addressing a crowd of night workers at 3 a.m. He had slept but four hours of the previous 36. But it was not enough. Bryan didn't make it into the White House, and he never tried again.

Theodore Roosevelt

It was Republican Theodore Roosevelt—ironically the first president to fly—who brought rail campaigning and presidential travel up from the level of private cars to entire dedicated trains beginning with his 1900 run for the vice presidency under William McKinley. Encoun-tering hot and dirty conditions, Roosevelt made 673 speeches over 21,209 miles. The Spanish-American War hero was partially shielded from the locomotives' big cinders by window screens, but still the soot and heat poured in.

Fresh from his military victory at San Juan Hill in Cuba, Roosevelt wore his "Rough Rider" hat and swept along the campaign hustings with dazzling success. The real exhibition of the whole trip seemed to be his shiny white teeth, which he bared prominently and to good effect to thousands all over the country. His schedule was monstrous. "They do not give me time to eat or sleep," he complained to aide Henry C. Payne.[265]

There was no lack of showman-ship either, for Roosevelt was thinking of 1904 all the while. He thought it well to be accompanied by a troop of Rough Rider veterans in South Dako-ta, and no audience was likely to for-get his heroics as he described the glo-ries of Republicanism. His endless energy and high spirits amazed thou-sands. "Has he been drinking?" asked an astonished Iowan as he watched Roosevelt grimace his way through hundreds of handshakes, telling sto-ries and cracking jokes. "Oh no," came the answer, "he intoxicates himself by his own enthusiasm."[265]

The West was William Jennings Bryan's territory, so TR faced some hostile crowds when campaigning there. At one gathering, where an old cowboy friend named Seth was in the audience, he expected a lot of heckling but to his surprise the people were unusually well-behaved. After the meeting was over, he complimented the chairman on the fact that there had been no interruptions. "Interrup-tions!" exclaimed the chairman. "Well, I guess not! Seth sent around word that if any son of a gun peeped, he'd kill him."[43]

One day in Illinois, Roosevelt's train was scheduled to stop for five minutes on the Chicago & Eastern Illinois at Bloomington. A reporter got off to buy stationery, and the spe-cial pulled out before he got back. Dismayed, the newspaperman ran at top speed, puffing and straining, but the gap between him and the last car kept widening. He was about to give up when Roosevelt, standing on the rear platform, leaned over the railing and shouted at the top of his powerful lungs:

"Come on! You can make it! Come on! You can make it!"

Teddy opened the car, stepped down and reached out his hand. The reporter said afterward, "I just had to make it, because Teddy expected me to. With a final spurt, I grasped his outstretched hand and was dragged up the steps. There I lay for a few minutes, utterly spent. But for Teddy's help, I would never have caught that train."[205]

After he became president when McKinley was assassinated, Roosevelt continued riding the rails. B&O con-ductor Charlie Pledge never forgot the day, for example, when TR rode his train while traveling from Wash-ington to Annapolis, Md. On the return trip, the president's daughter Alice rode in the locomotive, wearing long white kid gloves.

In 1903, TR made a safari throughout the American West via the Northern Pacific, Rio Grande, Col-orado Midland and the Colorado Springs & Cripple Creek, among other roads. At Pueblo, Colo., he spied a Civil War veteran in the crowd and hailed him with a familiar cheer of the day: "You who wear the button ..."[38]

Northern Pacific engineer A.E. Strand managed to keep a priceless souvenir that came his way April 7 just before he operated TR's special train. It was train order No. 42, a running order giving his engine, the 234, authority to leave Forsyth, Mont., at 2:27 a.m. April 8 and arrive in Billings at 5:25 a.m. with rights over all other trains.

"In those days," Strand recalled, "every effort was made by the railroad to conduct the presidential party safe-ly over its line."[309]

Engine 236 ran light ahead of the special as pilot with Jim Eckles at the throttle. The line was well-protected that night; men were stationed at strategic points, with lighted lanterns at switchstands, while others were hidden on high bluffs east of Billings where danger might lurk.

"It was an inspiring sight," Strand said, "to see the white lights blinking their advance signals as the train approached."[309]

Roosevelt was very much a rail-roader's friend. Perhaps no president was more popular with the rank and file than he. Many presidents posed in engine cabs, but Roosevelt was thor-oughly at ease in them. He often rode there, fraternized with the crews, and knew how to operate a locomotive. He once ran the *Atlantic,* the old B&O engine that pulled Andrew Jackson's original presidential train, and pronounced the trip "bully!"

Another time, he gave New Haven engineer Harry L. Grant a gold cigar cutter.

Theodore Roosevelt, William McKinley's running mate in 1900, campaigns at Chadron, Neb.

Nation's Hero!

TEDDY ROOSEVELT

—WILL BE AT—

ALLIANCE, OCTOBER 3

—1900, AT—

12-NOON!

A Grand Demonstration of Rough Riders.

Secretary of War.

GEO. D...

MEIKLEJOHN

WILL SPEAK AT 11 A. M.

SENATOR

J.P. DOLLIVER

Of Iowa, will also be present and continue the meeting. Come everybody and bring your family and friends. The only chance to see and hear the Hero of San Juan Hill. Our own Gallant assistant Secretary of War, Hon. Geo. D. Meiklejohn, and Iowa's great orator, Senator Dolliver. Let your boys and girls see these great men. Let the boys come on their horses : : : : : : : :

Special Train

leaving Scottsbluff at 8 a. m., arriving at Alliance at 11 a. m., one fare for round trip from Scottsbluff and all intermediate points where fare is more than $1.00. Return same day.

By Order of Committee.

This advertisement called all of Alliance, Neb., to go down to the CB&Q station for Teddy Roosevelt's political pitch on Oct. 3, 1900.

Teddy Roosevelt was a relentless campaigner, even when he was after only the No. 2 job in Washington. Here, he speaks to a crowd at Alliance, Neb., during a stop of CB&Q train 41 shortly after noon on Oct. 3, 1900.

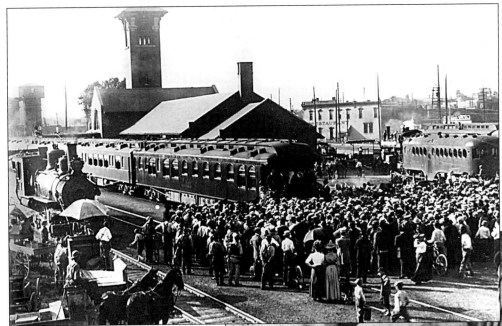

Left: *Theodore Roosevelt tells Fremont, Neb., how much he wants to go to Washington.*

Ever the politician, Teddy Roosevelt uses a stop in 1903, a year before his presidential campaign, to woo the people. The young man who has scaled the brass railing for a closer look seems to be concerned that the Secret Service is after him.

The "splendid engine," the old stereographic caption says, draws Theodore Roosevelt's train at Fairmont, Neb., in 1903.

As his AT&SF train nears Redlands, Calif., in May 1903, Theodore Roosevelt is where he wants to be—in the locomotive cab.

Below: Appropriately patriotic Southern Pacific locomotive No. 1453 awaits Theodore Roosevelt's train in Oakland, Calif.

John Draney, the Lackawanna engineer who rushed a heart specialist to McKinley's side in 1901, liked Roosevelt the most among the 10 presidents (Garfield through Coolidge) he met in his 42-year career.

"Seven of these men I knew personally," Draney recalled. "Teddy used to ride with me when he was governor of New York and later when he was president. He never failed to stop at my cab to shake hands and chat."[262]

In April 1905, Roosevelt traveled from Washington to New Castle, Colo., where he set out on another hunting trip. The Colorado Midland handled his train from Colorado Springs to New Castle. Engineer Jack Hickman remembered that day well:

"The day the special moved over the Colorado Midland, I was handling an eastbound freight. My orders were to go in the hole [siding] at Granite for his train. Of course, instructions in a general bulletin several days before the trip had ordered us to clear the

The little lady in the foreground seems contented enough as Theodore Roosevelt's train steams away from Colorado Springs, Colo.

LIBRARY OF CONGRESS

special train by 30 minutes.

"We arrived at Granite, pulled into the siding, and made very certain that the switches were all set for the main line. Not only we railroaders, but most of the residents of the village, were on hand to wave to Teddy when he went through. His special consisted of locomotive 15 [a 4-6-0 type built by Schenectady Locomotive Works], freshly

shopped, painted and decorated with flags and bunting, a combination baggage-buffet car from the B&O or some other eastern railroad, a sleeping car, and a private car in which the president rode. Presidential specials were smaller then—not the 10 or 15-car trains of later years. The Midland carried the president, his friends, his guns and camping equipment safely to New Castle.

Teddy Roosevelt makes tracks through the West on another hunting trip.

Freshly painted and gaily decorated, Colorado Midland Schenectady-built 4-6-0 No. 15 waits at Colorado Springs, Colo., to take President Theodore Roosevelt's special train to New Castle on April 15, 1905.

Teddy Roosevelt changes from iron horse to just plain horse right after arriving in New Castle, Colo., via the Colorado Midland for a hunting trip on April 15, 1905. The steed is "Bill," loaned to the president by expedition leader Jake Borah.

The party had a very successful hunt and later returned to Colorado Springs on the same train."[65]

The following month, the disconcerted president discovered that rail trips during his first term had cost $118,398, most of it borne by the Pennsylvania Railroad. Around that time, the public was agitated to find—in an article in the *Railway Gazette*—that Teddy's personal aide had requested a special car, porter and personal menus for a projected trip, and that when the PRR had complied fully and requested payment at $50 a day, the company was told that the service would not be acceptable to the president unless it were furnished free. Pennsy had backed down and charged the whole trip to advertising. The incident was particularly embarrassing in light of the fact that Roosevelt was pushing for railroad rate regulation, a policy PRR opposed.

WESTERN HISTORY DEPARTMENT/DENVER PUBLIC LIBRARY

Theodore Roosevelt may be relaxing on the Denver & Rio Grande at Glenwood Springs, Colo., but the telegraph wire strung to his private car, the Rocket, *indicates the president is still in contact with Washington.*

Theodore Roosevelt, whose life was associated with animals and the great outdoors, once crossed paths with a railroad dog named Roxie.

Roxie became acquainted with the railroad industry one hot day in August 1901, in the Long Island City depot of the Long Island Railroad. Among the passengers hurrying to board a train was a smartly dressed young woman carrying a bag and a parasol in one hand and a little mongrel pup under her other arm. She delivered the pup to the baggage car and told Baggageman Stryker to take good care of him until the train reached Roslyn. "He followed me onto the ferryboat and I've decided to adopt him," she explained.[193]

But the dog had other ideas. Evidently not used to baggage cars and eager to rejoin his new mistress, he broke loose at Floral Park and climbed onto a train going the other way. The conductor saw him in the coach and, unable to find his owner, turned him over to his baggageman. The pup wasn't happy in that baggage car either, and ducked out at Garden City. Station Agent Heaney found him outside the depot, took him in, and gave him his name.

Although he was treated well, Roxie was always ill at ease. He lay all curled up in the telegraph bay until a train came in, then he'd go out, sniff at the female passengers as if looking for his mistress, then return dejectedly to Heaney's office. Roxie even got to riding the Long Island's trains in search of his owner, but by that time Stryker had told the boys about the dog's background and everyone who

encountered him returned him to Heaney.

The agent even made a trip with Roxie to Roslyn, walking up one street and down another trying to find the young woman but to no avail. Eventually men at the Railroad YMCA in Long Island City bought him a silver-plated collar engraved "Roxie, the Railroad Dog." That collar virtually became Roxie's pass to ride Long Island trains at will; all the crews winked at the rule violation and tried to help the desolate little mutt. For years, Roxie took advantage of his privileges, visiting every station on the main line from Long Island City to Flatbush Avenue in Brooklyn, to Montauk on the eastern tip of the island, and all the branches in between, occasionally dropping in on Heaney. He was even welcomed in locomotive cabs, but much preferred coaches, where the young ladies rode.

Roosevelt met Roxie one day when a porter found the dog curled up on the president's bed in a private car that was to take him to his summer home in Oyster Bay. The indignant porter would have ejected the beast unceremoniously, but the conductor pointed to the collar and said that Roxie was a pet of all the trainmen. Roosevelt himself walked in right then, heard the story, and allowed the creature to stay.

Roxie continued riding trains and sniffing at young ladies' dresses for 12 years until one day he went to sleep at the Merrick depot and never awoke. They buried him on the station grounds, and a group of women paid for a granite marker on the site.

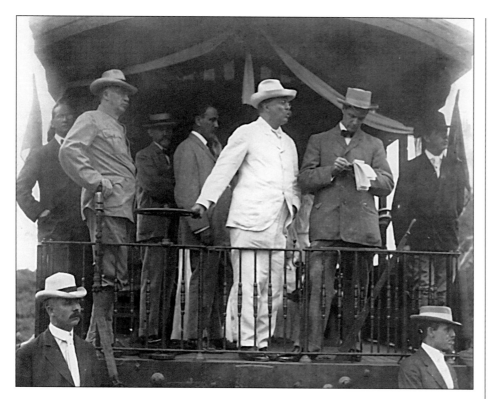

Teddy Roosevelt ventures onto the rear platform of his train in a white suit, but odds are that in the days of steam, cinders and open coach windows, the presidential finery didn't stay that way long.

As a result of the hue and cry, Congress passed a law on June 20, 1906, appropriating $25,000 a year for presidential traveling expenses. Ever since, presidents have never been beholden to the railroads for free rides, although charges didn't begin to cover all the costs of making such a complicated move.

TR wasn't afraid to laugh, even when the joke was on him. One time he detrained from a Southern Railway run at Red Hill, Va., where he would continue to a country home at Scottsville recently purchased by his wife, Edith.

According to his usual manner, the president stopped to shake hands with the train crew. He noticed a plainly dressed elderly lady trying to board the train and rushed forward to assist her. He caught her hand and gave it a regular executive shake.

The president was dressed in a rough-and-ready costume and the woman had no idea who he was. Snatching her hand away and eyeing him with wrath, she sputtered: "Young man, I don't know who you are, and I don't care a cent; but I must say you are the freshest somebody I've seen in these parts!"

She then entered the car on her own and the president turned away, convulsed with laughter.[387i]

Roosevelt made a southern tour in October 1905 and met a man who would be intimately connected with the White House for 30 years. At the time, Edmund W. Starling was a Louisville & Nashville special agent. Starling's friend, "Sleepy" Wright, with whom he had joined the Rough Riders in the Spanish-American War and who had become a great favorite of Roosevelt's, had taken a similar job. Wright wired Starling in Birmingham, asking him to meet TR's train in Atlanta and ride along with him. They would be helping the Secret Service—the new presidential security force formed as a result of William McKinley's assassination.

"We were to go from Atlanta to Montgomery and [back to] Tuskegee Institute," Starling wrote, "where the president was to meet Booker T. Washington, return to Montgomery, and from there go to Birmingham, where the president was to make an address at the fairgrounds."[363]

When Starling boarded the special in Atlanta, Wright took him back to Roosevelt's private car. "Teddy rose to meet me, a strong man with a good, courageous eye. I shook his hand—he had a forceful grip, and the flesh was warm. He radiated energy and conviction. His smile under his clipped mustache made me feel at home, despite his formal morning dress and my $18 blue serge suit and $6 Stetson hat. The most valuable thing I had was a pearl-handled Colt which the plain-clothesmen of the Birmingham Police Department had given to me."[363]

In the next few days, Starling saw a lot of TR and watched his personality go to work on the crowds. "I liked him. He was human and natural without effort. He talked with us about hunting and fishing and sports on a plane of complete equality ... as men we were all, in his opinion, equal. It was only as president of the United States that he differed. In this role I watched him with interest, and I remember saying to Sleepy, 'He's one of those dad-blamed practical idealists. He's willing to compromise anytime, so long as he wins his point.'"[363] Starling remembered that assessment 28 years later when he met TR's cousin Franklin and decided practical idealism must be a Roosevelt family trait.

The special agent's admiration for the chief executive reached its peak in Montgomery. During a farewell ceremony at Union Station, an extremely attractive young girl of no more than

18 stepped forward and gave the president an enormous bouquet of long-stemmed American Beauty roses. She was scared and trembling but game. Marching up to Roosevelt, she said, "Mr. President, on behalf of the women of Montgomery I want to present you with these flowers. My father was an officer in the Confederate Army. My mother was a daughter … ." Teddy stopped her. Removing his high silk hat, he swung it across his chest in salute, clicked his heels, bowed low, flashed his toothy smile, and replied: "Young lady, such a pretty little giver needs no introduction to the president."[363]

Three hours later, the train reached Birmingham and the special party was driven to the fairgrounds.

"The path of the president's carriage into the grounds had been carefully roped off," Starling wrote. "I walked on one side of the carriage, Sleepy on the other. There were two Secret Service men from the regular White House detail with us. One of them, Frank Tyree, was riding on the high seat in front of the driver.

Suddenly, a man jumped over the rope and ran alongside them, approaching dangerously close to the carriage. "Get him outside the ropes and keep him out!" Tyree commanded forcefully.

"I hustled the man over the rope," Starling recalled, "but in a minute he was back again. I began to sweat. Again I chased him over the rope. Again he returned, running close to the carriage. My nerves got the best of me. I picked him up and threw him over the rope and into the crowd like a sack of corn meal. This time he didn't come back." Later, Starling learned that the Secret Service combined firmness with tact, but his performance that day was good enough for a rookie volunteer.

An immense crowd had gathered when Roosevelt returned to the Birmingham station. "Getting the president through it was a problem. Finally we surrounded him, Sleepy on one side, I on the other, and W.W. Brandon, then adjutant general and later governor of Alabama, as the spearhead. We ploughed through the crowd by bulk strength, quickly and roughly. When we got him safely on the platform of the train Teddy rubbed his hands together gleefully and cried, 'Bully! That was great! Just like a football game!' I've never seen a president since who could stand that kind of treatment."[363]

Former President Theodore Roosevelt delivers his "Bull Moose" pitch as B&O train 710 pauses at Point Pleasant, W.Va., on April 4, 1912.

William Howard Taft

In the 1908 campaign, neither William Jennings Bryan nor William Howard Taft was eager to campaign at first, but eventually both took to the stump. Taft had been groomed for the office by Roosevelt, and although the victor of San Juan Hill had said he didn't care to run for a second full term, some thought he intended to keep controlling things through his old friend Taft.

The silver-tongued Bryan was good at campaigning, but Taft was clumsy. He read long, dull speeches and sometimes made tactless comments. Nevertheless, he stuck it out, making 418 talks on the road.

Even before the Tafts moved into the White House, the seeds were being sown for the destruction of his friendship with Roosevelt. Just after they arrived at the Homestead resort in Hot Springs, Va., for a rest, the president-elect wrote to Roosevelt dividing the credit for his victory between the Rough Rider and Taft's brother Charles, who had financed the campaign liberally. The letter backfired—Roosevelt didn't want to share the credit with anyone, and snapped that Will Taft "puts money above brains."[247] Dealings between the two began a steady downhill slide from that time.

Taft journeyed extensively in office. "There was the traveler," recalled White House travel officer E.W. "Doc" Smithers. "He went to Panama twice and made two or three Pacific Coast swings. Facilities were sometimes poor on the routes he had to take. Often his car had to wait five or six hours on a siding until some other train picked him up. He didn't mind as long as he slept well at night, and he saw to that. He had a special mattress made for himself. It lay in Union Station all the time, ready to go."[144]

On one trip via the Pennsylvania Railroad out of Washington's new station—opened in 1907—the president became downright distressed. One of his major difficulties was food. He loved it, and ate far too much of it. So once he arrived in the White House, his wife, Nellie, and his doctor were always after him to diet. He complied, but only when he couldn't escape supervision. Just after leaving Washington one night for his home in Ohio, Taft waddled into the observation room of his private car where White House Chief of Mails Ira R.T. Smith and Stenographer Wilbur Hinman were going through telegrams and letters.

"Anybody seen the conductor?" he asked.

The conductor came running.

"The dining car ..." Taft began shyly. "Could we get a snack?"

The conductor looked surprised. "Why, Mr. President, there isn't any dining car on this train."

The president's tanned face turned pink with a few splashes of purple, according to Smith. His prominent eyes seemed to bulge even more.

"Norton!" he called coldly. "Mr. Norton!"

The president's secretary, Charles D. Norton, emerged from a nearby bedroom. Smith surmised that Nellie had probably given him strict orders about controlling the

The town is Mitchell, S.D., and we know there will soon be a Vaudeville show at the Mitchell Corn Palace. Wonder if William Howard Taft feared being upstaged?

president's intake; perhaps there even was an ulterior motive in the selection of this train.

"Mr. Norton," Taft said, "there is no diner on this train."

The secretary agreed. He reminded his boss that they had had dinner at the White House, assured him they would not go without breakfast, and reminded him of the doctor's warnings about eating between meals.

The president turned back to the conductor. "Where's the next stop, d___ it? The next stop where there's a diner?"

"Harrisburg," the conductor believed. Taft glared at Norton and addressed the conductor.

"I am president of the United States, and I want a diner attached to this train at Harrisburg. I want it well stocked with food, including filet mignon. You see that we get a diner."

Norton protested, but was quickly silenced. "What's the use of being president," Taft roared, "if you can't have a train with a diner on it?"

Norton caved in. The diner was coupled on at Harrisburg in the middle of the night, and the president advised newspapermen traveling with him that it also was open to them. "He sat in his own car for a long time," Smith wrote, "partaking of refreshments. He seemed to be in high good humor."[356]

In 1909 Taft planned one of his major tours to the West for Sept. 15 to Nov. 1. One aspect of the journey, however, bothered him.

"If it were not for the speeches," he pointed out, "I should look forward with the greatest pleasure to this trip. But without the speeches there would be no trip, and so there you are."[247]

He planned to draft "about" four speeches—the "about" meaning he would try to get by with three. Parts of these master speeches could then be used in each talk he made and garnished with local color so as to appear completely fresh.

The trip started on the president's 52nd birthday from Boston following a 40-day vacation in Beverly, Mass. Taft headed west on the Boston & Albany and New York Central & Hudson River. An embarrassment occurred at Utica, N.Y., home of Vice President James Sherman, when the vice president boarded the rear of the private car

Oh, the things one must do to get votes. Here, at Northfield, Minn., William Howard Taft is no doubt bracing himself to become friends with a circus elephant.

William Jennings Bryan, wearing his characteristic wide-brimmed white hat, poses with the crew of CB&Q 4-4-0 No. 288 at Red Oak, Iowa, in 1908 while campaigning against William Howard Taft and Woodrow Wilson.

Mayflower and made for the presidential bedroom to present the chief executive with a birthday present. The problem was that the conductor wasn't aware of Sherman's presence. He gave the signal to proceed, and the train eased out of the station. Sherman screeched that he couldn't ride to Syracuse, dropped the 5-pound box of candy he had intended to personally give Taft, and jumped off.

The special party stopped at Winona, Minn., on behalf of a Republican candidate there. Taft made political history with one sentence. Said he, "On the whole, however, I am bound to say that I think the Payne bill is the best bill that the Republican Party ever passed."[247]

The next day he wired Nellie, "Speech hastily prepared, but I hope it may do some good." Afterward, he admitted he had dictated the speech—and that sentence—as he traveled between stations, "and glanced through only enough to straighten out the grammar." He concluded, "I said what I thought and there is that satisfaction."[247]

That turned out to be the only satisfaction. The Payne-Aldrich Tariff Act hadn't put Canadian wood pulp and newsprint on the free list and virtually every newspaper in the country turned against Taft overnight. Even Taft's brother Horace reserved comment about the Winona speech in a letter to the president "because my secretary is a lady and no language that suited that speech could be dictated. I will swear at you about it when I see you."[247]

A major destination of the trip was Gunnison, Colo., where the president would press a gold button set in a silver plate that would signal the opening of the great $3 million, 5.8-mile Gunnison Tunnel, one of the large-scale irrigation projects of the U.S. Bureau of Reclamation. Accompanied by a guard of Colorado sheriffs and civic dignitaries, Taft boarded a four-car Denver & Rio Grande special at Salida on Sept. 23 for the trip over Marshall Pass to Gunnison. There was some speculation as to whether the narrow-gauge equipment could handle the presidential tonnage and a special chair was installed in one of the business cars to accommodate his ample beam.[38]

Taft's trip to Gunnison proceeded

William Howard Taft offers a few kind words for Sen. Robert J. Gamble of South Dakota.

without incident, but the same can't be said about his stay in Denver. Anxious to experience the true feeling of Colorado's storied yesterdays, he tried to take a bath in the celebrated tin tub at the Windsor Hotel. The presidential aft became wedged in the narrow confines of the bath, and heroic measures—including a great deal of soaping and pulling by the management—were required to free him.

Taft's tour also included a special rendezvous with Mexican President Porfirio Diaz on the International Bridge between El Paso, Texas, and Juarez, Mexico, to discuss problems of importance to both countries.

President William Howard Taft's narrow-gauge Denver & Rio Grande special arrives at Gunnison, Colo., on Sept. 23, 1909, where the president will dedicate the 5.8-mile Gunnison Tunnel, the longest irrigation tunnel in the world at the time.

William Howard Taft takes a break from the rigors of campaiging in August 1908 on the porch of a cottage at The Greenbrier in White Sulphur Springs, W.Va. From left are Army Maj. Gen. Clarence R. Edwards (later commander of the famed Rainbow Division in World War I); Mrs. Taft; Rep. Joseph Holt Gaines, R-W.Va.; the candidate; and Mrs. Gaines.

President Taft offers a pleasant expression for the camera as he and his supporters arrive at Denver in 1911.

Engineer Carl Lathrop remembered the day well. He handled Diaz's pilot train.

"My engine at the time was [National Railways of Mexico] 645, a Brooks Ten-Wheeler," Lathrop said. "A sleek machine she was and quick as a cat on the throttle, but so defective in riding qualities that I often had to stand up and take her jolts through my knees. The brass hats decided to use this girl on the Diaz Special. For four days, they held me at Gomez Palacio, paying me a dollar an hour for loafing around town while she was being decorated.

"A fellow engineer, Jack Reese, was assigned regularly to another Brooks, the 644. Now I knew the 644 rode like a Pullman. She was a better engine than mine, but was up for an overhaul. The master mechanic didn't want to use her on the president's special. He gave Jack the 646, a locomotive of the same type. I was to pace the special which Jack would handle. But my friend was boiling mad. He said it would be a disgrace to put the 646 on the special and he demanded my engine for the run. So I made a deal. I agreed to let Jack use the 645 on the special, with the understanding that he keep her permanently and I get the 644 after she came out of the back shops. Jack accepted this condition although later he grumbled when I held him to the bargain. I handled the 646 that day.

"It was worth traveling miles to see those two Ten-Wheelers trimmed up. Green, white and red—the Mexican colors—covered every pipe. Flags were wrapped around the steam domes. The engine that was now Jack's had two small Mexican flags beside the headlight. Rods, tires, hubs, running boards and pilots were painted silver. Every inch of both girls had been cleaned and polished until they looked like an ad for the Gold Dust Twins. The running gear was floodlighted. …

President William Howard Taft's Northern Pacific special stops at Three Forks, Mont., in 1911.

"To honor the event, I dressed in my best bowler hat and new overalls. Behind the 646, which was now mine, stood Jack's 645. Everybody in town turned out to admire our engines and to greet President Diaz when his special pulled in from Mexico City. Our depot platform was a riot of color. Bands blared and flags waved. Senoritas cast provocative glances from coal-black eyes. It was quite an occasion. There was a quick change of engines; the 646 was coupled onto the pilot train.

"Mr. Alfred, the general manager, burst into my cab. 'Lathrop,' he said, 'we're late on our schedule. Can you pace us fast enough to make up the time?' I promised I would. Away we went, my shotgun stack blasting black smoke as we found our stride. The side rods on the 646 flashed a rhythm of speed. This was the way I liked to run: wind her up, then listen to the mutter of exhausts. We stopped at Escalone, some 125 miles up the line. We had made up the lost time. From there on to Juarez, I paced the trip in a more leisurely manner.

"Juarez is directly across the border from El Paso, Texas. Every building was gaily decorated. Never before had I seen a brilliant hot sun shine down on so pretty a scene. Fine-looking squads of U.S. Infantry drawn up in plain sight made me doubly proud of America. All of us railroaders strutted a bit that day.

"Surrounded by his braided and bronzed bodyguard and trailed by officials, the Hon. Porfirio Diaz strode to the center of the bridge. There he met the jovial, smiling and somewhat corpulent William Howard Taft. It was a meeting I will never forget."[262]

Taft's tour also included a side trip on the Yosemite Valley Railway from Merced, Calif., to Yosemite National Park on Oct. 6, 1909, returning Oct. 10. The excursion was arranged at the pleading of YV officials and paid off handsomely in publicity.

Taft made a second tour across the continent beginning Sept. 16, 1911, piling up 12,961 miles in 26 states, making it the longest single trip by a sitting president to that time. He left his special train in Michigan, making a four-day swing through that state in a self-propelled car. Memorable on that trip was a little girl dressed in white dancing on the track ahead of the president's car about three miles beyond Royal Oak on the Detroit United Railway. When the car stopped, the girl presented Taft with a big bouquet of asters, and he responded, "Thank you, my little maid." After they were under way again, the president turned to Norton and said, "Please get that little girl's name. Perhaps she would like a letter of thanks."[389m]

Typical of Taft's stops on this tour was his visit in Baldwin, Kan., on

In this retouched postcard view, William Howard Taft, center foreground, and his vice presidential running mate, James S. Sherman, on Taft's left, make a campaign stop at Utica, N.Y., Sherman's birthplace, during the 1908 campaign.

Left: *President Taft prepares to board an elegantly polished wooden coach for one of his many trips.*

Right: *Bending over the brass railing of a private car to shake hands must have been difficult for the rotund William Howard Taft, but if you want votes, that's what you do.*

The photographer has selected a rooftop vantage point as William Howard Taft addresses a crowd in a tight spot.

President William Howard Taft makes a campaign stop aboard his private car Colonial *on the Pennsylvania Railroad at Caldwell, Ohio, on Monday, May 13, 1912. In the next week, Taft and Bull Moose candidate Theodore Roosevelt will crisscross Taft's native state furiously, looking for votes in that state's primary. Taft and Roosevelt, once friends, are now bitter enemies. During the following night, both of their trains will spend a few hours together in PRR's Steubenville, Ohio, station, but the candidates will make no contact with each other.*

In his later years as chief justice of the United States, William Howard Taft —seen here being taken to his train at Washington Union Station in a wheelchair—had shed much of the girth of his presidential years. Could the Supreme Court be that much more nerve-racking than the White House?

Sunday, Sept. 24. He offered greetings to worshipers at the Methodist church, where a telephone rested on the pulpit with its receiver off the hook. The phone had been connected to about a dozen homes so shut-ins could hear. That afternoon, Taft donned an academic gown and hood to deliver the inaugural address for Wilbur Nesbitt Mason, the new president of Baker University. But, oh my, was it hot! When the sweating president arose to speak, he chuckled and said, "Having convinced you that I have the academic spirit, I hope you will pardon me for shedding a little of it,"[416] whereupon he took off the colorful vestments. In the evening, he enjoyed a turkey dinner at Dr. Mason's home, despite the fact that a nervous maid accidentally spilled cream down his back. Taft's jovial laughter rang out, saving the embarrassing moment, and others joined in.

An old ledger in the presidential travel office reveals that Taft set a White House rail mileage record—in spite of the fact that his administration was the first during which government automobiles were assigned to the White House. Altogether, he covered 114,559 miles during his term, touching every one of the 48 states except North Dakota. All of that was by rail except the two trips by sea to the Panama Canal Zone.

"My father was very fond of traveling," Ohio Sen. Robert A. Taft said years later. "I think he made a record in the number of miles traveled by presidents up to that time. I don't know whether or not he ever rode in an engine cab, but he made a practice of walking up and down the platform to greet the engineer and train crew."[262]

The presidential campaign of 1912 was a particularly caustic affair because of the split between Theodore Roosevelt and William Howard Taft. Perhaps either of them would have won for the Republicans. But when the party machine awarded Taft the nomination, Roosevelt bolted and formed his own party. The resulting divisiveness ensured victory for the Democrats and Woodrow Wilson.

Roosevelt had said he wouldn't run again. But, since this was the first presidential election to be influenced by primary elections, he was already on the road testing the waters by early spring. On a whirlwind 10-day, 17-state tour in March and April, he made many short speeches from the rear of his private car and generated much enthusiasm.

On this trip, he passed through Virginia, West Virginia and Kentucky on C&O's train 3, the *Fast Flying Virginian.* He didn't speak at Hinton, W.Va., because "the train came to a stop with the Roosevelt car just below the bridge and on account of limited space … it was impossible for the … people to get within hearing distance of the colonel," a newspaper recounted. "It was not until the train began to pull out of the station that the majority of the people were enabled to see him. There was considerable enthusiasm manifested by the crowd."

He did make speeches at Alderson, Thurmond, Fayette Station, Montgomery and Charleston. On his return from Cincinnati two days later, April 4, on C&O No. 6, the eastbound *FFV,* he got into a "machine"[387a] (automobile) at Huntington, W.Va., for a speech at the county courthouse while his car was transferred to B&O train 710 for a trip north to Parkersburg and beyond.

Roosevelt's visit proved to be too much for one Huntington woman. Maria Young, 42, ran two blocks from her home to the B&O station as Roosevelt was boarding his car. "So great was the excitement," a reporter wrote, "that the woman was overcome and with difficulty got back to her house." As she stepped through the door, she dropped dead of a heart attack.[387b]

As Roosevelt headed east from Parkersburg on the B&O's Baltimore-St. Louis mainline for appointments in Keyser and Martinsburg, W.Va., before doubling back on the Cumberland-Pittsburgh-Chicago main line, an alert engineer prevented a tragic conclusion to the trip. Stopping for water somewhere west of Clarksburg, W.Va., the engineer noticed that one of the rails ahead of his locomotive was loose. A single set of driving wheels on the locomotive of a freight train in front of them had derailed, and the train had continued for two miles before its engineer detected any trouble. For most of that distance, the errant wheel had clipped off the heads of most of the spikes holding down the rail. All Roosevelt suffered was a two-hour delay while the problem was remedied.

Meanwhile, the years of sparring between Roosevelt and Taft had reached a political Armageddon that brought on the final split. For a long time, Taft remained silent after being attacked by TR because of their years of friendship. Finally, in the spring of 1912, Taft relented and followed his advisers' counsel to speak out in his own defense.

This change of tactics received its first expression on a rail trip across Massachusetts from Springfield to Boston on April 25 prior to that state's primary. Taft's special train stopped at a string of small towns and cities that dotted the route. He stood on the rear platform or went into town at every one of them, including Palmer and Worcester, and exclaimed in anguish, "This wrenches my soul!"[247]

"I am here," he would say over and over again, "to reply to an old and true friend of mine, Theodore Roose-

CHARLES G. CHANEY COLLECTION/SMITHSONIAN INSTITUTION

PRR engine 5031 speeds President-elect Woodrow Wilson's train into Washington for his inauguration in 1913.

velt, who has made many charges against me. I deny those charges. I deny all of them. I do not want to fight Theodore Roosevelt, but sometimes a man in a corner fights. I am going to fight. Neither in thought nor word nor action have I been disloyal to the friendship I owe Theodore Roosevelt. ..."[247]

That night Taft spoke to an audience of 10,000 in the Boston Arena, repudiating meticulously each of Roosevelt's charges in a long, 11-point speech. Then he gave a condensed version of his defense at Symphony Hall and was driven back to the Boston yard where his special awaited for the return to Washington.

Louis Seibold, a *New York World* reporter who was traveling with the presidential party, entered the private car to ask the president a question. He saw Taft slumped forward on a lounge with his head in his hands.

Taft looked up. Seeing Seibold, he said despairingly, "Roosevelt was my closest friend."[247] Then he broke down and wept uncontrollably.

When Roosevelt's train followed Taft's into Massachusetts the next day, he threw away his prepared speeches and vented purple rage at Taft's outbursts. The gloves were off; the fight was on. Everyone, even the humorists, were shocked at the spectacle of a president and an ex-president carrying on so.

As the venom between them increased, so did Taft's propensity for saying the wrong thing. On the night before the Massachusetts primary, he called himself "a man of straw"[215] for refusing to fight for so long, and a few days later, May 4, in Hyattsville, Md., he likened himself to a "rat in a corner"[247] ready to fight. Campaigning in Ohio, he predicted that whoever won the primary there would secure the nomination in Chicago in June.

That statement made Ohio a watershed battlefield leading up to its May 21 primary. During the last week of campaigning, Taft crossed his home state twice from east to west and three times from north to south. In all, TR spoke about 90 times, Taft oftener.

Remembering that William Jennings Bryan was also crisscrossing the state is to realize that Ohioans of the day didn't have to go far or wait long to see a presidential campaign train.

The Republican struggle was highlighted by the icy silence that permeated Steubenville, Ohio, on the morning of Tuesday, May 14, when both GOP candidates' trains rested briefly in its Pennsylvania Station.

Taft had entered the state on the B&O at Belpre Monday morning and he had started his speech-making at Marietta. Continuing on the PRR, he stopped at Caldwell, Cambridge, Newcomerstown and Dennison, and switching back to the B&O, continued to Uhrichville, St. Clairsville, Bellaire and Bridgeport. Then taking the PRR to Steubenville, he delivered a major address in that city and spent the night on his car, the *Colonial,* in the station.

Roosevelt, meanwhile, had taken a Long Island train from Oyster Bay to Penn Station in New York City and had departed via PRR for the front lines at 6:34 p.m. Monday night on his private car, the *Oceanic.* He was decked out in a slouch hat and a worn overcoat because he would address "the plain people" of the blue-collar region, he said. When he arrived in Steubenville just before 6 a.m. Tuesday, Taft's train was still there. The president presumably was asleep, and there was no communication—friendly or otherwise.

One has to wonder if Taft was peeping around a window shade when his old buddy trundled in on a nearby track, but no one will ever know. The crowd that had gathered at that early hour was disappointed—there would be no street fight.

Roosevelt attended the Republican convention in Chicago, where he told a reporter he felt "like a bull moose."[215] When he was denied the Republican nomination, he formed a third party, called the Progressives, but forever nicknamed the Bull Moose party. That ensured a particularly divisive fight for the presidency.

Taft didn't want to campaign—he may have felt he was vindicated merely by wresting the nomination away from Roosevelt. Reluctantly, though, he did—becoming the first incumbent president to campaign, covering 34,446 miles.

There were marked differences between Taft's and Roosevelt's campaign styles. The contrast was most discernible when it came to remembering names.

One reporter saw both men in action. At a reception for Roosevelt in Wyoming, the reporter, seeing a great admirer of the Rough Rider approaching, asked TR in a low voice whether he remembered the man. "No," TR whispered back. "I can't recall him." "He's been at the White House and lunched with you," said the reporter. "His name is Watson." "Oh yes," said TR. "I know who he is now. How many children has he?" "Five, no, he has six—another was born just a few days ago." When Watson reached Roosevelt, the latter grasped both his hands, pumped them heartily up and down, and exclaimed, "My dear fellow, I'm so glad to see you again. I shall never forget the delightful hour we spent together in Washington. How are those five, oh no, I believe you have six children now?" Watson, who was popular and influential in Wyoming politics, left happy and smiling; and ended up supporting TR enthusiastically.

A few months later, the same correspondent went to Seattle with Taft and stood by his side as the reception line moved along. At one point he recognized an old Taft admirer approaching and quickly whispered, "Mr. President, there's a man approaching whom you certainly remember?" "No, I don't," said Taft. "What's his name?" The reporter told him. Taft repeated it reflectively and then said, "No, I don't seem to place him." When the man's turn came, Taft took his hand in a friendly way and beamed at him as he said, "They tell me I ought to remember you, but bless my soul, I cannot recall you at all." Extremely irritated, the man, a prominent politician in Washington state, left the reception determined not to support Taft.[43]

Roosevelt traveled 10,000 miles in 34 states. Lest the war be lost, he would still give his all in winning its battles. Catching sight of Taft badges in Springfield, Mo., he remarked, "They are the appropriate color of yellow."[247] TR began repeating remarks that went over well the first time. Whenever children flocked together on the tracks he would say, "Children, don't crowd so close to the car; it might back up, and we can't afford to lose any little Bull Mooses, you know." If a woman had a baby in her arms, he would say "I like babies; I'm in the grandfather class myself, you know."

After a 30-day swing, TR headed home and told reporters they wouldn't have to hear any more speeches. They began singing "We're going home, we're going home," and started tossing Roosevelt's stock remarks while imitating his voice, mannerisms and gestures. TR emerged from his compartment, saw what was going on, wagged his big forefinger at the reporters and began mocking himself in his high falsetto. The reporters agreed it wasn't his greatest speech, but it was one of his most successful.[44]

During a western tour, TR arranged a stop in Arizona so some of his Rough Riders from Spanish-

President Woodrow Wilson, gripping an end post of his private car Mayflower *for support, greets some of the thousands of fans who came out to see him.*

American War days could meet the train and shake hands with their old commander. When TR went into a huddle with his buddies, the moving-picture man in the party (whom Roosevelt called "Movie") saw a chance to get some good campaign shots and signaled to TR that he was cranking up the silent movie camera. The candidate lined up his pals and began orating. "Throw a little ginger in, Colonel," "Movie" shouted, and TR pretended to give a campaign speech by spouting any nonsense he could think of. "Barnes, Penrose and Smoot—do you remember the charge up San Juan?—Jack Greenway, one of the best men in my regiment—recall of judicial decisions—the man with the muckrake—Alice in Wonderland is a great book—Bob Evans took the fleet into the Pacific —" The Rough Riders gazed in astonishment, while

campaign workers behind the camera doubled up with laughter. "That'll be a corker, Colonel," "Movie" said when he stopped cranking. Then TR joined the others with roars of laughter. "By George," he gasped, mopping his brow, "I haven't had so much fun in a week!"[44]

TR campaigned with such fury that his voice gave way under the strain. The final straw was a talk delivered in a packed tent in Chicago, with flaps open to accommodate an overflow crowd and through which a raw October breeze blew off Lake Michigan. During a follow-up talk at the Chicago Coliseum, his voice sank to a painful, ragged whisper and he was unable to finish.

Doctors ordered him not to talk any more than absolutely necessary, but TR insisted on keeping a date in Milwaukee the next day, Oct. 14.

The train left at 3 p.m. and made several stops. Congressman Henry A. Cooper of Wisconsin did all the talking while Roosevelt pumped hands from the rear platform. Arrival in Milwaukee was at 6.

After the stop in Racine, the last before Milwaukee, members of TR's party met and decided that their boss shouldn't go immediately to the Hotel Gilpatrick as planned. Instead, to conserve his energy—and his voice—he would dine on the train and then go directly to the auditorium, where he would say a few words and have someone read the rest of his speech.

The welcoming committee in Milwaukee protested the change loudly and finally TR, wanting to be a "good Indian,"[247] surrendered. Dr. Scurry Terrell, a Dallas, Texas, throat specialist with the presidential party, agreed on one condition—that extra police be provided to save TR from the strain of pushing through the crowds.

Roosevelt, obeying the doctor only because of extreme weariness, did not stand up and greet the crowds along the mile-long route from the station to the Gilpatrick. He merely lifted his hat. He napped uncustomarily before and after dinner, then went down to a seven-passenger touring car waiting at the hotel door.

The committee kept its promise and did a thorough job—unfortunate-

NATIONAL ARCHIVES

President Woodrow Wilson exchanges some lighthearted small talk with a crowd from the rear of his train.

ly. The hotel lobby and streets had been totally cleared by extra police. Normally, TR would have been shielded by two men walking in front of him, but that precaution was now seen as unnecessary. Roosevelt walked alone, in the open, followed by his secretary, Elbert Martin.

TR, wearing a big brown Army overcoat, sat down in the car, but a cheer from the crowd caused him to pop right back up. As he faced the rear of the car and raised his right hand, holding his hat, he made a perfect target.

A former New York saloon keeper, John Schrank, was in the crowd that night. The bald, light-complexioned, stocky man, fairly well-dressed, had been following Roosevelt from city to city because he believed "any man looking for a third term ought to be shot" and he had imagined that William McKinley stood before him in a dream and said of Roosevelt, "This is my murderer; avenge my death."[247]

As Roosevelt waved to the crowd, he could not see Schrank in the darkness as he lifted his gun and fired at him. But a flash of metal caught Secretary Martin's eye. Reflexively, he dove over the side of the car.

The bullet's impact, which Roosevelt later described as being like the kick of a mule, made him stagger and sink into his seat.

"He pinked me," TR exclaimed. He arose and coughed. Quickly he put his hand to his mouth to see if there was any blood. When he saw there was none, he deduced that the bullet was in his chest and the "chances were 20 to 1 that it was not fatal."

Martin and other Roosevelt aides wrestled Schrank to the ground before he could fire another round. In the emergency, Roosevelt's voice returned and he ordered Martin: "Don't hurt him. Bring him to me."[247]

Martin arose, pulling the would-be assassin to his feet and twisting his face around so TR could see it. He didn't know the man. Still standing, he told the police to take the attacker into custody. Although the candidate had saved his assailant from Martin and the crowd, he later admitted, "I would not have objected to the man's being killed at that very instant, but I did not deem it wise or proper that he should be killed before my eyes if I was going to recover."[247]

After the crowd had been pushed away from the car, Dr. Terrell told TR he wanted to see the wound and ordered the driver to go to Emergency Hospital.

TR countermanded the instruction, telling the driver to take him to the auditorium.

"No, Colonel," one of TR's secretaries said. "Let's go to the hospital."

"You get me to that speech," TR shot back angrily. "It may be the last one I shall ever deliver, but I am going to deliver this one."[247]

Upon their arrival at the auditorium, someone noticed the hole the bullet had made in TR's coat. TR put his hand in his coat, withdrew it and discovered it was bloody.

Still, he said, "I don't think it's anything serious." But when Terrell asked again to see the wound, Roosevelt consented. By the time a few more doctors from the audience joined them in the dressing room, TR had opened his coat and vest and

94

pulled up his shirt revealing a wound about a half-inch below the right nipple that was bleeding slightly. It had made a stain about the size of a man's fist on his white shirt.

TR put his hands on his chest and took a couple of deep breaths. "It's all right, doctor. There's no perforation. I don't get any pain from this breathing."[247]

The doctors protested his lay diagnosis, but TR was adamant. "I will make this speech or die," he said. "One or the other." Overruled, the doctors fashioned a makeshift bandage from a handkerchief and TR strode out on the stage.[247]

Roosevelt advised the people as to what had happened and remarked that "it takes more than that to kill a Bull Moose!"[215] From his pocket he removed his metal spectacle case and his speech, transcribed on 50 heavy, glazed pages and folded double, only to discover that both had been penetrated by the bullet.

He held up the speech for all to see. "And friends," he said, "the hole in it is where the bullet went through, and it probably saved the bullet from going into my heart. The bullet is in me now, so that I cannot make a very long speech. But I will try my best."[247]

He was pale and unsteady when he finished his talk 90 minutes later, appearing oblivious to the applause. He told Terrell, "Now I am ready to go with you and do what you want."[247]

A half-dozen people mounted the stage to shake his hand. "Didn't they know," TR fumed later, "that it is impossible for a man who has just been shot to shake hands with genuine cordiality?"[247]

Three doctors accompanied him to the hospital, where he talked politics while awaiting the arrival of an X-ray machine. During the delay, it was decided that TR should make the short trip from Milwaukee back to Chicago, where he could be cared for

by Dr. John B. Murphy, the famous surgeon. The patient left the hospital at 11:25 p.m. under his own power and returned to his private car, the *Mayflower*. Once on board, doctors tried to persuade him to go straight to bed. TR wouldn't hear of it; he would shave first as always—humming as he made brisk razor strokes. Afterward, he still didn't lie down. He removed the studs and buttons from his bloody shirt and put them in a fresh shirt, thinking the task might be more difficult the next day if he became stiff.

He finally satisfied the impatient doctors by lying down. His activity on the train had further tired him, and a rapid heartbeat and shortness of breath had at last made him uncomfortable. After resting a short time, he finally turned onto his unwounded side and went to sleep.

Departure was arranged for midnight, but an X-ray picture that had just been developed indicated the wound might have penetrated the abdominal wall and therefore would have been serious enough to keep Roosevelt in Milwaukee. Just as the Chicago & North Western train was pulling out, the engineer was ordered to stop while doctors assessed the latest evidence. A team of surgeons was called to the North Western Station in Chicago in case they had to go to Milwaukee, and a special train was assembled for their use. But doctors in Milwaukee finally concluded the bullet was lodged in muscle they termed the "belly wall,"[389o] called off the surgeons' train, and allowed the candidate to leave at 12:50 a.m. His train included the *Mayflower* and the correspondents' car, Pullman private car *Sunbeam*.

The engineer made the run to Chicago as quietly and gently as possible in order not to disturb TR's sleep—no bells, whistles or sudden jerking stops or starts. The North Western Station was sedate when the

train arrived at 3:32 a.m., Tuesday, Oct. 15. The doctors let their patient sleep until 5:12. Then they awakened him, examined the wound once more, and let him leave the *Mayflower* at 6:16 to walk to a waiting ambulance beside the train.

Roosevelt was annoyed at the sight of the ambulance. He wasn't a "weakling to be crippled by a flesh wound" and he didn't like the idea of going to Mercy Hospital "lying in that thing."[247] But when the flashes of photographers popped all about him, his good humor returned. "Oh gosh," he exclaimed. "Shot again!" And to the crowd of about 400, he called out "Good morning!"[247]

Doctors found that the spectacle case and speech had indeed saved Roosevelt's life. They concluded that the case slowed the bullet; the heavy gloss sheets upon which his speech had been written deflected the projectile not into the "belly wall" as first surmised but into the fourth rib, cracking it, directing the bullet away from a trajectory between the fourth and fifth ribs and straight into the heart. Murphy decided not to remove the slug unless infection occurred.

The candidate ended up taking only a couple of weeks off, and being in the polite age they were, Taft and Wilson did too. Within a week TR was home, insisting he would keep his appointment to speak at New York City's Madison Square Garden on Oct. 30. And he did.

Wilson, the Democratic candidate, had a background that included the presidency of Princeton University and the governorship of New Jersey. With the objectivity of a professor, Wilson admired the progressive ideals of Roosevelt's new party and thus limited his attacks to the Republicans. But that wouldn't work; Roosevelt was ignoring Taft and firing his big guns at the main target. Wilson had to reciprocate.

He traveled about the country in an old wooden private car that got off to a slow start. His special train, leaving New York on Sept. 15, was not well handled by the railroads. It was often sidetracked and rarely kept its schedule. Consequently, Wilson had to pop out at odd moments, wave to a few people and deliver brief off-the-cuff remarks. Before he could establish any sustained communication with the sparse audiences, the train was moving again. Wilson initially came off as austere, but eventually developed a ready wit. At a station where crowds mounted boxcars to hear him, he said: "Fellow citizens, gentlemen in the boxes—"[44]

At one place he heard a man in the crowd shout, "He may be all right, but he ain't good-looking." Reporters asked Wilson's opinion of the man after they reboarded the train. The candidate smiled and said, "He may be all right, but he ain't good-looking."[367]

Wilson seemed too aloof to win a nickname on the stump and he later regretted this. Once, though, as he addressed devoted Democrats in the Middle West, the crowd applauded and someone yelled, "That was a good one, Woody!" Wilson beamed, and said afterward to reporter Charles Thompson: "Did you hear, Mr. Thompson? They called me 'Woody'!"[43]

The candidate came to enjoy campaigning despite its hazards. During an overnight trip from Gary, Ind., to Omaha, Neb., in October 1912, his car was severely damaged when it was slammed into by a runaway freight car. The car's observation platform was smashed and several windows were broken, but Wilson was not injured and continued the trip.

Wilson traveled 87,400 miles while in the White House. In the spring of 1914, he and his first wife, Ellen Louise Axson Wilson, journeyed on the C&O to White Sulphur Springs, W.Va., to enjoy a little Easter Weekend golf at The Greenbrier. Leaving Washington aboard private car *Philadelphia* on train 3 at 11:10 p.m. April 9, they arrived at White Sulphur at 7:40 a.m. the following morning. "Throngs of natives met the train," *The New York Times* said. "Prominent members of society showed keen interest."[389n] Leaving his wife at the resort, the president returned to Washington, going back for her the following weekend.

After a fall in the White House, doctors discovered Ellen Wilson had Bright's disease, an often-fatal kidney ailment. She died on Thursday, Aug. 6. Then, at 2 p.m. on Monday the 10th, after her funeral in the East Room, Wilson left aboard a funeral train to take his wife's remains to a hillside cemetery in Rome, Ga., where her parents were buried. The cortege consisted of a baggage car filled with floral tributes, a diner, a Pullman sleeper, a compartment car and the private car *National* for the president and his wife's body.

But presidential work—and travel—had to go on. On Friday, Oct. 8, 1914, Wilson traveled to New York City and back to Philadelphia the next day, where he took in the second game of the World Series and saw the Boston Red Sox whip the Philadelphia Phillies. Col. Edmund Starling, the former L&N special agent who had unwittingly been noticed by the Secret Service and was offered a White House job, went along, and described the return trip in a letter to his mother:

"At 11 o'clock [Saturday] we boarded a private car. … We landed in Phila[delphia] about 1 p.m. and were met at the station by a vast throng which the policemen could hardly handle. At 1:25 p.m. we rode out to the baseball game, 26 squares from the depot. I rode on the running board of the automobile all of the way and literally pushed the president and his crowd through the entrance of the ball park. The police seemed powerless to keep them back. In the ninth inning, I had to go along the aisle and request the people to keep their seats until the president and his party passed through. We hurried back to the depot, people yelling all the way, and it certainly was with a sigh of relief that I felt the train move forward in the direction of Washington, D.C. We were so busy with the president that we did not have time to eat our noon meal so we had to go to the game on empty stomachs. When I got settled down, after we started, I went back to the kitchen and had the cook give me a squab sandwich and I then went into a drawing room and enjoyed my first meal since 7 o'clock that morning."[363]

At 8 p.m. Saturday, Dec. 18, 1915, Wilson married again, to Edith Bolling Galt. They had been introduced by the president's cousin, Helen Bones, whom Wilson had tapped to serve as official White House hostess after his first wife's death. The ceremony took place in the bride's drawing room at 1308 20th St., N.W., and after a buffet supper the happy couple headed for their honeymoon train.

The boarding point and the destination were closely guarded secrets. Only three Secret Service men knew the plan—Starling; Joseph Murphy, chief of the White House detail; and Richard Jervis, their advance man. Starling tells the story:

"Everybody else was encouraged to believe the party would leave from Union Station. On the day of the wedding we loaded the two automobiles—ours and the president's—into the baggage coach of our special train. The two chauffeurs were told to report to Jervis at the stationmaster's office with their bags packed for a two weeks' stay. They were given no hint

Charles Evans Hughes, third from left, campaigns against Woodrow Wilson on the Milwaukee Road's Olympian.

as to what climate they would be in."

"The train crew didn't know the destination either. Suddenly they were ordered to depart, without the president. The engineer was told to pull into a [Richmond, Fredericksburg & Potomac] siding at the edge of the freight yards in Alexandria [,Va]. This was a spot I had chosen, and I was stationed there. It was remote from the activity of the yards, and easily accessible by automobile.

"Murphy was with the president and Mrs. Wilson. After leaving the 20th Street house, he directed the chauffeur street by street, timing his approach to Alexandria so that the car entered the yards at the same moment as the train. [Around midnight,] I winked my flashlight three times, the car slowed, I leaped aboard and guided the chauffeur to the side of the president's car. In a minute they were aboard, Murphy and I swung up

behind them, and the train pulled out. But even Murphy and Jervis didn't know where we were going. The engineer [of Chesapeake & Ohio No. 3, the westbound *'F.F.V. Limited,'*] was only then getting his orders from officials … who were aboard to see that all went well. Murphy and Jervis gasped when I showed them the clothes I was carrying in my bags. They had packed for all the possibilities, including Florida. When I confessed that I had known where we were going for nearly two months, they didn't know whether to commend me or cuss me out."[363]

White House Chief Usher Irwin Hood "Ike" Hoover, who rode in the Secret Service car, remembered the departure a little differently. He said the presidential limousine arrived at the Alexandria station a little ahead of the train and stayed in the shadows until it arrived. The Wilsons were

whisked through the baggage room to board their car, and a couple of people on the platform who recognized the president stood spellbound. Hoover also mentioned that the limousine had its shades drawn and the presidential crests on the door covered with black carbon paper—a subterfuge so successful that two carloads of newspapermen who guessed correctly the departure point went there, but returned empty-handed when they didn't spot the Wilsons' car.[185]

In any event, the ploy was successful. The limousine's chauffeur had dashed to trackside furiously to outdistance the press cars, losing all of the reporters, the police escort and almost all of the remaining Secret Service in the 15-mile jaunt.

Snow from the previous day's fall was still on the ground and the Wilsons thought it lovely in the clear moonlight. The private car was filled with flowers, and some sandwiches and fruit stood on a table.

At about 7 the next morning, the honeymooners had reached their destination—the Homestead Resort at Hot Springs, Va. Starling went into the presidential car, walked down the corridor flanking the bedrooms and "suddenly my ear caught the note of a familiar melody. Emerging into the sitting room I saw a figure in a top hat, tailcoat and gray morning trousers, standing with his back to me, hands in his pockets, happily dancing a jig. As I watched him, he clicked his heels in the air, and from whistling the tune he changed to singing the words, 'Oh, you beautiful doll! You great big beautiful doll …!' "[363]

The Wilsons' planned stay at The Homestead—which included an auto trip to the nearby Greenbrier—was cut short when the British passenger steamer *Persia* was torpedoed and sank in the Mediterranean Sea with considerable loss of life. Since many of the casualties were feared to be Americans, Wilson thought it best he return to Washington, so they ended their two-week honeymoon Jan. 2, 1916.

The president's historic 1918 trip to Paris for the League of Nations talks was taken partially by rail. The Wilsons boarded the *Mayflower* at midnight Dec. 3. They entered Union Station through the President's Entrance, the rooms of which he had turned over to the American Red Cross for care of homecoming troops.

"Here they had established a first-aid station, reading room and a canteen to which I had belonged," Mrs. Wilson wrote. "They were busy as ever, serving troops who were returning from, not going to, the front. We were 'the troops' who were going to the front. …"[447]

Because they were to be guests of the French government, Wilson held his personal entourage to a minimum to save expenses. The party included the Wilsons; Wilson's doctor, Adm. Cary Grayson; Miss Edith Benham, Mrs. Wilson's secretary; aide Gilbert Close; stenographer Charles Swem; and White House Chief Usher Ike Hoover.

The Secret Service detail included Starling, looking the perfect flatfoot with his square, seamed, big-nosed face, derby hat and clumsy booted feet; the comparatively inconspicuous Joseph Murphy; and a dapper little fellow with a cocked hat placed jauntily on his curly hair and a foxy face improbably named John Q. Sly.

Very early the next morning, the train jolted onto a pier at Hoboken alongside the liner *George Washington*. The party went up to the bridge amid bellowing foghorns, shrill whistles and airplanes cavorting overhead.

On the return trip, the party docked at Boston Harbor on the foggy morning of Feb. 24, 1919, and proceeded to Washington by train. Similar arrangements were made after a return visit to Paris that summer. By

THE WOODROW WILSON HOUSE/NATIONAL TRUST FOR HISTORIC PRESERVATION

President Woodrow Wilson, decked out in a straw hat, and his second wife, Edith, greet folks from the Mayflower's *back platform—complete with the customary gift of flowers—at Columbus, Ohio, on Sept. 4, 1919, during the first stop of their tour seeking support for the League of Nations.*

that time, the homesick couple commented that the *Mayflower* looked finer to them than all the royal trains of Europe.

Wilson had trouble selling Congress on permitting the United States to join the League. So he decided to appeal to Caesar—once again taking his case directly to the American people to get them behind it. It was one of Wilson's grandest tours—and his last.

On Wednesday, Sept. 3, 1919, at 6:40 p.m., they left the White House for Union Station—the Wilsons, Dr. Grayson and Secretary Joseph Tumulty. Two dozen reporters traveled with them, along with eight Secret Service men, a corps of aides, a valet for him, a maid for her and a double train crew. This time there was something new—four or five motion picture men to chronicle the trip in a way that hadn't been possible before.

The dapper president wore a straw hat, blue coat, white trousers and white shoes. His wife was decked out in a blue silk traveling dress and a small, close-fitting hat.

The president's blue *Mayflower* brought up the rear of the seven-car train; it would carry them 9,981 miles. The cars would operate as the second section of a regular train, as was the case leaving Washington, or as an extra with a pilot train in front. Every state except four west of the Mississippi was scheduled to be visited, as well as Ohio, Indiana, Kentucky and Illinois. The trip would take 27 days, with 26 major stops and at least 10 rear-platform speeches a day. Grayson and the first lady had pleaded for rest days—perhaps a week at the Grand Canyon—but the president would not hear of it. "This is a business trip, pure and simple," he said.[355]

Tumulty also was concerned about the absence of any rest periods as he stood on the car's platform and noticed how weary Wilson looked. During the New Jersey years, the governor was vigorous, agile, slender, an active man with hair only slightly streaked with gray. Now the president was an old man, gray and grim, like a warrior ready to fight until the end. "I am in a nice fix," Wilson told him. "I have not had a single minute to prepare my speeches. I do not know how I shall get the time, for during the past few weeks I have been suffering from daily headaches. But perhaps tonight's rest will make me fit for the work of tomorrow."[355]

Mrs. Wilson took this opportunity to describe the *Mayflower* in her memoirs: "Entering the car from the rear, one came first to a sitting room, fitted with armchairs, a long couch and a folding table on which we dined. Next came my bedroom and then the president's, with a door connecting. Each room had a single bed and a dressing table. Beyond this was a room my husband used as an office.

There was placed his typewriter, without which he never traveled, and there he and Mr. Tumulty worked whenever they could snatch a few minutes from the 'local committees' which were usually aboard.

"The next compartment was for my maid, on this trip a wonderful little Swedish girl named Siegrid [Larsen]. She carried an electric iron and all the necessary things for washing and pressing, which she had to do constantly. One more room was for Dr. Grayson. [Arthur] Brooks, the president's valet, slept on the leather couch in the sitting room. In the front of the car was the kitchen, presided over by a very fat and very excellent Negro chef named Green. Green's assistant, Lancaster, and a porter completed the staff."[447]

The four-person presidential party went into the *Mayflower's* sitting room and ordered cool drinks. Out to serve them came a tiny White House messenger, "Little" Jackson (sometimes "Major" Jackson), wearing a gigantic mushroom-shaped chef's hat almost as big as he. It sheltered him like a toadstool, the first lady thought. They all burst into laughter—which pleased Tumulty, who had gone to some trouble to get the hat made.[355] They departed via the Pennsylvania Railroad shortly after 7 that night of Sept. 3.

During a halt in the Baltimore yard, Red Cross workers gathered around to wish them luck and to offer cigarettes and sandwiches. The president declined the cigarettes, saying he never smoked; he also turned down the food because they had just dined on the train and he was "about filled up." Shortly after, they all went to bed.

In the morning, the reporters came for a press conference (a Wilson innovation), but they distressed the president. "They ask me such foolish questions,"[355] he sighed. During a stop at Dennison, Ohio, to swap locomotives, about 30 or 40 people gathered around the *Mayflower's* rear platform to hear the president say good morning, glad to see you, how are you, as he shook hands all around. An old man looked up and said, "I wish you success on your journey, Mr. Wilson. I lost two sons in the war; only got one left and I want things fixed up so I won't have to lose him."[355] The people applauded.

Another man in the crowd told Wilson that Dennison had voted against him in 1916, but would be for him in 1920. "Oh no," replied the president, laughing and shrugging his shoulders.[389p]

The train headed for his first speech, in Columbus, arriving before noon on Sept. 4. The "Columbus Welcomes You" sign at the station had been enlarged to include "Our President," and the city's schoolchildren had been given the day off. On Broad Street, hundreds of them were assembled to wave American flags. They broke ranks and came running through the police lines and the Army band that led the slow-moving automobile parade to trot alongside his car, where he stood waving a straw hat. Airplanes from Ohio State University zoomed overhead and dropped flowers on the crowd. At the hall where he would speak, he waited backstage for a moment while the first lady, in blue dress and Russian sable scarf and with a checkered coat over her arm, went out before the people. There was considerable applause when he followed her.

They departed Columbus after two hours, 10 minutes of which was spent beside the train greeting local dignitaries. They headed for Indianapolis, halting for a few minutes at Urbana, Ohio. "You will beat them," a man called out referring to the isolationists in Congress. "Their case is so weak they are not hard to beat," the president answered.[355]

After leaving Urbana, the president strolled into the club car and chatted with the newspaper correspondents. He discussed details of the trip and of the League treaty, sharing several humorous incidents connected with previous speaking tours.

They went on. Earlier, the day had been overcast, but now the sun came out, baking both the lush fields of 8-foot corn around them and the jolting cars of the train. At Richmond, Ind., he spoke from the rear platform for six minutes. Secret Service men stood in a semicircle to keep the people back.

Outside Indianapolis, a local reception committee boarded the *Mayflower* and Wilson talked with them in the lounge. They pulled in at 6 p.m. and went at once in a motorcade to the Indianapolis Coliseum. The Indiana State Fair was in session and the Wilsons proved to be just another attraction; the president had difficulty being heard above the unruly crowd.

They left at 10 for St. Louis, a pilot engine running two minutes ahead of them. They arrived at 4 a.m. on the 5th, and at 8 a dozen youths of the Junior Chamber of Commerce came and volunteered to carry baggage or anything needed. Behind them came a reception committee to greet Wilson with yells when at 9 he detrained in his straw hat. The party proceeded to the Statler Hotel in a motorcade. He spoke there that morning and again that night, and cigar smoke filling the ballroom made an intense headache he had had all day that much worse. From the hall they drove to the station, arriving at 9:15. Crowds gathered around the *Mayflower* and when Grayson and Indiana Gov. James P. Goodrich came out, the crowd shouted, "We want Wilson!" He came out to bow and when the train pulled out at 11 p.m. on the Chicago & Alton, people got

President Woodrow Wilson speaks with supporters from the Mayflower's *back step at Columbus, Ohio, on Sept. 4, 1919.*

another glimpse of him through the window of the car, sitting at his desk in the evening warmth typing on his next speech.

The New York Times was represented in the press pool, and made note of this advance in modern technology:

"On his private car … the president and Mrs. Wilson are well taken care of. Mrs. Wilson's maid came along and there is one of the White House cooks to prepare their meals. The president and Mrs. Wilson dine privately, but Mr. Wilson strolls back into the club car occasionally to chat with other members of the party ...

"One of the newspapermen, passing through the corridor of the *Mayflower*, saw the president beating away on his typewriter. The reporter stuck his head in the open door and said: 'May I come in and see you operate that machine? I have heard so much about it that I am curious.' The smiling president obliged, and remarked apologetically, 'I can do so much better than this when nobody is looking.'"[262]

The next morning, Sept. 6, the president was up early when the train stopped in Independence, Mo., to kill some time for an 8 a.m. arrival in Kansas City. Housewives came running from their homes when word spread that the president was there. Most of them wore big cottage aprons or Mother Hubbards. One apologized, saying they would have dressed up had they known he would stop, but he said he was glad to see them "just as you are." They asked for the first lady, and she came out to rousing applause. In Kansas City at 8, the heat was already quite intense and Wilson had to shout to be heard above the crowd gathered behind the train. There were flowers for Edith— "Oh, thank you, they're beautiful"[355] —and clicking movie cameras. The headache was back, and it was worse.

At noon they were back on the train. Wilson cupped his hands and shouted, "I've had a great time

here!"[355] Between smiles, reporters noticed, his face was serious. The headaches were continuous for most hours of the day.

They hurried north on the Chicago Great Western as the second section of a regular train. During a three-minute stop at St. Joseph, Mo., the crowd shouted for a speech but having been advised by Grayson to save his voice, Wilson only leaned over the brass railing—almost bent double—and shook dozens of hands. Reporters from Des Moines boarded to ride to their city, which was reached at 8 p.m. Wilson went to the Coliseum for his speech.

That night they slept at the Hotel Fort Des Moines, the first night off the train, and he told his people he felt like taking three baths to wash off the train grime. The next day, Sunday the 7th, the reporters went driving or headed for a golf course while Wilson complied with a tenet of his Presbyterian Church that there be no work on the Lord's Day.

They departed at midnight for Omaha via the Chicago, Rock Island & Pacific amid wheat fields bared by reapers. The plan was to arrive at 5 a.m. and remain asleep in the yard until the reception committee came at 9, but Grayson felt the president would rest better in a quieter place and so the train halted on a siding near Underwood, Iowa. They slept there beside a cornfield.

Amid the sirens, noisemakers and auto horns of Omaha on Monday the 8th, the president looked better. Reporters concluded the Sunday rest and the night by the cornfield had done some good. Around the train a crowd shouted for Wilson, and the president told the Secret Service to line them up so he could shake hands with several hundred of them.

By noon they were on their way north to Sioux Falls, S.D., via the

Chicago & North Western, stopping along the way as always for rear-platform remarks. After a two-hour stop there for a motorcade and speech was an overnight trip to St. Paul. Wilson tried to sleep, but it was difficult.

On the morning of the 9th in the St. Paul station, 1,500 girls of the War Camp Community Service burst into a nonsensical get-up-in-the-morning war song as soon as Wilson emerged: "Good morning, Mr. Zip-Zip-Zip, with your hair cut just as short as mine, rise up and shine, good morning, Mr. Zip-Zip-Zip, you're surely looking fine."[355] He stood with a fixed smile and then went to the automobiles for a trip to the Minnesota State Capitol.

Then it was on to Bismarck, N.D., and Billings, Mont., on the Northern Pacific.

As the train pulled away from Billings, some little boys ran after it. One reached up an American flag to the first lady. "Give it to him," he pleaded.[355] A boy running by his side had no flag, but he reached down into his pocket and then stretched out his hand with something in it. The child was running as fast as he could, holding out his hand, and Starling hooked a leg through the platform railing and leaned out to reach him. "Give him this," the boy panted. Starling opened his hand. A dime lay in his palm.[363]

"The widow's mite," Wilson often referred to it later.[355]

The train stopped at Coeur d'Alene, Idaho, home of isolationist Sen. William Borah. A woman held a baby up for the Wilsons to see. The first lady leaned over the platform railing and took the child. "It's a boy," the infant's father proudly said, "and his name is Wilson."[355] Here, the president's speech was made in a circus tent.

The crowds were getting more enthusiastic with every stop, but at night in the high, hot and dry air,

Wilson could hardly breathe. His asthma was returning. He tried to sleep sitting up in an easy chair in his compartment in the swaying train; that made it easier for him to catch his breath. Fighting the splitting headaches, he would sit with his forehead resting on the back of another chair and dictate by the hour to Charles L. Swem, his stenographer.

They made their way toward the state of Washington, moving slowly through wooded mountain country and under a drizzle and low-lying mist that turned the atmosphere suddenly cold. It was the chilliest spell for that season the area had experienced for years, and for the first time the train's heat was turned on. At Rathdrum, Idaho, the train stopped for an engine trade and a band played for Wilson. He went out on the platform very much bundled up to speak to the people, some of them Indians, standing by their muddy trucks. A mounted policeman put his horse through a bucking exhibition.

In Spokane, Wash., two hours later, the weather was stifling. Reporters came from the train in their pajamas. After the motorcade and speech, it was on to Pasco, Seattle and Tacoma. After his talk at Pasco, Wilson remarked to the little throng that theirs was a dusty area. Someone joked, "Yes, we have to have a lot of grit to live here." As the train pulled out, a man came dashing down the track. "Don't mind me," gasped the man. "I only promised to get the last look at you from Pasco and now I've done it."[355]

In Seattle the president made two speeches, reviewed the Pacific Fleet and rested over Sunday, Sept. 14, at the Hotel New Washington.

It was during that layover that disaster first struck. Traveling press representatives were taken on an auto tour along the Columbia River, and a collision killed Ben F. Allen of the

Cleveland Plain Dealer and injured Robert T. Small of the *Philadelphia Public Ledger*. Aides tried to keep the news from Wilson at first, but when he attended a Sunday luncheon given by the press and noticed several empty seats, he quickly learned of the tragedy. Immediately he went to see Small, who was not seriously hurt and was able to continue with them on the train that night. He was given a drawing room, and Wilson went to his car to see him every day. Edith said the man recovered fully and lived to write some "very unkind things" about her husband.[447]

The train made for Portland, then via the Southern Pacific into California over the Siskiyou Mountains behind three locomotives. The party stayed in San Francisco two days while Wilson made five major talks.

The Far West's weather was hot, steamy, draining—he seemed to be weakening by the hour, but there was no letup in the committees, politicians, bands and pushing and screaming crowds. Always there were more hands to shake, more people wanting just a moment of the president's time. "They mean so well—but they are killing me," he groaned.[355]

They went down to a stadium in San Diego, where with the assistance of a then-novel loudspeaker system, he spoke to more than 40,000 madly enthusiastic people shielding themselves with umbrellas from the sun. As they headed north to Los Angeles on the Atchison, Topeka & Santa Fe, Grayson had the train stopped so Wilson could get off and sleep in an inn. The doctor also insisted there must be no more rear-platform speeches and handshaking, but in the Los Angeles station a begrimed Mexican rail yard worker reached up to shake. Although the Secret Service men leaped forward to bar others from doing the same, the crowd set up three cheers and would not take "no" for an answer. So Wilson had to shake thousands of hands in a matter of minutes.

After a weekend respite in Los Angeles, the Wilsons headed north on Monday the 22nd via the Southern Pacific to Sacramento and east across the Sierras toward Washington at last.

Their train ran into forest fires that scorched the sides of the cars and filled the long tunnels with choking gas fumes. They stopped for a few minutes near Midas, Calif., got out and took a short walk along a high precipice overlooking the canyon of the American River. The fires were burning nearby, and several times during the afternoon the president's special car passed within a few feet of blazing trees. Once the train was stopped to make sure there was no danger from a fire, the smoke of which was blackening the sky.

Wilson could not sleep at all and the headaches, formerly located at the back of his head, now seemed to be moving to the very center of his brain. The sharp changes in altitude were the worst thing possible for his asthma, but even so the president kept his sense of humor. In response to shouts for Mrs. Wilson during the stops at Truckee, Calif., and Reno, Nev., he presented her with the remark, "This is the best part of the traveling show." At Reno a man below called, "Mr. Wilson, I would like to make a statement: I am very much pleased with your better half." Everyone laughed.[355]

When they moved out of the mountains into the dust of the Western desert, the twitching of his face was more pronounced and continuous for hours on end. The president's appetite was virtually nonexistent. At Ogden, Utah, the party endured a one-hour drive through the streets, then continued to Salt Lake City via Union Pacific's Oregon Short Line for a speech in the Mormon Tabernacle. The building was hot; Mrs. Wilson felt faint. Her maid saw her getting white and passed up some lavender salts, which she and the president used promptly. He was in agony from the pain in his head and choking from the asthma and poor air, and when they returned to a hotel his clothing was soaked through with perspiration. Dr. Grayson and Edith got him into some dry things, but within five minutes they too were sopping wet. All night on the train he could not keep dry.

The next day's itinerary on the UP included a stop at Cheyenne, Wyo., and arrival at Denver at 11 p.m. They requested as small a welcoming committee as possible, explaining that is was a security request from the Secret Service, but the plea was ignored and thousands escorted them to the Brown Palace Hotel. When he tried to sleep, he could not. Edith was terrified of the way he looked. "Let's stop," she begged. "Let's go somewhere and rest. Only a few days." "No," he said. "I have caught the imagination of the people. They are eager to hear what the League stands for. I should fail in my duty if I disappointed them." She was so downcast he tried to make light of the situation. "Cheer up! This will soon be over. And when we get back to Washington I promise you I'll take a holiday."[355]

After two more appointments there the next morning, Thursday, Sept. 25, they were on their way to Pueblo via the AT&SF by 11. They lunched on the train; Wilson ate little. As the train approached Pueblo shortly before 3 p.m., Wilson asked what arrangements had been made and was told there would be a drive to a fairground to greet a crowd before going to speak in the Memorial Auditorium. The idea of a long stand-up auto tour seemed too much for him. "Who authorized such an idiotic idea?" he snapped. Tumulty showed him that he himself had, signing an approving "W.W." The president sighed. "Any d—— fool who was stupid enough to approve such a program has no business in the White House."[363]

He said he wouldn't go to the fairgrounds but the reception committee insisted and he relented. It was blazing hot and the headache throbbed on. Still Wilson joked with the press corps: "This will have to be a short speech. Aren't you fellows getting pretty sick of this?"[355]

Later, entering the auditorium, he seemed to stumble at the single step and Starling almost lifted him over it. This time Wilson didn't object to the assistance as he usually did.

He began to speak. The voice was not strong, but he did well enough until he stumbled over a sentence. "Germany must never be allowed—" He stopped and was silent. "A lesson must be taught to Germany—" He stopped again and stood still. "The world will not allow Germany—" Reporters looked up from their notes. This had never happened before. Edith looked up with terror. Starling thought Wilson was about to collapse and edged forward to catch him. But the president gathered himself together and went on in a weak voice. He spoke of Memorial Day at Suresnes, France, of the soldiers alive and dead at the cemetery, and of how he wished that some of the senators opposing the League might have been there on that day. As he spoke of the dead boys in their graves at Suresnes, Tumulty saw men and women alike reaching for handkerchiefs to wipe their eyes. "There seems to me to stand between us and the rejection of this treaty the serried ranks of those boys in khaki, not only those boys who came home, but those dear ghosts who still deploy upon the fields of France." He halted. The people looked at him and he at them.[355]

The president of the United

President Woodrow Wilson bends over the brass railing of the Mayflower *to shake hands with fans at Columbus, Ohio, on Sept. 4, 1919. The man in the black hat to the president's left scanning the crowd may be Col. Edmund Starling of the Secret Service.*

States was crying.

He had come to the last words of his speech:

"I believe that men will see the truth, eye to eye and face to face. There is one thing that the American people always rise to and extend their hand to, and that is the truth of justice and liberty and of peace. We have accepted the truth and we are going to be led by it, and it is going to lead us, and through us the world, out into pastures of quietness and peace such as the world never dreamed of before."[355]

He turned away and Edith came to him. Their tears mixed.

They went to the train, but traveled only about 20 miles southeast of Pueblo when Dr. Grayson asked Wilson if he thought a stroll in the open air might do him some good. He said he would like that, and Capt. Dave Hardester, the conductor, was sent over the locomotive's tender to tell the engineer to stop. The 12-wheel locomotive panted impatiently as reporters were told that the Wilsons

and Grayson were going for a little walk. They had come down out of the mountain country and were in beautiful prairie land with no houses in sight and evening coming on. It was very pleasant. The reporters got off to lay in the grass, relax and watch the long, lovely September twilight.

The trio walked down a dusty road, with Starling idling behind at a little distance. They came to a bridge and paused on it, looking down at the thin Arkansas River, hardly more than a stream at that point. They went on in the comfortably warm Colorado air and saw a farmer driving his small flivver down the road. He stopped when he recognized the walkers and took out a head of cabbage and some apples, saying he hoped they would eat them "for dinner tonight." They thanked him and he drove off, raising a little cloud of dust. They came to a field cut off from the road by a fence. Some distance from the road was a frame house with a uniformed soldier sitting on the porch. The president said, "That fellow looks sick to me."

Grayson said, "Yes, he certainly is." They climbed over the low fence, went across to the boy and said "hello." The soldier's flustered mother, father and brothers came out and for a few minutes the visitors and farm people talked. Then they said goodbye and, carrying their cabbage and apples, strolled back toward the setting sun.

About an hour had elapsed when the reporters on the grass saw the four specks, three together and one in the rear, coming toward the train. When the group was about a hundred yards from the *Mayflower*, Grayson and the president broke into a dog trot and ran by the men in the grass. One reporter said, "Pretty good! I don't know whether I could do that myself or not." The president was smiling as he went up on the rear platform. Wilson seemed rejuvenated, enjoyed a happy dinner and even shook a few hands during a stop at Rocky Ford, Colo.[355]

That night, Mrs. Wilson's maid, Siegrid, came to her room as the train rolled toward Wichita, Kan., to brush her hair and give her a massage. The two spoke softly, since the president's room was next door and Edith thought he was asleep. But about 11:30, there was a knock on the intervening door and she heard his voice: "Can you come to me, Edith? I'm terribly sick." He was sitting on the edge of his bed with his head resting on the back of a chair. "I can't sleep because of the pain. I'm afraid you'd better call Grayson."[355]

When her maid located the doctor, he came but there was nothing he could do to ease his patient. The tiny bedroom oppressed the president; he said he must move about. They went into the room he used as a study and office. His typewriter stood on a Pullman table. They brought in some pillows and tried to make him comfortable, but he could not stay still and twisted about to try to find a position that would lessen the splitting agony in his head. About 5 a.m., sitting propped upright by the pillows, he fell asleep.

Edith motioned Grayson to go to bed and she sat alone opposite her husband, breathing as quietly as she could for fear she would wake him. Dawn came; the room grew light. He awoke at 7, stood, and said he must shave for soon they would be in Wichita. Grayson came in and spoke with Edith, then went to Tumulty's compartment. He knocked on the door and told Tumulty to get up and come quickly, the president was seriously ill.

The two men hurried through the train and as they moved, Grayson tersely said something was terribly, terribly wrong and that to continue the trip could prove fatal. Tumulty's support would be needed to convince the president. They joined Edith; a few minutes later Wilson came out of the bathroom, freshly shaven and dressed to Grayson's amazement. The men said he must cancel the tour, and Wilson said, "No, no, I cannot do it." As he spoke, saliva came down from the left side of his mouth and they saw that the left side of his face was fallen and unmoving. His words were mumbled and indistinct.

Grayson told him continuing was out of the question, but he said, "I must go on. I should feel like a deserter. My opponents will accuse me of having cold feet should I stop now." It was difficult to understand his words.

A grim-faced President Woodrow Wilson prepares to depart Chicago's old Union Station on Chicago, Milwaukee & St. Paul's Pioneer Limited.

Grayson argued with him. "I owe it to the country, to you and your family not to permit you to continue. If you try to speak today, you will fall down on the platform before the audience." Still the president insisted.

Tumulty urged him to obey the doctor. "My dear boy," Wilson replied, "this has never happened to me before. I don't know what to do."

"You must give up the trip and get some rest," Tumulty advised.

"Don't you see," retorted the president, "if we cancel this trip Sen. (Henry Cabot) Lodge and his friends will say that I am a quitter, that the trip was a failure. And the treaty will be lost."

Tumulty took both of the president's hands in his own. "What difference, dear Governor, does it make what they say? Nobody in the world will consider you a quitter. It is your life we must consider."

The president was sitting with Tumulty holding his hands; he tried to move closer but found his left arm

and leg refused to function. But he said, "I want to show them that I can still fight and that I am not afraid. Just postpone the trip for 24 hours and I will be all right." Grayson began to protest, but Wilson interrupted. "No, no, no. I must keep up."

It was his beloved Edith who convinced him. She said he must not let the people see him as he was this day, holding up a mirror to show him his sagging features and to convince him the fight was over. Ever afterward, she felt it was the hardest thing she had done in her life, to tell him the truth that morning even as the train slowed down in Wichita's outskirts. And when she said what had to be said, he finally understood. "I suppose you are right," he said. He burst into tears and the two men rushed out to tell the reporters.[355]

"This is the greatest disappointment of my life," Wilson wailed. Edith sat with her weeping husband and she thought, "I will have to wear a mask—not only to the public but to the one I love best in the world. For he must never know how ill he is and I must carry on."[447]

Starling had slept soundly in his bunk all night and was told about Wilson's illness early that morning by Brooks, the president's valet. "It's all over now," the faithful servant sighed. Starling rushed into the *Mayflower* while Grayson and Tumulty were conferring about how to proceed. The Secret Service agent had planned to detrain at St. Louis to go see his ill mother in Hopkinsville, Ky., but now

As Woodrow Wilson's League of Nations tour rolled through the northern tier of states, the party stopped for a few minutes to walk to a scenic view of some waterfalls. It was the president's first quiet exercise since leaving Washington.

When they returned to the siding, the Secret Service men made the usual check of the train and flushed out two hobos—complete with "bindles" and shaggy beards—planning to hitch a ride under one of the cars.

When the men found out whose train it was, one asked an agent, "Do you think he would shake hands with fellows like us?" The president stepped forward and did so, and even offered them a lift. But the hobos declined; they would not trouble him. He had troubles enough, and they would "hang onto" the "regular" when it came through. The first lady also shook hands with them and the train eased away.

Looking back, the president waved to the two and they bowed and waved their shabby hats in return. Starling glanced at the president, and seeing a wistful smile, thought to himself, he envies them.[363]

assumed he would stay aboard to Washington.

Tumulty addressed the reporters on board first.

"Gentlemen, we are not going to Wichita. The president is very ill. It will be necessary for us to start back for Washington as soon as the railroad arrangements are completed, and we will go through with no stops other than those that are imperative."

Then Grayson spoke.

"The president has suffered a complete nervous breakdown. It is altogether against his will that he give up his speechmaking tour. He did not wish to disappoint the people of Wichita. In fact, he was insistent that he would be able to take part in the parade and make his address. But my judgment as a doctor and the judgment of Mrs. Wilson and Mr. Tumulty is that we must not allow him to exert the slightest effort of any kind, and that we must get him, as soon as possible, into the restful atmosphere of the White House." The reporters scurried from the halted train to telephones.

Grayson headed for a nearby grocery store owned by Mr. and Mrs. W.B. Rankin, where he contacted the local telegraph office and started dictating telegrams to Washington and the president's daughters: Margaret was visiting in New London, Conn., and Jessie Sayre was at Harvard. Each was wired: "RETURNING TO WASHINGTON, NOTHING TO BE ALARMED ABOUT. LOVE FROM ALL OF US." He also wired daughter Eleanor McAdoo in Los Angeles and a niece who had planned to board the train at Memphis.

Meanwhile, neighborhood people clustered about the train. The Secret Service prevented them from approaching too closely and asked them not to make any noise. But when their numbers increased, it was decided to get the train under way again, moving slowly through the city

The President's Entrance, meant to be a private staging area for the chief executive's arrivals and departures at Washington Union Station, was rarely used as such. During World War I, President Wilson turned the area over to the American Red Cross for the care of homebound troops.

until the railroad could arrange a fast route east.

In Wichita itself, 15,000 people gathered at the auditorium were told there would be no speech. Most of them left and went to the depot to try to find out why. They were joined by many of the 100,000 gathered along the motorcade route.

Back on the train, Grayson was approached again by the reporters and asked for more information. He told them he hoped Wilson would need only a short rest and it was certain he was not seriously ill. He added that there was nothing organically wrong with the president's physical or nervous system. He would say no more than that.

After two hours of slowly moving through Wichita, the route was laid out, the track ahead was cleared, and the train picked up a pilot engine and headed for Washington, 1,700 miles away, via the AT&SF, Chicago & Alton and PRR. But the president seemed unwilling to admit the tour was over. Grayson urged him to sleep, but he answered: "I won't be able to sleep at all, Doctor, if you say I must cancel the trip."[355] He was unable to doze off, although the use of his arm and leg was returning, and so he sat with the first lady in the *Mayflower's* office compartment. She got out her knitting and tried to make small talk with him, but he could not be diverted and her chatting lapsed.

They roared on, faster than most expresses, the locomotive whistle moaning to warn back crowds that had hoped to see the president. All across Kansas and into Missouri crowds stood by and at the few necessary stops they peered in the *Mayflower's* windows. Their curiosity was unnerving and so the blinds were drawn. The darkened car was like a funeral cortege and the silence was oppressive after all the noise and cheering of the past weeks. As the president and first lady sat alone, his hands trembled.

In the club car up front, reporters broke out whiskey bottles—Prohibition notwithstanding—and celebrated their return home. For more than three weeks, they had lived out of suitcases and they were tired of it. Most thought the illness was indigestion or a reaction to the rigors of travel. Several argued it was a trick. "It's a fraud, a ruse; he's shamming," the *New York Sun* reporter said, but *New York Evening Post* reporter David Lawrence replied, "He's not feeling well; that's that. The doctor says he's sick; he must be sick."[355]

The writers passed the time by playing cards and singing. Grayson issued a bulletin to them and they dropped it off for station telegraphers to send to their papers: "The president has exerted himself so constantly and has been under such a strain during the last year and has so spent himself without reserve on this trip that it has brought on a serious reaction in his digestive organs." For later editions, Grayson issued: "President Wilson's condition is due to overwork. The trouble dates back to an attack of influenza last April in Paris from which he has never entirely recovered. The president's activities on this trip have overtaxed his strength and he is suffering from nervous exhaustion. His condition is not alarming, but it will be necessary for his recovery that he have rest and quiet for a considerable time."[355]

In the early hours of Saturday, Sept. 27, as they approached St. Louis, the first lady sent for Starling and told him neither she nor the president wanted all this to interfere with the agent's plans to get off at that point to visit his ailing mother. She said the president wanted to say good-bye and took the Secret Service man into the office, where the president, wrapped in a dressing gown, lay on a couch. The president offered his right hand. Starling took it and pressed it, but didn't shake it thinking the motion might be painful. "I want you to know how sorry I am," Starling said. "I will be praying for you until you recover and I am sure it will be

soon." Wilson smiled wanly. Only the right side of his face was moving. "Thank you, Starling," he said. "I want you to take something to your mother for me." He gave Starling a shawl; the first lady added two large boxes of candy.[355]

The agent was unable to speak. "The fact that they in their own grief should remember me and my trouble filled me with a sense of gratitude. I shook Mrs. Wilson's hand and departed."[363]

At 3:30 a.m. the train halted near St. Louis Union Station to change engines. The Secret Service detail—minus Starling—and local police roped off the area to keep it as quiet as possible, but the president couldn't sleep and the pain was as intense as ever. He could not force himself to eat and wanted only black coffee.

"In the yard I met R.S. Mitchell, chief special agent for the St. Louis Terminal," Starling recalled. "He was an old friend, a native of Bowling Green, [Ky.,] who had served with me in the Spanish-American War. He took me into Union Station, to the chief dispatcher's office. I had four hours to wait for my [L&N] train.

"I sat and looked at the big board, watching the little red light that was the president's train moving out of the yards and onto the main line. Suddenly I felt Mitchell's hand on my shoulder.

" 'What's the matter?' he said. 'What do you mean, what's the matter?' I answered. 'You're crying, you d— fool!' he said. 'Come on with me. You need a drink!' With the shawl over one arm and the boxes of candy tucked under the other, I followed him down the stairs."[363]

For the remaining day and a half of the trip, Grayson's bulletins were similar: "The condition of the president shows no very material change … he still suffers from headaches and nervousness … The president's condition is about the same …"[355] At every

brief stop, scores of inquiring telegrams were delivered, and Tumulty answered them vaguely. As they neared Pittsburgh, the train slowed up to save the *Mayflower* from jolting too strenuously around curves and through switches, and at 11 a.m. Sunday the 28th, 48 hours after leaving Wichita, Washington's Union Station was reached.

Perhaps a thousand people—and Wilson's daughter Margaret—were there. She linked arms with her father and together they walked down the long platform to where White House cars waited. He talked casually to his daughter, nodded to the crowd and smiled for photographers, but he was pale, his smile uneven and lopsided. When they came out into the plaza in front of the station, he got into an open car and they headed for the White House. Since it was Sunday, the streets were practically empty, but Wilson took off his hat and bowed as if returning the greetings of a vast throng. Rumors spread that the president was saluting empty sidewalks, that he had lost his mind.

A few days later, on the morning of Oct. 2, 1919, Wilson suffered a stroke that paralyzed his left side and left him a semi-invalid for the rest of his life. When he left office, he and Edith moved to a residence on S Street in Washington, the first former president to remain in the capital. He died Feb. 24, 1924.

Not long after her husband's funeral, Edith came across a little change purse that her husband had always carried in his pocket. She opened it and saw that in a special closed section of the purse there was an object carefully wrapped in tissue paper. She undid the paper and shook it out. Something fell into her hand. At once she knew what it was. It was the dime the little boy handed up as their League of Nations train pulled out of Billings, Mont.[355]

Warren G. Harding

Republican Sen. Warren G. Harding of Ohio and Massachusetts Gov. Calvin Coolidge ran against Ohio's Democratic governor, James Cox, and New York's Franklin D. Roosevelt—who served as Woodrow Wilson's assistant secretary of the Navy—in the 1920 presidential campaign.

Harding's was mainly a front-porch effort in Marion, Ohio, where he uttered platitudes and pleasantries to patriotic, professional and party groups making the pilgrimage to his home. Every so often, his managers sent him off with ghostwritten speeches for a bit of stumping. On one of those rare outings, Harding and his wife, Florence, embarked via the Pennsylvania Railroad on Sunday night, Sept. 26, 1920, on a three-day, five-state swing from Marion to Baltimore for a major speech. The trip was not without its troubles.

As his train passed through Pittsburgh during the night, a yard engine sideswiped one of the cars occupied by newspapermen and jolted Harding's private car, the *Ideal*, which was directly behind. The vestibule windows on the reporters' car were shattered, but no one was hurt. The train was running slowly at the time, and few on board were awakened. Railroad officials said the yard engineer had misunderstood a signal.

Harding's car was on the end of No. 34, the *Seaboard Express*, when it stopped in Altoona, Pa., at 7:15 the following morning.

"He had just gotten up when the train reached the city," a newspaper story said, "and when he appeared on the platform he had not completed his toilet and was without his collar and necktie."[8b]

The senator spoke to a crowd of about 4,000, tailoring his remarks to compliment railroad workers. They comprised most of the crowd since the stop was announced on short notice. The noise from several nearby steam locomotives made it hard for him to be heard.

After his talk in Baltimore, Harding returned westward on the Baltimore & Ohio via Grafton, Wheeling, Parkersburg and Huntington, W.Va., before taking the Chesapeake & Ohio to Ashland, Ky., and back to Kenova, W.Va.; the Norfolk & Western to

LIBRARY OF CONGRESS

A dapper Warren G. Harding poses before boarding a pristine wooden coach.

Columbus, Ohio; and the PRR back home to Marion. Ambling down the B&O's Ohio River Division on Wednesday, Sept. 29, more trouble was in store.

An equalizer spring on the *Ideal's* rear truck (a wheel-and-axle assembly) broke at Millwood, W.Va., and although B&O police officer Ernest Chapman pulled the emergency brake cord, Harding and his wife found themselves staggering about as the dancing car bumped along on the ties at between 30 and 40 miles an hour for 900 feet and across a trestle before stopping. Only a timber guardrail along the ends of the ties kept the bouncing car from falling 20 feet into Mill Creek below or into the adjacent Ohio River. The train stopped beyond the bridge just as the errant truck veered off the track entirely and buried itself in the gravel right of way.

The Hardings were in their bedrooms at the time, but came out to view the damage. The heavy steel car splintered ties and snapped off spike heads, crushing some ties on the trestle. Unhurt, they transferred to another car on their special train and, after 35 minutes, completed the trip without further incident.

For his trouble, Chapman earned the unofficial title of "master brakeman" and was in demand on POTUS specials for years afterward. [137]

The candidate had the presence of mind to incorporate the mishap into a speech at Mason City only a few minutes later. He likened his candidacy to the bridge's guardrail and offered to protect Americans against the Democrats' "derailments."[385]

At Ashland, the comparison was more refined. "The great car of state," he said, "going forward to the fulfillment of national engagements, somehow got off the tracks last year over in Paris. And it left things in very bad order. I think perhaps in crossing the trestle of internationalism, if it had not been for the guardrail on constitutionalism in the Senate to prevent us from completely leaving the track, we might have had a very serious wreck for the United States." The crowd cheered the allusion. [386a]

Cox, on the other hand, did some real campaigning. He traveled 22,000 miles and spoke to 2 million people in a valiant effort to attract support for the Democratic cause and the League of Nations. One of his trips was the longest campaign train journey on record, a swing through 18 states west of the Mississippi that consumed 29 days.

His train was historically significant in at least one other respect. Both Cox and Harding had newspaper backgrounds, but Democrat Cox put his to work during the campaign. As his train headed from Dayton, Ohio, toward the convention in San Francisco via the Cleveland, Cincinnati, Chicago & St. Louis Railroad (commonly called the Big Four), a four-page daily newspaper was published on board for the benefit of the train's 400 or so passengers. Prominent passengers furnished the copy for the seven editions of *The Big Four Daily*, while production—making use of a typewriter, a cabinet of type and a press—was carried forth in the baggage car. [311]

Harding won the election, and a railroad helped him celebrate. As president-elect, he—and his wife—rode the cab of Texas & Pacific 4-6-2 type locomotive No. 709 for 23 miles from Marshall to Longview, Texas, on Nov. 7, 1920, while it was pulling their seven-car special. Harding handled the throttle for several miles, "tried the air" (applied the brakes) and "blew for the board" (blew the whistle to request a signal from the ground). [423]

He went on to travel 32,228 miles while in office; his best known trip was his last. In the summer of 1923, Harding planned a transcontinental

rail vacation and speechmaking tour before going on to Alaska to drive the golden spike completing the Alaska Railroad on July 15. The president was distressed by rumors of graft and corruption among his associates and Republican losses in the 1922 midterm elections. The trip would be a "voyage of understanding"[131] that would give Harding a way to feel out the mood of the nation and present his ideas in preparation for a re-election campaign.

Planning the tour was Col. W.V. Shipley, B&O's assistant general passenger agent in Washington. Harding would go to the West Coast via the central route, head up the Pacific shore to Tacoma, and board a transport for Alaska. He would turn eastward to New York City via the Panama Canal and Puerto Rico. At 15,057 miles altogether, it would lack by only 20 miles the record for a single trip set by President Taft in 1911.

The Hardings were to ride the private car *Superb*. It would be equipped with a new invention that *The Pullman News* said combined "the highest developments in electrical science with a practical advantage that will be indispensable in American politics of the future"—a loudspeaker system. [240]

AT&T, Western Electric and the Pullman Company worked together on the project, the first such installation on a railroad car, and completed the project in 33 days at Pullman's Wilmington, Del., shop. The system included three portable transmitters mounted on the rear railing, a control room to house the amplifiers and accessory equipment such as batteries, five huge "voice magnifiers"[264] mounted on an extension of the car's roof, and a signal apparatus tying it all together.

The signals would permit observers in the audience to communicate with technicians on the plat-

form and in the control room. If the observer in the crowd thought more volume was needed, he could signal the platform man, who in turn would inform the control room—all without interrupting the speaker. As a bonus, the car was fitted with a telephone system that would link the president to any phone in the country during station stops.

The Hardings and a party of 70 departed Washington on their 10-car special shortly after 2 p.m. on Wednesday, June 20, 1923. At the start, crowds meeting the train were small and apathetic, but as Washington was left farther behind they grew in size and enthusiasm.

Harding soon wore himself out. He arose early and went to bed late, answering pleas by anyone and everyone to make speeches at all hours. His appetite remained strong; "He'd eat anything," Pullman Steward Billy Reid recalled. [76]

The president's first major speech was planned for St. Louis on Thursday afternoon, but it turned out that his first remarks were impromptu during a water stop at Martinsburg, W.Va., barely out of Washington. A few people gathered around the *Superb*'s rear platform as Harding stepped outside for a breath of air. "Hello, Mr. President," a little boy on a bicycle hailed him. "Hello, there," came the cheery presidential response. Several others, including railroad workers, crowded around the brass railing and wished him a good trip, receiving presidential handshakes for their trouble. [389a] A few miles later, Harding was still enjoying the view from the rear end. He spied a half-dozen boys swimming in a creek, whereupon he smiled and waved his cap at them. At each stop that day and the next, Mrs. Harding gave candy to all the children within reach, until it ran out much sooner than she expected.[387c]

The novelty of the loudspeakers helped draw larger crowds. Now thousands instead of hundreds could hear. At one stop, a railroad worker who didn't know about the apparatus remarked, "What a ... big voice that fellow has got."[240] The president also had speakers installed inside the cars so reporters could listen to his remarks without going outside. Some sources say he was fascinated with these new marvels of technology—adding that he often adjusted them personally—but others contend they distressed him. The system took some getting used to—Harding frequently uttered extemporaneous remarks and often paced back and forth on the platform, neither practice being amenable to voice amplification efforts. But he was now able to shout greetings to trackside observers while moving, and he liked that. He once called it a "lifesaver,"[240] and he was tickled to be able to use the telephone to talk to his sister in Massachusetts.

Only once did the loudspeakers cause a problem. Harding was scheduled to make a major address, and the stop was coming up quickly. Pacing back and forth in his bedroom, he called impatiently to his valet. "Where are my pants?" For a moment there was no answer. Then the valet appeared suddenly in the doorway. "Here," he fumed, throwing into the room a crumpled pair of trousers. "Why, they're not pressed," Harding protested. "I know it," the valet retorted testily, brandishing a cold iron. "You used up all the juice making speeches!"[353]

Indeed, instead of furnishing the respite the president had longed for, the tour made new demands on his waning strength. Between June 20 and July 29 he made 85 speeches, an average of more than two a day. Of the 19 major addresses planned, only seven of them had been written before the journey started, leaving little time for practicing and polishing.

Harding seemed preoccupied during much of the trip, realizing that sooner or later the treacherous and corruptive behavior of his "Ohio Gang" friends—which soon came to be known as the infamous Teapot Dome scandal—would come to public light. The mood on board changed all the time, "from heat to cold and back to heat again."[351] Harding didn't want to be alone, for when no one was around, he brooded. He played cards for hours at a time to take his mind off his troubles. And when he wasn't at the bridge table, he wanted to talk, which was most unlike him. He never remained long in his seat, moving about, peering through the windows, changing from one side of the car to the other.

Early in the trip, Harding made the revealing remark to one man that his enemies gave him little trouble; his chief worry was his friends. It was apparent the president was despondent and his health breaking.

"… The president was in a state of chronic jitters," a reporter wrote. "His one thought was to escape from thinking." To this end he organized a bridge game with Secretary of Agriculture Henry C. Wallace; Dr. Hubert Work, his new secretary of the Interior; Secretary of Commerce Herbert Hoover; Speaker of the House Frederick H. Gillett; and a naval aide, Admiral Hugh Rodman. "The president played to exhaustion 12, 14, and 15 hours a day, with brief time out for lunch and dinner … his nervous demoralization was painfully apparent. It reached a point where he felt the need for real relief. He sought out … Hoover. 'Mr. Secretary,' said he, 'there's a bad scandal brewing in the administration.' …"[1]

Haunted and frightened, the president muttered to himself and asked what should you do when your friends betray you. The Cabinet officers spelled each other at the card table; the pastime was becoming a chore for them. Harding said he was off liquor, but his friends said he needed it now, and collected bottles from the reporters. He was distraught, gray, collapsing, trying to fight off fear by dealing cards hand after hand.

Respites from presidential worry were few and far between. Speeding across the flatlands of Kansas early Saturday morning, June 23, on the Atchison, Topeka & Santa Fe, the train crew found themselves ahead of time and pulled onto a siding at Newton at 5 a.m. to let the schedule catch up. Harding, already up, saw wheat fields on both sides of the right of way as far as he could see, which he pronounced "beautiful!"[387d] He had a long talk with engineer S.H. Yokum, revealed his boyhood desire to be a locomotive engineer, and threw a broad hint that he would enjoy a cab ride. As far as the record shows, Yokum didn't pick up on it.

Once Newton was left behind, it became apparent that the train was running into a heat wave. Gen. Charles E. Sawyer, the president's physician, urged Harding to relax, but at every town and village where the train stopped, the president appeared on the back platform, spoke, shook as many hands as he could reach, posed for photographers, and stood bareheaded in the sun's glare. In sultry Hutchinson, Kan., after making a long address to a group of farmers, the president went to a hot, dusty wheat field owned by Chester O'Neal and drove a tractor pulling a binder. Thereafter, his fellow travelers noticed that he seemed to be failing.

The heat lasted all the way to Denver. There tragedy struck during the first Sunday layover. While Harding rested, politicians and pressmen traveling with him were treated to a lunch on top of Lookout Mountain,

President Warren G. Harding visits with supporters near Union Pacific locomotive 7016 at Ogden, Utah, on June 30, 1923, after coming forward to thank the engineer for a fine trip from Denver.

25 miles from Denver, hosted by the local press club. As the auto caravan was returning to the city, one of the vehicles plunged off the road through Bear Creek Canyon. Killed were Sumner Curtis, Washington representative of the Republican National Committee, and Thomas French of Denver, his driver. Two others were hurt; one of them, Thomas S. Dawson, died two days later.

The trip continued, however, to Cheyenne, Wyo.—where U.S. Mail airships flew above the train and dropped roses—and Ogden, Utah, via the Union Pacific and the UP's Los Angeles & Salt Lake line to Cedar City, Utah, for a 125-mile auto ride through Zion Park. The younger members of the crowd who saw Harding arrive were seeing their first

passenger train, for it was the first such occurrence since the last 35 miles of track had been completed from Lund to Cedar City. From that point, the president proceeded north—on UP lines and the Great Northern—to Pocatello and Idaho Falls, Idaho, and Butte and Helena, Mont. Butte featured another strenuous side trip—to a copper mine. Neither Harding nor his wife were holding up well. Finally, the special party dropped back to Gardiner, Mont., on the Northern Pacific for two days of Harding's first real rest in Yellowstone National Park.

After Yellowstone, the pace picked up again all too quickly. From Gardiner, the train speeded to Spokane on the NP and Chicago, Milwaukee & St. Paul railroads.

On July 2, Harding managed to

get his cab ride, boarding Milwaukee electric locomotive 10305 at Sappington, Mont., for a jaunt to Avery, Idaho.

"This is the most delightful ride I have ever known in my life," the president told the press. "[I] drank in inspiration from riding the train down the 20 miles in regeneration, storing up energy sufficient to pull another train up-grade."[368] Plaques commemorating his ride were attached to the locomotive beneath the cab windows, which the engine carried for the rest of its career.

At Meacham, Ore., on the UP, an Old West pageant was staged. Harding chuckled when the managers told him about one of their difficulties. One of the scenes was to be the holdup of a stagecoach by Indians. When Indians were sought to play the

Warren Harding poses in the cab of Chicago, Milwaukee & St. Paul electric locomotive 10305 at Falcon, Idaho, on July 2, 1923, during a head-end ride from Sappington, Mont., to Avery, Idaho.

role of savage redskins, the only ones willing were a few old fellows in jail on bootlegging charges. Amiably, the authorities granted temporary paroles in the interest of fidelity to historical atmosphere.

By the time the train proceeded to Portland and reached Tacoma on July 5, everyone was drained. They looked forward to the rest and cool weather during the four-day voyage to Alaska.

Members of the presidential party took the U.S. Navy transport *U.S.S. Henderson* from Tacoma to Alaska, arriving in the territory July 9 and spending several days in its lower part. On Friday, July 13, they docked at Seward and transferred to a special train provided by the government-owned Alaska Railroad—officially known then as the Alaskan Engineering Commission—for a 470-mile, two-day trip into the interior. Harding and his wife rode the wooden compartment-observation car *Denali*

—its regal olive green exterior with yellow trim matched inside with red plush upholstery, dark mahogany paneling and a nine-branched candelabrum.

Bringing up the rear of the nine-car northbound special was a flatcar coupled behind the *Denali*, but no one seems to have recorded its purpose. It may have been there to haul a speeder—a Dodge sedan fitted with railroad axles and wheels that the Hardings used frequently instead of the train, running just ahead of it. In fact, Mrs. Harding thought the automobile was "superior" to the private car.[87]

The special departed Seward at 2:35 p.m., July 13, and took its 70 guests as far as Anchorage. During the night, the train was run up the mainline to Matanuska and out a branch line to see the coal fields of Chickaloon. It isn't known whether members of the presidential party had trouble sleeping, but they could have

since the midsummer Alaskan sun never completely goes down.

After Saturday's breakfast on board, Harding, Work and Hoover detrained to inspect the U.S. Navy's first—and unsuccessful—venture at coal mining. Here, the incredible pace of the tour was further complicated by an exhausting ramble up a flight of 175 wooden steps.

Back on the main line, the presidential special proceeded north, passing glaciers, snowcapped peaks that jutted above the clouds and lakes set like emeralds in the tundra. It proceeded to Wasilla—where the Hardings, acting like children on their first train ride, mounted the cab of their locomotive, the 618. After a few instructions from engineer F.W. Brayford, Harding took the throttle and ran the locomotive to Willow, 25.9 miles up the road, consuming 51 minutes for the journey. Mrs. Harding rode in the fireman's seat. With the railroad being built and owned by the federal government, and with Harding as the head of government, one could say that the boss was running his own locomotive!

Brayford complimented Harding's operating skills, but the dining car steward took exception. He pointed out that one stop was so rough that 11 cups were broken.

While the engine took water at Willow, the president visited with some section men at work nearby. He helped them paint a new bunk house, wielding his brush vigorously. Discovering that young Leroy Harden—son of the section boss—was born on the day Harding was elected, the eminent traveler gave the lad a dollar bill.

Mrs. Harding was grateful for the railroad's hospitality. After her husband's death, she sent to engineer Brayford the white gauntlet gloves he had worn while running the 618.

The president and his party spent Saturday night on a siding at Broad

This closeup of Warren Harding reveals a president who should be delighted that he's enjoying a more-than-300-mile locomotive ride. Perhaps he's wondering when the corruption of his closest friends—the Teapot Dome Scandal—will become public.

Pass, near the top of the Alaskan range, easing through the switch just before midnight.

On Sunday, Harding detrained at Cantwell to watch some Eskimo herders drive by more than a thousand reindeer. A member of his party took advantage of the stop to visit a log-front store and purchase a handsome silver fox skin for $350.

The train reached North Nenana later that day after crossing the Tanana River on a 701-foot-long sin-gle-span overhead truss bridge. The span was a few hundred feet from the point where Harding would drive a golden spike completing the rail line from Seward to Fairbanks.

Charles Ross, who later would serve as Harry Truman's press secretary, recalled years later the discomfort of that day.

Admiral Rodman had advised the reporters to wear heavy shirts, heavy underwear, sweaters, galoshes and leggings. The latter was to protect them against mosquitoes and everything else would safeguard them against the cold. A reporter commented that the outfits qualified them "as characters in a wild Western moving picture production."[389r] It turned out to be quite warm—and mosquitoless—that day, and on Monday when Harding spoke in a baseball park in Fairbanks the temperature was 94 and three members of the audience collapsed from heat prostration. Ross wrote in his diary that those wearing heavy underwear threatened Rodman with bodily harm.

At North Nenana, Harding paid tribute to the pioneers of Alaska and to the builders of the railroad who had made settlement of the region possi-ble. Then he added:

"I am glad a generous government understood and carried to completion the construction of the Alaska Rail-road. It is not possible to liken a rail-way to a magician's wand, but the effect to me is the same. For the whole problem of civilization, the develop-ment of resources and the awakening of communities lies in transporta-tion."[135]

The president did better with the golden spike—tapping it once lightly while Gov. Scott C. Bone held it—than with the steel spike that was quickly substituted for it. He took one clumsy swing and missed, followed with another arc that hit the rail, and quickly added a third that drove the spike in nearly to its head. A fourth blow finished the job—at 4:50 p.m.

After the ceremony, Harding's train completed the journey to Fair-banks, a half-day's journey by auto-mobile from the Arctic Circle, arriv-ing late at night but with the sun still high in the sky.

"I don't know whether to address you people by wishing you 'good evening' or 'good morning,'"[78] Hard-ing quipped as he made his way to the Nordale Hotel, the only place where he would sleep off the train in Alaska.

The Alaskan travel was more of a strain than anticipated. The president and his wife grew more and more tired. Harding remained genial, beaming, a politician very much in his element, but candid photos showed lines of fatigue on his handsome, fleshy face. A plan to return by way of an automobile trip over the Richardson Trail and a ride on the Copper River & Northwestern Railway was given up in favor of retracing the upbound itinerary, which would more quickly return Harding to the peace and quiet of his ship.

Anchorage was reached at 2:30 p.m. on Tuesday the 17th, where area business leaders were scheduled to have talks with various Cabinet members on development problems. But Harding was in such a hurry to get back to his ship that the train was split into two sections. The Hardings departed Anchorage at 3:45 p.m. and the Cabinet secretaries and their aides departed at 1 a.m. on the 18th.

The return voyage was too short. Disembarking from the vessel again at Cordova for the Copper River & Northwestern ride and at Vancouver, the party nevertheless hurried back aboard the boat at each stop and landed at Seattle Friday, July 27.

Harding's attempts to respond to the tremendous crowd's enthusiasm were pitiful. While speaking bareheaded in a Seattle stadium, he suffered a sharp spasm of pain in his chest and faltered as if about to col-

President Warren G. Harding visits with a family during a stop in Alaska in July 1923.

President Warren G. Harding's Alaska Railroad special arrives at North Nenana, Alaska, on July 15, 1923.

Presidential excursionists enjoy the spectacular scenery of Alaska in this photo taken from a flatcar coupled to the rear of their Alaska Railroad special. Mr. and Mrs. Warren Harding are at left and Secretary of Commerce Herbert Hoover, a future president, is second from right.

The Harding presidential special—with the Alaska Railroad's track-mounted Dodge sedan just behind it—pauses at Girdwood, Alaska.

ALASKA RAILROAD COLLECTION/ANCHORAGE MUSEUM OF HISTORY AND ART

Warren Harding, on the platform with beret in hand, inspects the Curry Hotel at Curry, Alaska, where he and his party spent the night on their way back to civilization.

Above: *President Harding takes a swing at the spike ceremoniously completing the Alaska Railroad at North Nenana, Alaska, on July 15, 1923.*

Right: *Warren Harding has driven the spike completing the Alaska Railroad, and now the presidential party prepares to leave North Nenana.*

Warren Harding prepares to enjoy more cab mileage—this time in Alaska—as a serious-minded Secret Service man in the gangway scans the crowd below.

lapse several times. The president was rushed back aboard the train. He was obviously an ill man. Despite the advice of physicians and friends, however, he insisted on completing the scheduled program.

Harding experienced great pain that night aboard the train as it proceeded south on the Southern Pacific. Gen. Charles E. Sawyer, the president's physician, concluded he was suffering from ptomaine poisoning from eating rotten crabs on the *Henderson.* When no one else on the train became ill, the doctor's diagnosis was later interpreted as a plot to cover up the truth about the president's death. The public suspected a problem when Harding failed to appear on the back platform at Eugene, Ore. At Roseburg, an announcement was made.

Instead of advancing to Yosemite National Park via the SP to Merced, Calif., then via the Yosemite Valley line to El Portal, the train was diverted directly to San Francisco. On the way, Harding stayed in bed in his stateroom. He was repeatedly distressed because of the disappointment he was causing crowds by not being able to greet them.

The train reached San Francisco on Sunday, July 29. The weak and haggard president dressed himself and walked unaided through the station, but was half carried into the Palace Hotel and put to bed. He had a history of coronary problems, and doctors later agreed that he had suffered a heart attack in Seattle. Now, on top of that, he had bronchial pneumonia. A speech the following Tuesday was canceled and the president stayed put.

On the night of Thursday, Aug. 2, he was listening to Florence reading a favorable article about him by Samuel Blythe in *The Saturday Evening Post,* "A Calm Review of a Calm Man." When she paused to make sure he was not getting too tired, he said, "That's good; go on, read some more,"[43] and then gave a convulsive shudder. A sudden change came over his face and he slumped into the pillows. A nurse pulled back the covers and started rubbing his chest while Mrs. Harding ran screaming into the corridor for a doctor—but all was in vain. The president was dead. The doctors attributed it to a cerebral embolism, discounting rumors he was poisoned— by Florence to save him from the horrid Teapot Dome revelations ahead, or by he himself. Now the railroad cars that were to return him eastward would comprise a funeral train.

The Hardings disembark from their Alaska Railroad private car, the Denali, *to ride in the Dodge sedan following their train.*

Calvin Coolidge

Republican Calvin Coolidge's reluctance to spend money became painfully obvious even before he left home for Washington. On the morning of Aug. 3, 1923, just hours after his father had sworn him into office in Plymouth, Vt., Coolidge and his party motored to Rutland to catch the train that would take him to the nation's capital.

When he arrived at the depot, he spied a special train—garnished with red, white and blue bunting and punctuated with a private car owned by ex-Rutland President (and former Vermont Gov.) Percival Wood Clement —waiting for him with steam up.

Noticing that the regular 9:15 a.m. passenger train was still in the station, Coolidge became irritated. He sped past the reception committee and demanded to see the railroad's traffic manager. When the latter identified himself, the new president curtly ordered, "You're not running any special train for me! If you want me to ride in your boss's private car, you can hitch it on the regular train. But NO SPECIAL!"

The incensed notable escorted his wife, Grace, to a waiting-room bench, where he fumed while the switch was made. Several times, the president's young assistant secretary, E.C. Geiser, tried to speak to him, only to be impatiently waved aside. Two Secret Service men enroute from Washington hadn't arrived; but Coolidge couldn't have cared less. Soon the party was on its way, with much less fanfare than the president's fans had envisioned.

The Secret Service agents, having been stranded at Bellows Falls, talked their way into a caboose ride on a freight train proceeding toward Rutland. They made it to Mount Holly, a remote mountain stop, where the 9:15 paused for water and took on board the two very red-faced protectors.[445]

Coolidge traveled 35,594 miles while in office; notable among his trips was a pioneering effort that failed. When the frugal Vermonter found out how costly special trains and cars were, he put his presidential foot down. Planning a three-day trip to Chicago in December 1924 to speak at the Chicago Commercial Club and the International Livestock Exposition, he determined to ride as a regular passenger in a standard sleeper filled with other passengers.

Coolidge determined that a special train for the move would cost $6,000 and a special car attached to a regular train would cost $90 for the first day, $60 for each day thereafter, and 25 first-class fares to boot, for a

LIBRARY OF CONGRESS

A somber Calvin Coolidge disembarks from the Baltimore & Ohio's Capitol Limited *at Chicago's Grand Central Station on the morning of Dec. 4, 1924, perhaps realizing that if you're president, you just can't ride in a regular sleeping car.*

LIBRARY OF CONGRESS

Calvin Coolidge learned quickly that a president cannot ride in privacy and safety as a common passenger. After one such trip, now he and his wife, Grace, travel with Secretary of State Frank B. Kellogg aboard a private car on the Baltimore & Ohio's Capitol Limited.

117

President Calvin Coolidge's party prepares to depart Chicago for St. Paul, Minn., June 9, 1925, on the C&NW's Viking *for the Norse Centennial. From left are Secretary of State Frank B. Kellogg, Grace Coolidge, the president, Wisconsin Sen. Irvine L. Lenroot and presidential secretary Everett Sanders.*

total of $2,200. His idea, forcing the taxpayers to cough up only for those people traveling with the president, would cost a meager $400. He had preached economy to Congress and insisted on setting an example.

Coolidge and his wife rode from Washington to Chicago in a compartment aboard the 7-compartment, 2-drawing room sleeper *President Grant* on the first section of the Baltimore & Ohio Railroad's train 5, the all-Pullman *Capitol Limited*, on Wednesday, Dec. 3. Accompanying them were seven other people, including Secret Service agents and friends. Boarding at 3 p.m., Coolidge took a nap in his compartment while Grace and her friend, Mrs. Frank Stearns of Boston, took tea in the diner. The president quickly found that it was too hot to

sleep with the compartment door closed, but when he opened it all the passengers walked by for a look. At 7, the Coolidges ventured to the diner with Mr. and Mrs. Stearns for dinner. The president chose a $1.25 entree of clam chowder, oysters, turkey and ham.

Railroad officials were frantic. The thought of the president of the United States traveling on a regular train, taking his meals in the diner and attempting to fall into the routine of a regular passenger, horrified them. During dinner, Coolidge glared back at the people who stared at him. The waiters all had the jitters as they tried to work around the gawking passengers while serving the president. Richard Jervis of the Secret Service fretted about all the extra hazards. A waiter asked how he enjoyed his meal,

and the president—not noted for his verbosity—remained silent. As anxieties rose all around him, finally he smiled and said the dinner had filled his needs and was in every way acceptable.

At Connellsville, Pa., the president stepped onto the observation car's platform and acknowledged greetings from the ground. Afterward, things settled down for the night as B&O policeman Ernest Chapman guarded his presidential passengers—and the other clientele rooming in their car.

The special party returned eastward on the same sleeper, this time attached to B&O train 16, the *Chicago-Pittsburgh-Washington-Baltimore Express.* In one concession to presidential security, the train picked up its distinguished passenger at Brighton

While the Secret Service looks over the crowd in a Chicago yard on June 14, 1928, a workman scrubs the windows of B&O business car 97. The people are hoping President Calvin Coolidge—enroute to Brule, Wis., for a summer vacation—will make an appearance.

Park, a Chicago suburb, departing at 10:25 Thursday night. In another, the train was split at Willard, Ohio, and the two cars containing members of Coolidge's party, the regular Chicago-Washington sleeper and the observation car were operated from that point as a four-car first section.

Coolidge found that the members of his party were now practically the only passengers on the train, but if he worried that it would be considered a special movement, history doesn't mention it. On Friday, the president enjoyed three square meals in the diner, took his afternoon nap, and smoked and chatted with Stearns for a while in the diner.

At breakfast, the steward asked Coolidge if he liked his coffee."Delicious," the president muttered, and then as if by afterthought, he asked, "What did you think was the matter with it?"[389s]

The only appearance of presidential travel surfaced when Coolidge once again greeted the crowd at Connellsville at 1:10 p.m. Finally, when First 16 settled against the bumper post in Washington Friday night, a lot of people from the roundhouse to the White House began breathing easier.

But Coolidge's austerity did some good. The railroads got together and decided that the revenue wasn't worth the worry. They told the White House that henceforth, the president would be charged only for the space he occupied aboard his private car and that no guarantee would be required. The same rule would also apply to the rest of his train—and did so until the railroads gave the nation's chief executive his own car, U.S. No. 1, in 1942. One has to wonder if that was "Silent Cal's" motive all along. Of course the railroads lost money—but, after all, there is much publicity in carrying the nation's chief executive.

As for the president, he had learned a lesson. "However much he may deplore it," Coolidge wrote in his autobiography, "the president ceases to be an ordinary citizen. In order to function at all, he has to be surrounded with many safeguards. If these were removed for only a short time, he would be overwhelmed by the people who would surge in upon him. In traveling it would have been agreeable to me to use the regular trains which are open to the public. I have done so once or twice. But I found it made great difficulty for the railroads. They reported that it was unsafe because they could not take the necessary precautions."[89]

The problem was solved, he said, by running an extra section of a regular train for the exclusive use of the president and his party. This arrangement worked much better. The first section acted as a pilot train; newsmen and Secret Service agents aboard the second section bought regular tickets. Costs were low, while the benefits of safety, privacy and comfort were greatly improved.

Even so, the president and his wife preferred to eat in the diner rather than their private car. At such times, Mrs. Coolidge was more responsive to trackside crowds; her husband often ignored them. In June 1925, as the Coolidges returned from helping celebrate the first Norse immigration to the United States in St. Paul, Minn., their B&O train stopped at Willard, Ohio, as they were eating dinner. She spied youngsters running to the rear end from a nearby ball field. Without a word, she grabbed the president and pushed him to the back of the train so the kids wouldn't be disappointed. When they went outside, one of the children shouted in jest, "You spoiled our ball game!" A smiling Mrs. Coolidge answered, "And you broke up a perfectly good dinner."[389t]

On another trip, Coolidge found on his breakfast plate some muffins with currants in them. Carefully picking out a currant, he placed it on the side of his plate. "Look, Mamma," he remarked to Grace, "what I found in my food." The steward, thinking it was a dead fly or worse, turned pale and began apologizing. Then he began changing things on the table and shouting orders. When the president left the car, the steward was

President and Mrs. Coolidge greet well-wishers from the back of their train.

ready to collapse. "One more trip like this and they can put me in my grave," he fumed.[363]

The Coolidges' pets often traveled with them. There were two presidential collies, Rob Roy and Prudence Prim, and a raccoon, all of which were normally housed in the baggage car but which were often brought to the private car for feeding or simply companionship. Mrs. Coolidge also carried along some canaries. Prudence Prim, her collie, was white, and PRR's Washington passenger agent, Harry A. Karr, once noted that she always managed to rub a lot of grime off the baggage car floor. "I told my wife about it," Karr said, "and on my next trip she gave me a silken quilt she had made for the dog. I never knew if Mr. Coolidge approved of this luxury, but Mrs. Coolidge was delighted and so was her pet."[347]

The dogs caused some confusion on a vacation trip to the Black Hills of South Dakota in the summer of 1927. During a water stop at Capa, S.D., on the Chicago & North Western, valet John May thought he saw Rob Roy prancing smartly away from the train and, knowing the president would never leave without him, gave chase—irking the dog's real owner and nearly getting himself left behind. Mrs. Coolidge, seeing that Rob Roy was safely on board, had the faithful valet summoned just as he was disappearing from sight. The flustered May was grateful. "I don't know where I would have stayed out there tonight," he cooed.

Coolidge didn't say much while traveling, except to grunt "I thought so"[76] or some other such comment as he read the papers. He took a nap every afternoon, a practice that sometimes caused him to miss a chance to greet a crowd. In October 1925, as he was returning from an American Legion convention in Omaha, his Chicago, Burlington & Quincy train stopped for coal and water at a small town west of St. Louis and a crowd gathered to see him.

Col. Edmund Starling of the Secret Service went to the president's private car and found him seated on a big lounge, his elbows on a table and his hands cupped around his chin, sound asleep. Starling tapped him on the shoulder and said, "Mr. President, there are about 2,500 people waiting outside to see you."[363]

Without a word, Coolidge got up, smoothed his hair, straightened his jacket and followed Starling to the rear platform. He smiled; the people applauded. Then Grace came out and got an even bigger ovation.

The local master of ceremonies shouted, "Now you folks keep quiet. I want absolute silence. The president is going to address us." Silence followed. "All right, Mr. President," said the man to Coolidge, "you may speak now." Just then there was the hiss of air brakes being released and the train eased forward. The president, still smiling, raised his hand to the crowd and said: "Goodbye."[43]

Karr once told about a reporter—traveling with Coolidge in 1930 after he left office to another American Legion convention in Boston—who tried his best to break down the former president's reluctance to talk. Very early on the morning they arrived, the reporter slipped off the train and made his way to the waterfront, where he bought the two biggest and most succulent lobsters he could find. The train's chef prepared them with loving care and the steward presented them to the Coolidges as a special dinner treat.

"What's that?" asked Coolidge, eyeing his lobster coldly. Grace ate hers with obvious enjoyment.

"Who ate the other one?" an interviewer asked Karr.

"I did," he answered. "Mr. Coolidge had steak."[347]

New York Gov. Alfred E. Smith took his Democratic campaign to all parts of the country in 1928. His 11-car private train featured a shower and a barber shop, as well as a car full of duplicators to run off advance texts of his speeches.

But 1928 was Republican Herbert Hoover's party. And he took full advantage of railroad travel to crisscross the country between Washington, where he was secretary of commerce, and his home in Palo Alto, Calif.

A typical trip took the candidate south. On Friday, Oct. 5, he left Washington at 11 p.m. via the Southern and Norfolk & Western railways for appointments in the Elizabethton and Johnson City, Tenn., areas. He greeted a crowd of 5,000 at Bristol, Va./Tenn. at an early hour Saturday, and left the train at Childress, Tenn. He reboarded at 8:15 p.m Saturday for the return to Washington at 8 a.m. Sunday.

This trip registered some concern with Harry A. Karr, the Pennsylvania Railroad's division passenger agent in Washington, who wrote to George Akerson, Hoover's secretary, a few days beforehand to advise him the Southern Railway had no business cars available to the candidate for the trip. Southern had also advised Karr that even if they had, the trip would require 25 first-class fares plus a 10 percent surcharge, making the total expense $790.35. Apparently the promises made to Coolidge had been forgotten.

Karr had a suggestion, which apparently was accepted. "The following arrangements might be completed for this movement," he wrote. "Operate an extra section of any of their regular trains ... on the overflow basis, for an actual number of persons carried on the train. Train to consist of club car, dining car, necessary Pullman sleepers for the correspondents and picture men, and a three-compartment two-drawing room car for Mr. Hoover and his party. On this basis, the Pullman charge would be for the actual Pullman space occupied in the ... observation car, and the rail charge would be on the basis of two tickets for the occupancy of each room."[186]

Karr got to know Hoover well during his many campaign travels and came to like him. "He was up at 6 o'clock every morning," Karr recalled. "That meant still earlier hours for me as well as the Secret Service men. Often around sunup, Mr. Hoover would stroll back to the observation section [of his private car] to chat with us. He was a friendly man and quite a traveler."[347]

Hoover remarked that campaign travel was no luxury. For one thing, it was now the radio age, meaning that candidates could no longer use the same speech at each stop, adding a few comments to tailor them to the local situation. Each talk had to be new, because it would soon be beamed into millions of homes across the country. Maybe that's why Hoover was the last president to write his own speeches.

"The preparation of addresses is a job in itself," Hoover wrote. "And the pneumatic drill on one's brain of personalities, committees, crowds, messages, and incidents never ceases all the 18-hour day. Speeches must be spaced in each part of the country. The local committee at every depot must ride to the next station. Hundreds of thousands of people at train stops must have some sort of speech. Thousands of babies must be shaken by their plump fists."[187]

Then there were the gifts. The candidate accepted a 110-pound watermelon that, he was told, needed to be on ice for 30 hours. But he turned down offers of a free dromedary camel, a balloon ride over Kansas and a goat that ate Campbell's Soup for dinner every day—can and all.[60]

Causing the most pain, Hoover complained, were those who expected to be remembered by name. "In a reception line in Chicago a lady said, 'Don't you remember me?' and waited sternly for an answer. I try to be honest, so I replied, 'I am sorry, madam, but I would like to and no doubt could, if you will tell me where we met.' She said rather indignantly, 'Why I sat on the end of the third row when you spoke in Indianapolis, and you looked right at me.' "[187]

New York Gov. Al Smith, holding his characteristic brown derby, shakes hands with Colorado Gov. William H. "Billy" Adams in Denver Sept. 23, 1928.

Herbert and Lou Hoover pose on the back of the PRR's Manhattan Limited *with Vice President Charles Dawes, right, July 15, 1928. The Hoovers were guests in Dawes' home during a layover in Chicago.*

Another trial, he remarked, was signing autographs. "I am convinced that I have half a million in circulation," he wrote. "Certainly there is inflation in these issues."[187]

Hoover traveled 32,642 miles while in office, enjoying several refinements that had accrued to presidential travel by his day. Now telephone lines were installed between the head car and locomotive so members of the train crew could communicate with the engineer without climbing over the tender. On the ground, track patrols were so well staffed that no man had to observe more than 500 yards of trackage.

The chief executive and his wife, as others before them, traveled often on the B&O out of Washington. Notable among these trips was a journey to Detroit on Oct. 21, 1929, to help automaker Henry Ford celebrate his Light's Golden Jubilee at Greenfield Village, his model early American town at Dearborn.

The Hoovers' train narrowly averted being wrecked on the B&O after leaving Louisville two days after embarking from the capital. As they were preparing to depart the Seventh Street Station at 10 p.m., two men across the Ohio River were placing an automobile across the track at Sneder's Crossing five miles north of New Albany, Ind. Fortunately neighbors saw what was going on, and several of them came out and shoved the car out of the way. The Secret Service was

Arriving on the C&NW in Superior, Wis., on July 16, 1928, Republican candidate Herbert Hoover greets the throng before leaving his train to visit Calvin Coolidge at Cedar Island Lodge, that year's summer White House.

It's hard to say who goes through more anxiety in the politician-kisses-baby routine—the candidate or the infant. Here, as Hoover arrives in Palo Alto, Calif., on July 20, 1928, for the funeral of his father-in-law, he hands back a fussy child to an embarrassed mom.

called in—was it an attempt to wreck the presidential train? It turned out to be a less intriguing story. The owner of the secondhand Cadillac owed $35 on it. Not having the money to make the payment, he and a friend pushed it onto the track hoping a train would hit it and they would collect the insurance. They had no idea the president's train was the next one due.

Hoover found that presidential travel can have its embarrassing moments, too. One day that same year, his train stopped in Princeton, N.J., near a little school. The principal, anxious for his brief moment of glory, brought forward two little girls to present flowers. Then he turned about to lead his charges in three lusty cheers for Hoover. As he opened his mouth, however, no cheers were forthcoming. Instead, his false teeth went flying to the ballast while the president of the United States watched. [245]

The president often traveled by train to speaking engagements across the country. He left Washington at 10:55 a.m. Wednesday, Oct. 1, 1930, via PRR to North Philadelphia to

throw out the first ball at the Philadelphia Athletics-St. Louis Cardinals World Series game at Shibe Park, then headed west on an overnight jaunt to Cleveland to address the American Bankers Association convention.

He hoped that his presence at the game would display to the public his

calm confidence in the state of the Union and lift the nation's spirits as the Great Depression's grip became intolerably tight.

A photographer wanted shots of

Republican presidential candidate Herbert Hoover addresses a crowd in Gallup, N.M., on the AT&SF Aug. 19, 1928.

A nonchalant Herbert Hoover doesn't seem to have much to tell these folks.

the president throwing out the ball before the game, and Hoover posed for so many pictures that the game finally started without him. That evening, it occurred to a press association man that he had never seen the ball actually thrown. He went back to the president's private car, and sure enough, he was right. At some point while being photographed, Hoover had dropped the ball into his pocket; he never got around to making the ceremonial gesture. To reporter Richard L. Strout, the incident typified Hoover's good intentions but poor performance as president.[43]

When Hoover's seven-car train paused at 8:53 p.m. at Altoona, Pa., he greeted railroad men during the stop and a crowd at the station once he was under way again. The people noticed that his hair was much whiter than it had been when he passed through during the campaign two years before.

Secret Service agent Richard Jervis told a reporter the president had managed to maintain his neutrality during the afternoon's ball game, applauding the good work of both teams. And he had especially looked forward to seeing Pennsy's famous Horseshoe Curve by moonlight.

Fact is, Hoover didn't see the curve. His special veered off the main line at Altoona onto a mountain spur that connected with the old Allegheny Portage Railroad line so the president could get some sleep in the mountain quietness at Muleshoe Bend, four miles west of Duncansville, and avoid reaching his destination too early. No one around knew of the presence of their distinguished guest and when the train pulled onto the little-used siding, no one was there. Three crossties, lashed to the track with heavy chains, prevented the least possible chance of the train slipping back down the mountain even if its well-tested brakes failed. Switches leading to the siding were spiked and railroad police and Secret Service

guarded the train inside and out. Sometime during the wee hours, his train rejoined the mainline at Gallitzin, just east of the Allegheny Mountain tunnel and west of Horseshoe Curve.

The lack of payment for the Philadelphia-Cleveland trip caused some consternation in the Pennsy's executive offices. Two terse letters from PRR Treasurer George H. Pabst Jr. and an itemized statement written more than a year later reside in Hoover's White House files requesting "immediate settlement" of $252.71 in passenger transportation charges. In addition to various drawing room, lower berth and parlor seat charges for members of the party, the statement also included a fee of $2.30 for 6 ½ pounds of white fish delivered to the train in Cleveland.[186]

Apparently, there was some misunderstanding about who was supposed to pay the bill. One White House operative, N.P. Webster, understood that the bankers were going to spring for it, but presidential secretary Lawrence Richey finally answered him with a one-sentence

Herbert Hoover disembarks from Rock Island's Golden State *on Aug. 21, 1928, to spend three days campaigning in and around his birthplace, West Branch, Iowa.*

Local folks await the return of Herbert Hoover to his car on the Rock Island's Golden State *after a stop at his birthplace, West Branch, Iowa, Aug. 23, 1928.*

memo that said, "I think we will have to pay this."[186]

After another round of correspondence—in which PRR's Harry Karr tracked down a former presidential secretary, George Akerson, then with Paramount Publix Corp. in New York City—Akerson fired off a plea to Richey at the White House to pay the debt regardless of any promises made by the bankers:

"This bill should be paid right away to the railroad so that there be not a lot of correspondence either with the railroad or the American Bankers Association relating thereto. The amount is not a large one and the railroad company certainly has the money coming."[186] Apparently the White House complied. That was the last letter on the matter in the file.

A 1931 journey took the first family to Akron, Ohio, for the christening of the Navy airship *Akron*. It was on this occasion that Mrs. Hoover remarked, when told about B&O's historic blue china, "I knew a woman who had a hand in that."[380] She referred to Miss Olive W. Denis, B&O's engineer of service who suggested the historic equipment and

scenes depicted in the pattern devised by Enoch Wood of England to commemorate B&O's founding on its 100th anniversary in 1927.

Hoover embarked on a trip to the Midwest in June and it is apparent from his files that he traveled in an age when railroads still fought for the privilege of transporting the nation's

chief executive.

Alan B. Smith, PRR's general passenger agent, wrote a page and a half, single-spaced, to Richey on April 11 offering a beautiful train, fast running times and virtually anything else he wanted. Harry Karr followed up on May 18, using *The Liberty Limited* stationery, bragging on his road's double track, block signals, and willingness to park anywhere overnight. "With all the physical advantages favoring our line," he concluded heavy-handedly, "it will be a reflection upon me personally if this business is awarded to our competitor."[186]

Karr got his insult. The C&O's Walter Chamblin Jr., in the office of Assistant to the President L.C. Probert, wrote a letter nearly three pages long that outbragged Smith and Karr. C&O won the trip—in fact, the deal had been made before the PRR's Karr wrote his plaintive appeal. The eight-car special left Washington's Union Station at 7:35 p.m. Sunday, June 14, with the Pullman private car *Henry Stanley* reserved for the first

A crowd gathers as Herbert Hoover's train grinds to a halt, hoping to see the 1928 Republican presidential candidate.

PRR locomotive 5397 speeds Herbert Hoover back to Washington on Aug. 20, 1932, after a cross-country campaign trip.

Herbert and Lou Hoover greet PRR engineer Kogle and fireman Rapka on locomotive 5408 in Washington Union Station after returning from Des Moines Oct. 6, 1932.

family. The presidential party was picked up at Orange, Va., 25 miles from Hoover's fishing camp on the Rapidan River in the Blue Ridge Mountains.

Hoover's rail travels during his abortive 1932 campaign—after which he lost to Franklin D. Roosevelt— were extensive but counterproductive. He was in trouble because the nation blamed him for the Depression. Sometimes the public vented its anger at trackside.

The ugly mood in Detroit had Starling worried on an Oct. 3-6 trip to Des Moines, Iowa. "The area around the [Detroit] railroad station was cleared," he wrote, "but across the street a large crowd gathered. I decided to keep the president on the train [PRR business car 100] until the motor cavalcade was ready to start. I would then put him in his car and emerge from the cover of the station at a fast clip, taking the crowd by surprise and getting past it before a

demonstration could be staged. I had trouble persuading the members of the official party to get into their cars and to move into their place in the line. Despite their protests, I held the president until they had done as I asked. Then, with a pilot car leading the way, we swung out of the station. The crowd recognized the president. There were cheers. There were also other sounds. For the first time in my long experience on the detail I heard the president of the United States booed. All along the line there were bad spots, where we heard jeers and saw signs reading: 'DOWN WITH HOOVER'; 'HOOVER — BALONEY AND APPLESAUCE.' The president looked bewildered and stricken."[363]

Hoover received a 21-gun salute in Charleston, W.Va., on Oct. 22, but when the weapons went off, an old man in the crowd grunted, "Hrumph! They missed him!"

On the way back home to Palo Alto, Calif., a few days later, the pres-

Herbert Hoover addresses a crowd in Parkersburg, W.Va., on Oct. 28, 1932, enroute to a speech in Indianapolis. That's B&O police officer Ernest Chapman on the ground checking out the fellow holding aloft a microphone.

idential train was stopped near Beloit, Wis., where a man had been found pulling up spikes from the track. In St. Paul, Hoover made a reference to a Democratic prediction that mob rule would follow a Republican victory and stated, "Thank God we still have a government in Washington that knows how to deal with a mob." A ripple of boos rolled through the audience and Starling broke out in a cold sweat. A prominent Republican pulled him aside and asked, "Why don't they make him quit? He's not doing himself or the party any good. It's turning into a farce. He is tired physically and mentally."[363]

Hoover's private car was pelted with rotten eggs at Elko, Nev., and the state's governor refused to appear publicly with him. A senator did, and lost by 500 votes.

And there was word in Nevada of an attempt to wreck his train.

His SP pilot train was flagged at 8:55 p.m. on Monday, Nov. 7, at the 14th crossing west of Humboldt. Assistant Engineer Fish bore evidence of a severe fight and stated he had been shot through the hand by one of two trespassers he encountered at the west

PRR engine 5395 barrels toward Washington on May 30, 1931, returning President Hoover from Valley Forge, Pa.

President Hoover pauses on the B&O at Oxford, Ohio, Oct. 28, 1932, enroute to Indianapolis. It is late in the campaign, and Hoover is losing. When he reaches the Butler University field house in the Indiana capital, he will discard the aloofness that has characterized his earlier speeches and will deride Franklin Roosevelt's New Deal policies as "nonsense," "misstatements," "prattle," and other such uncomplimentary terms.

end of an overhead Western Pacific Railroad bridge. He also exhibited three cuts in his coat where he said he had been slashed during the fight.

"We found two sticks [of] giant 40 percent powder where fight occurred," a company report said, "and gunny sack with some 20 more sticks in it with no fuse or caps."[186]

Fish claimed to have fired four shots at the man, saying he didn't think they had any effect. The railroad left a detail of special agents to investigate three other bridges in the area and took Fish to a doctor on a motor car.

"Am leaving to your judgment as to whether best to leave to Cordon to handle rather than incur publicity which will follow if give to local civil officers," one SP agent telegraphed to another cryptically. "Recommend we handle ourselves as circumstances

Alton engine 5276 charges out of Peoria, Ill., on Nov. 4, 1932, with President Herbert Hoover's campaign special.

A grim Herbert Hoover makes the last radio broadcast of his 1932 campaign to the nation from the lounge of his private car at Elko, Nev., on Nov. 7, enroute to his home at Palo Alto, Calif.

appear suspicious."[186]

It turned out the agent was correct. Five days later, Fish confessed that the incident was a hoax, "perpetrated by him for publicity and possibly obtain financial assistance to help his family and to finance the publication of stories he was writing." The president would probably like to know that there was no attempt to wreck his train, he concluded.[186]

At a small town in California the next morning, Secretary of the Interior Hubert Work stepped in for the weary president, addressing a small crowd at the rear of the train. "The president was up very late last night," he droned, "and he is still asleep. I bring you his greetings, and while I am here I cannot miss the opportunity to say a few words for myself. I am myself from the West, and I have spent many delightful hours in your beautiful little city. In fact I see several faces out there that I know. It's a very genuine pleasure to find myself back here … "

He stopped suddenly and turned to Secret Service man Dick Jervis. Out of the side of his mouth, he growled, "Where in h— are we?" Unfortunately, a broadcast man was holding a live microphone against the rear of the platform and everyone within a quarter mile heard Work's plaintive plea. They roared with laughter as the embarrassed party left town.[363]

When the beleaguered candidate got home, he was described as a "walking corpse." One telegram that reached him there said "Vote for Roosevelt and make it unanimous."[60]

With his leg braces locked firmly in place, polio victim Franklin D. Roosevelt stands in a vestibule of his CB&Q special somewhere in the nation's midsection in October 1936.

The Golden Era is Born:

The Franklin Roosevelt Years

5

Franklin D. Roosevelt

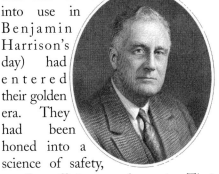

By the time Franklin Roosevelt began his 12-year residence in the White House, presidential campaign specials and trains labeled "POTUS" (the Presidential acrostic that had come into use in Benjamin Harrison's day) had entered their golden era. They had been honed into a science of safety, comfort, efficiency and security. Their circus atmosphere of bands and bunting, rousing speeches and declarations of principles stirred the imagination and presented the perfect way to bring the candidate or the president together with the people.

Nothing quite equaled the spectacle of 100 or so news correspondents, speechwriters, political advisers, press agents, secretaries, greeters, radio engineers and other assorted souls living for days on end in 10 to 20 heavyweight railroad cars. And nothing could unravel the complex and detailed planning by the men behind the scenes that went into safely routing such a cavalcade that necessarily disrupted railroads' regular schedules.

Yet Roosevelt's presidency represented a curious transition. No president traveled by rail more than he, amassing a record of 243,827 miles on 399 trips—the equivalent of 10 times around the world. But during his tenure came the earliest signs of technological change. He was the first president to travel on a diesel-powered train, on the Baltimore & Ohio Railroad between Washington and New York City in 1937. And he was the first sitting president to use an airplane for transportation—in 1943. Ironically, his peak annual rail mileage—55,422—also was tallied that year.

LAURA DELANO/ROOSEVELT LIBRARY

The presidency is a couple of decades away for Franklin Roosevelt as he and Eleanor prepare to board this train around 1910.

The star performer during the later years of the Roosevelt era, of course, was the presidential car *Ferdinand Magellan*, of which more will be said later.

A child of World War II and the need for extraordinary presidential security, the armor-plated Pullman weighed in at 285,000 pounds—easily the heaviest railroad passenger car in the world.

Planning for a POTUS special started months in advance—by the road upon which the move originated. Thus it was that Daniel L. Moorman, B&O's general passenger agent in Washington, or Harry Karr, his PRR counterpart, supervised many a Roosevelt special to the West Coast and other distant points.

Sometimes the facilities of 25 different roads were used on a single trip. Arrangements—especially during the war—were strictly confidential. Roosevelt liked rail travel. "I'm in no hurry," he once explained. "The sooner I get where I'm going, the sooner people will be wanting something from me."[452]

In fact, he often took a hand in planning his own trips. "He was well acquainted with the network of rail facilities across the nation," wrote Grace Tully, his private secretary, "and when he would initially line out a trip to the White House transportation officer, 'Doc' Edward W. Smithers at first, and later Dewey Long, the Boss usually had the routes and the required times pretty well laid out."[415]

FDR would call in Long, who came to his post from the Department of Agriculture, and the head of the White House Secret Service—first Col. Edmund Starling and later Mike Reilly—and not only tell them when and where he wanted to go, but also by what route. He particularly appreciated being routed over lines new to him. Most of the time, the chief executive even filled out diagram cards for his private car, allotting the sleeping space himself.

Roosevelt was superstitious. He tried to alter departures to 11:50 p.m. on the 12th or 12:10 a.m. on the 14th to avoid starting trips on the 13th. He also opposed embarking on Fridays.

FDR arranged to have his trains pull away just as he ended his rear-platform speeches—re-entering the observation lounge after receiving the crowd's cheers and remarking, "That's just great!"[288] That clever timing added to the drama but often strand-

Franklin Roosevelt waves to a crowd in Atlanta on Oct. 1, 1931, enroute to Warm Springs, Ga.

ed local politicians on the train and reporters on the ground.

Maintenance crews often wouldn't be finished icing or watering the train. Eventually, though, he became an expert at how long these operations took and timed his talks to the second.

Roosevelt ordered his trains to travel slowly during the day—various sources list the maximum speed at between 25 and 50 miles an hour. Reasons offered were as varied as the figures. The president himself said he liked to take time to see the sights and wave to the people. "I love this country of ours—every inch of it," he often told the B&O's Moorman, who rode with the president more than a hundred times. "And I want to take the time to really see it."[375] Miss Tully recalled that the chief's trips usually included a presidential commentary about the people, homes and crops of the territory being traversed.

Some attributed the polio-stricken president's slow-speed order to the fact that he would lose his balance while trying to navigate his leg braces and wheelchair at higher speeds or that the jostling hurt his lower back and hips. Whatever the reason, his trains were permitted to run much faster at night—after the president was safety tucked into bed.

FDR's most frequent destinations were his family homeplace, Springwood, located in the Crum Elbow area of Hyde Park, N.Y., and his "Little White House" at Warm Springs, Ga. Although the war cut into his travel down South, he continued making jaunts at least monthly to his New York home, mainly for extended weekends.

Usually, his Hyde Park trains followed the B&O to Philadelphia, the Reading Railway to Bound Brook, N.J., and the Central of New Jersey line to Claremont, N.J. At that point his train would take the National Docks Railroad (controlled by Lehigh Valley) for a short stretch to connect with New York Central's West Shore line at Weehawken, where it would continue to Highland, N.Y., across the Hudson River from Poughkeepsie. From Highland, the party would cross the Mid-Hudson Bridge and cover the last 12 miles to Hyde Park by auto.

An alternate route took Roosevelt's train from Washington to New York on the PRR, continuing via the New York Connecting and the New York, New Haven & Hartford railroads to New Rochelle. At that point it would back down a New Haven branch that connected with the NYC's Harlem Division at Woodlawn and continue backing to Mott Haven Yard in The Bronx. Then it would proceed on NYC's Hudson Division to a siding behind Roosevelt's home.

The PRR-NYNH&H-NYC route was more direct, but FDR always preferred the B&O routing. Some said it was because of B&O's down-home hospitality as manifested by B&O's New York General Passenger Agent Howard E. Simpson; others thought the president didn't like the Republican activism of PRR President William W. Atterbury; still others offered that PRR didn't like its four-track Northeast Corridor race track tangled up with FDR's slow POTUS trains or that B&O graciously pro-rated his fare, even when he was the only one aboard his car. Finally, the Secret Service was said to object to the direct route because of the security risks in crossing the Hell Gate Bridge spanning New York City's East River.

Between Washington and Warm Springs, Ga., Roosevelt traveled on the Southern Railway—making at least 50 trips during his presidency.

On board, FDR was the consummate country gentleman.

He loved to read his mail or play solitaire while the miles passed by, and anytime he arrived at an Army post he and his black Scottish terrier, Fala, would sit on the rear platform and enjoy the band music.

The president went out of his way to make his guests comfortable. His usual custom was to call in some companions just after a trip started for a round of soft drinks, but sometimes that didn't quite suit the mood of the customers. Secretary of the Treasury Henry Morganthau and his wife, who, like FDR, had a home in Dutchess County, N.Y., let it be known their tastes ran in different circles as one weekend trip home began.

Presidential Porter Henry W. Lucas showed up with the usual tray of orange juice. Morganthau looked disappointed and whispered to Miss Tully, "What does a fellow have to do around here to get a real drink?"

"What did Henry say?" the Boss asked his secretary.

"If you must know, sir," she responded, "the secretary doesn't think much of your choice of beverages."

ROOSEVELT LIBRARY

Franklin and Eleanor Roosevelt pose at Savannah, Ill., on April 19, 1932, as they head for Albany, N.Y.

"Ring for Lucas and tell him what you want, Henry," FDR told his guest. "We want you to be happy."[415]

During one trip, Pullman Special Agent P.C. "Pat" Darcey knew the train would be passing through Shipman, Va., where his mother lived. Dewey Long had received a telegram informing him that Darcey's mother was dying and shared it with the president. FDR advised everyone to keep quiet for the moment, but as they neared Shipman, he ordered the train stopped and told Darcey to go to his mother at once. He arrived at her side a half hour before she died.

"FDR was always kind to my husband," Pat's wife, Marian, recalled. "I never knew where Pat was—everything was such a secret, but the White House could get in touch with him in five minutes if I had to reach him."[288]

The president often sent his activist wife, Eleanor, to deliver lectures, visit slums, nursery schools, playgrounds and sharecroppers—to the tune of 40,000 miles a year. Roosevelt always questioned her closely when she returned; he gave her the Secret Service code name "Rover." When traveling alone, Mrs. Roosevelt usually occupied a Pullman drawing room in regular line cars, paying the same as anyone else.

Of paramount importance in the operation of POTUS trains was selection of crews—both by the railroads and the Pullman Company. The best people were handpicked—often from other regular assignments. Many were POTUS regulars who handled the specials for years over the course of several administrations. Roosevelt treated the railroaders well, and they couldn't do enough for him. "We were proud to clean and inspect the engines used on his train, seeing that every nut and bolt was safe," recalled Charles Householder, boiler inspection foreman at Southern's North Avenue passenger roundhouse in Atlanta. "We

even drained the water tank and thoroughly inspected it. Although the boilers may have been blown off, washed and inspected the day before, these jobs were done again, and cheerfully, not so much because our orders were to leave nothing overlooked but mainly because we loved Roosevelt."[262]

Bob Ackers, veteran chef on the *Crescent Limited,* always cooked on the president's special when it burnished Southern's rails. "President Roosevelt was the best man I ever worked for," said Ackers. "Never grumbled at all. If I cooked him a big plank steak or just a mess of turnip greens and other vegetables with country-style pone cornbread, it was the same with him, and he never left nothing on his plate. It was a pleasure to cook for that man!"[262]

The railroads always tried to cater to Roosevelt's cuisine. "Shortly after he began using our lines back in 1933," B&O's Dan Moorman recalled, "we made a special effort to learn what dishes he preferred and the way he liked them prepared. We did this by going into a huddle with Mrs. Roosevelt, his daughter, Anna, and his secretaries. From them we discovered that terrapin, pheasant, quail, trout, white fish and good coffee were among the president's favorites. No effort was spared to serve them up to his liking. We had railroad men and our friends all up and down the line on the lookout for good fish and game, and some of the B&O's most talented chefs were used to prepare them."[375]

Sometimes, as the special passed through the various states, a governor or some special friend would send the president a choice delicacy common to the region. One governor sent him a gift of selected fresh fish, swimming in a tank of water. Another once presented him with a crate of choice live quail. It was the job of dining-car crews to prepare these and many other fine food

Franklin and Eleanor Roosevelt pose on the back of their private car for well-wishers in the '30s.

gifts to grace the president's table.

L.P. Wesley, assistant district superintendent of the Southern in Atlanta at the time, said the Pullman Company also was very careful in assigning personnel to the specials. Henry Lucas, the president's porter at first, was a Georgian who started working for President Harding. Later, Fred D. Fair, another Georgia man, took over the job. Veteran W.A. Brooks was for years the presidential Pullman conductor on Southern rails.

Pullman service inspectors Dave Gahagan of the Philadelphia Zone and J.M. Darcey of the Yards Department were chosen as troubleshooters because of their reserved natures. These men stayed with the train during layovers until it was returned to Washington, while the rest of the Pullman crew members went back to their various runs until called again.

Pullman's Washington district superintendent, W.S. Jones, who had arranged presidential travel since the days of Woodrow Wilson and who personally supervised the handling of equipment and crews on every one of Roosevelt's POTUS trips, once reported that FDR's Pullman crew "all stacked up 100 percent as we did not receive a single complaint of any indiscreet talking on the part of any member of the crew during the 12 years."[452] On-board personnel achieved such a camaraderie with their presidential passengers that sometimes they crossed over and went to work for them in the White House. In 1945, porter Samuel Mitchell—who rode on 397 of Roosevelt's 399 trips—left Pullman to become a White House messenger. In that capacity he still rode the specials, in charge of Roosevelt's car whenever it moved with the president, his family, or any celebrity aboard at the president's invitation. He eventually returned to Pullman and worked for other presidents as well.

Porter J.W. Mays had made the same transition under President McKinley. B&O waiter William Brown made friends with FDR's valet, Chief Petty Officer Arthur Prettyman, and ended up as a White House butler.

The only problem porters found in POTUS service was with regard to tipping. In a day when their salaries were $72.50 a month—with a $25 bonus for work on private cars—tips meant much. But Fred Fair said there was no extra pay for working presidential trains and few tips as well.

"FDR, he didn't have any money to tip with," Fair once chuckled. He recalled that Roosevelt once asked an aide for money, saying "I want to tip these people."[67] Sam Mitchell's memory was that the president thought five dollars was sufficient enough a tip for a weekend trip to Hyde Park and

FDR enjoys a hearty laugh with a rear platform full of aides.

back. So Mitchell used his seniority in the Brotherhood of Sleeping Car Porters to have himself transferred to the press car, where each reporter tipped him a couple of dollars and he wound up with $40 or $50.[53]

Staff people riding presidential trains were there because the president needed them. Government business had to go on even though he was away from his office for a few days. That's why the White House secretaries, often several Cabinet members or other federal officers, telephone and telegraph men, radio men, newspaper reporters, cameramen and always a few invited guests were aboard. On the train were typewriters, dictaphones and telephones. The presidents and their staffs handled correspondence and carried on necessary work as though they were in Washington.

When B&O locomotive engineer

William E. Carroll—a descendant of Charles Carroll, the longest-surviving signer of the Declaration of Independence who participated in the laying of B&O's First Stone in 1828—retired after 50 years' service in 1952, he had chalked up 141 trips with Roosevelt. He also hauled Hoover and Truman, but FDR was his favorite.

The president was often wheeled up to the locomotive and "he would haul me down and ask me questions about what I was doing,"[74] Carroll recalled. Secret Service agents always rode the engine, he said. Sometimes the Roosevelt boys would come up for a ride, and once they brought Fala along.

Much had to be done when an occupant of the White House—or an aspiring one—was leaving town. Their trains had to be kept running smoothly and on schedule, even

though they were constantly shifted from line to line and often conflicted with regular streamliners. For months in advance, chief dispatchers were busy figuring out ways to satisfy government and political requirements without being called on the carpet for delaying their own bread and butter.

Advance paperwork was followed by the movement of a virtual army of railroad men. Watchmen patrolled long tunnels, bridges and canyons. A pilot train was always operated in advance of a POTUS special, and sometimes a "dummy train" would follow. Spare engines with steam up were spotted at strategic points, ready to take over in case of a breakdown. Sometimes an extra train crew would ride along in case illness should strike any of the regulars. At the least, trainmen along the route were alerted to take over at a moment's notice to prevent delays.

The Roosevelts leave Warm Springs, Ga., for Washington on Dec. 3, 1933.

Division superintendents or road foremen of engines rode in—or even operated—the locomotive while the train crossed their territory, sighing with relief when they stepped down to shake hands with the officer taking over. Railroad special agents were everywhere, cooperating with the president's Secret Service or the candidate's security staff. They usually occupied the second car from the rear, and screened everyone who came aboard. More than one politician with a bulging hip has been asked what he was carrying.

Most roads brought other trains—in either direction—to a stop 30 minutes in advance of the special, although a few permitted them to run on slow orders. The stop orders usually applied to everything—passenger, freight and yard switching—although passenger runs were sometimes permitted to keep moving slowly. Engines near the special were ordered to silence their bells and whistles or horns. Long memos—usually several single-spaced pages—were distributed to those officers needing them, calling for such measures as specially selected coal, inspection of the entire right of way by supervisors, master carpenters, bridge inspectors, track foremen and track walkers an hour before the special passed. Car inspectors were required to accompany the trains "with screw jack, bucket of packing, bearings, emergency knuckle, etc." and a telegraph lineman also rode "with portable telephone set and portable telegraph set and blueprint showing location of telephone and telegraph wires." [262]

Plainclothes agents would be assigned to every depot and coaling and water stations to watch for suspicious characters and prevent crowds from getting in the way.

Clearances had to comply with the dimensions of every car on the train, and the battery boxes, water tanks and charcoal boxes of each Pullman were rigorously checked. Comfort was never forgotten. Should

engineers use their whistles or horns needlessly or deviate for a moment from the speed they were told to maintain, reprimands were sure to follow.

By 1933, POTUS trains had grown to enormous—and complicated—proportions. Cars were lined up something like this:

- Behind the locomotive was a baggage car, which, more often than not, carried two or three late-model automobiles for VIPs to ride in while traveling between the train and civic auditoriums or hotels.
- Next on POTUS specials was a communications car designed to keep the president in touch with the White House and most capitals of the world. It also served as control point for communications with the locomotive cab and the other cars on the train. Beginning in 1942, this assignment was filled by B&O combination passenger-baggage coach 1401 under lease to the government. Ten years later, the combine was replaced by a former Army ambulance car fitted with the latest technology and renamed the *General Albert Myer*, and a companion sleeper for members of the Army Signal Corps.
- Press correspondents slept in the next three or four Pullman sleepers.
- Then came a working press car—usually a coach stripped of its seats and equipped with two boards at typing height, running lengthwise down each side. At one end was a darkroom for photographers and at the other an office for Western Union. The train agent there would alert all the branch offices along the route and pitch bags off constantly. Minutes after newspapermen had written their stories, they were on

the wire—often being handled by a telegrapher at some isolated spot. The press car's built-in public address system allowed correspondents to hear the rear-platform talks without having to walk to the rear end. They were usually handed mimeographed copies of major addresses, but had to stay on their toes for any significant revelations during off-the-cuff remarks at railroad operating stops.

- Next came the diner(s), one or two of them, furnished by whatever road the train was on at the moment. They were constantly being exchanged at interchange points. Open-ring hooks were spot-welded beneath the fireman's side of all of them so the communications cables keeping the locomotive and all of the cars in touch with one another could be quickly recoupled when the train was reassembled.
- A lounge car was usually next, for the staff and press.

- Then, two or three sleepers for the presidential staff—such as secretaries, speechwriters, political advisers, a nurse and a doctor, a radio engineer, a radio and television program director, a mimeograph operator, press agents, receptionists, the train manager and a paymaster. Also there were the VIPs—politicians who boarded when the train entered their state or congressional district and rode with the president or their party's candidate across their territory.
- Following was a sleeper for Secret Service, railroad special agents, the press relations boss, confidential secretaries and maybe political advisers.
- Finally, on the rear, was the president's or candidate's car.

Often the specials were shunted off on a lonely spur or spotted in the yard of some great city overnight, and then everyone used the train as a hotel. Telephone connections were plugged in, typists worked far into the

night, and there was all the hustle and bustle of any political headquarters. Sometimes the train continued moving through the night, especially in the West, where great distances had to be covered. But the normal procedure was to call a halt, so the candidate could start his day speaking in the next town on the route.

Campaign trains could cover 10,000 miles in 30 days, with the candidate giving 35 or 40 major speeches and 60 to 90 shorter rear-platform talks.

Richard L. Strout, then a reporter for the *Christian Science Monitor*, wrote in 1935 that campaign specials are "little worlds on rails, equipped with the last refinement of press and electrical broadcasting machines, in which journalism is carried on at high speed between station stops.

"The train generally carries 20 reporters, perhaps an equal number of cameramen and motion-picture operators, a crew of stenographers, mimeographers, electricians, and a retinue of political leaders besides the

A crowd gathers around the private car Robert Peary *to greet President and Mrs. Roosevelt at Columbus, Neb., Sept. 28, 1935.*

Presidential candidate Franklin Roosevelt holds a press conference in the dining room of his private car at Bellefontaine, Ohio, Sept. 13, 1932.

candidate's own family," Strout wrote. "It is a good deal like traveling with a circus." [338]

Gardner Bridge, an Associated Press correspondent, wrote in 1944 about the decor of GOP candidate Thomas E. Dewey's press car.

"On one wall was a large map of the United States, with the train's course traced in red crayon. Other walls were plastered with bulletins on arrival and departure times, copy 'drop-off' points, etc. One sign that puzzled members of the visiting press reads simply 'do not hate each other' in large type. It was a relic of a photographers' feud that sprang up early in the trip but soon died down. The sign was kept there just as a reminder." [338]

These long tours had another downside—the lack of clean laundry and access to shower facilities. Reporters and politicians often had to go for several days between showers and clean clothes. Atmospheric conditions aboard the cars became so unbearable that porters burned incense.

One train was making its way across a barren stretch of hot Texas countryside. It had not stopped in a major city for several days and all on board were anxious to take showers. As it approached a small refueling stop, the train pulled onto a siding directly beneath a water tank. All the occupants—except the candidate—got off the train, stood under the tank, and took a group shower—fully clothed—as the spout was opened and a torrent of water fell upon them.

Despite their rigors, reporters generally liked campaign trains. They not only could keep in touch with the candidate, but also had ample working, dining and sleeping facilities and could prepare their file copy quickly.

POTUS security was always thorough. Equipment and track were double-checked in advance and all hands were alerted for any possible contingency.

Key men from the operating, traf-

fic and mechanical departments rode along; detailed advance instructions told everyone what was expected. Once, Roosevelt's special was detoured without advance notice onto another railroad because there had been rumors of an attempted derailment. On another occasion, his train was saved from running over a bundle of dynamite on the track by an alert trackwalker in California.

By this time, campaign trips and POTUS movements had become an expensive proposition.

When presidents first started riding the trains, they paid the usual fare and rode in coaches. Many times, the railroads allowed them to ride free, redeeming the loss with the publicity value. But there was no clear-cut policy; sometimes the freebies were doled out according to the whim of conductors' politics.

By the time presidents began using business cars, they were charged the regular fare but nothing for the space they occupied or for their meals. Eventually the Interstate Commerce Commission investigated the use of business cars of one road on the tracks of another and made a recommendation—later covered by an order—that a minimum of 10 rail fares be paid for the car while on foreign lines; and in addition, a rail fare be charged for each non-pass holder, plus the equivalent of a sleeping section rate as well.

That more or less stopped the use of business cars for presidential tours. Then the Pullman Company came into the picture, agreeing to furnish a private car for the president on the same terms that it would a sleeper on an overflow basis. He would pay tariff charges for space occupied—room, berth or seat—as well as railroad transportation. On rare occasions, presidents rode as guests of railroad officials—but never on a pass. The official would procure the ticket his guest needed. Pullman was never known to grant the free use of cars to anyone except its own high officials or members of company founder George M. Pullman's own family.

After a while, these arrangements were found to be unsatisfactory, so the Association of American Railroads bought the *Ferdinand Magellan* from the Pullman Company and set it aside for the president's use in 1942. In 1946, the AAR sold it to the government outright for $1. It was designated U.S. No. 1.

Taxpayers, of course, shelled out for the presidential specials, but the politicians were nicked for campaign trains. By the early '50s, railroads demanded a minimum of 125 full fares plus Pullman rentals. Correspondents and VIPs paid their own

fares, but the candidate and staff members didn't. So a campaign train cost its national headquarters anywhere from $1,500 to $3,000 a day. Conductors aboard these specials reported no trouble with the correspondents but the politicians often tried to duck them, especially if they were riding for only a day or two. After one 10,000-mile journey, a conductor fumed that he had worked harder as a detective than at his job. The railroads themselves were often stalled on their pay for up to four years if the party was broke, as the Democrats were in 1932 when Franklin Roosevelt was first elected.

But in spite of the poor credit, political confusion and chaos, the nation's railroaders kept those specials

running smoothly, taking politics directly to the people—to cowpunchers in Arizona who had ridden miles for the event, to miners in West Virginia clustered around a drab depot, to farmers in Iowa who had left their fields for a few moments, to lonely folks in Montana who had walked far to reach the tracks, and to great mobs in the big cities. And no one will ever know just how many mothers have held their youngsters high, pointed to a special train and said, "Now you've seen the president of the United States."[152]

Roosevelt traveled extensively during the 1930s, starting with 13,000 miles during the 1932 presidential campaign. Unlike Hoover's dreary and plodding style, he

696. PRESIDENT ROOSEVELT AND PARTY IN COLUMBUS, NEBR. SEPT. 28, 1935

Mr. and Mrs. Franklin Roosevelt bid a fond farewell to the folks in Columbus, Neb., Sept. 28, 1935.

enlivened his speeches with catchy phrases and homely tales. The candidate was accompanied by his son James and his daughter-in-law Betsy Cushing Roosevelt. He liked to have his children with him, and was especially fond of Betsy, who was pert, vivacious and enjoyed coquetting with her irresistible father-in-law. From time to time Eleanor flew out to join the train, and she was in Chicago when the whole family attended a World Series game between the Cubs and the Yankees. She was not a model of attentiveness, Jimmy later claimed, having slept through most of the game in which Babe Ruth and Lou Gehrig each hit home runs.

From his rolling platform Roosevelt faced the crowds with his running mate, "Cactus Jack" Garner of Texas, while his son sat on the railing and waited to be introduced. "This is my LITTLE boy James," FDR would say. "I have more hair than he does!"[153]

The campaign was hectic. "We broadcasters were quartered at the front of the train," recalled CBS newsman Robert Trout. "Clyde Hunt and I—he was presidential engineer for CBS and had invented the clamp-on arrangement that held the microphone in place at the back rail of the observation platform—we had to run from the front of the train to that rear platform to get set up. Then we had to unclamp, grab our gear and leg it back to the front of the train after FDR's remarks fast enough to avoid being left standing on the tracks in the wake of the train."[411]

The campaigner remained cool through it all. At Deer Lodge, Mont., he told the crowd from the back platform that he fondly remembered visiting there 12 years before when running for vice president. "Why, when I was here in 1920," he recalled, "I had one of the finest fish dinners I ever had in my life." The problem was that

Franklin D. Roosevelt enjoyed the fruits of his New Deal labors on Saturday, Feb. 23, 1935, when he left Washington for Hyde Park via Boston. It was the first presidential trip on the PRR's Washington-New York line after it was electrified—with large infusions of Public Works Administration money. The locomotive, GG-1 type 4800, set a speed record, too—hauling seven cars in two hours 53 minutes from Union Station's Track 30 to Penn Station's Track 11 for an average speed of 78.6 miles an hour.

he referred to a dinner in which the cocktail hour had taken precedence over the fish, and Roosevelt had enjoyed himself so much that he wisely canceled his speech and took a nap instead. The crowd now before him stirred uneasily, then from somewhere in the rear came the shattering reminder. "That isn't all you had, either," the voice shouted. Roosevelt looked down, grinning. "Now, there," he said while the crowd roared, "is a man who speaks the truth." [353]

FDR's first trip after taking office was a 4 ½-hour sprint from Jersey City to Washington on April 21, 1933. But it wasn't until June, on a trip to Hyde Park, that B&O's Dan Moorman met the new president.

"I'll never forget my first introduction ... " Moorman recalled. "Marvin McIntyre, presidential secretary, took me into his car and presented me with this disconcerting sendoff: 'Mr. President, I don't know whether to bring this fellow in here or not. He's been running around the country with Hoover.' President Roosevelt seemed to enjoy the quip immensely and extended his hand warmly in greeting." [375]

In August 1934, a B&O train went to Portland, Ore., to take the chief executive back through the drought-stricken Northwest after a

Hawaiian vacation. It was on this trip that Secretary of the Interior Harold L. Ickes caught a rare glimpse of the Roosevelt family's youthful irreverence in a private moment at dinner: "It resolved itself into a debate between the members of the Roosevelt family, with all of them frequently talking at one and the same time," Ickes wrote. "Mrs. Roosevelt precipitated the discussion by raising some social question and her three sons at once began to wave their arms in the air and take issue with her. She expressed belief in a strict limitation of income, whether earned or not, and the boys insisted that every man ought to have a right to earn as much as he could. The president joined in at intervals, but he wasn't president of the United States on that occasion—he was merely the father of three sons who had opinions of their own. They interrupted him when they felt like it and all talked to him at the same time. It was really most amusing. At one stage when they were all going on at once, I raised my voice and observed to the president that I now understood how he was able to manage Congress. Sen. [Burton K.] Wheeler [of Montana] followed my remark with the observation that Congress was never as bad as that. That was about the sum and substance of outside contribution to the dinner that night, but it was all very interesting and very amusing." [228]

The Roosevelts returned to Washington on Friday, Aug. 10, on a run that made the B&O especially proud. In Chicago the evening before, the carrier had received the special late from the Chicago & North Western, then put up with immense crowds through Indiana and Ohio until well after midnight. Despite that, the trip was made in 16 hours 29 minutes, beating the *Capitol Limited's* running time by an hour and 8 minutes. "This is a remarkable record,

Franklin Roosevelt and his party look hale and hearty as they return to Washington Oct. 24, 1935, after a fishing cruise down South. From left are the president, son James Roosevelt, first lady Eleanor Roosevelt, Secretary of the Treasury Henry Morgenthau, Secretary of Commerce Daniel C. Roper and Secretary of State Cordell Hull.

considering the slow orders through crowded sections, and the fact that the entire run was made smoothly and without a single jolt, either in starting or stopping," the company boasted. [304]

On Sept. 26, 1935, Roosevelt started a trip to the West Coast: Washington to East St. Louis on the B&O, to Council Bluffs, Iowa, on the Chicago, Burlington & Quincy, and to Ogden, Salt Lake City, Boulder Dam and Los Angeles via the UP. He returned via the Panama Canal.

E.A. Klippel, UP's assistant general passenger agent in Omaha, wrote to one of his superiors, Assistant Passenger Traffic Manager C.J.

Collins, outlining their road's part in the move.

All hands were warned that the private car *Robert Peary* was not equipped with telephone connections and that at each stop telephone companies would have a hand phone set with enough cord to allow it to be taken on board the private car from the front end if needed. "[The *Peary*] will be manned with one porter, and it will be necessary for our dining car crew to serve the president in his car from our diner," Klippel wrote. "There is a small dining room in the *Robert Peary*. ... I am informed that the president is allowed a wide range in his

diet, hence the diner should be well-stocked, the market's best, local to our line."[339]

"All cars," Klippel added, "except the baggage and dormitory, should be cooled at Boulder City, Nev., and Yermo, Calif. [at 'a quiet place,' apparently a nocturnal stop of several hours], and Los Angeles." Klippel's letter called for a "drum sign" reading "Special UNION PACIFIC Train." And, "twelve vestibule rugs or mats should be available at Council Bluffs to replace B&O rugs."[339]

The White House questioned a scheduled service stop at Council Bluffs. "I explained that this would save a back-up switch and unavoidable delay at Omaha, and that work would be done at the UP Transfer, not in the Council Bluffs station, and that we would endeavor to have none but railroad workmen near the train."[339]

Klippel advised his boss to figure on midnight lunch menus and a healthy bar sale. "Popular whiskeys with the local men who will make the trip are Old Grandad, Mount Vernon Rye, and Vat 69 Scotch."[339]

Roosevelt left the railroad up in the air regarding the return trip."(As to) your inquiry regarding disposition of equipment upon arrival Los Angeles—the answer is somewhat indefinite," Klippel wrote. "The train should be held in the Central Station until 10 a.m. Oct. 1. The president and some of his party are expected to board the cruiser *Houston*, however, should his plans change, he might require the equipment to return to Washington by rail."[339]

Roosevelt got in dutch on this trip, bringing upon himself a dressing down by Secret Service agent Edmund Starling once he reached Los Angeles.

Starling, working as advance man, had set up every detail of FDR's westward advance. In Los Angeles, reporters asked him about rumors that the Boss had gotten lost on some mountain road near Las Vegas.

"I knew nothing of this," Starling complained. "The committee at Boulder Dam had informed me by telephone that the party had left there on time. Officials of the Southern Pacific told me that the train had pulled out of Las Vegas late [on the Union Pacific], but was now enroute to Los Angeles with everyone on board."

Starling met the train when it arrived at 8 a.m. the next morning and spied agent Henry Taggert, whom he had placed in charge of the White House detail. "What happened at Las Vegas?" Starling asked him.

Taggert was so mad he spat out the words: "Key Pittman [senator from Nevada] and Harry Hopkins [federal relief administrator] got the president to drive up a narrow mountain road just to see a CCC [Civilian Conservation Corps] camp and the whole party got stuck and had to turn around on a dime. We had a mountain on one side and a drop of about a mile on the other."

Starling couldn't understand why Pittman and Hopkins had interfered with the Secret Service's arrangements, all of which were timed to the second. "Why did you let them change our plans?" he asked Taggert.

"I didn't," the exasperated agent sighed. "I went to Marvin McIntyre and told him we had made no arrangements for a side trip up Mount Charleston. I said it was foolish and unnecessary and a big risk. He went to

RAILROAD MAGAZINE/CARSTENS PUBLICATIONS

President Roosevelt enjoys the view and the crowd from the rear platform of the Pullman private car Marco Polo *during a stop in Colorado's famed Royal Gorge July 12, 1938. Notice that the Baltimore & Ohio tailsign is still in position all the way out West.*

Trip of
The President
to Johnstown, Pennsylvania
Cleveland, Ohio
Chautauqua, New York
Binghamton, New York
Scranton, Pennsylvania
Wilkes-Barre, Pennsylvania
and Hyde Park, New York
August 13-15, 1936
Pennsylvania Railroad

Luncheon menu on a Roosevelt campaign special through the northeastern states in August 1936. This meal is for the 15th, the last of three days on the road.

A la Carte

BROILED SIRLOIN STEAK 1.75; WITH POTATOES OR BACON 1.90
BROILED MINUTE SIRLOIN STEAK, HASHED BROWNED
OR FRENCH FRIED POTATOES 1.40
GRILLED LAMB CHOPS (2) 90; WITH BACON 1.00
BROILED HAM OR BACON 70; HALF PORTION 35
BROILED HAM OR BACON WITH EGGS 70
A CASSEROLE OF BAKED NAVY BEANS WITH HAM 40
EGGS—BOILED, FRIED OR SCRAMBLED 35; POACHED ON TOAST 40
OMELETS: PLAIN 50; WITH BUTTERED ASPARAGUS TIPS 65

VEGETABLES

STEWED SUGAR CORN 25   BUTTERED BEETS 25
STRINGLESS BEANS IN BUTTER 25
POTATOES: HOME FRIED OR PARSLEYED 25

COLD DISHES, ETC.

CHILLED PEELED TOMATO STUFFED WITH CHICKEN SALAD 60
SLICED SUGAR CURED HAM AND CHICKEN WITH POTATO SALAD 80
HEAD LETTUCE OR LETTUCE AND TOMATO SALAD, FRENCH DRESSING 45
HEAD LETTUCE, THOUSAND ISLAND DRESSING 45   SALAD PRINCESSE 45
COMBINATION SALAD 45   LETTUCE AND EGG SALAD 45
HAM AND FRIED EGG SANDWICH ON TOAST 60
BACON AND SLICED TOMATO SANDWICH ON TOAST 60
HAM SANDWICH 35   CHICKEN SANDWICH 50
AMERICAN CHEESE SANDWICH 35

DESSERTS AND CHEESE

FRESHLY MADE PIE (BAKED ON CAR TO-DAY) 25; WITH CHEESE 30
CARAMEL CUP CUSTARD 25
CHILLED MELON 30   ICE CREAM 30   SLICED FRESH PEACHES 35
CHILLED PRUNE JUICE 25   SLICED BANANAS WITH CREAM 20
ORANGE MARMALADE 25
ROQUEFORT OR SWISS GRUYERE CHEESE, TOASTED WAFERS 35

COFFEE, COCOA OR CHOCOLATE (HOT OR ICED): POT FOR ONE 25
TEA: ORANGE PEKOE, GREEN, ENGLISH BREAKFAST (HOT OR ICED):
POT FOR ONE 25
POSTUM, KAFFEE HAG OR SANKA COFFEE 25
SWEET MILK OR BUTTERMILK (BOTTLED) 15

BREAD

WHITE, WHOLE WHEAT, RAISIN OR RYE 15   TOAST 20

August 15th

Luncheon

ONE DOLLAR AND TWENTY-FIVE CENTS

CHOICE OF ONE:

CREAM OF TOMATOES, CROUTONS   CONSOMME

JELLIED BEEF BROTH

————

CHOICE OF ONE:

FILETS OF FRESH FISH, SAUTE MEUNIERE BUTTER

OMELET WITH BUTTERED ASPARAGUS TIPS, BECHAMEL SAUCE

BAKED VEAL AND HAM PIE, PENNSYLVANIA

CREAMED MILK FED CHICKEN EN CASSEROLE, WALDORF

COLD BAKED SUGAR CURED HAM, PICKLED BEETS

POTATOES, LYONNAISE   BUTTERED BEETS

————

ASSORTED BREAD

————

P.R.R. MIXED SALAD WITH CHEESE

————

CHOICE OF ONE:

CARAMEL CUP CUSTARD

ICE CREAM   CHILLED CANTALOUPE

————

TEA—COFFEE (HOT OR ICED)   MILK

the president's automobile and told him the Secret Service was against the trip. Before the president could answer, Senator Pittman interrupted and said the road was perfectly safe. Hopkins butted in and said the trip ought to be made. So the president overruled me."

The gravel road wound around shoulders of rock on the edge of a precipice, with just enough room for a single car to pass. The grade was so steep that the wheels of the cars slipped in the gravel and their radiators boiled over. One of the newspapermen's cars stalled and had to turn back. Finally, Taggert stopped the Secret Service car, which was in the lead, and went back to tell Roosevelt that the camp was still several miles away and that road ahead was impassable. To his relief, FDR agreed that they should turn back and told his driver to turn around at the first possible point.

"This was not easy to find," Starling explained later. "When a spot was finally chosen, it was necessary for the chauffeur to jockey the car back and forth on a narrow ledge. The president stayed in the car, and Marvin McIntyre was so frightened that whenever the rear wheels approached the edge of the precipice he gripped one of the back mudguards, prepared to hold it up by main strength if it slipped over. This was too much for the president's sense of humor— McIntyre weighed scarcely 100 pounds—and he burst into laughter."

The about-face was finally accomplished and the caravan trundled down the mountain. Taggert told Starling they left Las Vegas two hours late.

Starling, aggravated, headed for the *Peary*. Irvin McDuffie, the president's valet, stuck his head out when he knocked. The president, he said, was dressing. Behind McDuffie, a voice called out.

"Come on in, Ed," FDR chimed.

He was laughing when Starling entered. "Have you heard about our mountain adventure?" he asked.

"Yes," Starling answered in measured tones, "I have heard all about it.

That's why I am here. I don't think you were fair to me or to the Secret Service or to the country to go up that mountain last night. You took an unnecessary chance. I know it is hard to realize that you have no right to endanger yourself, but you haven't. Your life isn't your own to give or to take now. It belongs to the people of the United States. That's why I am paid to look out for you. If anything had happened last night, my whole life would have been ruined, not to mention what would have happened to the country."

Roosevelt stopped smiling and a grave look came into his eyes. He was being bawled out, but he was taking it like a man.

"I am sorry, Ed," he finally said. "You're right, and I will square you with the Secret Service. I'll ... assume personal responsibility for an unwise act." Just then Mrs. Roosevelt emerged from an adjoining bedroom and appeared in the observation room's doorway. "I couldn't help overhearing Colonel Starling's plain talk

Franklin Roosevelt concentrates on staying vertical as he pulls his stricken limbs down a ramp from the rear platform of his private car.

to you, Franklin," she said. "I endorse everything he said. I think it is only fair for you to promise him that you will adhere rigidly in the future to the itineraries he approves."

The president raised his eyebrows. "Apparently the majority is against me," he said. "Very well, I'll promise." 363

FDR, a natural campaigner, took to the stump again in 1936 in the Pullman private cars *Marco Polo* and *Pioneer*—but even a natural campaigner has to rest once in a while. So while his train rumbled through Arkansas on the Missouri Pacific, Roosevelt summoned White House usher William D. Simmons to his car. When Simmons—who was about the same size as his boss—walked into the lounge, Roosevelt regarded him stern-

ly. Then, in a voice that seemed prompted to rise from profound thought, asked, "Bill, how would you like to be president for a while?"42 Simmons looked as if the Boss had gone mad. "Only for a little while," Roosevelt went on, ignoring his usher's apprehensive eyes. "Maybe an hour or two."19

FDR rolled his wheelchair away from the window and instructed Simmons to pull up a chair and sit at the vacated spot. He removed his pince-nez glasses, clamping them on Simmons' nose, and leaned back to peer with a critical eye. "Fine! Fine!" Roosevelt exclaimed, and began to laugh heartily. Then he announced he was tired of sitting there waving to crowds in every passing town. With a

flourish, he turned over his cigarette holder to Simmons and showed him how to wave a big, open-fingered hand in the Rooseveltian manner and how to smile a big, open-jawed smile. "Fine! Fine!" the president said again. "Now every time we pass a town, just sit there and wave. I'm tired. I'm going to take a nap." And he wheeled out of the lounge. 42

All across Arkansas, Simmons sat by the president's window. At each town the train slowed just enough so the local townsfolk could experience the incomparable thrill of seeing that fine, open-handed wave and the magnificent smile that one man, and one man alone, could thrill them with.

The campaign trips were long and grueling, but reporters noted they

Franklin Roosevelt hated these types of photos. It shows him about to drag his crippled legs down a ramp from his special train to board the destroyer U.S.S. Monaghan *at Port Everglades, Fla., to begin his annual fishing trip in southern waters March 24, 1936. Eldest son James Roosevelt is preceding his father down the ramp.*

were more comfortable when traveling with an incumbent instead of a mere candidate. Richard Strout of the *Christian Science Monitor* described his relatively plush surroundings on Roosevelt's train:

"The car is air conditioned, cool and fresh. The compartment is like a ship's stateroom (with) wash basin, toilet bowl under a seat, a ventilating fan which is not required with the air conditioning, green plush covers, a green metal door (and) carpet on the floor. The berth is wider than normal and moderately comfortable." [338]

The atmosphere aboard the train was confident and calm. The Roosevelt children and their spouses often went along, and Eleanor herself favored the voters with fleeting glimpses of the incumbent's family. That is, when she was not ensconced in her bedroom busily dictating sections of her autobiography to her personal secretary, Malvina "Tommy" Thompson. Crowds were "simply fantastic," wrote Associated Press correspondent Douglas Cornell. "They pressed against ropes and barriers, and people were actually maimed." [153]

Roosevelt won a second term handily and continued riding the rails. One such trip was a nine-day midterm stumper that left Washington on Thursday night, July 7, 1938, and meandered to the West Coast on the B&O, MP and Denver & Rio Grande Western.

Virginia Tanner, writing for the *Baltimore & Ohio Magazine,* was impressed with the sight of B&O's gleaming passenger diesel lashup, headed by unit 55, idling at the head end of the special on Union Station's lower-level track 30 minutes before the 10:30 p.m. departure.

She was impressed with the security, too. Noting a few grim-faced plainclothesmen gathering when Roosevelt was preparing to board Pullman private car *Marco Polo*, she remarked to the B&O's Dan Moorman that she had no trouble getting down the stairs to the platform—and this surprised her.

"Well, don't fool yourself on that," Moorman told her. "First place, you had a pass. Then I shook hands with you as soon as you got down here. And just a few seconds after that the head of the Secret Service detail asked who you were and what you were doing there." [376] Then Mrs. Tanner began noticing more of them—agents standing around, unobtrusively, on the platforms, on the tracks, on the train, not drawing attention to themselves but vigilant and ready to act nonetheless.

"Wait till you see those government fellows tomorrow," volunteered Howard McAbee, manager of dining car and commissary. "They've got no cinch running alongside the president's automobile."[376]

After midnight, with the train well on its way, Moorman took Mrs. Tanner through the cars. Some reporters had gone to bed, others filled their compartments with the staccato keystrokes of stories in the making. The spot news of Roosevelt's departure had been filed before leaving town; now features, color sidebars, etc., were in production so they could be wired from the next stop.

In the diner, a half-dozen congenial groups were enjoying midnight snacks. Presidential Secretary Marvin McIntyre and two newspapermen asked Moorman and Mrs. Tanner to sit with them, and small talk followed. Steward J.B. Martin and his crew were busily serving up generous portions of bacon and eggs, three-tiered club sandwiches and other delectables. He told Mrs. Tanner at breakfast six hours later that his last guest had left the diner at 4:30 a.m. and that the first contingent of Secret Service men came in at 5:15 for their breakfasts. Martin expected to be on duty continuously until his diner was removed from the train about 36 hours later—a brutal shift of catering to the appetites of a hundred people and with only a few minutes off at a time for a shave and change of uniform.

Noted rail author Morris Cafky was in his teens when this 1938 Roosevelt special—still with its B&O drumhead attached—rolled toward the Royal Gorge on the D&RGW through his hometown of Florence, Colo., 35 miles west of Pueblo.

"The train passed through town at around 10 a.m.," Cafky recalled. "First came the pilot train: a newly painted 4-8-4 of the 1700 series (Baldwin, 1929) and a fine old wooden business car. Ten minutes later the special itself came. The engineer shut off and allowed the train to coast past the station crowd.

"First came the locomotive, engine 1800, a Baldwin-built 4-8-4 just a few months old, beautifully painted and polished as you might imagine. Leaning out of the gangway with his watch in his hand was a man wearing suitcoat and hat but coveralls below—I imagine the road foreman of engines.

"Behind 1800 were about 15 cars. The first was a Baltimore & Ohio baggage car; both doors on the station side were open and men seated on boxes were eyeballing the crowd—Secret Service operatives, without doubt. Then came several standard Pullmans; some had the upper 'dutch doors' open with Secret Service men leaning out and looking us over.

"Midway of the train was a Baltimore & Ohio dining car. Then came more Pullmans and then finally ... FDR's car. He was seated on the station side (right side of the train) just behind the bulkhead separating the car from the open platform. He smiled and waved at us. One man was on the platform, leaning against the railing on the left side of the car. Another Secret Service man, without doubt, who gave us a good looking over. As soon as (the train) cleared the last of the station crowd, the engineer began working steam on the 1800 and whistling for the Main Street crossing."[66]

Cafky noted that FDR's train made a 10-minute stop in the gorge that summer day—as all D&RGW daylight passenger trains did—to let him see it close up.

Before boarding his Naval cruiser on the West Coast, Roosevelt spent July 15 on the Yosemite Valley Railroad. Roosevelt's special arrived at Merced, Calif., via the Southern Pacific at 3:15 a.m. and was spotted on a siding under bright floodlights while a crowd of 100 local residents waited in vain for him to appear. At dawn the special was transferred to the YV and headed out for the valley.

Under the able hand of YV senior engineer Jack Shoup, the train arrived at El Portal at 8:40 a.m., 35 minutes early. Mogul-type locomotives 29 and 26, appropriately decorated by a Fresno caterer, hauled it to Briceburg, where engine 25 was added for the last miles.

Roosevelt toured the valley and had lunch at the Mariposa Big Trees Grove in the open. His special reached El Portal at 6 p.m. and Merced at 10:45 p.m. It left town on the SP within 30 minutes, disappointing a crowd of 2,000 who had hoped for a speech.

By 1939, war clouds were looming, especially in Europe. On Easter Sunday, April 9, Roosevelt left Warm Springs for Washington and wisecracked a prophecy from the rear platform: "I'll be back in the fall if we don't have a war."[166]

The visit that summer of King George VI and Queen Elizabeth of Great Britain—the first time British royalty had visited the United States—was overshadowed by these fears. The royal couple's 12-car blue and silver train carried them into Niagara Falls, N.Y., at 9:43 p.m. Wednesday, June 7, after a three-week tour of Canada, then brought them overnight to Washington on the PRR. The Roosevelts met their royal guests at Union Station when they arrived at 11 a.m. Thursday and hosted them during two days of sightseeing, swims in the White House pool and a state dinner.

At 11:30 Friday night, the royal train departed Washington via PRR for Red Bank, N.J., where the king and queen would motor to Sandy Hook and board the destroyer *Warrenton* for the rest of the journey to New York City's Battery Park. Ahead was a Saturday filled with sightseeing and a stop at the New York World's Fair. Shortly after they left Washington, the Roosevelts' train departed on the B&O, bound for Hyde Park.

The president had planned for everyone to travel together, but Ed Starling of the Secret Service once again put his foot down. FDR had called in his Secret Service agent, now head of the White House detail, and said, "Here are my plans for the visit of the king and queen to the World's Fair and their motor trip to Hyde Park. We will leave here on the same train at night, and drop the king and queen off along the New Jersey shore the next morning. A boat will take them to New York and on the way they can see the skyline. After visiting the fair they will come to Hyde Park, where Mrs. Roosevelt and I will be waiting. "That's fine," Starling said, "except for one thing. Let's not put all our eggs in one basket. At this point in history I don't think the heads of the two greatest nations on Earth ought to be on the same train, with everybody in the world knowing about it. Suppose you let the king and queen go on one train, and then, a little later, you and Mrs. Roosevelt leave on another one, over a different road. If anything happened to the king and queen, England would never forgive us, and if anything happened to you I couldn't set foot in Kentucky [his home state] again."

Roosevelt smiled and cocked his cigarette holder toward the ceiling. "You're probably right," he said. "We'll use two trains."[363]

After their day in New York City, the king and queen motored the 80 miles to Hyde Park for a quiet Sunday at the president's home, then departed for Canada on their train that night.

RAILROAD MAGAZINE/CARSTENS PUBLICATIONS

Southern Pacific Ten-wheeler 2284, appropriately festooned, awaits Franklin Roosevelt's train at Tracy, Calif., in 1938.

Roosevelt was always gracious, even on those rare occasions when things went wrong. Take, for example, the president's weekend outing to Hyde Park April 6-9, 1940, when things turned sour on the return trip at Claremont, N.J.

"As usual, [we] were trying to put on our best show for him," Moorman reminisced. "One of our big, new Diesel engines had been assigned to his train. It had, of course, just undergone rigid inspection. Nevertheless, at the moment of our scheduled departure, the engine's fuses blew out, rendering it helpless. We were held up 30 or 40 minutes until a steam engine could be brought up to move the train, Diesel and all. It was just one of those unpredictable things that couldn't be helped but that was certainly enough to give any railroad man a very red face." [375]

Reporters got wind of what happened and started kidding Moorman—they even composed a song on the subject that they sang in mock seriousness from one end of the train to the other. Roosevelt heard them—and sent word for Moorman to come back to his car, the *Roald Amundsen*. The chagrined railroader didn't know what to expect.

"Dan," the sympathetically smiling president told him, "the only thing that worries me about this delay is that you and members of the crew may be disturbed by it. I don't want you to worry. The important thing is that you always take me where I'm going and bring me back safely and comfortably. I'm turning out work right here and it doesn't make a bit of difference what time we get back to Washington." [375]

It was also in 1940 that an important member of the Roosevelt clan joined the traveling party. He was a shaggy Scotsman, known in the books as "Murray, the Outlaw of Falahill," but commonly referred to simply as Fala. The terrier was a gift from Margaret Suckley, a cousin and close friend of the family.

"Fala considered himself thoroughly eligible for all presidential trips," Grace Tully, FDR's personal secretary, wrote, "and he sulked quite obviously if he found himself left behind. He ... became a regular commuter to Hyde Park ... and to Warm Springs." [415]

By the time of Fala's arrival on the scene, another presidential election was drawing near. Had there been no world crisis, Roosevelt would probably have retired to the life of a country squire at Hyde Park. As it was, he felt this was no time to change horses, so he ran for an unprecedented third term. He did choose a new running mate, however, since John Nance Garner had broken with him over New Deal policies and tried to get the Democratic nomination for himself. FDR chose his secretary of agriculture, Henry A. Wallace, for the No. 2 spot on the ticket.

No matter how tired Roosevelt became during the race, he kept his sense of humor. Miss Tully revealed a story about Judge Samuel Rosenman, a speechwriter. "One of his consuming passions is a taste for chocolate ice cream sodas," she wrote, "and most of his wagers were in terms of this so-American concoction. Sam was often not present on the train when some of his finely turned phrases he had conceived were delivered by the Boss and this was the case during one of the 1940 campaign trips. On the train, during a well-kibitzed bridge game that involved Harry Hopkins [then Secretary of Commerce] and some of the correspondents, it was decided Sam should be rewarded. Accordingly, a telegraphic order for delivery of a chocolate ice cream soda by a singing messenger was dispatched to New York." [415]

Tully said an acknowledgement

Vice President and Mrs. John Nance Garner board the C&O's George Washington *in the nation's capital enroute to their home in Uvalde, Texas.*

caught up with the party sometime later.

" 'Flavor was swell but ice cream was melted and singing was terrible. Thanks and regards.' " The Boss liked it. [415]

Roosevelt's Republican opponent was Wendell L. Willkie of Indiana. "Bring on the Champ!" [44] Willkie cried as he launched an energetic campaign against the man he always referred to as "the third-term candidate." [44] Then he traveled on speechmaking tours that covered 34,000 miles by train in 34 states, making more than 500 speeches.

Willkie's 16-car special had its moments of difficulty. On Oct. 3 near New Castle, Pa., the coupler drawbar on the front of the sleeper *Banavie* broke as the train was stopping at Lawrence Jct. on the PRR to back into New Castle. The drawbar tore loose steam heat connections on the tender of the second locomotive, K4 Pacific 3773. A nearby freight engine was commandeered to couple to the other end of Willkie's train, now the only end with a working coupler, and pull it backward—minus the disabled sleeper—to New Castle. A yard engine then removed the *Banavie* from the main line, and Willkie's steam locomotives exchanged places so the train would still have steam heat. The problem was solved in about an hour. An Erie & Ashtabula Division road foreman who was at the throttle of the lead K4, the 3766, was blamed for the accident. He applied the brakes for Lawrence Jct., then seeing he was stopping short, released them before reapplying them. The company concluded that the drawbar broke because the last application was made before brakes on the rear cars had fully released.

C.F. Wilmington, supervisor of agencies for the Railway Express Agency in Chicago, offered a detailed five-week glimpse of life on the Willkie train. He first boarded in Chicago at 7:30 a.m. Sept. 13, after the special movement made an eight-hour jaunt via B&O-Indianapolis-PRR from Willkie's home in Rushville, Ind.

The candidate was leaving on a two-week, 7,200-mile tour of 18 western states on 10 railroads. Wilmington had signed on for this tour and stayed with the train through much of the rest of the campaign. As soon as he started making his way through the cars, passengers began asking about REA services: air and rail shipments; money orders; cashing travelers' checks; forwarding telegrams; information on connections; furnishing supplies such as address labels, wrapping paper and twine; as well as delivery of air mail at airports when air express was forwarded.

"The bulk of the shipments forwarded consisted of moving picture films, flashlight photos, sound records, magazine scripts and personal shipments of Mr. and Mrs. Willkie and the staff," Wilmington wrote.[444] But the

NORTHERN PACIFIC RAILWAY/*RAILROAD MAGAZINE*/CARSTENS PUBLICATIONS

Republican Wendell Willkie of Indiana tries to snag some votes during the 1940 presidential campaign.

job became more burdensome.

"As we approached the western states, Mr. and Mrs. Willkie were given fruit, candies and livestock, which they requested be forwarded to their friends and relatives, as well as to their home. ..." he explained. "While we were enroute between Worthington, Minn., and Sioux City, Iowa [on the Chicago & North Western], Mr. Willkie was presented with a 42 ½-pound live turkey which he admired to such an extent that his secretary sent for me asking me to see that it be sent by express to his farm. Due to the turkey's enormous size, it was neces-

sary that I have his legs tied. When we arrived in Sioux City I arranged with our agent to crate properly and forward same." [444]

Sometimes Wilmington had to use a little ingenuity to get his job done.

"On Oct. 29, the local committees of 20 counties in Ohio arranged for a gathering of 65,000 people to meet in an open field in Taylor, Ohio (near Columbus on joint B&O-PRR trackage), where Mr. Willkie was to deliver a speech. This was such a huge success that we received 10 air express shipments. Due to the fact that we

FDR relaxes with Fala on the rear platform of his special.

had no air connections in Taylor, we were obliged to take these shipments to Huntington, W.Va., where a plane departed at 4:10 p.m. Our train was not due in Huntington until 4:30 p.m. Mrs. Fred Willkie, sister-in-law to Wendell Willkie, was leaving the train at Ironton, Ohio [N&W], to taxi to Huntington to catch that plane which would take her to Cincinnati, her destination. I asked Mrs. Willkie if she would take these shipments with her to Cincinnati and she kindly consented to do so. ... All connections were made properly and all shipments arrived at destinations on time." [444]

FDR won—and kept on riding.

In early 1941, a change of location for Herbert H. Harwood meant he would be spending much of his time on Roosevelt's trains. Harwood, a New York Central passenger representative, had started riding with the president in 1938 while a junior officer in the New York headquarters. It had become his responsibility to ride the trains once they reached NYC trackage at Claremont or Mott Haven. "My senior colleagues—jaded by years of caring for celebrities—preferred a night's sleep to stumbling around a railroad yard at 2:30 a.m. in Jersey City. At 34, this was an exciting assignment for me, [for] which I was willing to miss some sleep." [165]

The change took place when Harwood was sent to Washington to open an office there. Afterward, Dewey Long, the White House transportation officer, invited him to ride from that point. In all, Harwood figured he made between 100 and 125 trips with the president.

"This meant on the many Hyde Park trips staying with the group at the old Nelson House in Poughkeepsie until the return," he recalled. "It was, indeed, an intimate group with gatherings every afternoon at about 5:30 p.m. in [switchboard operator] Louise Hackmeister's suite, known as 'The Children's Hour.' The children consisted of [Assistant Press Secretary] Bill Hassett with endless stories of his interesting readings, experiences or anecdotes, Grace [Tully], Dorothy [Brady, Tully's assistant], Dewey [Long], Hackie [Louise Hackmeister], usually [United Press correspondent] Merriman Smith and perhaps one or two others of the newsmen …and some of the others. …Then it was dinner with one or several in the group. …The White House staff was a tight little group, and those of us from the outside were accepted as friends but never quite in the circle. Occasionally, they would have their private parties, and it was made clear we were not included. … They were all wonderful people. Those days were certainly among the most interesting of my entire career. It was long hours of work and responsibility that we all shared together and developed a certain unique camaraderie." [165]

Press Secretary Steve Early lost his famous temper with the Boss himself shortly after Roosevelt boarded the *Amundsen* on Aug. 3, 1941, for what was supposed to be a vacation. He had told the Boss he didn't want to know any secrets lest he inadvertently reveal them to the press. But as war grew closer, he changed his mind and believed he should know about all the president's secret movements.

It turned out that FDR took his train to New London, Conn., where he boarded a cruiser for the so-called Atlantic Conference with British Prime Minister Winston Churchill "somewhere in the Atlantic," actually off the coast of Newfoundland, where the two leaders formulated the document later called the Atlantic Charter in which their postwar hopes for the world were outlined.

Miss Tully told what happened: "When the story finally broke out of London and it was further revealed

that Churchill had three thinly disguised authors along with him, Steve 'blew his top,' threatened to quit and otherwise raised a fine ruckus around 1600 Pennsylvania Ave. He knew about the subsequent conferences—in advance." [415]

Japan attacked the United States' naval base at Pearl Harbor in Honolulu on Dec. 7, 1941. The next day, Roosevelt asked Congress for—and quickly received—a declaration of war, thrusting the nation into World War II. Now Roosevelt's rail travel would be shrouded with utmost secrecy.

The first "blackout trip" that was undertaken with the strictest of secrecy in force was to Hyde Park on the night of Tuesday, Jan. 6, 1942.

FDR's assistant press secretary, William D. Hassett, found out about the trip at 5:30 that evening. He left to go home to pack, but on the fortunate advice of an associate, he stopped on the way at Hausler's on 17th Street and bought a notebook in which he could jot down a few notes on the trip. He kept taking these most valuable notes during the rest of the Boss's tenure.

Hassett quickly returned to the White House and the traveling party departed for the train at 10:30. "With the president were Harry Hopkins [an intimate adviser of Roosevelt's then living in the White House] and Grace Tully," Hassett noted. "I rode with the Secret Service men in the car immediately behind the president's." [166]

Tonight the train would depart from Silver Spring, Md., instead of Union Station for the president's protection. "We went out 16th Street to Silver Spring," Hassett explained. "A bitter cold night with sharp wind, not very cozy in an open car. Our party was not recognized as we made our way through traffic congested in spots." [166]

Roosevelt boarded the *Amundsen*

at once and the train pulled out at 11 p.m., "leaving one bewildered railroad man completely in the dark as to what was taking place," Hassett said. "Hackie also along. While this was to be an 'off-the-record' trip, Hackie said that in the middle of the afternoon [Secretary of the Navy] Frank Knox's secretary phoned to inquire casually whether the president had already left for Hyde Park. Snack on the train with Grace Tully and Harry Hopkins and soon to bed afterward." [166]

The press aide duly recorded that the party had a quiet arrival in Highland on a "snappy, cold morning. The president in fine spirits; told me to guard against any publicity through press or radio concerning his arrival and stay at Hyde Park." [166]

On Saturday the 10th of January, Hassett noted that FDR ordered the train in readiness for his return to leave Highland at 11 p.m. that night. "He pleased with complete privacy of his visit home, which has not been mentioned by press or radio anywhere; said he will adopt this mode of travel in the future. …Weather bitter when we pulled out …for Silver Spring. Reported 16 below at Rhinebeck. The president, as usual gloveless, coming up the ramp to his car, had to grasp metal rails with bare hands; nearly froze his fingers. A snack with the president, Grace and Harry, and then to bed." [166]

The train reached Silver Spring at 8:30 a.m. Sunday.

"The president, remembering experience last night, did not demur when I offered him my gloves. Halfway down he shouted: 'Wait till I send the gloves back to you.' What a lot of tripe has been written and bellowed about the 'dictator.' Dictators don't talk that way. An unobserved trip back to the White House through quiet Sunday morning streets, the first blackout trip a complete success." [166]

Another such jaunt followed on

Saturday afternoon, Jan. 31: "The president, as usual the perfect host, in rare form, kidding, full of wisecracks. For himself he had ordered only a salad, to be followed by cheese; for the others, steaks. The president said he had eaten pretty well of the hors d'oeuvres. He seemed a trifle tired to me, but he was in excellent spirits."[166]

After the meal, the discussion turned to the sprawling 1898 mansion of Frederick W. Vanderbilt, the Commodore's grandson, an Italian Renaissance masterpiece near Roosevelt's Springwood. By then, the mansion had become a national monument where FDR decided his staff would stay during his Hyde Park trips to avoid publicity.

"He [had] said Hackie must occupy Mrs. Vanderbilt's Marie Antoinette room (with chicken fence around the bed), sleep under black satin sheets, have black satin negligee with blue ribbons, also blue ribbons on bedroom chinaware. …I told him that a certain piece of bedroom china, and the cupboard to keep it in, used to be called a 'convenience' in Vermont. 'They called it something else in Virginia,' said [Appointments Secretary Maj. Gen. Edwin M.] 'Pa' Watson."[166]

Which moved Roosevelt to share a story on himself.

"The president told us about a German governess he had when he was a little boy. This was in the age when ladies were easily shocked, easily upset. He stole a Seidlitz powder [a laxative] from his father's private cabinet and put the contents of the blue and white packets in the convenience in the governess' room. He listened at the bedroom door, as no good little boy should do, and was rewarded by a startled cry from the governess, who in the morning reported to his mother that she was ill."[166]

More discussion ensued, covering everything from Vanderbilt family history to the artificialities of the Victorian era. "The president recalled that gentle ladies were supposed to faint on proper occasions with very slight provocation and that young ladies received instruction in the art of fainting gracefully. In those days, he said, ladies who had fainted were sometimes revived by burning feathers under their noses. A sofa pillow might be broken open for the purpose. 'What kind of feathers?' asked Dottie Jones [Brady]. 'Horse feathers, possibly,' replied the president."[166]

Hassett recorded that around 8 p.m., Roosevelt resumed work on his "basket" of mail and other paperwork with Dottie Jones, until the train arrived at Highland shortly after 9:30. "This time the staff did not go to the Nelson House. Apparently unobserved, we crossed over the Poughkeepsie bridge and turning left went by a side street to the Albany Post Road and direct to the president's home. … After the president went into the house, we drove on through Hyde Park village and entered the Vanderbilt grounds by the north gate. Rain had frozen on the roads, which were icy. …"[166]

The rain had turned to snow and back to rain, Hassett recalled, when they took the train from Highland to Washington on Thursday night, Feb. 5. "The president, in good shape and good spirits but reluctant to go back, went immediately to bed. Margaret Suckley returning … with us. Left the train at 9 o'clock (Feb. 6) at point near Catholic University where we took it last Saturday. The president had breakfast on the train in anticipation of a press conference scheduled for 10:30. He told the correspondents he had had a cold for two days, but did not disclose that he had been away."[166]

Roosevelt's blackout visits to Hyde Park continued, his operatives experimenting with departure points. Trips variously left from Silver Spring, the Catholic University in

MARGARET SUCKLEY/ROOSEVELT LIBRARY

President Franklin Roosevelt wiles away the hours during his secret 1942 inspection tour by playing solitaire in the Roald Amundsen's *lounge while friend and former law partner Harry Hooker watches from the rear platform.*

Brookland, Bolling Field Army Air Corps Base, the PRR's 14th Street Yard and the Arlington Cantonment. Finally, beginning with a trip to Hyde Park on Oct. 30, Roosevelt used a new terminal facility under the annex to the U.S. Bureau of Engraving and Printing on the east side of 14th Street that remained the permanent choice. A new two-car high-level platform, built next to an underground siding where the bureau received its supplies, permitted automobiles to be driven close enough to require only a half-dozen steps for the president and his staff to board the private car and a Secret Service sleeper.

They were joined to the rest of the train in PRR's 14th Street Yard. Hassett and Miss Tully continued to offer tantalizing glimpses of life aboard the Hyde Park trains. "Raised the curtain in my berth," Hassett wrote on June 2, "at 6:15 just below Cornwall [N.Y.] in order to enjoy the early morning view of the Hudson, always lovely and particularly so now with all the freshness of the new foliage."[166]

Then, after a June 17 nocturnal departure: "The president asked me to bring the girls in for a drink—Hackie; Lois Berney, Harry's secretary; and Grace Tully—we were having lemonade when we reached Anacostia Jct. and stopped to change power at 10:25. We heard [an air raid alarm signaling the beginning of a blackout] clearly; saw to it that all of our curtains were down. The president said, 'Bet the headlight is on!' The headlight of another train was visible back of us. We moved away at 10:31 and all to bed soon after. … Dan Moorman on this trip and everybody happy. The president prefers all trips by B&O in the future."[166]

British Prime Minister Winston Churchill, making his second secret wartime visit to the United States,

returned with the president on Saturday, June 20. "I was sitting with him and the Boss in the president's car," Miss Tully wrote, "when the Churchill valet, a little baldheaded man who always traveled with him, came into the car with the Churchillian-initialed slippers, leaned down and started to take the prime minister's shoes off. 'Not here,' Churchill sputtered in obvious embarrassment. Retreating hastily into his own compartment, he made the change and came back—slipper clad."[415]

Everyone catered to the president's whims on these outings—and even more so on a trip that left Washington on Thanksgiving Day.

"The ever faithful Dan Moorman had stocked the B&O larder with good things the president likes, particularly wild duck and terrapin, and some choice wines," Hassett wrote. "Dan asked me to find out the Boss's preference. Told him the president left the Thanksgiving dinner table to take the train and I doubted he would eat very heartily, and so it turned out. Caught him just as he was getting ready to take his nap. 'Tell Dan,' said he, 'that I've just had Thanksgiving dinner and have got to lose 4 pounds in the next five days.' So he selected only some cream of oyster soup and some cheese. Dan was disappointed and implored me to tell Mrs. Roosevelt what he had aboard. But she and Jim Forrestal (later secretary of the Navy) were equally frugal in their selections. Dan, not to be circumvented in dispensing hospitality, ordered four of the ducks, with wild rice and a jar of terrapin, sent to Hyde Park to be served when the president desires. Dan personally conferred with Mary Campbell (the cook in the Roosevelts' family kitchen on the top floor of the White House) as to the care and safe custody and delivery of his precious ducks. So at least two feasts are in store for the Boss. My

own Thanksgiving dinner on the train as the guest of Dan the bountiful—marvelous dinner, soup, Maryland terrapin (not in the Yankee tradition), fine roast turkey; stopped short at the pumpkin pie."[166]

On the next Hyde Park trip, 10:30 p.m., Friday, Dec. 18, 1942, Roosevelt rode for the first time his rebuilt, armor-plated *Ferdinand Magellan*. "Immediately upon coming aboard, the president inspected the car from end to end and gave it his approval. It contains four sleeping compartments, instead of five as in the *Amundsen*. This permits the enlargement of the observation space by 3 feet and the dining space toward the forward end of the car by the same amount. It relieves congestion in both these compartments, a very decided improvement. The decorations are quiet and subdued on the green-gray order and blend harmoniously with the green-and-buff upholstering of the chairs. Nothing elaborate, but plain, comfortable and serviceable. The rear door, of armor steel and bulletproof glass, weighs 1,500 pounds. This glass and all the window glass is 3 inches thick, although it appears to be of only ordinary thickness. John Pelley [head of the Association of American Railroads] came down to turn the car over to the Boss and accompanied him on his tour of inspection. Dan Moorman had champagne cooled for the christening. FDR smiled at the thought of champagne before going to bed and stuck to orange juice. He retired soon after the train pulled out. Alas, I did not, but sat up talking with Grace Tully, Hackie, and Roberta Barrows until 3 a.m."[166]

Wartime restrictions began to make things tight by 1943—even in the seat of power. "No dining car on the president's train tonight," Hassett wrote March 4. "Unusually heavy troop movements have diverted all rolling stock, and 300 soldiers can be

Darkness has descended on the evening of Sept. 19, 1942, as Roosevelt engages in some solitaire on board the private car Roald Amundsen. *Presidential cousin Laura "Aunt Polly" Delano looks bored.*

fed by our dispensing with the diner for this trip. For the use of the president of the United States (and those with him), the incomparable Mrs. [Henrietta] Nesbitt[, who was in charge of the White House kitchen,] allowed 14 teaspoonsful of coffee."[166] Mrs. Roosevelt had brought Mrs. Nesbitt to the White House as housekeeper in 1933—from her Hyde Park kitchen where she had sold homemade baked goods to the Roosevelts when FDR was governor.

"Arrived as usual at Highland," Hassett wrote, "prepared to leave the train without breakfast. Surprised and grateful when [Henry] Lucas, the president's porter, gave me a cup of coffee made from Henrietta's scant allowance."[166]

Hassett noted on the return that he was invited to have lemonade with the president before he went to bed. "I ditto in Compartment A for my first sleep in the new private car. ... No diner on return trip either, but Lucas managed to give me a cup of coffee despite Mrs. Nesbitt's frugal allowance." [166]

Restrictions were still in force on the next Hyde Park venture April 1.

"The president asked for orange juice for himself and friends; but Lucas, the faithful porter, said there were not enough oranges if the president was to have a glass of juice in the morning. Frugal La Nesbitt had carefully counted out for the trip not a dozen oranges but 10. So all went without. ... Detrained at Highland at 8:30 (Friday morning, April 2) and scattered in all directions for breakfast. Again no diner on our train. Troop movements very heavy during the past week to camps adjacent to embarkation points in New York and New Jersey—all available dining cars necessary for the well-being of the soldiers. ...Early arrival [back at the Bureau siding April 6] after miraculous cup of coffee provided by Lucas." [166]

Utmost secrecy surrounded Roosevelt's departure on Jan. 9, 1943, for his summit with Britain's Churchill in Casablanca, Morocco, to determine the future course of the war. "Our personal baggage was being picked up surreptitiously at our homes," wrote Miss Tully, who was going as far as Miami. "I asked Capt. John McCrea to spirit a well-loaded briefcase into the equipment without letting it be seen all over the office wing. Unfortunately, he laid it momentarily on the table in the corridor outside my office just long enough for Toi Bachelder, who was helping out in my office at the time, to see it and to realize that it meant a trip by somebody to somewhere. I had asked Toi to take the president's dictation that afternoon, which itself was a bit of a giveaway, and started people wondering if the president was leaving town. When Toi had finished working with the Boss, she stopped at my desk and inquired, 'Are you going to be here on Monday, Grace?' 'Certainly,' I replied. 'I'm expecting a quiet weekend.'" [415]

Miss Tully also had had a tangle with her mother, who thought she was packing for just another jaunt to Hyde Park. "She became quite firm at my failure to include enough warm clothes for January in New York State," Miss Tully recalled. "When I hinted that we might be going to Warm Springs instead, it made no difference. 'You know very well, Grace, that it can get very cold at night in those Georgia mountains. You put in some more warm things.' So I did—for a quick ride to Florida and back." [415]

Because of the small number of people in the party, Dewey Long ordered only a five-car train. The rebuilt *Magellan* had been delivered without its name displayed on the sides of the car; for this trip, the names of the other cars were painted out, too.

Baggage, food and other supplies had been stowed on board an hour before the 10:30 p.m. departure time. As always the crew was specially selected, but there was a major difference. Except for the engineer and fireman, who could hardly be expected to determine the identities of their passengers, all regular railroad and Pullman employees had been told their services would not be needed this time. Rail and Pullman officials had spent the day instructing five Filipino messmen from the *U.S.S. Potomac*, the president's ship, on the technique of making up berths and catering to the appetites and other wants of their 30-some passengers. Food for the party would be supplied from the *Magellan's* kitchen. Tray service was provided for all who were not actually "messing" [429] with the president.

At the appropriate hour on Saturday night, a small cavalcade of limousines eased away from the south portico of the White House, turned right on 15th Street and headed for the Bureau siding. Following Roosevelt into the *Magellan* was Miss Tully; Secretary of Commerce Harry Hopkins; Dr. Ross McIntire, the White House physician; and a glittering staff of generals and flag officers.

The train headed north on the B&O as if bound for Hyde Park. But at Fort George G. Meade, Md., it turned and headed south for Florida, via PRR, RF&P, Atlantic Coast Line and Florida East Coast. "We made up our berths and ate K rations," Miss Tully groused. [415]

After speeding down the East Coast, the special arrived at Military Jct. in Miami at 1:30 Monday morning, 27 hours later. Twenty-two hundred pounds of luggage and 900 pounds of bottled table water for the planes—the *Dixie Clipper*, FDR's craft, and the *Atlantic Clipper*, for his staff—were unloaded into Army vehicles and dispatched to the Pan-American Airways base on Dinner Key, three miles south. The train stayed hidden in the woods until shortly after 5 a.m., then proceeded to S.W. 27th Avenue and Dixie Highway in Miami where Roosevelt and his party detrained at 5:45 for an automobile ride to their planes and the historic flight to Casablanca. Dewey Long went along to approve the communication setup in the president's plane. After Roosevelt took off, Long and two Secret Service men took a taxi back to the spot where they had left the train—but to their astonishment it had vanished. "It isn't often anyone mislays the president's train," he said afterward, "but they'd done it this time. Somebody had moved it over half a mile from where it was supposed to be. And with the security of the president involved, it wasn't funny. Nobody was supposed to know that train was there, and I didn't want to go around asking people if they'd seen anything of my train." [224]

With the two agents, Long set off on his quiet search. They found the train, but not without some embarrassment. "It was daylight by then," he

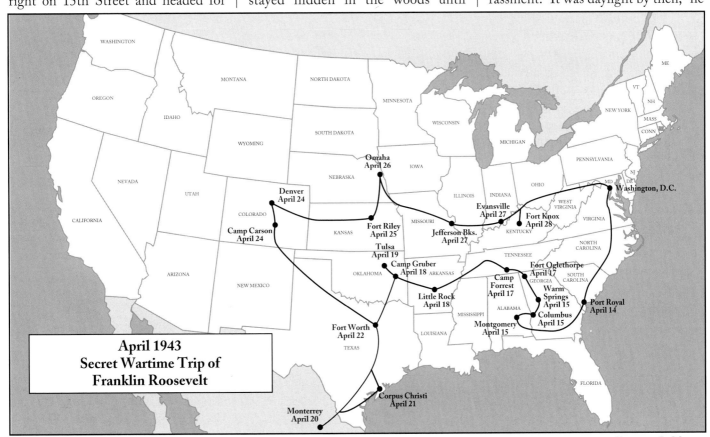

April 1943
Secret Wartime Trip of
Franklin Roosevelt

KENNETH L. MILLER

said, "and the boys were sort of conspicuous carrying those machine guns. There isn't much you can do in the way of hiding a machine gun, and the early workers of Miami didn't linger long in our vicinity."[224]

Roosevelt wasn't much of a flyer, not because it scared him but because he felt it boring. He hadn't been aloft since flying to Chicago to accept the Democratic nomination in 1932; but the world was changing. Soon he would have a new plane, the *Sacred Cow*, especially outfitted for him with an elevator and special cabin facilities that would follow his train around the country during the latter part of the war in case he needed to hurry back to Washington.

The nearly empty special left Miami at 12:20 p.m., arriving Jacksonville at 8:40. It was tucked away on an abandoned spur in a wooded area of the Yukon Air Base until 11:30 p.m. on the 25th, when it returned south to pick up Roosevelt. The train arrived Miami at 8 a.m. the 26th, and departed at 6 p.m. on the 30th for home, quietly easing into the nation's capital at 6:30 p.m. Jan. 31. It was a successful trip; a Pullman officer noted on his report: "Only minor defects—repaired enroute."[149]

Roosevelt made a secret wartime inspection trip across the country April 13-29, 1943. The president's official chronicler, Navy Ship's Clerk William M. Rigdon, and Everett L. "Tommy" Thompson of the B&O went along—the latter producing one of his many magnificent logs that provided succulent operating details of the kind that rail historians devour. He dutifully recorded the class, number, tractive effort, cylinder stroke, driver size and steam pressure of the steam locomotives that hauled the train, as well as the horsepower of the few diesels that took part. Of the 67 locomotives that handled the train, Thompson missed identifying only

one. He meticulously recorded the times at every station and water stop along the way—to the second!

And each page carried, perhaps as an offhanded apology, this notation: "This was a special train for the accommodation of the president of the United States. The schedule was purposely made quite slow."[400]

Roosevelt had made an earlier such jaunt on Sept. 17-Oct. 1, 1942, covering 8,396.5 rail miles in 24 states.

(It was during that venture that the Southern Railway insisted on a security act hard to follow. Southern didn't like to operate pilot trains, saying that the heavy rush of regular business on its main line provided ample opportunity for advance movements. So six soldiers were placed along every mile of right of way, meaning that a total of 7,848 men went on duty at trackside many hours before the special was due.

"I never saw anything like it," recalled Southern engineer Jess Davis, who was on the lead engine of the extra train that picked up these men between Atlanta and Greenville, S.C.

"Our train was doubleheaded by two light Pacifics, the 1209 and 1219. I had the 1209 and Jack Gossett the second engine."[262]

(Davis said they stopped the train more than 560 times in the 153 miles between Atlanta and Greenville to pick up the soldiers. "There were two at each crossing, and one at each end of all the bridges," he explained. "They had been on duty so long that they were groggy for sleep. Two of them sat down on the crossties, went to sleep, and were killed by trains that followed the special. Some grabbed shuteye beside the track. Others sneaked off into the woods. I remember we had a heck of a time finding some near Ayersville. We failed to locate one at Alto. Later I heard he'd stayed there two days."[262])

Whereas the 1942 trip skirted around the rim of the nation, the 1943 tour made a smaller circle—7,243.7 miles on 23 roads—through the country's heartland. The trip commenced on a cool and windy Tuesday, April 13, the afternoon after Roosevelt had dedicated the Jefferson Memorial.

The all-important first leg of the journey—all 6.9 miles of it—was on the B&O. The advance section left Silver Spring, Md., at 1:15 p.m., behind class P-7 Pacific No. 5319, the *President Arthur*, and proceeded to Union Station with seven cars.

After a 13-minute stop to swap the P-7 for RF&P 4-8-4 steamer 610, the special ambled to PRR's 14th Street Yard, where the Secret Service sleeper *Conneaut* and the *Magellan* were coupled on at 2:10. Among the 48 passengers were Madame Chiang Kai-shek, wife of the president of China. The first stop of this super-secret run was a brief pause just across the Potomac River in Virginia—to pick up some horse meat for Sister, an Irish Setter belonging to Roosevelt's cousin, Miss Laura "Aunt Polly" Delano, that had been overlooked in White House packing that morning.[321] The horse meat was swiftly driven south in a White House vehicle after the "tragedy" was discovered. Thompson ignored that stop, but groused about several other delays:

"Slow order from Dunlop to North Petersburg [Va.] account double-tracking the [Atlantic Coast Line]. Slow at Enfield [N.C.] to secure orders to watch out for pole blown down by storm which was encountered at Emporia. Flagged near Whitakers [N.C.] to watch out for tree on track, then slow for some time. Ran out of rain at that point."[400]

Roosevelt's first stopover was Wednesday the 14th at West Port Royal, S.C., for a look at the Marine barracks, air station and hospital at Parris Island. Thompson noted it was "impractical" to turn the train at West Port Royal while the party was off, and so it backed around the Charleston & Western Carolina wye after leaving with all on board. "This move was made unusually slow since there was no buffer [coach] to ride on the rear."[400]

Next was a stop at Maxwell Field, Ala., on Thursday the 15th for an aerial review and visit to an athletic field. "Fala, always a great favorite with the crowds wherever he goes, almost stole the show from his master about this time," Rigdon wrote. "When[ever] Miss Suckley took him from the car for a limbering-up walk, he was immediately recognized and a din of 'oh's' and 'ah's' went up."[321]

That afternoon, the party proceeded to Fort Benning, Ga., home of the Army's parachute and infantry schools and the 10th Armored Division. The president saw a platoon attack demonstration—with machine guns and mortars firing live ammunition—that was so realistic one soldier was wounded.[321]

From here, members of the party motored to Warm Springs, where the train had proceeded without them. "The motor ride, although dusty in places, was a most pleasant change after three days' close confinement aboard [the] train," Rigdon opined.[321]

Curiously, FDR spent the night in the *Magellan* rather than in his Little White House on the grounds of the Warm Springs Foundation. The party departed Warm Springs Friday night, April 16, 1943, enroute to Fort Oglethorpe, Ga., home of the Third WAAC Training Center. Roosevelt emerged from the train at 10 Saturday morning. "All cars in the official caravan, except the president's car, were driven by WAACs, who did excellently," Rigdon noted a little chauvinistically in his report.[321]

FDR continued on a midday Saturday schedule to Camp Forrest, Tenn., near Tullahoma, home of the 80th Division, for an inspection of troops in bivouac. Next followed an overnight haul to Camp Joseph T. Robinson, near Little Rock, Ark., for a Palm Sunday morning visit. Thompson noted that when pulling up a steep grade into the camp at 7:11 a.m. Sunday, Missouri Pacific class P-73 Pacific 6614 stalled. A pre-arranged whistle signal summoned MK-63 class Mikado 1253, which chuffed down from the camp and assisted, pulling at 7:33 and cutting off at the yard switch at 7:42, four minutes before the train finally came to a stop in the camp. "Driving rain from Bald Knob [Ark.]," he recorded ruefully, pinning blame for the snafu.[400]

While at Camp Robinson, Roosevelt visited the Branch Immaterial Replacement Training Center, which offered basic training for recruits destined to any of several Army branches. He also attended a Palm Sunday worship service.

Sunday afternoon, Roosevelt continued to Camp Gruber, Okla., for a look at the 88th Infantry Division. The president had supper with a selected group of soldiers. He ate what they did—lettuce and radish salad, chili, crackers, macaroni, candied carrots, french fried potatoes, bread, butter, coffee and cinnamon rolls—and said he liked it: "I want to pay special tribute to your cooks. I don't get as good a meal as that in the White House. I only get butter for breakfast—one little pat at that. You are very lucky to be in the Army."[321]

The train laid over there until Monday morning. On tap next was a visit to the Douglas Aircraft Co.'s Tulsa, Okla., plant, which built and assembled A-24 Dauntless dive bombers and B-24 Liberators from components made at Ford Motor Co.'s Willow Run plant in Michigan. "The running from Claremore [Okla.] to the … plant was very, very slow," Thompson complained about the Frisco run: "The engineer just dawdled along."[400]

The train continued that afternoon to Fort Worth, Texas. The president held his first press conference of the trip somewhere enroute, reminding journalists they could release no dispatches until their journey was over. Thompson fumed about an engineer: "While running along nicely in spots, [he] apparently let his speed fall too low over several of the hills, with the result that he was occasionally dropping time."[400]

At Fort Worth, Mrs. Roosevelt; her daughter-in-law, Mrs. Elliott Roosevelt; two of her grandchildren; her secretary, Miss Malvina Thompson; and several others joined the train for FDR's historic foray into Mexico to visit with Mexican President Manuel Avila Camacho.

Shortly after the party departed Fort Worth at 8:04 p.m. April 19, Steve Early and Dorothy Brady had dinner with Miss Tully. "Steve suddenly asked Dorothy if she had her passport," the Boss's secretary wrote. "She said in a frightened tone, 'No, am I supposed to have one? Nobody told me anything about it.' We had no rehearsal on this but knowing how Steve liked to kid Dorothy, I joined in with, 'Oh, I'm so sorry, Dorothy, I guess in the excitement of last-minute work I forgot to remind you to call Mrs. Shipley and arrange to get yours.'"

"Do you have one?" she asked Miss Tully. "Why, certainly," she answered with a straight face. "We all have them." By this time, Mrs. Brady was in a tizzy. "Well, what do I do, Mr. Early? Do you mean to say that after traveling all this distance I can't be in on the big doings? Can't you fix it up for me?" Early thought a minute, then suggested Mrs. Brady go get her notebook so he could dictate a telegram to the White House asking that a passport for her be sent down in the next mail pouch. "Dorothy typed out the message and while she was preparing it, we let the telegrapher in on the joke and told him to accept the wire and assure her it would go right off." Mrs. Brady was still worried the passport wouldn't arrive in time, so Early said, "I tell you, Dottie, what I would do if I were in your shoes, and I think we can arrange it. I'd get off at some stop down the way and Guy Spaman can wire ahead to have a car meet the train and assign a Secret Service man to drive you. Of course, it means driving all night but you won't mind that." Early instructed Spaman, who left dinner to carry out his orders. "We kept Dorothy on the anxious seat for some few hours," Miss Tully wrote, "and then she looked so unhappy and worried that I insisted we tell her it was all in fun, that no one had passports, and let her relax." The next day, Mrs. Brady still hadn't gotten over the shock. "When she saw the president, she regaled him with the story. He howled with laughter and said he wished he could have been there. 'Silly goose, didn't you know they were pulling your leg?' he asked. She admitted she didn't but assured him she would be on her guard in the future."[415]

Roosevelt arrived at Laredo at 11:01 a.m. Tuesday the 20th, departing at 11:26 a.m. (Central War Time, same as Eastern Standard) via the National Railways of Mexico and in the charge of a Mexican railroad crew. After crossing the border at 11:34, the train paused at Sanchez Crossing to pick up the Mexican foreign minister and the U.S. ambassador.

"The trip south from Laredo to Monterrey was uneventful and through interesting country," Rigdon recorded. "Occasionally we passed an adobe village (they were usually dilapidated and deserted-looking) but the country in the main was desert land and populated only by mesquite trees.

The route of our train was guarded by very widely dispersed mounted cavalrymen." [321]

Roosevelt's train arrived at Monterrey's Military Field at 4 p.m. (Mexican time, an hour behind CWT).

President Avila Camacho's train was already there, on a siding, headed north toward Laredo. (At Tanque San Diego, FDR's train had been ordered to delay its arrival from 3:35 until 4, "consequently running very slow from there in,"[400] Thompson noted, probably to ensure Avila Camacho would arrive from Mexico City first). Roosevelt's special pulled by, then backed onto the same siding so that the two presidents' private cars were end-to-end, with only a street over which the automobile caravan into town would pass separating the two.

The big shots went into town to visit the governor's palace, review troops, witness a mass demonstration by schoolchildren and attend a seven-course dinner. Both presidents made 10-minute radio speeches to the Mexican people before returning to Roosevelt's train that night.

Thompson once told the author that he nearly got himself in a mess during the layover. He got off the train for some purpose long since forgotten, only to realize that he spoke no Spanish. He had "a devil of a time" convincing Avila Camacho's security men to let him back on the train. [400]

The same night Dewey Long nearly got himself killed when an overzealous Mexican guard charged at him with a bayonet. "I got off the train to rig up a field telephone when this character came at me," Long recalled. "Every time I'd try to go for my credentials, he'd come at me with that bayonet. He finally prodded me up to his commander and it was straightened out, but it wasn't funny there for a while."[224]

Avila Camacho planned to pay a

return visit to the United States quite soon—he returned with Roosevelt to Corpus Christi, Texas. Avila Camacho's private car and one other car on his train were cut into Roosevelt's train ahead of the rear two cars to give the presidents more time together and to provide for tighter security than would have been the case with two presidents on two trains.

FDR's train, now with 11 cars, started north at 10:34 p.m., followed a few minutes later by the Mexican train. Thompson noted a 13-minute delay at 12:27 a.m. because the pilot train emptied one of two plugs at a water stop. The train "could not move to the other until after [helper engine] 2520 had cut off and cleared up."[400]

Another unscheduled stop of the type that give security men ulcers was made at 2 a.m., Miss Tully and Long recalled. Long, "who always slept like a fireman with his gear close at hand,"[415] jumped out of bed, hauled on his pants, and with Secret Service man Mike Reilly went charging out to see what was happening. He encountered no train crew members and felt a surge of panic. Finally they found the Mexican trainmaster. It was calmly explained that the stop was being made to permit the crew to eat its customary midnight snack—off the train.

"But they can't do that," Long protested. "There's a couple of presidents on board." [224] But doing it they were. "Looking out on the black and desolate wasteland," Miss Tully wrote, "Dewey then asked in some bewilderment where a train crew, or anybody else, could find anything to eat except on the train. His attention was directed to a flickering light about a half-mile distant. After resolving some doubt … that flagmen had been sent out to guard the front and rear approaches to the … train, Dewey [and Reilly] set out for the overland light. They discovered it to be a little hut where the entire train crew was lolling about while a blanket-clad Mexican woman fried up a spot of supper"[415]—sandwiches and tequila. "Presidents or no presidents," said Long, "they were following their custom. I think they thought we were nuts."[224] Concluded Miss Tully: "Conversation in neither English nor [Spanish] could prevail upon them to return to the train until they had finished their meal."[415]

Roosevelt's train crossed the border at 4:21 a.m. (5:21 a.m. CWT) on Wednesday the 21st, returning him to U.S. soil and ending his precedent-setting day in Mexico. The enlarged train, with its Mexican counterpart closely behind, set out for Corpus Christi.

Thompson noted some confusion over which of two Texas Mexican Railway 2,400-horsepower Baldwin diesels would pull which train. TM put the 601 on FDR's train at Laredo yard, then replaced it with the 600 at the International-Great Northern station a few minutes later. He attributed some of the delay to officers wrestling with the question of adding a Mexican diner to Roosevelt's train, which apparently was not done

He penned a scary note referring to the 11:01-11:04 a.m. stop at Robstown, Texas. "No stop scheduled at Robstown, but (Gulf Coast Lines) train 12 due on the same track at 11 a.m. (and we were) permitted to go ahead!!!"[400]

The presidential train was pulled backward from Flour Bluff Jct. to Flour Bluff for arrival at the Corpus Christi Naval Air Training Center at 12:28 p.m. The Mexican train pulled in right behind it.

Both presidents enjoyed a lunch—of steamed smoked sausages (the press called them frankfurters) with Spanish sauce, string beans, mashed potatoes, mixed green salad, celery and olives, bread, rolls, butter,

limeade and lemon meringue or blueberry pie—with about 400 cadets. Roosevelt's train departed from the air station at 4 p.m., with Avila Camacho aboard. The Mexican president's train, with his two cars back where they belonged, had left 10 minutes before. The plan was to stop alongside each other on the Flour Bluff Jct. wye, about 19 miles from Corpus, for photographs in a most dramatic setting before Avila Camacho returned to his train. Once the pictures were taken, each train departed—Avila Camacho's for Mexico via Brownsville, Roosevelt's for Ben Brook siding near Fort Worth. Thompson fumed about the train's tardiness as it neared San Antonio on the Missouri Pacific: "No particular effort was made at recovering time as the track does not ride very good and the run was through the dinner hour."[400]

Arrival at Ben Brook was at 9:45 a.m. Thursday the 22nd, where the president made for the Dutch Branch Ranch of son Elliott to spend the day. "Cars were on hand at Ben Brook siding to transport the other members of the party to Fort Worth," Rigdon wrote, "where we spent the day cleaning up, souvenir buying, and resting from the effects of our 10 days' confinement to the train. The cars, meanwhile, were sent to the railroad shops [he doesn't say which railroad] for servicing and for repairs to flat wheels on the [*Magellan*]."[321]

Security remained tight, to the extent that even long-distance telephone calls in the area were monitored by the Secret Service. Two Texas businessmen got the shock of their lives when, during their telephone conversation, one of them happened to mention that Roosevelt was traveling through the area. At that point a strange voice broke in and admonished him politely to shut up.[224]

The train returned to the siding at 6:30 p.m. and the president boarded

at 9:25 to continue west. Mrs. Roosevelt and her party stayed behind.

What could have been a major incident occurred just west of Amarillo when a man rushed toward the standing train and tried to board it. He was quickly halted; but local police officers who were known to railroad special agents recognized him as a town drunk, and he was led away to spend the rest of the night in confinement. This time, the Secret Service wasn't even involved. [224]

Rigdon enjoyed the "32-hour lazy train ride" into the foothills of the Rocky Mountains. "We passed through the Texas Panhandle country and began the long ascent," he wrote. "Our train was guarded along this section of the route by motorized units, which followed the train from station to station along highways that generally paralleled the railroad. This section, once the worst part of the 'dust bowl,' was quite green today and looked like anything but a dust bowl. … It was beautiful … in the Rockies in the springtime and also a bit cool to those of us who only so recently had been in more southerly climes. For the day, everyone was observed to have donned his heavy clothes." [321]

Next in line were several visits in the Denver area on Saturday, starting with Camp Carson, near Colorado Springs. Thompson noted a 32-minute stop 30 miles beyond Trinidad, Colo., to repair a stubborn air pump on CB&Q O-2b Mike 5252. The tardy train was pulled backward from Kelker into Camp Carson by a yard engine, with the road engine helping when the grade got tough, and finishing the job when the yard engine cut off in the yard for a 3:07 a.m. arrival. The president detrained at 10. Among the sights he saw in the lofty shadow of Pike's Peak was a new secret weapon—the bazooka. Then it was off to Denver

Presidential secretary Grace Tully smiles for the camera while she looks at the paperwork she's going over with the Boss on the Roald Amundsen *Sept. 20, 1942, during Roosevelt's first nationwide defense inspection trip.*

via the Colorado & Southern. Thompson noted:

"Snappy run was made from Kelker to Denver, and the time from Palmer Lake in was very good, with speeds in the high 60s in places."[400]

After transferring to the UP, the party made stops at the Fitzsimmons General Hospital, Remington Arms Ordnance Plant and Lowry Field, all in the Denver area. Soldiers assigned to protect the president as he passed from the hospital to the Remington plant on a 30-minute drive attracted a fair contingent of civilians. Rigdon overheard some of their comments: "It's the president! Did you see him?" "Looks just like him!" "Well, I guessed right. It IS the president!"[321]

Thompson kept scribbling: "Pulled back from Sable to Bunell (when arriving). ... Slow from Bunell (when departing) to let 1/38 pass, then pulled through Sable siding."[400]

The party continued to Fort Riley, (Whiteside) Kan., where it arrived at 7:47 a.m. Easter Sunday. A Union Pacific dispatcher's train sheet shows that the nine-car POTUS train was preceded 30 minutes earlier by a three-car pilot train. The dispatcher on duty that night in Salina, Kan., marked the two secret trains as *FDR Spls* at the top of their columns, despite the fact they were known officially only as MAIN (Military Authorization Identification Number) 18345. He also noted on the back—ruefully, one supposes—that the specials delayed the *Pony Express*, westbound UP train 37, for 57 minutes at Sand Spring and a local passenger run, No. 39, for an hour and five minutes at Chapman.

On the agenda at Fort Riley were an Easter service and luncheon with about 400 officers and OCS cadets. When the president returned to the train in early afternoon, Sergeant A.C. Green of Brownfield, Texas, gave him a beautiful handmade wooden nameplate for his desk. Green said his grandfather had given one to Woodrow Wilson and that he was carrying on a cherished family tradition. The president's train stayed put while he signed official mail and rested. For a half-hour before his 6 p.m. departure, he and his immediate party—including Fala—gathered on the rear platform to enjoy music by the post band. Then it was off to a Monday tour of the Glenn L. Martin Co.'s Nebraska bomber plant, maker of the B-26 Marauder, 10 miles south of Omaha.

The special was routed from Fort Riley to Menoken, thence via the Grand Island line to Marysville and the Beatrice branch through Valparaiso, Neb., to Valley, the present Cheyenne-Omaha main line to Lane, then the old main line to Gilmore Jct., where the Missouri Pacific took over.

Union Pacific archives still contain a lengthy memo regarding movement on its lines of Roosevelt's train. It stated the overall length of MAIN 18345 was 710 feet, and mistakenly referred to the president's private car as the rebuilt *Marco Polo* rather than *Magellan*. A coded telegram dated April 13 fine-tuned the schedule between Denver and Gilmore Jct. (translations in brackets): "Lv Denver 130PM 24th for BAJBIS BASWET BAQZOF BANDYM [Fitzsimons] Lv. BAJBIS BASWET BAQZOF BANDYM [Fitzsimons] 430PM ar. LAMQIX [Fort Riley] 8AM 25th Lv. 6PM via Manhattan and Marysville Ar. Valparaiso 1230AM 26th. DUKJUS FOMDIH FOZMAV KISFIS AM [Park train until 7 a.m.] Wye train LIZVOW [Valley] Ar. LAPGAH DIDDAL [Gilmore Jct.] 930AM where train will be delivered MoPac for further handling. B-26.

The trek included a layover at Valparaiso from 12:30 to 7:30 a.m. Monday. All the operator/agent knew was that the special would "hold [stop in]" the siding.[339] The first sign that something was going on was the arrival of Army soldiers on Sunday afternoon who set up camp in the yard near the depot. When FDR's blackened-out train arrived, it pulled in on the far end of the siding, south of town. The soldiers were assigned to surround it and not let anyone near it or to stop on the road beside the track.

At about 7 a.m., the train moved up to the depot area to service its power, UP two-unit EMC diesel 8-M-1/8-M-2. Residents nearby thought it was "just another troop train,"[339] except for the few who noticed a man in a dress coat exercising Fala. Then they knew whose train it was. This breach of security was becoming quite a problem, as the young ruffian demanded exercise in this manner at virtually every extended stop—often at the hand of FDR's valet, Arthur Prettyman. Secret Service agent Mike Reilly gave him a code name, Miss Tully said: "The Informer."[400]

The train proceeded north to Valley. There, Thompson noted, the diesels were cut off and the train was pulled around a wye westward toward North Platte by a UP Consolidation. Once the train was in position, the steam engine was uncoupled from the front end of the train and the diesels—with a buffer coach—were reattached, this time to the rear of the *Magellan*, ready to pull the train backward toward the East. The special had been positioned for a 25-mile reverse move to Gilmore Jct., on UP's double-tracked old main line—which looped southward from Lane, then north again into Omaha—so it would be properly pointed when it left the defense plant for Kansas City on the Missouri Pacific.

The move was indeed complicated. In Omaha, Missouri Pacific conductor Walter G. Slaybaugh had been told to take his westbound (actually southbound) Fort Crook local down the UP (upon which MP had trackage rights) to Gilmore Jct., where two tracks diverged to the left from the UP's eastbound (actually northbound) main: first, a CB&Q track heading into the plant, and second, the MP line to Kansas City. Slaybaugh was further instructed to deliver his train past the Gilmore Jct. tower to a siding in the plant and return his locomotive—diesel switcher 4102—to a position north of the tower and through a crossover to the westbound UP main. There, the 4102 would couple onto Missouri Pacific class MT-73 Mountain steamer No. 5339 and wait for the special, now approaching on the eastbound main from the south. Behind the two MP locomotives while they waited was yet a third, MP class P-73 Pacific No. 6407, which had cut off from its freight train moments earlier. Once the POTUS special arrived and stopped north of the crossover, its UP power was removed from the backward-facing train and dispatched to Omaha. The 4102 and 5339 crossed back over to the eastbound main, coupled onto its head end and pulled it into the bomber plant for the tour. The 4102 was then released to do its work at the post. Once the visit had concluded, the special—with the 5339 still attached to its head end—was pulled backward out of the plant by the 6407 and five idler freight cars to keep the steam engine from working inside the grounds. Then the 5339 started the special south toward Kansas City and the next stop, an hour-long pause the next morning at Jefferson Barracks, Mo.

The Auburn, Neb., paper reported that the operator/agent there knew only that an "extra southbound"[339] was enroute from Omaha to Kansas City. About midmorning, a number of Army soldiers arrived and spaced themselves every quarter-mile along the track outside of and through town and over and under a viaduct north of town. Several were on the station platform and allowed no one near as the train approached at 2 p.m. Even the soldiers thought it was just a training mission. Once the train passed through, the article said, "all left their posts of duty as unceremoniously as they had taken them."[284]

Thompson recorded a 34-minute operating stop at Jefferson City, Mo.—from 11:29 p.m. to 12:03 a.m.—and Rigdon explained why they were there so long. "Overzealous guards would not permit anyone, including the Secret Service, to leave or board the train," he wrote. "After some discussion between Mr. [Frank J.] Wilson, Chief of the Secret Service, and the colonel in charge of the guard here, this situation was clarified." He added that this was the first and only difficulty with U.S. Army guards who protected the route.[400]

Dewey Long encountered some difficulty when the same guards forced him and a couple of Secret Service agents back on their car when they tried to get off. "They meant business," Long recalled. "They thought we really were krauts [German prisoners], and they'd have shot us in a minute."[224]

The president hastened on to a Tuesday afternoon visit to the Republic Aviation Corp. plant at Evansville, Ind., maker of the P-47 Thunderbolt fighter.

"We arrived ... to find a large crowd gathered at the railroad station and along our troop-lined route out to the Republic plant to see what was coming off," Rigdon wrote. "Since leaving Denver the size of the crowds of interested citizens had been steadi-

Military personnel and a color guard wait for President Roosevelt to detrain from the private car Roald Amundsen *at Fort Lewis, Wash., Sept. 22, 1942, during the president's first secret tour of military installations and defense plants around the country.*

ly increasing, almost to a number that would cause us to suspect that we might have had an advance publicity agent. One little girl, when told she couldn't see Roosevelt, was heard to reply, 'I don't care if he is a military secret, I WANT to see him!' " [321]

Mrs. Erma Drain, an employee in the electrical assembly department, presented Roosevelt with a model of the P-47 and talked with him at length. She "told him that she has two sons in the Army Air Forces, one of whom (a bombardier in a Flying Fortress) is now a prisoner of war in Germany. She asked the president if he thought her son was going to be all right there. The president told her that he thought he would ... but he wouldn't say the same about Japan. Mrs. Drain then told the president she felt much better about her son's safety now that she had his assurance and that if she wasn't too excited over meeting him today, she might be able to sleep tonight for the first time in a

long time." [321]

The president left Evansville for an overnight trip on the L&N to the government's gold bullion depository at Fort Knox, Ky. Thompson noted a 20-minute delay at Cloverport, Ky., because the pilot train had not cleared up at Irvington: "This particular stretch is manual block, and there was apparently some misunderstanding as to how far in advance that train would run. It consumed 62 minutes on the (26-mile) run Cloverport-Irvington." [400]

Roosevelt arrived Fort Knox at 3 a.m. Wednesday, although he didn't leave the train until 10:05. He saw the depository, which contained 80 percent of the world's gold bullion supply, and witnessed an attack demonstration by a reinforced armored battalion. "At 12:35 p.m.," Rigdon noted, "our train pulled out of Fort Knox for Louisville and the overnight haul to Washington and home." [321]

Operator R.O. Barclay, working at New Albany, Ind., across the Ohio

River from Louisville, was impressed with the B&O's planning. "A trainmaster called Friday afternoon [the 23rd] and said the train would pass me at 2:25 p.m. [Wednesday]. I handed up orders to both engines [Pacifics P-5a 5206 and P-5 5207] and the conductor and flagman—four sets in all—as he came slowly around a tight [10-mile-an-hour] curve. I OS'd him by [reported the departure to the dispatcher] at 2:27 p.m.!" [28]

The party was delayed at Cincinnati because B&O No. 2, the eastbound *National Limited*, which was due out at 6:10 p.m., was late, and the special was held to follow it. "Engineer[s Hesson and Polen] worked rather slowly," Thompson wrote, "to let it get out of the way, since it stops at Winton Place and Oakley." [400]

Out of Grafton, W.Va., Thompson noted: "With two large engines [S-1a 2-10-2 6179 and 4-8-2 Mountain 5501 Grafton to Keyser], it would have been interesting to note some of the times had the train been late. As it was, it was necessary to drag and drag to keep from running ahead of time ... Ordered not to exceed 55 mph; however, this was lifted after Point of Rocks [Md.]. ... Eased off after passing Kensington, and took plenty of time from there to Washington, coming down very slow at the north end of the platform to pick up a pilot for the run through the tunnel [at Union Station]." [400]

"After a very bumpy ride from Cincinnati," Rigdon concluded, "our train arrived at Washington, D.C., at 9:50 a.m." (Thursday, April 29, 1943). [321]

Roosevelt left on the night of Friday, July 30, 1943, for a day at Hyde Park before leaving for a 10-day off-the-record fishing trip on the Canadian side of Lake Huron. The party, traveling via Albany and Niagara Falls, would live on the train.

Dewey Long and Mike Reilly had done their usual reconnaissance and settled on Little Current, on Manitoulin Island in Georgian Bay, where they found reports of good black bass fishing and a railroad spur running close to the water.

A small dock was built near the track for the convenience of the anglers and a communications headquarters was established at Birch Island station, Ontario. Arrangements were made for twice-daily air-mail service and telephone and telegraph connections with the White House.

"Dorothy and I were never more surprised than when the president invited us to accompany him on this fishing trip," Miss Tully commented. "Of course, he would have work to do but somehow I didn't expect to be asked because it seemed to me that a woman might be out of place in a group of men who intended to spend most of the time in fishing boats. We were thrilled to be included." [415]

She recorded that the party included Appointments Secretary "Pa" Watson; Rear Admiral Ross T. McIntire, the White House doctor; Admiral William D. Leahy, chief of staff; Jimmy Byrnes, director of the Office of War Mobilization; Admiral Wilson Brown, Naval aide; and, later in the stay, presidential adviser Harry Hopkins.

"To accommodate the party two boats were needed, so the first day I went in the president's boat and the next day Dorothy had the honor," Miss Tully wrote. "On the third day the Boss emerged from his room and rolled into the observation end of the train where Dorothy and I were reading the morning papers. We were not in our fishing regalia and the president noticing that we were 'dressed up,' as he put it, asked, 'Aren't you children going fishing today?' We thanked him and said that we thought they might have a better and more comfortable time if we stayed home. He smiled and said, 'Well, if you will turn me down there's nothing I can do, I guess.'

"That was a wonderful 10 days of relaxation for all of us. The president was in especially good form and everyone was careful not to bother him with any matters unless they were urgent. In the evenings over an old-fashioned cocktail we listened to all of them tell about the big fellows that got away. They weighed their catches and kept track of the number so they could see who won the pool." [415]

The trip wasn't a vacation for everyone. When some high-speed telegraph equipment failed, Dewey Long and his staff took over the telegraph office in the local Canadian Pacific Railroad station, patched one of its wires across the border into the White House and for 30 hours handled encoded messages to and from the train just as it had been done in Lincoln's time. "We communicate the

horse-and-buggy way if necessary," Long quipped later. "That's why we carry blinker lights, semaphore flags, telegraph instruments, spare wire and telephones." Then he added, "I've never used smoke signals—not yet, anyway." [224]

"The last day of our stay was my birthday," Miss Tully wrote, "and the captain of the Navy ship, which was anchored nearby, had somehow got wind of it and had his cook bake me a birthday cake. It was huge and beautifully decorated. Everyone on board had a piece and the president had ordered a special dinner for the occasion and champagne to give it the added party touch." [415]

As the 1944 campaign neared, Roosevelt was tired, and looked it. Most of those around him were convinced he didn't want to run again, and even he wrote Democratic National Committee Chairman Robert E. Hannegan that "all that is within me cries out to go back to my home on the Hudson River." [246] But if there was a need to stay in office in 1940 because of the war in Europe, certainly there was now.

Roosevelt would end up running against Republican New York Gov. Thomas E. Dewey, although in the spring Wendell Willkie also tested the waters. The effort brought on a flap when Willkie tried to procure a private railroad car for his campaign. Henry McCarthy, associate director of the division of traffic movement for the Office of Defense Transportation, ruled that he was entitled to one because, McCarthy explained, "that's the kind of country I like to live in."

The declaration brought a stern rebuke from Traffic World magazine, chiding that the opinion meant that anyone, anywhere would be entitled to the use of such a precious wartime resource. "Especially in these days of the radio," the magazine wrote, "the country can very well forego the privilege of seeing and hearing in person all of the candidates who seek office. The conservation of transportation facilities is a whole lot more important."[407]

Roosevelt started a 35-day cross-country trip at 10:45 p.m. on Thursday, July 13, 1944, that took him to the Marine Base at San Diego. From there he set sail to inspections and high-level war strategy conferences in Hawaii and Alaska before returning to the train at Seattle.

As might be expected, he spent the first night of the trip Dewey called "Mr. Roosevelt's holiday" at Hyde Park before continuing across the continent. The itinerary called for a 30-minute stop in Chicago on Saturday the 15th, for any last-minute political plotting before the Democratic convention convened. He would not appear before the delegates, but would broadcast the acceptance of his nomination for a fourth term from San Diego a few days later. A little conference occurred on the *Magellan* in Chicago that shows how world history can turn on a single petty political decision—not necessarily by the president, but by those near him.

"There had been no personal rift between Mr. Roosevelt and [Vice President] Henry Wallace," Miss Tully wrote. "The Boss wanted the Iowan to continue with him in office ... but ... he was told again and again by those who spent nearly full time in preoccupation with party political matters that the National Democratic Convention would not accept the choice." [415]

Wallace had neglected his duties and needlessly bruised some of the congressional leadership; he was now a liability.

Hannegan had huddled with Roosevelt a few days before the president left Washington and told him Wallace wasn't acceptable. The names of Jimmy Byrnes and Alben Barkley were batted about, and the president suggested Supreme Court Justice William O. Douglas. Hannegan proposed Sen. Harry S. Truman, who was from his home state of Missouri and who had distinguished himself as chairman of a special Senate committee investigating war expenditures and contracts.

Roosevelt was too busy with the war to quibble. He had finally agreed to accept either of the latter two, and, at Hannegan's request, had written a letter to that effect.

"The letter, naming Douglas and Truman in that order, was addressed to Hannegan just before the convention met," Miss Tully recalled, adding that Roosevelt scheduled the clandestine Chicago stop—that stretched to two hours at Hannegan's request—to further discuss strategy. [415]

His train was moved awkwardly from Englewood to the Rock Island's 51st Street coach yard. A telephone was placed aboard. Finally, a perspiring Hannegan arrived, along with Chicago Mayor Edward Kelly. The *Magellan's* observation room was cleared for a private pow-wow.

"Hannegan had a lengthy palaver with the Boss," Miss Tully said, "and when he came out of the president's sitting room he was carrying in his hand the letter naming Douglas or Truman as an acceptable running mate. He came directly to me. 'Grace, the president wants you to retype this letter and to switch these names so it will read "Harry Truman or Bill Douglas!"'

"The reason for the switch was obvious. By naming Truman first, it was plainly implied by the letter that he was the preferred choice of the president. The convention took it that way and Truman was nominated. By that narrow margin and rather casual action did one man rather than another, perhaps one policy rather than another, eventually arrive at the head of American government in April 1945." [415] Miss Tully didn't reveal whether she ever wondered if the order had come from the Boss, or whether Hannegan merely said so. She did search White House files for a carbon copy of the original version after Roosevelt's death, but never

President Roosevelt transfers to an automobile to tour Fort Lewis, Wash., on Sept. 22, 1942, during his first wartime inspection tour of military installations around the country. B&O police officer Ernest Chapman is second from left.

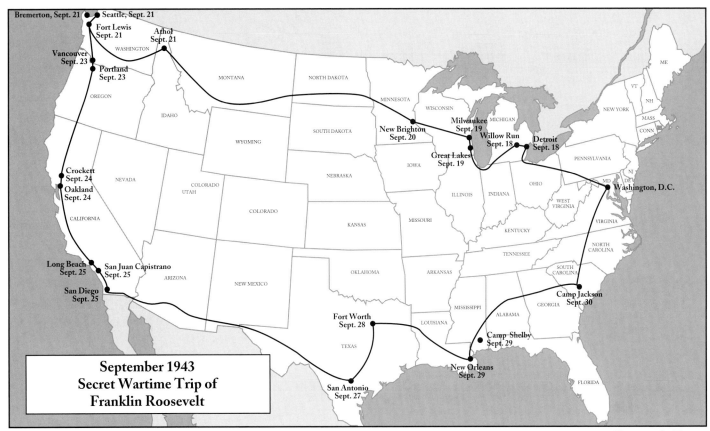

KENNETH L. MILLER

found it and assumed that Dorothy Brady threw it away.

"First drafts of letters which are amended before sending are never retained," she concluded, "but (this) is one case in which an original would have had great historical interest." [415]

Meanwhile, the train rolled on. Somewhere out West, Porter Fred D. Fair probably saved a man's life, his friends said, even if it did mean disturbing the president. A Secret Service man had taken a position outside on the rear platform of the *Magellan*. "Fred, we're heading for a long tunnel," the agent's chief said. "Our man can't survive with all that smoke in the tunnel. Fred, can you help us?"

The president was the problem. He was seated in his favorite spot in the rear of the car, with his legs stretched out across the back door. No one was willing to disturb him.

Except Fair.

Without a word, he approached the president, who was engrossed in his reading, and carefully moved his lifeless legs just enough to permit the door to be opened so the grateful agent could slip inside.

"The president never took his head out of his newspaper," Fair said. "Perhaps he didn't even know I moved his feet. He didn't have to worry about me—he was used to me being around." [284]

The business of the presidency continued despite the fact the Boss was on the road. As his train rumbled southward on the Chicago, Rock Island & Pacific toward El Reno, Okla., he was sitting at a window in the *Magellan,* with his blind up, busily working away. That proved to be a problem. The special pulled into a siding to let a regular passenger train pass. Dewey Long, in the car ahead of Roosevelt's, watched as the cars eased by. He could see the expressions on their faces. They were goggle-eyed; they had recognized FDR.

When the special arrived in El Reno, fully 2,000 people were on hand. "Get him out!" they yelled. "We know he's there!" [224]   The blind had been drawn by then, but Long knew that word had passed down the line upon which they were traveling. That wouldn't do for a secret wartime movement.

"So we lost ourselves," [224] Long recalled, explaining that the schedule was changed then and there. Instead of proceeding south then west as planned, the train was diverted to the west then south, on another Rock Island line to Tucumcari, N.M., then to El Paso, Texas, on the Southern Pacific. They just vanished. That did the trick; the crowds vanished, too.

Roosevelt's habit of tinkering with schedules was evident in his planned arrival in San Diego on the 19th. He goofed. San Diego could have easily been reached on the 18th; FDR simply miscounted the days.

Because of this, during daylight hours his train was throttled down to 18 to 25 miles an hour and sometimes when FDR was asleep the train was

President Franklin Roosevelt visits with John Nance Garner, vice president during FDR's first two terms, during a stop at Uvalde, Texas, on Sept. 27, 1942, during the president's first wartime inspection trip.

sneaked onto sidings to kill time. The slow speeds and inactivity made it impossible for the cars' generators to keep their batteries charged and thus allow the air conditioning to work properly.

"As a result," Miss Tully wrote, "the train was halted for four hours one night in [Fairbank,] Arizona [on the SP] to permit recharging by stationary equipment." [415] But FDR never knew he had made a mistake.

Just before arriving at San Diego, FDR asked the B&O's Dan Moorman for his help. "Dan," he said, "there's a favor I'd like you to do for me."

"Why certainly, Mr. President, if we can," Moorman replied.

"Well sir, there's nothing I'd like more right now than a good Abalone steak," the Boss declared, referring to a large sea snail common on the Pacific Coast. "Do you suppose you could arrange to have one prepared for me?"

Moorman quickly went into action. His dining car steward, Edward De Graves, rounded up one,

but none of the chefs, who hailed from the East, knew how to cook it. No problem. Moorman simply borrowed a Southern Pacific chef who turned it out "fit for a president." [375]

The last leg of the trip was via the SP's InterCalifornia and San Diego & Arizona Eastern subsidiaries. A train order pounded out at Calexico, Calif., reveals that the pilot train was pulled by Southern Pacific class T-31 4-6-0 steam locomotive 2360, Roosevelt's by sister engine 2362.

At San Diego, the press began to kick about the secrecy imposed on the trip. The government relented to the point that the three press men in the party could file stories through Navy facilities there, but they had to carry Washington datelines. Miss Tully was assisting as a press secretary for part of the trip, so when Merriman Smith of United Press exploded, he exploded to her.

"Everybody at the convention knows the Boss is on the West Coast," he bellowed. "Thousands of people have seen him or some of the party while crossing the country. If we put

'Washington' on our stories, it won't be security, it will just be a d___ lie!" Miss Tully liked the reporters and approached the president, whose reaction was immediate and positive. "It's completely ridiculous, child," he answered. "I'm saying in the speech that I am talking from a West Coast Naval base. Of course it doesn't have to be written 'from Washington.'

"Will you see Smitty yourself, Mr. President?" Miss Tully asked. "I think he will feel better if he has a chance to discuss the difficulty with you personally."

"Of course. Ask him to come in a minute." When Smith came out of the *Magellan*, he was grinning broadly. "That'll learn those admirals," he cracked. The stories were datelined "A West Coast Naval Base." [415]

Back in Chicago, the vice presidential flap was nowhere near resolution, with several men counting on the Democrats' nod. Truman had been approached by the party hierarchy, but had stubbornly refused to go along, saying he was pledged to support Byrnes. Hannegan had to arrange a little presidential pressure to force the proper puzzle piece into its slot. He arranged to talk to the president by phone from the Blackstone Hotel, making sure Truman was in the room. Roosevelt, not sold personally on the Missourian, nevertheless played along for the sake of party unity.

"Have you got that fellow lined up yet?" FDR asked from his private car parked on the California coast. "No," Hannegan replied. "Well, tell the senator that if he wants to break up the Democratic party by staying out, he can. But he knows as well as I what that might mean at this dangerous time in the world ..."

Truman, too politically loyal and patriotic to buck his commander-in-chief in wartime, capitulated. He allowed his name to be placed in

Eleanor Roosevelt, on the train at left, waves to Mexican President Manuel Avila Camacho's party on the adjacent special at Flour Bluff Jct., Texas, on April 21, 1943, as the presidential convoys prepare to go their separate ways. The historic visit took place during President Roosevelt's second secret World War II tour of the nation's military installations and defense plants.

nomination. [42]

Roosevelt was nominated on Thursday, July 20. As spotlights in Chicago focused on a huge portrait of him, the president's voice boomed into the convention hall "from a Pacific Coast naval base." He repeated his desire for "the quiet life," but "you in this convention have asked me to continue." He would be "too busy to campaign in the usual sense" so he hoped for re-election on the basis of "experience vs. immaturity." There was thunderous applause and a demonstration. [42]

The president sat with two of his sons and their wives as he spoke from the *Magellan's* lounge. An AP photographer was allowed to take his picture, and it received wide attention—perhaps because it was a bad one. FDR looked haggard; his eyes were encased in dark sockets. His thin shoulders sagged in an oversized jacket. His mouth hung open listlessly; his legs under the desk were splayed awkwardly. Now the people as well as the politicians came to view Roosevelt as a sick man.

Meanwhile, his health showed more signs of failing. That day he complained from what he called the "collywobbles" and stayed on the train. When son Jimmy came to get him Friday morning to watch an amphibious landing by the Fifth Marine Division, he said he felt tired but otherwise all right. Suddenly his face was drained of all its color. Writhing with his eyes closed, he gasped, "Jimmy, I don't know if I can make it—I have horrible pains." [42]

His son wanted to cancel the appearance, but the president, recovering after several minutes, overruled him. Jimmy said he would call for the doctor, but his father offered that it was probably indigestion and he'd be all

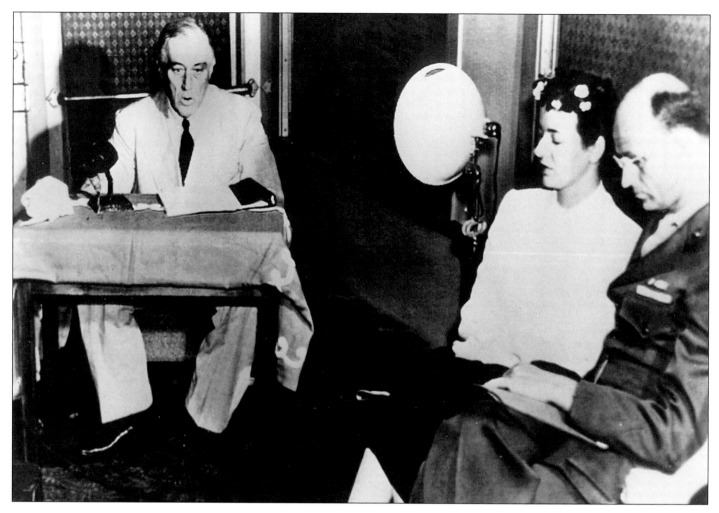

A haggard, weak-looking Franklin Roosevelt accepts the Democratic Party's nomination for a fourth term as president of the United States from the lounge of the Ferdinand Magellan *while spotted at the San Diego, Calif., Naval base as son James Roosevelt and his wife listen. It was this July 20, 1944, picture that revealed to the world how sick FDR was.*

right if he could stretch out for a few minutes. Jimmy helped him out of bed and onto the floor of his room, where he lay for about 10 minutes. Gradually the color returned to his face and his breathing returned to normal.

"Help me up now, Jimmy," he directed. "I feel better." [44]

In his wheelchair, FDR seemed like his old self—for the time being. Lt. Cmdr. Howard Bruenn of the U.S. Navy Reserve, a cardiologist who had examined the president at Bethesda (Md.) Naval Hospital the previous spring, was never told about the episode, which was probably an attack of angina pectoris.

As the campaign heated up, the president answered one particularly vitriolic attack by invoking the name of one of his most precious traveling companions—Fala. "The Republican leaders have not been content to make personal attacks upon me—or my wife—or my sons—they now include my little dog, Fala," FDR intoned on a nationwide radio hookup. "Unlike the members of my family, Fala resents this. When he learned that the Republican fiction writers had concocted a story that I had left him behind on the Aleutian Islands and had sent back a destroyer to find him—at a cost to the taxpayer of 2 or 3, or 8 or 20 million dollars—his Scotch soul was furious. He has not been the same dog since. I am accustomed to hearing malicious false-hoods about myself, such as that old worm-eaten chestnut that I have represented myself to be indispensable. But I think I have a right to object to libelous statements about my dog." [166]

Even Republicans smiled at that, but although the crack was shot through with political hype, it carried a grain of true sentiment. Roosevelt was devoted to his dog. "I would get Fala's food from the chef and take it to the president," Pullman porter Fair said of one of his priority assignments. "First, I would hand the president a napkin and then the food. Only the president could place food in front of Fala. That privilege was reserved for him." [284]

Meanwhile, the train carrying

Thomas Dewey, the Republican candidate, began crisscrossing the nation. Sixty-three reporters went along and reported everything the precise prosecutor/governor said. They also noted that if his train was about to arrive at a stop early, Dewey would order it to slow down or stop so it would arrive exactly on time.

Although Roosevelt's campaign train had no difficulties, Dewey's did. At 11:45 a.m. Pacific time on Tuesday, Sept. 19, 1944, his 14-car Great Northern Railway special was passing Castle Rock, Wash., on its way to Portland Ore., where the candidate had a major speech scheduled. Gardner Bridge and Jack Bell, the Associated Press correspondents aboard the train, were seated, reviewing an advance text of the speech. According to Bell, "Suddenly we weren't seated at all. With a tremendous crash the train stopped dead and typewriters and chairs flew in every direction." [338]

The night before, a through freight had sideswiped a local freight trying to pull out on the main line at that point, killing a trainman. As a result, Dewey's departure from Seattle was delayed from 4:50 to 8 a.m., putting his train behind a 22-car passenger and troop train. Its conductor, L.J. Agnew, said he had orders to stop at the wreck scene, and E.A. Wells, engineer on Dewey's train, apparently ran up on Agnew's train before its flagman had time to walk back. Wells said he saw the train sitting still as he rounded a curve doing 55 miles an hour, and got his special down to 30 before they hit.

"I should like to say that when we picked ourselves up groggily from amid our first train wreck," Bell said, "we thought first of the presidential candidate and his lady and our duty to get off a story on this unprecedented happening to a campaign special. But we didn't." [338]

Instead, they made their way to the bar, where miniature bottles of whiskey now covered the floor. "Automatically, Gardner and I reached out, picked up a miniature each, uncorked it, and swallowed the contents. Fortified with another of these windfalls, we made our way back through the train to find that Dewey and his wife had survived the wreck without major mishap." [338] The candidate was only shaken, having narrowly missed being hit on his head by a bouncing Pullman water bottle in the bedroom of his private car. Mrs. Dewey had been thrown against the side of the compartment, hitting her head and causing a severe headache for several hours.

At least four people on the train, two Pullman porters and Bell and Bridge, who both suffered broken ribs, were taken to hospitals, as were about a dozen from the passenger and troop train. Railroad doctors and Army and Navy first-aid men aboard both trains treated something like 50 people for cuts and bruises. Only the first car on the campaign train, the baggage/darkroom car, was seriously damaged—but there was broken glass throughout. Dewey calmly shaved himself and dressed before walking the length of his train and inquiring about the injured. Then he walked forward to check on occupants of the other train.

After several hours' delay, state police cars and those of passing motorists were commandeered to get the campaign party the remaining 59 miles into Portland, where it was supposed to spend the night anyhow.

Another engine took over for the disabled one the next day enroute to San Francisco, and Dewey didn't miss a speech.

To commemorate the incident, the candidate, his staff, and the traveling reporters formed the "Castle Rock Survivors Association," and had their official group portrait taken at the depot in Tulsa, Okla. For several years they relived their harrowing experience with an annual dinner in the comparative safety of the National Press Club in Washington.

Claims settled by the Great Northern eventually totaled around $10,000. Warren Francis, a correspondent covering the campaign for the *Los Angeles Times*, was awarded $10 for a pair of pajamas his roommate grabbed and pressed to his face to stop some bleeding. The man had been shaving at the moment of impact.

Bill Hassett recorded a trip to Hyde Park Oct. 5-11 that included as a passenger young George Elsey, who would eventually join President Truman's speechwriting staff. Roosevelt was preparing for the eventuality of losing to Dewey and had decided to arrange for the movement of his personal papers and files from Washington to Hyde Park.

"I was then on duty at the White House as a Naval aide," Elsey recounted to the author, "and he took me with him ... to inspect the library and to see what changes might have to be made to provide a secure facility to the top-secret materials relating to the war that he had in his White House possession."

Elsey assumed he would be just another passenger on the train. "But ... lo and behold, I was told to go to the president's car," he said, "and I found myself the only passenger in the *Ferdinand Magellan* with FDR himself, which was quite an experience for a young Naval Reserve lieutenant."

Elsey explained that there was "nothing momentous" about the trip. "I boarded before he did ... he came along shortly thereafter and asked if I cared for a drink. We had one drink [in the lounge], and then he said 'It's time to go to bed' and that was it." [129]

Elsey said he and the president

didn't have breakfast on the train. They disembarked at Highland, N.Y., motored to Hyde Park and ate in the Roosevelt mansion. The Naval aide finished his work in a few days and returned to Washington on regular trains ahead of the president.

Roosevelt's second 1944 campaign trip departed from the underground Bureau terminal at 10:30 Thursday night, Oct. 26. As was the custom, it traveled in two sections until it reached Alexandria Jct.—the rear three cars from the Bureau siding and the front 10 cars from Union Station—where they were combined. The rear section was retrieved from the Bureau siding by a PRR engine and forwarded from Anacostia Jct. to Alexandria Jct. by B&O P-5 Pacific 5209. The front 10 cars were brought from Union Station's lower level track 30 to Alexandria Jct. by B&O passenger diesel 59.

A 15-page B&O transportation order survives from this trip, listing instructions only for the Washington-Philadelphia portion of the journey. Preserved by its flagman, C.C. Bredehoeft, its detailed explanation of the combining of the sections at Alexandria Jct. and a rest stop at Aikin, Md.,—73 miles farther up the line—from 1:31 to 10:15 a.m., reveals the depth of its detail.

"On arrival of head portion of train, it will be pulled east of Riverdale station siding switch on No. 2 track, stopping with the rear end 200 feet east of siding switch. Rear portion of train from Anacostia Jct. will be crossed out to No. 2 (two) main track at Alexandria Jct. tower to Riverdale, stopping with rear of engine clearing siding switch. Engine 5209 will be detached and backed into station siding to clear. Diesel yard engine from Washington Yard will be stationed in eastbound passing siding west of east leg of wye and after passage of rear portion of special from Anacostia Jct.,

will cross out to No. 2 track and follow this train carefully to Riverdale where it will couple to rear of train and then couple these three cars to head portion of train. Required air test will then be made by road engine.

"On arrival at Aikin, special train will pull into the eastward passing siding and stop east of station siding switch. Assistant Trainmaster Miller will locate at point cab of engine is to stop, identifying himself with white flag. Relief engine with buffer coach attached to east end of engine will be located in eastward station siding clear of eastward switch, and after special train stops, will couple carefully to rear of train, and after proper air test is made, pull train westwardly back into station siding to west end of tangent track, after which relief engine and buffer coach will be detached from train and move west three car-lengths and remain in that location until departure of special." [50]

After a stop at Wilmington, Del., and a day-long tour of Philadelphia, the president returned to the latter city's B&O station and was off for Chicago at 10:15 Friday night. The train was transferred to the Reading Railroad at Eastwick, then to the Pennsylvania Railroad at Grays Ferry for its trip west.

"All hands slept late, since our first platform stop was at Fort Wayne, Ind., at 1:30 p.m. (Saturday)," Hassett noted. "When I raised my curtain, we were passing through a monotonous prairie country and presently went through Mansfield, Ohio. It was interesting to see here and there little groups or individuals outside their homes who knew the president was passing."[166]

As the flat Ohio farmland whizzed past his window, the president slept through the clacking of typewriters. He had called his speechwriters together once he had left

Philadelphia and said he wanted thorough revisions on the speech he had given there touting the Allies' military successes and statistics.

Sam Rosenman was fearful. The revised speech had not been checked for corrected figures. He had left a draft with his associate at the White House, Isador Lubin, with orders to recheck everything. Lubin sent the corrections directly to Rosenman via the Army Signal Corps car on the train. Longer messages were sent by telegraph and placed aboard the train as it passed various stations.

"Lube's" corrections were formidable. Rosenman fired back questions of his own. The trip to Chicago required a night and a day, but Lubin was awake during every minute of it. Two fresh drafts were typed before the president registered his approval.

The train slowed down through Lima, the nearest it came to a stop in Ohio. A nice crowd assembled below the station platform in Fort Wayne, Ind., where a stand had been erected to allow the president to address the people. Then it was on to Chicago, where the train pulled onto a track in the Dearborn Station yard at 6 p.m. on a bitterly cold and windy Saturday evening. Outside Roosevelt's window, plumes of steam from other trains rose tall and railroad men were boxing their ears—the temperature was 14 above.

The president rested until it was time to go to Soldier Field, only 10 minutes' ride from where the train was parked on Illinois Central tracks.

"Outside the field was an enormous crowd," Miss Tully wrote. Within Soldier Field Stadium was a crowd said to be 110,000—the capacity of the place—with, it was estimated, twice that number outside ... the largest crowd, it was said, ever addressed in person by one speaker—surely the largest the Boss ever faced." The president said later he was in "a difficult spot."[166] The auto ramp from which he spoke was at least a city block away from the nearest spectators; he had an uphill fight trying to appeal personally to such a throng.

Things were a bit laid back the next day as the train hurried back eastward.

"No reason to get up this morning and all remained in their bunks," Hassett recorded. "Passed through a dreary and desolate countryside as we moved [on B&O] toward Clarksburg [W.Va.]—wretched hutches for human dwellings, not much different than those which shelter cows and horses from the weather. Reached Clarksburg at 12:30—Louis Johnson's [secretary of defense 1949-50 under Truman] home town. Louis and some West Virginia politicians came aboard and stood around the president while he spoke from the rear platform to a large crowd— 10,000 or 15,000—on trees, a rather wordy discourse inspired by the hillsides he had been watching during the forenoon journey."[166]

The candidate's last campaign trip was a swing through New England, climaxing with a speech in what he called "cold, roast Boston."[415] He arrived there without incident on Saturday, Nov. 4, but was delayed an hour and 15 minutes past his scheduled 10 p.m. departure to Hyde Park. To turn the long train after it had arrived, the Boston & Albany had had to pull it in reverse from Beacon Park Yard 11 miles back out to Riverside, then return it to Beacon Park via the Highland Branch through Newton and Brookline.

The problem was that there were engine restrictions on the branch; NYC passenger rep Herb Harwood said one of B&A's suburban tank engines was used. It was probably one of the 400-series heavy 4-6-6T types, but the train still proved too much for the struggling switcher and it became

bogged down. When FDR's advance men arrived back at Beacon Park and wanted to know where the train was, a red-faced officer reluctantly confessed that it was in the Chestnut Hill section of Brookline. Harwood's diary noted only that the train was turned "with delay," and explained—somewhat cryptically—that Dewey Long was "mad, as president just made it after being held up by radio."[165] Roosevelt's aides had made as much of the situation as they could—they used the delay as an excuse to parade their boss around a few more areas of Boston in his open touring sedan to the delight of the local populace.

Roosevelt won the election— again. Now in his fourth term, he departed secretly on Monday night, Jan. 22, 1945, for a historic summit with Churchill and Soviet Premier Josef Stalin at Yalta in the Crimea. The president quietly boarded his train for the Norfolk Navy Yard at Newport News, Va., where he boarded the cruiser *U.S.S. Quincy* for the trip across the Atlantic. "Few have been told the place of the meeting," Hassett fumed, "and I am not among that limited number."[166]

At precisely 10 p.m., the president was wheeled out of the White House to his limousine. He was wearing his old gray campaign hat and his dark flowing Navy cape. Once inside the well-lighted *Magellan* with shades drawn, the president told his conductor he wanted to "go slow."[42]

At 10:47 the private car began to move, and shortly two big steam engines were rocking down RF&P rails toward the C&O at Doswell, Va., and the connection for Newport News. The president slept well.

It was still dark at 6:25 a.m. Tuesday when the train slid under the covered Pier Six. Perhaps the brakes squealed a little, because several passengers awoke and raised their shades to view the long gray silhouette of the

Quincy. A deck crew in blues and pea-jackets stood at attention near the starboard gangway. Someone slipped off the train and advised officers of the vessel that the president was still asleep and might not disembark for an hour or two. He slept until sunup, while others aboard were having breakfast. He finally emerged, smiling, surprised to see the track was depressed so that the cruiser's two-stage loading ramp fitted precisely to the *Magellan's* rear platform.

Thus his wheelchair could glide effortlessly onto the quarterdeck. After proper introductions and handshakes, but no formal honors at FDR's request, the *Quincy* sailed at 8 a.m.

The president was filled with grief when he returned to the United States on Tuesday night, Feb. 27. Maj. Gen. Edwin "Pa" Watson, his close friend and adviser for years, had suffered a stroke as the *Quincy* started home and died two days out of Algiers. The loss seemed to affect him deeply and accelerate his own physical decline.

When Navy tugs shoved the *Quincy's* port side against Pier Six, two admirals came aboard. Roosevelt invited them and two or three others to a farewell dinner on the *Magellan*. Muffled in his Navy cape and huddled under the gray fedora, he was wheeled down the *Quincy's* specially built ramp and into the railroad car. He had directed that Watson's body not be transferred until he was on the train.

Arrival in Washington the next morning was muted further by a cold pelting rain. Watson's body was removed in the 14th Street yard, where Mrs. Watson and Eleanor were waiting. Mrs. Roosevelt wanted to see her husband, but was told he was still asleep. That wasn't true. He was up, bathed and dressed, grieving behind lowered shades. He had left word that he would attend Watson's burial service at Arlington National Cemetery at noon, but he

Franklin Roosevelt campaigns at Bridgeport, Conn., Nov. 4, 1944, enroute to what he calls "cold, roast Boston."

didn't want to witness the removal of the casket from the train. On the Bureau siding, he waited until everyone else had left. Then he was carried to his automobile.

The next day, Thursday, March 1, when he reported to Congress on the Yalta summit, he remained in his wheelchair, acknowledging for the first time in public the bothersome weight of his leg braces. He rambled through a long speech, slurring several lengthy ad libs and generally alarming everyone who heard him.

The war was progressing well—

landings had been made on many of the Philippine Islands, the flag had been hoisted over Iwo Jima, and Okinawa had been attacked. The United States First Army was ready to cross the Rhine at Remagen. But Roosevelt seemed increasingly weary. His eyes, in stark contrast to his thinning face, appeared larger. His appetite was fading and at times his mind appeared to be elsewhere.

The presidential party arrived in Washington from Hyde Park Thursday morning, March 29, a few days after heading north. "Hope he

responds to the good air and quiet," Hassett remarked.[166] The plan was to continue to Warm Springs.

When Roosevelt was wheeled into the Oval Office about 11 a.m., Miss Tully hadn't seen him for several days. But she could tell that the respite had failed to erase the fatigue on his face.

"Did you get any rest at Hyde Park, Mr. President?" she asked. "Yes, child, but not nearly enough," he answered. "I shall be glad to get down South."[415]

Shortly after 1, the president went

"over to the house" for lunch and returned at 3 to tackle some mail before catching the train at 4.

"When he was wheeled in, I was so startled I almost burst into tears," Miss Tully said. "In two hours, he seemed to have failed dangerously. His face was ashen, highlighted by the darkening shadows under his eyes and with his cheeks drawn gauntly." [415]

Jonathan Daniels, a press secretary, and Archibald MacLeish, assistant secretary of state, showed the Boss a statement concerning the Soviet demand that it have three votes in the proposed U.N. General Assembly and the U.S. reaction to it. Roosevelt suggested only minor changes in the statement, then turned to a great pile of mail and bills that Miss Tully had laid on his desk.

"I had never had much luck previously in dissuading him from going through this kind of chore," Miss Tully wrote. "He liked to know what people were writing him and he enjoyed answering—but today I knew without any doubt in my mind that he was not up to it. 'Mr. President,' I said gently, 'there is nothing urgent here except the top bill with the red tag on it. Mr. Latta (the executive clerk) said it should be signed today. All the rest can wait until we get down to Warm Springs.'

" 'All right, Grace,' he replied in a quietly grateful tone." [415]

Anna had planned to go south with her father, but had changed her mind. She did see him off, however, and once he was aboard the *Magellan*, she asked Miss Tully to come outside.

"Grace," she said, "I wish you would try to have father work a little bit each day on his mail. If he doesn't, he'll get terribly behind and I think it is good to keep him busy." [42] Miss Tully disagreed but nodded and promised to try to keep things moving, at least slowly.

Despite the chief's appearance,

optimism was in the air; after a rest of more than two weeks, he was scheduled to return to Washington April 18 and leave on the 20th for San Francisco to open the United Nations Conference April 25.

The party was smaller than usual. With the president were cousins Margaret Suckley and Laura Delano, who had come down from Hyde Park; Leighton McCarthy, Canadian ambassador who was a board member of the Warm Springs Foundation and an old friend of FDR's; and "Doc" Basil O'Connor, FDR's former law partner. Of the staff: Grace Tully; her aides Toi Bachelder, a former Warm Springs patient; and Dorothy Brady; Bill Hassett and his secretary, Alice Winegar; and Hackie, the White House switchboard operator.

Dr. Ross McIntire didn't go because of a commitment to testify before a congressional committee in his capacity as surgeon general of the Navy, but he sent a heart specialist, Commander Howard G. Bruenn, in his place.

Regulars Mike Reilly, Dewey Long and Lt. Commander George Fox, Roosevelt's masseur, were aboard. Merriman Smith of United Press, Bob Nixon of the International News Service and Harold Oliver of the Associated Press went along, although no stories would be filed until the return.

Miss Tully brought aboard the 10-car train a big stack of paperwork to be dribbled out to the president in small doses. He had packed his usual leisure-time enjoyments, including his stamp collection, and had sent ahead a box of books to autograph for the Hyde Park library and other repositories.

Just after the train left, Roosevelt suddenly called for Hassett, Miss Tully and Mrs. Brady. It had just occurred to him that the next day would be Good Friday.

"You three are the Catholics

around here," he said. "Don't you think you ought to get off the train at Atlanta and attend services? You can join the rest of us at Warm Springs." [42] The trio exchanged glances. This was the sort of consideration that endeared him to those around him. They took turns explaining that Good Friday is not a Holy Day of Obligation, and it is not compulsory to attend services. In fact, there would be no service at all, except what was called the Three Hours of Devotion—more meditation and prayer than sermon. The president still thought they should go, but didn't insist.

It was apparent he was very tired when he went to bed early without dinner. Prettyman and Reilly helped him get into his pajamas and he fell back on the pillow, nodding to have all lights extinguished except the tiny night light. "Now don't let that engineer set any speed records," he told Reilly. "Tell him to take it easy." [42] Reilly and Prettyman understood the president's wish. They knew he was gaunt and flaccid. He had lost so much weight that there was no longer a cushion of muscle to protect him from pains in his hip bones as the train took curves. For the most part, the trip south was uneventful. "We worked just briefly at some mail," Miss Tully recalled. [415]

The entourage arrived at its destination after lunch on Friday, March 30, 1945. Jim Bishop and Bernard Asbell beautifully described the scene in their books *FDR's Last Year* and *When FDR Died.* Warm Springs was a typical sleepy southern town of 600. The crowd that collected around the station in little congealed groups and stared down the long, curving single track could see the faint green grass growing in the ballast. On a hill overlooking the left side of the track, the wisteria was fading from long arching fingers of yellow to green. They weren't tourists, they were old friends who saw their first citizen only once or twice a year. Dr. Neal Kitchens, 80, smiled as he stared around the curve. He had once entertained Roosevelt at dinner. Ruth Stevens, manager of the whitewashed hotel across the track, wiped her hands on an apron and hung it up. The salesmen had been fed their lunch; the dishes were done. She would watch for the train. Frank Allcorn, the hotel's owner and mayor of Warm Springs, took his place along the right of way. A woman turned the key in her ladies' emporium and locked it for the day. The Methodist minister stuck his long legs out of his old car and said, "Well, he's here again." [42] A car almost hit Mabel Irwin, wife of a doctor. She had to park a few blocks away and had hurried down the street, fearful she'd be late. Turnley Walker, a patient at the foundation, watched from his wheelchair. Minnie Bulloch hurried to the little gabled railroad station, which still sported "white" and "colored" waiting rooms. Inside, Agent C.A. Pless sat, jetting tobacco juice into a can. The man who was coming was his old friend.

At 3 p.m., Pless lowered the crossing gates and stood at trackside. The flasher signals blinked red; and a steel hammer hit a bell repeatedly. The several dozen or so "old friends" pressed closer without crushing for space like tourists do. A boy with his bare foot on a rail announced Roosevelt was close by just as a black plume shot to the sky from around the hill. The big green Southern locomotives eased by the depot, hissing and squealing. As the train lumbered past, an iron-wheeled cart waited where the second baggage car would stop. As the *Magellan* came into view, barely moving and then stopping, clerks along the main street hurried out of their stores to watch. Distinguished-looking passengers began to disembark; the Secret Service got off the *Magellan* and

fanned out into an ellipse. They peered suspiciously outward, seeing a sea of smiles. The rear door opened and a wheelchair emerged. "There he is," they whispered. "That's him." [42] Prettyman pushed the Boss onto the elevator and slowly it lowered him to ground level. Reilly ordered two agents to open a path to the big car 10 feet away. Everyone gawked. This is where he always waved. He didn't. Those closest saw a figure slumped in a wheelchair, a gray hat pulled over his eyes. The old friends waved; the figure's hands stayed clasped on his lap. Pless pushed his way through for a closer look. "Just like setting up a dead man," he muttered. [42]

Ruth Stevens grabbed Merriman Smith when he swung down from another car. "Honey, is he all right?" she asked. "Tired to death," Smith responded. "But he'll pull out of it. He always does." [42]

Reilly reached down into the wheelchair as he had done for years. The auto's back door was open; the jump seat was waiting. Roosevelt had always reached back to the door with both arms, and, as Reilly held him, yanked his body toward the door and onto the jump seat. Then, with a twist, he would swing himself onto the back seat. This time Reilly tugged. There was no response. He strained and puffed, barely able to get the president up. He had to be lifted into the seat. "I never remember him being that heavy," Reilly said. [42]

Mayor Allcorn stepped up. "Welcome home, Mr. President."[42] The gaunt face, half covered by his fedora, came up. "Why," said the soft voice, the face tilting into a smile, "His Honor the Mayor." [42] He lifted a palsied hand to move the hat upward but missed and struck his pince-nez. The glasses fell off, an agent picked them up and FDR impatiently pinched them back in place. He extended his hand feebly to the

mayor.

His gray eyes scanned the crowd, stopping on the face of Dr. Kitchens. There was a flash of recognition that quickly faded. The doc turned toward home. Mabel Irwin stepped forward and took FDR's hand in both of hers. "I saw you back there, Mabel," gesturing in the direction from which the train had come. "I was looking out of the train and I saw you in your old Buick—back there along Raleigh Road," he smiled. "I guess the old eyes aren't so bad." She had not been back there. She stepped away, swallowing repeatedly.

The motorcade crossed the track and disappeared on the lower dirt road toward the Little White House atop Pine Mountain two miles away, where he remained for the rest of the day. "Hope he gets the rest which he so much needs," Hassett wrote.[166]

Roosevelt's train was returned the 80 miles back to Atlanta the day after he arrived. With instructions to be ready for the return trip, Pullman Conductor Walter Brooks and all Pullman crew members except the president's attendant, Walter E. Lupura, Porter Fred Fair and two service inspectors returned to Washington and reported for their regular runs. The train was cleaned, inspected and restocked, except for ice, in Atlanta. Charlie Hicks, Pullman yard foreman, inspected the train every day, testing all lights and other equipment, going so far as to take the gravity readings of the batteries, to be sure nothing went wrong. Fair and the waiter, E.C. Calloway, who remained with the *Magellan* wherever it was when away from Washington, cleaned and dusted each day. Ready to go almost at a moment's notice, the train stood in the yard for nearly three weeks without anyone but a handful of Southern Railway and Pullman Company officials and employees knowing it was there while Georgia's

President Roosevelt offers one of his trademark hearty waves during a campaign stop.

adopted son was at the Little White House.

Hassett collared Dr. Bruenn during their first evening in Warm Springs for a talk about the president's health. "He is slipping away from us," Hassett predicted, "and no earthly power can keep him here."

"Why do you think so?" Bruenn asked.

"I told him I understood his position," Hassett wrote, "his obligation to save life, not to admit defeat. Then I reminded him that I gave him the same warning when we were here last December. He remembered. I said: 'I know you don't want to make the admission and I have talked this way to no one else save one. To all the staff, to the family, and with the Boss himself I have maintained the bluff;

but I am convinced that there is no help for him.'"[166]

Both men were on the verge of emotional upset. Bruenn guessed Hassett had talked to "Doc" O'Connor. Hassett told Bruenn that both of them had given up hope before the election.

The Boss was indifferent after the convention, as if he didn't care who won the election. Only after Dewey's vicious attacks did he get "his dutch up"[166] and come out swinging. "I could not but notice his increasing weariness as I handled his papers with him," Hassett lamented, "particularly at Hyde Park, trip after trip. He was always willing to go through the day's routine, but there was less and less talk about all manner of things—fewer local Hyde Park stories, politics,

books, pictures. I mentioned his feeble signature—the old boldness of stroke and liberal use of ink gone, signature often ending in a fade-out. The old zest was going."[166]

Hassett and Bruenn said goodnight with heavy hearts. Soon the nation would join them.

Franklin Roosevelt departed Washington Sept. 1, 1944, for a Labor Day weekend at Hyde Park by a strange route that was never repeated: PRR-Phillipsburg-Lehigh & Hudson River-Maybrook, N.Y.-NYNH&H. No one knew the reason for the detour, even when the train paused all day at Allamuchy, N.J., on the L&HR.

As the train rocked along out of Washington that night, those aboard who stayed up late to play cards noticed they were not on the regular B&O route. In the morning, with the sun barely up, they eased to a stop on a rusty siding that appeared to be in the middle of nowhere. An auto pulled up alongside the *Ferdinand Magellan*, and a few minutes later a clean-shaven FDR descended from the private car on his elevator. A few on the train were jolted awake by the stop and glanced at the station sign. "Where ... is Allamuchy?"[42] they wondered, assuming there was a hotbox or some other minor problem. With Secret Service agents trotting alongside, the president's auto followed a sleepy country road to a huge gate leading to a snow-white mansion.

The real reason for the stop went back a long way. Eleanor Roosevelt had employed Lucy Page Mercer as a social secretary during the winter of 1913-14. She was an efficient worker and a charming person, and, as they say, one thing led to another. Miss Mercer and the president became involved romantically, and had quite a thing going until Eleanor found some of their correspondence in 1918 and confronted her errant husband. He promised to break it off, but didn't. He nurtured the relationship down through the years,

even after Lucy married wealthy industrialist Winthrop Rutherfurd. He saw her whenever he could; he even invited her to the White House when Eleanor was away, with the quiet cooperation of the children and staff. Now Lucy's husband was dead, and even though she lived most of the time on his estate in Aiken, S.C., today she was staying at their home named Tranquillity—in Allamuchy. The president was stopping over to see his girlfriend! Imagine keeping a secret like this—with the press on board—these days!

The president entered the building; those with him remained outside. Agent Howard Anderson guarded the front gate, Jim Griffith was told to watch the rear entrance. The train became hotter and hotter. The engineer and fireman stood beside their locomotive and told newsmen they had no idea why the train had been stopped. "Orders."[42] That's all.

Noon arrived, and luncheon was served. The afternoon was slow and distressing. Some said it was cooler to sit in the shade of the old railroad station and hope for a breeze across the beautiful countryside; others remained tieless and shoeless on the train. It was a long day.

Those who knew what was going on protected the president's privacy. "I can distinctly remember taking a walk with Bill Hassett," NYC's Herb Harwood wrote. "(Hassett's) exact words: 'Now isn't this just like this great man with all the affairs of state will take the time to come here to see his less fortunate relatives and help with their financial matters?' "[165] Harwood found out the real reason for the stop [25] years later and concluded that the coy Hassett intentionally misled him. Dewey

Long explained the stop by saying that the president wanted to visit some old friends on his way to Hyde Park."[224]

Finally, in midafternoon, Roosevelt's car came over a rise with Secret Service men on the running boards. The train departed for Poughkeepsie, the president anticipating questions from his wife when she met the train and noticed it was coming from an unusual direction. Wartime security requires varying the route, he would tell her.

At 5 p.m., long after the president had departed, Lucy Rutherfurd took a walk in her back yard. She noticed a man sitting in the wicker rocker.

"Are you part of the president's party?" she asked. "Yes," he said, standing. "Well," she said, smiling, "they all left about an hour ago."[42]

Agent Griffith uttered a polite farewell and ran, fuming, to the front of the house. They had indeed left him behind. It would take him the rest of the evening to catch up with the train.

Hassett scribbled two pages about the visit in his diary, then destroyed them, leaving only an all-business analysis of the detour.

"Told the president the Secret Service satisfied with the Pennsylvania-Lehigh route, especially so as an alternative to exclusive use of the B&O, which we have used exclusively for more than two years to avoid the hazards of Hell Gate Bridge. Besides appeasing the Pennsylvania system, travel by this route would do away with a switching charge of $100 at Anacostia Jct. He said he would consider it; but he still wants another trip over Hell Gate—said he didn't believe the bridge would be blown up during his transit."[166]

A passenger in Franklin Roosevelt's party mugs for the camera in Allamuchy, N.J., while two colleagues relax on the Ferdinand Magellan's *brass railing.*

Members of the presidential party stretch their legs during Franklin Roosevelt's clandestine stopover at Allamuchy, N.J., Sept. 1, 1944, to see his lady friend, Lucy Rutherfurd.

Left: *What is there to do in Allamuchy, N.J., while the president is off romping around some estate up the road? Take a walk and chat with old friends, we guess. The man on right may be Meriman Smith of United Press.*

Press representatives and presidential aides kill time around the Ferdinand Magellan's *rear platform while they try to figure out what Franklin Roosevelt is up to a little ways up the road.*

President Harry S. Truman shakes hands with B&O engineer Harry Beltz after riding in his locomotive cab for about an hour in the Pittsburgh area Oct. 27, 1952, during his lame-duck campaign for Adlai Stevenson against Dwight D. Eisenhower.

The Golden Era Matures

Truman's Whistlestopping

Harry S. Truman

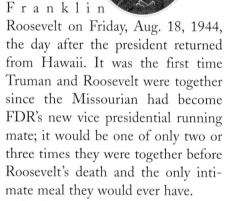

The fact that Democrat Harry Truman used trains during his national political campaigns—and traveled 77,170 miles by rail while in the White House—can be traced to a luncheon date he had with Franklin Roosevelt on Friday, Aug. 18, 1944, the day after the president returned from Hawaii. It was the first time Truman and Roosevelt were together since the Missourian had become FDR's new vice presidential running mate; it would be one of only two or three times they were together before Roosevelt's death and the only intimate meal they would ever have.

As they munched on roast sardines on toast, a salad of peas, beans, tomatoes and asparagus and pickled clingstone peaches under the Jackson magnolia tree on the White House lawn, Truman became worried. It was one of Roosevelt's bad days; he looked terrible, his hand shook so badly he couldn't get the cream in his coffee, and he talked with difficulty.

"Physically, he's just going to pieces,"[100] Truman thought. They hardly discussed campaign strategy, let alone conduct of the war. Truman was told nothing about the Manhattan Project, which was at that moment developing the first atomic bomb. Just one directive was given.

"I want you to do some campaigning," Truman said Roosevelt told him.

"I don't feel like going everywhere.

"All right," Truman said he answered. "I'll make some plane reservations to go around over the country anywhere you want me to go."[255]

"Don't fly; ride the train," Truman said the president told him. "Can't both of us afford to take chances." Other sources add that FDR also gruffed "one of us has to stay alive"[100] or "this time we may need you"[42] as if he knew how precarious his health was.

So Truman launched his campaign by rail. He had already been armed with a taste of the benefits of such a time-honored contact with the people just after he and Roosevelt won the election. Truman was returning to Washington from his home in Independence, Mo., after the convention that nominated him. He wrote back to his daughter, Margaret—with a touch of panic—about an interesting encounter with Tom Dewey, the Republican presidential candidate, in St. Louis. "I was going into the Union Station to take the B&O as Dewey came out," Truman told his daughter. "There were not 10 people there to meet him. More people came and spoke to your dad accidentally than came to meet Mr. Dewey on purpose. That can't be so good … This little 'deestric attorney' will try to hit me by being nasty to my family. You must remember that I never wanted or went after the nomination, but now that we have it … we must win and make 'em like it. Maybe your dad can make a job out of the fifth-wheel office. …"[100]

Truman campaigned aboard two Pullman cars attached to regular trains. He and his staff rode the

Pullman private car *Henry Stanley*; the other was reserved for the press. The Democrats won; but Truman was vice president for only 82 days before FDR died and the Missourian inherited the White House.

The first rail trip Truman made back to his home state as president took place in March 1946 when he took Winston Churchill—then between terms as Great Britain's prime minister—to Fulton, Mo., to speak at Westminster College.

The appointment came about after Franc McCluer, president—and graduate—of the tiny school, visited one of his old classmates, Brig. Gen. Harry Vaughan, a White House military aide. Dr. McCluer, who was nicknamed "Bullet" because Vaughan said his 5-foot frame was shaped like a projectile, wanted Churchill, whose Conservative party was then the opposition back home, to speak as part of the school's John Findley Green lecture series. Vaughan took McCluer in to see Truman. The general read him a letter of invitation to Churchill that McCluer had prepared, and the president penciled on the bottom of it: "This is a fine old school out in my state. If you come and make a speech there, I'll take you out and introduce you."[100]

"We all were rather amused at it—the chances of his getting Churchill there," presidential special counsel Clark Clifford told the author years later. "We thought they were about one in a million. But it struck President Truman as being very intelligent. He wanted to know Churchill better. He had met him at the Potsdam Conference … but [that visit] was cut short because of an elec-

Presidential aide Brig. Gen. Harry Vaughan peeps between his boss, Harry Truman, and British Prime Minister Winston Churchill as the world leaders prepare to depart Washington for Fulton, Mo., March 3, 1946, where Churchill will deliver his historic "Iron Curtain" speech.

tion that had been held back in Great Britain in which Winston Churchill had lost. So Churchill had to leave the Potsdam Conference and his successor [Labour's Clement Attlee] came and took his place."[84]

Truman sent the letter on to London. "Churchill wrote right back," Clifford recounted, "and said it was a capital idea and he accepted and he came on over."[84]

The president wanted to make the trip by train, Clifford explained, to give the two more time to visit: "The plane trip only took two and a half hours or so. He couldn't get much of a visit that way."[84] Truman also scheduled a speech for himself on their return, before the Federal Council of the Churches of Christ in Columbus, Ohio.

Government and railroad officials showing up at Washington's Union Station an hour ahead of departure—at 2 p.m. on Monday, March 3—

found a glistening B&O diesel, No. 68, ahead of 10 sparkling cars. Steps on every one of them had been given a special coat of white paint.

"Up and down the length of the train, B&O, Washington Terminal and Pullman employees buzzed with last-minute activity," Virginia Tanner wrote for the *Baltimore & Ohio Magazine*. "Between tight-lipped Secret Service men standing guard alongside the train, car inspectors darted in and out, making their final check of journals. Truckloads of ice were put on. Baggage arrived, and J.A. Hodges, district mail, baggage and express agent, was ready—with space diagrams in hand—to direct porters in placing every piece of it."[377]

More than 60 press, radio and newsreel men began claiming their spaces, and photographers took their positions behind the *Ferdinand Magellan*—standing on boxes pyramid-style—to await Truman and

Churchill. Finally, a long White House limousine with Secret Service men hanging all over it swept into view, coming straight across the concourse and stopping almost at the steps of the private car. Truman stepped out, sporting a black Chesterfield overcoat and gray hat; Churchill stepped forth dressed smartly in black, clenching his customary black cigar between his fingers. Greeting them and other members of the presidential party was veteran presidential Pullman Conductor Walter Brooks, with pressed uniform and polished buttons.

The distinguished travelers got no farther than the back platform when the photographers shouted for them to stop. "Right there, Mr. President, if you please! Let us get you there! Make the 'V' sign, Mr. Churchill!" The world leaders complied good-naturedly for several minutes before ducking inside.

As soon as they were settled in the lounge, the B&O's Dan Moorman and George Drescher, head of the Secret Service, brought B&O President Roy B. White aboard, who wished them a nice trip and pointed out that inscribed copies of Edward Hungerford's 1927 history of the railroad had been placed aboard for each of them as mementos of the trip.

As soon as the train pulled out, Truman had drinks served to his guests in the sitting room, Clifford recalled. "As was his wont, Churchill drank scotch with water, but no ice, which he viewed as a barbaric American custom."[85]

Truman turned to his guest and said, "Mr. Churchill, we are going to be together on this train for some time. I don't want to rest on formality, so I would ask you to call me 'Harry.'"

The former prime minister agreed, but only if Truman would call him "Winston." It was agreed.[85]

Moorman asked Drescher if he

President Truman shakes hands with well-wishers in St. Louis Union Station on the morning of March 5, 1946, as he escorts British Prime Minister Winston Churchill to Fulton, Mo., for Churchill's "Iron Curtain" speech.

thought the president would enjoy a ride in the locomotive. Moments later, much to the surprise of press people getting settled in the cars ahead, the smiling president came through, poking his head into open compartments in the sleepers, halting at tables in the diner, greeting old friends all around with folksy pleasantries and earthy banter. Photographers grabbed their cameras and reporters reached for their notebooks, joining the procession.

In the club car, the door opened and Truman entered briskly as two reporters were having a drink. "Don't get up," he cracked. "I'm just making an inspection of the train to see if there's any gambling going on"[280] It didn't take long to find some.

On he moved through the swaying car, followed by Vaughan, Moorman and Drescher. At the other end, United Press' Merriman Smith was playing poker with several of his buddies as soft-spoken waiters darted from table to table with highballs and sandwiches.

"It was a crucial moment at our table," Smith explained. "The man across from me had an ace showing and was raising heavily. I had kings back to back and, with the occult ability found only in poker players, was about to decide that he had aces paired and that I was wasting my money."

At that moment a soft voice came over his shoulder. "Why don't you raise him?" the voice asked. When Smith whirled around to caution his uninvited adviser to mind his own business, he stared into the face of a grinning president. Then Smith remembered. This chief executive wasn't confined by paralysis to the rear car. He dropped his hand and fumbled for his notebook.[358]

Up in the cab of the 68, Engineer James L. Rock got the surprise of his life when someone asked him if he would mind giving his seat to the president for a few minutes. While Rock applied the air for a slow order, Truman was helped along the catwalk inside the diesel units' engine rooms.

"Here's your seat, Mr. President,"[377] Rock said as Truman entered the cab. Beaming like a 10-year-old, he sat down and put his hand on the throttle. Rock stood over his shoulder to make sure he did the right thing. The president was at the controls for five tingling minutes, watching the rails vanish under him at 60 miles an hour. Photographers crowded around; they must have asked Truman to switch sides for better light because surviving pictures show the president's gloved hand on the cab heater switch while seated on the fireman's side of the locomotive.

After Truman started back to the *Magellan*, Moorman asked him how he liked the diesel. "I think I'll buy the thing,"[377] he beamed happily. Stopping under a pin-up of a half-naked beauty in communications combine 1401, he grinned and told Signal Corps personnel "That's a good prop."[280]

Meanwhile, Churchill remained in the *Magellan*, putting finishing touch-

WIDE WORLD/TRUMAN LIBRARY

Press photographers told the world they snapped pictures of Harry Truman "at the controls" of his B&O special as it raced through southwestern Ohio on the way home from Fulton, Mo., March 5, 1946. What they did not reveal, however, was that the president was seated on the fireman's side of the cab and he had his gloved hand on the heater switch.

Former British Prime Minister Winston Churchill makes sure his hat is on straight as he and President Harry S. Truman leave their train at Jefferson City, Mo., enroute to Fulton for the P.M.'s speech. The ever-vigilant B&O patrolman Ernest Chapman, below, keeps an eye on the crowd.

Churchill had expressed a desire to see Barbara Frietchie's home and challenged Roosevelt to recite John Greenleaf Whittier's poem about the Union heroine's defiance of Jackson. When FDR couldn't, Churchill did, in full. He repeated the challenge to Truman and received the same response.

So Churchill repeated the literary feat for his delighted audience: "Up from the meadows rich with corn,/Clear in the cool September morn,/The clustered spires of Frederick stand/Green-walled by the hills of Maryland," he began, with perfect British diction.

The quiet resolve with which Churchill spoke the line that most people remember, "Shoot if you must this old gray head,/But spare your country's flag,' she said," crescendoed into a dramatic fervor when he got to Jackson's response: " 'Who touches a hair of yon gray head/Dies like a dog! March on!' he said."[439] Truman nodded with enjoyment.

The discussion turned to affairs of state. The president confided in his guest that he would soon return the body of Mehmet Munir Ertegun, Turkish ambassador to the United States, to Turkey aboard the battleship *USS Missouri*. Ertegun, who died in 1944, had been buried at Arlington National Cemetery until the war was won and his body could be shipped home. Truman further explained that the battleship would be accompanied by a Naval task force that would remain in the Sea of Marmara indefinitely to impress the Soviets with the importance America attached to Greece and Turkey. Churchill was gratified that Truman had shared this with a "private citizen"[85] and although the president didn't know it, the promised show of force fit right in with the Briton's speech theme at Fulton.

Finally, Truman succumbed to the

es on his speech. When the president rejoined his guest, Churchill was still hard at work. So his host practiced his Columbus speech for a while on a dictating-recording machine. Finally Churchill's press relations man got the Missouri manuscript away from his boss so he could mimeograph it. Then the two notables began to relax and enjoy the scenery.

Crowds were gathered along the right of way. Schoolchildren carrying American flags were lined up with their teachers, and more than one school band could be heard serenading the president with the "Missouri Waltz."

The former prime minister startled and delighted Truman with his intimate knowledge of American history. When the president told his guest they were passing through Harpers Ferry, W.Va., Churchill replied, "I know. That's where (Gen. Stonewall) Jackson seized (Gen. George) McClellan's stores." [389]

He then recalled for the party seated in the *Magellan's* lounge that he had once made a motor trip with President and Mrs. Roosevelt to Shangri-la (the presidential retreat now called Camp David near Thurmont, Md.) during which the party drove through Frederick.

temptation to read Churchill's speech, even though he had intended not to so he wouldn't have to say he had endorsed or approved it in advance. It was a brilliant and an admirable statement, Clark Clifford said his boss told Churchill, and would "create quite a stir."[85] It also presented the president with a dilemma; he was not ready to take such a hard line against Stalin although events of the next year and a half would prove Churchill correct. "Still hoping to keep open channels of communication with Stalin, the president instructed me to put into his introduction of Churchill some positive words about Stalin that might make this possible," Clifford wrote later.[85]

The chief executive assigned Vaughan to keep Churchill supplied with his favorite liquid refreshment, Margaret Truman learned later. "When the general delivered the first drink," she wrote, "Mr. Churchill held it up to the light and said, 'When I was a young subaltern in the South African war, the water was not fit to drink. To make it more palatable, we had to add whiskey. By diligent effort I learned to like it.'"[100]

He must have applied himself to his studies. Before dinner, the portly Briton downed his customary five Scotch highballs.

Perhaps it was this trip that a railroad detective referred to when he recalled some time later being taken in to Churchill and introduced to him by Scotland Yard's Inspector Thompson. "Would you like some whiskey?" asked Churchill. The detective replied that he couldn't drink on duty, but after Churchill put in his order, two drinks arrived. The detective noted the extra drink and reminded his host again that liquor was not for him while on duty. Churchill looked up from his chair, took off his glasses and growled amiably, "And who the 'ell said it was yours?"[138]

B&O dining car Supervisor R.E. Dasch, Steward D.T. Rusch and their staff of chefs, cooks and waiters took care of the distinguished party's culinary needs. Reporters chuckled when they learned that the men feeding Truman and Churchill their steaks were named "Dasch" and "Rusch," and asked if the Russian-sounding names meant anything.

As they were going to dinner, Truman showed Churchill the redesigned presidential seal on the wall of the *Magellan*. "This may interest you," he said. "We have just turned the eagle's head from the talons of war to the olive branch of peace."[85] Churchill studied the seal a moment, then dryly suggested that the head be on a swivel so that it could turn either way depending on the occasion. Then he teased that the berries on the olive branch looked like atomic bombs to him.

In several compartments up ahead, typewriters clattered out the story of the journey as it unfolded. When the speedy special took the Patterson Creek cutoff around Cumberland, Md., and stopped at Keyser, W.Va., for its first crew change, stories and dozens of rolls of film tagged with captions were handed off to Western Union representatives, who dispatched them all around the nation. Truman spent the short stop chatting on the back platform. Even on this trip, he was a politician. At several stops, he was spotted waving from a window of the *Magellan*.

Churchill's speech, titled "The Sinews of Peace,"[386b] made history the next day. He called for a strong British-American alliance to protect freedom from an "Iron Curtain"[85] that had descended across Europe "from Stettin in the Baltic to Trieste in the Adriatic," thus adding a powerful phrase to the language that held sway for more than 45 years. Its import was sinking in for members of the press even as they scanned advance copies finally placed in their hands.

Tristram Coffin, CBS news analyst, was at his typewriter immediately. "How's this for a starter?" he asked a group standing nearby as he read from the typewritten sheet: "It was an eerie feeling to be racing through the night as our train sped westward, knowing that the contents of this speech would produce charges and countercharges around the world on the morrow!"[377]

After dinner, the presidential party settled in for a good game of poker. "Churchill said he read in the press that he knew that President Truman had played poker," Clifford recalled. "The president said, 'Yes, I've played a good deal of poker.' Churchill said, 'I learned to play poker in the Boer War.' The president said, 'Well, that's been a good long time ago.' And so Churchill said, 'You think there's any possibility, Mr. President, on this trip, that we might play some poker?' The president said, 'I can guarantee it.'"[84]

Sure enough, right after dinner, the attendant began putting a green baize cover on the dining room table. Churchill excused himself and the president turned to his aides—Clifford, Press Secretary Charlie Ross, Gen. Vaughan and Col. Wallace Graham, Truman's doctor. "Men, we have an important task ahead of us," the president announced. "This man has been playing poker for more than 40 years. He is cagey, he loves cards and is probably an excellent player. The reputation of American poker is at stake, and I expect every man to do his duty."[85]

Churchill returned dressed in his famous World War II zippered blue siren suit and the six men squared off for the game. The tart-tongued Briton soon had the poker-playing Missourians doubled up with such comments as "I think I'll risk a few shillings on a pair of knaves," Margaret Truman wrote.[100] To him, a straight was a "sequence."[85] The

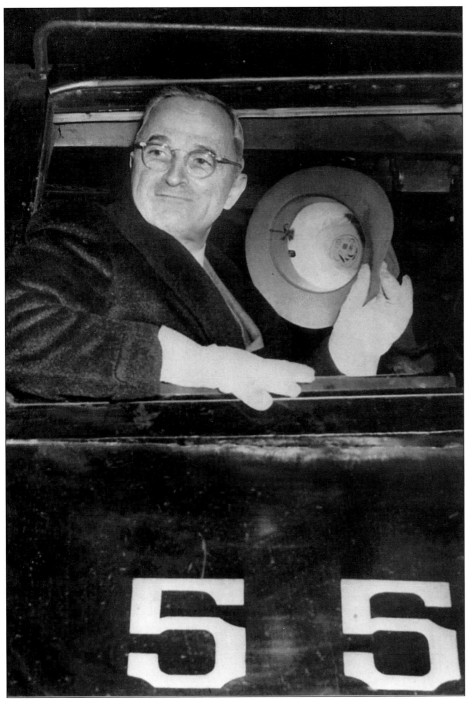

Harry Truman poses in a locomotive cab before leaving Chicago April 7, 1946, after an Army Day speech at Soldier Field.

British terminology kept Vaughan busy stifling a belly laugh. "It turned out after a while that Churchill was not a very good poker player," Clifford remembered. "So about halfway through the evening, why, he excused himself to go to the men's room and the president leaned over and counted his chips and turned to the rest of us and said, 'Men, you're not being very kind to our guest. He's lost $350.'" Gen. Vaughan spoke up and said, 'Well, boss, there isn't anything we can do about it,' he says. 'This guy is a pigeon—and,' he said, 'before we're through with this game, we're going to have his underclothes.' And the president said, 'Well, we can't do that; we've got to be nice to him,'"[84] and directed his companions to engage in what Vaughan called "customer poker."[85]

"Everybody eased off," Clifford laughed.[84] "Churchill 'won' some splendid pots, lost some others. At one point, I dropped out of a hand of stud poker, and noticed that Charlie Ross, who was sitting next to me, had an ace showing and an ace in the hole. I watched Ross raise Churchill and raise him again. Churchill, with only a jack showing, stayed right with him. Then, at the end, Churchill bet a substantial amount of money, perhaps a hundred dollars, right into this ace. Charlie studied what he knew had to be a winning hand, with its two aces, looked over at the president, gave what I thought sounded like a sigh, and folded.

"When the dust had settled and we tallied up, Churchill had lost about $250. He had enjoyed himself thoroughly, but he had dropped just enough money so that he could not go back to London and, as Vaughan put it, 'brag to his Limey friends that he had beaten the Americans at poker.'"

When the train reached St. Louis at 8:45 a.m.[85] Tuesday, Truman was on the back platform immediately in a double-breasted powder blue suit, shaking hands with some of the 5,000 people who had managed to get around the glass barricade that restricted most of the others to the concourse. The crowd was disappointed when Churchill stayed in his room; his valet said he wasn't dressed. He finally emerged near the end of the 15-minute layover—in a dressing robe.

The biggest laugh of the morning came when Truman tried to get 3-year-old Lynn Mason of Decatur, Ill., to wave to him. He waved again and again, but the lad stared straight ahead and didn't respond. Finally the child shouted, "I don't like him"[280] to his grandmother and Truman roared with amusement. He leaned over the railing and shouted to Republican Mayor Aloys P. Kaufmann: "That little boy refuses to wave at me. I think he must be a Republican!"[377] The boy's grandmother said Lynn's father was indeed a Republican. "But Mr. Truman needn't worry. His mother happens to be a Democrat."[377]

The train continued to Jefferson City via the Missouri Pacific Railroad, and on arrival there at 11:20, Missouri Gov. Phil M. Donnelly presented 50 of Churchill's favorite long black de Cabana cigars to the former prime minister and a 20-pound hickory-smoked ham to Truman. From there, the party embarked on a 25-mile automobile trip to Westminister College, where Churchill was entertained at McCluer's home and spoke in the school gymnasium during the afternoon.

That evening, everybody reboarded the train to return east at 6:45 p.m. This time, it veered off the B&O's Baltimore-St. Louis main line at Midland City, Ohio, and continued to Columbus for Truman's Wednesday appointment.

Waiter Charles Adderly overheard a conversation over the dinners he carried to the *Magellan's* dining room that night.

"How do you manage to get such tender roast beef in this country?" Churchill asked Truman. "Why, haven't you heard?" the chief executive chuckled. "It's that good Missouri corn our cows are fed on!"[377]

The poker game resumed as the train headed east, and after another carefully calibrated loss for the guest, most of the party retired for the night. But Churchill, in a convivial and mellow mood, felt like talking, Clifford noted. "Charlie Ross and I sat with him, listening to him with a sense of incredible privilege."[85]

Ross, an old newspaperman, referred to Churchill's early career as a journalist.

"I was never a journalist," Churchill corrected him pointedly. "I was a war correspondent."[85]

The three discussed how the design of their lives had been shaped by the accident of birth. "If I were to be born again," the former prime minister said suddenly, "I would wish to be born in the United States. Your country is the future of the world. You have the natural resources, the spirit, the youth, the determination which will steadily increase your global influence. Great Britain has passed its zenith. We must adjust now to the enormous pressures in the world which have brought such dramatic changes. I believe your leaders must confront this responsibility head on, and it is my hope you will assume the leadership of the free world." He added with a smile and a puckish look, "I say this despite the fact that you Americans have some barbaric customs."

"Like what, Mr. Churchill?" Ross asked.

"For one thing," Churchill replied, eyes twinkling, "you stop drinking with your meals."[85]

The world leaders appeared on the back platform to a crowd of 1,500 at St. Louis that night, Churchill clad in his siren suit and Truman in striped pajamas with a topcoat over his shoulders. Someone shouted, "Where is your cigar, Winnie?" to which his only response was "God bless you all."[386c]

Early Wednesday morning, Truman stirred about the train before many of the others awakened. Since not all the photographers could be accommodated in the locomotive on Monday, the president agreed to borrow another set of gloves and make a repeat performance at the throttle for their benefit (and likely his). In the diesel this time as the party neared Columbus was Engineer Bob Polen. "It was a case of two good Democrats getting together,"[377] recalled Polen, who had

served in the Ohio General Assembly as well as working for the railroad 36 years. "The president stepped on it while he was at the throttle," Polen said, "and he appeared quite amazed when I pointed to the speed indicator and he read that we were going 65 miles an hour." The affable engineer was asked if Truman had any mechanical ability. "I guess a man who can hold the throttle on the U.S. government ought to be able to master a diesel locomotive in a short while."[377]

With Truman at the controls, his train raced through Bloomingburg, Mount Sterling and Derby at a 60-mile-an-hour clip while cameramen had a field day. A reporter asked the president if he'd get in trouble with the union. "Oh, they gave me a card," Truman smilingly replied. It was true—he was an honorary member of the Brotherhood of Locomotive Engineers.

Truman was careful to return the gloves to their owner, Supervisor of Locomotive Operation Harlan T. Clark of Baltimore, as he had Monday to Baltimore Division Supt. T.C. Smith. "Yes, sir," Smith had chuckled. "We've got an honest president!" The Ohio episode delayed Truman's train 11 minutes, probably because it slowed down to allow him and members of the press to safely cross from the combine car to the diesel and back.

Arriving in Columbus at 10:19 a.m., the train was pulled backward by class Q-1b 2-8-2 type steam engine 4206 into the Naghten Street siding adjacent to B&O's freight station at 10:41. Here the special party detrained for the Hotel Deshler-Wallick. In his speech, "The Place of Religion in American Democracy,"[387c] Truman called on the church to lead America as it led the postwar world. "Oh, for an Isaiah or a St. Paul to reawaken a sick world to its moral responsibilities," he cried.[280]

At 1:05 p.m., Truman rushed back

to Washington on his plane, the *Sacred Cow*, for a 3 p.m. appointment he didn't disclose—leaving Churchill behind on the train even though the Briton's B-17 awaited him at the Port Columbus airport. The former prime minister rested aboard the *Magellan* all day without making an appearance.

During the afternoon Churchill spent in the B&O yard, Elizabeth Claffey, a trainmaster's secretary, was asked to call the phone company and order a telephone for installation in the *Magellan*. Churchill wanted to call his wife. When told who the set was for, a woman on the other end of the line gasped and the request was passed higher up five or six times before it was approved.

Churchill left Columbus on the train at 6 p.m., returning to Washington on an uneventful overnight trip via Wheeling, Pittsburgh and Cumberland.

Memos gleaned years later from Charles W. Van Horn's files showed that the B&O's vice president in charge of operation and maintenance was kept informed of the train's progress throughout its journey—several of the dispatches reaching Van Horn in Chicago in care of business car 97. The special operated on time virtually all the way, with one of the few delays being two minutes at St. Louis on the return trip to remove a generator belt from the Pullman 12-section, drawing-room crew sleeper *Merlin*.

Costs were closely watched. Every category on every division was listed, even down to the $6.03 in overtime wages consumed in cleaning locomotive 4206. The revenue received amounted to $5,374, but expenses came to $15,631, leaving a deficit to the B&O of $10,257. Of that figure, the operation of dining car 1064 lost $957.66—despite revenues of $1,237.28 from the sale of meals, beverages, cigars, cigarettes, etc. The

diner's deficit would have been worse, but since it went all the way through, Missouri Pacific was billed $111.09 for its share of the loss. The big item here, a memo explained, was crew time, which amounted to $648.72, which ate up more than half the revenue. "We have to pick a special crew," Manager Dining Car and Commissary H.O. McAbee complained to Van Horn, "particularly the two men who wait on the presidential party in the rear car, who are familiar with what is required, having taken care of this duty on the many trips of former President Roosevelt. Furthermore, the diner on the special is kept open until an early morning hour to accommodate the newspaper people, photographers, etc., who sit up to play poker, eat and drink."[27]

Later, Churchill sent Harry Vaughan $50 to be divided as a tip for the chef and two waiters who had served him.[413]

As the 1946 midterm elections loomed, Truman's political fortunes were at a low ebb. He hadn't yet established himself as his own man, he had bungled the handling of a railroad strike, and Congress refused to pass any legislation he wanted. The country was dissatisfied with him and as the Republicans' fortunes brightened, Democrats turned loose from their president's coattails. He regretfully accepted the advice of Democratic National Chairman Bob Hannegan not to campaign. When he went home on a six-car special train in November to vote, he made no back-platform talks.

"Even in Missouri, where the train stopped three times, he only came out on the rear platform and shook hands with local politicians," Margaret recalled.

"At Jefferson City, schoolchildren were let out of classes for an hour to meet the train. The kids begged him to make a two-hour speech. But Dad

only wagged his finger at them, and clamped his hand across his mouth."[100]

The only problem enroute occurred on the B&O at Hayden, Ind., when an air hose broke on the front of 6-compartment, 3-bedroom Pullman sleeper *Times Square* at 4:54 a.m. Nov. 1, forcing an emergency application of the air brakes. The delay stretched to 19 minutes owing to the difficulty in getting the flagman back on board because he saw the headlight of freight train 91, which had followed the special out of North Vernon's Whitcomb Yard. The lost time was recovered by Vincennes, where the train passed on time at 7:15. Officers were careful to inform B&O President White that the sudden stop from 70 miles an hour resulted in no flat wheels and "no bad effects … on Car No. 1."[27]

Truman awoke on the train returning to Washington on Wednesday, Nov. 6, to discover that he had a Republican Congress—and a bad cold to boot. At Union Station, only one man met him—Undersecretary of State Dean Acheson. He and Truman weren't close, but the president was delighted to see him. When he invited Acheson back to the White House for a drink, it was becoming clear that he knew he had to widen his circle and start feeling at home with politicians outside the ranks of his old Missouri cronies.

The politicians and press were quite complimentary of the journey. A memo from McAbee to Van Horn quoted a report by Dining Car and Commissary Department Supt. W.R. Morten: "I talked to eight or 10 of the newspaper men, all of whom complimented the B&O dining car service very highly. …Mr. Charles Ross, press secretary to the president, told his luncheon guests yesterday [Nov. 6] that the meals on the B&O were remarkable, the best in the country, and

Delaware & Hudson Railroad's 4-8-2 type No. 304 pulls President Truman's Ottawa-bound special out of Albany, N.Y., on June 10, 1947.

added that the Pennsylvania service was 'lousy.' … President Truman walked through the train about 30 minutes after it left Independence, Mo., and seemed in a most jovial mood. In fact, he spent about 20 minutes in the club car [B&O diner 1049] talking to newspaper men and others. One of the newspaper men insisted that he have a drink, which he accepted."[27]

Meanwhile, railroad personnel were discovering they had quite a different passenger than they cared for when Roosevelt was aboard. For one thing, Truman was an early riser.

"I was sitting in my room (about daylight) smoking my pipe," recalled porter Fred Fair. "I looked up and there he was—President Truman—standing at the door. He asked for coffee, which I got in about 10 minutes. From that day on, coffee was ready at 5:30."[284]

The Trumans were relaxed and very much at home in the *Magellan*. Truman washed his socks and underwear himself and hung them up to dry in the presidential bedroom. Bess, his wife, and daughter Margaret did their laundry in the first lady's bedroom.

"He always said that that was one thing everybody had to do himself, wash his own socks and his own underwear," Mrs. Tom Evans, a family friend, once commented. "And I believe he always did—even after he became president."[101]

Headwaiter Billy Reid said Truman was one of his favorites among the presidents he served—from Harding to Eisenhower.

He "was my pet," Reid explained. "He got up every morning at 6, and we'd stop the train so he could take his walk."[76]

FDR was the lightest-hearted of the two. He loved to wisecrack while discussing travel plans, Dewey Long noted, while Truman was all business.

Roosevelt loved bull sessions and would come wheeling in on the White House people at odd hours on long trips, frequently bringing his own whiskey. "We always had a jug," Long said, "for those who wanted a little nip, but the president would bring his own. He always said he wanted to be sure he got a drink."[224] Truman didn't come to the bull sessions so much, but liked to have people in for lunch on the car more often

than did FDR. B&O police officer Ernest Chapman said he went broke trying to beat Truman at poker.[173]

Crews always fondly remembered the Truman family as gracious people who appreciated even the smallest courtesy. Charles R. Van Horn, B&O's regional passenger sales manager in Washington and the operating vice president's son, once received a letter from Mrs. Truman advising that she had forgotten to tip the redcap who handled her baggage on a trip. Enclosed was a check, which she asked Van Horn to pass on to the redcap.

Truman liked to fly; Roosevelt hated to. Truman liked speed; Roosevelt didn't. "Mr. Truman doesn't care if the train goes 80 miles an hour or more," Long once said. "In fact, he seems to prefer it."[224] Even the crowds were different. Roosevelt's were more demonstrative, Truman's quieter. "I don't know why," Dewey Long said at the time. "Maybe it's because they think they know Truman better and feel they don't have to make a lot of racket."[224]

Truman's most memorable campaign was that of 1948, when he covered 29,432 rail miles and delivered 343 hard-hitting speeches on seven rail jaunts heard by at least 6 million people in 35 states—a record. Clearly the underdog because of nationwide strikes, inflation, a meat shortage and the onset of the Cold War, his ardent campaigning is credited with turning the tide in his favor—even though Republican foe Thomas E. Dewey traveled quite a bit himself.

Strategists felt Truman's best shot would be to take his case to the people. "(The president) must …resort to the kind of trip which Roosevelt made famous in the 1940 campaign—the 'inspection tour,' mused Clark Clifford and James H. Rowe Jr. in a 1947 memo.[85]

But the Democratic party was nearly broke. If only there were a non-political reason for the president to travel in the line of duty, Clifford and Rowe figured, the taxpayers would have to pick up the tab. The opportunity came when Dr. Robert Gordon Sproul, president of the University of California at Berkeley, called his old friend, Undersecretary of the Interior Oscar L. Chapman, to see if he could get Truman to deliver the school's commencement address.

"I jumped two feet out of my chair," Chapman recalled. "I told him to hold the line, that I thought I could get him an answer right away. With Sproul on the 'hold button,' I picked up my direct line to the White House and got through to the president. I told him this was just the thing we were looking for; that here was an unassailable prestige invitation that would take him all the way to the West Coast. The president seemed pretty pleased, too. I asked him to speak directly to Sproul. He agreed. So I just switched the call from my phone to the president. He and Sproul completed the deal right on the spot, with an honorary LL.D. for the president thrown in."[292]

Berkeley was 2,500 miles from Washington. The trip would offer a slew of opportunities to visit with the people and acquaint them with his programs. The politicians had all been staking out their protective positions, but Truman had a hunch that "everybody was against me except the people."[292] This trip would help him test that hunch.

Chapman arranged for a 17-car train on a 15 ½-day, 18-state, 9,504-mile itinerary that called for five major speeches and 68 other talks. The bills would be paid from Truman's annual $30,000 travel allowance.

Two problems remained. One was Truman's stiff speaking style. His eyesight was poor; he had to stare intently at prepared texts and read flatly in his high-pitched monotone. Administrative Assistant Charles S. Murphy saved the day, however, when he prepared the president's speech before the American Society of Newspaper Editors on April 17. Murphy wrote it in outline form and gave Truman the choice of simply reading it or using it as a springboard for extemporaneous remarks. Polite applause ensued as long as Truman read, but the editors went wild when he lifted his eyes off the paper and began to speak his mind and heart in his own vocabulary and humor. "He was suddenly a very interesting man of great candor who discussed the problems of American leadership with men as neighbors," Truman speechwriter Jonathan Daniels wrote.[171]

The other difficulty was the Democrats' complacency after four Roosevelt victories. The party was ill-equipped to provide the facts and figures needed for meaty speeches, so Truman established a research unit to pull together background data on all the issues. It also stockpiled "local color"[171] items about each town Truman would visit that would make him sound familiar with all of them.

The last piece of the puzzle was in place.

Departure from Union Station was set for Thursday night, June 3, 1948. A blue velvet curtain was hung outside the rear door and windows of the *Ferdinand Magellan,* apparently to provide a cleaner background for photos and newsreel films. The 125 people permitted on board included 60 media representatives, 13 White House staff and 11 members of the president's party. Conspicuously absent were big-shot Democrats—after all, this was a non-political trip.

Chapman went out a week ahead to contact Democratic leaders and make sure crowds turned out. Clifford and Murphy came aboard from the presidential special counsel's office, as did Press Secretary Charlie Ross and Appointments Secretary Matthew J. Connelly. Three military aides were there, as was Dr. Wallace Graham, Truman's physician.

The president exuded confidence as he boarded. "If I felt any better, I couldn't stand it,"[329] he told reporters, who noticed that Truman's zest wasn't shared by his staff.

The train departed at 11:05 p.m. on the PRR. At breakfast the next morning, Walter Fitzmaurice, who covered the White House for *Newsweek* and who wrote about his presidential travel experiences for the March 1949, *Trains* magazine, ran into the Pennsy's Harry Karr. He asked if there was a pilot train.

"Nope," Karr answered, lighting a cigar. "A pilot train would be a nuisance here where we can pick up a regular passenger train every hour or so. Right now, 20 minutes ahead, one of our fastest trains (he lowered his voice and named a famous limited) is piloting for us; chances are, the passengers probably don't know it, of course."

"Look there," Karr said, pointing to a man on a slope, barely visible between the passing girders of a bridge. "And there," he continued, the cigar nodding toward another Secret Service agent knee-deep in weeds beside a culvert. "Every bridge, crossing and culvert has been under guard for hours," he explained. "Every switch has been spiked, every freight train stopped, every opposing passenger train switched one track away. Expensive? Sure it is. But we're running a POTUS operation."[137]

The train stopped at noon next to an embankment east of Crestline, Ohio. Truman had difficulty maintaining the "non-political"[171] fiction when he chuckled to a crowd of 1,000 and mentioned that "on this non-partisan, bipartisan trip we are taking here, I understand there are a whole lot of Democrats present, too."[329] He introduced former Ohio Gov. Frank J. Lausche as "the next governor of Ohio"[171] and later told a crowd at Gary, Ind., that he hoped he would get a new Congress in the next election "that will work in the interests of the common people."[329]

Truman seemed genuinely pleased. "How intriguing it is," he said, "for the president to get away from the White House and get to see the people as they are. The president, you know, is virtually in jail. He goes from his study to his office and from his office to his study, and he has to have guards all the time."

At Fort Wayne, Ind., at 2:20 p.m., Truman indulged in local pleasantries, then dived into a lecture on how to keep the world at peace. Later, at Gary, he berated Congress for not controlling inflation.

Murphy wrote the shorter speeches. "This material was ordinarily furnished in the form of a brief outline," he recalled. "Sometimes it was only a few rough pencil notes which I wrote early in the morning and handed to the president before most of the people on the train had gotten up."[171]

It was soon apparent to the Republicans that Truman's jaunt was a disguised political coup, and lit the fires of criticism. The president's aides, admitting privately that yes, indeed, this trip was very political, advised him to become more pointed in his attacks. He did, especially when he got out West and learned that people there were holding him responsible for Congress lack of action on housing, high prices and slashes in funds for flood control and rural electrification.

Newsweek's Fitzmaurice managed somehow to wangle a cab ride in the green and yellow two-unit Chicago & North Western diesel as the overnight run to Omaha began between Chicago and DeKalb, Ill. "Engineer Larry Martin shook his head when another head popped in the door" of

Two Pennsylvania Railroad K-4 class Pacific-type locomotives, led by the 3743, pause at Buffalo, N.Y., June 13, 1947, while returning President Truman from a conference in Ottawa.

Kearney, Neb., rolls out the red carpet for President Truman June 6, 1948, as he makes his way to a speech at Berkeley, Calif., on a "non-political" trip across the country.

the cab already crammed with officials, Fitzmaurice wrote. "However, press credentials proved persuasive."

"The run began smoothly, the reluctant rear-end mastodon balking only slightly as the train threaded through the Chicago terminal yards," Fitzmaurice wrote of the heavy *Magellan.* "From signal bridges ahead, lights glowed yellow, then green. The diesel picked up speed, empty suburban streets passed by, and then the rails stretched toward open country.

"As the miles whisked by at 73 miles an hour, bathed in the rhythmic blobs of a Mars headlight, General Railway Signal's Elton Legg explained automatic train control to the new guest. Martin momentarily ignored a yellow light and the system bonged a reminder that if he didn't reduce speed, it would.

"And it would, too," Legg nodded. "Within 30 seconds."

Legg's next words were swallowed up in a roar as diesel inspector A.C. Buran went into the engine room for a check. He returned shortly to report "everything lovely back there."

Just then a culvert sounded a sudden thunder beneath the wheels, and then a bridge strummed a longer, deeper chord. Road Foreman Albert Hitchcock, without consulting his watch or the view outside, announced that a village would be coming up in two minutes 30 seconds. A red station flashed by at precisely the right moment. "Two minutes, 30 seconds," Fitzmaurice declared. "But how is it done without landmarks or a timepiece?" he asked. Buran exchanged a smile with Hitchcock and explained. "Remember the culvert and the bridge? When you've ridden a road as many years as Hitchcock has, you can wake up in your berth at night, listen a little while and your ears will tell you

just where you are."

Just as the special neared DeKalb, a brake inspection stop, Fitzmaurice thought of a question. "What device caused that first brief brilliant gleam as the train moved into automatic control?"

"Device? Gleam?" Legg looked perplexed, then his face cleared. "Oh! Gleam. You probably saw the headlight reflected in a rabbit's eye. Guess we ran over one back there."

A glance at the locomotive's blood-spattered frame as Fitzmaurice climbed down the ladder at DeKalb confirmed the guess. "The 1944 campaign had seen human faces cut and bones cracked when the Dewey train collided with another at Castle Rock, Wash.," he wrote, "but this rabbit was the only casualty in President Truman's ... campaigning."[137]

There were several blunders on this campaign shakedown cruise. Some

Crowds at Pennsylvania Station in Baltimore often were the first or the last Harry Truman saw when he ventured from Washington. Here he pauses as he winds up his "non-political" June 1948 trip, late on the morning of the 18th.

were minor, such as stenographer-typist Jack Romagna listening to the president refer to Republican "moss-backs" and transcribing it as "moth bags."[171] And Democrats who thought Truman had agreed to draft Dwight Eisenhower showed up at one stop with homemade signs reading "IKE FOR PRESIDENT! HARRY FOR VP!"[246]

Other slips were more serious.

Saturday, June 5, started out as a fine day for Truman's parade in Omaha. Bess and Margaret joined the train there after taking Bess' ill mother home to Independence, Mo. Truman always enjoyed introducing Bess to the crowds as "the Boss" and Margaret as "the one who bosses the boss."[100] Then, referring to one of his honorary degrees, he joked about how Margaret worked four years for a "diploma[sic]" from George Wash-ington University, but on the same night she got hers, he got one "for nothing."[239] Also, the president was

B&O diesel 80 leads President Truman's train into Keyser, W.Va., July 4, 1948, as the chief executive accompanies the president of Venezuela, Romulo Gallegos, to Bolivar, Mo., to dedicate a statue to South American liberator Simon Bolivar.

delighted to see fellow veterans of Battery D of the 129th Field Artillery, his World War I outfit, during a reunion of the 35th Division that day.

But that evening the roof fell in. A rally at the 10,000-seat Ak-Sar-Ben Coliseum, during which Truman delivered a major farm speech, drew only a handful of people. This was partly because it was billed as a military reunion and not for the public, and partly because most of Omaha had already seen the president earlier in the day. Press photographers who thought Truman couldn't win anyway had a field day taking pictures of the nearly empty auditorium and editors enjoyed splashing them all over the nation's front pages. Truman's comments were virtually ignored.

The exuberant candidate tried to recover with down-home statements that shattered presidential dignity as he traveled across Nebraska on the Union Pacific Railroad. Given a pair of spurs at Grand Island, he exclaimed, "These spurs are wonderful. When I get them on, I can take the Congress to town." Presented with cowboy boots in Kearney, he remarked, "I can really take Congress for a ride now." In North Platte, he noted 900 members of the Lions Club were in town for a convention, and quipped, "You ought to have some cages. I hope nobody gets clawed."[329]

Trouble returned at Pocatello, Idaho, on Monday morning. The chief executive did well with his speech, using a "prop"[171]—a copy of a Bureau of Reclamation report on the Columbia River basin—to drive home his support of western power and reclamation projects. But he blew it with an ad lib at the end. He pointed out that the press was always throwing accusations at him, and he countered: "I have been in politics a long time, and it makes no difference what they say about you, if it isn't so. If they can prove it on you, you are in a bad fix

indeed. They have never been able to prove it on me."[171]

The remark seemed to link Truman to the graft of Missouri's Pendergast machine, and the press had a field day with it. Reporters in the press car who liked Truman personally couldn't help laughing about the blunder.

More trouble followed at Carey on Tuesday morning as the special party returned to the train by auto after a day of fishing at Secretary of Commerce W. Averell Harriman's resort at Sun Valley. Carey's mayor had called, asking that Truman detour to his town and help dedicate an airport. Such an impromptu invitation is a formula for disaster, and this one proved to be no exception. Apparently, Press Secretary Ross—who had closed the Sun Valley bar in the wee hours with his newspaper friends—was still asleep when the call came. It was taken hurriedly by a Secret Service agent, who relayed to Truman through Harry Vaughan that the airport would be named in honor of "Wilmer Coates."[171] Truman agreed to go without allowing time for the customary research.

Robert G. Nixon, the International News Service correspondent, recalled that he was just sitting down to Harriman's sumptuous six-course breakfast of pheasant and other delicacies when White House receptionist Bill Simmons came tearing down the hallway into the breakfast room shouting that the president was ready to go. Without having taken a bite, Nixon was herded into a car with other newsmen; the groggy Ross was dragged to the motorcade with shaving cream still on his face.

Thirty or forty miles to the southeast, the party came to Carey, a hamlet of several hundred people. Charles Murphy, riding a few cars behind Truman, looked up to see a line of automobiles parked beside the road next to a "cow pasture"[171] with a

mountain on the far side of it. The "cow pasture" was the airstrip.

The president's car stopped and a microphone and wreath were thrust into his hands. Nobody told him anything, but he saw Legionnaires and other veterans lined up as an honor guard and concluded that Wilmer Coates was a war hero.

"I'm honored," he began, "to dedicate this airport and present this wreath to the parents of the brave boy who died fighting for his country...."[115] There was a rumble in the crowd; a tearful woman pulled on his coattails and told him he was honoring a young woman. The garbled telephone message had apparently referred to a "Wilma Coates."[171]

Truman cleared his throat and started again. "Well, I'm even more honored to dedicate this airport to a young woman who bravely gave her life for her country."[115] He now assumed the woman was a WAC, WAVE or WAF who had died in the service. Why else would all those vets be there? There was more whispering and more coattail-tugging. "No, no," Mrs. Coates wailed. "Our Wilma was killed right here!"[329]

Wilma Coates had had no military service; she was a 16-year-old who had been killed in a civilian plane crash while hedge-hopping with her boyfriend. A disconcerted, red-faced president apologized to the bereaved parents and got out of there as quickly as he could.

Truman rode in grim silence to Idaho Falls, where the train was waiting. When his motorcade stopped in the town square, he spoke on the merits of municipally owned power plants. But when he reached the station, he spied another crowd waiting behind the *Magellan,* a meeting the local committee had billed as the event of the day but one that caught Truman's staff completely by surprise. Truman mounted the back platform, rattled off a few inane sentences, and told his staff he wanted to see them upon departure.

Before leaving town, he made a weak stab at humor, indirectly complimenting the citizens for their handling of the surplus potato problem: "I understand you grow a lot of potatoes here. … You also have a very loyal citizenship. During the war I was up in Presque Island [Isle], Maine, making an investigation of an air field up there, and I heard that there was an Idaho boy in the guardhouse. I inquired as to why he was in the guardhouse. I was told he had been on kitchen police and refused to peel Maine potatoes."[417]

All the gaffes made the train's 12:01 p.m. scheduled departure nearly 45 minutes behind. Truman called the staff into the *Magellan's* dining room for what Murphy expected would be a dressing down. "But," said the aide, "when the time came for him to do that, he couldn't quite manage to scold us."[171] Instead, he said the president—never raising his voice—gave specific assignments to each staffer to head off repetition of the blunders.

Dewey Long remembered the meeting differently.

"He read us the riot act," Long recalled. "He told us he was going to make the blank-blankedest campaign on record and that from there on out he wanted no nonsense. Said we'd have to produce, or else."[224] The errors, embarrassing as they were, served to ensure that the rest of the campaign would be one of the most thoroughly researched and accurate ever.

Truman felt better after a thunderous welcome in Butte, Mont., where 40,000 greeted him downtown and another 10,000 filled a stadium for his speech. Once again he assailed the "do-nothing 80th Congress"[115] in general and Sen. Robert Taft, R-Ohio, in particular, who had called on Americans to fight inflation by eating less. "I guess he would let you starve, I don't know," the president remarked.[171]

Three days later Taft counterattacked on nationwide radio, digging himself in deeper and inspiring the addition of a new term to the American political dictionary. Speaking before the Union League Club in Philadelphia, Taft berated Truman for "blackguarding Congress at every whistle station in the West."[171]

Truman and his staff loved it. A few days later in Los Angeles, he nailed Congress again and joked that the city was the biggest "whistlestop" he had visited, editing slightly Taft's "whistle station" and permanently planting in the public mind an apropos description of his style of campaigning.

The Democratic committee caught the cue and telegraphed 35 cities along the train's route to ask the mayors how they liked being referred to as whistlestops. Taft was bombarded with criticism:

"Must have wrong city," responded Mayor Earl McNutt of Eugene, Ore.[292]

"Characteristically, Sen. Taft is confused," wired back the president of the Laramie, Wyo., Chamber of Commerce.[292]

"Very poor taste," echoed the mayor of Gary, Ind.[292]

From the West Coast: "Seattle is not a whistlestop, but everyone who sees her stops and whistles, including presidents and senators."[417]

From Nebraska: "Grand Island was never a whistlestop. Third largest city in Nebraska with 25,000 of the finest people in the Midwest; first sugar factory in the United States here; largest livestock auction market in the world."[417]

"Rather misleading," fumed Crestline in Taft's own Ohio. "Forty-two passenger trains make regular scheduled stops here daily. … "[417]

From Los Angeles: "The term hardly applies to the Los Angeles metropolitan area in which presently live one-thirty-fifth of all the people in the United States, considerably more than half the population of Ohio. … "[417]

Late Tuesday night at Missoula, Mont., the president appeared on the back platform in his pajamas and robe. "I understand it was announced I would speak here," he smiled. "I am sorry I had gone to bed. But I thought I would let you see what I look like, even if I didn't have on any clothes."[246]

But Truman's temper was still on edge in Spokane, Wash., Thursday morning. Sen. Warren G. Magnuson, D-Wash., who was accompanying him at the moment, handed him a copy of that morning's Spokane *Spokesman-Review.* Magnuson remarked that the paper was just as Republican as the *Chicago Tribune.* Actually, its play of political news that morning was fair, and the editorial page carried a friendly welcome to the president. But Truman never looked at it; he took Magnuson's word. When the president stepped from the train, reporter Rhea Felknor asked him, "How do you like being in a Republican stronghold?"

"Do you work for this paper, young man?" Truman countered. Felknor said he did, and Truman snapped: "The *Chicago Tribune* and this paper are the worst in the United States. You've got just what you ought to have. You've got the worst Congress in the United States you have ever had and the papers—this paper—are responsible for it."[115]

He turned to the crowd before making a motor trip to the Grand Coulee Dam and said the Republicans "are going down to Philadelphia in a few days and are going to tell you what a great Congress they have been. Well, if you believe that, you are bigger suckers than I think you are."[239]

Later that day, Truman apologized

to Felknor. He didn't need to be caustic; the shakedown tour was beginning to prove the worth of campaigning by rail for the underdog.

Truman wasn't the only one operating on a short fuse that day.

A young woman working for a Spokane paper boarded there to ride to Seattle. When the conductor came to collect her fare, INS correspondent Nixon remembered that she became indignant. "She was astounded that this wasn't a free ride," Nixon explained. "She said, 'Fare? What fare?' She said, 'Aren't all these reporters riding free? Why do I have to pay a fare?' It was then explained to her that we were not riding free, that we were making the campaign train possible by the fare that we paid. ... She couldn't believe it. It was just preposterous to her."[282]

Truman continued through the Northwest and down the Pacific Coast via the Northern Pacific, Great Northern and Southern Pacific, making major speeches in Seattle and Portland. He visited the region at a time when floods had caused severe damage, and his folksy, informal approach convinced the friendly crowds that the lack of flood control was the fault of Congress for not appropriating enough money. The crowds began to grow.

The president's humor was much improved at Albany, Ore.

"You're close enough to see your dimples," a woman exclaimed.

"Not dimples, they're wrinkles," Truman said. "You don't have dimples at 64."[115]

Clifford and Murphy concluded that the people were beginning to believe that the president "wasn't nearly the bad person the newspapers made him out to be." He was being perceived as one of the common people, speaking "the language of the courthouse steps, the Baptist Church, the businessman's table at the Busy

ABBIE ROWE, NATIONAL PARK SERVICE/TRUMAN LIBRARY

Enroute to Bolivar, Mo., with Venezuelan President Romulo Gallegos to dedicate a statue to South American liberator Simon Bolivar, Harry Truman's B&O special train crosses the Ohio River at Parkersburg, W.Va., on the afternoon of July 4, 1948.

Bee Cafe," one analyst wrote. "He was fighting their battle with high prices, with a stubborn Congress, with Russian Communism. There were no tricks about this fellow; he was down to earth, on the level, called a spade a spade. They warmed up to him."[292]

Only occasionally would he put his foot in his mouth now, but when he did it was a doozy. At Eugene, Ore., on Friday the 11th of June, where his train was transferred to the SP, he rambled about his pursuit of peace and mentioned the 1945 Potsdam Conference where he met the Soviet Union's Josef Stalin. His next comment sent newsmen scurrying to their typewriters.

"I like Old Joe!" he declared. "He is a decent fellow. But Joe is a prisoner of the Politburo. He can't do what he wants to. He makes agreements, and if he could he would keep them; but the people who run the government are very specific in saying that he can't keep them."[417]

Of course, Stalin ran the Politburo, and his regime was the most brutal in Soviet history. Merriman Smith of United Press realized he had a scoop on his hands as they headed for "the boondocks of Northern California"— if he could just get his story filed ahead of the pack. He told a United Press regional reporter that the only way was to jump off the train at the next station. "Press pool folklore eventually had it that I wrapped the man in pillows and personally shoved him out the door," Smith said. "but this is an exaggeration. Actually, we were simply operating on an old principle—the theory of the expendable reporter. United Press got about a 45-minute beat on that story." Smith didn't explain exactly how his colleague detrained.[338]

Newsman Robert J. Donovan was close behind with his copy. When the train stopped at a junction in the Cascades, there was only the telegraph operator. "It was already around 10 p.m. in New York. Everyone was battling everyone else to have his story put on the top of the pile," Donovan said. "The futility was obvious. The only hope was a telephone. Even if I could get to one first, I would not have time to dictate my story. But someone else might do it for me. When I finished my story, I attached two things to it. One was a note of instruction on how to call the [New York] *Herald Tribune* telegraph desk to explain the situation and to read the story. The other was a $20 bill. I had an instinct that it would be wisest to give the story to a woman. And when we pulled into the station and jumped off the train, there she was. She seemed to be in her mid-40s and was neatly dressed in a green sweater and gray tweed skirt.

"As I rushed up to her, she was taken aback; I explained as quickly as I could talk. She wanted to give me back the $20 bill, but I wouldn't take it. I jumped back on the train amid a bunch of reporters all hollering at Western Union. The train started. I knew that woman would not let me down. In San Francisco the next morning, I received a telegram from the paper, saying the Stalin story had made the big press run."[384]

Clifford and Charlie Ross had the dubious distinction the next day of telling the president he had made a mistake.

Ross started off. "Mr. President, we just have to tell you, frankly, that your 'I like Old Joe' remark is not going over well. We are going to get hammered for it; we know you understand, and we know you will not want to repeat that phrase."[85] Clifford then summarized several angry telephone calls from the State Department in Washington.

Truman listened quietly, then after a moment said, "Well, I guess I goofed."[85] There was no more affectionate talk about Stalin.

The president never seemed perturbed by his bobbles, because there was little doubt his tour was pleasing the people. From early in the morning until way after bedtime, he was always out on the back platform, pugnacious, peppery, down to earth. Between stops, he amazed his staff at his ability to drop off and take a sound nap as though he didn't have a care in the world.

So as Truman neared Berkeley on Saturday, June 12, he felt better.

"My grandfather [Solomon Young], you know, owned the site of Sacramento," he commented when he got to town. "He was a freighter from Westport, which is now part of Kansas City, Mo., to Salt Lake City and San Francisco. They made a deal one time and obtained 27 Spanish leagues of land in the Sacramento Valley on a part of that site that Sacramento City is upon." Then his grandfather's partner, he said, had decamped with the assets of the freighting company and the Sacramento ranch had to be sold to pay grandfather's debts. "Now think of that! I probably would not have been president of the United States if the old man had kept that valley. …"[329]

He joked with the crowd at Davis, Calif., about his upcoming educational honor: "I am going down here

to Berkeley to get me a degree."[115] After a few drinks, newsmen composed an original ditty to the tune of "Oh, Susannah!" combining a poke at that comment and the slip in Pocatello.

"They can't prove nothing
"They ain't got a thing on me
"I'm going down to Berkeley
"To get me a degree."[171]

In the academic atmosphere of Berkeley itself, the president shifted gears and delivered an unusually sober, thoughtful and dignified oration on foreign policy. The speech was well received by the stadium crowd of 55,000 and praised editorially around the country.

Ever the fast reporter, Merriman Smith leaned out of a Dutch door to catch a glimpse of the crowd as the train pulled in. But he leaned too far, lost his balance, and fell off the train, landing on a steel guy wire. Alarmed members of the reception committee thought he was dead, but Smith recounted that "to get me out of the way, they stuffed me into a telephone booth at the station. It turned out to be the only telephone within miles and we got a 10-minute beat on the story."[338]

Even though pollsters said Truman didn't have a chance, everyone who saw and heard him was impressed. Close to a million people lined the five-mile parade route from the station to the Ambassador Hotel in Los Angeles on Monday the 14th. They threw confetti and waved flags while a skywriter spelled out "Welcome President Truman."[115] Dinah Shore serenaded the president with "You Made Me Love You" before he addressed the Greater Los Angeles Press Club.

The small "Missouri mule" with the thick glasses and high-pitched voice had scored some telling points and made many wonder if a Republican victory in the fall would be all that automatic. His asperity toward the 80th Congress, mixed with his humor and informality, continued to score points as he started east from California via the Atchison, Topeka & Santa Fe.

In San Bernardino, someone gave him a basket of eggs. "At least they didn't throw them at me," he joked. Someone called out: "What about throwing them at Taft?" To which Truman shot back: "I wouldn't throw FRESH eggs at Taft."[329]

Past midnight on Tuesday morning the 15th, his train nosed into Barstow, Calif. The crowd was dismayed to see the *Magellan* buttoned up for the night, but suddenly Truman appeared on the back platform attired in a blue dressing gown and blue pajamas. He was met with a roar of surprise and pleasure.

A woman asked if he had a cold and he denied it. "But you sound like it," she insisted. Truman grinned. "That's because I ride around in the wind with my mouth open."[329]

By now it was becoming apparent that the underdog who had entered the White House through the back door now had his finger firmly on the nation's pulse. "I have seen, I imagine, about two and a half millions of the people," he told the audience in Dodge City, Kan. "I have talked to a great many people, and a great many people have talked to me, and I think I have found out what the country is thinking about. I think I have definitely fixed the issues which are before the country now. It is merely the fact: Are the special privilege boys going to run the country or are the people going to run it?"[329]

He continued home via Warrensburg, Mo., transferring to the Missouri Pacific, and to the PRR at East St. Louis, Ill.

A curious incident took place about 15 minutes east of Columbus, Ohio. The low lubricating oil alarm sounded

Only once did posterity record a sour note between President Harry Truman and a train crew member. C.C. Bredehoeft, a B&O flagman, was one of the men regularly chosen for POTUS trips.

"Dad was told not to talk much about the presidential trips because of the security," Wayne Bredehoeft related about his father. "But he said one day he was on the back platform smoking his pipe when Truman came out and asked him if he knew the score of some ball game then in progress.

" 'I don't have any idea,' Dad snapped at him.

" 'You're not very American,' Truman joked with him, trying to make him feel better.

" 'How can I have time to listen to ball games when I'm out here running up and down the railroad babysitting you all day?' my dad retorted.

" 'Well!' the president exclaimed, and went back inside."[50]

in the first of the two Baldwin "centipede" passenger diesels pulling the train, the 5832, indicating that one or more engines in the units had shut down. After a stop, officers found that indeed the No. 2 motor on the lead unit and both motors on the trailing unit had died. The culprits were shutters on the three affected motors' radiators, which had been manually closed, and a cleaning water drain valve that had been left about a half-turn open. Once the valve was closed, the shutters reset for automatic operation and the motors cooled off, they were restarted without difficulty. A company report concluded that since the diesels had given no trouble all the way from St. Louis, one of several railroad employees who were on the engines during the 25-minute stop in Columbus must have deliberately sabotaged them. The records don't reveal

if the guilty party was identified and prosecuted.

Anyone who might dispute the president's hold on the country could not argue the fact that he had found an effective political style. "Without that June trip," Clark Clifford wrote later, "I doubt the whistlestops would have succeeded in the fall."[85]

Truman's fall itinerary included a Labor Day kickoff in Michigan, a 16-day transcontinental train trip, a three-day sweep of the Northeast, a week-long foray into the Midwest, a single hop by air to Florida, a one-day trek into Pennsylvania, and an eight-day finale of New England and the Northeast.

"I went by train," Truman said years later. "I wanted to talk to them face to face. I knew that they knew that when you get on the television, you're wearing a lot of powder and paint that somebody else has put on your face, and you haven't even combed your own hair."[255]

The procession officially got under way at 3:40 p.m. Sunday, Sept. 5, when his 16-car special departed via PRR from Union Station for a one-day tour of Michigan. Aboard were more than 80 reporters and photographers, a dozen White House aides and secretaries, and the president and his daughter (Bess was attending a christening in Denver).

The *Truman Special* rolled onto a siding at Grand Rapids at 7 a.m. on Labor Day ("We were up at 6:15,"[101] Margaret groaned), with several hundred people cheering and shouting from the station platform. Local leaders and politicians—including an ambitious newcomer to Democratic politics in Michigan, G. Mennen Williams, who was running for governor—packed into the *Magellan* for handshakes and coffee. Although it was early, 25,000 jammed into the town square, where Truman had gone to speak. "It is a great day for me. It is

Purcell, Okla., sports a banner across Main Street near the AT&SF station to welcome President Truman on Sept. 28, 1948.

a great day for you. I am just starting on a campaign tour that is going to be a record for the president of the United States," he announced exuberantly.[329]

Within an hour the train was under way again on Chesapeake & Ohio's ex-Pere Marquette Railway, headed by class E-7 passenger diesel 102, whizzing past knots of people at crossings and way stations who waved and hoped to get a wave in return. Several times it stopped at stations where a crowd had gathered—such as Lansing—for brief remarks and some handshaking. The crowds responded warmly.

Next was Detroit, where the train arrived about noon. This was labor's city, labor's holiday and labor's candidate—and everybody had a terrific party as a motorcade wound its way to Cadillac Square for Truman's 1:40 p.m. speech. Everybody, that is, except Undersecretary of the Interior Oscar Chapman, still Truman's advance man.

Chapman had spent a week making plans for the visit. All seemed in order until Saturday morning, when the radio network that would broadcast the speech told him it would have to have its $50,000 fee up front. This was the first wrinkle of a worrisome maze of financial problems that plagued the

Democrats all fall. Chapman called New York for Sen. J. Howard McGrath of Rhode Island, the Democratic national chairman

"We haven't got that kind of money," a frantic McGrath snapped at Chapman. "If the labor boys out there can't raise it, you'll just have to cancel."

Chapman had already checked with the Congress of Industrial Organizations and had turned up nothing. He brooded in his hotel room for about an hour before thinking to call his old friend, Gov. Roy Turner of Oklahoma—a loyal Truman Democrat and a wealthy man with several oil-wealthy friends. "Governor,"

Chapman whined, "I'm in the tightest spot I've ever been in in my life."

"Of course you can't cancel," Turner boomed reassuringly. "Stay in your room and I'll call you back in an hour."

Two hours later he called back.

"You're in business, Oscar," the governor said. "I've just cleared the whole thing with the network. I've laid down $50,000 with their station here, and everything is checked out all the way up the line. You tell those ... that if they don't put this show on the air Monday, I'll wreck this ... station of theirs here before sundown."[292]

After the Detroit rally, Truman continued via Grand Trunk Western and C&O to Hamtramck at 2:45, Pontiac at 4, Flint at 7:15 and a final rear-platform appearance in Toledo at 11:55 p.m. The president made much use of his new speaking style, using instead of ponderous manuscripts more than 300 outlines—short sentences separated by three lines of space—prepared by George Elsey. Clark Clifford, Elsey's boss, and Administrative Assistant Charles Murphy rode the train and prepared the longer texts.

Already the press noticed Truman's confidence. Two reporters collared Clifford and dragged him into their compartment. "Now look, Clark," they began. "The president talks about winning. He is very optimistic; he's very sanguine. Does he really believe he's got a chance to win this election?"

Clifford laughed. "We don't know. It's a wonderful thing for the staff. We all feel we are on our own goal line and we've either got to punt or pass or do something desperate, but the boss doesn't seem worried, and it's very morale-building for us."[417]

Truman was energetic. He was "making speeches before Dewey was up in the morning and often [was] still entertaining crowds along the way after Dewey had retired at night," wrote presidential biographer Robert J. Donovan.[115]

The chief executive's enthusiasm failed to build a fire under the traveling correspondents at first. "The excitement was along the way, not in the press," recalled George Tames, a *New York Times* photographer. "The assumption was that the trip[s were] hopeless, that Dewey had the election locked up. The reporters stayed in their car playing poker, and wouldn't even listen to the speeches. But we photographers were out there at each stop, and we saw the crowds."[389a]

Truman headed back to Washington from Toledo on the B&O. The trip proved to be memorable for P.R. "Pete" Cordic of Pittsburgh, supervisor of locomotive operation on B&O's Central Region.

"Gotta ride 5 [the '*Capitol Limited*'] to New Castle to pick up the special," Cordic told his son Rege on Monday night. "Wanna give me a ride down to the [Pittsburgh &] Lake Erie station?"

After a hearty "breakfast" around midnight, Cordic was ready to go with his black hat, black "B&O business suit," a fistful of fresh Marsh Wheeling stogies and his ever-present grip, Rege recalled. Son needled father a little, wondering if the president would experience some rough handling through Cordic's region.

"Don't you worry about that d——d Truman," the portly company man snapped. "He'll get the best ride of his trip on the B&O. And, he'll be in Cumberland [Md.] right on the mark!"

Cordic made it to New Castle and came back east in the spit-and-polish diesel cab of the POTUS special. Soon a Secret Service agent joined him to check things out. "Harry wanted a ride on the engine," Rege Cordic related. "That was that. No questions. No discussion."

The elder Cordic had always been a firebrand of a Democrat, but he had become soured at Truman when the president threatened to take over the railroads a couple of years back as a nationwide strike loomed. Now the two would meet—two strong wills thrust together shortly after sunrise by the vagaries of a whistlestop itinerary.

"Since the power was in an A-B-B-A configuration, the diesel nose at the rear represented a hazardous gap between the locomotive and the train," Rege explained. "And, as Pete swung open the small door beneath the headlight ... there in the swaying lead car stood the diminutive leader of the Free World, hanging onto his hat, bracing himself against the pitching and rolling.

"I'm Harry Truman. What's your name, sir?" he shouted. "I'm Pete Cordic, Mr. President," the officer boomed. "Well, Pete, you'd better get me across here in one piece or we'll both be in trouble." They laughed.

Despite a few concerned looks from protectors behind him, Truman leaned on Cordic's hefty arm and landed lightly on the A unit's deck. A strong handshake followed as two Secret Service agents were left to fend for themselves. "Pete, let's see what you've got here." No photographers came forward; it was too early.

"Through the roar of the engines and generators and pumps, the party made its way toward the lead unit, pausing along the way for bellowed questions and answers on the finer points of diesel locomotion," Rege Cordic recalled.

Conversations were easier in the cab as introductions were made. Truman said he'd always felt at home with railroaders; the Missouri Pacific fellows had helped him a lot in his early political days. Then Cordic asked if his guest would like to try his hand at the throttle.

Truman grinned boyishly. "You

aren't gonna let me run us all into the ditch, are you, Pete?" Laughter ensued all around as the engineer eased out of his seat, guided the president's foot to the dead man's pedal, settled him into position and replaced his fedora with an engineer's cap.

"Now, Mr. President, you've got a couple of crossings to whistle for."

"Tell me when, Pete." Truman leaned on the horn through Coraopolis and West End along the misty Ohio River. Somehow the word spread and photographers on the ground snapped pictures of the honorary engineman. "He really didn't do much running," Cordic said later. "We kept a pretty good eye on things. But he looked like he was having a … good time." Too soon, it was over. Truman had to go back to the *Magellan* for breakfast. "Pete, you run a fine railroad," the smiling chief executive declared with another handshake. "If you're ever in Washington, stop by the house."

Cordic's loyalty to the Democratic party never suffered any setbacks after that. "He called me Pete, y'know."[90]

The first major tour commenced Friday morning, Sept. 17, but it almost didn't. As the family was packing, party treasurer Louis A. Johnson called some wealthy Democrats to the White House and Truman got up on a chair in the Red Room to inform them that if they didn't come across with $25,000, the train wouldn't get beyond Pittsburgh. Two men immediately pledged $10,000 each, and the show was on.

Trimly attired in a tan double-breasted suit, the president was animated and confident as he bade goodbye to Secretary of State George Marshall; his running mate, Sen. Alben Barkley of Kentucky; and a smattering of Democratic loyalists on the platform of Union Station's Track 15. "Go out there and mow 'em down, Harry!"[115] Barkley boomed. Truman

grinned. "I'm going to fight hard," he vowed. "I'm going to give 'em h——."[329]

With nothing to write but the departure story after the 17-car PRR special left Washington, reporters gave space to Truman's daring slogan, which caught on across the country despite Margaret's chiding her father for using it.

Walter Fitzmaurice described life aboard the special.

"You go to the press car, knock off your stint, and then go back to your compartment where the reading lamp throws an inviting glow over your made-up berth. However, the hour is still early and the lounge cars are still open so you wander back to the one just ahead of the *Magellan.* No news, just politicians there. The young man sitting just inside the rear door … declines a highball, pointing with a smile to the Secret Service button in his lapel, and you know that Capt. Ernest Chapman of the Baltimore & Ohio police [on board by White House request even though the train was on the Pennsy], sitting just across the aisle, doesn't drink. So you talk about the *Magellan,* its occupants and long-past presidential trips."

The brakes slowed for Baltimore and the *Magellan* gave the press car a sharp spank, channeling the conversation to the comforts of the unwieldy and heavy private palace. "And the family's just as comfortable as the car," Fitzmaurice quoted the unnamed Secret Service agent. "I mean to work for. We never get any orders from back there; only requests."[137]

The exchange with Barkley had set the tone of the tour. Crowds everywhere shouted Barkley's challenge to the president, and if they hadn't after about a minute, Clifford or Dr. Graham, now a brigadier general, would slip off the train, melting into the crowd and "priming the pump"[384] themselves. For their efforts, they earned the label of "carnival shill"[115]

from *New Yorker Magazine* writer Richard H. Rovere.

"Of all the things I ever did in government, this may have been the least dignified," Clifford remarked. "But, after all, we were shorthanded on the train, and very far behind in the polls. And, to tell the truth, I rather enjoyed it."[115]

Once again, Truman made appearances from dawn to midnight—even taking his famous "constitutional" on station platforms or through yards at the first stop of the day. "I'd get off and take a walk," the president chuckled years later. "And, of course, they had to hold the train as long as I wanted it held. I was president."[255]

Less was left to chance this time. Advance men—Oscar Chapman and presidential Administrative Assistant Donald S. Dawson—ensured that June's disasters were not repeated. Also, local politicians were allowed to flock aboard the train.

The first two days of the trip, Sept. 17 and 18, were so taxing they nearly hospitalized the president. In Pittsburgh, he helped celebrate the first anniversary of the American Freedom Train, which was carrying original copies of the Declaration of Independence, Constitution, Gettysburg Address and other historical treasures around the nation. He followed that up with a whistlestop talk at Crestline, Ohio, at 10:30 p.m.

The politicians were so welcome that when the train reached Chicago at 2:15 a.m. Saturday the 18th for transfer to the Chicago, Rock Island & Pacific, Truman was awakened to greet Cook County Democratic leader Jack Arvey—who had tried to convince the convention to dump him—and his delegation. The conciliatory president received the group in pajamas and bathrobe, sitting on the edge of his bed. Arvey told reporters they exchanged greetings and he wished Truman well. "He looked sleepy," Arvey concluded, "and I felt like a heel getting him up."[329]

The wee-hours visit didn't sap Truman's energy, however. As always, he was at his best during the rear-platform talks. He headed straight into Republican country—a master political stroke—and began his Saturday schedule at Rock Island, Ill., at 5:45 a.m. ("I don't think I have ever seen so many farmers in town in all my life.")[329] He also included four more stops before 9 a.m. ("I'm only a synthetic alumni,"[330] he modestly misspoke when introduced as the most distinguished graduate of Grinnell College in Grinnell, Iowa.) In all, Truman spoke 13 times that day, concluding at Polo, Mo., at 8:10 p.m. ("I didn't think I was going to be able to do it but the railroad finally consented to stop.")[329]

The steamy Saturday's major speech was at midday at the National Plowing Contest at Dexter, Iowa, a community of 635 persons 35 miles west of Des Moines. To an audience of farmers, bankers, mortgage holders, equipment sellers and produce buyers gathered on Mrs. T.R. Agg's model farm, he skillfully enunciated an effective farm policy that won him many votes in the region. The papers listed the crowd at 80,000, but Truman disputed that.

"Nobody asked me, but I could have told 'em," he bragged. "There were 96,000 people there."[255]

A writer asked him how he knew.

"There was 10 acres, and the place was jammed full. Now figure two to the square yard and you'll see how many there were. Figure it out for yourself."[255]

Quickly getting down to business, the president recalled how the New Deal had wiped out the horrors suffered under the Republicans and the great crash of 1929. Labeling the Grand Old Party as "gluttons of privilege,"[239] he declared that the

Thomas E. Dewey greets a supporter at Providence, R.I., during his 1948 campaign.

Republican Congress "has already stuck a pitchfork in the farmers' backs"[329] and pledged to reverse a shortage of storage bins that forced farmers to sell all their grain at depressed prices (since January, corn had dropped from $2.46 to $1.78 a bushel, wheat from $2.81 to $1.97). Truman chuckled and looked behind him after reading the "pitchfork" line, as if he were seeing a speechwriter's creativity for the first time. Clifford later winced at the sledge-hammer phraseology, but approved it at the time.

After he inspected the plowing and some tractor exhibits for a couple of hours and sampled some of the prize-winning cakes and pies, Truman returned to the *Magellan's* platform and talked informally about his early days as a dirt farmer back in Missouri.

He could plow as straight a furrow behind a pair of mules as the next man, he crowed. "A prejudiced witness said

so—my mother. I used to sow a 160-acre wheatfield without a skip place showing in it."[100] And he joked about how well the Iowa farmers must have prospered under Democratic rule, pointing to the 50 private planes tied down in an adjacent field that many of them had flown to the contest.

He carried on for quite awhile about the differences between mules and machines. "The most peaceful thing in the world is riding behind a mule, plowing a field," he said. "And while there's some danger that you may, like the fella said, get kicked in the head by a mule and end up believing everything you read in the papers, the chances are you'll do your best thinking that way. ... A tractor will never be as ... satisfactory as a mule. It makes a noise, for one thing, and noise interferes with a man's thoughts."[255]

Soon it was over. The presidential

Harry Truman meets the press aboard his whistlestop special in October 1948.

party was driven away in a brand new fleet of convertibles—with their tops down—to catch up with the train, which had backed from Dexter to Des Moines. The dust the farmers kicked up with their plowing damaged the presidential throat. For at least a week, Dr. Graham had to spray Truman's throat before every speech. The president was the only one surprised by the damage.

"Dr. Graham just sprayed, mopped and caused me to gargle bad-tasting liquids until the throat gave up and got well," he wrote to his sister, Mary Jane Truman.[171]

In the press car of the special that evening as it continued south through the Iowa countryside, a score of reporters wrote for their papers that Truman appeared to have "hit the mark" or had "touched a sensitive nerve."[292]

Truman's impromptu talks fell into a set pattern. Someone would give him something of local manufacture— from apples, peaches or corn to a mess of celery, a piece of cheese or a miner's hat. And always a key to the city. The speeches usually contained a plug for the local Democrats, a reference to the local school, baseball team or sausage factory, a brief exposition on some local or national problem the Republicans had managed to mess up, and a plea to register and vote. They never defined policy, but were always rehashes of previously announced programs couched in local terms provided by careful staff work. Finally, he would introduce Bess, who had joined the train at Des Moines, and Margaret, having refined his "boss" lines a bit.

"And now, howja like to meet my family?"[330] he would ask after an intentional pause and a puzzling glance over the crowd. He would cock his head slightly to catch the response. Said one writer, "He has the appealing look of a man who wouldn't be surprised if the answer was 'no' but would be terribly hurt."[330] Always the response was favorable. "First, Mizz Truman,"[330] he would announce, and the blue curtain behind him would part and the first lady—like her husband, more relaxed in small crowds with no photographers present—would come out and stand by the president's right side smiling. "And now I'd like to have you meet my daughter, Margaret," or in southern states, "Miss Margaret."[417] She was an object of great curiosity because of her singing career. Then the president would refer to his wife as "the boss," winking to the men in the crowd. Sometimes Bess would sass back that "they'll never believe that."[384] Then he would again call Margaret "the one who bosses the boss."[100] Margaret, who called the show a "vaudeville act,"[101] usually stepped into the picture carrying an armful of roses. While she tossed one or two of them into the crowd, Truman would bend over the railing and start pumping hands. He often consented to hold or hug children, but kissing them was out. "Babies can't talk," he explained. "And how do I know they wouldn't object?"[403]

Once the womenfolk flanked the president, a railroad official behind the curtain would telephone the engineer to leave town, going easy for four car-lengths or so to ensure stragglers a chance to reboard. The Trumans would clasp their hands high in the air, wave briefly, then when the ladies went back inside to fix their hair for the next curtain call, Truman would keep waving until the last brakeman in the yard had seen him.

Bess grew tired of the "boss" references. "You know, I don't think Mother really likes you calling me her boss," Margaret told her dad confidentially. Truman thought about it for a second, obviously calculating risks and advantages. "It gets a good laugh," he finally answered. "I remained the boss's boss," she sighed.[101]

Sometimes hecklers interrupted the president, but he always knew how to handle them. Once some 12- and 13-year-olds were particularly persistent. He waited until they shut up, then pointed to them and said, "I think it's time you boys went home to your mothers." The crowd roared, and they vanished sheepishly.

All in all, the crowds warmed up to Truman—and he to them. "All over the country they call me 'Harry'," he said. "I like it. I believe when you speak to me like that you like me."[403]

There was always an element of danger at stops when the long train's slack ran out as the brakes released. Secret Service agents bellowed to the crowd to stay at least 6 feet away on the sides and 30 feet to the rear but no one ever obeyed.

"They would surge right up under the wheels," Margaret wrote. "Once I tugged on an emergency brake that was on the rear platform to prevent a rollback. I was quietly reprimanded. Dad pointed out I was liable to start a panic in the crowd."[100]

Later Saturday, the train dipped into Missouri, where the president spoke briefly in Trenton, Polo and Independence, his home. On Sunday, the Trumans went to church and in the afternoon the president borrowed a car and visited friends and relatives nearby. That evening, his train pulled out of Kansas City for the West behind gleaming Union Pacific 4-8-4 No. 835.

Margaret offered a tantalizing glimpse of life in the *Magellan's* lounge as it raced across Kansas after making the 11:05 p.m. whistlestop at Junction City.

"My father … was seated opposite me, reading a speech that he would make the following day in Denver. My mother sat beside me, reading a

B&O engines 68, 62B and 68A pull President Truman's 15-car whistlestopper into Gary, Ind., Oct. 25, 1948.

murder mystery. It was a typical Truman family evening. …

"The engineer let the throttle out all the way. Dad was scheduled to speak at noon the following day … and it was to be broadcast over a national radio hookup. Maybe someone had told the engineer to take no chances on arriving late. At any rate, from the sound of the spinning metal wheels alone, I could tell that we were traveling at an unusual speed.

"Then I noticed Dad's eyes rose from the page he was reading, and he stared for a moment at the wall just above my head. This was very unusual. One of the most remarkable things about my father is his power of concentration. He has always been able to read a book or a memorandum with the radio or phonograph playing, and my mother and me conducting a first-class family argument. I am convinced that the world could be coming to an end, but he would not look up until he got to the bottom of the page he was reading.

"My mother went into the dining room to discuss the menus with [Sam] Mitchell, the [White House] steward [and former Pullman porter] who ran the car. Dad let his speech fall into his lap and stared almost grimly at the wall above my head. 'Take a look at that thing,' he said.

"I twisted my neck, remembering that there was a speedometer up there. … At first I could not believe what I saw. We were hitting 105 miles an hour!

"Like most 24-year-olds, I considered myself indestructible, so this discovery only excited me. 'Wow,' I said, and rushed to the window to stare out at the black blur of landscape whizzing by.

"I glanced back at my father and saw something very close to disgust on his face. I had obviously missed his point. 'Do you know what would happen if that engineer had to make a sudden stop?'

"Only then did I remember that the *Ferdinand Magellan* weighed 285,000 pounds. … Its base was solid concrete, reinforced by a section of steel track imbedded in it. It also carried 3 inches of armor plate and the windows were bulletproof. The goal was the safety of the president of the United States. But it made for problems on the right of way.

" 'If he had to stop suddenly,' Dad said in the same calm, matter-of-fact voice, 'we would mash those 16 cars between us and the engine into junk.' He heard the car door opening and quickly added, 'Don't say a word to your mother. I don't want her to get upset.' The person coming through turned out to be not Mother but Charlie Ross. He wanted to find out what the president thought of the latest draft of tomorrow's speech. The president said he thought it was fine. Then, almost casually, he said, 'Charlie, send someone to tell that engineer there's no need to get us to Denver at this rate of speed. Eighty miles an hour is good enough for me.' " The engineer was told, and complied.[100]

As Truman's train moved through the mountain states, he spoke about conservation and reclamation. Public power projects were on the agenda in Denver on Monday and Salt Lake City on Tuesday. Thrown in for good measure were references to the high cost of living, the housing shortage, the need for federal aid to education, a national health insurance and expanded Social Security. His voice was husky from a cold but still full of fire.

A fleet of 22 Kaisers and Frazers and eight Fords met the party in Denver, and a reporter's curiosity prompted him to ask his driver if he had lent his car to the president out of party loyalty.

"Nah," he said. "This isn't my car. I'm just helping out a friend of mine here. He's the Kaiser-Frazer distributor in town—Northwestern Auto Co., they call it—and I guess he came out first in this agency fight. Got mostly Kaisers and Frazers here. Lucky for him. The 1949 models just came in yesterday, and he's getting a chance right off to display them."[330] Not a bad deal, and it was repeated in every major city on the tour—free transportation for free advertising.

The president reminisced at Salt Lake City. He recalled how his grandfather, Solomon Young, had driven an ox-train load of merchandise to that city and had difficulty disposing of it. Brigham Young advised him "to rent space down on the main street, … place his goods on display, and he would guarantee that my grandfather would lose no money, and he didn't."[329]

The president mentioned his grandfather so often that one reporter commented dryly: "According to a Pennsylvania Railroad representative on the Truman train, this campaign trip is just about the most elaborate tour ever made of this country. I suspect that he is referring only to railroad trips and has conveniently overlooked, for the sake of rail propaganda, those wagon-train trips made by Grandfather Young."[417]

The crowds grew in the West, and so did Truman's confidence. He began lacing his folksy informality with raw invective.

On Monday evening, the train left Denver via the Denver, Rio Grande & Western, and the president lectured the audience in Colorado Springs, Colo. "In 1946, you know, two-thirds of you stayed at home and didn't vote. You wanted a change. Well, you got it. You got the change. You got just exactly what you deserved. If you stay at home on November the 2nd and let this same gang get control of the government, I won't have any sympathy with you."[329]

Another talk—at Canon City—ran

Harry Truman greets onlookers as he leaves the B&O station in Gary, Ind., to get into an automobile.

a little long and dusk was falling. It had turned to deep night by the time the train entered the fabled Royal Gorge. "From the windows of the Pullman compartments, even with the lights out, the (rock) walls appeared as vague shapes, very close but indistinct," wrote Fitzmaurice. "The vestibule doors on the other side of the car weren't locked but two newspeople who opened one were at once reminded of the risk by a trainman."

The cooperative crewman led the pair through a door into the diner's darkened pantry, closed it, then opened another to the outside and let

down an iron bar across the frame. "There," he said. "Lean out on that and you can see everything."

"Below, so close you wanted to peel off your shoes and dangle your feet it in, rushed the Arkansas River, indigo blue except where the water foamed white against big boulders," Fitzmaurice recalled. "The track curved and the Pullmans ahead, their golden windows glowing against the overhanging immensity of the walls, shrank to model-train size. ... The green [marker] light of the *Magellan*, shining steadily at the rear, and a searchlight, darting its beam here and

there along the walls, dispelled the illusion."[137]

About the same time, the *New Yorker's* Richard Rovere ran into the PRR's Harry Karr, the man in charge. He had been doing this since the days of Harding, Karr said, and it had left him a "nervous wreck."[330]

They were deep into the gorge as the slight, tense man talked.[362] "Just look out that window," Karr declared. "Makes you sweat blood even to think of taking a president through here. Let a few boulders roll down that thing and we'd all be shooting the rapids. Believe me, we thought long and hard before we agreed to bring this train down through here."[330]

Karr said the scheduling for this trip had been arranged almost without a hitch. But he did reveal that one passenger train, an express between Kansas City and Denver, was seriously delayed by the POTUS move. The superintendent of one division wanted to sidetrack Truman—who was always stopping to talk—and let the express pass. But during a conference Sunday in Kansas City it was decided not to let the train by.

"There was just the tiniest chance that a piece of flying steel or something like that might have hit the president's train," Karr explained. "Of course, nothing could have hurt the president in his armored car."[330] As it

was, the express arrived in Denver only 45 minutes late.

With a "feed-mill"[330] informality, Truman urged the crowd in Provo, Utah, on Tuesday to exercise "that God-given right … to go to the polls on the second of November and cast your ballot for the Democratic ticket—and then I can stay in the White House another four years."[329] In Ogden, he suggested that the voters can "keep me from suffering from a housing shortage on Jan. 20, 1949."[329] This statement upset his staff because they figured people wanted to know what Truman could do for them rather than vice versa. But he kept on using it. It worked, at least in Ogden. The president was appointed an honorary captain in the Weber County

sheriff's posse, and Miss Utah put a boutonniere in his lapel.

In Truckee, Calif., on the Southern Pacific on Wednesday the 22nd, Truman bragged that he was glad so many had come out to see the next president. West of the Sierra Nevada Mountains in Roseville, he informed the crowd that the Republican Congress "tried to choke you to death in this valley"[329] by cutting off appropriations for publicly owned power lines.

By this time speechwriters were feeling the pressure. Enduring a hectic work pace, their outlines began to show frequent deletions and corrections, usually in pencil. A note in Elsey's handwriting appeared on the outline for Sacramento: "This was

E.L. Thompson/B&O Historical Society

While Harry Truman presses the flesh in the Gary, Ind., station, Everett L. "Tommy" Thompson snaps a quick shot of the head end of the president's train.

done in about 2 hrs. It was to be a speech on 160 Acre farm limitation—then was completely altered to be about Public Power!"[417]

Another crisis followed close behind. Elsey scribbled to Clifford: "Outside Sacramento less than three hrs before speech with no one having seen it! Is there any possibility of detaching you to look at San Francisco outline?" The note was signed "GME" and carried an R.S.V.P.: "I'm standing outside in corridor." Clifford's response: "Hold it. Will get to it later. CMC."[417]

Bess spent most of her time on the train with her husband. "She let the staff take care of greeting the numerous politicians who got on and off," Margaret recalled. "She felt it was more important to keep her eye on the president, to make sure he didn't go over the edge into total exhaustion. She also functioned as a quiet cheering section and subtle critic, telling him how she thought the latest speech had gone over and suggesting small ways to improve the routine."[101]

Mrs. Truman also played mother to the staff.

"As we approached San Francisco … Elsey came into the car with [the] speech that Dad was supposed to make. … He had not yet had time to go over it. We were having dinner and George was very apologetic about interrupting us. But he was also more than a little frantic. 'Mr. President, you've really got to read this as soon as possible, in case you want any changes —' he began." Elsey explained to the author he had "very hastily whipped up a text" on the accomplishments of the United Nations, since its charter was signed there. "The train was within 20 to 25 minutes of Oakland before I had something I could take back to him."

"George," Mrs. Truman said. "You look frazzled. Have you had any dinner?"

Elsey shook his head. He had thought she was looking "real cross" at him. "No ma'am, nothing to eat," he politely replied. "I've been busy."

"Eat this," Bess commanded, pushing her apple pie and a cup of coffee across the table.[101]

Truman read the speech and Elsey ate his meager dinner. "By the time I finished," the aide said, "we were slowing down to arrive at Oakland."[129]

Sometimes tempers flared when Democrats back in Washington tried to run things on the train.

A wire from party researcher William L. Batt Jr. to Clifford noted that during a radio address the "rattling" of paper could be heard by radio listeners. "Would it be possible to use either linen or parchment paper?" Batt asked. The suggestion elicited a one-word rejoinder in Elsey's handwriting: "Nonsense."[417]

In the same memo, Batt criticized sentences that were too long and involved, with too many dependent clauses. The penciled response: "He can't talk kindergarten all the time."[417]

In Merced on Thursday, Truman invoked Scripture when he said the Republicans were hoarding the big incomes and letting "a little of it trickle down off the table like the crumbs fell to Lazarus."[329] In Fresno, he declared about Republican Bertram W. Gearhart that: "You have got a terrible congressman here in this district. … He is one of the worst obstructionists in Congress. He has done everything he possibly could to cut the throats of the farmer and the laboring man. If you send him back, that will be your fault if you get your throats cut."[171]

Later, a reporter was banging away on his story in the press car. "I felt somebody behind me," recalled Edward T. Folliard of *The Washington Post*. "I looked around and it was the president. 'Oh, Mr. President, I was just writing what you said about Congressmen (Gearhart).' He said, 'Well, probably, I've just re-elected the son of a ———.' "[171]

He hadn't; Gearhart lost.

The president had to make his major Los Angeles speech at Gilmore Stadium because the Republicans had rented the Hollywood Bowl to rehearse lighting effects for Dewey's speech there the next night. On the platform with Truman were entertainers Humphrey Bogart, Lauren Bacall, George Jessel and a left-wing Democrat actor named Ronald Reagan.

This time the Secret Service had rebelled at the new model cars, refusing to let the president ride through this unpredictable city in a car without

One passenger wouldn't have made it back aboard Harry Truman's train in Los Angeles had it not been for Dewey Long's alertness. A weary veteran newsman had tried to drown his boredom in the local bistros and turned up missing as departure time neared. Long sent out an alarm while other journalists covered for their missing buddy.

The Los Angeles police finally found the errant writer sleeping in a bus filled with members of a church choir. The singers were clad in angels' robes "with gossamer wings attached to their shoulders" and were trying to figure out what to do with their uninvited slumberer when the law arrived.

Upon being awakened and beholding the seraphically clad group, the gentleman became a might turbulent. He was returned to the train, where Long helped administer proper restoratives and put him to bed.[224]

One of the more unusual gifts Harry Truman received on his 1948 whistlestopper was an Angora goat, appropriately labeled as a jab at Truman's opponent, Thomas E. Dewey. The president said he wanted to use the critter to keep the grass trimmed at the White House, but had to leave it behind as there was no place to house it on his train.

running boards for them to stand on. A search had been made, and they had found a 1934 Lincoln touring car owned by Cecil B. De Mille. The movie mogul planned to vote for Dewey, one writer said, but his patriotic impulses were stronger than his party loyalty.

Leaving Los Angeles on Friday the 24th, Truman's train was routed via the SP to San Diego, then AT&SF to Colton. It left Colton at 2:15 p.m. via the SP again, as Extra 6000 East, a surviving train order reveals. "Make careful inspection of cars in train and on adjacent track," the long order read, "to see that no hazardous conditions exist giving particular attention to lumber and other objects that might be protruding from open top cars and carefully noting that all refrigerator car doors are closed and securely fastened."[145]

The president quickly covered New Mexico on Saturday, speaking only at Lordsburg and Deming. By now the train was really taking on the appearance of a carnival. At Lordsburg, a National Guard company saluted Truman's arrival and Indians gave him purses for Bess and Margaret. The Bataan Veterans Association gave him a letter opener in the form of a totem pole. The mayor of Deming gave him an inscribed, specially made silver belt and his wife and daughter received leather-bound albums engraved with 46 views of area ranches and industries. The Deming Lions Club distributed small bags of Mimbres Valley pinto beans to everybody on the train, and 300 Mescalero Indians boarded and talked with the president.

By 11 a.m., Truman was in El Paso to start an intensive four-day Texas tour via SP to San Antonio, the Missouri-Kansas-Texas to Fort Worth, the Texas & Pacific to Dallas, MKT to Bells, T&P to Whitesboro, MKT to Gainesville, and Santa Fe toward Oklahoma City, Okla. Truman spoke about public power, then addressed five more whistlestop crowds in the next 10 hours.

He was in a jolly mood. "It has been an education to see these bright and shiny faces," he told the crowd in Valentine. "Everybody seems to be happy and everybody seems to be interested in the welfare of the United States because you have come out to meet your chief executive and look him over and see what you think of him." The Republicans, he said, "are on the run now! We've got them scared and we want to keep them that way."[329]

The president arrived in Uvalde, Texas, at 6:50 a.m. Sunday to have breakfast with 79-year-old John Nance Garner, FDR's first vice president. Margaret recalled that arising at 5 a.m. didn't bother her dad, who thought that's when every right-thinking American gets up. "The rest of us were practically comatose," she fumed.[101]

Garner, the high school band and some 4,000 citizens were on hand at the railway station. So was an Angora goat, clothed in a gold blanket with red lettering bearing the legend "Dewey's Goat." Truman loved it. He posed for pictures with the frisky critter, telling the press, "I'm going to clip it and make a rug. Then I'm going to let it graze on the White House lawn for the next four years."[100] He was forced, however, to leave it behind. The train had no facilities for it.

The president's visit to Uvalde was billed as a social affair, but it was a shrewd political coup. If the old conservative "Cactus Jack" Garner found Truman palatable, he was clearly no threat to democracy. At his home, Garner gave him a tremendous Texas breakfast of white-wing dove and mourning dove, bacon, ham, fried chicken, scrambled eggs, rice and gravy, hot biscuits, Uvalde honey, peach preserves, grape jelly and gallons of coffee.

"As we finished this feast, Dad gave Cactus Jack a small black satchel,"

Margaret revealed. "He said it contained 'medicine, only to be used in case of snakebites.'[101] It was the same expensive Kentucky bourbon the vice president used to invite Sen. Truman to share when he visited Mr. Garner's Capitol "dog house" in his Senate days."[100]

Truman gave Garner his gift in his home library, Truman aide Donald Dawson told the author. "Garner looked at it and he said, 'Well, this is too good for company; I'll just put it up here for private use.' And he climbed up the ladder there and put it [on a] shelf behind the books." (Years later, Dawson said Truman was again present in Uvalde when Garner celebrated his 90th birthday. "I spoke to President Truman on the telephone," Dawson said. "And I suggested that he ask about that bottle of whiskey. And that I would bet that it was still up on the shelf behind the books. Truman did that, and sure enough, Garner got up there and the books were still in front of the whiskey—untouched.")[107]

After the repast, Garner introduced Truman to the crowd outside as an "old and very good friend,"[329] a comment that guaranteed the president the votes of numerous Texas conservatives. Truman replied: "Mr. President —that's the way I used to address him in the Senate—I haven't had such a breakfast in 40 years. ... John Garner and I have been friends for a long time and we are going to be friends as long as we live. I'm coming back for another visit sometime. I fished around for another invitation and got it."[329]

Mrs. Truman broke her customary silence and told everybody: "Good morning and thank you for this wonderful greeting."[101] Then, before the train left town, Garner urged every-

B&O engine 51 pulls a Truman special.

one to go to church.

On Monday, the northbound special was required to stop—by law—in Temple, Texas.

"It's a good thing President Truman scheduled a campaign stop here,"[417] a newspaper article said, recalling that Theodore Roosevelt had intended to pass through in 1904 without stopping but was prevented from doing that when City Council passed an ordinance requiring all presidential trains to stop for at least five minutes. "The city marshal and county sheriff halted Mr. Roosevelt's train," the article continued, "climbed aboard and served papers on the engineer. Mr. Roosevelt made a speech, complimenting the city on its nerve. The ordinance has never been repealed, but it never has been needed since."

Truman laughed. He was going to stop anyway, he said, because "your congressman says I promised him to come here."[417]

Continuing north through Texas, Truman launched attacks on Dewey's bland calls for national unity. He said the Republicans wanted "the kind of unity that benefits the National Association of Manufacturers. ... They don't want unity, they want surrender."[329]

Large and friendly crowds were everywhere—15,000 in Waco, another 15,000 outside the station in Fort Worth, 20,000 at Rebel Stadium in Dallas. Dawson had wanted to hold the rally at the station, fearing that the stadium would look empty. He was wrong.

The aide had his hands full in the Lone Star State. The anti-Truman Texas Regulars had rigged things so they would be in the spotlight at all the stops. "I had to rearrange all the people (who) came onto the back platform and shook hands with the president ... so that the voters ... could see Truman."[107]

A young Democratic congressman named Lyndon Johnson, who was running for the Senate, boarded the train at San Antonio and stayed all day, "talking to everyone he could corner," Clifford said.[85] But he was "as low as he could be" because he thought he was going to lose, Dawson recalled. "He was by himself in the last car—not gregarious at all—but Truman would call him out every time we stopped at the end of his speech and say, 'Now here I want you to meet your next senator,' and hold (Johnson's) hand up. I'm satisfied that that was one of the great contributing factors to Johnson's election."[107]

At Dallas, before Truman spoke, Attorney General Tom Clark introduced him at some length, winding up with: "And I was with him when he stopped Joe Louis in the courts." His misstatement pitted the president against the nation's heavyweight boxing champion instead of the fiery, bushy-browed head of the United Mine Workers of America. Truman was still laughing when he got to the microphone. "Tom, you give me too much credit," he said. "It wasn't Joe Louis I stopped, it was John [L. Lewis]. I haven't quite that much muscle."[329]

It was in Dallas that Truman addressed his first integrated crowd in the South—a very daring venture for that day, planned by Dawson. But all went well. "It worked so smoothly that the black newspaper reporters who were on the train didn't even notice it," Dawson recalled. "We had to go to them later and tell them all about it so that they would print it."[107]

The staff followed the same integration policy all the way across Texas. Once, there was a tense moment when Truman shook hands with a black woman and the crowd booed. But he didn't back down and told the hecklers that blacks had the same rights as whites. "In some towns," Dawson said, "they didn't even want the black voters to come down to the train. We just told them they were going to come. The president wanted them there."[107]

It was also in Dallas that Truman spied an orphanage and ordered the train to stop so he could talk to the children.

"I thought that, well, being spoken to by the president of the United States was something they'd remember all their lives," he explained later. "It's a very lonely thing being a child. It was for me, and I had a family, including ... 39 first cousins, and I was the only one they all spoke to."[255]

The highlight in Bonham was a reception arranged by its native son, Speaker of the House Sam Rayburn. Truman endured bitter cold to speak at an outdoor meeting, then stood for hours in an indoor receiving line at Rayburn's home to greet what seemed like half of Texas.

"It was an old-fashioned Southern house, with a central hall that ran from the front door to the back door," Margaret remembered. "Suddenly Mr. Sam exclaimed, 'Shut the door, Beauford [Texas Gov. Beauford Jester], they're comin' by twice.' But that didn't discourage anybody. People just kept on streaming out the back door and in the front door again."[100]

The frantic pace for speechwriters continued. A talk prepared for Dennison, Texas, had been readied for Tuesday but instead Truman spoke without preparation from a platform at Sherman. "No preparation for this," Elsey noted. "Our route was changed"[417] (from MKT to T&P between Bells and Whitesboro, for unexplained reasons).

The president's free-swinging style came through at the first stop in Oklahoma—Marietta—where he found a hot Senate race going between former governor and oil producer Robert S. Kerr and Sen. Edward H. Moore. "We need a man like Bob Kerr to take old man Moore's place," Truman declared. "He never was any good in the first place. I know old man Moore. I served in the Senate with him for quite a while, and if he ever did anything for the people it was by accident and not intention."[171] It was the kind of line no ghostwriter could have dreamed up.

At Aardmore, Okla., the president's farming background came in handy again.

"A young man on a very skittish horse was among the crowd," Margaret wrote. "The train terrified the animal, and he was obviously close to bolting. There was a real danger that he might have hurt or killed the rider, as well as many other people in the crowd. While White House aides and Secret Service men wondered what to do, my father stepped down from the rear platform, strode over to the jittery animal and unsteady rider, and seized the bridle. 'That's a fine horse you've got there, son,' he said. He opened the horse's mouth and studied his teeth. 'Eight years old, I see.' Calmly, he led the animal over to one of the Secret Service men, who escorted him a safe distance from the train."[100]

"Who'd [have] thought that the president of the United States would know about horses?" the young rider muttered.[44]

Truman's quip in Dallas about "muscle" must have come to haunt him in Oklahoma City. Indeed, it seemed as if he had no muscle at all when it came time to leave. The Chicago, Rock Island & Pacific Railroad refused to move the train out of the station until past charges for transportation were settled. Oklahoma Gov. Roy Turner and W. Elmer Harber, another rich Democrat, gave a party on the *Magellan* and raised enough money not only for the rest of that trip but for the next one as well.

"For a time," wrote Jack Redding, who was the Democratic National Committee's publicity director, "it seemed possibly the whole party might have to alight and get back to Washington the best way they could."[292]

Entertainer Perle Mesta had done her part to keep the train rolling. INS correspondent Robert G. Nixon said she went into the special guests' car after the train had left Bonham. "She told them what a predicament that the train was in. She flashed a check, $5,000, her own check."

The singer said that to keep the train from being stalled, "here's my check for $5,000," which she held up. The gesture was effective; several bigwigs came across on the spot. "Interestingly enough," Nixon recounted, "I was told by a member of the president's staff later that Perle ... tore up her check. ... Perhaps she had earlier made her own contribution."[282]

A memo to Clifford from Stephen J. Spingarn, an occasional speechwriter for Truman, illustrates that it wasn't only important what the candidate said, but where and when as well. In discussing the timing of a major address on communism, Spingarn said: "My opinion is that this speech should be made as far East as possible, and in any event, not West of the Central Time Zone. I say this because I think it is the type of speech that should have the widest possible radio audience. I believe it will be the kind of fighting speech that will have more impact on the air than in print. Because of the three-hour time difference, relatively few people in the East would hear the speech if it were given in California. At the same time, I think the speech should be made as early in the campaign as reasonably possible. I think Mr. Batt is right when he says that the Middle West is the place where the cries of Communism are doing the most damage. ... In all the circumstances, I think that Oklahoma City would be an appropriate place for the speech."[417]

The timing became all the more important when Dewey attacked the administration for calling the search for communists in government a "red herring"[171] at his Hollywood Bowl appearance. Clifford knew the counterattack had to come quickly; so the struggle against communism provided the backbone of Truman's speech at the Oklahoma State Fairgrounds. And the speechwriters aboard the train wrestled with every phrase up until the moment of delivery. For instance, Murphy wired the train from Washington about one sentence that read: "I charge that the Republicans have impeded and made more difficult our efforts to apprehend communism in this country." He suggested that the word "apprehend" be changed to "cope with," and the change was made.[417]

After all that, a snafu nearly unraveled everything.

"The speech was to go on the air at 1 p.m.," Nixon recounted. "The train was (40 minutes) late. ... The president and everybody else piled off the train and into cars at the station. We had motorcycle police, and we went roaring through downtown Oklahoma City at 80 miles an hour, sirens screaming. Why somebody wasn't killed you often wonder. We roared into the fairgrounds with the dust flying, brakes screeching and tires skidding. The president got to the rostrum where the microphones were with less than a minute to spare, but he made it."[282]

The chief executive continued through Oklahoma and into Missouri, via the Rock Island to McAlester, the MKT to Tulsa, and the St. Louis-San Francisco (Frisco) to St. Louis, delivering 16 speeches between 7:35 a.m. and 11:15 p.m. Wednesday, most of them from the rear platform.

Thursday's itinerary routed Truman out of St. Louis via the Louisville & Nashville. He talked at Mount

Harry Truman has introduced his wife and daughter at Mount Sterling, Ky., on Oct. 1, 1948; his "vaudeville act" is done again.

Vernon, Ill., then got in an automobile for a 141-mile trip through southern Illinois, during which he spoke nine times in 5½ hours. By late afternoon, he was rolling through Kentucky, heading for a major speech in Louisville.

The last stop before Louisville was Irvington, Ky.,—population 790—which was visited in a three-week period by Truman, Dewey and Dewey's running mate, California Gov. Earl Warren, each on his own L&N campaign special. Try THAT kind of coverage in a Boeing 747!

The Louisville & Nashville Employees Magazine covered the passage of Truman's train between St. Louis and Louisville: "He ... made brief talks at Henderson, Owensboro, and Irving-ton, as well as at Hawesville, Ky., and at several cities in southern Illinois. After spending the night at Louisville in back of the general office building in his private car, President Truman's special left the next day for Lexington, Ky., with stops enroute at Shelbyville (one-time home of all four of his grandparents), Frankfort and Midway."[300]

In Shelbyville, the president returned to family history. He delighted the crowd with a story about how his grandfather Anderson Shippe Truman had eloped with a local farm girl, incidentally a descendant of President Tyler's brother. Fearing her father's wrath, they moved to Missouri; not until three or four years later when the in-laws wanted to see their first grandchild was a reconcilia-tion effected. But this time Truman went a little far. "You all know my daughter Margaret," the president said jovially. "She was down here several years ago, looking up the records to see if my grandparents were legally married." The train then pulled away; soon afterward Press Secretary Ross fled to the correspondents' car to assure everyone the president was joking.[329]

In Lexington, the train switched to the C&O. The president was deep in racing country and his immodest optimism drove him to compare him-self to Citation, a horse that often won despite slow starts. "It doesn't matter which horse is ahead or behind at any given moment," he told the crowd. "It's the horse that comes out ahead at the finish that counts. I am trying to do in politics what Citation has done in the horse races."[171]

The train, pulled by two C&O class K-4 2-8-4 steam locomotives, entered Ashland a half-hour late. Noted railroad photographer and author Gene Huddleston, then a 17-year-old with a paper route, was in the crowd, but didn't take his camera. "I knew that if I got out on the line to get an action shot, I would probably be arrested by one of the many law enforcement officers patrolling the line," he said. "In 1948, anyone with a camera around a railroad was still highly suspect."[195]

The procession got to Huntington, W.Va., at 4:30 p.m., 45 minutes late. Speaking to 10,000 people, Truman endorsed M.M. Neely.

"If you people don't elect Matt Neely to the Senate, you don't know which side your bread is buttered on."

Neely slapped the president on the back and responded, "And if you folks don't vote for this man, you won't have any bread to put butter on."[171] The show continued to the state capital of Charleston for an evening radio address at the Municipal Auditorium. Truman left town without his glasses case, but a WCHS Radio employee turned it in and as soon as it was known who the owner of the thick-rimmed spectacles was, the case was returned. The last whistlestop of the tour occurred at Montgomery at 10:43 p.m.

Robert R. Young, the C&O's impresario chairman, provided a movie preview in the forward diner that night. Word spread that the Trumans might attend, Walter Fitzmaurice wrote, but when the lights went out none of the three was

there. The crowd concluded no snub was intended; the family was either busy or tired. The special continued to Washington via C&O to Orange, Va., Southern to Alexandria, and the Richmond, Fredericksburg & Potomac, sighing to a stop in Union Station Saturday morning after an overnight trip through the Mountain State and the Old Dominion. On this lap, Truman had covered 8,300 miles, spoken at least 126 times ("No one could ever determine the exact number," Clifford stated),[85] and, by the president's estimate, been seen by 3 million people.

For all the hoopla, most people still thought Truman would lose the election. Crowds on this swing had been large, curious and good-natured, but not particularly enthusiastic. "Nobody stomps, shouts or whistles for

With daughter Margaret still on the rear platform of the Ferdinand Magellan *and a photographer lounging on the brass railing, Harry Truman keeps waving until he passes the last well-wisher as his train departs Mount Sterling, Ky., Oct. 1, 1948.*

Truman; everybody claps," wrote the *New Yorker*'s Richard Rovere. "I should say that the decibel count would be about the same as it would be for a missionary who had just delivered a mildly encouraging report on the inroads being made against heathenism in Northern Rhodesia. This does not necessarily mean that people who come out to hear him intend to vote against him—though my personal feeling is that most of them intend to do just that."[329]

This tour was a marked improvement over the June shakedown as far as public appearances were concerned; but life on board was still lacking. There were the usual bruising ordeals brought on by the crowds and speeches and parades and motorcades and bands. By this time, Truman was sick of "The Missouri Waltz." There were incessant deadlines, the pressure of too little sleep, cold meals, warm drinks—and of too many people living too close together for too long.

Sometimes the train was so crowded people had to take turns sleeping in the same berth. "Not very sanitary," Dewey Long remarked, "but necessary."[224]

There was another problem concerning personal hygiene. "The president can take a bath," Long lamented at the time, "but no one else can." He said the problem was solved one hot night in western Kansas the same way earlier campaign troopers had tackled it. At a stop to water the steam engine, all the permanent party from staff and Secret Service to the press stripped and stood under the spout. "Must have been quite a sight," Long commented, "all of us running around out there stark naked."[224]

There were also problems inherent in the Truman operation. Prepared texts were often available only an hour or so before delivery; speechwriters had gotten behind in preparing the Dexter, Iowa, speech and that threw everything else late as well. This meant that for principal speeches on the West Coast, texts were distributed too late to be printed in Eastern newspapers' first editions.

"It was high-pressure work," typist Marian Norby said. "We'd have a manual typewriter sitting on the table and we're typing away on a speech just as the train hits a curve. Zoo-o-o-o-t goes the carriage. The whole line of type is ruined and you have to do it all over again while they're standing there waiting for it."[384]

Reporters criticized the lack of a loudspeaker in the press car, which compelled them to dash to the rear end even at the briefest stops to catch the president's words. They were not allowed in the last three cars, so they were cut off from valuable interviews with presidential staff and local politicians. There were no arrangements for baggage and laundry; when the train stopped overnight in a city, it was every man for himself.

"Sometimes we were burning the 4 a.m. oil because the next day's speech was not given to us on time," groaned reporter Nixon. "When we finally got it, we had to immediately read and digest the contents and write a news story about it to be put on the wire at the next train stop on a release-on-delivery basis the next day. Then we were confronted with the fact that the president gets up at 6 o'clock in the morning. If we were parked in a rail yard, he took his morning walk. So, it was the newsmen who got haggard. Their day just didn't seem ever to end. … There were occasions when we would be so exhausted that if we sat down in the club car between whistlestops, we would immediately fall asleep."[282]

One morning out West, Truman was off the *Magellan* at 6 a.m. talking to a Spanish-speaking section gang, porter Fred Fair recalled. "I don't think they fully understood what he was saying, but that didn't stop the president. He enjoyed lambasting the 80th do-nothing Congress."[284]

Occasionally there were clashes aboard the train. One day Clark Clifford approached Dewey Long, who didn't know him well, and abruptly announced that he didn't think the stops were being handled right as far as crowd control was concerned.

Long was stung. "I've studied crowds," he snapped. "You haven't. Suppose you tend to speechwriting and let me take care of the train."

Clifford smiled and tried to defuse the situation. "OK," he said. "And if you have any criticism of the speeches, let me know."

"Now what can you do when a guy's like that?" Long asked. They became fast friends and everyone worked all the harder.[224]

Tom Dewey ran a shorter, more efficient, overconfident campaign. As the expected victor, he garnered more press attention; there were 98 correspondents aboard by the time his *Victory Special* reached California, more than twice the number traveling with Truman. Some 35 writers who had applied late were left behind. Dewey's train, like Truman's, had 17 cars—but his personal staff numbered 43, compared to Truman's 20-some. It included two doctors (a medical doctor and an osteopath who gave him daily rubdowns), five speechwriters, a researcher, a large secretarial staff and various expediters and odd-chore men.

The press was more impressed with the Dewey operation. Paul Lockwood, in charge of the train, would signal the railroads when to leave stations. James Hagerty, the efficient press secretary, had speeches mimeographed a day ahead of time; often they were published in the papers back home before the candidate ever spoke. Hagerty's press car and the diners were equipped with loudspeakers. He was so thorough that when the train was pelted with tomatoes, he would soon afterward run to the press car to report how many were thrown. Ed Jaeckle shepherded local politicians in and out of the governor's presence. Housekeeping was taken care of, too. Laundry was dispatched and returned within a few hours. The train's schedule was listed in minute detail and was rarely more than 20 minutes late.

One correspondent who rode both caravans wrote that to transfer from Truman's to Dewey's was "like leaving a casual free and easy theater stock company on tour to join up with a sleek New York musical."[417] Another made an even more graphic comparison: "the difference … is, I calculate, 30 or 40 years. It is the difference between horsehair and foam rubber, between the coal stove griddle and the pop-up toaster. Dewey is the pop-up toaster."[417]

Dewey's train covered much of the same territory as Truman's, with a loop through Oregon, Washington, Montana and Idaho subbing for Truman's swing through the Southwest, Texas and Oklahoma. Sometimes the two foes were only a day or two apart, but nearness didn't provoke Dewey into starting a debate. In keeping with his carefully calculated strategy to win by not making a mistake, he rarely acknowledged Truman's existence and never mentioned his name.

The dignified, dapper New Yorker made whistlestop talks, but only about half the number of Truman's. He tried to be folksy, but crowds discerned that it was forced. Like the president, he boosted local candidates and introduced his wife, Frances. But he couldn't shake devastating comments like the one by Alice Roosevelt Longworth that he "looked like the little man on a wedding cake."[384] Herbert Brownell and other aides tried to get him to shave off his priggish, pencil-thin

DR. RICHARD L. LANE/DR. WENDELL H. MCCHORD COLLECTION

Chesapeake & Ohio K-4 type locomotive No. 2787 and a sister engine lead Harry Truman's train into Mount Sterling, Ky., Oct. 1, 1948.

mustache to improve his newsreel image, but Frances put her foot down.

Sometimes he flubbed. At one stop, he said he was glad to see so many children in the crowd and that they should be grateful because he got them a day off from school. Cried one kid: "Today is Saturday!" The throng roared.[44]

Truman took only a four-day rest before returning to the hustings. On Wednesday, Oct. 6, his 15-car train departed behind B&O passenger diesels 68-58B-68A for a three-day tour of Delaware, Pennsylvania, New Jersey and upstate New York. There were no surprises; the president had no need to vary his routine. In Philadelphia, 12,000 cheering, foot-stomping partisans nearly filled Convention Hall; 500,000 filled the

streets to watch the president's motorcade.

Financing problems persisted, but they weren't the only headache. While Truman rolled through upstate New York on Friday, stories broke about his plan to send Chief Justice Fred Vinson to Moscow to engage in private discussions with Joe Stalin. The idea was to moderate Cold War tensions over the Berlin blockade by having the chief jurist of the land approach Stalin personally, and also to stop a leakage of votes to Progressive candidate Henry Wallace over his "peace" issue.

When the subject came up on the train, Clifford and Elsey put up the strongest possible arguments against the mission.

"[It] caused enormous tensions

Above: *Crowd awaits President Truman's train at Mount Sterling, Ky., Oct. 1, 1948.*

Below: *President Truman, having been introduced by Hiram Redmon, owner of the Redmon Printing Co., addresses the crowd at Ashland, Ky., Oct. 1, 1948, as the omnipresent B&O police officer Ernest Chapman, on the ground, glances over his shoulder.*

Above: *The Mount Sterling, Ky., crowd ignores the long row of heavyweight sleepers as President Truman's train pulls in on Oct. 1, 1948, waiting to see the president on the rear.*

Right: *Aides make sure the crowd is in place before Harry Truman makes his appearance at Mount Sterling, Ky., Oct. 1, 1948.*

217

within the staff," Elsey recalled. "Clark and I argued vigorously—almost violently—against it. This was the only matter in which I ever tried to slug it out toe to toe with Matt Connelly, who defended the idea because it had come from [speechwriters David M.] Noyes and [Albert Z.] Carr."[171]

Secretary of State George Marshall vehemently opposed the plan because it didn't go through proper channels and such a unilateral move would upset U.S. allies. So Truman canceled the trip. The problem was that Charlie Ross told the press about it before the cancellation, then had to hurriedly call all the reporters back and tell them about the change. All this, of course, was in confidence—but someone leaked the story anyway, and Truman came into a persistent and stinging round of criticism.

The president decided to cut his trip short and call Marshall home from talks in Paris to soothe his feelings and figure out how to explain the bungled affair. The train had been scheduled to leave Buffalo at 11:30 Friday night. It would have traveled via the Delaware, Lackawanna & Western to Taylor, Pa. (including a 4 ½-hour sleeping layover at Bath, N.Y.); CNJ to Bethlehem, Pa; Reading to Philadelphia; and B&O, arriving in Washington at 8:45 p.m. Saturday. But a direct overnight trip via PRR was hastily substituted.

The B&O's ever-vigilant "Tommy" Thompson recorded that NYC diesel switcher 577 pulled the train backward for 1.3 miles from Buffalo to NYC Jct., where PRR class K-4s Pacifics 12 and 3749 took over for the run to Renovo, Pa. Sister engines 5344 and 5369 advanced the train to Harrisburg; model E-7a passenger diesels 5855 and 5859 to Baltimore; and GG1 electrics 4916 and 4870 to Washington. Only operating stops were made; arrival was at 9:46 Saturday morning.

Truman's meeting with Marshall didn't work. The president realized he had made a big mistake, but too late; the leak had badly damaged his credibility. The Vinson affair was still filling the headlines on Sunday, Oct. 10, when he and Dewey each set out on the next legs of their quests for votes.

Dewey departed from Albany that night for Pennsylvania, Kentucky, southern Illinois, Oklahoma, Missouri and Michigan. The chief executive's 15-car special left at 6 p.m. Sunday, Oct. 10, for a trip through Ohio, Illinois, Minnesota, Wisconsin and West Virginia. His initial route was B&O, his power passenger diesels 68-62B-80A. It was a "straight-away run," Thompson noted, but "with No. 19 scheduled approximately 10 minutes ahead all the way to Patterson Creek, and stopping at Silver Spring, Martinsburg and Harpers Ferry, engineer (Adams) laid back around those points so as to insure [sic] clear signals."[400]

B&O class T Mountain 5501 doubleheaded Truman's train over the rugged West Virginia mountains from Keyser to Grafton, and Thompson labeled it a "fine run."

"Eased along after (Altamont) most everywhere," he penned, "and as a matter of fact poked so much that eventually dragged by East Grafton [a minute] late."[400] The party—sans helper locomotive—slowed considerably at Clarksburg to throw off press wires and stepped out lively toward Parkersburg to avoid delaying train No. 4, the *Diplomat*, too much at Jackson.

Meanwhile, the GOP's Dewey got into trouble as his L&N special suddenly lurched backward toward the crowd in Beaucoup, Ill., on Tuesday, Oct. 12. Dewey lost his temper, exclaiming, "That's the first lunatic I've had for an engineer. He probably ought to be shot at sunrise but I guess

we can let him off because no one was hurt."[171] The Democrats inflated the remark and charged again and again that it proved Dewey was unfeeling and hostile to the working man. New York Times writer James Reston cracked in his column: "And then the train pulled out of the station with a little jerk."[338]

What had happened? CSX Transportation executive Tim Hensley, writing for CSX News 40 years later, explained what Engineer Lee H. Tindale told reporters who followed him to the register room at the East St. Louis roundhouse. Tindale had been on the first of two L&N class K-5 Pacifics pulling the special. The locomotives had to take water at Beaucoup, and Tindale overshot the water tank by a few feet when he was easing the second locomotive into position.

"There was a lot of mist and smoke in the air and I couldn't see the 'spot'," Hensley quoted Tindale as explaining. "I was backing so slowly that anyone could easily have gotten out of the way. I gave the proper signals."

He was asked what he thought of the term "lunatic."

Tindale, a staunch Democrat, answered: "I think as much of Mr. Dewey as I did before—and that's not much." Later, he said: "He ought not to have said that because he didn't know what it was all about. It was just a lot of hot air."[181] In fairness to Tindale, Hensley noted that he had rarely pulled a passenger assignment up to that time. He had spent much of his career on yard engines, and even when running road freights, their engines would cut off the trains before taking water.

Three days later, Truman told a rear platform crowd at Logansport, Ind., "I was highly pleased when I found out … that the train crew on this train are all Democrats. … We have had wonderful train crews all around the country and they've been just as kind

New York Gov. Thomas E. Dewey and his wife receive flowers on Oct. 12, 1948—the day Dewey lost his cool at Beaucoup, Ill.

to us as they could possibly be."[329] In a nationwide radio broadcast Oct. 21 sponsored by the International Ladies' Garment Workers' Union, Truman declared, "We have been hearing about engineers again recently from the Republican candidate. He objects to having engineers back up. He doesn't mention, however, that under the 'Great Engineer' [Herbert Hoover] we backed up into the worst depression in our history." [171]

Privately, Truman was more direct. "The trouble was [Dewey]'d forgot what it was like to have to work for a living, and it showed on him."[255] Railroaders reacted with predictable anger; freight cars all over the country sprouted derogatory chalked slogans about Dewey.

Tindale became an overnight sensation, Hensley wrote. He was inundated with thousands of letters and telegrams that praised him, criticized him, and even threatened to kill him. The engineer became disgusted and perplexed, and despite being cleared in a company investigation, took some time off to sort things out.

Why did the usually nonplussed Dewey blow his stack? Hensley reasoned that perhaps the candidate was alarmed because his personal secretary, Lillian Ross, was standing in the crowd and would have been "the first to go." He may have been skittish because of the wreck of his 1944 campaign special at Castle Rock, Wash. Or he may have been in a foul mood because some mischievous young boys had scored a direct hit right between the politician's eyes with an overly ripe tomato—also splattering his wife—at Mount Vernon, just 21 miles before. After the Beaucoup tirade, he was booed and

J.F. Doolan, NYNH&H/Truman Library

Harry Truman poses with New Haven Road Foreman of Engines Robert L. Acker in Yard 17 at Providence, R.I., on Oct. 28, 1948, as the president prepares to board his special for the last lap of his upset whistlestop campaign. Whether or not Truman is about to score another cab ride is lost to history, but sharp eyes will note the clean pair of gloves in his hand.

further pelted with rotten eggs.

Hensley revealed a longstanding controversy about how far the train actually backed up. "It couldn't have been more than 2 feet," said Tindale's brother, Carl, who was the special's flagman and was standing right there.[181]

Just a few days later, B&O patrolman Ernest Chapman's trained ear picked up the same ominous slack rumble while Truman was speaking on his back platform. Chapman reached up—without speaking a word or turning his head—and grasped the brake valve. A sigh of air stilled the rumble and the president went on speaking.

"Chappie sure earned himself a medal that day," a Secret Service agent chuckled.[137]

On Dec. 11, long after Truman's victory, both the president and Dewey were toasted at a dinner of the Gridiron Club—a usually off-the-record Washington shindig run by D.C. newsmen at the Statler Hotel. Radio commentator Ned Brooks put on a skit based on the Beaucoup incident. The revelers lustily sang a spoof written by Brooks to the tune of the Georgia Tech drinking song:

(Verse:)

"Oh come, you wise Republicans and listen to all my strain,

"And never trust yourselves again aboard a Victory Train.

"I hope you've learned your lesson, the meaning is mighty clear,

"I'm a rambling wreck, but what the heck, I'm a lunatic engineer.

(Chorus:)

"I'm a rambling wreck from Georgia Tech, and a heckuva engineer,

"A heckuva, heckuva, heckuva, heckuva, heckuva engineer,

"Like all good jolly fellows, I like my whiskey clear,

"I'm a rambling wreck from Georgia Tech, and a heckuva engineer."[172]

"They ribbed Dewey unmercifully,"

Truman wrote later in a letter to his sister Mary. "Had a lunatic engineer act that was a scream. ... Of course when I came to speak—the last thing on the program—I couldn't be the least bit elated, triumphant or overbearing. I told them ... the country is theirs not mine but they'd have to help me run it. Complimented Dewey on being a good sport and sat down."[133]

Truman's crowds on his Midwest tour rivaled those on his swing through the Northeast. In Ohio on Monday, Oct. 11, 50,000 had come out in Dayton and 100,000 lined the streets of Akron.

Administrative Assistant Donald Dawson's political instincts came to the rescue again.

Frank Lausche, the Democratic candidate for governor of Ohio, was loathe to tie his candidacy to a loser's coattails, but reluctantly boarded the Truman train anyway at Hamilton, north of Cincinnati, for the short B&O ride to Dayton. A crowd of more than 6,000 saw them off, and larger throngs were on hand at the next two stops. Then came Dayton, where folks were practically standing on each other's shoulders. "Is this the way all the crowds have been?" Lausche asked. "Yes, but this is smaller than most states," the president asserted. "Well," responded Lausche, "this is the biggest crowd I ever saw in Ohio." He stayed on board all day.[329]

"We talked with ... Lausche ... coming from Willard into Akron," Dawson told the author more than four decades later. "[I] arranged a meeting with the rubber company executives on the train before the meeting in the armory [downtown]. It had previously been scheduled by the local people for the Rubber Bowl, which was out in the country a little ways then, but the weather was too cold and it was too far out in my judgment to get a crowd at night. And so

I just switched it to the armory."[107] The reluctant Lausche endorsed Truman at last, and Dawson concluded that the rally was a turning point in the race.

At Richmond, Ind., the first stop on Tuesday, Clifford emerged from his "little cubby hole"[452] on the train in search of the Oct. 11 issue of *Newsweek*. The magazine had announced it would publish a poll of the nation's 50 leading political journalists on Truman's election-day chances.

"I slipped off the train early in the morning—about 8 o'clock—and went into the station to see if they had a newsstand," Clifford told the author. "And so they did. And the woman was just opening the newsstand.

"And I said, 'Has *Newsweek* come in?' She said, 'Well, I haven't unwrapped it. There it is. You can unwrap it.'"

Clifford anxiously clipped the string that held the issues together and flipped through the top copy. Finally he found the "Periscope Preview" on Page 20, with its big black headline: "Election Forecast: 50 Political Experts Predict a GOP Sweep."[17]

"There it was," Clifford said. "The result of the poll was devastating. Out of the 50 experts, all of them responded, and 50 of them said that Dewey was going to win. Not one thought that Truman could win." That Dewey was favored hardly surprised Clifford, but the shocker was the 50-to-0 vote. A wave of nausea gripped the special counsel.

"It was very upsetting because it was going to have a lot of impact on the electorate. So I bought a copy ... and got back on the train. ... I had to (board) on the president's car and I thought I might run into him. So I had this *Newsweek* under my coat.

"So I walked in and sure enough, he was up, sitting on the couch. He had been reading the papers.

"I said, 'Good morning, Mr.

President.'

"And he said, 'Good morning, Clark.'

"I said, 'Well, we've got another busy day ahead of us.' 'Yes,' he said, 'We certainly do.' And then he said to me, 'Uh, what does it say?' I said, 'Now what's that, Mr. President?'

"He said, 'Well, I saw you go into the station and you disappeared for a while and I think what you were doing was probably going in there to get a copy of the *Newsweek* magazine. And the way you're holding your left arm against your side, I think you may have a copy of that magazine under your coat.'

"I said, 'Well, OK.' ... I hauled out the magazine. ... He took a look at it and I remember his remark. He said, 'I know every one of those 50 fellows,' he says. 'Not one of them has enough sense to pound sand in a rathole.'

"And that was it. ... He just tossed it off ... and went ahead as though it hadn't happened."[84]

The polls consistently showed Truman was losing the race; one of them even stopped sampling weeks before the vote. "Sleeping polls,"[171] Truman called them, and charged that they were lulling the electorate to sleep.

There was one survey, however, that predicted the president would win. Leslie Biffle, secretary of the U.S. Senate, disguised himself as a chicken peddler and circulated through the crowd at many of the whistlestops. "Now listen, Harry, you don't have to worry," Truman quoted Biffle as telling him. "The common people are for ya."[255]

Departure from Chicago's California Avenue stop via the Chicago & North Western was at 3:28 a.m., Wednesday, Oct. 13, behind diesels 5016A and 5016B. Tommy Thompson noted that the engineer had trouble holding the train back on some 100-mile-an-hour stretches, and took some heavily banked curves on C&NW subsidiary Chicago, St. Paul, Minneapolis & Omaha near Wyeville, Wis., so slowly "that it was actually uncomfortable inside the [leaning] train."[400]

Pesky problems cropped up occasionally—twice on that day.

"It was a crisp ... morning after a night of frost," Fitzmaurice recalled. "The western Wisconsin forests blazed with color; the president's off-the-cuff talks in the little woodland towns along the line had made no news. ... Musing over the scenery or their poker hands, the newsmen shrugged off the *Magellan's* jolts when the brakes went on for [Altoona,] a whistlestop east of Eau Claire, and resumed their reveries or recreation. Few even bothered to look up the name of the town on the schedule."

As Truman had closed his five-minute pitch with the housing shortage gag, the Omaha Road's general superintendent, H.P. Congdon, sitting in the Pullman *Waldameer*, just ahead of the *Magellan*, picked up his train phone and said, "Go ahead."

The train didn't budge. Three minutes, five minutes, eight minutes passed. Newsmen running back for a look found Truman still on the back platform, his smile now forced.

"What's he waiting for, Mom?" piped a tot in the crowd. "Why don't they start up?"

By now Congdon knew. A sharp-eyed inspector had spotted a broken leaf spring under the rear of the second of two blue-gray C&NW diners borrowed from the *Overland Limited*. Detaching the car would deprive half the passengers of lunch; letting it stay on the train might cause a derailment. The solution was to repair it in place. The car was jacked up and a thick plank jammed between the frame and the springs—a little untidy but secure, and a precious few 20 minutes lost.[137]

After lunch, another snag developed. The president spoke at Superior, Wis., motored to Duluth, Minn., spoke again, and headed back to the train. "His pennanted car came first in the parade," Fitzmaurice wrote, "with Mrs. Truman and Margaret in a Cadillac six cars behind, and a long line trailing afterward."

The motorcade picked up speed on a deserted highway in the Superior docks area paralleled by a railroad track. The rusty rails must have fooled the Secret Service; the agents didn't protect the point where the track crossed the road just ahead. Nor did anyone show concern when the Truman auto passed a Soo Line switcher chugging in the opposite direction a minute or so past the crossing. Across a dividing ditch, the president and the engineer exchanged a toot and a wave as Truman headed for the Superior station and the engineer proceeded toward the crossing.

Those in the press automobile, fifth in line behind the president's and just ahead of the Truman ladies' car, turned their heads and watched as the engine and its rattling string of freight cars rumbled across the crossing, cutting the procession in two. The newsmen discovered to their dismay that the parade was no longer following. A leaking tire had compelled the family car to stop just before the crossing, giving the engine a chance to proceed across it and block the passage of Bess and Margaret's Cadillac and the cars behind it. At a traffic light five miles later, someone in the crowd shouted, "Hey, Mr. Truman, where's Margaret?" The president looked back, saw the dismembered line, and repeated the query to the Secret Service men. The answer came as the lost cars appeared around a turn and Margaret waved reassuringly. The parade moved on. A later investigation cleared the engineer, who recognized Truman but didn't know he had cut off the ladies.

However, the Secret Service detail drew a reprimand anyway for separating the first family.[137]

That afternoon the special headed for St. Paul on Great Northern track, still behind the C&NW diesels. A switcher had to assist the start.

While the press doubted that Truman's large crowds would translate into a margin of victory, the president was confident he'd come from behind and win. Aide George Elsey also was sure of that. On the way to the Twin Cities, Elsey took four speeches back to the *Magellan* for Truman to look over. He found him alone at the dining room table, his work place. "Sit down," the president said, and he began going through the pages. "Well, let's get out your paper and pencil," Truman ordered, and Elsey scrambled for a mimeographed transcript of the chief's remarks at Duluth.

"He started dictating the states to me, with their electoral votes," Elsey told the author, and the aide dutifully scribbled on the back of the manuscript. "Maine, Vermont, New Hampshire, Massachusetts, Rhode Island, Connecticut, etc., and in each case he'd call out from memory— 'cause he knew them all by heart—the electoral votes and then his prediction of who would win that state. And he came out with a very clear indication that he was going to win the election by a very substantial number of electoral votes. I still have that piece of paper—it's the only documentary evidence that can prove that Truman really thought he was going to win. If there had been a big audience or a lot of politicians around, you could have said, 'Oh, he was just trying to keep everybody's spirits up.' The fact that it was just the two of us, utterly alone, there was no pretense, no play-acting there, that was what Harry S. Truman personally, deeply believed."[129]

The president's forecast showed 340 votes for Truman, 108 for Dewey, 42

for Dixiecrat Strom Thurmond, and 37 labeled "doubtful" (four votes were accidentally omitted from the calculation). He was only a little overly optimistic; the final total gave him 303 electoral votes, Dewey 189. A lot of pollsters wished they had written it.

Reporters traveling with the train noticed crowds were getting larger, but they refused to believe it could change the outcome of the election. "I think the president's message is getting through," Clifford would say to the regulars on board, trying to stimulate more coverage. They would answer, "Well, certainly something is happening. It's too bad for you guys that it didn't start earlier."[85]

At St. Paul, Clifford gave himself a night off—dinner with friends—and nearly got into trouble.

"By 1948, I drank quite rarely—I had learned over the years that alcohol did not agree with me—but that night I felt that if I did not give myself a break I might explode from the pent-up pressure and strain," he recalled. "We had a few drinks before dinner and then listened to the president's speech on the radio while we ate and drank some more. Suddenly the president was no longer speaking, and I realized that if I did not get back to the St. Paul rail yards quickly I would miss the train. Driving wildly, we made it to the station just in time, but as I lingered, making prolonged and fond farewells about 50 or 60 feet from the train, it began to pull out. Running directly behind it on the tracks, I clambered on board at the last possible moment, in full view of several amused and cheering local reporters. If the president was aware of the incident, he never mentioned it."[85]

Back on the CStPM&O, the special left St. Paul at 11:36 p.m. Wednesday, the diesels moving B-unit-first (in effect, backward) for an incredible 84.6-mile run to the Mankato coach yard. There, the diesels were turned

and continued via C&NW to a Thursday evening arrival in Milwaukee and a 3:28 a.m. Friday arrival at Chicago's 51st Street Yard.

Five hours later, the campaign train left on the Erie, behind diesel 804, and transferred to the PRR at Kouts Tower, near LaCrosse, Ind., where it was placed in charge of diesels 5849-5854B-5855A. From there it was handed to the Nickel Plate (H-5b Mike 510) at Kokomo ("engineer seemed scared to death of the crowds," Tommy Thompson said),[400] the NYC (J-1d Hudsons 5384 and 5391) at Indianapolis, and the B&O (diesels 68-62B-68A) at Cincinnati.

Saturday morning's pull over the Appalachian Mountains was accomplished with a spectacular combination of steamers 4404 (class Q-4 2-8-2) and 5501 (class T 4-8-2) and passenger diesels 68-62B-68A that yanked the special from Grafton up to Terra Alta, W.Va., in 71 minutes, only 5 minutes longer than the light, speedy *Cincinnatian's* schedule. Arrival in Washington was at 3:57 p.m. Saturday.

Before he got off, Truman told reporters: "Never felt better in my life. I have been highly pleased with the trip. I was agreeably surprised in Ohio, Minnesota, Wisconsin, Illinois and Indiana. … In fact, I don't think we have had a dud on the trip." Asked whether he thought that "your stock has gone up as a result of this trip," he answered, "Well, now, that's what you're along for. That's your job. I am the candidate. The candidate is not going to comment. He's optimistic!"[329]

The B&O's Thompson, proud of his railroad's impressive show of motive power over the mountains, praised the operation in a report to his colleague Dan Moorman. "Just picture 15 cars blasting up Cranberry Grade, around Salt Lick Curve, in broad daylight with a Q-4 Mikado, a T Mountain and a big, powerful

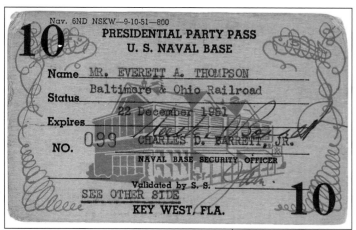
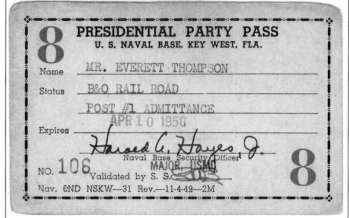

Passes are typical of the ones handed out to railroaders and press representatives traveling on POTUS trains in Harry Truman's day. These belonged to B&O passenger rep Everett L. "Tommy" Thompson.

three-unit diesel locomotive on the head end! If you can't picture this, rest assured that most of the passengers on the presidential train could, for they were frequently observed watching the upward progress."[63]

The Trumans' final tour began when they left Union Station at 9:30 p.m. Sunday, Oct. 24, their 15-car train behind B&O passenger diesels 68-62B-68A. Major speeches were scheduled in Chicago, Cleveland, Boston, New York, St. Louis and Independence.

The crowd who came to send them off was not encouraging. "Mother glowered at the tiny band of mostly White House staffers who were waving goodbye," Margaret wrote. "It was not a presidential sendoff."[101]

Thompson was also out of sorts, for a different reason. "Slow schedule. Engineer [Adams] just played with the train."[400]

In Chicago, on Oct. 25, 50,000 people marched in Truman's parade from the Blackstone Hotel to the Chicago Stadium, with 500,000 more lining the route. Brass bands, fireworks, Roman candles and aerial bombs added to the festivities. Another 23,000 were in the stadium.

Margaret despised the fireworks, which went off just as the motorcade was crossing a bridge. "I hate noises,"

she announced. "I thought the bridge was coming down. Above us a tremendous series of explosions created a fiery image of the candidate. As an old artillery captain from World War I, Dad was not bothered in the least—in fact he loved every bang."[100]

Dewey was bland and boring to the last. It's not that he wanted to be—Truman's invective was discussed long and hard on the Dewey train as it headed toward Chicago. Now the governor was angry; he wanted to make a vigorous rebuttal. He stayed up half the night revising his Chicago speech but in the end bowed to the wishes of his staff—and the reporters traveling on the train—that a change in tactics now would be tantamount to a confession of weakness.

Truman kept slugging as he departed Chicago behind NYC passenger diesels 4019 and 4018 Tuesday morning the 26th. In South Bend, Ind., he charged that 90 percent of the country's newspapers were against him. Somehow, Truman's staff scored a publicity coup at Holland, Mich. At 1:10 p.m. they arranged for his train to pass Dewey's special. No word survives as to whether the candidates waved to each other.

In Sandusky, Ohio, Truman hit the press again, and in Cleveland, where NYC diesels 3503, 3601 and 3502

took over, he accused the Republicans of rigging the polls "to prevent a big vote on Nov. 2 by convincing you that it makes no difference whether you vote or not."[329]

Somewhere in northern Ohio, rebellion reared its ugly head.

"Mother told the candidate that if he called her 'boss' once more, she might get off the train," Margaret recounted. "Dad surrendered. By that time he was getting tired of it, too."[101]

Leaving Cleveland at 10 p.m. Tuesday, the special proceeded to Buffalo and Albany, where it transferred to the Boston & Albany early Wednesday morning. The train had been delayed through the night because train 66, running ahead of it, had hit an automobile at a grade crossing. The entourage made a late-morning sweep from Springfield, Mass., to Hartford, Conn., and return, with NYNH&H diesels 0767 and 0766 pulling the train backward on the southbound move. Once back in Springfield, the NYC power was reattached.

In Boston that night, Truman declared to a crowd of 250,000 that the communists wanted the Republicans to win, following up with equally caustic rhetoric during 13 speeches in the New York City area on the 28th and 29th. He sprinkled his Madison Square Garden address with characteristic humor, revealing that he had complained to his doctor that everywhere he went, somebody was following him. "The White House physician told me not to worry. He said: 'You keep right on your way. There is one place where that fellow is not going to follow you—and that's into the White House.' "[171]

The last whistlestop, at Mattoon, Ill., at 5 p.m. Saturday, Oct. 30, was made melancholy by a gloomy autumn drizzle before only a fair-sized crowd. The mood was captured well by Press Secretary Charles Ross as the train started on its last lap toward St. Louis. "Win, lose or draw," he told reporters, "we'll be going down to Key West, [Fla.,] right after the election."[115]

The speechwriting staff got together that afternoon and pooled what they called "their gems"[100]—their best and brightest phrases—and poured them into a climactic speech for St. Louis' Kiel Auditorium at 9:30. They hadn't had time to even think about putting it together until they left New York.

"Meanwhile," Margaret said, "my father for the first time showed he was at least capable of getting tired, and took a long afternoon nap."[100] As always, he dropped right off and was refreshed when he awakened for dinner.

Clifford and Murphy joined the Trumans, Ross, Connelly and other aides in the *Magellan* for a quiet family meal. The president didn't seem to have a care in the world.

Only when the train was almost in St. Louis did the team present Truman with their "wit-encrusted, diamond-bright, verbal tour de force," as Margaret called it.[100] Truman glanced through it, and then said, "I'm sorry, boys, but I just haven't got time to get all this into my head."[100] He threw it aside and excused himself to his bedroom, where he scribbled out about two pages of notes. The Kiel Auditorium speech was completely extemporaneous, and was hailed as one of his best.

It also was his angriest tirade. "Of all the fake campaigns," he said, "this is tops so far as the Republican candidate … is concerned. He has been following me and making three speeches about home, mother, unity and efficiency. … He won't talk about the issues, but he did let his foot slip when he endorsed the 80th Congress."[329]

Once again, he predicted victory. "I have been all over the United States from one end to the other, and when I started out the song was—well, you can't win—the Democrats can't win. Ninety percent of the press is against us, but that didn't discourage me one little bit. You know, I had four campaigns here in the great state of Missouri, and I never had a metropolitan paper for me that whole time. And I licked them every time!"[85]

The enthusiastic crowds had convinced Jack Sowers, PRR's general passenger agent in Washington, who had gone along. He warned his colleagues to not be too sure Dewey would win.

When the train departed St. Louis at 11:30 p.m., Clifford stayed behind. Planning to visit his mother for a couple of days, vote in his home precinct and fly back to Washington to be with his family on election night, he bid goodbye to the president on the platform.

"He was relaxed and smiling," Clifford recalled. "I had mixed emotions as I said goodbye to them, but on one point I was not nostalgic: watching the *Ferdinand Magellan* pull away and knowing that I did not have to be on it, I felt a wave of joyous relief, as though a prison sentence had been lifted."[85]

Clifford returned to Washington so exhausted that he actually fell asleep at least once while standing in a reception line. "Months after the … campaign was over, I still woke occasionally in the middle of the night with nightmares that I was trapped on that train." He was glad to be rid of those "unstately staterooms."[85]

"Our hegira ended at 7:25 a.m. Oct. 31 … when our train clanked into the Missouri Pacific … depot at Independence," Margaret recorded. " 'It's grand to be home,' Dad told the crowd that welcomed us. It was a sentiment Mother and I heartily endorsed."[101]

Truman had put on an amazing show from June to November. Dewey Long recounted that 18,000 meals had been served aboard, tons of garbage removed, and bales of bed linens, blankets and towels handled. Even supplying ice and soap was a major chore, he groused.

One writer said the expression most frequently heard on Truman's train was "Hey, Dewey!"[224] as everybody from the president to reporters and railroad crews called the White House transportation chief for yet another chore. Because of the name of Truman's opponent, the cry never failed to startle visitors.

Considered the underdog all the way, the president won the upset victory on Nov. 2 that he was always so confident of. When his train left Independence Thursday morning, Nov. 4, to take him back to Washington behind MP diesel 7015, it was christened a *Victory Special*.

When it reached Union Station in St. Louis that afternoon, the waiting crowds pushed aside police barricades and swarmed over the tracks. From the rear platform of the *Magellan*, Truman delighted his admirers by holding aloft the previous day's early edition of the *Chicago Tribune* that a jubilant Bess had thrust into his hand. Its banner headline read: "DEWEY DEFEATS TRUMAN"; the photographs taken of that scene are some of the best known in American histo-

Harry Truman disembarks from his special in Chicago early on the morning of May 8, 1950, to take his morning stroll—through a railroad yard.

ry. "That's one for the books," the president chuckled.

"The reason I am so happy," Truman told the throng, "is because my home state stood by me so well. You must continue to stand by me, because I have got the biggest job in the world now."[329]

The train was besieged by anxious Democrats who, only a few days before, seemed to have forgotten that they were members of the party. "Fairweather pals were milling around like women waiting for a department store to open on bargain day,"[224] Long complained. It did them no good; the White House travel officer wouldn't let them board.

Margaret missed much of the fun. "I crawled into a berth and got the first real sleep I had encountered in 48 hours," she wrote. "So I have to rely on other eyewitnesses for what happened enroute. … Humility did not preclude a little private crowing, especially over the red-faced pollsters and journalists. Mother … chortled when she heard that Drew Pearson had filed a column for the day after the election, analyzing "the closely knit group around Tom Dewey who will take over the White House 86 days from now."[101]

B&O diesels 68A-62B-68 did the honors when the president left St. Louis at 2:30 p.m. Once again, steam locomotives 4404 and 5501 assisted the run over the mountains of West Virginia and Maryland. Tommy Thompson recorded medium to heavy fog between Smithburg and Bridgeport, W.Va., in the wee hours Friday morning and the fact that the 4404 wasn't originally scheduled to help. "But to play safe in the event of slippery rail or other failure, they … put them all on."[400]

Dawson went back to see his boss Friday morning before arrival in Washington.

"He was having breakfast by himself when I went back," Dawson told the author, "and he reached under the table and pulled out the *Chicago Tribune* paper. 'I'm going to have a lot of fun with this today,' he said, and he did."

Truman's train encountered what came to be called "Wednesday Democrats" and "Johnny-come-lately boys"[207] all the way across the long B&O route to Washington—party leaders and big businessmen who had sat on their hands and checkbooks, but now wanted to make it clear that : "We were with ya, Harry, all the time." When they backed into Union Station at 10:56 a.m. Friday, Nov. 5, an estimated 750,000 people were waiting to greet them on the motorcade route to the "Great White Jail,"[100] as Truman called the White House.

"Remember how many came down to see us off last month?"[101] Bess asked Margaret in glee as she stared out the window of the *Magellan* and saw the wildly smiling faces and frantically waving hands. "It's nice to win," Margaret yelled to her mother above the din once outside. "You bet it is," Bess replied.[101]

Truman—and most of his staff—credited his come-from-behind victory largely to the fact that he used a train to roam around the country.

"You get a real feeling of this country and the people in it when you're on a train, speaking from the back of a train," Truman said. "And the further you get away from that, the worse off you are, the worse off the country is. The easier it gets for the stuffed shirts and the counterfeits and the fellas from Madison Avenue to put it over on the people."[255]

It was clear at that fall's Army/Navy football game that the president had put one over on the pollsters. He saw underdog Navy fight its way to a 21-21 tie with Army. As the president switched from Army's side of the field to Navy's at halftime, he chuckled when some midshipmen hoisted a huge sign reading, "GALLUP PICKS ARMY."[171]

The most extensive speaking trip of Truman's full term was his tour to the Pacific Northwest that began Sunday, May 7, 1950. New speechwriter Ken Hechler went to work preparing presidential talks in early March.

"Elsey came over from a presidential staff meeting lugging a collection of timetables and brochures and threw them all on the black leather couch in my office," Hechler recalled. " 'You are now our local color man,' he said simply. 'The president is taking a trip out to the West Coast in early May, and you are nominated to pull together an analysis of every city and town he will visit. Here's the tentative schedule,' " he said, indicating a list of some 30 or 35 stops.[171]

The trip's major purpose was a May 11 return to Washington state's Grand Coulee Dam for a formal dedication, but staffers successfully urged that Truman make several speeches in southern Idaho and other stops as well. The schedule was frequently expanded until it called for 57 speeches.

"I found a beautiful quotation in an old *Congressional Record* for Jan. 26, 1936," Hechler said. "A Republican congressman from New York, Francis D. Culkin, told his colleagues: 'But I say to you, Mr. Chairman, that up in the Grand Coulee country there is no one to sell power to except the coyotes and jack rabbits, and there never will be.' The president got a great kick out of the phrase, and decided right off the bat to use it at Grand Coulee."[171]

The White House staff worked on developing a theme for the trip. A "non-political" trek that put too much heat on Congress would be branded as too political. Recalling a congressman's "stockholder report" from the 1930s, Hechler suggested that the trip be billed as "sort of a profit-and-loss

NORMAN DRISCOLL, *PATHFINDER MAGAZINE*/B&O HISTORICAL SOCIETY

The Trumans depart Washington May 7, 1950, for a tour of the Pacific Northwest. B&O police officer Ernest Chapman, standing beside his company's new tail signs, stands guard.

President Truman walks back to his train after his constitutional through a Chicago railroad yard on the morning of May 8, 1950.

report of the president's stewardship." Initially dismissed as "pretty tame," the idea was eventually adopted for the president's "report to the people."[171]

"Assembling the background material was an eye-opening experience," Hechler remembered. "It involved contacts with every federal department and agency affecting the area through which the president traveled. It required original research on the interests of cities and towns. ... I went up to Deck 10 of the Library of Congress annex every evening to leaf through all the published information in the local history collection. At the newspaper room, I made notes on recent articles covering the areas the president was to visit."[171]

Since Washington is a virtual melt-ing pot of residents who grew up in towns all over the country, Hechler found knowledgeable people who had lived in each area the train would traverse. He talked to them, drawing out reams of local color.

He distilled his gleanings into a two-page analysis for each whistlestop that covered local economics, political conditions, background history, personalities and current issues. The succinct summaries also came equipped with the latest figures on employment and nearby federal projects. At a glance, Truman could see if the local congressman had supported his legislation and how the area had voted in every presidential election since 1896.

"The White House carpenter shop built a small box and bookcase, which fit snugly into a train compartment," Hechler recalled. "In it, the staff placed basic reference materials, including six volumes of the *Dictionary of American History*, all of the president's messages to Congress and economic reports, party platforms and folders on every conceivable subject that related to federal projects and local interests—even down to the grasshopper situation in Wyoming."[171]

Hechler talked to so many folks around the capital that he inadvertently drew attention to himself. A Scripps-Howard reporter got wind of his research and asked him about it. Realizing White House staffers were supposed to stay out of the newspapers, he stammered out a response

Harry Truman greets the folks at Burlington, Iowa, on May 8, 1950, his 66th birthday.

that by his own assessment was "amusingly stupid"[171] and discouraged the story, which is the last thing one should do to minimize coverage. Confronted by the reporter on the telephone, Hechler blurted out, "Well, I'm really not here. You see, this is very—how shall I put it?—sub rosa."[171] The syndicated story caused some raised eyebrows among his bosses, but the disarming quote minimized the embarrassment to the White House.

As in 1948, the president spoke from three- or four-page triple-spaced outlines at the five-minute stops and five- or six-page studies at the 10-minute stops. They were written in such a way that Truman could read them as speeches, use them as outlines by expanding on any point he saw fit, or take a theme from them and speak totally "off the cuff."[171]

After weeks of preparation, Truman's 13-car special left Washington at 3 p.m. Sunday, May 7, 1950. It was pulled by B&O diesels 78, 62B and 78A. Contrary to custom, the B&O diner would operate all the way through at the request of the White House. The company scored another public relations coup, too. For the first time since a new presidential seal had been affixed to the rear platform of the *Magellan*, the railroads were permitted to attach tail signs, too. The B&O prepared two attractive inserts reading *B&O Special* with a Capitol dome on the side and attached them on either side of the platform railing with the seal in the middle. Other roads were permitted to do the same, but when some of them didn't, the B&O signs were used.

Among delays noted by Tommy Thompson was three minutes at Pittsburgh that evening because someone forgot to take down a blue flag and a slowdown from Newton Falls to Ravenna, Ohio, to allow the eastbound *Columbian* to pick up a

school party without endangering anyone with the passing POTUS train.[400]

Once again, the B&O handed the train to the CB&Q at the Rockwell Street yard office in Chicago, which coupled on a three-unit diesel headed by the 9961. Departure was at 6:10 a.m. Monday, on time.

The schedule was showing slower times now to accommodate Truman's whistlestops and slowdowns to wave. He spoke at Galesburg, Ill., in Iowa at Burlington, Ottumwa and Creston, and bypassing Omaha via Plattsmouth, Neb., headed for Lincoln.

U.S. Sen. Paul H. Douglas, D-Ill., was present when Truman rolled into Galesburg, Ill., at 8:50 a.m., recalled speechwriter Hechler. Expecting crass politicking, Douglas was agreeably surprised by the president's reasoned analysis of the dangers of isolationism, strong United Nations support and eloquent exposition of the paths to world peace.

"Truman also captivated the audience completely by ad-libbing that Mrs. Truman had a great uncle who was a graduate of Knox College 'and one of our great circuit judges in Jackson County, Mo.,' " Hechler noted. "The crowd of 8,000 knew he wasn't just reciting a rehearsed, ghost-written speech when he folksily referred to 'my first sashay into politics' in 1892 when he wore a white cap labeled 'Cleveland and Stephenson.' He got a big laugh by recalling that 'some big Republican boys took my cap away from me and tore it up, and the Republican boys have been trying to do that to me ever since.' "[171]

A chilly rain greeted Truman's arrival in Iowa at Burlington, but 15,000 well-wishers crowded around the back platform anyway. Sleek cattle, fat hogs and rich farmland stood as visible evidence of the Truman prosperity he bragged on all the way across Iowa. Thirty-five thousand

people squeezed around a special platform erected beside the train at Ottumwa, surprising even Victor Johnson and Philip Willkie, who had been sent by the Republican National Committee in a private plane to follow and keep tabs on the president. Johnson called the train a "traveling medicine show," but admitted to reporters that "nobody hates him."[171] Johnson was startled when Truman spotted him in the audience and invited him to ride the train if he would buy a ticket.

The president celebrated his 66th birthday aboard the train. Margaret entered the following Monday entry in her diary: "They gave Dad a huge cake at Ottumwa. He's had 13 or 14 cakes today. We got off in the pouring rain at Lincoln (at 4:51 p.m.). I got soaked but it was warm anyway. The crowds have been tremendous even in the rain. They have smiling faces and are very enthusiastic."[101]

Dewey Long recalled that it was only seven cakes, but they were massive. "Each of 'em [was] so big it took three or four men to carry. There must have been a ton of cake on that train."[224]

The cakes, the many pounds of candy, flowers and nuts were put off the train at the nearest convenient stop and sent to hospitals anonymously. "Not that the president doesn't appreciate the gifts," added Long, "but a ton of cake— "[224]

After Truman's major farm speech at Lincoln, departure at 5:30 called for a yard engine to pull the train backward past Baird Tower to clear a home signal before the forward movement could begin. It was all done extremely slowly because of a terrific storm, which had doused the Trumans despite the fact they were on a canopied speaker's stand and which caused flooding in Lincoln that night. Thompson said the engineer "just dwaddled along"[400] after that to keep

CB&Q train 29—with engine 9935B—passes Harry Truman's special at Casper, Wyo., May 9, 1950.

Crowd at Boise, Idaho, gathers around the Ferdinand Magellan *for a look at President Truman on May 10, 1950.*

from arriving at Grand Island too early.

Thompson must have drifted off to sleep somewhere beyond Broken Bow, for his log shows a gap of several hours. He was on duty again at Guernsey, Wyo., at 4:06 a.m. Tuesday, and found that the train had swelled to 14 cars and was being pulled by a three-unit diesel headed by the 9951. At Wendover, the special headed around the south leg of the wye and the engines ran around the train to pull it from behind into Casper. At that point, the engines were again placed on the head end for the run back to Wendover, where that 14th car was removed, and on to an afternoon stop at Cheyenne Jct.

Here the train was transferred from the Burlington's Colorado & Southern line to the Union Pacific by a yard engine that attached to the rear and pulled it back into town. After Truman's talk, the special left behind diesels 905, 905B, 901B and 910.

Thompson was impressed with the evening run to Rawlins.

"Although leaving early, drifted easily and dropped back gradually on schedule, as there were many trains to be met going up Sherman Hill," he wrote. "As it turned out, the time was too sharp up the hill for the heavy train, but drifted down the other side in good shape. Slowed at Bosley trying to kick off brakes which were sticking, coming down to perhaps 25 mph. Slowed to 15 mph through Hanna to permit president to wave;

however, broke much too soon, and took the whole train through the town at that speed, instead of just the rear end. No other delays, and a good run was made on a first-class main line."[400]

On Wednesday, the special proceeded through Idaho and Oregon, adding a three-unit helper (1551, 1550C and 1554) between Huntington and Elcina, Ore., in the early afternoon. The 37.5-mile run took 71 minutes, faster than the schedules of the *Portland Rose* but slower than the *Idahoan, City of Portland,* and even mail and express No. 25. "Even with seven diesel units, did not make much time on the hill," Thompson wrote. "But engineer really did roll them from Baker to North Powder, averaging from the dead stop approx-

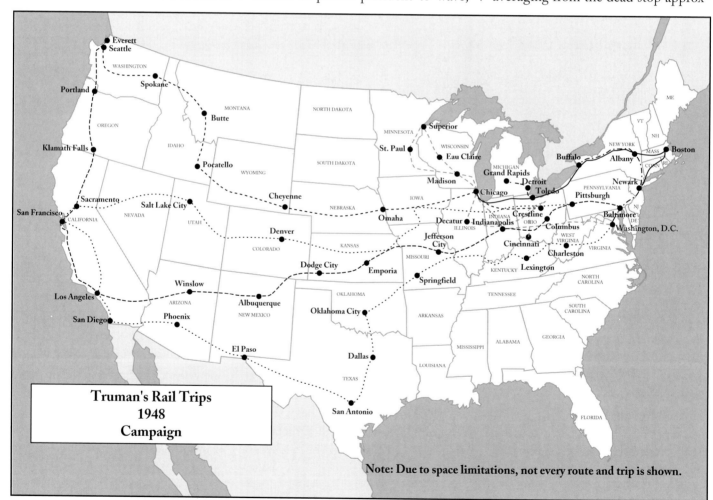

Truman's Rail Trips 1948 Campaign

Note: Due to space limitations, not every route and trip is shown.

KENNETH L. MILLER

President Truman's 1948 Campaign Map reflecting the many different trips and stops.

"Tommy" Thompson finds a convenient dutch door and snaps this image of his own train—President Truman's special—crossing the Snake River from Idaho into Oregon May 10, 1950.

imately 73 mph. One mile was clipped at 89½ mph with stop watch."[400]

Another helper (1556 and 1560B) joined the head end from La Grande to Kamela, this time allowing the special to beat all schedules except that of the *City of Portland*. "Definitely not a line as far as Pendleton for making any time," Thompson complained. "Even streamliner only averages 31.1 as far as Reith."[400]

The special headed north at Hinkle and transferred to the Northern Pacific at Spokane. With an extra car added to the consist, diesel 6508 pulled it to Coulee City. Arrival was at 8:16 a.m. Thursday.

Once the presidential party had detrained for the motor trip to the Grand Coulee Dam, the train backed out to Odair and the engine ran around it. The equipment was deadheaded to Wilbur, where the party was picked up after the dedication ceremony for a 1:46 p.m. departure. Everybody piled off again at Cheney at 3:48, after which the special backed to a wye, then headed back to Spokane. Departure from there was at 6:29 p.m., a minute early, with 14 cars.

At Missolua, Mont., early Friday morning, Truman used a metaphor Hechler dreamed up in a speech offering a tribute to Rep. Mike Mansfield. Impressed with the clarity of Mansfield's thinking, Hechler asked in a letter to Sam Rosenman why Mansfield "can look at some things and see the broad future while others see only the narrow past? It seemed to me like an acorn; some people could look at an acorn and all they would see would be the acorn; others like Mansfield would see the oak."[171]

When the president arrived shortly after 7 a.m., Mansfield boarded the *Magellan* to introduce him to a waiting crowd. Truman responded, "After that introduction, I will have to deliver the goods, won't I?" Commenting on the early hour, he joked, "Of course, we farmers think this is pretty late in the day." Then he launched a Mansfield commendation, using the acorn/oak line. Papers across the country were complimentary.[171]

Hechler wryly noted the favorable reactions may have been in part because of two hindquarters of a freshly butchered elk and 175 newly caught trout that were placed aboard the train at Missoula. The president shared his generous gifts with the press and other passengers.

Butte was attained at 10:44 a.m., still a minute early. The special proceeded from that point—with a 15th car to make steam—on the Great Northern, behind a four-unit diesel headed by No. 456.

"Even by using freight diesel[s], the climb up the 2.2 percent grade to the Continental Divide was very tough, and there were times before reaching Mountain Spur where it seemed the engine would stall," Thompson noted. "On arrival at East Switch, a diesel switcher was attached to the rear, and pulled the train [backward] into Helena."[400]

The freight diesels continued to Havre, where the steam car was dropped and the freight diesel traded for a three-unit passenger lashup headed by No. 354. Thompson signed off for the night, but recorded a departure from Glasgow at 9:30 a.m. Saturday.

"Train was originally scheduled to start from Nashua," Thompson said, "but a last-minute switch in plans caused the … departure to be observed from Glasgow. Due to pilot train getting out late, No. 1 [the *Empire Builder*], which went in siding for pilot train at Nashua, did not get over to Wheatley in time to clear this special, and some considerable delay [ensued] while [the special] drifted along awaiting it to clear."[400]

The special made a "good fast run" through North Dakota, although Thompson fumed that it "bounced like a rubber ball"[400] between Genoa and Munster. Train orders that survive reveal the pilot train ran between Minot, N.D., and Breckinridge, Minn., as the first section of No. 28, the *Fast Mail*, with engine 225. The POTUS move, with engine 354, was Second 28, and the regular train—powered by the 350—was Third 28. A meet order directed the westbound *Fast Mail*, No. 27, engine 356, to take siding at Brantford, N.D., for the first and second sections, "with all doors and windows closed."[452]

Minneapolis was reached at 3:26 a.m. Sunday, May 14, four minutes early. From there the train continued on C&NW, behind a two-unit diesel headed by the 5018. A long stop was set at Madison, Wis., from 10:28 a.m. to 3:54 p.m. There, Truman attended church, spoke at the University of Wisconsin field house and dedicated the new international headquarters of the Credit Union National Association.

Arrival at Chicago's Grand Central

CB&Q diesel locomotives 9961C, 9961B and 9961A pause with President Truman's 13-car train in Casper, Wyo., May 9, 1950.

Station was at 8:31 p.m.

Departure from the Windy City was at 10:28 p.m. Monday, behind B&O diesels 78, 62B and 78A. "Situation was well in hand at all times" across Indiana and Ohio on his home railroad, B&O's Thompson commented, on "some very favorable track." A strike on the PRR required the special to run for a while Tuesday morning on the westbound track of a shared double-track segment between Warwick and Akron Jct. (B&O owned the westbound track; PRR the eastbound), and a heavy fog caused problems seeing signals.[400]

Hechler and two other staffers had just mailed Truman's speech for Cumberland, Md., to the train from Washington when he suggested they pile into a car and drive over to witness the noon Tuesday address.

"Unfortunately, when Truman spoke, the wind kicked over one of his pages, and I'm sure some of our pearls of wisdom were lost to history," Hechler wrote. "But we all felt it personally as, in the final words of his 7,000-mile, 16-state tour, he looked out over the audience and said, 'You have welcomed me at the end of what I think has been a most successful tour to make a report to the people of the United States as president of the United States.'"[171]

Hechler and his companions renewed acquaintances with their traveling counterparts amid much back-slapping. Murphy took him aside and invited him to ride back on the train, to which he readily agreed.

"Tired and worn though they were," Hechler explained. "Murphy's crew (was) optimistic and enthusiastic. The president was overjoyed with the results he had achieved and made no secret of it. Wandering forward to the press car, I found the bedraggled newsmen full of admiration for the performance of Truman and his staff."[171]

On the leisurely home stretch, they swapped stories about funny incidents that had occurred along the way:

- Bill Bray, an aide to Assistant to the President John R. Steelman who helped Appointments Secretary Matthew J. Connelly with the reception of local politicians, drew laughs one day as he emerged with a huge Dewey button attached to his coattails by Associated Press correspondent Tony Vaccaro.

- At the Spokane stockyards, when the head of the livestock show pinned a huge purple livestock champion's ribbon on the president's lapel, Truman cracked, "Am I the grand champion pig or cow?"[171]

- A reluctant lamb noisily protested having a blue ribbon pinned on him by the president, until Truman called him a "Republican sheep" and the animal miraculously subsided.[171]

- In Casper, Wyo., the president interrupted a major address to tell his audience in the high school auditorium that he remembered his mother telling him about the time the grasshoppers were so bad they ate the handles off the pitchforks.

- Columnist George Dixon said, "He doesn't miss a local trick. I'm glad we're not going to Alaska on this trip, as he would undoubtedly come up with a batch of tasty recipes for cooking whale blubber."[171]

- They remembered the sturdy farmer who, when the president made his last speech of the day, after 10 p.m. in Broken Bow, Neb., yelled with great fervor, "Thank you, Harry!"[171]

- In Baker, Ore., he enchanted the crowd by saying he had come out "so that you could see me and find out if I have gone 'high hat' since you elected me in 1948." All agreed he had not.[171]

- Murphy's favorite press story involved a young lady who wrote about the effectiveness of the White House staff work, and "said that if the train stopped in a little town out there somewhere for five minutes, and if they had crooked cue sticks in the pool hall, that we would know about it and the president would say something about it."[171]

Thompson noted using No. 2 track from Patterson Creek and the Magnolia Cutoff because the B&O's Baltimore Division had so many trains coming west. "Planned to go slowly through Brunswick yard, and did, then had to stop in Point of Rocks tunnel for three minutes a/c brakes sticking on head car. A lively run after that until, passing Silver Spring, began easing. Stopped at F Tower to attach back-up hose, and then backed in very cautiously."

Union Station was reached at 2:38 p.m. Tuesday, May 16, 1950, two minutes early. Truman had a right to be pleased. All along the way, he had enjoyed friendly, good-sized crowds. "There was none of the tension, the frantic pace of the '48 campaign train," Margaret wrote. "Mother had a smile on her face most of the time."[101]

Dwight D. Eisenhower's campaign special stopped at Salisbury, N.C., early on the morning of Sept. 26, 1952, for servicing. Noticing a crowd of railroad workers outside, Ike and Mamie donned bathrobes over their pajamas and trekked to the rear platform of their office car to wave their greetings. One photographer was awake—International News Service's Frank Jurkoski—and snapped a prize photo. The rest of the traveling press corps, caught asleep on the job, persuaded the Eisenhowers to restage the event at Winston-Salem later that morning lest their bosses be upset they missed a glorious opportunity. This photo is the re-enactment. "The gratitude of the group was gratifying," Ike wrote. "Every man implied that he was going to vote Republican."

The Golden Era's Sunset Years: 7

The Eisenhower Presidency

Dwight D. Eisenhower

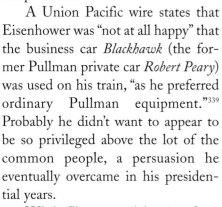

A 14-car Chicago, Burlington & Quincy special eased out of Denver Thursday morning, July 3, 1952, taking Gen. Dwight D. Eisenhower and his wife, Mamie, to the Republican National Convention in Chicago. The train stayed overnight in Omaha and stopped over in Boone, Iowa, so the Eisenhowers could spend the Fourth with Mamie's family. Arrival in Chicago was on the 5th, two days before the convention opened at the International Amphitheater.

A Union Pacific wire states that Eisenhower was "not at all happy" that the business car *Blackhawk* (the former Pullman private car *Robert Peary*) was used on his train, "as he preferred ordinary Pullman equipment."[339] Probably he didn't want to appear to be so privileged above the lot of the common people, a persuasion he eventually overcame in his presidential years.

While Ike was celebrating freedom at Boone, much of the drama that would hand him the presidential nomination was being played out on a train heading eastward from California. After lunch on July 3, Gov. Earl Warren and his party boarded a special train christened simply *The GOP* at the old Western Pacific terminal in Sacramento. Warren was hop-ing to secure the nomination for himself in the event of a deadlock between Ike and Ohio Senator Robert Taft.

The sleepers had been sitting in the hot California sun all day; boarding them, one delegate said, "was like walking into an oven."[269] Insurance executive Frank Jorgensen, lawyer Patrick Hillings, rancher Ray Arbuthnot and Harrison McCall, a former campaign manager for Richard M. Nixon, the state's junior senator, soon opened the partition between their rooms to make one large compartment. They "bribed the porter,"[269] as one said, to bring a tub of ice, and stripped down to their shorts to sit and drink.

Even when *The GOP* slowly pulled out of the hot Feather River Canyon into the Sierra Nevada Mountains, the cooler air gave little relief. "The cars just baked all night,"[269] Jorgensen remembered. Still, everyone was hopeful "even exhilarated; many of the men put on gold shirts with "Warren" in blue block letters stitched on the back. Someone began playing a piano in the lounge car, and the suntanned Warren daughters—each wearing a bright orange baseball cap emblazoned with a "W" —danced with delegates to repeated renditions of "California Here I Come."

Meanwhile, politics had begun to stir in the corridors elsewhere on the train. Publisher Joe Knowland told everyone who would listen that his

UNION PACIFIC

General and Mrs. Dwight D. Eisenhower board UP office car 102 in Kansas City enroute to a gala homecoming in Abilene, Kan., the general's boyhood home, on June 21, 1945, after the Allies' World War II victory in Europe.

RAILROAD MAGAZINE/CARSTENS PUBLICATIONS

Dwight Eisenhower's popularity after World War II was unmatched in modern political history. Both parties wanted the hero; his celebrity status was trumpeted everywhere. Here, the general poses in the GG-1 cab of Pennsylvania Railroad's General *stream-liner at New York City's Pennsylvania Station in a postwar publicity shot.*

Dwight D. Eisenhower whistlestops in California, having been introduced by the Golden State's governor, Earl Warren, at right.

son—California's senior senator, William Knowland—should refuse the No. 2 spot on the ticket that everyone thought Eisenhower or Taft would offer him and hold out for the No. 1 position. Splinter meetings and caucuses were taking place among Jorgensen's group, all of whom would have been pleased to see the presidential nomination go to Nixon.

Another Nixon man, Bernard Brennan, felt an awkward, cold silence as he passed through the swaying doorways of the cars telling everyone "Hello." Several days before, as secretary of a committee formed to select convention delegates, Brennan had secretly replaced Warren supporters with Nixon backers just before he

took the list to the printer—a maneuver that had put many of his fellow cronies on the train. But he was hypocritically still making noises for Warren—and many of his friends froze him out that night.

The passengers celebrated the Fourth with small ladyfinger crackers and still more dancing and singing in the lounge car. Despite the hushed meetings of the night before, the mood was light. "You stay up all night and you drink a lot of liquor and you eat a lot of food," Jorgensen recalled, "and you don't accomplish a blessed thing except to enjoy yourself."[269]

Then at Grand Junction, Colo., on the Denver & Rio Grande Western, a report reached the politi-

cians that Nixon himself was flying out from Chicago to board the train in Denver that evening. Warren was stunned; he refused to arrange a meeting with the senator that his men said he wanted, but said he'd be in his car if Nixon wanted to talk.

Brennan, having lost patience with the petty gesturing, issued an ultimatum to one of Warren's secretaries. "You tell Earl that as soon as Dick gets on the train, I'm going to take him back to that car and I'm going to press that button. If he wants to see Dick, he'll open the door. If he doesn't, he won't."[269] He reminded her there were a lot of Eisenhower and Taft people aboard, as well as several newspapermen.

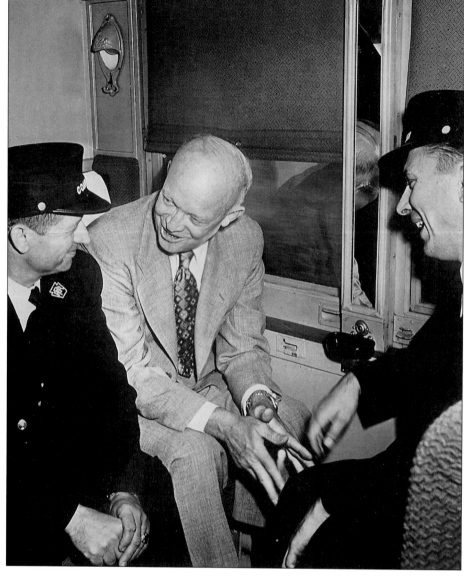

Ike enjoys a visit with PRR conductor W.D. Waldrop, left, and flagman J.R. DeHaven as his campaign train crosses Pennsy's Fort Wayne Division in Indiana Sept. 15, 1952.

When Nixon boarded, he went straight to Jorgensen's enlarged bedroom and reported that Eisenhower had won several delegate fights over Taft. He talked to his four friends for "quite some time"[269] and mentioned the possibility of his own vice-presidential candidacy. The fact that he was on board and talking with his own men behind closed doors tensed up the whole train, and Warren's circle was incensed that Nixon talked to his friends before paying a courtesy call on him. "They managed to stir up considerable commotion," Jorgensen said.[269]

Brennan finally walked back and offered to escort Nixon to Warren's car. On the way, they tarried for a snack in the diner, and when they arrived at the rear of the train, they were received "at once."[269]

Warren was "pleasant and casual," Brennan said, and Nixon went on to assure the relieved governor of his support "one hundred percent." But after the visit was over, the wind changed. Nixon began pumping hands all through the delegate cars as if he were the candidate. He told those in the press car that rumors of his own vice presidential nomination

were "ridiculous," then arranged a series of meetings in the compartments and aisles of cars largely occupied by his own faction to convince everyone that Warren, in fact, had little chance at the nomination and that everyone should jump on the Eisenhower bandwagon. The reward for California of such a defection from Warren would be the vice presidential plum for Nixon.[269]

Warren loyalists rushed to the governor and asked what should be done. His recollections reveal a barely constrained rage as he calmly stated that the delegation was obliged to vote for him on the first ballot at least. Privately, he was angrier than anyone could remember. It was clear Nixon and his people were running through the train asking everyone to violate their oaths.

Nixon's defiance hurried through the cars as *The GOP* raced across the prairies on the CB&Q. "If you're on the front end of the train, you have to run pretty fast before the statement gets to the back end," Jorgensen said.[269] Alternate Tom Bewley, seated in one of the last cars, knew his old law partner and protege was a few cars away politicking for the state's 70 votes—"a hullabaloo," Bewley said, "over who would run the delegation."[269] Nixon seemed to avoid only those delegates he knew were irrevocably committed to Warren; he had done his homework well. The powwows continued into the night.

Nixon's men were with him in a compartment near some roomettes occupied by Warren supporter Thomas Mellon and his family. The hour had grown late as the car's air conditioning malfunctioned and compartment doors were flung open for air. Mellon overheard a "big discussion"[269] in which Nixon's men were pressing the Senator to break openly with Warren no matter what the other Californians decided. "They were

Ike greets the crowd at LaPorte, Ind., Sept. 15, 1952.

working on Nixon … to cut Warren up … really putting the heat on him. They kept hammering Nixon to be sure that he didn't weaken his position in being for Eisenhower."[269] Nixon was probably arguing for caution, Mellon thought, because he had worked out a deal with the Eisenhower camp for the No. 2 spot. But his men were adamant. "Hillings was pretty ruthless; Jorgensen was very ruthless about it," Mellon remembered. "The arguments were so loud through the night that their words could be overheard up and down the car."[269]

Once they reminded Nixon how important they and their friends were to him. "Well, after all, I am a United States senator," a wounded Nixon responded. "We don't give a d—-

what you are," they answered brutally. "You wouldn't be anybody if it wasn't for us."[269]

The next morning, Nixon maintained for the press that Warren was still in charge, and had an excellent chance at the nomination in the event of a deadlock. But before he could be questioned closely, he got off the train at Cicero, Ill., and hitched a ride the last few miles into Chicago. Warren partisans gave the story of "the great train robbery"[269] to the press, but it was so captivated by the Eisenhower-Taft fight that the leak was largely ignored. On the surface, Warren's arrival at Union Station was attended by much hoopla, as was Ike's arrival at North Western Station later in the day.

After Ike secured the nomination, he planned a grueling campaign.

Discussions of rigorous schedules, long hours and family partings gave cause for pause. For weeks, it was drummed into Ike's head that the Republicans lost in '48 because of "over-confidence and lethargy."[124] He was determined it wouldn't happen to him. "I invited our daughter-in-law (Mrs. John Eisenhower) to participate, just for the experience, in one trip on the campaign train," the general wrote, "but Barbara's reply was a laughing 'No, thanks!' Afterward she did accompany us on one trip through Pennsylvania and the East."[124]

The itinerary relied heavily on the railroads, but mixed in was more air travel than ever before. In all, he would travel a total of 51,376 miles in 45 states, speaking at 232 stops. Even during the legs that took him to an airport instead of a depot, Mamie stayed with the train.

Ike's was the last and one of the best whistlestop barnstorming trains, assessed biographer Stephen E. Ambrose. "All the hoopla of American politics was there. The train would stop; the local Republicans would have the crowd waiting; Eisenhower would appear on the rear platform accompanied by Mamie; he would deliver a set speech that concentrated on cleaning up the mess in Washington and asking the audience to join him in his 'crusade'; the whistle would sound; they would be off again. Between stops, Eisenhower conferred with local Republican candidates, all of whom wanted their pictures taken with the general."[11]

Ike's first rail trip of the campaign was a New York-Philadelphia sprint Sept. 4, and the first extensive tour began Sunday evening, Sept. 14. The 4,000-mile route called for 70 speeches in 12 states, seven of them major addresses. All of the 18 immaculate cars on his *Look Ahead, Neighbor Special* —excepting the diners provided by each road—were freshly painted Pullman-pool two-tone gray; the last of them, reserved for the Eisenhowers, was New York Central business car 17. It was the former Pullman private car *Roald Amundsen*; NYC had bought it from Pullman when the latter divested in 1947.

The party's instructions for rear-platform appearances were explicit. Just before each stop, Sen. Frank Carlson of Kansas brought to the rear persons to be introduced. After the stop, a local spokesman introduced them one by one, after which each retired to the "rear parlor." At the longer stops of 15 minutes, a local campaign leader had two or three minutes to talk; then the general was introduced five minutes before departure. He first introduced Mamie, then spoke four minutes on a "local refer-

ence" (one minute), a recapitulation of "principal issues of crusade" (two minutes) and a "specific instance for the day" (one minute). Party aide Lou S. Kelly and speechwriter Robert Cutler timed him. Three minutes into the talk, Kelly blew his police whistle once; one minute later the train started without further signal. Mamie then rejoined the general on the platform and both waved to the crowd. Only Kelly could prolong the stop.[125]

The railroads' plans were equally detailed:

- All sleeping car rooms were on the engineer's side for safety and to minimize noise from adjacent trains.
- The Pullman Company removed the furniture from its lounge *Sungold* and the PRR installed tables for the press along the sides of the lounge and solarium that extended 23 inches into the aisle on each side. Folding chairs accommodated reporters.
- Pullman lounge *Calverton*, home for local politicos traveling from one town to the next, was stripped of its dining tables, leaving 16 straight chairs and 26 lounge seats, plus the drawing room.
- Pullman lounge *Sunlight* kept its furniture and was stocked with the usual refreshments.
- Some rooms in the last four cars were equipped with telephones, and Pullman 6-compartment, 3-drawing room sleeper *Franklin Square* always had to be next to Ike's car. The phones were to be connected to public lines at each stop.
- The ladies' washroom in Pullman 12-section, drawing room crew sleeper *McClanahan* was converted to a photographic darkroom, with the door latch on the inside.
- RCA installed a public address system on the rear platform and through the rear seven cars, as

well as an "inter-communicating system" between certain rooms in those cars. They were to remain coupled at all times.
- Both diners served meals, and one had snacks available around the clock. Occupants of the rear car ate in that car. Menus were headed *Eisenhower Special*.

The first leg of the itinerary included PRR from New York City to South Bend, Ind.; NYC to Englewood, Ill.; and the Rock Island to St. Paul. At this point, on Tuesday the 16th, Ike flew back to New York to address the American Federation of Labor. The train backtracked to Rock Island, Ill., where Ike rejoined it Wednesday evening. He continued via CRI&P to Omaha, arriving there Thursday night.

At 8:30 a.m. Friday, the train continued on the MP to Falls City, Neb.; Burlington to Kansas City; and MP to St. Louis, where it laid over from Saturday afternoon, Sept. 20, to Monday morning the 22nd.

Up to this point, only minor glitches were noted.

Columnist George Dixon reported that the "rumpots" aboard didn't like crossing the Mississippi River westward from Illinois into Iowa because the latter state was dry. During the night when the train had laid over in the Quad Cities area, there was a dispute over whether it should be spotted in Rock Island, Ill., or Davenport, Iowa. Dixon contended the train was moved back and forth across the Mississippi no less than five times, with the bar opening on every eastbound run, closing on every westbound one.[396]

Sometimes, there were problems with mail. Ike was handed a letter from Tennessee that carried this address: "General Dwight D. Eisenhower, care post master, Omaha, Neb., attention Mr. Postmaster: General Eisenhower is now on a political tour and will stop overnight in Omaha, Thursday, Sept. 18. Hotel unknown by sender: Should be easily learned. Please locate, deliver to desk with instructions this be delivered to General Eisenhower in person. Thanks."[396]

As the special continued via L&N to Cincinnati, it overshot a waiting crowd at Carmi, Ill., by several yards. Listeners had time to hear Ike say merely, "I'm sure sorry—"[389y] before he was gone. Ironically, the engineer was Cecil Tindale, brother of the engineer who allowed Tom Dewey's train to nearly back into a crowd at Beaucoup, Ill., in 1948.

At Evansville, Ind., another engineer—Owen Allen—took over. But in his zeal to avoid Tindale's error on his own run through Kentucky, he stopped the train short at Henderson and Owensboro. Candidate and crowds finally got together, and Ike remarked, "I guess the engineer didn't quite get his signals right."[389x]

Allen actually redeemed himself with the Owensboro stop. He made an emergency application of the brakes on a bend two blocks short of the station because some schoolchildren were scampering across the tracks. The general, badly jolted, pulled himself together as stoically as any commuter and sent Allen a message:

"I have just heard that as we entered Owensboro this morning, our train would almost certainly have injured some children except for your alertness and quick action. I congratulate you on your efficiency and give thanks from the bottom of my heart that we did not become involved in a tragedy. I'm sure the parents of those children—if they knew of the incident—would join me in this statement. With best wishes—and my appreciation of a fine ride on the L&N.— Sincerely, Dwight Eisenhower."[127]

Meanwhile, Mamie was having the time of her life. Local Republicans

WEIRTON STEEL/EISENHOWER LIBRARY

Although no speech was scheduled in Kenova, W.Va., after the Norfolk & Western delivered Eisenhower's train to the B&O, the crowd mills around New York Central office car 17 hoping for a glimpse of the candidate while his train is being iced. They were not disappointed; Ike offered a few impromptu remarks.

presented her with a mink stole at one stop, and photographers caught her in the private car trying on several hats to see which one best went with it.

From Cincinnati, the special rolled via NYC to Cleveland and back to Columbus; at that point it picked up B&O diners 1025 and 1028 and left town behind two of N&W's streamlined class J 4-8-4's, 611 and 613. At Kenova, W.Va., a yard engine carefully transferred the special to the B&O, pulling it backward through the N&W yard and shoving it onto

B&O's interchange track, stopping short of a month-old F7 quartet of EMD diesels, 959A-957X-959X-959.

Moments after the N&W switcher cut off, Eisenhower suddenly stepped onto the rear platform and said a few words, even though no speech was scheduled. At age 61, with ruddy complexion and disarming grin, the dapper Ike looked presidential. A crisp brown suit showed off his military bearing; his hairless head capped a face America had grown accustomed to—and loved.

Several women important in local Republican circles visit with Mamie Eisenhower, fourth from left, in the dining room of New York Central business car 17.

From this point up along the Ohio River to Wheeling, the train was operated by D.J. Ferrell, regional supervisor of locomotive operation, instead of assigned engineer Clem Parr.

"It was a long and heavy train," Ferrell explained to the author. "You had to keep 10 pounds of air on it at all times to keep the slack from running out. I determined if anybody would get in trouble, it would be me. I could answer for myself."[132]

The other Wheeling Division crewmembers were fireman Harry Nixon, conductor C.F. Branham, brakeman I.P. Smith and flagman W.M. Dunham. They would have to follow more meticulous instructions formulated by J.J. Sell, B&O's Wheeling Division superintendent, who wanted them "followed to the letter" and "surrounded with safety in the superlative degree."[340]

As Eisenhower spoke, the four-unit diesel was coupled to his train to allow as much time as possible for an air test and inspection before the scheduled 11:10 a.m. departure for Wheeling. Twenty extra men had been deadheaded in on train 77 from Parkersburg; other personnel, including section gangs and freight house hands, were called out of Huntington and Kenova to water and ice the train "with a minimum of disturbance to passengers, particularly with regard to the private car"[340] and resupply the diners under the master mechanic's watchful eye. The sleepers had ice-activated air-conditioning, the diners B&O's York system. If the men weren't finished with their duties by the time the train was ready to leave, they were told to ride the 8.2 miles to Huntington and finish the job there.

Train orders were distributed in triplicate: one set to the engine crew, one to Branham in midtrain, and one to Dunham on the *Franklin Square*. Opposing trains were safely tucked away in sidings 30 minutes before the special was due and all adjacent switching ceased as it passed.

Departure from Kenova came, in fact, two minutes late at 11:12 a.m., and arrival in Huntington was eight minutes late, at 11:38. Despite flag protection at two crossings with C&O, the long train had to negotiate trackage up the middle of 2nd Avenue, and a crowd of 20,000 had gathered for a ceremony that started at 11 a.m. A two-square-block area of the B&O yard was cleared to accommodate them.

Signal Maintainer Walter J. McElfresh stood with a "clean white unfurled flag"[340] at the precise spot the diesels were to stop—without signal—so Ike's speaking platform would be 10 feet east of 12th Street.

More than 25 local politicians, civic and religious leaders, and nearly a dozen West Virginia newsmen who had boarded the train at Ironton, Ohio, detrained. They had joined about 40 staff, speechwriters and advisers plus 40 wire-service newsmen and photographers who were traveling on the train, which could sleep 223.

These "short hauls" were replaced by a like number of local leaders on the Huntington-Parkersburg leg. Lists that today repose in the Eisenhower Library indicate this is the way it was throughout the trip, probably making the *Calverton* the most jammed car on the train.

The Huntington folks getting off had, in 20 brief miles, gathered up memories that would last a lifetime.

Mrs. P.O. Duncan had tea in car 17 with Mamie, who "charmed" her.[122]

Jack Havens had been a supporter of Taft for the Republican nomination, but he easily shifted loyalties once Eisenhower was chosen. "I was struck by his eyes," Havens declared. "He almost took you over with those piercing blue eyes. You had to have confidence in him."[168]

Mrs. Martha Campbell Dwight had been Ike's neighbor in Abilene and had a brother, George Campbell, who played high school football with him. George's son, Charles Eugene Campbell who owned a flower shop in Huntington, made Mamie a cor-

244

Ike loved to wade into a swarm of railroaders, as he did here on the B&O enroute from Kenova to Wheeling Sept. 24, 1952. We don't know which yard this is—Parkersburg or Benwood, perhaps. Know any of those grimy faces?

sage. Years later, Mrs. Dwight was said to have called the White House, somehow managing to be put through to Mamie so she could assure her she was praying for her husband during his illnesses.

"He was straight as an arrow, yet gracious and friendly," recalled Paul Humphreys. "He could have been a relative—and he was that way with everyone."

Humphreys had a good chance to see for himself. He was supposed to detrain at Huntington, but he and local newspaper publisher William

Birke ended up riding all the way to Wheeling—with only a few dollars in their pockets.

"The conductor never entered our car," Humphreys said. "Nobody said anything to us. We just didn't get off."

Humphreys said it never occurred to them how they would get back. "Our enthusiasm set aside our judgment," he said. "We were as happy as if we were going to our own weddings."[196]

Huntington's response was typical of hundreds of other towns. C&O employee Bob Harris held two fingers

aloft in the V-for-victory gesture; Ike returned it and snagged another vote. Niceties provided to the travelers included 50 copies of that morning's *Herald-Dispatch* to compartment "A" of *Sunlight* for distribution throughout the train, and the delivery of a dozen ash cans purchased from a local hardware store five days before. As ordered, an agent-operator had scrawled *Eisenhower Special* across the Huntington station's train bulletin. Six high school bands were on hand, as were hundreds of students who had been excused from school on written

No doubt when he glanced out the windows where West Virginia highway 2 paralleled the railroad up the Ohio River Valley, Tommy Thompson saw a 1949 Dodge, in the days before rail fan pacers, tearing alongside the Eisenhower train. Driving that Dodge was Herb Little, a junior Associated Press staffer from Charleston, W.Va., who served as the link between the AP's veteran national correspondent Jack Bell on the train and the outside world.

"The train didn't linger; each stop lasted only long enough for Ike to make a brief rear-platform speech," Little said. "There was no time for reporters aboard to file before the train left for the next stop.

"Between Stop A and Stop B, Bell would bang out a lead aboard the train about Ike's speech at Stop A. I would meet the train at Stop B, grab the copy from Bell, dictate it over the nearest telephone, then drive to catch up with train at Stop C to snatch Bell's new lead about the speech at Stop B. My participation required a heavy foot on the accelerator but no journalistic skill whatsoever."[234]

Standing and smiling in the center of the picture is West Virginia Republican gubernatorial candidate Rush Holt as he hobnobs with the party faithful on the Calverton, *Ike's car reserved for guests, on Sept. 24, 1952.*

request of their parents.

Ike's customary speech was broadcast live on the local television station, and the general posed for pictures with Mamie after the couple was given a pumpkin pie.

Mamie, whom the general often introduced as "Mrs. Ike," was an asset to the campaign. She hated crowds and was uneasy with politicians, but she was at her husband's side at every stop, smiling and waving, her bangs fast becoming a fad.

Fifth-grader Bill Hartz was close enough to hand Ike his history text to autograph. But the train started, and the apologetic general handed it back without a signature.

The command to start the train was in the hands of Lou Kelly, or in his absence C.H. LaFond of the Republican National Committee. The chain of command flowed from Kelly to Superintendent Sell to conductor Branham, who gave the highball. The train crawled for about four or five car-lengths to permit any stragglers on the ground to board safely. Taking slack and executing backup movements were strictly forbidden.

Departure was at 12:01 p.m., 16 minutes late. No doubt the commands of printed memos rang in Supervisor Ferrell's head: "It is imperative we make schedule. Exact-minute arrival is desired."

Sell's staff wanted a neat right of way, too. A work train was ordered to work east of Parkersburg for two days, picking up bridge timbers and rail, and another worked for three days—including the day the special operated—picking up rail west of

Parkersburg. A third was ordered out of Huntington to pick up old rail, replaced just four days before, using a laying-over passenger engine out of Kenova.

Protect engines included two P-5 Pacific-type steam locomotives at Kenova with short-notice crews; the Baden district run's engine and the work train engine, both with crews, at Point Pleasant, 42 miles distant; a three-unit diesel (from the Monongah Division) at Parkersburg, another 78.9 miles; a district run engine and Short Line helper engine at Brooklyn Junction, 55.8 miles farther; and a three-unit diesel at Benwood Jct., 4.4 miles below Wheeling.

On up the river the gleaming special trod; Guyandotte, 12:10; Glenwood, 12:36; Apple Grove, 12:42; Gallipolis, 12:53.

Although the schedule called for no Point Pleasant stop, the train halt-

General Eisenhower's train arrives at the B&O station in Huntington, W.Va.

ed there from 1:06 to 1:21 p.m., throwing it a total of 31 minutes behind. Through Mason City, Hartford, New Haven, Millwood, Ravenswood, Belleville and into Parkersburg it continued. Ferrell managed to make up 18 minutes, but gave two of them back, leaving at 3:30 p.m., 15 minutes late.

The Point Pleasant stop was arranged at the last minute by local politician Bartow Jones, who was riding from Huntington to Parkersburg.

"They didn't want extra stops," Jones recalled. "I had my men stationed near the stockyard with a bulldozer, ready to put the thing on the track if it came to that. Turned out we didn't have to."

Jones was asked to introduce Ike, throwing him into a nervous tailspin about what to say. He labeled the candidate "a fighting son-of-a-gun who doesn't know how to spell 'defeat.' " Afterward, Mamie hugged him. "You couldn't have said anything that would have pleased us better," she crowed.[213]

Railroad officers aboard included B&O's Tommy Thompson. He had spent weeks with Democratic opponent Adlai Stevenson on his train and had arrived at Silver Spring, Md.,

when a superior told him to turn back and meet the Eisenhower operation in Kenova.

Thompson rode Ike's train from Kenova to Baltimore and back to Washington, and penned enough entries in his log to fill six single-spaced typewritten pages. Among his notes was an entry that the four-unit diesel had "40-inch drivers" and a tractive effort of 247,500 pounds to pull the 1465-ton, 18-car train.[400]

The special was never able to make up much time, running a maximum 32 minutes behind leaving Benwood. The day was clear and mild, with temperatures between 60 and 70 degrees, Thompson noted, but the speed limit on the Ohio River line was only 45 mph, and there were a great many slow orders and snail-paced travel through towns because of the crowds. The top scheduled speed was 42.8 mph. Thompson groused that in addition to the scheduled platform speech at Parkersburg and the extra halt at Point Pleasant, impromptu one-minute stops at St. Marys, Sistersville, New Martinsville, and Benwood Junction were finagled by local politicians.

Even at that, a slowdown at Ravenswood and extra stops at Paden

City and Moundsville were overlooked.

Ike apologized at Parkersburg for being too slow to get to the rear platform at Ravenswood, and promised to send wires to the folks in Paden City and Moundsville. But New Jersey lawyer Bernard Shanley, a campaign worker who kept a diary of the trip, reported that the behind-the-scenes atmosphere aboard the special was hotter.

"It was particularly peaceful because the West Virginians led by Walter Hallanan were a much subdued group of chicks after the chewing Ike had given them ... when they pushed him into making the additional stops by naively stating that they had just heard that a large group of people were to be at different railroad stations. It was an old trick. They weren't pulling anything new that we hadn't learned. Ike finally lost his temper."[343]

The political posturing, so evident in the campaign speeches and whispered deals on the platforms, permeated the train too, Shanley wrote.

"Lou Kelly always took good care of me and gave me a phantom roommate named Edgar Nathan. It was luxurious to have my own bedroom. During the first week or so the girls were very unhappy as they were bunking two in a room. With all the clothes they had and with the hours they were keeping, it was just impossible and the morale went down awfully hard. So I went to [Nebraska Sen. Fred] Seaton and [New Hampshire Gov.] Sherm[an] Adams and suggested to them that many of us would be tickled to death to double up. I felt something had to be done about putting these girls in a single room, especially the top secretaries. Somehow the girls knew that I had been responsible for this and from then on, of course, I was a great

His pitch completed, Dwight Eisenhower leaves Huntington, W.Va., for Parkersburg and Wheeling on Sept. 24, 1952.

favorite of theirs. There were a few people who kicked like steers at this, but they disappeared from the train as many others did. It was an interesting thing to see this happen because many people came aboard but didn't stay aboard too long, but there was never any fuss or feathers about it. Somehow Ike was able to get rid of them without any seemingly hard feelings or notoriety about it."[343]

But yet, to Shanley, the posturing was mild.

"The most amazing thing to me was the politicians jockeying for position. [But] to see this team working together with no one doing this was a reminder of the [Harold] Stassen group who also worked together on the same basis of mutual respect—no knifing—which was something almost unheard of in the political game."[343]

There was no doubt Ike was in charge. Those on board were his organization and his team. He told Gov. Adams he wanted a Jew and a Catholic aboard; Adams found them. He said he wanted a close associate to Republican National Committee Chairman Arthur Summerfield; Adams provided one. He demanded a detailed schedule because "advance preparation saves wear and tear on the nerves."[11]

Shanley's life aboard the special wasn't all peaches and cream. He reported getting stranded twice in the same day. This had happened to others, and they decided to organize "The Left Behind Club."

"I was unanimously elected the Grand Left Behind," Shanley wrote, "and [Rachel Adams, Sherman Adams' wife] subsequently had certificates printed which I signed and also insignias in the form of a tie clasp with L.B. on them to designate our

organization. The press was also included, and finally before we finished the campaign there were some 35 in all in the club, and I over a period of time signed the certificates for each of them, which they were very proud of."[343]

As Ike's train rolled along the Ohio River, it was heading for a historic climax at Wheeling. Just days before, the *New York Post* had bannered a revelation about an expense fund of $18,235 contributed to Nixon by California business figures. The money, meant to help him take care of many of the necessary expenses not covered in a senator's salary, was never a secret but hadn't been ballyhooed much either. The story was a political plant, inspired by a disgruntled Warren Republican and ignored by most papers. But Nixon's overreaction to it and the pump-priming of the Democrats escalated the issue into a

Dwight Eisenhower waves from the left side of the rear platform as his train picks its way up the street at St. Marys, W.Va.

full-scale crisis, with many demanding that Eisenhower drop Dick from the ticket.

The mood had been festive when Nixon's 11-car whistlestop special made its lavish televised departure from Pomona, Calif., at 8:59 p.m. Wednesday, Sept. 17. The candidate had found out a reporter was planning to do a story on the fund just before departure. At first, he felt it wouldn't be damaging, but the mood aboard the train—despite an opulent private car with "large beautiful beds for the candidate and his wife"[269]—took on an increasingly dark and desperate tone

as it wheeled northward.

The first sign of concern wasn't long in coming. After just a few miles, the *Nixon Special* took refuge on a siding in Southern Pacific's Mission Yard in Los Angeles for the night, so it could star in another dramatic station scene in Bakersfield Thursday morning. It was about midnight when a staff man from the Los Angeles GOP headquarters hurried across the darkened yard and clambered aboard with a report that the *Los Angeles Daily News* would publish a story on the fund in the morning that "might cause trouble."[269] Nixon called a strategy

meeting in his bedroom for 1 a.m.; even then, everyone decided that the fund was on the up-and-up and that any stories about it should be simply ignored.

The *New York Post* hit the streets of Manhattan at 10 Thursday morning with the story played to shock. In Bakersfield, Republican conservative Keith McCormac met the Nixon train at its 9 a.m. stop, and once the train was rolling he handed the nominee a United Press summary of the story headlined "Nixon Scandal Fund."

"Have you seen this?" McCormac asked, but Nixon was unable to answer. He slumped in his seat and stared at the page. Campaign Manager Murray Chotiner and aide Patrick Hillings hurried in and helped him back to his room. "So when I handed him that paper, he almost needed intensive care," McCormac remembered. "They almost had to take him off the train."[269]

In the little more than an hour before the next stop at Tulare, they composed the candidate and "finally got him unshook," McCormac said. Outwardly dismissing the story, Chotiner nevertheless bounded for a telephone and called GOP headquarters in Los Angeles, trying to set up a conversation between Nixon and Eisenhower at Fresno, the next stop. The train pulled out while Nixon was still speaking, and the crowd followed him a ways down the track.

Afterward, Nixon furiously upbraided his friend Jack Drown for allowing the crew to start too soon, but William P. Rogers broke the tension by pointing out the excitement of the crowd moving after the car and Nixon seemed pleased. He laughed self-consciously.[269]

The respite was brief. Reporters who had heard about the *Post* story jumped aboard at Tulare, spread the word and waited for a statement. Press Secretary Jim Bassett answered that the candidate would say nothing for the time being. At Fresno, aides tried again to talk to Los Angeles, but there was no answer. "Ike was in the weeds," McCormac remarked.[269] Nixon spoke, retreated inside, and Bassett told the press they were barred from the car until further notice.

In Washington, Robert Humphreys, the party's publicity director, was becoming concerned with the dispatches he was seeing. He put in a call for the Nixon people to contact him as soon as possible, and the return call came from Madera at 4 p.m. Eastern Time. Chotiner said they knew of the *Post* story and downplayed Nixon's state of mind. Thinking Nixon's people were too calm, Humphreys admonished Chotiner that the story was "going to be much bigger than we dreamed" and advised the candidate to go on the offensive.[269]

By this time, notables were starting to demand Nixon's resignation from the ticket. Humphreys called Eisenhower's campaign chairman, Arthur Summerfield, reaching him as Ike's train rolled into Des Moines, Iowa. He urged a solid front of support for Nixon.

While things were heating up in California and Washington, little news about the fund had penetrated the Eisenhower train. Bundles of the *Des Moines Register* had been thrown aboard that morning as the *Look Ahead Neighbor Special* trundled across Iowa. Few passengers were alarmed about the small story on Page 8.

Humphreys' call threw Eisenhower's staff into a turmoil, but they decided to handle the situation without bothering Ike about it. After his Des Moines speech, the candidate took a nap. Even after his major address in Omaha that night, Eisenhower went to bed still unbriefed. The cars hummed with speculation, though, and Summerfield tried to reach Nixon for an explanation. Back on Nixon's train, Chotiner and Rogers prepared a statement in response to Humphreys' call and to forestall the press demands that were mounting with each stop. The single-page release belied the anxiety on both trains; it argued that the fund was proper and actually saved public money by taking care of many legitimate senatorial expenses with private donations. Nixon still avoided the press, walking quickly through the lounge car to meet boarding politicians and then returning briskly to his compartment to bone up "on the local color,"[269] as he said later. The state-ment was released about 1:30 p.m. West Coast time, just before the Merced stop. Although most papers still didn't make a big deal about it, Nixon feared they would. All afternoon, he stayed hidden away in his room, nursing a smoldering resentment that would stick with him for years that the press was against him. At Stockton and Sacramento, his aides scrutinized all the papers, looking in vain for some word of defense from Eisenhower. The growing story was traveling by telephone faster than the train, and now politicians were hanging back from having their pictures made with Nixon.

On a side trip by plane to Reno, Nev., Nixon was "gloomy and angry" and hotly dismissed the story as "a political smear" when reporters were lucky enough to get close enough to him to ask about it. When the party returned to the train near midnight, an agitated Nixon had sleepy reporters rousted from their berths and lashed back in an impromptu statement in the tone Humphreys had suggested. As he returned to his car, Nixon was once again confident, relieved by his counterattack. "When I turned off the light in my stateroom that night," he said, "I was still convinced that because the attack was entirely partisan, it would not stand on its merits. I thought it would eventually run its course and be forgotten, provided I continued to play it down."[269]

Anxiety was still mounting on Ike's train Friday morning. Bernard Shanley remembered being awakened in his sleeper at 2 a.m. to find "terrible turmoil and grave concern" among campaign aides. They decided to tell Eisenhower about the flap at an 8 a.m. meeting in his car. The general listened calmly to conflicting advice, then said, "Let's find out the facts before I shoot my mouth off. I don't believe Dick did anything wrong." Press Secretary Jim Hagerty could give some statement, but they should play for time. Ike then retreated to a corner of the car and quickly wrote out a private message to Nixon, crossing out and interlining as he went, instructing him to make an immediate and fully documented disclosure of the sources, amounts and disposal of donated money. The long telegram was dispatched to California, and after Ike's train left Omaha, Hagerty read a statement to the press saying the candidate believed "Dick Nixon to be an honest man" and intended to talk to him personally "at the earliest time we can reach each other by telephone."[269]

Unwittingly, the Eisenhower statement ignited the real bonfire by adding legitimacy to the issue. All day long, the clamor for Nixon's sacrifice grew louder.

As the Californian's train started to leave from Marysville, an hour north of Sacramento, a voice in the crowd interrupted Nixon's last sentence, demanding he tell them about the fund. Nixon reacted instantly. "Now I heard a question over there— Hold the train! Hold the train!" The cars stopped a hundred yards up the track, and Nixon let the heckler have it. "They tried to say that I had taken money," he wailed in a lengthy discourse. "What I was doing was saving you money, rather than charging the expenses of my office, which were in excess of the amounts which were allowed by the taxpayers and allowed under the law. ... What else would you do? Take fat legal fees on the side?" In his rambling response, Nixon wrongly evoked the Red bogey, saying communists were responsible for the accusation, and misrepresented the fund again as a substitute for public money. Once more he felt relieved. "I walked back into my private compartment feeling better," he wrote.[269]

At Chico, another hour north, he launched another volley at "the smear"

C.T. STEELE/*RAILROAD MAGAZINE*/CARSTENS PUBLICATIONS

Vice presidential candidate Richard Nixon's campaign train has just departed Marysville, Calif., Sept. 19, 1952, when a heckler demands to know about the "secret fund" that had just come to light in the press. So Nixon orders that the train stop again so he can level both barrels in defense.

and delayed departure for a half hour while aides took calls from the Eisenhower train. It was clear that Ike wasn't committing himself. Nixon continued his counterattack at Red Bluff and Redding as arrangements were made for the disclosure Ike wanted. Assurances that the accounting would show nothing improper brought some relief, but still the tension was unbearable aboard the train as it wound its way through the thickly forested isolation of northern California.

Passengers on the *Look Ahead Neighbor Special* also were troubled as it wound along the bluffs of Missouri. Copies of the local paper thrown on at St. Joseph showed that smaller papers were paying attention to the story now, and at Kansas City Ike and Mamie were greeted by signs such as "DONATE HERE TO HELP POOR RICHARD NIXON." Audience reaction to the general's speech there was restrained, and shortly a call went out to William Knowland—on a speaking date in Honolulu—to come back and board the train. He would be a handy vice

presidential replacement just in case.

As Nixon's train neared the Oregon line, he convened another staff meeting. Reporters were clamoring for more information. They had been rushing to telephones at each stop for the latest revelations, even knocking on doors of nearby houses if station phones were tied up. Each time they had returned with more news about how serious the problem had become.

It was after 9 p.m. when the train reached Medford and Chotiner was given the shocking word that the *New York Herald Tribune* and The *Washington Post*, both staunch Eisenhower backers, were calling for Nixon's departure from the ticket. They tried to keep the word from Nixon, but the train was spotted on a siding near Roseburg for the night and a reporter asked Nixon for a comment on the editorials as he returned to his compartment.

"What editorials?" he asked, and the reporter spilled the beans. Nixon shook his head and said nothing but hurried back to his bedroom for yet another conference with Chotiner and

WIDE WORLD/*RAILROAD MAGAZINE*/CARSTENS PUBLICATIONS

General Eisenhower introduces Jimmy Waldzak, 7, to the folks at Bay City, Mich., Oct. 1, 1952. The boy had run alongside the train for a mile as it entered the city and was eventually hauled on board to meet the Republican standard bearer.

Rogers. It was after 2 a.m. when they left their boss, and he turned to his wife, Pat. Waking her, he described the *Tribune* editorial and his speculation that Ike's aides were undermining him. "Maybe I ought to resign," he sighed finally. "You can't think of resigning," she flashed. "If you do, Eisenhower will lose. Look, if you get off, you will carry the scar for the rest of your life. He can put you off the ticket if he wants ... but if you ... do not fight back but simply crawl away, you will destroy yourself. Your life will be marred forever and the same will be true of your family, and particularly, your daughters."

Once again during this emotional, weeklong roller coaster, Nixon was shored up.[269]

Meanwhile, Chotiner and Rogers summoned Nixon's secretary, Rose Mary Woods, and her aide, Marge Acker, and secretly left the train for a second-rate hotel in Grants Pass where they could find some telephones and gather ammunition with which to refute the charges. As the two men and two women approached the desk clerk in the dingy hotel and asked for a couple of rooms with phones, he shot back, "Phones?" Usually, two couples coming to his hotel couldn't care less if their rooms

were so equipped. "The beds were never slept on," Chotiner assured an interviewer later. The rooms had phones, but they were wall phones, so for several hours the four stood at the walls with each man holding a phone while the women listened to the cocked receivers and took notes. Dawn was breaking as the four struggled back to the train, their notebooks crammed full of data about the fund and their arms and legs aching.[294]

Humphreys awoke in Washington Saturday morning with the idea that Nixon should go on television to defend himself. But while he was making arrangements to fly out and meet Ike's train to sell the idea, the mood aboard still matched the gray and rainy day. At Jefferson City, an obviously troubled Eisenhower ran into the station in a downpour and called his old Army buddy, Gen. Lucius Clay, for advice. Clay urged caution and delay, at least until GOP operative Herbert Brownell could meet the train in Cincinnati Monday and talk things over.

Proceeding east, the train was deluged at each stop with bags of letters and telegrams, at least half of them calling for Nixon's removal. Reporters took their own poll and voted 40-2 that the nominee should be dumped. It was clear that Ike would have to talk to the press, although it was arranged he would meet them informally "on background" and not for attribution—as if there was any doubt who "the highest source on the campaign train" was.[269]

At 4 p.m., drinks were poured in the press car and Ike strolled in to smiles all around. Did he consider "the Nixon thing a closed incident?" With a deep, wrinkled frown that would become famous in future press conferences, Eisenhower shook his head heavily and launched a strikingly candid rendition of his dilemma. He was disturbed Nixon was making statements without checking with him, but he felt his running mate had done nothing wrong. Then he leaned forward earnestly and told them, "I don't care if you fellows are 40 to 2. I am taking my time on this. Nothing's decided, contrary to your idea that this is a setup for the whitewash of Nixon. ... Of what avail is it for us to carry on this crusade against this business of what has been going on in Washington if we, ourselves, aren't as clean as a hound's tooth?"[269]

Meanwhile, in Oregon, Nixon began to see his train "like a prison with its inexorable schedule."[269]

Hecklers were in evidence at Roseburg and Eugene, and as the train departed the latter, protesters were assaulted by Nixon supporters. The travelers enjoyed a warm welcome at Salem, and Rogers burst into Nixon's room after departure, saying "I think the tide has begun to turn."[269]

Robert Taft, of all people, had issued a statement saying he could see no reason why senators shouldn't receive such assistance. But it was a thin silver lining in a very ominous cloud, and the mood wasn't lifted much as the train neared Portland.

After a parade, Nixon retreated to the Benson Hotel and received a message to call Sherman Adams on Ike's train in St. Louis. Angry, he said he would talk to no one but Eisenhower. After a speech that night in Portland's Grand High School, Nixon returned to his room with close aides for a strategy session that included a call from Humphreys. He had lined up the Eisenhower train behind the TV idea, and before Nixon went to sleep at dawn, he agreed it was the only thing to do.

Both trains stood still that Sunday, but telephone calls continued all day between Ike's headquarters in New York and Washington, St. Louis and Portland. Tom Dewey—then governor of New York—called Nixon

and advised him to appeal on his TV broadcast to the American people to decide whether he should stay aboard. After a troubled flight to St. Louis, Humphreys met with Summerfield and Adams in the latter's drawing room. They hotly debated the issue, with Adams insisting Nixon was a liability. Humphreys challenged Ike's contention that he intended to talk to Nixon, saying the American people could hardly be convinced the general hadn't had a chance to reach his running mate by now. Adams, instead of rebelling, picked up the phone and ordered a phone call to be arranged that night between the two after Ike returned from dinner with friends.

Nixon was in his room at the Benson being examined by a doctor because of a persistent rigidity in his neck when Ike's call finally came through. Nixon recalled later that Eisenhower seemed to be fishing for a resignation although he didn't say so. Nixon vulgarly told him he should make up his mind quickly, but Ike insisted he would wait until three or four days after the telecast to gauge public reaction. The truth is, he didn't want to be blamed for the dump. The Republicans arranged for Nixon to speak to the nation at 9:30 Monday night following the popular "I Love Lucy" program to ensure a big audience. Nixon objected, saying that didn't give him enough time to prepare. So the talk was reset for the same slot Tuesday, shortly after Milton Berle's "Texaco Star Theater."

Leaving his train in the hands of Sen. Harry Cain for its stops in Washington State, Nixon flew back to Los Angeles on a chartered DC-6 Monday morning for the broadcast.

At the same time, as Eisenhower's train rumbled through Illinois east of St. Louis, Ike appeared again, unexpectedly, in the press car, slouching on a small red couch and telling the reporters about his call to Nixon. "I do

not want to nag ... (or) prejudge him," he commented.[269] Off the record, he was uncertain whose place it would be to remove him from the ticket; maybe it would be up to the Republican National Committee. As he talked about what he would do with a "secret" fund, wired press summaries continued to pour into the train, including one that said more column inches were now being devoted to Nixon than to Eisenhower and the Democratic nominee, Illinois Gov. Adlai Stevenson, combined.

Herb Brownell met the train in Cincinnati and sat down with Ike and Adams in car 17, "with the shades ... carefully lowered."[269] Brownell calmly advised them to do nothing until after Nixon made his address to the nation. Telegrams were running 3-1 against Nixon; there were reports that the Democrats were ready to reveal a new twist to the story because of a shady loan to Nixon in his 1950 Senate campaign; Eisenhower-Nixon clubs were losing heart and slacking off in their efforts.

As the Eisenhower train rumbled toward Cleveland on the New York Central, the press was notified that Ike would soon make a third visit to the press car. Bob Clark, working for International News Service, was just sitting down to lunch in the diner, but he left his plate and hurried back for the sudden news conference. The next stop, the first opportunity for Clark and the others to file their stories, was two hours distant, so after Ike finished talking and left the press car, Clark decided to return to the diner and eat his lunch before writing his story.

When Clark came back to the press car, Charlie Brown—Western Union's No. 2 man on the train—was there. "What's going on?" Clark asked. Brown told him the railroad had arranged an emergency drop of wire copy so stories about the meeting with Eisenhower could be dropped off—and it was coming up in five minutes!

Clark was frantic. The Associated Press correspondent had written five pages and had given them to Brown for the drop. Clark had written nothing. He collared the conductor and asked if the train would stop. He was told it would not, but would slow down to about 20 to 25 miles an hour. Although he didn't recommend it, the conductor told the frustrated reporter it might be possible to get on the lowest step of one of the cars and jump off to file the story.

Clark was desperate; he had to try. He jumped, and fell into a "cinder bank," rolling and tumbling to a most uncomfortable stop. His hands were cut and bleeding. His relatively new suit was torn to pieces, its knees ripped open. "And just as I was picking myself up and brushing myself off," he told the author, "I looked up. The train had stopped!"

Clark limped to a telephone booth and dictated his story to INS without the benefit of notes. But the train had paused for only two minutes; he had to hitchhike from the town (whose name he can't remember) to another where he could catch a bus to Cleveland and catch up with the train.[82]

There were a couple of bright spots that Monday. The report came back that the fund was "absolutely clean" legally and morally.[269] The money was raised and spent properly; in the years that it had existed it never was a secret. And in another gratifying development, the spotlight on Nixon's fund persuaded Stevenson to reveal that he too had such a stash, and it was considerably richer than Nixon's.

But the momentum in the other direction was strong. Bill Robinson, an executive with the *New York Herald-Tribune*, boarded the train

somewhere in Ohio and was seen walking back to Ike's car. Congressman Charles Halleck became alarmed and at the first opportunity called Summerfield, who had returned to Washington. Once again, Summerfield felt the need to intervene and prop up the ticket, so he summoned Humphreys and the two of them flew to Cleveland in time to meet Ike at the Carter Hotel after a parade.

After a half-hour wait, Humphreys was called into Eisenhower's suite, where the general was half-reclining on a bed. Several advisers were there, and had been checking "various rumors about the Nixon finances," one said.[269] They asked Humphreys about a report that Pat Nixon had paid for an interior decorator's job with $10,000 in cold cash. Not true, Humphreys declared; but as soon as he was ushered out, Eisenhower ordered an aide to call Dewey and ask him to call Nixon to persuade him to resign after his broadcast. Ike would still hold the option of taking back his young running mate; this arrangement would give him ultimate control.

Dewey waited out stubborn aides in California who finally put Nixon on the line. The nominee was stunned at Ike's directive, and exploded at the New York governor who had the most to do with his political rise. When Dewey asked him what he was going to do, in angry defiance he snapped that he didn't know. If they wanted to find out, they would have to watch just like everyone else.

Nixon's speech, broadcast live from the El Capitan Theater in Los Angeles on Tuesday, Sept. 23, 1952, became famous for its down-home references to "Checkers," the cocker spaniel puppy someone had given the Nixon girls, and Pat Nixon's "cloth coat."[269] He worked in the dog angle after remembering how well Franklin Roosevelt—in his bitter 1944 cam-

paign against Dewey—had accused the Republicans of attacking "poor Fala" [see Page 168]. Nixon offered no resignation, but challenged listeners to write to the party about what he should do. He was so rattled by Dewey's 11th-hour call, however, that he neglected to give the national committee's address. He thought he'd failed miserably; but the outpouring of support that swelled up around the nation from that moment turned the situation around.

Ike and his aides had been watching from the manager's office of the Cleveland Public Auditorium, where the candidate was to speak. When Nixon finished, some of Ike's aides were weeping softly. Ike himself was angry; Nixon had tried to take the decision out of his hand, and by promising to reveal his finances and challenging Stevenson and Democratic vice-presidential nominee John Sparkman to do likewise meant that Ike would have to as well. It wasn't that he had anything to hide; he merely felt that his finances were a private matter. The slap ruined forever whatever chance the two men had of becoming close friends.

Now Bill Robinson and virtually everybody else with Ike wanted to keep Nixon. The crowd downstairs, who had heard the talk on a public address system, went wild for him. Ike hurriedly revised his speech to throw in a few compliments to the beleaguered candidate, but—still reserving the final decision for himself—sent Nixon a complimentary wire but nevertheless asked him to meet the Eisenhower train in Wheeling the following night for a face-to-face meeting.

The telegram got lost in the torrent of cables descending on Nixon, but he got wind of the Wheeling meeting in a news wire bulletin. He was livid; he insisted he would not "crawl on my hands and knees to him." Pat Nixon cried out, "What more does that man want?"[269]

Nixon had had it. He was through. He drafted a telegram of resignation on the spot, but Chotiner intercepted it and tore it up. He huddled with Nixon long enough to secure a promise to go to Wheeling as long as Ike promised him in advance he would stay on the ticket. When Summerfield called from Cleveland thinking everything was all right, Chotiner delivered that ultimatum and broke off the call, saying they had to rejoin their train at Missoula, Mont. Chotiner and Nixon's other aides intentionally refused several other calls from Cleveland until they had flown back north, letting Ike's supporters sweat awhile. The delay meant Summerfield and Humphreys had to stay behind when Ike's train left Cleveland at 2 a.m. Wednesday to keep trying to prevent the ticket from shattering. Sitting in their pajamas at the Carter Hotel, they finally reached Nixon in predawn Montana, but the nominee stuck to his guns. Now they had to get a call through to Eisenhower—wherever he was.

Summerfield caught up with Ike at Portsmouth, Ohio, at midmorning Wednesday. After Ike made his rear-platform talk, he and Adams squeezed into a telephone booth in the N&W station, and with Adams holding the receiver, Summerfield laid out the deal. Once again, the decision was being taken out of Eisenhower's hand, and observers reasoned that had Ike been a seasoned politician, Nixon "would have been slapped down and slapped down hard."[269] But Eisenhower had had enough; his telegram to Nixon was now public, and Wheeling was just a few hours away. The military hero who had brought World War II's Axis Powers to their knees and had secured the adoration of the Free World capitulated. He shrugged and nodded his head.

Ike must had been genuinely relieved that the die had been cast. Scores of children who had followed him to the station door swarmed around him when he came out. He encouraged them to gather around and walk with him back to the car, signing autographs, shaking hands, smiling and greeting as many of them as he could. Once he lifted a small tot from the throng and gave him a special greeting. The telephone call delayed departure 10 minutes; few on the scene knew its historic importance.

So as Ike's train neared Wheeling, the nation—especially the Republicans—wondered if they still had a coherent ticket. Telegrams flew thick and fast, some delivered in mail sacks to the train at Parkersburg. Advisers on both sides of the issue tugged at Ike's intellect. Staff members on the train, not knowing a deal had been made, were split 50-50.

Ike had hinted what his decision would be during the Point Pleasant stop when he told a crowd of 5,000 that Nixon was the victim of an "attempted smear."[387f] But he saved the final drama for prime time.

The train approached B&O's impressive, four-track elevated brick-and-stone Wheeling terminal amid considerable road-crossing flag protection. As it trundled onto the trestle spanning Wheeling Creek and eased under the umbrella sheds, people were everywhere.

Arrival was at 6:29, 29 minutes late, on the terminal's track 3. As locomotive supervisor Ferrell threw up his hand to George Reith, WR Tower's second-trick operator, and began looking for Crossing Protection Supervisor Jim McElroy with his unfurled white flag, he sighed with relief, knowing his delicate task was nearly finished. Early the next morning, the special would retrace its steps to Moundsville and head out the Monongah Division's original main line to Grafton.

The train stopped with the Eisenhowers' private car short of the platform. Ike and Mamie walked ahead three car-lengths and detrained on the right side.

Once Ferrell had come to a stop and cut off, he finally turned the road engine over to its assigned crew, dismounted from the cab, and started walking back toward the station. He was introduced to the Eisenhowers. The general, expressing thanks for a "pleasant ride," gave him a silver pin that spelled IKE.[132]

As soon as the official party had waded through the sea of well-wishers and negotiated a set of stairs down into the waiting room, yard power eased against the rear of the train and pulled it back to Benwood for turning. The road diesels followed, and the Wheeling Division crew members laid up there at 8:40 p.m. They would catch train 77 as it paused at Benwood at 11:56 p.m. for a three-hour deadhead trip back to Parkersburg.

For his part in furthering history during those two days more than four decades ago, fireman Harry Nixon claimed $21.12 plus $4 expenses for the 132-mile deadhead move from Parkersburg to Kenova, $32.20 for the 230-mile special movement from Kenova to Wheeling and back to Benwood, and another $13.97 plus $4 expenses for the deadhead return from Benwood to Parkersburg.

Meanwhile, the train was looped on the circular approach to the Benwood-Bellaire (Ohio) bridge and returned to the Wheeling terminal. The rear eight cars were spotted on No. 1 track, the next eight on No. 2 track, and the two head cars tucked in Hempfield Yard's office-car track east of the station, with the entire train remaining on steam. Servicing was immediate and thorough; two redcaps stayed on duty all evening.

Supt. Sell's memos emphasized that the entire depot area must be well

PRR locomotive 6925 forwards running mate Richard Nixon's train northward as it approaches Spartanburg, Pa., Oct. 10, 1952.

lit, quiet, and secure.

The plan for Wheeling called for Eisenhower to leave the station at 7:10 p.m., stop at the McLure Hotel from 7:20 to 8:10 to greet 300 local supporters, deliver a major speech at Wheeling's Island Stadium from 8:25 to 9, and return to the train at 9:20.

The late arrival, but mostly Nixon's debacle and hastily arranged rendezvous, rearranged everything.

Amid an enthusiastic crowd, Eisenhower, now in a light blue suit, was given a key to the city, a presenta-tion few saw or heard because there was no public address system. The general headed for the street, with spectators perched on waiting-room benches and filling the plaza out front.

His automobile raced through a cool and misty evening and stopped outside the McLure, but as if Ike or someone realized time was running out, sped back to the station while aides pacified disappointed supporters at the hotel. He picked up Mamie and, about 9, the two of them went 12 miles out of their way to the airport instead of to the stadium.

The Republican standard-bearers sparked a sensation among 4,500 unexpected locals, including jubilant bobby-soxers, who had gathered at Stifel Field to welcome Nixon, but ended up greeting Ike and Mamie too when they arrived at 9:25. The couple waited in their automobile for Nixon's chartered DC-6b, a United Airlines "Mainliner," largest craft to land at Wheeling up to that time.

When the plane, bringing the vice presidential nominee in from Mis-soula, Mont., landed at 9:56, Ike, pro-tected by a gray overcoat and red scarf, bounded aboard for a moment or two of private conversation with his run-ning mate.

Press accounts paint Nixon as bewildered that Ike himself showed up at the airport, to which Ike replied, "Why not? You're my boy."[11]

The reply assured a "completely vindicated"[396] Nixon—and the nation—that he was still on the ticket and that Ike hadn't been herded by Nixon, the public, the Democrats, the Republicans, or anyone else. Politically, at least, he had made up his mind, deliberately and slowly, remind-ing everyone he was able to lead.

The pair went on to the stadium to address a half-frozen crowd of 8,000 that had waited two hours, with Nixon not taking the podium until about 11 p.m.

Newspapers the next day quoted the Californian as saying "it made me realize that all you have got to do in this great country of ours is to tell the truth and not keep anything from the people,"[396] a lesson he would have done well to remember during the Watergate scandal 20 years later.

Returning to the station, Eisenhower and Nixon ensconced themselves in a second-floor confer-ence room before posing on the now-turned train's rear platform for pic-tures. Nixon himself, in a letter to the author, recalled that they "had a long conversation in his special car and made some plans for the balance of the campaign."[283]

The visit on NYC car 17 was not merely social. Ike brought up again the charges that Humphreys thought he had laid to rest in Cleveland about Pat's interior decorator. Angry and barely controlled, Nixon denied the story and lectured Ike on politics: "This is just like war, General. Our opponents are losing. They mounted a massive attack against me and have taken a bad beating. It will take them a little time to regroup, but when they start fighting back, they will be desperate, and they will throw everything at us, including the kitchen sink. There will be other charges, but none of them will stand up. What we must avoid at all costs is to allow any of their attacks to get off the ground.

The minute they start one of these rumors, we have to knock it down just as quickly as we can."[269]

Eisenhower's special had forced several changes in routine operations. In 1952, Wheeling was still a major passenger terminal for B&O, with trains fanning out in five directions. While Ike was in town, five trains were due to arrive or depart, including three within 10 minutes.

Train 245 was due out for Chicago at 6:20 p.m., 20 minutes after the special was due and 10 minutes before it actually arrived. No one remembers if 245 was held until the special arrived or was allowed to proceed on double track toward Benwood to be stopped again just out of the terminal while the eastbound extra passed.

A bottleneck was scheduled a couple of hours later, with No. 72 due in from Kenova at 8:20, No. 441 for

Grafton due out at 8:25 and No. 238 due in from Cincinnati, bound for Pittsburgh, at 8:30—a bottleneck now compounded because only two of four terminal tracks were available. Again, no one remembers how the trains were handled. One memo called for a storage mail car normally moving on the rear of train 72 from Kenova to Wheeling, then on to Pittsburgh via train 238 the next night, to move instead at the head end of 72 on Wednesday, being forwarded on 238 the same night without stopping over.

With Nixon's place secure on the ticket, history's course had been set in Wheeling for several years to come. With everybody back on board, snoozing or sipping, soil cans were removed from the sleepers and a yard crew doubled the special together at 1 a.m. for the outbound move. The four-unit diesel road locomotive, with

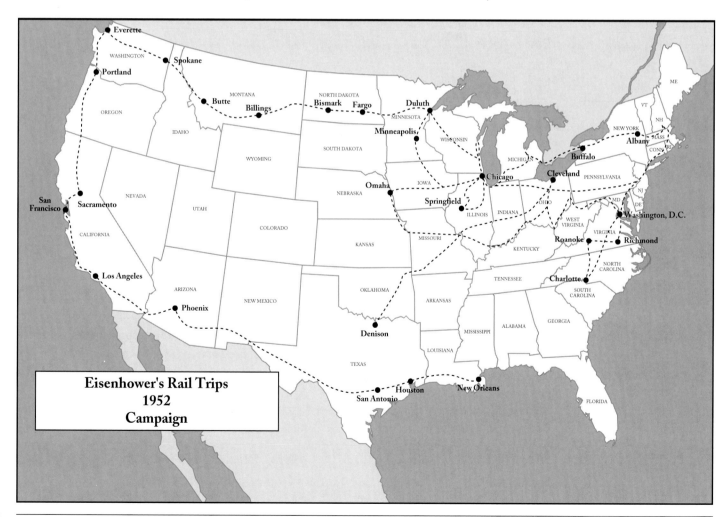

Eisenhower's Rail Trips
1952
Campaign

the 959 in the lead, was back from Benwood by that time with a Monongah Division crew and nosed against the train for an air test.

The weather was clear at 50 degrees, with occasional fog pockets, as the special departed Wheeling on time at 1:45 a.m. for Grafton. In fact, the ever-faithful Tommy Thompson recorded that the departure was 30 seconds early, but there were two unscheduled stops: 10 minutes at Cameron for a sticking brake and one minute at Fairmont to put off Western Union messages.

Eisenhower's train went on to Baltimore and back to Washington on the B&O, then took the candidate on his second excursion into the solid Democratic South via the Southern Railway.

The train drew up for servicing at Salisbury, N.C., at 6:45 a.m. on the 26th of September, where it would reverse direction and back on to Charlotte. Most of the general's staff were asleep, but Ike heard a clamor outside his car and ducked out in his bathrobe to greet about 50 railroad workers, women and children. They called for Mamie, and in a moment she popped out in pink pajamas and dressing gown with a ribbon around her hair. Shouted a male voice, "Boy, Mamie sure does look good, even in the morning.' "405

"The men of the press, sleeping eight or 10 cars ahead of ours, had always before been completely unaware of or had ignored the unscheduled stops and meetings," Eisenhower recalled in his autobiography. "But in Salisbury a wakeful photographer had a feeling that something unusual was going on and came to the rear of the train. The photographs were most informal and unusual, but we had become so adjusted to the ever-ready, ever-present cameras that we thought no more of the incident until Jim Hagerty

came to us a few hours later with a request from all the other photographers on the train—actually an earnest and prayerful petition—that we pose for pictures duplicating the one they missed earlier in the day. Otherwise, they said, their employers might accuse them of more than negligence.

"Because of our friendship with the photographic group, we complied," Eisenhower wrote. "At a convenient stopping place they herded back to the rear of the train while we solemnly donned bathrobes over our normal clothing and posed until they got the scene recorded on film. The gratitude of the group was satisfying; every man implied that he was going to vote Republican."124

The train continued to Charlotte, then headed north to Winston-Salem on the Southern and got on the N&W again.

Between Martinsville and Bassett, Va., Ike popped into the conference car and began his greetings by pumping the hand of a *Norfolk & Western Magazine* representative near the door—with a hearty clap on the shoulder for good measure. He was in great spirits and obviously enjoyed greeting those aboard, but had to hurry back to the NYC 17 so he could wave to the crowd at Bassett.

At Roanoke, Class J steamers 612 and 613 were substituted for the 600 and 604, which had replaced Southern power at Winston-Salem. At Bedford, east of Roanoke, the candidate was back in the conference car, shaking hands again with the magazine rep. "I know someone on your railroad," he said. "Freeman Jones— his brother-in-law is going to introduce me tonight at Petersburg."199 He was referring to Lt. Gen. Leonard T. Gerow (retired), who served under Ike during the European campaign in World War II. His brother-in-law was a retired N&W general freight

agent then living in Petersburg.199

Ike's people aboard the train began to relax now that the Nixon trouble had been settled, and even started to joke about it. Typical was the incident that ensued after someone came to Bernard Shanley in Lynchburg and told him he should meet an old Harold Stassen supporter who was then vice chairman of the state GOP committee. "I had noticed a very attractive blonde standing around … and I was brought over and introduced to her. She didn't look a day over 25. She told me she started in politics because of Harold Stassen and then married and moved to Virginia three years ago. In this short space of time she had become vice chairman of the state committee. That in itself was a remarkable feat. … 343

"In the late afternoon of a very relaxed day … the 'Tippin Club' convened with the following members present: Sen. Fred Seaton, Tom Stephens, Walter Swann and myself; and as we were preparing our stateroom for it, this young girl passed by and I asked her in for a drink. During the course of the conversation Tom Stephens, who had known her before, in a discussion of the Nixon television program, said, 'There was just one thing left out of the program which was the best part of it all.'

"This young girl said, 'What was that?' Tom proceeded to tell her that it was the portion where Checkers, the Nixon dog, crawled up on Dick's lap and licked the tears off his face. Tom, who has a wonderful sense of humor, has the faculty of hitting the nail on the head and this certainly was it, because the program was so corny; the story was more than apropos."343

During a crew change at Crewe, Ike was resting up for his Petersburg speech and the crowd had to settle for Mamie. Ike sent a telegram of regret to the mayor. "At that," he wired, "you saw Mamie—that is the better part of the Eisenhower family."[199]

From Petersburg, the special traversed the Atlantic Coast Line to Richmond; the Richmond, Fredericksburg & Potomac to Washington; and the PRR back to New York.

Eisenhower had his first brush with an accident as he was finishing his talk at Richmond. A temporary platform in front of the old capitol collapsed; Ike fell 5 feet, went to his knees, stood up unhurt, grinned and brushed himself off.

By now Ike was a seasoned campaigner, and could provide telling recollections of whistlestopping: "The candidate … steps blithely out to face the crowd, doing his best to conceal with a big grin the ache in his bones, the exhaustion in his mind. Armed with a card on which he—or an assistant—has written three or four words to remind him of the particular subjects he must mention, and the local candidates for whom he wants to express support at this stop, he awaits cessation of the crowd's clamor—which he fervently prays will consume at least two minutes of his allotted seven [sic]. Then he launches into a talk that he is convinced, by his battered memory, must certainly fail because it has been delivered over and over again, never-ending and tiresome. But quickly he feels within himself a transformation. Although as he came out to the platform he was bored, resentful, or even sorry for himself, invariably the excitement generated by the crowd buoys him up—suddenly he is anxious to make his planned points; he strives for new thoughts; he speaks enthusiastically for Congressman Blank; he seeks for lucidity, conciseness, and logic in the exposition of his policies. He seems to feel that he owes it to these people to expose to them his beliefs, his convictions, his hopes and aspirations for our country. He almost wishes he could have those two minutes back, to share his wisdom more generously with the audience.

"At the appointed time the train slowly moves out. Now, as he calls his goodbyes, he feels a genuine regret that his stay has been so short. Then, out of sight once more, he stumbles back into the car, to an inviting couch where he tries, for a moment, to revitalize himself for the next chore.

"During his seven-minute appearance, a number of people have boarded the train. They will travel only as far as the next stop. These are political figures of the territory the train is now entering; they consider it important to their prestige in the upcoming town to be seen debarking from the same train that carries the candidate. Moreover, each needs a picture—which the local paper will print—of himself talking or shaking hands with the presidential candidate. The picture-taking goes on in the train's 'conference car,' the only one with sufficient space to accommodate group photography, and usually located about three cars ahead of the candidate's 'office.' After two or three minutes of rest the candidate starts forward to meet his political allies.

"By this time the train is rushing ahead—indeed, at a maximum, jolting, and almost terrifying speed. To negotiate the three car-lengths of narrow passageways, constantly guarding against injury from the lurching, jerking, unpredictable motion of the surging metal monster, is an ordeal. At its end, introductions are futilely made by the chairman of the visiting committee, whose voice, no matter what its carrying power, is drowned out by the clatter and din of speeding wheels and the groaning of the car's structure. As each visitor steps forward, the photographer obligingly flashes his light, and soon the deed is done. When the last visitor records his smile for posterity—and his constituency— the nominee, trying his best to look

WIDE WORLD

Three-year-old Mark Mitchell just isn't cooperating as his dad tries to take his picture with Democratic candidate Adlai Stevenson at Pittsfield, Mass., Oct. 25, 1952. The frustrated father gave up when a flashbulb refused to fire. Fortunately, The Associated Press didn't.

happy and hospitable, has now to repeat the ordeal of passage, this time to, rather than from, his car. (Even yet, I try to figure out which was worse in politics—coming or going.)

"Invariably, reaching the office car in the rear, the candidate is visited by two or three of the staff who have several services to perform on his behalf.

"First and most important is a recitation of the subjects likely to excite the deepest interest of the people in the town next to be visited. Whether it is a bridge, a dam, agriculture, national defense, an anniversary, or a favorite son, it is the candidate's business, according to the pros, to demonstrate an awareness of each of their civic problems (and explain what he proposes to do about them) and share their civic pride."[124]

Ike wrote that a staffer would

scan newspapers for reactions to his speeches. If he came across as tired, vague, indifferent, rash or inaccurate, the candidate had to find a way to correct such errors.

"Throughout the day, whenever there was a moment, I was always writing and correcting—at times missing a meal as a result. Only at the last possible minute was any speech ever finished, to be turned over to the typists and hurriedly mimeographed for the press.

"The moment this happened, I normally began the process of preparing the next address. And about the time I could settle down to this, the whistle would blow for the next stop.

"And every night there was a platform talk to be delivered, formal or informal." [124]

Though the routine, repeated day after day, was grueling, Eisenhower wrote that there were too many unusual happenings along the way, serious or amusing, to class the experience as monotonous.

"One time a teleprompter operator, failing to notice I was extemporizing, got so far ahead of me that I never could catch up. On another occasion a motorcycle policeman, eager to get me to my hotel, took me on a short cut—away from my own motorcade." [124]

The press perceived Ike's speeches as a little bland. His generalities led reporters to refer to him privately as "the extremely General Eisenhower," and one of them noted that when he "utters the most obvious platitude, [people] look at that serious face as if they had heard something that ought to be graven on stone and passed on to the third and fourth generation." One newspaperman on the train asked "Where are we now?" His companion sighed, with the recent division of Korea in mind, "Crossing the 38th platitude." [44]

Eisenhower took to the air again on Tuesday, Sept. 30, for a flight to Columbia, S.C., and then to Cleveland, where his train left from Linndale Station at 11 that night. He ventured along the NYC to Bay City, Mich., where his whistlestopping began the next morning. The political novice made a lot of points when he hoisted 7-year-old Jimmy Waldzak up to the back railing and into the nation's spotlight after he ran a mile to catch up with the train. The general continued on his route toward Chicago, encountering some difficulties. The train lost precious minutes; by the time his diesels pulled up at Saginaw, the crowd of 20,000 had trampled wires to the public address system. After emergency repairs, the train's auxiliary power system was turned on, and Ike barely had time to say "Ladies and gentlemen" before engineer Glenn L. Stevens started the train rolling, endeavoring as any good hogger would to keep his train on schedule. A state policeman assigned to keep the crowd under control sprinted down the track, but didn't catch the train. "Whoops!" Ike cried to the astonished crowd as the train lurched forward. "They're taking me away." [389z]

Half an hour later at Lapeer, Mich., Stevens' quick hand once again interrupted Ike by inching the train toward the Grand Trunk Western connection. Again helplessly fleeing his public, the nominee called back to the waiting throng, "I was supposed to have three minutes to talk to you people —" [389z]

For all his trouble, Ike secured Stevens' promise that he would vote for him, saying it was "time for a change." [205] The apologetic engineer had gone for Truman in '48.

That didn't end the day's annoyances. The train halted again in one town for a crew change and Ike and Mamie started signing autographs. "This train has been acting oddly all day," Ike told a fan. "I just think it was an honest mistake; I don't know what happened." As it eased forward again, Ike caught Mamie handing a pen down to an autograph seeker and cried out in anguish in a live mike, "No, no, Mamie. That's MY pen." [389z]

At Lansing, the train returned to the NYC from the GTW; Ike left it at Jackson to motor into Chicago. The next morning, Oct. 2, he struck out again on the train, traveling south on the Illinois Central to Champaign and Tolono, Ill. At Champaign, the engineer overshot the spot by 30 feet. The intended stopping place would have put car 17 on top of a viaduct near where two streets intersected; missing by even such a short distance meant that many of the 15,000 who had gathered saw little and heard nothing.

At Tolono, the general turned westward on the Wabash to Springfield, where he thanked candidate Stevenson for giving state employees the day off so they could see him and also made a pilgrimage to Lincoln's tomb; then he went northeast on the Gulf, Mobile & Ohio to Bloomington and west on the NYC's Peoria & Eastern subsidiary to Peoria. That night, the train departed from Peoria's Rock Island Station for Wisconsin via the Rock Island line to Chicago and the Chicago & North Western. Friday morning he stumped at Green Bay and worked back to Milwaukee.

Rough handling broke a coupler in Chicago as the party slept, and Ike bumped his head. "I have felt groggy all day," he told reporters later. "I was lying down and then the train stopped suddenly. I banged my head against the wall." [389aa] His mother-in-law, Mrs. John Doud, also suffered a hard bump on her head, but no doctor was summoned.

A quirk in Wisconsin law forced the *Look Ahead Neighbor Special* to play a role in a tragedy that day. An 18-month-old baby girl had been killed by a regular C&NW train running ahead of the special on a parallel track between Appleton and Neenah. The impact threw the tot's body onto the track Ike's train was on, but Wisconsin law stipulated the body could not be moved until the coroner had completed his investigation. The train was held short of the accident scene for several minutes until someone determined its passage would not touch the remains, then it was allowed to proceed over them. Neenah was reached about 15 minutes late; Ike didn't know what happened until later.

The events that unfolded on that leg of the tour could have spelled disaster for Eisenhower. The problem was Sen. Joeseph McCarthy, the Wisconsin senator who was finding a communist under every government rock. His extremism was repulsive to the moderate Eisenhower, and yet he had to embrace him for the sake of party unity. McCarthy had boarded the train at Peoria and was much in evidence on the back platform, always ducking inside when Ike began talking about their different methods of ridding the government of incompetents, crooks and subversives.

In Green Bay, Ike flinched, refusing to pose for pictures with McCarthy and infuriating him. But the candidate inched closer to McCarthy in Appleton when he called for election of a great Republican "team" in Wisconsin, "from the governor himself through the Senate and the House."[389aa]

The strain would only get worse. McCarthy and his minions had denounced Gen. George Marshall, Ike's commander in the Army, as a traitor and a friend to communism. Eisenhower owed much of his military career—indeed, his World War II allied command—to his friend, and

yet to compliment him would be tantamount to repudiating McCarthy.

Feeling belligerent when his Milwaukee speech was being planned, Ike had said to speechwriter Emmett Hughes, "Listen, couldn't we make this an occasion for me to pay a personal tribute to Marshall—right in McCarthy's back yard?" The appropriate phrase was crafted and included in advance press releases. But Wisconsin Gov. Walter J. Kohler had boarded the train in Peoria with McCarthy and worked through the night to convince Ike's aides that the tribute would split Republican strength in the state. When Sherman Adams and military aide Wilton B. "Jerry" Parsons approached Ike, he said, "Are you trying to suggest that I take out the paragraph on Marshall?" Adams replied, "That's right, General." Ike said, "Well, take it out. I covered that subject thoroughly in Colorado a few weeks ago."[239] Some said the excision was McCarthy's price for riding the train.

Actually Eisenhower hadn't disposed of the issue. Praising Marshall in Colorado wasn't the same as nailing McCarthy in his home state. The fact that Ike didn't recognize the difference only exposed his political naivete; but Truman, Stevenson and the Democrats bitterly denounced Ike's deletion—public knowledge because of the advance texts—as cowardly and compromising.

Friday's overnight ride was to Minnesota, where the candidate spoke at Duluth on Saturday, then caught a plane for points west.

He rejoined the train—and Mamie—at Fargo, N.D., Saturday afternoon and proceeded toward the West Coast on the Northern Pacific. Whether early in the morning or late at night, huge crowds turned out; in the cities there were showers of tape, and people sometimes lined the curbs five deep. Newsmen on the train (who

stood 24 for Stevenson, 7 for Ike in an on-board poll) admitted they had seen nothing like it since Franklin Roosevelt's greatest days.

With the difficult political maneuvering through Taft country and the tensions with McCarthy behind him, Ike seemed more at ease. He worked hard, going through half a dozen speech drafts with his advisers before he was satisfied. He tried to get in bed by 10:30 or 11, but his aides were used to hearing his knock on their compartment doors at 2 a.m. when he had thought of something he wanted to thrash out at once.

Ike, Mamie and several members of their staffs attended a 25-minute Episcopalian worship service in a lounge car as the train thundered between Big Timber and Livingston, Mont., on Sunday, Oct. 5. An invitation to the Rev. A.W. Symm, pastor of the St. Andrew Episcopal Church in Livingston, had been wired ahead at Eisenhower's behest, and the train made an unscheduled stop at Big Timber to pick him up. Symm wore the traditional white vestments of his office as he stood at one end of the swaying car and conducted the service.

In the early afternoon, Ike made an unscheduled stop east of Whitehall to have his picture made with 30 horsemen in cowboy garb who had ridden to trackside, then sped past a larger crowd at the station.

His train reached Spokane late Sunday night and laid over until Monday morning the 6th. Continuing on the Great Northern, it overnighted again at Seattle, then on Tuesday continued down the GN and Southern Pacific through Oregon. Arrival at Oakland's Sixteenth Street Station was at 1:35 p.m. Wednesday. It arrived with, of all things, Stevenson stickers plastered to several car windows. Kids had stuck them on at Sacramento and the schedule was so tight workers didn't get a chance to remove them.

The Eisenhowers motored to San Francisco, then the next day Ike flew to several California stops, returning to Mamie and the train at Los Angeles late Thursday night to continue on the SP to Phoenix. Campaign aides presented 2-year-old Ronald Welch of Long Beach with a 5-inch "I Like Ike" button to replace a smaller one he had swallowed. As they pinned it on him, they assured his parents this one was too big to follow. A hospital said the metallic morsel would be taken care of "by nature."[389ab]

Once again, Ike took to the air, returning to the train at New Orleans Monday night the 13th to backtrack to Houston overnight. The 14th was his 62nd birthday; friends brought a huge cake to the train.

"The cake was the largest example of the confectioner's art that I had ever seen—almost large enough for us to eat it and have it, too," Ike wrote. "But the entire company of campaigners feasted on it (one of them, I believe, accidentally sat in part of it), and the cake disappeared."[124]

Eisenhower flew all over Texas on Tuesday, pleased that he was in the state where he was born (at Denison). He returned to the train at San Antonio for an overnight run up the Missouri-Kansas-Texas and the Texas & Pacific to Fort Worth and Dallas.

During an operating stop in Austin at 2 a.m., a crowd of students began serenading the Eisenhowers. Tousled and sleepy-eyed, "we had to reach for our robes, hasten to the platform, and join in singing 'The Eyes of Texas are Upon You,'"[124] Ike wrote.

At Dallas, a coupler broke on the train, and both halves came to a jarring halt. The Eisenhowers were badly shaken up, furniture was overturned and Mamie's cosmetics were smashed. But the general recovered enough to leave his private car and

begin walking the half-mile to the station. The first few cars were still intact; he boarded one of them and rode the rest of the way.

It was because of such incidents that James P. Shields, grand chief of the Brotherhood of Locomotive Engineers, sent Eisenhower the following telegram: "Any interpretation of these incidents as implying opposition to your candidacy is based on misinformation or slander. As one of the few major labor organizations which have not issued political endorsements, we have no intention of attempting to influence a campaign by less obvious means."[205]

At Dallas, Eisenhower left the train for good on this tour. With Mamie still on board, it left Dallas at 10:45 p.m. Wednesday and arrived in New York at 6 a.m. Friday.

On Friday, Oct. 17, Ike began another swing, but rode his train only from New York to Wilmington via the PRR. He finished the day motorcading through New Jersey.

Then, on Monday the 20th, he boarded once again for a foray into New England via the New York, New Haven & Hartford. Motoring from New Bedford to Taunton, Mass., he concluded the day at Worcester and headed back to New York.

Leaving again Wednesday, Ike flew to Hartford, Conn., then reboarded the train to continue to Springfield, Mass., on the New Haven and proceed west on NYC. Early Friday morning, the train switched to the Grand Trunk Western in Detroit for Michigan whistlestops in Pontiac and Royal Oak before returning to Detroit for a major speech.

It was there that the general dropped the bombshell that, if elected, he would personally visit Korea in an effort to end the military stalemate there. The announcement was ridiculed by the Democrats but

moved several reporters to conclude that he had won the election right then and there. The train returned him to New York late Saturday morning for a long day of appearances.

Sunday night, he was off again by train, rolling to Philadelphia on the PRR for an overnight stay followed by whistlestops across Pennsylvania to Pittsburgh and a return to New York Tuesday morning.

After motorcading in the New York area during the latter part of the week, Ike flew to Chicago on Friday the 31st, returning Saturday.

The last sweep was by rail, leaving Grand Central Station's Track 27 just after midnight, Monday morning, Nov. 3. Detraining at South Station, he motored to several Boston points and reboarded on Track 3 at Back Bay Station for an overnight return to New York.

"Mamie and I, for the first time during all those weeks of travel, instead of going immediately to our beds after the day's work, went to the conference car to enjoy two or three hours of companionship with the staff. Fred Waring and his orchestra were with us that night and they entertained the entire company. Work was a thing of the past; everybody present was gay and thoroughly happy—even though sleepy."[124]

They arrived in New York City at 6:25 a.m. Election Day. The Eisenhowers, exhausted, voted and went home to bed.

Nixon's role on the '52 campaign trail was to cover out-of-the-way places while Ike visited the big cities, an arrangement that put the vice-presidential nominee on some odd routings down isolated branches and on some of the best Eastern mountain railroading.

The "secret fund" debacle—and the resulting flight back to Los Angeles for the "Checkers" telecast—interrupted Nixon's first tour at

Portland, canceling the candidate's scheduled Sept. 21 jaunt to Seattle behind NP 2626, the "Four Aces" 4-8-4 that was originally numbered 1111 and was noted as the original Timken roller-bearing locomotive. He rejoined the train at Missoula, Mont., only to leave it again and fly to Wheeling for the fateful meeting with Ike that announced to the nation he was still on the GOP ticket.

Nixon's second tour, a seven-day trek, left from New York Sunday, Oct. 5, via the New Haven. After overnighting at Berlin, Conn., the special was switched to the Boston & Maine at Springfield, Mass., and stopped at Greenfield and Fitchburg before returning to New Haven rails at Atlantic. Monday night was spent on the train enroute to Steubenville, Ohio, via NH-New York-PRR, and Tuesday was spent on the Pennsy to Zanesville and the Nickel Plate Road's ex-Wheeling & Lake Erie line to Canton. (One wag in Justus, Ohio, quipped that "they finally brought Nixon to Justus.")[32] The train then transferred to the B&O for an overnighter to Wapakoneta, Ohio. Wednesday's itinerary followed the B&O to Sidney, NYC to Columbus, C&O to Dundas, and B&O to Parkersburg, W.Va.

Nixon flew to Pittsburgh for evening appearances while the train deadheaded there. Then he reboarded for an overnighter on the PRR to York, Pa. Thursday's trip covered the PRR to Harrisburg, the Reading to Allentown, and the Lehigh Valley to Wilkes-Barre. Overnight, the train continued to New Castle (the route is uncertain). On Friday, it traveled on the Erie Railroad to Oil City, then PRR to Erie. The overnight leg headed for Jamestown, N.Y., via PRR-Corry, Pa.-Erie. On Saturday, the candidate covered the Erie to Binghamton and overnighted to New York.

Trip 3, a four-day, 14-car jaunt, started from Detroit on Wednesday, Oct. 15, and proceeded via NYC to Allegan, Mich., and C&O to Muskegon. It ventured overnight to Logansport, Ind., via PRR. On Thursday, the candidate headed out on the Wabash to Lafayette, NKP to Kokomo and back to Cayuga, and the Chicago & Eastern Illinois to Evansville. The overnight leg covered C&EI to Chicago and the Illinois Central to Freeport, Ill. Friday's jaunt backtracked on IC to Chicago, then the train deadheaded to Cleveland via NYC while Nixon attended campaign functions in the Windy City. He flew to the train, rejoining it in Cleveland at about 1:45 a.m. Saturday and overnighting to Ithaca, N.Y., via NYC-Buffalo-LV. Saturday's leg covered the LV to Geneva and NYC to Utica, where Nixon flew back to New York.

Trip 4 began in Columbus, Ohio, at 1:30 a.m. Monday, Oct. 20, for an overnight trip via B&O to Olney, Ill. Monday's trek started at Olney on the IC, changed to the Southern at Browns, C&EI at Mount Vernon, IC at Marion, and Southern again at Centralia, all in Illinois. The party spent Monday night in St. Louis Union Station, then on Tuesday headed down the Frisco to Cape Girardeau, Mo.

Trip 5 began at Ottumwa, Iowa, the following day, and proceeded to Cedar Falls on the Rock Island and Sioux City on the IC. It overnighted to Moorhead, Minn., via the Great Northern and on Thursday backtracked to Willmar and proceeded to St. Paul. Thursday's overnight leg continued to Superior and then on Friday via C&NW to Beloit, Wis. The schedule called for Nixon to overnight from Beloit to Fort Wayne, Ind., via C&NW-Chicago-PRR and work back to Chicago Saturday, but no record of the trip seems to exist

and some speculate the tour ended in Chicago Friday night.

Diesels were used most of the time on the 1952 campaign specials, but there were notable exceptions. Eisenhower's train, for example, was pulled by N&W's famous streamlined class J 4-8-4s during its two hitches on that road. Nixon's troubled romp up the West Coast was handled by various SP steamers, presumably Daylight-class 4-8-4s. Campaign workers remembered the "old-fashioned" steam whistles on that trip because they would mimic the "hoot hoot" proceed signal at each stop.[294]

Nixon's tour was forwarded by steam at least three other times. Out of Lafayette, Ind., it was pulled by Nickel Plate 2-8-2 587, which went at least to Frankfort, Ind., and may have continued to Kokomo and back to Cayuga. His short stint on the NKP's ex-Wheeling & Lake Erie line in Ohio was hauled—except for the last mile—by NKP Berkshire 815 (ex-W&LE 6415). The train was backed into the yard at Canton with such finesse that an old brakeman exclaimed, "That'll show 'em we still know how to handle varnish [railroad slang for passenger trains] on this line."[32] Finally, Pennsy M1 4-8-2 6925 was on the point from Oil City, Pa., north to Corry and Erie.

As far as anyone remembers, the rest of the tours were diesel-powered—even if the railroads had to go to some trouble. On Nixon's Oct. 20 trip from Marion to Centralia, Ill., IC arranged to pull assigned E units off regular Train 25 at Centralia in the wee hours and forward it to Memphis behind steam while the diesels deadheaded to Marion for the special. Train 4 returned with steam the next day from Memphis to Centralia and picked up the diesels to complete its run to Chicago.

Nixon liked campaign travel, his aides said. "It was easier to campaign by train than by plane," Chotiner recalled. "He found it better to talk with the party brass. It gave him a chance to firm up his contacts, and he'd have a chance to talk with his staff people." Chotiner agreed with his boss' assessment. "I still like a good train campaign. There's still nothing better to build campaign morale and momentum than a campaign train. It's infectious. A train was really very effective."[294]

There were only minor operating glitches. Nixon's private car was equipped with a wood cook stove, and sometimes the rear of the car would fill with smoke. In one incident, a local official miffed that Nixon wasn't stopping in his town pulled the emergency brake valve as the special wound through its outskirts. The train screeched to a halt in front of a crowd at the station, and Nixon had no choice but to give a hasty impromptu speech.

Stevenson did his share of whistlestopping, and his journeys were not without incident. He met up with a lively spectator at Elkhart, Ind., on the New York Central at 11:40 a.m. Wednesday, Oct. 22. Iola Bankhart, a 20-year-old waitress from Oakley, Mich., threw an egg at the dignified contender. It splattered on the canopy of his private car, the yolk landing on campaign aide William Galvin, who was standing in the crowd. "I just wanted to throw an egg," she told the police who seized her. "I'll throw one at Eisenhower, too."[387g] She was released after questioning.

On Friday the 31st, Stevenson's train suddenly backed 15 to 20 feet into a crowd at Silver Spring, Md., on the B&O, bringing shouts and screams but no injuries because the people backed up with the train. *The New York Times* quoted a B&O statement that stubborn brakes had taken too long to slow the special and it

stopped out of range of some TV cameras. Baltimore Division Supt. William M. Murphey at first refused requests from TV crews and staffers on the train to back up, then gave in and ordered the track behind to be cleared for a 60-foot back-up move. Before the move could be made, a campaigner on the train told everyone it would not back up and beckoned everyone to come closer. That's when the train began backing. Murphey, horrified, jumped under a car and pulled an emergency brake valve that stopped the train after it had backed about a third of the intended distance. Stevenson missed all the excitement; he had left the train at Pittsburgh to fly home to Illinois to deal with a prison riot. Sen. J. William Fulbright of Arkansas substituted for the candidate on the rear platform until Stevenson rejoined the train in New York.

B&O's Tommy Thompson's log ignored the incident, except to note that the stop consumed 35 minutes. Murphey came out of it as a hero, but others were somehow caught in the middle. Engineer Frank Mewshaw was fired and Road Foreman J.S. Stewart was demoted. Their colleagues always thought they got a bum rap.

Although President Truman was eligible to run again, he didn't care to—referring to Jan. 20, 1953, the day he would leave office, as the Millenium. But he said he would campaign for Stevenson. Truman's effort this time around was clearly the sideshow, but the president served as a good complement to the candidate. He provided the rough stuff when he thought Stevenson was too mealy-mouthed.

Truman made a rare foray into the South on a two-day Arkansas trek to dedicate two new dams—Bull Shoals across the White River and Norfolk across the White's North

Fork. He traveled mostly by air, but still managed to spend nearly 24 hours on a train.

He flew into Little Rock about 6:30 p.m. on Tuesday, July 1, 1952, leaving 30 minutes later on a Missouri Pacific special for the dedication the next day. The train, with a three-unit diesel and about 12 cars, headed up the Arkansas Division to Newport, with two railroad officers preceding it in a rail-mounted Jeep. For the occasion, a crew brought the North Little Rock wreck train to Newport and kept it there until the move was completed.

During the late evening stop at Newport, population 6,262, Truman made some impromptu remarks. "This happens to be the No. 1 whistlestop of 1952," he croaked, raising his voice because there was no loudspeaker. "There are going to be a lot more of them."[389w]

Then the president proceeded up the White River Division to Norfolk, where his train was spotted on a siding at 1 a.m. Wednesday, July 2. Truman, riding Missouri Pacific business car 2 instead of the *Ferdinand Magellan*, spent the rest of the night on the train, then left via a motorcade at 8:45 for the two dams.

With the train rearranged so the office car was still on the rear but improperly pointed, it deadheaded on to Cotter, where the presidential party reboarded shortly after 1 p.m. The special returned to Newport shortly before 4, where Truman left the train and boarded a flight for Washington. In addition to the two dedications, he had spoken at Newport in both directions and at Batesville on the return, slowing down at several other places so the crowd could catch a glimpse of the president waving through the windows.

Working now under Special Counsel Charles S. Murphy and Administrative Assistant David D.

Lloyd, speechwriter Ken Hechler began churning out two-page outlines after the 1950 pattern for Truman's Labor Day swing through the states of Pennsylvania, Ohio, Wisconsin and West Virginia. This time Hechler went along for the whole trip. And he learned what whistlestopping was all about.

"One of the first things I discovered … was that I was cut off from my customary sources of information and intelligence," Hechler wrote. "I couldn't switch on radio or television to find out what was happening in the world. There is scarcely time during a 10-minute stop to jump off and get a newspaper. If the president wanted a fact or figure checked before using it, I couldn't pick up a telephone and go right to an accurate source—I had to take enough material along to supply the answer immediately."[171]

At some stops, Hechler would jump off the train and make a beeline to a phone for a quick long-distance call to verify some fact, carefully listening for the "beep-beep" signal of the air whistle that operating people used to signal the train was about to leave.

That signal saved Hechler—and others—many times, but once it almost didn't.

"I still shudder and break out in a cold sweat when I recall the worst example, at a town whose name I cannot remember," Hechler said. "For a speech on small business, I made an unusually lengthy phone call to my friends in the Department of Commerce and other agencies who had up-to-date records. I heard the warning signal, but the phone was located a little distance from the train, and by the time I had run down the track, the train was already pulling out. The president and the governor of a state I cannot even remember were still waving to the crowd, when down the track came this staff assis-tant huffing and puffing with a look of desperation. A football-muscled Secret Service man reached down and helped me pull up onto the rear plat-form, where the president got a great kick out of the genuine burst of speed I had mustered in the final 50-yard sprint."[171]

Even the fact that the Army Signal Corps had updated its commu-nications network by replacing radio car 1401 with two converted Army ambulance cars and state-of-the-art equipment, being out of touch caused problems for the president as well as his staff.

Truman had greeted a crowd in the warm noonish sunshine at Crestline, Ohio, on Monday, Sept. 1, and the train was roaring toward Milwaukee, where he would give his evening Labor Day radio address.

"Murphy, Lloyd, [Press Secretary Joseph] Short and I sat together in one of the train compartments in what seemed like a relaxed moment," Hechler said. "The Milwaukee speech had been frozen [finished]; the text had already been released to the reporters on the train. … We started to get out the long yellow pads and pencils for some serious drafting work."[171]

Suddenly the foursome heard Capt. Harvard Dudley, chief of the Signal Corps team, running in the hallway toward them. Breathlessly, he handed Short a message and gasped, "Cordell Hull is dead!"

The drafting ceased immediately. This had been expected; Roosevelt's longtime secretary of state was 81, he had had a stroke and news accounts circulating before the train left Washington the day before indicated his condition was grave.

Short said the president would want to issue a news release and send his condolences to Mrs. Hull. Lloyd put Hechler to work on both of those.

Hechler waded into the long, ponderous statement that had been beamed to the train from the State Department and found it seriously lacking. While he was busy redrafting it, someone else sent the sympathy message to Mrs. Hull. Hechler finally finished the release, datelined "ABOARD TRAIN ENROUTE TO MILWAUKEE," and distributed it to the press.

An hour or so later, *The New York Times'* White House correspondent Anthony Leviero poked his head into Hechler's compartment.

"This was unusual because the compartment was by custom off-lim-its to the press," Hechler explained. "Evidently Leviero had something serious on his mind, because he said it was very important that he talk to Short."

Leviero got right to the point: "My desk tells me that Cordell Hull is still alive and didn't die."

It was true; somehow a mistake had been made. Hechler was not overjoyed, he admitted, to find that Hull was still among the living. The release was corrected, an explanation and apology sent to Mrs. Hull, and the former Cabinet member lived for almost another three years.[171]

Truman enjoyed tremendous crowds as his train rolled across West Virginia the next day, Tuesday, Sept. 2. By that time, the speechwriters had their craft down to a science: Murphy and Lloyd produced the major addresses and Hechler the whistlestop outlines.

In Parkersburg, 3,500 people heard the president denounce Republican boasts that they would liberate peoples behind the Iron Curtain. The talk was intended most-ly for national consumption via the press coverage, but the local crowd liked two points in particular.

Just before they pulled into Parkersburg, Truman had asked Hechler for a Bible. "Anything special

President Truman leaves his train at Norfolk, Ark., to dedicate two dams.

I could find for you, Mr. President?" the aide asked. "Thank you very much," Truman answered. "I know exactly where it is: Gospel according to St. Matthew, Chapter 6."

The president flipped the pages quickly and started reading with feeling: "And when thou prayest, thou shalt not be as the hypocrites are: for they love to pray standing in the synagogues and in the corners of the streets, that they may be seen of men. … But thou, when thou prayest, enter into thy closet, and when thou hast shut thy door, pray to thy Father which is in secret; and thy Father which seeth in secret shall reward thee openly."

Truman remarked that Republicans like John Foster Dulles, Eisenhower's foreign policy adviser, were posing as self-righteous defenders of the captive people of Eastern Europe. He read the passage at Parkersburg and passed along advice his grandfather had given him: When you hear someone praying loudly in public, "you had better go home and lock your smokehouse."

Then Truman sent reporters looking for a dictionary when he declared that the Republican "snollygosters" should read the New Testament and be governed accordingly. He turned to the puzzled press corps, chewing their pencils at trainside, and admonished them, "Better look that word up; it's a good one." Short later told them it refers to "a pretentious, swaggering, prattling fellow."[171]

The president went on to see enthusiastic crowds in Clarksburg, Grafton, Keyser and Martinsburg, W.Va. Even the fact they were running quite late worked to their advantage.

An advance man contacted the approaching train from a station in the Mountain State and said about 3,000 people were waiting. "We said, 'Tell 'em to go home and come back. We won't be there for three hours; we don't want to have 'em standing around,' " Administrative Assistant David Stowe told the author. "We debated whether to tell them to go home. We figured they'd be mad at us if they stood three hours waiting for us. And we figured we lost our crowd. And when we pulled in there, instead of 3,000 there were about 5,000!"[371]

Things were getting a little ragged as the tour approached its conclusion. At Grafton, several hundred grimy railroaders and coal miners met the train. Hechler handed Truman the last speech in the can—one on soil conservation. His audience was perplexed at the subject, staring blankly at the speaker. Afterward, Truman reprimanded Hechler: "Please don't pull another Grafton on me."[261]

Hechler was impressed with Truman's fighting form. "I had a feeling that despite a few 'bugs,' the whistlestopping was going to be almost as enjoyable as it would have been if the president had been a candidate."[171]

Asked about it a few days later, Truman confirmed such outings were for him still a delight. "To tell you the honest truth, I always enjoy it. I had a good time coming across West Virginia the other day." A reporter answered, "We enjoyed it, too. Thank you, sir."[171]

A more strenuous trip began for Truman on Sept. 27, a 15-day epic that took him to California, Oregon and Washington. Its stated purpose was to dedicate a new dam at Hungry Horse, Mont.

While Eisenhower was ridiculing Stevenson's use of humor in his whistlestop talks, Truman defended his colleague with another Scriptural quote: "Be not, as the hypocrites, of a sad countenance" (Matthew 6:16). He also proved he could dish out his own quips, telling listeners in Troy, Mont., that the GOP stood for the "General's Own Party."[207]

"There's a lot of truth in that," the president went on. "The Republicans have General Motors and General

Electric and General Foods and General MacArthur and General Martin and General Wedemeyer. And they have their own five-star general who is running for president. … I want to say to you that every general I know is on this list except general welfare, and general welfare is in with the corporals and the privates in the Democratic Party."[207] He refused to create a circus atmosphere on the train, however, vowing not to stock supplies of confetti and balloons as Eisenhower's staff had planned to do.

But Truman did have fun, as evidenced by his comment at one stop after leaving California: "I can't remember when I've ever enjoyed a day's ride on a train as much as that trip up the Feather River Canyon."[47]

Hechler enjoyed himself, too, especially when he produced Truman's remarks for Helper, Utah, on the D&RGW shortly after 1 p.m. on Monday, Oct. 6. He boned up by conversing with railroad people on the use of helper engines on the rugged Rocky Mountain grades. The president told his audience: "I have always been interested in the way your good town got its name. They tell me that Helper was named for the helper engines that pull the trains up these wonderful mountains you have around here. You know, I think the Republican Party needs some helper engines. It would take a whole roundhouse full of these helpers to get them elected this fall, with their terrible record holding them back. As for their candidate for president, I don't think helper engines can get him out of the trouble he is in now. With the crew he has got around him, I don't think he will ever be elected. …"[171]

At Colorado Springs on Oct. 7, Truman leveled his biggest guns at Ike for deserting Marshall to placate Joe McCarthy. Years later, when *Washington Post* correspondent Edward Folliard asked Truman what

President Truman concludes a whistlestop tour of Arkansas at Newport.

had caused his famous feud with Eisenhower, Truman answered: "Oh, Eddie, I wouldn't call it a feud. But I'll tell you what made Ike mad. It was a speech that I made at Colorado Springs. You go back and look up that speech, and you'll see that I skinned old Ike from the top of his bald head to his backside."[171]

By Thursday the 9th of October, the president and his party had been

on the road 12 consecutive days. Hechler described the routine:

"Starting sometimes before 7 a.m., and frequently not giving his last speech until shortly before midnight, the president thrived on the rugged pace. Even without his customary two-mile brisk early morning walks, he still managed to feel fit, and he was able to drop off to sleep quickly despite the swinging and swaying of

267

President Truman tells Parkersburg, W.Va., about "snollygosters" and the Bible during a whistlestop. Secret Service agent Henry Nicholson is at Truman's right and speech-writer Ken Hechler smiles on the ground.

the train. For the major speeches, we received a supply of fairly good first drafts from Washington, and Murphy and Lloyd were hammering them into shape in time to enable the release of an average of one major prepared speech per day. Meanwhile, [Richard E.] Neustadt and I fed whistlestop drafts to Murphy for final clearance. Sometimes the drafts for the following day were not completed until the small hours of the morning, after which Murphy would work them over and meet with the president early in the morning before the first whistlestop speech. If Murphy got more than two or three hours of sleep a night, he was lucky. The rest of us worked well into the early morning hours and then got up about 8:30 a.m."[171]

"I ran the president's car, deciding who would come in to see him and who didn't," Truman aide David Stowe told the author. "In 1952, [since] he wasn't running for anything … it wasn't like '48, where they were hanging from the rafters and consumed all his time between stops. In '52, we sent 'em forward to a visitors'

car after they'd had a chance to shake hands and say a few words."[371]

There were always minor glitches. One railroad president—Stowe couldn't remember the road—was supposed to ride with Truman but couldn't be found. "We couldn't figure out what happened to him." After some anxious moments, the staff learned that the missing president was riding in the cab of the pilot train.[171]

"I remember one time," Stowe said. "The person who was doing the advance used to leave things under my door about 5 o'clock in the morning so I'd know who to let on the train and who not to let on at each stop, and it must have been 5:30 in the morning and the train was stopped somewhere. The Secret Service [agent] knocked on my door and said, 'Dave, the president's about to make a speech.' I said, 'He's not supposed to make any speech here.' They said, 'Well, he's up and he's back there, and he's got a crowd back there.' So I got up and tried to get in my clothes—I think I got both legs in one pant leg—so finally got back there and he'd gotten a bunch of railroad yard workers together, and he was going to make 'em a speech. Course, we wanted a record of everything he said. It's just luck somebody called me, 'cause he would have made that speech and we would have never known what went on."[171]

Sanitation was also on Stowe's mind. "The only showers on the train (beside the *Magellan's*) were up in the Signal Corps car, and we sorta made a rule that the secretaries who were working night and day on the train had the rights to those. So the rest of us used to have to wait until we got into a town—either overnight or even if we weren't staying more than an hour or two—just to run up to a hotel and get a shower."[171]

Hechler had no fun at all after an unfortunate stop in Anderson, Ind., on the New York Central. "In preparing the two-page background summaries for the president and for other speechwriters, I furnished the names of the congressional incumbents and Democratic candidates," Hechler recalled. "We had just passed through Democratic territory in Missouri where the congressman in office was also the Democratic candidate. We then entered Indiana, having Republican congressmen and Democratic challengers."[171]

The inevitable happened. A young speechwriter rushed a draft to Truman with the name of the Republican incumbent jotted down in the place where the Democratic challenger should be. The process was running late; draft after draft went unchecked; the error slipped into Truman's speech draft and he read it.

Hechler and the young writer were slumbering in their compartment when Murphy appeared at the door. They awoke fast as Murphy announced, "The boss is a little upset. He just endorsed the Republican candidate for Congress! In fact, it was the present Republican congressman!"[171]

Hechler couldn't figure how his roommate's correct data became garbled enroute to the president. And he dreaded what the press would say about the goof.

"Staggering into the dining car shortly after 9 a.m., I listened closely to the newspeople discussing the president's speeches. I wondered how long it would be before they discovered the slip. I was amazed to find out that not a single one of them had bothered to get up that early to listen to the president. They ribbed me with comments like: 'When are you going to stop making every whistlestop so full of meat that we have to cover them all?' "[171]

Most of the correspondents seemed groggy after 12 days' travel. None of the wire services reported the

Western Pacific Railroad/*Railroad Magazine*/Carstens Publications

Harry Truman prepares to greet a California crowd Oct. 5, 1952.

J.J. Young

The B&O has delivered President Truman's train from Pittsburgh to Wheeling and Benwood, W.Va., where the train was looped and now returns to Wheeling Oct. 22, 1952.

Western Pacific Railroad/*Railroad Magazine*/Carstens Publications

An artist has magically airbrushed some of the foliage away to highlight President Truman's train as it leaves Sacramento, Calif., on Oct. 5, 1952.

Anderson mistake; Hechler checked later and found that not one local paper or radio station did, either.

Margaret got even with her father for some merciless ribbing on that trip. While speaking from the rear platform at Hungry Horse, Mont., Truman interrupted himself to ask, "Where's Margaret?" Turns out the first daughter had committed the unpardonable sin of not getting up that morning.

"I was teased unmercifully all the way across the rest of the country," she wrote. "But I got even with him in Ohio. ... There, Mike Disalle, who was running for the Senate, introduced Dad as "Margaret Truman's father."

Always able to dish it out, the president responded ruefully, "I'm a back number already."[100]

On another swing through New England, Truman caught a stiffer put-down from Margaret with a stinging reference to her singing career. Aide David Stowe believes that it was after her father had received a stirring reception by the townsfolk of Brockton, Mass. "He had 'em going

real good," Stowe related. "They were hoopin' and hollerin' and jumping up and down and he came into the car and he turned to Margaret and said, 'Margaret, when you get a crowd as enthusiastic as that, you'll know you have arrived.' And she looked at him and said, 'Well, Daddy, when you get a crowd to pay $8.80 a seat, then you'll know YOU'VE arrived!' "[371]

Hechler contributed a statement to an Altoona, Pa., whistlestop speech Oct. 22 that tickled the local people. Said Truman of Ike: "The General has contradicted himself on so many issues that you can't tell exactly where he does stand. He meets himself coming back—worse than a train going around Horseshoe Curve."[171] The local paper liked that.

The president played to the railroaders gathered round. "In 1928, the hourly pay for the railroad worker was 93 cents an hour and today, under the Democrats, it is $1.86 per hour. It is true that much of this increase has been taken up by the increase in the cost of living, but that wouldn't have been so if the Republicans had helped put in and keep price controls."[9c]

Local newsmen riding the 12-car train into Altoona asked Truman if he ever wearied of campaigning.

"No, I don't get tired of talking to the people," he said. "It is a source of great pleasure to me and I enjoy every minute of it."[9c]

The reporters found a different atmosphere in the press car—boredom. Reporters were passing the long hours by playing cards, snoozing or talking shop. They sipped their drinks with indifference, barely noticing the news handouts they were offered.

"There's one thing that's really handy on the special train," the Altoona writers beamed. "You can eat in the dining car almost 24 hours of the day."[9c]

During his last lap that started Oct. 27 and included a tour of Ohio, Indiana, Minnesota, Iowa, Michigan and Illinois, Truman cabbaged another locomotive ride, staying with B&O engineer Harry Beltz for about an hour in the Pittsburgh area. "I had a lot of fun up there," he told reporters.[452]

Spoofing a remark by Eisenhower in Boise, Idaho, that the government

Congressional candidate Robert Richardson enjoys the view from President Truman's coattails as they campaign for the Democratic ticket at St. Joseph, Mo., Oct. 9, 1952.

did "everything but come in and wash the dishes for the housewife,"[171] Truman read some Hechler-inspired lines designed to win over the votes of employees of a dishwasher firm in tiny Troy, Ohio: "We have made it possible for many housewives to get cheap electricity so they can afford to have electric dishwashers to do the dishes. ... The Republicans are more interested in the problems of big corporations than they are in the problems of people who have to wash their own dishes. They are too busy trying to open up loopholes in the tax laws for the special interest lobbies to spend much time trying to make life easier and better for the ordinary citizen. I am afraid that the Republican candidate is going to lose the dishwasher vote. I think he will lose the vote of the KP's who have had to wash dishes in the Army, too."[171]

That night in Cincinnati, Taft's hometown and home of Procter & Gamble, he was in rare form. "Now I honestly think they ought to let Bob Taft have the nomination. He was the best representative of their party, and what it stands for, and he deserved that nomination. But the advertising experts said 'no'. ... Then they had to have a slogan for a sales drive. 'Back to McKinley'? No, that may be the right kind of slogan but it doesn't have the right kind of ring to it. ... "Ninety-nine and $^{44}/_{100}$ percent pure'? Well, they were using that for a while; and then somebody started asking questions about their vice presidential candidate, and some of the other great crusaders, so they dropped it. ... So they decided on this one: 'It's time for a change.' Whatever soap you are now using, they tell you, switch to our new brand. If you do that, you will have no more problems. Use an entire package, and you can clean up all the fears

of depression and unemployment. You can wash away the whole problem of Korea with one simple application."[171]

On Saturday, Nov. 1, the last day of the campaign, Truman started speaking at 7:20 a.m. at Vincennes, Ind., after which the 16-car special was transferred to the Chicago & Eastern Illinois.

The railroad company magazine touted the move as the line's first-ever presidential movement, until C.R. Phleger, a retired fireman, wrote in that he had seen William McKinley's train go by the old C&EI depot on Collett Street in Danville, Ill., more than 50 years earlier. His father, T.F. Phleger was conductor on the 100, the pilot engine.[64]

Truman whistlestopped all across Indiana and Illinois. In Danville, where the train was switched to the Wabash at 10:35 a.m., he held aloft a copy of the local Republican paper

Followed by former press secretary Roger Tubby, Harry Truman strolls through the cars of B&O's National Limited *on his way home from Washington on Jan. 21, 1953. "Don't get up," he smiles. "I'm no longer president."*

that called for a Republican victory on grounds that it was time for a change. Truman pointed to a "Do you remember" column right across from the editorial, which said "the lowest price for wheat in the history of the Chicago Board of Trade" had been recorded in 1932 at 44 cents a bushel. He asked if that was the kind of change being demanded.[171]

In Granite City, Ill., at 3:40 p.m., the last whistlestop of Truman's last campaign, he summed up his political philosophy—including an implied salute to whistlestopping: "My experience in 1948 proved something I had always known in my 40 years of politics. If the people get the truth, they can be trusted to look out for their own welfare, and the welfare of their great country. That is the basic principle I have followed in my seven years as president of the United States."[171]

Hechler was given a unique assignment for the Kiel Auditorium speech in St. Louis. The address had just about been "frozen"[171] for mimeographed release when Truman decided he wanted to dramatize the way Republicans jumped on the bandwagon of Democratic issues just before the election. He wanted to do a parody of the poem "Just before Christmas I'm as good as I can be." To do so, he had to verify the original wording of the poem.

"None of the materials I had along for research purposes, including *Bartlett's Familiar Quotations*, included the poem," Hechler recalled. "When the train arrived in St. Louis, we had only a few hours before the speech. I tried a few libraries, which were closed on Saturday afternoon, but finally located one where I could check the precise dialect used in Eugene Field's poem. The president wowed the crowd with his rendition, which included the lines, 'Jest 'fore the election I'm Fair Deal as sure as sure can be' and 'Just 'fore election I'm fer the people as strong as strong can be.' "[171]

He wound up his address—and the campaign—with an attack on Eisenhower for deserting his former principles and contrasted his behavior with Stevenson's "courage and dedication to duty,"[171] which led him to the interruption in his campaign during which he quelled the Illinois prison riot. David Stowe offered his own assessment of Truman's style:

"He definitely was at his best on the train. He'd get the people and he'd bring 'em in there and he was a marvelous one-on-one kind of talker. And he'd get a little group on that train and, riding from stop to stop, he'd talk to them all face-to-face. You can't do that on an airplane."[371]

After the election, the lame-duck president learned how fleeting fame is when he and Bess went home to Independence for his mother-in-law's funeral. When their nine-car special paused in Cincinnati at 6:40 a.m. Sunday, Dec. 7, Truman disembarked from his car (again, the *Magellan* was not used) for a walk through Cincinnati Union Terminal. He and a couple of Secret Service agents walked down the platform, up a ramp and through the nearly deserted station concourse without being recognized. Even Eileen Kinerian, the newsstand operator from whom he bought a newspaper, didn't recognize him at first. He fumbled around for some change, then presented her with a crisp new dollar bill he had autographed to give to a child. When she turned to get his change, he smirked, "That'll be worth $50 to a collector." She glanced at the bill, wheeled around and recognized the smiling president. "I have poor eyesight," she apologized to the press later for the snub.[386d]

The White House changed hands on Jan. 20, 1953. Ike left New York on Sunday the 18th and rode to Washington on PRR business car 90. After his inauguration, the Trumans attended a luncheon at the Georgetown home of outgoing secretary of state Dean Acheson. Later that afternoon, Truman sneaked in a nap at a

White House staffer's home. Then that evening, they went to Union Station for a final trip on the *Magellan*—courtesy of the new president—to Missouri on the B&O, the line Truman referred to affectionately as "my road."[382] Margaret saw her parents off and headed back to New York. It was the first and only time, seasoned observers say, that a private car was ever allowed to deface the rear of B&O No. 1, the *National Limited*, during its heyday.[110]

"We were amazed at the mob scene," Margaret wrote. "At least 5,000 people were in the concourse, shouting and cheering. It was like the 1944 and 1948 conventions. The police had to form a flying wedge to get us to the *Ferdinand Magellan*. Inside, the party started all over again. Newspaper men and women who had spent eight years tearing Dad apart came in to mumble apologies and swear they never meant a word of it. Half the executive branch of the government seemed to be trying to shake his hand, or, in the case of the ladies, give him a kiss. He soon had lipstick all over his face. We finally had to call a halt to it, so the train could get out of the station on something approximating its schedule. Dad went out to the old familiar rear platform and gave them a farewell salute: 'May I say to you that I appreciate this more than any meeting I have ever attended as president or vice president or senator. This is the greatest demonstration that any man could have, because I'm just Mr. Truman, private citizen, now. This is the first time you have ever sent me home in a blaze of glory. I can't adequately express my appreciation for what you are doing. I'll never forget it if I live to be 100.' "

He paused momentarily, leaned forward to chop the air with that familiar awkward gesture that had become a trademark, and added: "And that's just what I expect to do!"[100]

"He did not seem down at all," Administrative Assistant Donald Dawson told the author four decades later. "That night he just had a rousing good time saying nice things to people who were saying nice things to him."

"I got off the train," Margaret wrote, "and stood beside Mrs. Fred Vinson [wife of the chief justice of the United States] as it pulled out. Everybody in the station started singing 'Auld Lang Syne.' It was absolutely thunderous. Beside me, Mommy Vinson was weeping. But I didn't feel in the least weepy now. The tremendous outpouring of affection for Dad was too wonderful. It made all those years in the Great White Jail almost worthwhile."[100]

Small crowds populated station platforms all along the B&O in West Virginia, Ohio, Indiana and Illinois—even through the night. A big crowd showed up at St. Louis early Wednesday afternoon, and one of the people who got to shake hands with Truman was Bob Wilson, the engineer of his train west of Washington, Ind. He had hauled Truman many times, and the staunch Republican railroader was crying at the knowledge that this might be the last. Truman told his friend he had had a "fine trip—a smoother one he'd never had" and hoped the B&O would continue to offer good service, Wilson's daughter told the author.[154]

It was at 8:15 p.m. that evening when they reached Independence on Missouri Pacific No. 15, the *Royal Gorge*. Typically, Truman had gotten off to get a haircut at one of the Missouri stations.

Big crowds showed up at St. Louis and Independence. There, 10,000 people cheered at the station as the Kansas City American Legion band played "The Missouri Waltz" and 1,500 more flocked around the family homestead at 219 N. Delaware Ave.

The *Magellan* was dismissed to return riderless to Washington—and virtually to oblivion, because Ike used it but three times and Mamie once before it was declared surplus federal property in an air age.

According to White House travel officer Dewey Long, Truman piled up 77,170 rail miles during his term, behind only Franklin Roosevelt and William Howard Taft. His annual high was 32,574 miles in 1948, the low 426 in 1951. The 1952 total was 20,687.

By any yardstick, 1952 proved a transition in political campaigning. "The train, the automobile, and the podium served as in the past," Eisenhower commented, "but the plane and television extended the range as never before. 1952 was the last year when whistlestopping was the major mode of electioneering."[239]

For Stevenson, the whole thing had been an ordeal. "You must emerge, bright and bubbling with wisdom and well-being, every morning at 8 o'clock just in time for a charming and profound breakfast talk, shake hands with hundreds, often literally thousands of people, make several inspiring 'newsworthy' speeches during the day, confer with political leaders along the way and with your staff all the time, write at every chance, think if possible, read mail and newspapers, talk on the telephone, talk to everybody, dictate, receive delegations, eat, with decorum—and discretion!—and ride through city after city on the back of an open car, smiling until your mouth is dehydrated by the wind, waving until the blood runs out of your arm, and then bounce easily, confidently, masterfully into great howling halls, shaved and all made up for television with the right color shirt and tie—I always forgot—and a manuscript so defaced with chicken tracks and last-minute jottings that you couldn't fol-

With President Eisenhower safely aboard Chessie 29, *the Chesapeake & Ohio's business car serving as his private car, a special train prepares to return him from White Sulphur Springs, W.Va., to Washington on March 28, 1956.*

low it, even if the spotlights weren't blinding you in the eye every time you looked at them …

"But the real work has just commenced—two or three and sometimes four hours of frenzied writing and editing of the next day's immortal mouthings so you can get something to the stenographers, so they can get something to the mimeograph machine, so they can get something to the reporters, so they can get something to their newspapers by deadline time. … Finally sleep, sweet sleep, steals you away, unless you worry—which I do."[239]

By the time Eisenhower became president, duties of the office had become much more complex and the White House decreed the chief executive's time to be so valuable that he couldn't spend much of it riding trains. POTUS trains used by Ike during his first term can be counted on the fingers of one hand, and there were even fewer during his second term.

Among the first-term trips were those to:

• **New York City, May 7-8, 1953.** Intending to fly, Ike resorted to the Pennsylvania Railroad for a whirl-wind trip to speak at twin $100-a-plate GOP fund-raisers at the Astor and Waldorf-Astoria hotels. Since the party was picking up the tab rather than the taxpayers, the president had planned to use a chartered commercial airliner rather than the White House plane. Bad weather changed his plans, however, and he opted for the train ride. Leaving the *Magellan* at home— also to spare the taxpayers—Ike rode a PRR private car. He arrived at Penn Station at 8:40 p.m., dressed nattily in an "electric-blue homburg and tuxe-do."[389ac] After motorcading to his appointments, he departed for the capital late that night, again on the Pennsy.

• **State College, Pa., May 8-9, 1953.** The night after he returned from New York, Eisenhower took his wife and mother-in-law to Pennsylvania State College for the weekend, where his brother Milton was president. This time the *Magellan* was used, for the first time by Ike as

president. The special traveled most of the way on the PRR, but the last 18.5 miles was on the Bellefonte Central, a short line built to haul iron ore that hadn't seen a passenger train in five years. The overnight journey ended at 7:20 a.m. Saturday; whereupon Ike and Milton went golfing and fishing. After attending a church service on campus Sunday morning, Ike motored 55 miles to the Blair County Airport near Martinsburg, Pa., and flew home in the *Columbine II*, the four-engine propeller-driven Lock-heed Constellation that had succeed-ed Truman's Douglas DC-6 *Independence* as the presidential plane. He left the *Magellan* with Mamie and her mother at State College. The first lady crowned Miss Penn State on Monday night to kick off the school's Spring Weekend, then the ladies returned to Washington in the presi-dential private car.

• **Defiance, Ohio, Wednesday, Oct. 14, 1953.** Ike departed at 11:30 p.m. for a 12-hour ride to Defiance College on the B&O, where he par-ticipated in the laying of the cornerstone of its Anthony Wayne Library. The trip was a favor for Kevin McCann, the school's president and a former Eisenhower speechwriter. Someone on the president's staff believed the ultraheavy *Magellan* suffered too much whiplash and ordered it to be positioned platform-first at the head of the 10-car train, separated from the locomotive only by a buffer car. Despite railroad officers' protests that it was the cars in the middle of the train that took the beating, the staffer was insistent. So it rode backward that day and Eisenhower greeted onlookers during a brief stop Thursday morning at Willard, Ohio, sandwiched in the narrow space between the *Magellan* and the buffer. A president never rode like that again.

In the early afternoon after Ike's speech, the train was routed from FC Tower at Defiance over the Wabash, Toledo Terminal and PRR lines to the Toledo Municipal Airport, where Ike boarded a plane for home. On the one hour, 40-minute Wabash leg of the trip, the *Magellan* was on the rear, properly pointed, and of course the buffer had been removed. Power included diesels 56-54X-55 on the B&O and diesel 1008 on the Wabash.

• **Ottawa, Nov. 12-15, 1953.** In his first trip to a foreign capital after his inauguration, Eisenhower visited Canada to cement good relations between the two countries and to address the Canadian Parliament. He and Mamie departed from Union Station at 5:35 p.m. Thursday, routed on the PRR to New York City, the New Haven to Woodlawn, N.Y., the New York Central to Troy, the Delaware & Hudson to Rouses Point, and the Canadian Pacific. The train sat in New York's Penn Station from 9:35 to 10 p.m. while carmen replaced a generator belt on the White House staff car, and it was delayed again for the same reason at NYC's 138th Street Station in The Bronx. It

departed at 12:11 a.m., 41 minutes late. Ike stopped at Rouses Point at 7:40 a.m. on Friday the 13th, 30 minutes late, where two carloads of Canadian dignitaries and red-jacketed Royal Canadian Mounted Police were added to the train. He stepped to the back platform in blue pajamas and a maroon silk bathrobe and apologetically greeted a crowd of about a hundred who had shouted, "Hi, Ike."

"Hi, back there," he responded. "Sorry I'm not dressed. I wish I could stay longer—it's a cold morning."[389ad]

Arrival in Ottawa was at 11:45 a.m., when the train backed into Union Station at Confederate Square and Wellington Street 15 minutes late to a red-draped and -carpeted, flag-bedecked platform. He was met by Canadian Prime Minister Louis S. St. Laurent, whose visit to the United States he was repaying.

The Eisenhowers started back to Washington at midnight Saturday. The president slept until 8 the next morning and enjoyed a leisurely breakfast. Then he passed the miles by talking with Henry Cabot Lodge Jr., the United States' ambassador to the United Nations, and taking care of other accumulated business. Mamie celebrated her 57th birthday on Saturday, and spent the day showing off a gold presidential seal her husband had given her. It was in the form of a pendant, attached to her bracelet and engraved "D.D.E. to M.D.E. 1953."[389ae]

On arrival at the 138th Street Station in The Bronx at 11:20 a.m., Eisenhower and Lodge could be seen talking in the *Magellan's* observation room. During the unexplained half-hour wait until a New Haven Railroad engine coupled to the rear to pull the train backward up NYC's Harlem Division to Woodlawn Jct. and on the New Haven to New Rochelle, Ike stepped out on the platform for "a breath of air"[389ae] and posed amiably

for photographers. Power (and direction) was changed once again at New Rochelle and Ike proceeded across the Hell Gate Bridge and onto the New York Connecting Railroad in Queens, then to the Long Island line and under the East River to Penn Station. A PRR locomotive was coupled on there as officials gave Mamie a bouquet of birthday flowers and Lodge left the train. The Eisenhowers departed at 1:05 p.m. Reporters noted that the meandering route from the NYC's Hudson Division to Penn Station had consumed an hour and 45 minutes.

Although no one knew it, the trip was historic for another reason. When Ike stepped off the *Magellan* at Washington Union Station at 4:50 p.m. that Sunday, it was the last time a president would ride the car for almost 31 years. Mamie used it one more time, enroute to Groton, Conn. on April 21, 1954, to christen the atomic-powered submarine Nautilus. The *Magellan* and one other car were attached to PRR's *Federal*, a Washington-Boston passenger train, for that trip.

• **White Sulphur Springs, W.Va., March 25-28, 1956.** Eisenhower was involved in a top-drawer rail operation in 1956 when he traveled 245 miles on a Chesapeake & Ohio Railway train from Washington to White Sulphur Springs, W.Va., to host a three-way summit at the C&O-owned resort hotel *The Greenbrier* with Canada's Prime Minister St. Laurent and President Adolfo Ruiz Cortines of Mexico.

Ike boarded the 14-car train shortly after 10 p.m. on Palm Sunday, March 25, 1956. It was headed north on Washington Union Station's upper-level track 20 despite its southerly destination because the Secret Service had demanded that it run nonstop. Lower-level loading apparently would have complicated

There's no rear platform, so this will have to do! President Eisenhower and his brother, Milton, left, greet well-wishers from the back door of C&O President Walter J. Tuohy's private car Chessie 29 *at Clifton Forge, Va., as a C&O special returns them from White Sulphur Springs, W.Va., to Washington March 28, 1956.*

Eisenhower's boarding, and the train was headed the wrong way so it wouldn't have to back out, stop and reverse direction.

Pulled by an A-B-B combination of FP7 8008 and F7B's 8504-8506, the special carried a combine car, two U.S. Army communications cars (USA 87325, designated SC-1 *General Albert J. Myer*, and USA 87426, which contained sleeping berths and mess for personnel), four Pullman sleepers, a twin-unit C&O diner, a C&O five-bedroom lounge, three more sleepers and office car *Chessie 29.*

It left Washington at 11 p.m., with instructions to run a slow schedule and arrive on the minute at 7:30 the next morning.

The 8008's cab was crowded. A Baltimore & Ohio engineer and fireman took charge as the special proceeded north on the B&O main to Hyattsville, Md., turning east on the Alexandria Jct. wye, then south on the Alexandria branch, passing Anacostia Junction at 11:40. As it entered Pennsylvania Railroad trackage, a PRR crew took the controls. Once Virginia Tower was attained at 11:52, C&O crew members took over because they had operating rights on Southern Railway trackage.

The train crews had intentionally crawled, intending not to pass Virginia Tower before 11:50 to allow Southern's southbound *Pelican* to clear RO Tower at Alexandria, Va.

One by one, the B&O and PRR crewmen dropped off as the special eased past Alexandria's station platform at 12:08 a.m., leaving only the C&O men on board.

The operation was flawless, with POTUS security in effect over the entire route. Railroad special agents guarded every bridge and tunnel. The special passed Charlottesville at 2:55 a.m. and Clifton Forge at 6:07 a.m., slowing down each time to pick up clearance cards and drop off railroaders whose tours of duty were ending. New engine crews waited in the combine car for their territories.

Exact-minute arrival at White Sulphur Springs was achieved, but Ike made about 200 well-wishers at the station and another 200 at the hotel wait 45 minutes while he finished a steak breakfast on car 29. Before his honored guests arrived by air that afternoon, Eisenhower enjoyed 18 holes of golf with *The Greenbrier* pro Sam Snead, two aides and his doctor during an icy rain.

The largely unstructured "Little Summit" was Ike's idea to allow the three leaders to become better acquainted. He likened it to having the next-door neighbors over for dinner. The meeting included dinners on Monday and Tuesday nights and a formal session Tuesday morning. All of it took place in the West Virginia Wing's Presidential Suite.

An impromptu telephone directory typewritten by *The Greenbrier* shows that 59 people were included in the three national delegations.

The most exciting development of the trip was ballyhooed by area newspapers and ignored totally in an article in C&O's *Tracks* magazine.

The *Chessie 29*, assigned to C&O President Walter J. Tuohy, had left Cleveland fully stocked several days before the trip and stopped over at Huntington, W.Va., for a mechanical check. It was to proceed to Washington Thursday night, March 22, to join the special. That evening, a mechanical officer in Huntington allowed nine members of his own family to visit the car. The chef gave them all cocktails. Some detected a cloudy look or bad taste and set the drinks aside. Three drank their glasses dry and became ill.

The incident resulted in a big flap, with charges that someone was trying to poison the president, local papers downplaying the embarrassment to West Virginia and railroad P.R. types issuing lengthy explanations to cast their employer in the best possible light. Tests were conducted, thorough to the point of having section gangs look for empty bottles tossed off the car enroute to Washington that night, and the car was restocked when it arrived in Washington.

Eisenhower laughed off the poison stories at breakfast with Tuohy Tuesday morning.

"They're making a great to-do over this ... business, aren't they?" he asked the C&O president. "Who are they trying to get, you or me? It must be you, because you're the pop-drinker. I haven't drunk pop in years."[387h]

Another chef said years later the

DANA SNOW

Powered by B&O freight diesels, Vice President Nixon's special enters the Pennsylvania yard at Marietta, Ohio, on Nov. 3, 1956.

problem was traced to cleaning fluid often stored on board in club soda or ginger ale bottles. Apparently the party was accidentally served from a bottle containing the cleaner.

After Eisenhower saw his guests off on Wednesday, March 28, his special departed White Sulphur at 9:30 a.m. with the 413-member White Sulphur High School student body seeing him off. This time, it made operating stops at Clifton Forge and Charlottesville, arriving back at Washington Union Station at 3:17 p.m.

Ike had planned to fly back to Washington, but stayed with the train after thunderstorms were forecast. He turned the trip into an improvised whistlestopper with his second term in view.

About 50 townsfolk were surprised at Clifton Forge when Ike appeared in the open rear door of the *Chessie 29*, smiling, waving, and shaking hands. He made small talk about his golf game and told the crowd his mother was born at Mount Sidney, Va., about 50 miles northeast of Clifton Forge.

Not only was *The Greenbrier* meeting supposedly the first between three heads of state on U.S. soil, it was touted as the first time a C&O train had passed the division points of Charlottesville and Clifton Forge without stopping. Moreover, it probably holds the record for the most on-duty engineers and firemen in a single locomotive cab.

Because Eisenhower traveled so infrequently by train during his presidential years, memories of his habits by those who served him are scarce. Headwaiter Billy Reid's only recollection: He didn't want any scrambled eggs; he'd seen enough of them in Europe.

Eisenhower occasionally snuck away for outings at the Augusta National Golf Club in Augusta, Ga., traveling on the Richmond, Fredericksburg & Potomac and the Atlantic Coast Line because of Mamie's aversion to flying. At least once he made the trip with ACL President Thomas Rice on Rice's private car—No. 308.

Mamie often traveled via B&O and Missouri Pacific to Colorado Springs, Colo., to visit her ill mother in 1954 and 1955. She always rode B&O office car 100 and started her trip on train No. 1, the *National*

Limited. Even though she was first lady, she was not accorded POTUS standards, and since nothing was permitted behind No. 1's observation car, the 100 was spliced between the Railway Post Office car and the baggage-lounge combination car. Secret Service men could be seen peering out of the combine's baggage door; Mamie could be seen winking at railroad patrons from the 100's dining room. From St. Louis, she continued to and from Colorado Springs on MP Nos. 11 and 12, the *Colorado Eagle.* The arrival time of MP 12 back in St. Louis meant she finished her trips on B&O No. 4, the *Diplomat,* which had no such stringent conditions, and her car was gladly accepted on the rear.[110]

America's fixation for air travel had virtually supplanted the whistlestop train by 1956, only eight years after the term was coined during Truman's upset campaign. Even though *The New York Times'* political writer James Reston wrote that "there is something about a railroad political caravan that no flying machine or magic lantern can replace," railroads were called on by then only for brief trips that served primarily as photo opportunities. And the primary reason was to satisfy television's insatiable appetite rather than as a means to get to the people.

As a result, Eisenhower traveled very little by train when he campaigned for his second term. One trip took him from Washington to New York via PRR on Thursday, Oct. 25, 1956, where he arrived at Penn Station at 12:14 p.m. After speaking that night at a Madison Square Garden rally, the president flew back to Washington. A week later, Nov. 1, he rode the B&O to Philadelphia to address an overflow crowd of 18,000 at Convention Hall and millions more by radio and television, hastening back that night. A later trip to Boston was canceled because of the Suez Canal crisis.

Adlai Stevenson, again the Democratic nominee, campaigned mostly by air. But he did run a whistlestop train through New Jersey, Pennsylvania and West Virginia Wednesday and Thursday, Oct. 3-4—traveling on the Delaware, Lackawanna & Western from Hoboken, N.J., to Scranton and Northumberland, Pa.; the Pennsylvania to Pittsburgh; the B&O to Belington, W.Va.; and the Western Maryland to Elkins, W.Va. His train was nicknamed the *Joe Smith Express* to rib the Republicans, one of whom had thrown the fictitious name into the vice presidential ring to liven up a dull convention.

The attraction at Elkins was the annual Mountain State Forest Festival. Speechwriter Ken Hechler went along, and remembers well Stevenson's stop at Belington, W.Va., 17 miles short of Elkins, at 10:40 Thursday morning. The candidate was greeted by about a hundred schoolchildren. "How many of you would like to run for president?" Stevenson shouted to the kids, and all of them raised their hands. "How many candidates would like to be a school kid again?" he asked, then raised his own hand. The railroad operation ended in the small town of Elkins, a most unlikely spot, when Stevenson was flown back to New York in a five-seat plane; everyone else in the party was bused back to Pittsburgh.[172]

Two weeks later, the Democratic hopeful whistlestopped through Michigan and Ohio, leaving from Chicago at 5 a.m. on Wednesday, Oct. 17. The 13-car train traveled along the New York Central, stopping in Niles, Kalamazoo, Battle Creek, Lansing and Flint, Mich. After an overnight stop in Detroit, it continued along the NYC to Toledo, Elyria and Cleveland, switching to the B&O for the run to Akron and Youngstown, Ohio.

It was this trip that *Washington Star* columnist Mary McGrory found so pleasant, terming whistlestopping as the "poetry" of campaigning. "The train meanders through the russet landscape of autumn, idling before the appointed entry into towns by meadows where brown cows graze and gaze incuriously. Now and then a low-flying pheasant skims over the corn shocks. The glory is gone from the oaks and maples, but the sumac and the bittersweet still blaze. Along the fences, there is the gossamer white of milkweed and purple patches of wild aster."[250]

Miss McGrory felt that the ride had a therapeutic effect on her fellow passengers. "These scenes of muted, pastoral beauty come pleasantly to the eyes of weary campaigners who have had nothing but bird's-eye views for weeks gone by. Now they can watch boys playing football and children scuffling through leaves on their way to school. ... The trains were also fun. You could roam up and down the aisle in some sort of comfort, have a snack, and look out the window."

But she was not oblivious to the fact that times were changing. "The whole affair is made somehow more poignant by the thought that by the next go-round [the train] will be obsolete. This prospect is a sad one. Campaigning at its best is a time of discovery. The voters discover their candidates, and the candidates, riding in a train through the autumn mists, can discover America."[250]

Nixon, the incumbent vice president, made two trips during the 1956 campaign, the first covering Michigan, Indiana and Illinois and the second traversing Pennsylvania and Ohio. They came late in his race, Oct. 22-24 and Oct. 31-Nov. 4, with nearly the first couple of months blanketed by air travel in a reversal of the

1952 strategy.

Virtually nonexistent now were several nights of sleep on a campaign train parked on isolated sidings. Being lost to history forever was the convenience of moving whole campaign organizations overnight as they slept. Getting a good start was the hassle of arranging transportation and lodging for hundreds of travelers each and every night.

Also nearly extinct were campaign trains pulled by steam. The only iron horses to haul Nixon were N&W Class K 4-8-2s 113 and 119 from Chillicothe to Columbus, Ohio, on Saturday, Nov. 3, the last day of the race.

The Illinois Central was prepared to use steam for Eisenhower and Nixon, but never did. "Engine handling president's special, whether diesel or steam, must be carefully selected and must be thoroughly inspected by master mechanic personally," the road's instructions stated. "If steam engine (is) used, quality of coal must be known to be grade A."[294]

One glitch has survived history's purge. At one stop, an engineer mistook a five-minute warning for a signal to start, and began pulling out as a mayor was giving a speech, flanked by Nixon and a local beauty queen. With his mike still on, the mayor began shouting, "Stop the train. My wife's on the platform and she won't like me with this girl!" Nixon ordered the train stopped, but the mayor had to walk a half-mile back to his wife.[294]

During his second term, Eisenhower ventured to Baltimore by train on Oct. 31, 1958, as the midterm election loomed. The five-car special left Washington at 7:45 p.m., arriving in Baltimore's Mount Royal Station at 8:30. For staff and press, the diner offered a choice of broiled Chesapeake Bay fish with lemon wedge or a golden omelet with sauteed mushrooms for $2.50 or a

CHARLES F. TOMASTIK

Richard and Pat Nixon greet the folks at Chillicothe, Ohio, on Nov. 3, 1956, before their train is transferred from the B&O to the N&W.

broiled sirloin steak for $4. Complementing the selections were french fried potatoes, B&O's "Help Yourself" salad bowl and bread and butter. Also on the menu were assorted a la carte dishes, salads, sandwiches and desserts. The stop at Mount Royal was so smooth, Baltimore Division Supt. William M. Murphey picked up a portable telephone and

told engineer Daniel L. Adams, "You did that perfectly. Couldn't have been better."

After Eisenhower's nationally televised speech from the Fifth Regiment Armory, he returned to Washington. Ike shook hands with Charles R. Van Horn, B&O's general passenger agent there, and said he was "well pleased" with the trip.[392]

279

President John F. Kennedy boards PRR business car 120, the Pennsylvania, *in Philadelphia after the Army/Navy game Dec. 2, 1961, for a quick trip back to Washington.*

Modern Times

8

John F. Kennedy

By 1960, whistlestopping was largely a fading memory. People must have been wondering if America had lost a tradition, because the *Baltimore & Ohio Magazine* polled several candidates about "the return of" of campaign trains.

"Since I have mentioned that should I be the nominee I intend to use a campaign train," Vice President Richard Nixon said, "I have noted that the press also shares this feeling. It almost seems to me that more reporters have commented on trains than on some of the issues."

Nixon intended to offer an image of "unhurried solidity" during the campaign, one newspaper said. "The sedate train provides a much better frame for presenting such a picture than does rushing about in jet planes. It is also a far better way of transportation for any candidate who wants to keep continually in touch with his advisers. And even more important, it is the best way of getting from city to city when the problem is to touch many middling cities rather than a few vast ones."

Sen. John F. Kennedy, D-Mass., who had secured the Democratic nomination, agreed.

"Television may reach more voters at one time," JFK remarked, "but from the rear platform of a campaign train there is no chance to use gimmicks to dress up a candidate. The campaign train exposes him as he is. I believe 1960 will see the return of the campaign train."

Sen. Lyndon B. Johnson, D-Texas, who was Kennedy's running mate and ended up inheriting the presidency from him in 1963 and winning his own term the next year, concurred: "It seems to me [the campaign train] is an excellent way of getting close to our people."[381]

Kennedy backed up what he said. On Wednesday through Friday, Sept. 7-9, he rode a Southern Pacific special from Portland, Ore., to Bakersfield, Calif., making rear platform speeches at stops along the way. His 11-car train carried 64 in the official party and 59 members of the press.

Then on Friday, Oct. 14, he whistlestopped through Michigan, boarding a nine-car special at Ann Arbor for a 14-hour, 10-city tour of heavily Republican areas of the Wolverine State. He traversed the New York Central to Kalamazoo, the Pennsylvania to Grand Rapids, the Chesapeake & Ohio to Lansing, the NYC to Saginaw and the Grand Trunk Western back to Detroit.

Johnson rode the *Cornpone Special* through Dixie to help convince his fellow Southerners to vote for Kennedy. The five-day, 3,812-mile trip is noted for the senator's line at Culpeper, Va., on the Southern Railway: "And remember," he yelled, "when you go to the polls, think of this: What did Richard Nixon ever do for Culpeper?"[338] His wife, Claudia, nicknamed Lady Bird, added a touch of down-homeyness at various stops in Alabama, where her parents were from, by recognizing and calling by name no fewer than 18 "kissin' cousins."[389af]

Nixon made one trip—a five-day tour on Oct. 24-28 that began in Washington and covered Pennsylvania, West Virginia, Ohio, Michigan and Illinois. Routing was via the PRR from Washington to Pittsburgh; the Baltimore & Ohio to Cincinnati; NYC to Columbus; C&O to Marion; Erie to Lima; B&O to Toledo; NYC to Kalamazoo, Mich.; PRR to Muskegon; PRR and Wabash to Tolono, Ill.; and Illinois Central to Carbondale.

Fireman A.E. Tribbett showed up for work in a mischievous mood the day he worked on the Nixon special between Wheeling and Parkersburg, W.Va. "I was wearing a Kennedy button," he grinned. "When [Supervisor of Locomotive Operations] Jack Ferrell saw me, he said, 'That's disgraceful!' I told him, 'We'll give [Nixon] a smooth ride today, but we'll nail him in November.'"[408]

Nixon noticed that Friday's audience at Centralia, Ill., was mostly railroaders and chatted about his early experiences with trains.

"I recall that occasion in particular," said Clifford Massoth, an IC public relations officer. "I gave [Nixon publicity aide] Herb Klein some information about Centralia being the center of the IC employees with its car shops there ... I was quite awed by how quickly he incorporated my remarks into a talk that had immediate appeal in the railroad community."[294]

Nixon gave his stock speech, then added: "I can't resist as we come through Centralia, which is a great railroad center, telling you what I really wanted to be when I was growing up. You know, they have asked my

Above: *Sen. John F. Kennedy begins a day of whistlestopping through Michigan Oct. 14, 1960, at Ann Arbor. He is aboard business car 10, assigned to NYC President Al Perlman.*

Right: *When John Kennedy returns from the Dec. 2, 1961, Army/Navy game, he will ride in splendor back to Washington aboard PRR business car 120, the* Pennsylvania.

A POTUS special waits in Philadelphia for President Kennedy's return from the Army/Navy game Dec. 2, 1961.

mother many times, 'Now, Mrs. Nixon, when the vice president was a boy, what did he want to be?' Well, actually, I certainly had no idea I'd ever be running for president, I can assure you of that. You know what I really wanted to be? Right alongside our house ran a railroad track [a long-gone four-mile AT&SF branch through Yorba Linda, Calif.], and I used to hear the whistles at night and I used to think of all the places those trains were going. And I wanted to be a railroad engineer so that I could travel through America and through the world. I didn't make that, of course, but I got to travel anyway. But may I say to those who run the nation's railroads: Remember, it's a wonderful service you're rendering."[294]

Nixon was pestered by an on-board practical joker—California Democrat Dick Tuck—who donned a trainman's cap a couple of times and gave the engineer a signal to start just as the candidate was beginning to speak.

Kennedy won that election, and it was during his brief term that the U.S. chief executive first was assigned his own jet aircraft. Perhaps it was indicative of the ongoing metamorphosis in presidential travel that JFK rode a train only twice while in office—returning from the annual Army/Navy football games in Philadelphia on Dec. 2, 1961, and Dec. 1, 1962. In each case, he flew up from Washington early Saturday afternoon while a trainload of government dignitaries and press rode the train.

The 1961 POTUS train left Washington's Union Station at 9:05 a.m. and arrived at what a White House memo called the "Special Train Yard,"[218] a five-minute walk from the Philadelphia stadium, at 11:45 a.m. The Army hosted a luncheon and refreshments on the train; men from the Navy mess served in Kennedy's car, even when the president wasn't on board. The rest of the service for working staff and VIP guests was provided by the PRR and paid for by the Army. Each of the passengers paid for his or her own ticket, including, by his own wish, Kennedy himself.

With the president on board after the game, the special departed Philadelphia at 4:06 p.m. for Washington and arrived at Union Station at 6:45.

Incidentally, Navy won, 13-7.

Vice presidential candidate Lyndon B. Johnson campaigns for the Democratic ticket at Culpeper, Va., Oct. 10, 1960.

When Democratic President Lyndon B. Johnson of Texas began thinking about the 1964 campaign, he remembered the advice Harry Truman had given him.

"You may not believe this, Lyndon," Truman had said, "but there are still a h___ of a lot of people in this country who don't know where the airport is. But they d___ sure know where the depot is. And if you let 'em know you're coming, they'll be down and listen to you."[73]

Johnson heeded the advice as he had in 1960, only he sent his wife—also a Texas native—in his place. She journeyed into the deep South, traveling right into the lion's den months after Johnson had pushed his landmark civil rights legislation through Congress. The *Lady Bird Special*, planned as a four-day 1,682-mile, 47-stop whirlwind tour from Washington to New Orleans, was the first whistlestop journey undertaken by a first lady on behalf of her husband.

On Tuesday morning, Oct. 6, 1964, Lady Bird's party of 300 boarded a glistening 19-car special on Washington Union Station's lower-level track 26. The *Queen Mary*, PRR parlor/observation car 7125, provided Lady Bird's speaking platform. It had been refitted inside and repainted red, white and blue on the outside. A red-and-white striped tin canopy garnished the rear platform, and a speaker system had been installed that would blare the strains of "Happy Days Are Here Again" and a political version of "Hello, Dolly"—"Hello, Lyndon"—as the entourage entered each town. Hostesses—a group of Southern-born beauties in their 20s and 30s—were decked out in bright blue shirtwaist dresses, white gloves and white roll-brim hats and carried Lady Bird pennants, balloons and "All the Way With LBJ" buttons.

The president decided to ride, too—all of 8.2 miles to Alexandria, Va. On arrival, he escorted his wife to the back platform and shushed the crowd so she could speak.

"I wanted to make this trip because I am proud of the South, and I am proud that I am part of the South," she drawled. "I'm fond of the old customs—of keeping up with your kinfolks, of long Sunday dinners after church, of a special brand of gentility and courage. I'm even more proud of the new South, the spirit of growth, advances in economy and progress in education, and I share the irritation when unthinking people make snide jokes about us. None of this is right. None of this is good for the future of our country. We must search for the ties that bind us together, not settle for the tensions that tend to divide us."[73]

The president let it be her show. He said a few words, introduced daughter Lynda (she and sister Luci would split the trip to avoid missing too much school), gave them goodbye kisses and left the train. Lady Bird was on her own. With a pilot train running 15 minutes ahead, Richmond, Fredericksburg & Potomac passenger diesels rolled the special southward—a crowded and confining convoy. The diners remained open continuously and offered such specialties as the "LBJ Steak Platter" ("Please specify: raring to go, middle of the road, or all-the-way.")[73] The three sleepers reserved for White House staff and hostesses also carried all the campaign material—including two helium tanks to inflate the balloons. One of the press cars was equipped with a Western Union filing desk. Southern private car 14, placed ahead of the *Queen Mary* for Lady Bird and her closest staff, had the only bathtub on the train. And the *Queen Mary* was equipped with a mailbox and carried an array of colorful postcards of the train that VIPs wrote home on between stops.

"The political talk emanated from Car 3 [PRR 6-double bedroom lounge sleeper *Sassafras Falls*, ahead of the Southern car]," wrote Liz Carpenter, Lady Bird's press secretary.

"Mrs. Bill Brawley [wife of the Southern regional campaign director] dispensed warmth and hospitality. I think she and [John Ben] Shepperd [a veteran Texas politician], the master of ceremonies, stood in the center of that car all the way from Virginia to Louisiana. It was a trip that swelled shoe sizes more than heads."[73]

Mrs. Carpenter concocted a "Dixie Dictionary" for a large press bulletin board. Some of the entries:

- Yawl—not a boat, but more than one Democrat.
- Tall cotton—what the Southerners walk in, because of Johnson prosperity.
- Grits—only staple available during Hoover depression.
- Kissin' kin—anybody who will come to the depot.
- Beri-beri [pronounced Barry-Barry, for Sen. Barry Goldwater of Arizona, the Republican nominee]—a disease wiped out in the South.
- Yankee—object of good neighbor policy.
- High on the hawg—the gross national product under the Democrats.[73]

She also warned the press: "A whistle will blow two minutes before the train starts moving. We hope we won't be scattering you over the countryside, but the train does not wait. In case you get left, look for the advance

Richmond, Fredericksburg & Potomac E unit 1014 leads Lady Bird Johnson's campaign train into Alexandria, Va., Oct. 6, 1964.

Rep. Hale Boggs of Louisiana warmed up the crowds. "How many of you-all know what red-eye gravy is? Well, so do I. And so does Lyndon Johnson!"[73]

Lady Bird smiled, said her howdy-dos and thank-yous, and bragged about each town and its Democratic candidates. She turned over to her personal secretary, Mary Rather, handfuls of notes and telegrams pressed into her hand at each stop. One woman on the back of a wagon shouted, "I got up at 3 o'clock this morning and milked 20 cows so I could come to see you, Lady Bird."[73] The first lady blew her a kiss.

Inside again, Mrs. Johnson was ecstatic. She liked mingling with the homefolks. "I love it," she beamed. "I'm like Br'er Rabbit in the brier patch."[73]

The train filled up with gifts: hams and beaten biscuits at Richmond, peanuts at Suffolk, hosiery in the mill towns, a jar of May haw jelly at Valdosta, Ga., and roses, roses, roses.

At Raleigh, N.C., the first overnight stop, the president rejoined the party long enough to escort it to a downtown rally. During the confusing transfer by automobile, two press people got into a fight. A CBS photographer broke a tooth of *Life* magazine's Stan Weyman, and Mrs. Carpenter had to spend all evening locating Dr. Janet Travell, the train's physician. Behind the bleachers Dr. Travell administered pain-relieving Novocaine and someone called ahead to make a date with a dentist at the next overnight stop, Charleston, S.C.

"Stan brought the dentist and his family down to the station and lined them up for a picture with Mrs. Johnson," Mrs. Carpenter recalled, "a method I strongly suspected that Stan used to aid the expense of his dental bill."[73]

The press secretary lightly

man. He can easily be identified as the happiest man at the depot because all of his problems have just left. See if he can work out your transportation to a nearby town. If he can't, just take out residence, register and VOTE!"[73]

The *Lady Bird Special* rolled merrily down the track with its Southern accents and Dixieland music—via the RF&P to Richmond, Va.; Atlantic Coast Line to Petersburg; Norfolk & Western to Norfolk and back to Suffolk; ACL to Selma, N.C.; Southern to Charlotte, N.C., and Charleston, S.C.; ACL to Drifton, Fla. (reverse movement with buffer from Thomasville, Ga., to Drifton);

Seaboard Air Line to Chattahoochee; and Louisville & Nashville to New Orleans. From the crossroads villages of Virginia to the tobacco fields of North Carolina and bayous of Louisiana, bands played, pennants waved and huge crowds turned out. "Into town they came from the back roads and the coves, and the forks of the creek, the sand hills and the river bottoms," Mrs. Carpenter wrote. "There, from the back of the train, standing in the depot, is where the government and the people meet. It is politics, U.S.A., served up … with the flavor of fried chicken and mustard greens and cornbread."[73]

accused Dr. Travell of dispensing more drugs than she did press releases. There seemed to be an epidemic of laryngitis and sprained ankles. Reporters jumped off at each stop, raced to the rear, scribbled their notes and beat it back to their car—sometimes calling their offices first if deadlines loomed. Cinder and slag ballast mutilated their tennis shoes; Mrs. Carpenter had advised the informal footwear to ease the strain on feet. The staccato of typewriters aboard never stopped, serving as continual background sounds for TV commentators producing their footage.

It wasn't all work. The railroads furnished a free daily happy hour from 4 to 5 p.m., and White House staffers would serve the Southern dish of the day—beaten biscuits and ham in Virginia, hushpuppies in the Carolinas and shrimp and avocado dip in Florida.

Another medical crisis occurred when Doris Fleeson, covering the trip for United Features Syndicate, suffered a stroke at Charlotte. Mrs. Carpenter's husband, Les, volunteered to accompany her back to Washington by plane. As she waited on the station platform beside Miss Fleeson's stretcher for an ambulance, Mrs. Carpenter tried to be cheerful. "You're the only woman in the world, Doris, whom I could trust flat on her back with my husband."

Miss Fleeson uttered an expletive and replied, "I'll never be THAT sick!"[73]

The first trouble reared its head at Columbia, S.C. Introduced by Gov. Donald Russell, Lady Bird came to the mike and before she could begin talking, a group of boys started beating a drum and chanting, "We want Barry! We want Barry!" With one hand raised gently, the first lady scolded, "My friends, in this country we are entitled to many viewpoints. You are entitled to yours. But right now, I'm

JOHNSON LIBRARY

Lady Bird Johnson and her hostesses pose on the rear platform of PRR parlor car 7125, the Queen Mary, *during her whistlestop at Alexandria, Va., Oct. 6, 1964.*

entitled to mine." It worked. The heckling stopped, and Lady Bird continued unruffled.[73]

In Orangeburg, S.C., 5,000 blacks cheered Mrs. Johnson. At a distance, a gathering of white men eyed the adoration suspiciously, but did nothing. In Charleston, the hecklers showed up again—some of the same ones who were in Columbia. This time they wouldn't be silenced, but Lady Bird's bread-and-butter message got through. When a reporter asked one man who he'd vote for, he responded: "Johnson, because I'd rather stand beside a Negro in a factory than stand behind a white man in the soup line."[73] The atmosphere was equally frosty during a horse-drawn carriage ride through historic Charleston the next morning.

In Savannah, Ga., daughter Luci, who had taken Lynda's place aboard, took on the hecklers. "It seems to me," she said, "that it is easy to holler a lot and make a lot of noise when you're not the one having to handle the prob-

lems." She was only 17, but the crowd shut up. "We're the generation that is going to have to handle the problems later on," she poured it on. "All the emotion in the world isn't going to help us when the time comes for us to lift up our banners and take the reins of government."[73]

Congressman Boggs and others became so indignant at the heckling that they began striking back. Lady Bird urged caution in a hastily called meeting in her private car. "Look," she said, "I appreciate your kind words, but the effect is simply this. We are doing more talking about the hecklers than about the candidates. So, really, I can handle any ugly moment, and I do think it would be best if we each ignored the hecklers as much as possible in speeches."[73]

Boggs decided the best way to deflect the critics was to use a lighter approach instead of so many facts and figures.

"You know what we had on this train this morning?" he would grin.

"Hominy grits. About noontime we're gonna start servin' turnip greens and black-eyed peas. Later on, further South, we're gonna have some crawfish bisque, some red beans and rice, and some creole gumbo."[73]

The crowds ate it up.

Then he'd slip in his commercial: "You're not gonna turn your back on the first Southern-born president in a hundred years?"[73]

As always, cleanliness on board was a problem. The press cars were littered with newspapers and leftover happy hour snacks. Advance man Bill Gates, in Tallahassee preparing for the next overnight stop, was startled by a wire from the train: "Press stinks. Please reserve three rooms and 150 towels for bathing period at nearby hotel."[73]

One reporter—The *Chicago Tribune's* Mary Packenham—brought a makeshift tub with her. "It was a large plastic sack that she filled with water, slipped into and swished about, emerging better than before," Mrs. Carpenter wrote.[73]

At the first stop of Oct. 9, Flomaton, Ala., half a dozen of Lady Bird's cousins boarded. And there was another surprise—a large bouquet of roses from Gov. George Wallace, certainly no LBJ supporter. But since Lady Bird had several family ties with Alabama, Wallace didn't want to ignore her. So he sent Mrs. James Allen, wife of the lieutenant governor, to give her the roses. Mrs. Allen boarded at Flomaton, then made a public presentation at Mobile.

At this point the overefficiency of the *Lady Bird Special* nearly caused a political incident. The train couldn't hold all the gifts the first lady received, so a quiet operation was set up to dispose of most of them. Once Mrs. Johnson received flowers, Mrs. Rather would take them, wait a decent number of towns, then walk them or have someone walk them 19

cars through the train to the first vestibule door behind the locomotive. By previous arrangement, a police car would be waiting; Mrs. Rather would toss the flowers into the cruiser with some nicely written notes from the first lady and the flowers would be dispatched to the nearest hospitals.

When the train reached Mobile, Mrs. Allen asked Mrs. Carpenter where her roses were.

The press secretary glanced around nervously. "They were right here. They must be here somewhere."

"I just laid them down here," the lieutenant governor's wife snapped nervously. "I've got to have them." Mrs. Carpenter rushed to find Mrs. Rather, suspecting what had happened. "Where are Gov. Wallace's roses?" she demanded.

Mrs. Rather turned ashen and sprinted in a dead heat to overtake an emissary she had just dispatched to the front of the train. In what seemed like hours later as the train slowed for Mobile, she returned—breathless but with the roses. She had snatched them just as they were being tossed out the door. The crowd's cheering response when Lady Bird "received" her flowers confirmed Wallace's political cunning—and Mrs. Carpenter's luck.[73]

That crisis past, Lady Bird thoroughly enjoyed the visit with her cousins from several Alabama towns "that are filled with memories of watermelon cuttin's and pallets on the floor."[73]

Johnson joined his wife again as her special trundled into the Union Passenger Terminal in New Orleans, where he would speak that night.

"Our trainload of bedraggled reporters and staff—and an exhausted first lady—packed our tumbled suitcases, took one last deep breath, and mustered enough strength for the final appearance," Mrs. Carpenter wrote. "We stood there on the back platform waiting for the president to

join us. I could see the president pushing through the crowd, taller than anyone, stopping to shake a hand or give a hug to the newswomen whose bylines he had been reading so avidly and proudly during our trip. ... When he reached the train, he kissed Luci and enveloped Mrs. Johnson in his arms. She happily yielded the microphone and speechmaking to him. He was buoyant, glowing in praise of all the dignitaries who were there, trying to get the message over to Gov. John J. McKeithen who timidly stood back in a corner."[73]

It was an unusual sight. Thousands of blacks mixed with whites behind the *Queen Mary's* rear platform, chanting, "We want Lyndon."[73]

"I'm going to repeat here in Louisiana what I have said in every state of the Union," he drawled. "As long as I am your president, I'm going to be president of all of the people. And your president is going to protect the Constitutional rights of every American."[73]

The crowd—black and white alike—went wild. Sen. Allen J. Ellender, D-Louisiana, certainly no supporter of civil rights, got caught up in the euphoria. But in his excitement, he got his tongue twisted and yelled: "All the way with LJB!"[73] The crowd roared.

Once the party had departed for the Jung Hotel, porters began sweeping out the accumulation of trash, copy paper and carbons from the resting railroad cars. A reporter, her bags packed and waiting beside her, finished her story: "NEW ORLEANS, Oct. 9—Together, the president and the first lady made an assault on the heart and the mind of the South that must be the most remarkable joint campaign effort in American political history.

"Perhaps they changed some votes; perhaps they had altered none.

But they had given it everything they had."[73]

After the president's well-received civil rights speech, the first family flew on to the LBJ Ranch in Texas. An exhausted Lady Bird said she felt "like cooked spaghetti," but the president was beaming with pride. "Now, Liz," he laughed to Mrs. Carpenter, "that's the way to run a railroad!"[73]

Meanwhile, Republican Barry Goldwater set out on Monday night, Sept. 28, on a six-day trip from Washington to the Midwest on his own 18-car train. B&O office car 100 sported a drumhead that encircled a heart enclosing the inscription, "In Your Heart You Know He's Right."

The Arizonan's special—made up of lightweight and heavyweight cars from five railroads—was officially named *Baa Hozhnilne*, Navajo for "to win over."[434] Thirty political aides and 85 radio, television and newspaper people were housed in the sleepers; the press worked in lounge cars.

B&O operator Esther Morrow never forgot the passage of Goldwater's train. Armed only with a telephone in a small temporary building, she was stationed at Debar Crossing just east of Parkersburg, W.Va., to keep track of train traffic for a flagman protecting the private road. It was being used by a contractor building nearby Interstate 77. On that terribly foggy Tuesday morning, the senator's train was due but a slide had knocked out signals on the line. Concrete mixers were ready to go to work; but no one—including Mrs. Morrow, the flagman or the dispatcher in Grafton—knew where the special was. Mrs. Morrow told the flagman to walk a good distance east of the crossing so the train wouldn't surprise them. After phoning the dispatcher, she walked to the contractor's shanty and told him no trucks could cross the track until Goldwater's spe-

JEFFREY H. MADDEN

Barry Goldwater's 18-car B&O special, Baa Hozhnilne, *pauses at Athens, Ohio.*

cial came—then stood guard at the crossing with her lantern to enforce her edict. Finally, the flagman heard the engine's horn and returned to the crossing. With the two of them protecting each side, the special passed without incident. They were relieved to see its markers disappear into the gloom.[270]

Goldwater made Ohio stops that day in Marietta, Athens, Chillicothe, Blanchester and Oakley. "This is the first time I've ever whistlestopped," he said in Blanchester. "And the more I do it, the better I like it. It gives me a chance to get close to the people."[341]

By the end of the week, segregation had taken a curious form aboard the special. Murray Schumach groused in The *New York Times* that Republicans were confined to the VIP car and the press was denied access to them.

"On the doors of the Very Important Persons car are printed signs reading, 'Press may pass through VIP car but it would be appreciated if they do not remain there,'" Schumach wrote. "Politicians gather over drinks in armchairs or standing while they wait to be called forth to share the rear platform … with Goldwater or … to shake hands with the candidate when he makes a quiet visit to the VIP car before or after a speech."[389ag]

Schumach noted that the frivolity of past junkets was lacking on the Goldwater train. "The poker and dice games, once so characteristic, are now just nostalgic memories. … An attempt was made last night to return to tradition. A poker game was started, but it lasted only about half an hour and had to be disbanded for lack of a quorum. The game dissipated into a political discussion. A game of checkers on a pocket board outlasted the poker session."[389ag] A railroad man on the train whose experience reached back to 1932 said campaigners had become "too serious. We used to mix freely with visiting politicians, and press conferences were held with the candidates. [Wendell] Willkie, for example, used to hold press conferences sometimes at 3 o'clock in the morning."[389ag] Others thought air travel contributed to the new atmosphere. Faster travel meant more speeches and more writing, revising and polishing.

Columnist Russell Baker wondered in *The New York Times* how effective whistlestop trains were when Goldwater's public address system in Frankfort, Ind., was too weak to allow most of the crowd to hear what he said. They cheered wildly anyway.

"All the evidence of the last week suggests that the intimate whistlestop campaign … may be better for the candidate's morale than for anything else. All polls tell Mr. Goldwater that he is in deep difficulty, but all through Ohio, Indiana and Illinois his trainside crowds have been big. Not enormous and not tumultuous, to be sure, but large enough and sympathetic enough to cheer a candidate with the suspicion that the polls might just possibly be wrong."[389ah]

Baker wondered if the kids were cheering the Republican or the fact that they were out of school to see him. He asked if the adults believed in what he was saying or were caught up in the current euphoria. "Did you like his speech?" he asked a woman in Crown Point, Ind. "It was wonderful," she exclaimed. "What did you like about it?" The woman looked puzzled, turned to her companion, shrugged, then smiled and answered, "Everything!"

He was curious even about the hecklers. One woman in Indiana heaved apples at the train, crying, "That's what you'll be selling if he's elected." Did these people really have a cause, or were they the result of an efficient Democratic drive to demoralize the candidate? "It is a mystery," Baker concluded, musing that a single TV appearance would accomplish more than the train trip did.[389ah]

Dick Tuck, the Democratic practical joker, slipped aboard Goldwater's train, too—and this time he brought a friend, Moira O'Conner, along. They began distributing a newsletter called *The Whistle Stop* to keep passengers "advised, informed, protected, and, with considerable assistance from the senator himself, amused." For example, the newsletter announced that "fluoride has not been added to the water on this train," a jab at ultraconservatives who had claimed fluoride was dangerous. As the train moved from the Eastern to the Central Time Zone, the newsletter said Goldwater "has decided to use Washington time, George Washington, that is." Before the couple gave up, they fired a parting shot: "We wish we could say that Goldwater's speeches speak for themselves, but they don't."[44]

Somewhere enroute, Goldwater donned an engineer's cap and went up front to ride the locomotive cab. "He drives a train very smoothly," the skeptical Baker wrote. "Should he fail to become president, he would certainly make an adequate train driver."[389ah] The rest of the time, he noted wryly, Goldwater never ventured outside his office car to hobnob with others on the train. The trek still struck Baker as an odd way to earn votes.

"It is the strangest thing," he wrote. "The train rolls through the cornfields while the politicians sit inside drinking coffee and listening to 'The Stars and Stripes Forever' on squawk boxes. Every hour or so, the thing stops and all the coffee-soaked politicians are put off and another shift is put aboard.

"Everybody else jumps off the train and runs to the rear. The man who wants to be president comes out the back door, and everybody shouts, 'We want Barry! We want Barry! We want Barry!' 'Well, you have him,' says the man who wants to be president, and the crowd laughs."[389ah]

Before long, the crowds began to look the same to Baker. "The train is stopping again. … The last shift of local politicians is disembarking and the new one is getting on. … Everyone is racing to the back. The crowd is at it again. … 'Well, you have him.' The crowd is laughing. That eerie crowd. There is the woman carrying the sleepy baby. There is the old fellow with leathery ears. … the jeering adolescent with (an) LBJ placard. … Could we be carrying the crowd in the baggage car?"[389ah]

Sometimes the candidate seemed quite real, he opined.

"He hailed the local Colgate toothpaste plant and declared that if government would stop harassing teen-agers and young married people, 'there can be millions of these Colgates started across the country.' A man kept walking through the train asking where the country would get enough teeth to keep them all in business, but he was finally restrained and told to go easy on the coffee.

"It is curious here. Very curious. One has these fantasies, especially after nightfall. Perhaps it is the coffee and too much 'Stars and Stripes Forever,' but one has the gnawing suspicion that we are all doomed on this train—doomed to roll forever through the cornfields, listening to Barry say, 'Well, you have him,' seeing the old man with leathery ears day after day, week after week, year after year. And at night there are the dreams. Millions of toothpaste factories turning out billions of toothpaste tubes. It is a curious way to make a president."[389ah]

History records one other whistlestop train for Goldwater—a one-day, 245-mile jaunt across Pennsylvania from Harrisburg to Pittsburgh on Thursday, Oct. 29, 1964. He rode PRR private car 180.

Richard M. Nixon

In 1968, Richard Nixon tried again for the presidency; that time he was successful. His campaign featured one day—Tuesday, Oct. 22—of whistlestopping from Cincinnati to Toledo, Ohio. The route was Penn Central to Columbus, C&O to Marion, Erie Lack-awanna to Lima and B&O to Toledo. The Detroit, Toledo & Ironton became involved in a small way when EL used a DT&I wye at Lima to point the train the right way for transfer to the B&O.

By then, U.S. rail passenger service was in decline. The Association of American Railroads' Paul Marshall and Nixon aide Booth Turner had a tough time scraping up enough acceptable equipment. Turner inspected some Penn Central office cars in New York and rejected them all. He looked over Southern's fleet in Washington and found it acceptable, except that the cars were a drab green—and didn't fit the light mood of a whistlestop train. Finally, he settled for C&O 15, assigned to that road's Assistant Vice President Transportation Erle Rucker. A C&O official told the author that Rucker convinced the Nixon staff to use his car—even though it was not the most desirable—to put one over on Rucker's boss, C. Vernon Cowan, vice president of C&O's operating department. Aside from it and C&O tavern/lounge 1903, the 15-car special was composed of stainless-steel PC cars.

Nixon's stop on the B&O at Deshler, Ohio, catapulted this short train ride into the national consciousness when 13-year-old Vicki Lynn Cole held a sign aloft. Speaking of the divisiveness of the Vietnam War, it said, "Bring us together again," and became the theme of his presidency.

"I saw many signs in this campaign," Nixon said in his victory statement. "Some of them were not friendly and some of them were very friendly. But the one that touched me the most was one I saw in Deshler, Ohio, at the end of a long day of whistlestopping—a little town, I suppose five times the population was there in the dusk—but a teen-ager held up a sign, 'Bring us Together.' And that will be the great objective of this administration at the outset. …"[44]

Nixon rode a train only once while in office—a short Metroliner hop from Washington to Philadelphia on Jan. 24, 1970, to attend a concert. His Penn Central special carried two snack bar coaches for the press, a Metroclub car for the Secret Service and communications, and another Metroclub for President and Mrs. Nixon.

The extra work and security involved may help explain why POTUS trips have gone the way of the stagecoach. The Metroliner cars were sealed and checked by the Secret Service. Ten seats were removed from the first press car to make room for television equipment, and a special communications enclosure was built in the Secret Service car. Communications were seen as a problem, too—they would have been readily available on *Air Force One*. A policeman or state trooper was stationed at every crossing, bridge, culvert and tunnel. A helicopter followed a beacon on top of Nixon's train. Secret Service agents were jammed in both the train and the helicopter; all other trains stopped while Nixon's passed. Most of the planners involved felt that television, airplanes and heli-copters had made presidential travel much more secure. In all, it took an army of policemen, technicians and railroaders to put this president on a train—and nobody wanted to pay that kind of a price anymore.

Constantly at Nixon's side in seat 16 was a red telephone, but it never rang. Mrs. Nixon sat nearby in seat 20, and the only other occupants of the car were a Secret Service man, PC Assistant Director of Passenger Service Clifford Alban, and the two Metroclub attendants, Emory A. Nauden and W.S. Crawford. Other PC personnel included engineer instructor George Smeltzer at the throttle, conductor Frank E. Brown, rear brakeman Kenneth B. Goodson and standby conductor E.A. Fisher.

The president's train left from Union Station's Track 17 at 5:17 p.m., arriving at 30th Street Station in Philadelphia at 6:55, 98 minutes later. The president ate from the standard Metroclub fare—Cornish hen.

The special party spent the next few hours at the concert of the Philadelphia Symphony Orchestra that marked the 70th anniversary of the symphony and the 70th birthday of director Eugene Ormandy. The group returned to the train later than expected and left 30th Street, where the equipment had been turned, at 11:33 p.m. Arrival back in Washington was at 1:10 a.m. on the 25th. As with the northbound trip, the southbound sprint—made a minute quicker—made no intermediate stops, slowing only for the station platform at Wilmington and the tunnels at Baltimore. The northbound run had averaged 98.5 miles an hour, the southbound 99.2.

The only problem encountered was a heavy snow at Perryville, Md., on the return. An NBC film crew took advantage of the storm by filming considerable footage of the train's oscillating headlight playing in the whirling

Robert Kennedy, John F. Kennedy's brother, whistlestopped four times in the spring of 1968 in his pursuit of the presidency. He didn't receive the Democratic nomination, but most likely would have had he not been cut down by an assassin's bullet on June 6, so he merits a mention here.

His four trips included:

Logansport to Peru, Ind., via Norfolk & Western's Wabash line on April 23.

Cheyenne, Wyo., to Omaha, Neb., via the Union Pacific on April 27.

Portland to Eugene, Ore., via the Southern Pacific on May 18.

Fresno to Sacramento, Calif., via the SP on May 30.

After Kennedy's untimely death in California, his body was flown to New York City for funeral services on June 8, then taken to Washington, D.C., on a Penn Central funeral train for burial in Arlington National Cemetery. The Kennedy tragedy was compounded when two people who got too close to the train at Elizabeth, N.J., were killed by the eastbound *Admiral*, and when 17 people on top of a boxcar in Trenton were injured when one of them touched an 11,000-volt overhead wire.

LOU SCHMITZ

Robert F. Kennedy campaigns for the Democratic presidential nomination aboard Union Pacific office car Arden *at Fremont, Neb., April 27, 1968.*

Richard Nixon campaigns for the presidency at Dayton, Ohio, Oct. 22, 1968, on C&O business car 15.

snowflakes as the track rushed toward them at 120 miles an hour.

Nixon loved his ride. "It's like night and day when you think of the old trains,"[293] he remarked in Philadelphia. Steve Bull, Nixon's trip planner, figured travel time was less than taking *Air Force One* when transit time to and from airports was included, and about the same as a helicopter trip. "Very nice," Bull concluded. "It's also quieter than an airplane."[293]

The press was reserved, but even cynical writers seemed pleased. United Press International's Merriman Smith, who could remember when presidential travel meant weeks in heavyweight cars and an "old-fashioned good" diner, called the Metroliner "impressive in that it's new equipment and more comfortable. But at high speeds you certainly are aware of it if you walk around. When you're in your seat, you can't believe you're going at 120 miles an hour. [But] a lot of coffee was spilled when we were standing up."[293]

In all, Penn Central managed the evening flawlessly. Howard Gilbert, manager of PC's news bureau who made the trip, was elated and relieved. "It was a smooth, completely routine trip," he declared.[293]

Nixon made no rail trips during his 1972 re-election campaign, but Democrat George McGovern of South Dakota did. His seven-car UP train made a 570-mile round trip from Omaha to North Platte and back on a rainy Saturday, May 6, just before the Nebraska primary.

McGovern's train was a further commentary on changing times. It was operated by the UP as an Amtrak special, the first campaign operation of the nation's new quasi-public rail passenger carrier. All equipment except the locomotive and one car were owned by Auto-Liner and leased to Amtrak. There was no diner; riders ate peanuts, chips and beverages.

The candidate's car, Auto-Liner open-platform sleeper/lounge 100, was the first car with Amtrak colors to operate in Nebraska. It was beautifully equipped with telephones and television.

James Taylor, writing for a rail enthusiasts' newsletter, revealed that the exit from Omaha was a little inglorious, with a Burlington Northern switcher pulling the train backward out of the station and onto the UP's Missouri River bridge for the trip west. Departure was 30 minutes late, almost time to stop for the first speech at Fremont. But in spite of a 70-mile-an-hour restriction, the party was back on schedule at Grand Island.

Between Columbus and Grand Island, Taylor was granted an interview with the candidate in compartment U of car 100.

"The senator stated that we felt it is really too early to tell about Amtrak," he wrote, "but that rail service must be saved and in many areas is not now adequate."[388] McGovern was very much aware that his home state had no passenger service at all.

At Grand Island, ham sandwiches were put aboard. Several more stops were made, uneventful except for the rainy ending, Taylor wrote. McGovern and his party detrained at North Platte and continued through the rest of the state by air while the train deadheaded back.

At 11:45 p.m., Omaha was reached. Again, the special stopped on the bridge and a UP switcher coupled onto the 100 and pulled the train back into Burlington Station track 3, from whence it had come.

In the wake of the Arab oil embargo of 1973, White House aides apparently contemplated other rail trips for Nixon after being stung by critics of his costly jet travel. A Dec. 8, 1973, newspaper article predicted he would ride Amtrak's *Blue Ridge* to and from Brunswick, Md., enroute to

Camp David, his retreat in the Catoctin Mountains. A Dec. 13 *Washington Star* dispatch said the president would take an after-Christmas vacation at his Key Biscayne, Fla., home and unnamed sources said he and a small staff would travel in a "few cars, possibly only three," at the rear of a regular Washington-Miami train. "White House communications officials are installing new gear in a presidential car that Nixon will use," the *Star* said. "He is expected to leave here Dec. 26 for a weeklong stay."[395]

As these revelations were unfolding, The *Huntington* (W.Va.) *Advertiser* of Dec. 10 reported in an exclusive story that Chessie System 15, the office car Nixon rode in 1968, had been refurbished for the president's use in C&O's Huntington shops the previous Wednesday. Expenses for electrical work alone amounted to several hundred dollars, an anonymous source claimed, and several men involved in the work drew overtime pay.

Chessie was confronted with what *The Advertiser* had been told and was prodded for a statement. On Dec. 11, a terse response was forthcoming: "Business car No. 15, which is assigned to Central Regional Manager G.S. Harris and Western Regional Manager A.W. Johnston, received routine maintenance for operating purposes only."[387j]

Beyond that, the White House and Chessie referred reporters to each other. Amtrak would only note that the White House abruptly dropped plans for any train trips and wouldn't say why. Meanwhile, the Huntington shop informant said the refitted car left Huntington for Washington on an Amtrak train the day after it was worked on, but was dispatched again to Regional Manager Johnston's headquarters in Cincinnati three days later.

Gerald R. Ford

President Gerald R. Ford and wife, Betty, rode a seven-car Amtrak whistlestopper from Flint to Niles, Mich., on Saturday, May 15, 1976, just before the Michigan primary. With its lead unit of the *Presidential Special* painted to honor the nation's bicentennial and appropriately numbered 1776, the train was routed GTW-Battle Creek-Conrail.

Rain didn't seem to dampen the enthusiasm of the Fords or the crowds, estimated to total 50,000. The special often slowed so Ford could wave to large groups; each of the Victorian-style stations at the stops—Durand, Lansing, Battle Creek and Kalamazoo—were decorated with patriotic bunting and permeated with band music.

Security met the usual POTUS standards; a high-rail vehicle served as the pilot train.

At one stop, the president called the trip, "A train ride to victory in Kansas City [the Republican convention site] and in November."[14a]

At Durand, the Fords walked through a rain shower to shake hands. Back on the rear platform of Amtrak private car 10000, he said, "I need your help on Tuesday. I won't let Michigan down. Don't you let me down."[389ai]

Between Durand and Lansing, the candidate strolled through the train and talked with newsmen. "It sure is good to be traveling with you rather than on another plane," he chuckled. In response to a question,

he declared, "I couldn't feel better. I think it's great." One of his aides later told the press Ford was "having the time of his life."[14a]

A jazz band and young ladies decked out in Ford hats circulated through the train, adding a festive air. Mrs. Ford came through and said, "The train is lovely and the trip is great. I think we'll take it again in the fall."[14] She did a little dance in the car where the band was playing.

Next was Lansing. "Just a few years ago," Ford said, "Harry Truman won with a whistlestop campaign. President Eisenhower won with a whistlestop campaign and now President Ford is going to win with a whistlestop campaign."[14a] He told the press he came up with the idea of a special when he saw pictures of Ike's train at Grand Rapids, Ford's hometown.

After his Lansing talk, Ford went to a downtown restaurant, "The Depot," to meet with newspaper publishers and editors. CBS newsman Walter Cronkite boarded at Lansing, saying he hadn't been on a presidential train since 1940 and was enjoying himself immensely. "It's about time the country started paying more attention to public transportation and stopped putting all of its money into the highways," he commented.[14a]

Three reporters were invited into the 10000 to detail its furnishings. They described its handsome dark wood paneling, rose-tinted windows, stuffed yellow chairs and gold carpeting. "It sure beats first-class air travel," they concluded.[14a]

Ford lost his temper in Battle Creek. He was telling the crowd what he had done to reduce unemployment, perhaps forgetting that Michigan's rate at the time was 12 percent. A young man near him shouted, "You blew it!"

Ford responded promptly. "We blew it in the right direction, young man," and the crowd cheered. Then, his voice rising and his face turning red, he added, "If you go out and look for a job, you'll find one!"[389a]

Shortly before arriving at Niles, Ford invited three railroad officials—David A. Watts Jr., Amtrak's vice president and general manager; Rich Tower, Amtrak's Detroit district superintendent; and B.L. Strohl, general manager of Conrail's northern region—into the presidential car for a short visit.

EMERY J. GULASH

GTW diesel 1776, patriotically garbed in honor of the nation's bicentennial, leads Amtrak engines 203 and 214 in pulling President Gerald R. Ford's campaign special into Lansing, Mich., May 15, 1976.

Gerald and Betty Ford wave to well-wishers as their whistlestop train begins its journey at Flint, Mich., May 15, 1976.

President Ford thanks the engine crew for a fine trip as he prepares to leave his train at Niles, Mich., May 15, 1976.

Ford told them how much he was enjoying his trip and thought it had gone well. Tower pointed out that the Amfleet equipment on the train was scheduled to go into service the next week in Michigan. Tower also explained that the Chicago-Detroit corridor was the fastest-growing on the Amtrak system. Ford asked the running time, and Watts said it was 5½ hours but would be cut another 30 minutes when track work was finished.

At Niles, Ford walked up to the 1776 and thanked engineer Dick Zane for a good ride. He climbed into the engineer's seat, stuck his head out the window and shouted, "Are you ready?"[14a] He then gave the horn a couple of hard blasts. From Niles, the president flew to Holland for the city's annual tulip festival.

Tower noticed there was a visible change in the president's attitude during the day. "At Flint that morning, he seemed to be down, but by the end of the day his delivery had picked up and he seemed to be in excellent spirits. He really was enjoying himself."[14a]

"It was a tense day for Ford," Watts told the author, explaining that the candidate was in a do-or-die battle with Ronald Reagan for the GOP nomination. But Watts added that he was much more relaxed during the discussion around the private car's dining room table. "Ford lit his pipe and for the next half-hour he talked as if he wanted conversation on how nice railroad travel is, not how nervous he was about the election. He is a thoroughly decent human being."[424]

Ford beat Reagan in Michigan by a two-to-one margin. "[The train] was very beneficial," he told the author.[140]

Betty Ford's prediction was on the mark; she and the president rode Amtrak again during the general election campaign. This train, dubbed The *Honest Abe*, operated from Chicago to St. Louis on Saturday, Oct. 16, and Amtrak provided the same office car for the Fords.

The first couple had flown to Chicago the night before and motored to Joliet, where they boarded the train. They rode the Gulf, Mobile & Ohio Railroad from Joliet to Alton, stopping at Pontiac, Bloomington, Lincoln, Springfield and Carlinville. Entertainers Chuck Connors, Hugh O'Brien and Peter Graves and ex-astronaut Alan Shepard accompanied the politicians.

At Lincoln, Ford detrained to attend a luncheon with members of the Illinois Publishers Association. The affair took longer than planned, and the train departed late. At Alton, they left the train and motorcaded to an appointment in St. Louis before boarding *Air Force One* for Washington.

Presidential Press Secretary Ron Nessen praised Amtrak's equipment, especially the Amdinette cars, whose tables held several typewriters, mimeograph machines, stenotype equipment and banks of telephones. "It was a great trip," he said, "even better than the last one."[14c]

Ford's assessment? "Again, very productive," he told the author.[140]

Watts commented that POTUS trains were so infrequent by then that the Secret Service had to be retrained each time. "They were familiar only with air travel," he explained, "and there was a lot more that needed to be checked out on the ground."[424]

Railroad officers never knew how long candidates would speak, so "huge amounts of fudge" were thrown into the schedule, Watts noted. "At Springfield, Ford not only got off and started shaking hands, he walked a good block away from the train and was gone an hour. My fudge factor saved the day."[424]

Jimmy Carter

Democrat Jimmy Carter, the victor over Ford, rode trains twice during his 1976 campaign. In late May, he boarded Amtrak's Metroliner at New York and rode to Trenton to campaign in New Jersey. He returned on a Metroliner to Newark.

On Sept. 20, Carter boarded a 13-car Amtrak/Conrail special at New York to launch a two-day, 904-mile whistlestop swing through New Jersey, Pennsylvania, Ohio, Indiana and Illinois. The candidate spoke from the rear platform of his *Train for a Change* at several stops. Carter got off the train at Pittsburgh, but the next day it continued to Chicago with wife, Rosalynn, and vice presidential nominee Walter Mondale and his wife still aboard.

"We expect this train will do the one thing Jimmy Carter likes to do better than anything else," Democratic Party Chairman Robert Strauss remarked, "campaign at the grass roots where the people are." The run was Strauss' idea. "Lord, I'm happy about this," he said. "It's been one of my dreams for a long time."[14b]

Carter spent his time aboard in conference with local politicians riding between stops. Carter, Mondale and their wives walked through the cars, shaking hands and getting to know press people, local dignitaries and Amtrak employees. Democratic secretary Dorothy Bush made announcements over the train's public address system, giving a short history of each town where the train would stop and warning members of the press to get off and on carefully.

Austin Noll, manager on-board operations, was pleased.

"The foreign press in particular liked the train," he said. "They thought the food service was excellent, the equipment beautiful and the ridability of the cars as good as anything in Europe."[14b] Crews served 1,100 complete meals during the two days and countless sandwiches. The trip consumed nearly 3 tons of ice cubes.

"I may do this again sometime,"[14b] Carter commented as he neared Altoona, Pa.

Joe Margolis of the *Chicago Tribune* perceived the odd blending of past and present.

"The whistlestop trip was a sort of

Vice presidential candidate Walter Mondale greets the public at Massillon, Ohio, on the 13-car Democratic Whistlestop *Sept. 21, 1976. Running mate Jimmy Carter had disembarked at Pittsburgh.*

Walter Mondale's campaign train crosses the Tuscarawas River after leaving Massillon, Ohio, Sept. 21, 1976.

President Carter looks over paperwork aboard Amtrak Metroliner No. 104 between Washington and Baltimore Aug. 7, 1979.

historical balancing act itself," he wrote. "The built-in nostalgia of a train trip was combined with the futuristic characteristics of this particular train, which seemed more like an airplane than the trains of Harry Truman's day. The backs of seats reclined individually, little tables could be dropped down in front of each seat and the facilities were so modern that passengers did not have to refrain from flushing toilets while the train was in the station."[14b]

Mrs. Carter and the Mondales were met in Chicago by Mayor and Mrs. Richard J. Daley. "This is a good way to end a great day," Mrs. Carter beamed.[14b]

"Everywhere we went, just as was the case for Harry Truman, we met the American people,"[14b] Mondale declared.

The only anxious moments for the Secret Service came in automatic block signal territory on an ex-PRR Conrail stretch in Indiana. The westbound mainline had a 30-mile-an-hour restriction, but eastbound trains could hit 50. "So the railroad gave the crew train orders to run against the current of traffic on the wrong main,"

Watts told the author. "This meant they saw no signals, since they now faced the wrong way. The Secret Service about had a heart attack."[424]

Carter rode a train at least once while in office, taking a Metroliner from Washington to Baltimore on Tuesday, Aug. 7, 1979. He and Rosalynn were scheduled to visit a solar-energy demonstration house and fulfill several other appointments in the city.

Leaving from the South Lawn of the White House at 7:43 a.m., the Carters arrived at Union Station at 7:55 and boarded the last car, a snack bar coach, on a regular train. It departed at 8:01, stopping at the Beltway Station along I-495 for more passengers, and arriving in Baltimore at 8:37. The Carters sat in the front left seat, the president next to the window. Their party included Press Secretary Jody Powell, sitting behind them; Attorney General Benjamin Civiletti, who was from Baltimore; Moon Landrieu, nominee for the secretary's post of the U.S. Department of Housing and Urban Development; Sen. Charles Mathias, R-Md.; Judge John Sirica; Rep. Mario Biaggi, D-N.Y.; Geno Baroni, an assistant HUD secretary; and White House staffers David Rubenstein, deputy domestic adviser who was also from Baltimore; speechwriter Henrik Hertzberg; and Jerry Rafshoon, assistant to the president for communications. The press sat in the section behind the snack bar.

Dignitaries including Maryland Gov. Harry Hughes met the Carters at Baltimore's Pennsylvania Station and escorted them during the day. At 1:18, they departed on a returning Metroliner and reached Washington at 1:56.

Rosalynn returned to Metroliner service at least once, on Oct. 20 when she rode to Philadelphia to help New Jersey Gov. Brendan Bryne's re-election campaign.

Ronald Regan

Republican Ronald Reagan rode one whistlestop train during his 1984 re-election campaign when the *Heartland Special* plied 133 miles of the Chessie System's B&O western Ohio line from Dayton to the Toledo suburb of Perrysburg. The Friday, Oct. 12, run—which included  stops at Sidney, Lima, Ottawa and Deshler—was especially notable because it resurrected the armor-plated *Ferdinand Magellan* from the Gold Coast Railroad Museum in Florida.

Gold Coast had been trying to have the *Magellan* declared a national historic landmark by the National Park Service, museum member John Forbes McLean explained. Meanwhile, the American Association of Private Railroad Car Owners scheduled its annual convention in Washington later in October, so Gold Coast took the car up there to show it to the Park Service during the convention. With this trip in mind, members had invited Reagan to speak from the car's rear platform. The administration responded with a request to use it in the campaign! The landmark status was conferred in February 1985—the *Magellan* being the first railroad passenger car in history to receive it.

The "cream of the operating crop"[352] was selected to comprise crews for Reagan's special movement. Handling the POTUS train would be engineer Lucius "Sackhead" Eyler, fireman Don Brooks, conductor Roy

Moon and flagman Bob Tirey. Selected for the pilot train were engineer Bob Scheidler, fireman Coy Wells, conductor Bill Kilburn and flagman Ken Rogers. The following train would have engineer Jim Sampson, fireman Dave Christopher, conductor Randy Napier and flagman Bob Watt.

On Thursday, Oct. 11, 36 years to the day after the 66-year-old Eyler hauled Truman on the same route, the *Heartland Special* and its escort trains made an exhausting 16-hour "dry run"[352] with 300 reporters on board.

Some journalists boycotted the ride—because it would cost them $1,000 apiece. "It sounds like the great train ride is turning into the Great Train Robbery,"[397] cracked one editor who declined to be identified. The White House had said it expected 200 reporters on board and figured the total cost of carrying them at $200,000—with $150,000 of that eaten up in telephone costs. Billy Dale of the White House Travel Office defended the figures, saying the cost of covering the president had skyrocketed after the breakup of AT&T, which used to offer phones to the White House as a courtesy.

The practice run reached the North Street crossing in Sidney about 10:40 a.m., where a speaking platform was being assembled. Even though the station was closed, it sported a new roof, brickwork, paint and station signs. The phone company was hooking up an extensive network, the utility companies were running all kinds of lines and security—military and civilian—was tight. Six loudspeakers were installed on the *Magellan* at Sidney, even though the aluminum framework for them had been attached at Dayton. The speakers were to be mounted there, too, but someone got impatient and ordered the train to leave before the work could be finished. Workmen had to

MARK PERRI

A window washer gets in a few last licks on the historic Ferdinand Magellan *as Chessie System railroaders wait with the press and politicians for President Ronald Reagan's arrival at Dayton Union Terminal Oct. 12, 1984.*

drive to Sidney to complete the task.

The press was allowed to tour the *Magellan* for an hour and a half. One writer was critical; he said the interior had "the musty smell of a seldom-used cottage." Adding that it appeared "worn" and "austere," the writer went on to complain that "the curtains are faded, the carpeting is well-trod [and] the walls are an outdated shade of green."[406]

Later Thursday, a high-rail truck ventured up the line and installed hundreds of large black and white numbers between the rails. They served as locators to enable the throng of security agents flown into Dayton's Wright Patterson Air Force Base and forwarded to the right of way on unmarked Air Force buses to find their assigned sectors. Most of them wouldn't know in advance where they were headed.

The railroad cleared all adjacent tracks. "Someone goofed at Piqua and left five loaded stone cars on the scale track," wrote rail fan Scott Trostel of Fletcher, Ohio. "Boy, you should have heard the roar the next morning."[410]

The FBI called Chessie Road Foreman John Baker and said that the railroad's operating people could not use their hand-held radio sets during the trip. "When [our people] raised them to their mouths, Secret Service agents couldn't tell whether they were going for guns or what," Baker remarked. "So the railroad ordered 50 Motorola lapel mikes and they were delivered overnight."[25]

The mood was subdued on the train as it returned to Dayton for the real thing. Nine exhausted and silent men—Secret Service agents, railroad technicians and Reagan advance people—watched a debate between Vice President George Bush and Democratic vice presidential nominee Geraldine Ferraro on a small-screen television. Sometimes the viewers dozed, but their snoozing was restless because they knew most of their work lay ahead. In other cars, men slept fitfully, curled up in reclining seats. Some played cards in a brightly lit lounge. A Secret Service agent read a spy novel. Chessie waiter James Sembly, still in white jacket, strolled through the train offering refreshments. Secret Service agent John Baffa was stumped by some of the train's most elementary technology. "Hey Jack!" he yelled from the restroom of an Amtrak coach. "How do you flush this thing?"[410]

Once back in Dayton at 1 a.m. on Friday the 12th, the train was turned, cleaned, watered and refueled. Chessie provided vacuum cleaners for carmen cleaning the coaches, and Amtrak brought in a power washer to take care of the exteriors.

President Reagan's Heartland Special, *headed by Chessie System diesel No. 4444, approaches Troy, Ohio, Oct. 12, 1984.*

Bill Hart, Chessie's assistant to the vice president-transportation, and Bob Stender, general manager of Chessie's Western Division Business Unit, were given FBI-registered American and presidential flags—each fastened to a black staff with a gold eagle on top—to install on B&O diesel 4444's cab roof ("We insisted that a Chessie locomotive pull the train"[352] in front of the Amtrak units, said Dan Sabin, manager operations at Cincinnati). The poles were too thick to fit in the unit's flagstands, but Dayton carman Eddie Miles used a hacksaw and metal grinder to whittle them down to size. They still wouldn't fit until the husky Miles muscled them into place.

At 2 a.m., the White House told Hart to place fiberglass discs bearing the presidential seal on the engine. This task required a ³/₈-inch drill bit, which was nowhere to be found at that hour. General Mechanical Foreman John Childers came to the rescue, and the job was done by 3. "An awful lot of people didn't get any sleep," Hart said.[352]

The private car *Virginia Dawn*, another Gold Coast holding, posed a more serious dilemma. Used on the trial run, it developed truck spring problems and had to be replaced by standby former Seaboard private car *Virginia*. This required disconnecting and reattaching temporary communications cables as big as a man's arm strung along its sides. A Cincinnati electrical crew was called in and supervised by Jim Barron, manager-passenger equipment maintenance. The electricians spent six hours rewiring the power while White House technicians rewired government equipment. "It was crucial," Barron stressed. "Without this rewiring, there would have been no power to Mr. Reagan's car." Dayton carmen worked all night to clean the *Virginia*.

John Scott Jr., chef on C&O private car 7 and assigned to the company's track inspection train, will never forget that day. It would be his privilege to fix Reagan's lunch.

"We had taken the Secret Service over the territory on the geometry train," Scott recalled to the author. "They stopped and looked around everywhere. Nothing was said until I got a call one morning at home. My boss said car 7 would be used by the president."[335]

Scott and car 7 traveled on Amtrak's *Cardinal* from Huntington to Washington a few days early, he recalled, so the special communications gear could be installed. The car then moved to Dayton on the special train with the *Magellan* and *Virginia Dawn*.

"They made us leave the car unlocked all night, so the city police, state police and Secret Service would have constant access," Scott said. "The day before the trip, I went with the Secret Service to buy food at random—no one knew we were coming."

Scott said agents put the food in a different automobile, though he couldn't figure out why. "Those people don't talk too much."[335]

At one store, a clerk asked Scott if he would be riding the presidential train. When Scott replied, "Yes, ma'am," a glowering agent elbowed him and politely told the woman, "He's kidding."[335]

The chef was impressed with the train's appearance.

In addition to its flags and fiberglass presidential seals, the 4444 sported a patriotic red, white and blue bunting draped from the pilot at running board level. Under the cab windows, the B&O lettering had been covered with glossy black paint and white lettering that said "HEARTLAND SPECIAL—PRESIDENT REAGAN'S OHIO WHISTLE-STOP." From just behind the cab to the far end of the engine compartment was a large blue sign with red letters proclaiming that the candidate was "BRINGING AMERICA BACK, PROUDER, STRONGER AND BETTER" that was topped by eight or 10 more flags. The *Magellan* carried red, white and blue bunting along the end sill under its rear platform.

As Friday dawned everyone was ready—but there were the usual last-minute bugs. A persistent fog, traffic jams and hitches in security clearances threatened to keep Chessie President John T. Collinson from meeting Reagan at the Dayton airport, but he made it just in time. Proper introductions were made and Reagan hurried to a rally at a mall before continuing to the station.

Meanwhile, back at Dayton Union Terminal, Chef Scott went downstairs to find out why the flowers he had ordered were late. He forgot his I.D. badge, and an agent had to be summoned from the train before he could reboard.

Security impressed the chef. The flowers, bags of ice and food and beverage supplies were sniffed by dogs before being allowed on board. The Secret Service checked each car—every cabinet had to be unlocked. Then the German shepherds followed.

A Chessie carman from Troy, Ohio, had problems getting close enough to make a predeparture air test. He had been cleared several days before by the Secret Service, but the paperwork got misplaced and he was stopped as he approached. By the time someone with enough authority to admit him was tracked down, security personnel blanketed the ground and nearby rooftops to the extent that he was afraid of putting his hands in his pockets lest he be shot.

Security was so tight that editors of the *Dayton Daily News* had to obtain a special dispensation from the police to deliver early editions of their afternoon paper. The company's production facilities were inside a secured area downtown that surrounded the station, and original orders prevented delivery trucks—or any other vehicle—from leaving the area.

"My boss called, wanting to know what the luncheon menu was," Scott said. "They told me not to say until after the president had eaten."[335]

When Scott heard a band playing "Hail to the Chief," he positioned himself on the observation deck as the president boarded shortly after noon.

"That music—it does something to you," he said. "It was a great feeling."[335]

Once the special departed, Scott and Sembly controlled their awe and rolled up their sleeves. It was time to work.

"I prepared dinner for 12, including Mr. Reagan," Scott explained. "Three of his people ate on car 7, including the bagman [the high-ranking Naval officer with a black bag full of instructions in case the country was attacked], [Chief of Staff] James Baker and [Dr. Daniel Ruge,] the president's private physician."[335]

The classified menu was beef broth with vegetable soup, seafood salad plate, asparagus spears, red beets, dinner rolls, heart of palm with vinaigrette dressing, macedoine of fresh fruits and cookies. A framed copy was mounted in car 7's dining room until it was given to Scott when the car received its CSX Transportation livery during the winter of 1986-87.

"The beef broth was the only hot item," he noted. "They wanted mostly a cold platter because the president would stop eating at every town for speeches."[335]

The only other food Scott prepared for the presidential party was an array of hors d'oeuvres at 3 p.m. including a cheese plate, sliced tenderloin and cubes of chicken breast with orange sauce.

"I was so nervous the orange sauce turned out lumpy," he remem-

WAYNE BRODERICK, CHESSIE SYSTEM/JOHN B. CORNS COLLECTION

Ronald Reagan enjoys the view from the rear of the venerable Ferdinand Magellan *as his* Heartland Special *nears Troy, Ohio, on Oct. 12, 1984.*

Chessie System 4444 heads Amtrak 276 and 275 in hauling President Reagan's train out of Sidney, Ohio, Oct. 12, 1984.

Chessie System chef John Scott found himself nervous on Oct. 12, 1984, the day he fixed President Reagan's lunch, but he did fine anyway.

bered. "They came in the galley and said, 'The president is waiting for this,' and I threw in the corn starch without putting it in cold water. I apologized and asked what I should do, but they answered, 'Can't help it, we gotta go with this.'"

As the train glided northward, crowds were waiting. In Vandalia, Tipp City and Troy, through corn-fields and tiny country crossroads, they waved, held placards and shouted with enthusiasm. Men in coveralls and caps stood on flatbed trucks or leaned against John Deere tractors.

"This wasn't the sophisticated East," Chessie's Hart mused. "I real-ized that as we drove through the heartland and saw flags and heard the national anthem."[352]

Somewhere in Miami County, the Secret Service eyed with suspicion a tractor alongside the right of way. A manure spreader was attached, piled high with a load. "Mondale's farm policy," the spreader was labeled.[114]

Trostel described Reagan's pas-sage at Piqua. At the Statler Road crossing at 9 a.m., it was still extreme-ly foggy, but a security man was already seated with a white box in front of the railroad scale house. He told Trostel he was part of the massive airlift of more than 700 armed federal security agents charged with the pres-ident's safety. The white box was a lunch given to him at Wright Patter-son Air Force Base.

Other agents who showed up said they had come from all over the United States. They had departed from Washington at 2:38 a.m. on mil-itary cargo planes and were at their posts by 5:30 a.m. They were sta-tioned 250 yards apart and at every crossing, bridge and building—rail-road and non-railroad alike. Any structure near the railroad was

This is what whistlestopping is all about, the photographer says. Small children, awed with the aura of the presidency, wave at President Reagan's train south of Ottawa, Ohio, Oct. 12, 1984.

searched and some public buildings were closed.

A fuel truck driver stopped to see the train, but wasn't permitted to stay. Three advance high-rail trucks passed Piqua at 11; the first put wooden switch blocks in the points of all mainline switches. They stopped occasionally to check questionable situations, including the loads of stone at Piqua. They climbed over and crawled under all of them. That was when a B&O agent showed up and tried to call a local freight to come pick up the cars. Finally the security people declared them secure and denied Chessie permission to move them. Dump trucks blocked all public crossings at 1 p.m. Those sitting on cars close to the tracks were ordered away; doors on nearby vehicles were opened.

At 1:20, a Marine helicopter made the first of two passes over the Piqua area, and at 1:30 the pilot train arrived and slowed to about 5 miles an hour. Sightseers were ordered to the far side of adjacent tracks just as Secret Service agents became visible in its

cabooses. The pilot train accelerated rapidly beyond the crossing. At 1:35, the *Heartland Special* passed under Interstate 75 and slowed to a crawl. Reagan was on the rear platform, speaking and waving to the crowd. The following train was close behind, using its horn and bell liberally. It was all over for Piqua by 1:40 p.m.

Trostel drove to Sidney in hopes of seeing the train at speed and wasn't disappointed. It roared past Mason Road at 2:35, with two Secret Service agents on the back platform.

Sidney also was the first stop. There, 17,000 people turned out— "That's not advance work," Hart commented. "That's the whole darn town."[352] Those who planned to view the president had to walk through metal detectors into a sealed-off area. Shopkeepers were advised not to try to take advantage of the view from their second-story windows or roofs. Secret Service men blanketed the area, all wearing firefighters' hats provided by the Sidney Fire Department. That apparently was a trick the Secret Service used to look inconspicuous,

but locals knew Sidney didn't have that many firefighters.

Engineer Eyler missed his spot by about 10 feet and no one bothered to place a stepbox under the *Magellan's* bottom step even though two police sharpshooters wearing bulletproof vests were crouched at the rear wheels. Reagan had to make a long hop down and walk a few steps back to the walkway.

The president waved to four little girls wearing frilly gowns and carrying parasols. They stood in front of an old-fashioned mural freshly painted on a cinder block wall; Reagan crossed the track and initialed it. White House aides, thoroughly enjoying themselves, crossed over too, and had their pictures taken. Boy Scouts and schoolgirls lined a fence nearby, waving small flags. Christie Knowles, 7, of Lima stood on an empty barrel for a better view, raising her Cabbage Patch Doll, Edie, so it could see, too. An Albion, Ind., couple said they had driven in from out of state "for the fun of seeing a president."[33]

"We are on a train bound for

President Reagan addresses the crowd at Ottawa, Ohio, from the rear platform of The Heartland Special *Oct. 12, 1984.*

glory," the president told the crowd, "to demonstrate that our government is once again on the right track and our national renewal is not going to be derailed."[301]

He invoked the memory of Truman's trip of 36 years and one day before; the crowd loved it. Democratic presidential nominee Walter Mondale later fumed that Reagan was "grave-robbing"[389ak] by invoking the name, but nobody paid any attention to him.

Lloyd D. Lewis, Chessie's media spokesman who busily distributed press kits to the throngs of nationally known reporters on board, recalled that Reagan's Sidney speech was almost word for word what he said at all of the trip's other whistlestops.

Trostel called it a day at Sidney.

"We observed the USMC helicopter at the Sidney airport on the way north and while President Reagan was delivering his address [there]," he wrote. "As we started back home on I-75, we passed the presidential limos going north with a three-car patrol escort."[410]

Trostel and his friends drove the back roads closer to home and ran into about 25 federal security agents sitting along the tracks waiting to be bused back to Wright Patterson.

"I stopped and struck up a conversation. Their sidearms were plainly visible and the box lunches were being eaten. They didn't have any water so I offered my water jug. Boy, there was an instant lineup and the conversation loosened up. One fellow said he was from Miami, Fla., and had never seen the presidential private car and just learned that it was within a few minutes' drive of his home. He said he intended to go see it when he got back."[410]

The agents gave them several bags of snacks in appreciation for the water just as the bus approached to take them away.

Trostel walked the tracks later and noticed that the guards even picked up all their security post numbers. The only sign of anything out of the ordinary were the wooden switch blocks lying in a ditch.

Reagan spent most of the day on the *Magellan's* platform. But the venerable old car's water system wasn't working, so he had to make a few visits to car 7, placed just ahead of it. The *Magellan's* air conditioning was operational at first, but soon quit. One source said Chessie had wanted to refuse use of the car, but the Secret Service, impressed with its armor plating, insisted.

"I saw him walk down the hall once, going to the bathroom," Scott said. "And he used a telephone to talk to some astronauts in space."[335] Reagan conversed with Katherine Sullivan, riding 147 miles above the train aboard the space shuttle *Challenger,* just after she became the first American woman to walk in space.

The chef was struck by Reagan's charisma.

"It was a great honor, regardless of politics, to be with the No. 1 man in the world. For his age, he was neatly built, very spry, with a fast, peppy walk and a nice smile. He looked like a president."[335]

At Lima, Reagan climbed onto another makeshift platform for his speech. On a nearby siding sat a Chessie boxcar providing cover for the Secret Service. Draped in red, white and blue, it appeared to be part of the campaign hoopla, but periodically an agent would pop out and scan the crowd.

By the time the special arrived at Ottawa at 6:20, it was 45 minutes late. Nearly 10,000 people, many of them just getting off work, heard the president speak. Some onlookers hopped a security rope and stood in the center of the track, but all they wanted was a better view.

In the crowd at Deshler was 29-year-old Vicki Cole Gray of Findlay, Ohio, with her daughter in her arms. In 1968, it was Vicki Cole who, at 13, had raised her plea aloft in that town for Richard Nixon to "Bring Us Together Again."[301]

Don Knipp, working his regular shift in the venerable two-story dispatcher's tower across the tracks, had the best seat in the house. He brought his camera to work the day before, then backed out when he had his chance. "I'll have Secret Service agents all over me," he fumed.[33]

It was dark by the time the *Heartland Special* arrived at Perrysburg. As Reagan finished his speech, fireworks boomed overhead. A throng of 30,000 waved flashlights, green fluorescent tubing and torches. As Reagan turned toward the local high school band, it began to play "God Bless America" and the crowd, without any prompting, began to sing. Inside the train, Barron's spine tingled.

"It was hard to describe. I felt proud to be there. There was nothing any of us wouldn't do to make his trip a success."[352]

Not everyone was happy. The authorities had closed two main streets leading into town, irking Perrysburg High School students who feared the detour would make them late to Friday's 7:30 p.m. football game across the river with rival Maumee High. "This is the biggest game of the year," moaned 17-year-old senior LeAnn Witzler.[33]

At this point, Reagan disembarked, shaking hands with several Chessie officers. Stender gave him a braided engineer's hat and Hart presented him with some jelly beans, the favorite presidential snack. "When he saw that, he hesitated long enough for the White House photographer to snap a picture," Hart recalled. "He had a grin on his face from ear to ear."[352]

Bedroom A in car 7 had been reserved for Reagan's overnight use, but he headed back to Washington. "I was on the deck and he waved at me," Scott beamed. "I wanted to take a flash picture, but was afraid I'd be shot."[335]

Scott was taken aback by the beautiful White House china. "The plates were white, with the presidential seal in the center. There was a blue band with a small seal near the edge, and another gold band outside of that. When we were finished with them, they loaded them back into a steel casing. I asked if I could keep one out, but they said 'No.' "[335]

Scott was given some precious mementos, though: a gold tie clip with presidential seal and signature; napkins with the seal; a white book of matches with the seal and Reagan's name on the front and an embossed White House on the back; and even a white pack of presidential cigarettes (which will never be opened, he said), with the seal on front and a flag on the back. Later, he was presented a certificate showing he was on board.

JOHN B. CORNS, CHESSIE SYSTEM

A Secret Service man keeps his eyes on the crowd as Ronald Reagan speaks to the people at Ottawa, Ohio, Oct. 12, 1984.

Late that night, the train dead-headed back to Dayton, arriving at 5 a.m. on Saturday the 13th. On the way back, Chessie people relaxed and reminisced. "I was still high," Hart said. "For a seven-hour train ride, Mr. Reagan looked great. He trotted up to platforms all day, and at the last stop he didn't look tired at all. I was more tired than he was."[352]

President Reagan's train arrives in Deshler, Ohio, Oct. 12, 1984.

Ronald Reagan greets the crowd at Deshler, Ohio, Oct. 12, 1984.

"We spotted [the] platter of white chicken cubes, one of Reagan's favorites," Chessie P.R. chief Milton B. Dolinger recalled. "When he left the train, we polished them off."[114]

Dolinger also noted that case upon case of Chessie merchandise—ornaments, badges and engineer hats—delivered to the train had been confiscated by Secret Service agents. "For weeks afterward, anywhere in the world, Secret Service agents could be seen wearing Chessie hats," he chuckled.

Everyone was complimentary. "I never heard one complaint," Stender said. "It was Chessie teamwork at its best."[352] Reagan himself called Sabin and reminisced about his post-World War II train experiences.

"For a number of years after the war," the president wrote to the author, "all my travel was by train and frankly I enjoyed it that way. When the opportunity came … to do an old-fashioned whistlestop, I was delighted. I enjoyed that ride through Ohio and have nothing but happy memories of it."[316]

Washington Post writer David Hoffman compared the train favorably with campaigning by air. "Most of the time we fly on an airplane, get off, are bused to a speech site, hear the (candidate) speak, file the story, get back on the bus, then get back on the plane and go to the next site. You repeat that a hundred times."[338]

But Hoffman was under no delusion that presidents would return to the rails in any significant way. "I don't think anybody lost sight of why they were there. Nobody got so wrapped up in it that they thought it was 1948."

ABC newsman Sam Donaldson certainly enjoyed himself.

"The whistlestop train hasn't been effective politically in a campaign in decades," he commented, "but it's colorful, and in this age of television, that's important. In any age, it's a lot of fun."[301]

George Bush

The triumphant Democratic nominee in 1988, Massachusetts Gov. Michael S. Dukakis, rode on three Amtrak campaign trains:

- A five-car *Presidential Special Unlimited* on Conrail from Pittsburgh to Altoona, Pa., and return on Sunday, April 24, 1988.
- A nine-car consist from Belleville, Ill., to Walnut Ridge, Ark., on Friday, Aug. 19, 1988. The trip was to continue to San Antonio, Texas, the next day, but was canceled by the Democratic National Committee for "logistical reasons."[13] It was routed from Belleville to St. Louis on the Norfolk Southern and on to Walnut Ridge via Union Pacific. During a stop at Bismarck, Mo., Dukakis departed from his prepared remarks to compliment Amtrak on the operation of its train and the railroad industry in general.
- An eight-car special on Southern Pacific's San Joaquin Route from Bakersfield to Stockton, Calif., on Sunday, Oct. 30, using all Superliner equipment except for the candidate's private car, *Sunset* (SP 150).

Vice President George Bush, Dukakis' GOP foe, never set foot near a train during the '88 campaign. Amtrak explored a couple of possibilities—from Washington and Baltimore to Harrisburg and Harrisburg to Philadelphia and Washington—but they were never carried out. Bruce Heard, Amtrak's senior director special projects, wrote to his friend Ed Mead that a steam locomotive should not be used "as that would occupy more attention than the candidate."[13]

Nevertheless, Bush won. And in a sign of the times, the president took delivery in 1990 of a new *Air Force One*—a wide-bodied Boeing 747, further restricting the number of airports where he could land, and increasingly isolating him from the people. As far as most Americans were concerned, the name *Magellan* referred not to a famous explorer or a fancy railroad car, but to the spacecraft launched in April of that year to map the surface of Venus. So it was a surprise that Bush's 1992 race reversed the trend momentarily.

His vice president, Dan Quayle, launched the race with a 76-mile, one-day whistlestopper on Tuesday, Aug. 25, via the Norfolk Southern from Charlotte to High Point, N.C., with stops at Salisbury and Lexington. The two-car train featured a sleeper/dome owned by furniture maker Jerome Bollick of Conover, N.C., and the private car *Doris*. The latter car, built in March 1917 for tobacco magnate James B. Duke and named for his daughter, was borrowed from the North Carolina State Transportation Museum at Spencer, N.C.

Viewing the day with mixed emotions was Fred Corriher, president of the North Carolina Transportation History Corp., whose lot it fell to accompany the *Doris*. Corriher was a former Democratic Party chairman of his state's 8th Congressional District, and he viewed the outing as strictly business.

"The vice president is paying full price," he told the *Salisbury Post*. "It's a charter, not a gift."[333a] Corriher, tapped to make sure nothing happened to the car and that everything worked all right, rode it from Spencer to Charlotte the night before and spent the night on it. Action picked up quickly early Tuesday morning.

"The Secret Service came on board and looked through every drawer and cabinet," Corriher told the

WAYNE HINSHAW, *THE SALISBURY POST*

Vice President Dan Quayle, at left on the rear platform of the private car Doris, *greets the folks at Salisbury, N.C., Aug. 25, 1992.*

Post. "They had people looking underneath the car, and they brought a dog on that sniffed through everything. All he found was a pair of dirty socks under my bed."[333b]

When Quayle entered, Corriher was one of the few people already on board. "I welcomed him … and asked him to sign our guest book," Corriher recalled. Then—"I made myself invisible … and I had to bite my tongue quite a bit during the day."[333b]

The Secret Service gave Corriher a pin that gave him free run of the car, but he holed up in one of the bedrooms most of the day.

"Quayle spent a lot of time with his speechwriters in the room that I slept in the night before," Corriher explained. "He and [Lt. Gov.] Jim Gardner spent a lot of time together, and [8th District congressional candidate] Coy Privette was along. I thought there would be a lot of politicians going back and forth, but about the only people on the car were the vice president and lieutenant governor and their staff."[333b]

A big shoulder of barbecue was brought aboard at Lexington and, of course, examined by the Secret Service. "Everybody jumped on that pork shoulder and ate quite a bit of it," Corriher told the *Post.* "Later, when I was cleaning up the car, there was a fair amount of pork left. I brought it home, and so my family ate some vice presidential leftovers. I hate to tell you, but we all got heartburn!"[333b]

Even though Corriher saw his guest often during the day, the initial greetings were the only words spoken between them until Quayle disembarked at High Point. "I asked him how he enjoyed it, and he said, 'Great'."[333b]

Quayle's boss took to the rails in a big way as he mounted an unsuccessful effort to overcome his sagging popularity. Bush rode campaign trains for five days in six states—more than

any other POTUS candidate since Barry Goldwater in 1964 and more than any other incumbent president since Harry Truman.

CSX Transportation was selected to operate the first Bush trains, Sept. 26-27, 1992, from Columbus, Ohio, to Grand Blanc, Mich. Equipment belonging to several owners was assembled in Huntington, W.Va.

Chosen for Bush's use was CSX office car *Baltimore,* built as Seaboard Air Line No. 1 in 1924, the year the president was born. The campaign staff had considered using the *Ferdinand Magellan,* as Reagan did in 1984. It's generally believed that option was ruled out when Hurricane Andrew tore through the Gold Coast Railroad's Miami museum on Aug. 24, collapsing an aluminum and steel shed on top of the *Magellan* and several other treasures. The truth is that Bush's campaign people checked with Gold Coast earlier in the summer. They found that the car was due for its 40-year inspection, and the costs and time necessary for repairs prevented its use.

Motive power was assigned from CSX's newest acquisitions, month-old General Electric safety-cab CW40-8 units 7812 and 7810. The former received an appropriate patriotic blue-and-yellow paint scheme and a new number—1992—at the company's Waycross, Ga., shop. The unit sported new black-and-white number boards, and a large "1992" emblazoned on its yellow nose. The blue sides were garnished with painted American flags and trimmed with two horizontal thin white stripes bordering 29 white stars. On the sides of the cab was lettered in white script, "Presidential Whistle Stop Tour 1992," and along the top of the hood's sides, in larger letters, *The Spirit of America!* Just below the cab windows were four silver bolts to hold the presidential seal once Bush was on board; the railroad's reporting marks

appeared only on the rear.

When the POTUS special pulled out of the Huntington W.Va, shop on Friday the 25th for the deadhead move to Columbus, it paused at the division headquarters building for fueling and watering of the coaches, drawing a considerable crowd. Several noticed that the 1992 carried a cryptic greeting on its right rear flank matching the flowing script on the rest of the unit: "With regards for President Bush, James L. Holly." It turned out that the salutation was a practical joke directed at the campaign official overseeing the event, but the stunt backfired because the man's name was Hooley, not Holly. When he saw it just before departure, he had his name painted out.

Union Pacific diner *Overland's* roof had been adorned the day before with four huge white dishes resembling giant L'eggs hosiery eggs, drastically limiting where the car could go but keeping the president in touch with satellite communications. Government technicians hit a snag with UP officers when they wanted to drill holes in the *Overland's* roof, but after considerable talk the matter was resolved when the existing cap strip was unbolted and replaced. A long, curved whip antenna adorned the adjoining CSX conference car *Indiana,* which was hard-wired to the *Overland* for the duration.

Private car *Selma,* UP Corp. Chairman Drew Lewis' car, had been fitted with speakers identical to the *Baltimore's* as a presidential backup. The *Baltimore* had received armor plating over its brass railing and similar plating and rocket-resistant window glass in its observation room. It would receive its bunting and presidential seal the next morning. CSX private car *Washington,* which, as C&O car 7, was Reagan's backup car, was the designated crew rider (perhaps the finest ever operated), isolated

President George Bush's Spirit of America *special prepares to deadhead from Huntington, W.Va., to Columbus, Ohio.*

from the rest of the train by CSX power car *Kentucky* and pointed backward to serve as a Bush backup car in case an emergency forced the chase train to couple to POTUS and pull it in reverse.

The special left Huntington at 12:10 p.m., pausing briefly at Russell, Ky., for a crew change while workmen mounted a heavy 3- by 5-foot American flag on the left side of the 1992's cab. The day's only difficulty delayed the combined pilot/chase deadhead run: a smoking brake on RF&P baggage car 28 forced a quick stop at NJ Cabin just before the train crossed from Kentucky into Ohio. The special arrived in Columbus' Parsons Yard at 4:45 p.m.

The route approved for Saturday included Conrail's Indianapolis Division—Western Branch to Darby,

The presidential seal has been affixed to CSX Transportation's office car Baltimore *and all is in readiness for George and Barbara Bush's arrival in Columbus, Ohio.*

311

George Bush waves off the right side of the Baltimore's *rear platform to the folks in Marysville, Ohio, Sept. 26, 1992.*

Scottslawn Secondary to Ridgeway, Toledo branch to Toledo's Stanley Yard—and CSX's Detroit Division—Toledo Terminal and Saginaw subdivisions—to Plymouth, Mich. Sunday's trek—approved just three days before the trip—continued northward to Grand Blanc (suburban Flint) on the Saginaw line.

On Friday morning, the president began two days of ingratiating himself to the heavily Republican precincts of northwestern Ohio and southeastern Michigan—and the railroaders therein—on his class-act whistlestopper. The presidential seals had been applied, left and right, and the American flag moved to the right side of the 1992's cab to make room for a presidential flag of identical size on the left. Rumor had it that three of the POTUS pennants—each stitched with gold thread—were made for this trip at a cost of more than $6,000 each, but the campaign countered that while such flags existed, cheaper and reusable nylon boat flags were used.

The glistening 19-car POTUS special—designated as No. 602—was resplendent in the early autumn sun on a Conrail track adjacent to CSX's old Mound Street Yard. The coaches offered their own variety of autumn splendor with UP's Armour yellow and the blue variations of CSX and American European Express equipment. Up front, the CW40-8's burbled impatiently on Conrail's Scioto River bridge—manned by an engineer, road foreman and two Secret Service agents—as the last of the press representatives, many equipped with laptop computers and cellular telephones, boarded their coaches.

Just ahead was the pilot train—No. 601—and, ahead of it, two high-rail vehicles. Behind POTUS was the chase train, No. 603, and, last but not least, CSXT cabooses 16632, 16624 and 904051 were on hold in the yard as backups. An extra crew would follow in an automobile lest a crew member fall ill.

The railroads spent $10,000 to landscape an open area between Conrail and CSX tracks, and while the area looked nicer, the freshly turned, black cinder-based gook readily affixed itself to the shoe soles of press representatives who unwittingly tracked it onto freshly vacuumed carpeting on CSX press lounge *Tennessee*—much to the consternation of its attendant.

Then the politicking started, being piped through the train so everyone could hear without leaving their comfortable seats.

"You know, my granddad knew how America was blessed, and he lived here in Columbus," Bush crowed after he and wife, Barbara, boarded the *Baltimore* for their 233-mile ride in full view of a flag-waving crowd and high school bands. "His company, Buckeye Steel, made couplings for the railroads."[62]

The transportation puns started

The presidential seal and presidential flag mounted on CSX Transportation's diesel 1992 (7812 in disguise) let everyone know this is no common, ordinary train. Eighteen cars back, George Bush addresses a crowd in Marysville, Ohio, Sept. 26, 1992.

immediately and kept coming, all directed at Bush's opponent, Democratic Arkansas Gov. Bill Clinton and his wife, Hillary, who did most of their campaigning by bus. "Another candidate for president has been tearing down the United States of America, running the country down," Bush declared. "Maybe he's inhaling too many of those bus fumes! Well, let's get that bus off the side of the road, because on this train trip we're going to blow the whistle on Governor Clinton. I am tired of his lousy record in Arkansas."[62]

Departure was at 10:25 a.m., 10 minutes late. As the train rolled slowly across the Scioto River, crossed CSX's route to Toledo and Conrail's Cincinnati line, and gathered speed beyond Scioto Tower, rail enthusiasts fanned out to find good photo spots—a problem in light of the awesome security.

The boarding area had been roped off for blocks around; powerful searchlights had held the trains in their gaze all night. At departure time, everyone approaching—to ride or to behold—had to pass through a magnetometer, placing their cameras and other metallic objects on a table for closer inspection.

At every road crossing, cruisers or fire trucks with flashing lights blocked traffic until the trains had cleared, with yellow tape holding the crowds at bay. Overpasses were emptied and patrolled. Vehicles on parallel roads were chased away, lest any be carrying a car bomb.

Security helicopters constantly circled overhead, and one of them chased away a small aircraft that had strayed into Bush's air space. The Secret Service had wanted to place a helicopter on a flat car on the pilot train in case of emergency, but clearances were too tight. Security men in the cab of the pilot train were in constant touch with officers on the ground, and could dispatch them to any trouble spot ahead of POTUS in minutes. (They could also advise the president's train about the size and location of crowds that would merit a slowdown.)

Back on the *Selma*, Huntington Division Assistant Superintendent of Operations Wayne Mason wandered into a bedroom and stopped short of a Secret Service SWAT team with bloused trousers and combat boots. Draped across an exercise bike was a machine gun.

Other rail movements were

The Bushes wave to well-wishers along the Conrail right of way in northwestern Ohio on a sunny Sept. 26, 1992.

embargoed four hours ahead of the specials, both on the track ahead and in the nearest blocks of intersecting foreign roads. Facing point switches were spiked; derails were installed on intersecting tracks. No adjacent moves were permitted and those tracks were cleared wherever possible. Cars carrying hazardous materials were kept at a distance. Every railroad building, signal, signal box, battery box and electric lock was inspected and secured with numbered fluorescent orange seals to show they had been checked (at one location a signal problem required a box to be opened, a procedure that was closely monitored on the railroad radio).

Pacing photographers grumbled that it was next to impossible to take pictures, but there were two notable exceptions.

Rail photographers David Goodheart of Chicago and Victor Hand of Washington, D.C., approached a grade crossing near Kileyville and found five sheriffs, a junior high school band and a crowd of onlookers. "We asked a sheriff if we could step forward of the grade crossing so we could get a good picture of the train without the people and a signal box in view," Goodheart recalled. "He looked at my large video camera and our other camera equipment and asked where we were from. [Hand] quickly answered that he was from 'D.C.,' which he was, and the sheriff said we could go out in front of the crowd if we wouldn't get close to the tracks. I think he thought we were D.C. press."[150]

Goodheart and Hand thus had a ringside seat for the whole procession. First, Goodheart said, was a helicopter 30 minutes ahead with some kind of roving eye—checking for hidden bombs maybe, or buried devices under freshly turned earth. Then, 10 minutes later, the first high-rail vehicle followed, occupied by four men in suits. Then, maybe 500 yards behind, the second high-railer. Another 10 minutes passed, and a second helicopter came into view, circling and swinging back and forth, with men peering out its open doors with binoculars.

Goodheart noticed the change in nomenclature during radio transmissions. Yesterday's deadheading train was called Extra 1992, while today the pilot train was No. 601, Bush's train

George and Barbara Bush enjoy the view as they leave Marysville, Ohio, Sept. 26, 1992. Perhaps they are searching for the cemetery where Mrs. Bush's grandparents are buried.

It looks as if the whole town of Holly, Mich., has turned out to greet George and Barbara Bush on Sept. 27, 1992.

No. 602 or simply "POTUS," and the chase train No. 603.

Five minutes later, the pilot train eased past with several well-dressed men eyeballing the crowd from CSX theater car 318. A sign in the bottom of the huge rear window said, "President on next train."[150]

Another five minutes and Bush's train approached. The crowd clapped and waved for its entire length, since they didn't know where Bush was. Finally, the Bushes were spotted on the rear platform, leaning out to look forward and wave at the approaching crowd. Standing behind them in the partially opened door were two Secret Service types. It turned out that the back of the train was a favorite spot for the president—and for television reporters, too. Most of the press (with red I.D. tags) weren't allowed in the rear seven cars, but the TV people (with green tags) were. And they enjoyed it.

A few more minutes passed and the chase train showed up. The parade was over. Goodheart and Hand departed as fast as they could in the traffic to find a new photo location.

CSX Transportation's C.C. McClain prepares to run President Bush's train out of Plymouth, Mich., Sept. 27, 1992.

The first whistlestop of the day was at 11:30 at Marysville. In what proved to be a pattern for both days, the press disembarked from their forward cars and followed a freshly graded and graveled pathway—at some towns they would walk on a freshly poured asphalt lane. The path was roped off with police tape and guarded by agents with explosives-sniffing German shepherds—and led to risers behind the *Baltimore*. Unknown to the riders, one of the Secret Service helicopters had touched down moments before the train's arrival to check out the precise spot upon which Bush's car would rest.

By the time most newsmen had reached their perch, the chase train had closed in, keeping a respectable distance and shutting down its locomotive so the politicians could be heard. A local functionary had finished firing up the crowd and had introduced Ohio Gov. George Voinovich and his wife, Janet. Next was an exception to the pattern—Voinovich introduced first lady Barbara Bush, who offered remarks of her own because her mother was born and reared in Marysville. Indeed, this stop was rumored to be the reason why the route was changed from CSX to Conrail at the last minute.

Then Bush, smiling and waving, emerged with a few local comments to convince the crowd he knew where he was. "May I salute the Monarchs, the Wildcats and the Panthers," he said of the three Union County high schools, and after wild applause, "I couldn't help but notice the sign down the street—on McCullough's Hardware. It says, 'All I want for Christmas is a new Congress.' Not a bad idea. Let's get this country moving forward."[62] More applause. Then he rattled off his agenda—making his pitch for "family values"[62] and railing against Clinton's economic, taxation and environmental policies. All, of course, interspersed with cheers: "Clean the House!—Four more years!—Hit him again!"[452] Newsmen snapped their shutters, then made for a bank of phones behind the stands to file their stories. Once finished, the president ducked inside while the correspondents retraced their steps to their cars. As the train eased away at 12:25, the Bushes returned to the rear platform—which Mrs. Bush called in her memoir "the caboose"—to wave. Minutes after departure, White House Press Office staffers strolled through the train, handing out copies of the president's remarks. Following close behind was Gary Wright of the White House Transportation Office, checking the names of each passenger to ensure all on the train belonged there.

A half-hour up the line, Barbara Bush called the *Marysville Journal-Tribune* from the train to express her pleasure with the welcome and to talk over old times. She correctly observed that the train passed the cemetery where her grandparents are buried.

Crowds often gathered to wave and cheer, holding up flags or signs of various political persuasions. Supporters toted gems such as "Hillary wears combat boots," "Abortion is not a family value" or "Thanks for stopping Saddam"[452]—a reference to the Iraqi leader who had invaded Kuwait and precipitated the 1991 Persian Gulf War. A dairy farmer affixed a greeting to his tractor that said, "I'm pulling for you."[109] The Clinton crowd was there too, with jabs such as "Four more months," "Clinton and broccoli, not Bush" (the president's dislike of the vegetable was well known), "Get off your caboose and debate" or "Make an appointment with Kevorkian"[452] (the doctor who was helping terminally ill people die). Occasionally, POTUS slowed down before passing schools or shopping malls while authorities kept the throngs at a safe distance.

Goodheart and Hand, racing north on a highway, soon found themselves sandwiched in between eight Ohio Highway Patrol cruisers—and realized the authorities were leapfrogging ahead to set up new positions. At the crossing they chose for their second shot, the "Washington, D.C." answer worked again, and they walked down the track away from the crowd. This time, a helicopter circled them several times, no doubt wondering how they had gotten there.

The special paused at Arlington from 2:01 to 3:10 so the Bushes could visit a picnic in a ball field to celebrate the town's centennial.

Goodheart and Hand found security in Hancock County tighter. Vehicles—and people—were kept at least 75 feet from the tracks. No doubt Bush would not have wanted that—close contact was the name of the whistlestop game. Indeed, at one crossing where the crowd was closer, Goodheart saw the president wave to one man who turned to his friends

and declared, "Well, he's got my vote!"[150]

An "unscheduled" stop followed at Findlay from 3:30 to 3:45, where the Bushes greeted the crowd and got off to shake a few hands. Goodheart was close by; he and his friend had befriended a bored policeman who seemed to appreciate the company. When the pilot train went by that time, a Secret Service agent was sitting on the steps outside the cab. Soon, someone on the policeman's radio reminded the officers to watch the people, not the train.

At Bowling Green—where POTUS stopped from 4:55 to 5:35—rain had chased away the sun but failed to dampen anyone's enthusiasm. Goodheart and Hand had scouted ahead and found an open field where the pilot train was waiting. The agent who had been sitting outside the cab came out three times to look them over with binoculars. "I'm not sure," Goodheart said, "but I think he actually cracked a smile when he saw me at one of the photo locations on Sunday."[150]

Bush and his gubernatorial host frequently invoked the name of a Democrat—Harry Truman—as if the '92 train was riding on the blocks of Truman's come-from-behind marathon 1948 journey that saved the day for him. (CSX's press kit even included copies of Walter Fitzmaurice's epic on Truman's travels that appeared in the March 1949 issue of *Trains* magazine). The comparison—and the appropriation of some of Truman's phrases—aroused the public ire of Margaret Truman Daniel, the feisty Missourian's daughter, who wrote in *The Washington Post* that her dad would have been "flabbergasted" to learn he was the role model for Bush's campaign. "Personally," she wrote, "I have always found President Bush to be a friendly, pleasant man, invariably courteous to me. I never suspected

that behind this Ivy League facade there was a political plagiarist. ... The Republicans are just lucky that [Dad's] no longer around to shoot back."[452]

By midafternoon, when it was apparent that the operation was proceeding without a hitch, personnel began to relax. A young Secret Service agent, conspicuous by his communications earpiece and rectangular lapel pin, was asked if the number of government people involved was classified. "Certainly is," he replied with a stone face. Then he smiled, shrugged his shoulders and added, "Besides, I don't know." His colleague piped in with, "Let's say there's one too many. Can I go now?"[452]

Another agent, engaged by a reporter in a discussion of the pressures on a president, sighed. "It has to be the most stressful job in the world. If Clinton gets it, in four years they'll be yelling at him, too. I'm glad it's not me."[452]

Leaving Bowling Green, two agents shared a bargain pizza that a reporter had snapped up on the ground for $1, sat down in the press coach beside him and went to sleep.

Chef Ted Kelly, roaming through the train enroute to his assignment in the CSX diner *Greenbrier*, related that earlier he had strolled through the more sensitive cars near Bush and asked an agent timidly if he could walk on. The agent examined the green tag around his neck and replied, "Sir, you can go anywhere on this train you want to."

"How about that?" Kelly, who is black, chuckled. "This is one time I don't have to go to the back of the bus!"[452] Kelly's boss, Senior Chef Amos Robinson, had to plan menus for the VIPs without much notice. "The only thing we knew about President Bush is he doesn't like broccoli," Robinson said. "Other than that, we didn't know much about what the president likes."[454]

There was no cause for concern, however. Kelly whipped up crab cakes that "I think went over really big,"[454] he said, explaining that he did his cooking on the *Greenbrier* and the president's chef took the food back to his boss on the *Baltimore.*

"This guy came and got some," Kelly told the author, "and then came back and got some more. He said the president really went crazy over those crab cakes. I think the whole crew ate them; at the end of the day they were all gone."[452] A highlight of the trip for Kelly was a visit to the *Baltimore,* where he had his picture taken with the Bushes.

Goodheart's favorite security story involved a friend in Ohio who had dinner plans with his wife and friends for 6 p.m. Saturday, but who wanted a picture of the train first. It was determined he would get dressed first, go shoot the train, then meet everyone at the restaurant.

The friend was uncertain about the train's schedule, so he arrived at a bridge over the tracks quite early, Goodheart related. He had left his car about a block away, out of sight, when it started to rain. Even though he was wearing a trenchcoat, he decided to wait under the bridge until he saw a headlight.

While he waited in his dry sanctuary, two policemen and a Secret Service agent showed up. When the pilot train loomed into view, he stepped out from under the bridge and came to the top. The next sounds he heard were the cocking of two shotguns and an order to raise his hands and turn around slowly.

One of the helicopters descended so close that this friend could feel its rotor wash. The Secret Service agent talked into his radio while one of the troopers questioned him—peering intently at the bulge his camera was making in his coat. Eventually, they

DAVID GOODHEART

Wooden blocks spiked between the outside rail and open switch points, as they were along the Conrail and CSX Transportation rights of way in Ohio and Michigan before President Bush's train traveled over them, ensure that a switch cannot be thrown by unauthorized personnel in front of a POTUS train.

let him go—but he missed the chance to snap his photo.

The special transferred from Conrail to CSX at Stanley Yard near Toledo without stopping. The hand-picked CSX crewmembers—engineer C.C. McClain, conductor J.R. Bengston and brakeman E.W. Browne—had boarded at Bowling Green, and their Conrail counterparts—engineer J.B. Adams and conductor T.H. Bartee—would stay on

board to Plymouth.

A White House press advance spokeswoman contended the Bush caravan snubbed Toledo because a stop would have delayed a General Motors parts train rushing to a plant struggling to recover from a strike. But a more cynical—and probably more accurate—source maintained it was because Toledo had been hard hit by the recession and was heavily Democratic. Indeed, the train passed back yards of a neighborhood blighted by crime and hard times, and the few people at trackside were anything but friendly. "Booed in Bowling Green and mooned in Toledo! What else can happen?" an agent fumed as he walked between coaches.[452]

At Plymouth, the POTUS special turned eastward onto the Detroit Subdivision and stopped adjacent to the old passenger station at 8:19 p.m., 49 minutes late. Here, as at every stop the next day, the Bushes were introduced by Michigan Gov. John Engler and his wife, Michelle. After the president's speech and a stunning fireworks display, the first couple left in their limousine for the Marriott Hotel in nearby Livonia. The chase train coupled to the *Baltimore* to drag POTUS back to the wye to turn it and restock it for Sunday.

Here the changes from Truman's day were most apparent; while the 1992 train was a splendid example of what railroads can field when they put their minds to it, it was void of many of the amenities of yesteryear. While the politicians ate well in diners, the only on-board food for the press were box lunches and snacks. Moreover, this train carried coaches, not heavyweight sleepers. It would not roam a vast stretch of track overnight to reach another politically sensitive area, nor would it stay on the road for days or weeks at a time. No one occupied it overnight except a few railroad operating officers, dining car crews and the Secret Service. An early scenario had the Bushes staying on board, but the idea was discarded. The press, campaign aides and most of the railroaders were bused to hotels.

Although Sunday's dawn was soggy, the clouds soon parted. Once again the sun made the train sparkle as the Bushes arrived after attending the early service at St. Andrews Episcopal Church and returning to the Marriott dining room—to the

delight of hotel guests—for breakfast.

CSX accommodatingly spotted the head end of POTUS adjacent to CSX's Detroit Division headquarters building in Livonia, where the Bushes boarded their car, so they could see the train as it pulled by. There was talk of Bush greeting Engineer McClain. But as the cars lumbered by, the president was looking the other way—working the crowd.

The second day of whistlestopping began with departure at 10:35 a.m. Retracing its route to Plymouth, the train once again turned north on the Saginaw Subdivison.

Goodheart and Hand were on the road again, this time pausing for a photo at Novi. A city policeman pulled them over, but after checking Goodheart's story and his driver's license, pointed out some great locations farther up the track. This was the only time they were stopped. At the crossing they selected, they noticed that the officers there—contrary to procedure—turned their backs on the crowd and saluted Bush's train from the first diesel to the rear car.

"This was the worst security we saw," Goodheart said, "but it made a nice picture."[150]

Stops were made at Wixom (11:20-12:10), Milford (12:25-12:35, "unscheduled"), and Holly (1:05-2:45). In the latter town, the Bushes attended a luncheon at the adjacent Holly Hotel and a Veterans of Foreign Wars post offered the press a complimentary buffet lunch. Here security was breached, with the public jamming in against the press platform. Everyone reboarding the train had to be "magged" again. As always, each time a vestibule door was opened, Secret Service agents were on the ground, eyes roving over the terrain. But this time their stares were more piercing.

The tour ended in Grand Blanc,

33 minutes late at 3:18, before the largest crowd noted during the two days—10,000. After a final round of speechmaking, cheering and fireworks, everybody pulled up stakes quickly. The Bushes were whisked to *Air Force One* at Flint's Bishop International Airport; they were back in the White House at 5:30. The press abandoned its story-filing center in a public works building and boarded shuttles to the airport. Workers removed telephones by 7 p.m. The pilot and chase trains once again were combined for a quick sprint back to Plymouth-area hotels, and the POTUS equipment was soon broken up and dispatched to Chicago and Huntington (the communications cars were returned to the Huntington shop and kept under guard) to await word on more possible POTUS moves.

The operation was virtually flawless, the only jolt coming a week later when press representatives received bills for their ride. The White House Travel Office tapped one reporter who traveled both days for $692.81, after he had been assured the trip would cost no more than $370. Probably not as many press as expected rode—the coaches were less than half-full—and the cost was pro-rated to those who did. Even the phone banks thoughtfully provided at each stop proved to be no bargain. Installation charges were included in the bill. Officially, payment for the POTUS special came from the president's re-election campaign fund—but the press covered a big hunk of it. The other trains were billed to the Secret Service, and communications to the White House Communications Agency, so the taxpayers picked up those tabs.

The president seemed to be pleased. He spent a lot of time on the back platform while rolling past scenic farmlands, gripping an overhead grabiron and shouting greetings such as "Good to see you," "Yo, man" and "How you doing there?"[452] Television crews (and ONLY television crews) were permitted to interview him there, much to the chagrin of the print media. Bush referred in his speeches to "this wonderful train," "this magnificent train ride" or "this fantastic journey" and, posing for pictures with railroad officers in the *Baltimore*, opined that it had been "a very enjoyable trip."[452]

He must have meant it. On Tuesday and Wednesday, Oct. 20-21, while Vice President Quayle bused through Ohio, the president duplicated much of his running mate's earlier whistlestop jaunt with a 436-mile Norfolk Southern trip through Georgia, South Carolina and North Carolina. The first day, he covered the territory from Atlanta's Armour Yard to Spartanburg, S.C., continuing the next day to the state fairgrounds at Raleigh, N.C. Makeup of the trains was similar to the Ohio-Michigan movement.

The president seemed to gather energy from the sight of the crowds closing in around his private car. "I can't tell you what this has done for my spirits,"[452] he remarked in Cornelia, Ga. The next day, in Gastonia, N.C., he elaborated. "I love the American people, and this train trip is fantastic. You get outside of that Beltway, you take your case to genuine Americans."[452] He clearly enjoyed rolling on the rails and gazing at small-town America, noting in Thomasville, N.C., a furniture-making town, that he was speaking close to "The World's Largest Chair,"[452] a monstrous armchair atop a concrete pedestal.

Bush and his son Marvin put a Waffle House restaurant in Spartanburg on the map when he stopped there Wednesday morning for a breakfast of waffles, scrambled eggs, bacon and coffee, saying Clinton would turn the White House into a Waffle House if he were elected. He chatted with patrons (one in French), swapped riddles with them and even paid for some of their meals. The Clinton campaign countered two days later by saying the White House was already a Waffle House under Bush, even producing menus featuring "Read My Lips Service" (a reference to Bush's infamous 1988 no-new-taxes pledge that he later broke), "Jobs on the Short Side" and "Pay Raise Souffle."[452]

A fifth-grader struck a blow for freedom of expression when Bush stopped in Salisbury. Ten-year-old Nathan Harrill and the rest of his Knollwood Elementary class were scheduled to watch the train pass, but he elected to stay home when Principal Bill Shive ordered him not to wear his Clinton button to the event. "They're making us hold up Bush stuff," Nathan complained.[452]

Operation of the NS specials was similar to the CSX/Conrail operation. A high-rail vehicle ran about three hours ahead of the specials, "sweeping" the track. The pilot train was designated No. 056, POTUS was No. 042, and the chase train was R56. Security precluded normal crew change points, so the Atlanta-Greenville crew rode to Spartanburg while the Greenville-Spartanburg crew boarded at Cornelia. Likewise, the Spartanburg-Linwood crew rode on to Thomasville, while the Linwood-Raleigh crew boarded at Kannapolis. The advance and following trains changed crews normally at Greenville and Linwood.

The president's staff arranged a final trip for a cold and rainy Oct. 31 via the Wisconsin Central between Burlington and Chippewa Falls, Wis., with stops at Sussex, Oshkosh and Stevens Point. At 279.5 miles and 12 hours, it was the season's longest presidential travel for a single day. Again, consists were similar to the prior moves, but the fact that it was Halloween dictated some changes. The huge satellite dishes atop the *Overland* were disguised to look like jack-o-lanterns, and the Bushes' grandchildren—in costume—tricked-or-treated their way through the cars to the delight of the passengers.

There were visual alterations as well. WC and the campaign committee commissioned a Stevens Point artist to further adorn the *Baltimore* with *The Spirit of America!* in 18-inch-high flowing script matching the 1992's, and to add a row of 80 stars to each of its sides. Another 6-inch *The Spirit of America!* adorned the front of the 1992's cab sides.

Bush tailored his messages to suit the day. Clinton was "trying to scare America," he warned at Burlington. "Under him, every day is going to be Halloween—fright and terror." And at Chippewa Falls, "Governor Taxes and the Ozone Man (a jab at the environmental stance of Clinton running mate Al Gore)—they'll give you a trick and not a treat."[452]

Once again, signs waved by the multitudes were of any and all political persuasions. "Read my lips, no new president," a supporter's said. Opponents signaled "George, you're on the wrong track" and "Happy retirement, George." A small plane somehow managed to circle the train, toting a Halloween banner that charged, "Iran Contra haunts you," a reference to fresh accusations that Bush knew about a secret arms-for-hostages deal worked out with Iran while he was vice president.[452] Bush defended himself against new revelations in this matter all day long.

The *Milwaukee Sentinel* wondered why Bush was staying so long in Wisconsin with so little time left before the election. White House Political Director Ron Kaufman

CSX Transportation's powerful new locomotives rest while George Bush engages the people of Holly, Mich., Sept. 27, 1992.

countered that the train was smarter politically than jetting around the country during the home stretch. The president "can do 30 interviews while he's on [the train] if he wants to," Kaufman declared. "If you're doing 10 states in a day up in an airplane, you lose all that time."[452]

After the gala arrival in Chippewa Falls, the equipment of all three trains was bunched together for return to Stevens Point as a single train. After everyone got off at the depot, it was taken to Track 28 and "locked in"[449] until the government stripped the cars of their special equipment. Then the foreign-line coaches made their long journeys home via Chicago—12 UP and two C&NW cars to C&NW at Proviso, CSX's conference car *Indiana* and the *Baltimore* to connect with a CSX intermodal train out of Brighton Park, and New Georgia office car 300 and St. Louis Car Co. diner *Cuivre River* to Amtrak at 14th Street.

The 1992 departed Stevens Point at 6:30 p.m. Nov. 3 (Election Day) in style—on the point of a DM&IR/WC/CSX taconite ore train bound for Birmingham, Ala. This was no accident—WC and CSX had just agreed on this run-through arrangement and WC President Ed Burkhardt wanted to commemorate it in grand fashion. Back home, the 1992 was often sighted in freight service—with its original number restored but still decked out in its *Spirit of America!* dress—well into 1996.

Clinton won the election, meaning that Bush's whistlestop strategy didn't work. The grandest display of campaigning by rail in decades didn't do for him what it had done for Truman. Of the six states Bush's trains called on, he carried only North Carolina. And how much the train helped him there cannot be quantified.

"I hope this doesn't mean an end to whistlestopping in favor of bus trips,"[52] lamented Peter A. Briggs, who handled WC's public relations, in a letter to the author. Indeed.

It was also during the '92 campaign that Ross E. Rowland Jr., chairman of the Steam Locomotive Corp. of America in Lebanon, N.J., tried to interest on-again, off-again independent candidate H. Ross Perot in running a 21-state, 40-day tour using a 20-car train pulled by Rowland's ex-Chesapeake & Ohio 4-8-4 Greenbrier-type passenger steamer 614; but nothing ever developed.

Bill Clinton

Arkansas Gov. Bill Clinton, the Democratic contender, rode a train once during the 1992 campaign, taking an Amtrak Metroliner from New York to Philadelphia on Monday, Aug. 10. He and Tennessee Sen. Al Gore Jr., his vice presidential running mate, had appeared on the "CBS This Morning" show earlier and, when Gore left for Connecticut to campaign, Clinton boarded No. 113 at noon for a one-hour, 10-minute trip to an afternoon rally outside Independence Hall. But on all other occasions when Clinton used ground transportation, he and Gore traveled by bus.

As president, Clinton rode a Maryland Area Rail Commuter train on CSX rails from Washington to Baltimore on Monday, April 5, 1993, to throw the opening pitch at the American League season opener and to see the Texas Rangers whip host Baltimore Orioles 7-4. MARC train 902's regular consist was swelled to two locomotives, four coaches and Amtrak private car *Beech Grove* (10001) for the occasion, and its 10:45 a.m. departure was delayed 25 minutes because of Clinton's late arrival. The president spent little time in his private car, however, choosing to walk through the train and shake hands. The train delivered him to B&O's venerable Camden Station, adjacent to Orioles Park, at noon—but the convenience wasn't good enough to hold him. He returned to Washington by helicopter.

First lady Hillary Rodham

SAM P. CALICIOTTI, AMTRAK

Democratic candidate Bill Clinton models the conductor's cap given to him by Amtrak passenger services as he boards a Metroliner in New York City's Pennsylvania Station for a quick jaunt to Philadelphia on Aug. 10, 1992.

Clinton rode Amtrak to Baltimore and Philadelphia two or three times during the spring of 1993 out of necessity. The White House helicopter fleet had been involved in a fatal accident, and the Secret Service was skittish for a time about air transportation.

The week after Christmas 1995, Mrs. Clinton treated her daughter, Chelsea, and her mother, Dorothy Rodham, to a two-day vacation in New York City. The trio rode from Washington to New York on Wednesday, Dec. 27, via Amtrak No. 84, the *New England Express*, and returned the next day on No. 68/189, the *Adirondak*.

1996

As press time neared for this book, the 1996 presidential race had already seen two campaign trains.

On Friday, Dec. 8, 1995, Sen. Robert J. Dole, R-Kan., rode a Guilford Transportation Industries train 34.3 miles on Boston & Maine trackage from Nashua to Concord N.H., to file in that state's primary.

The same day, his wife, Elizabeth, rode her own train 18.4 miles on the New England Southern from Tilton to Concord— a former B&M line.

CLEVELAND & ERIE RAIL ROAD.

TIME CARD

For Special Train, Friday, April 28th, 1865,

CONVEYING REMAINS OF ABRAHAM LINCOLN,

LATE PRESIDENT OF THE UNITED STATES,

AND ESCORT.

STATIONS.	Miles.	Miles.	Pilot Engine.	Cortege Train.	
			LEAVE	LEAVE	
Erie			2.15 A. M.	2.25 A. M.	
Swanville	8¼	8½	**2.42**	**2.52**	Pilot Engine & Cortege Train meets Stock Express No 1.
Fairview	11	2½	**2.49**	**2.59**	Pilot Engine & Cortege Train meets Stock Express No. 2.
Girard	15½	4½	3.05	3.15	
Springfield	20¼	4¾	3.17	3.27	
Conneaut	27¾	7½	**3.39**	**3.48**	Pilot Engine & Cortege Train passes Fast Freight No. 3.
Kingsville	35¼	7½	3.59	4.09	
Ashtabula	41	5¾	4.17	4.27	
Saybrook	45¾	4¾	4.30	4.40	
Geneva	50¼	4½	4.42	4.52	
Unionville	53½	3¼	4.51	5.01	
Madison	55¾	2¼	4.59	5.09	
Perry	61	5¼	5.13	5.23	
Painesville	66½	5½	5.31	5.41	
Mentor	72¾	6¼	5.47	5.57	
Willoughby	77	4¼	5.58	6.08	
Wickliffe	81¼	4¼	6.10	6.20	
Euclid	86	4¾	6.22	6.32	
Cleveland	95½	9½	6.50 A. M.	7.00 A. M.	
			ARRIVE.	ARRIVE.	

This Train and the Pilot Engine will have the POSITIVE RIGHT OF ROAD, and all Trains must be kept entirely out of their way.

Train and Pilot Engine must be run strictly to card time as possible.

Strict carefulness is enjoined upon Agents, Train Men, and all Employes. You must be on duty, and know that every thing is right when Pilot Engine and this Train is due.

Supt's Office C. & E. R. R., Cleveland, April 26, 1865. **H. NOTTINGHAM, Sup't.**

SANFORD & HAYWARD, PRINTERS, CLEVELAND

BILL JERNSTROM/*RAILROAD MAGAZINE*/CARSTENS PUBLICATIONS

This special timetable details the operation of Abraham Lincoln's funeral train and pilot over the Cleveland, Painesville & Ashtabula line from Erie, Pa., to Cleveland, Ohio, April 28, 1865. Curiously, the CP&A is referred to here as the Cleveland & Erie, by which name it was known briefly before the Civil War.

The Last Miles

9

William Henry Harrison

The presidential funeral train tradition began with William Henry Harrison in 1841, when his remains went home to Ohio part of the way by rail. They were placed in Washington's National Burial Grounds for more than two months after his April 4 death. On June 26, they departed Washington on a B&O train for Baltimore, accompanied by a delegation from Cincinnati. "Comparatively few of our citizens witnessed its passage from the railroad depot to the City Hotel," a Baltimore newspaper wrote, "guarded by the Independent Blues, National Guards, Independent Greys. ..." [251]

The special departed on June 28 from the Baltimore & Susquehanna's North Street depot, at Eager Street and the present Guilford Avenue bound for Columbia, Pa., via the B&S, York & Maryland, and Wrightsville, York & Gettysburg railroads.

The presidential party faced the ordeal of traveling by canal boat, rail and cable-wound inclined planes across Pennsylvania to the Ohio River. It went up the Juniata Canal to Hollidaysburg, Pa., in a packet boat, where a funeral train was made up to cross Allegheny Mountain and reach Johnstown on the 36-mile Allegheny Portage Railroad. This operation included slow winching up and down inclined planes, five on one side of the mountain and five on the other.

On an 11-mile stretch near Johnstown, Capt. Robert Lowry stopped the train and inspected the trucks. A wheel under the baggage car carrying the body was found to be badly cracked. This car was at the rear of the train, and since there were no bell ropes, Lowry mounted the top of the car and watched, the fireman keeping him in view to catch any signal he might make. The train arrived at Johnstown without incident, and the casket was placed on the packet boat *John Hancock* and conveyed to Pittsburgh.

John Quincy Adams

The next president whose remains were carried home by train was John Quincy Adams. On Monday, Feb. 21, 1848, Adams collapsed in the House chamber—where he had served with distinction for 17 years after leaving the Executive Mansion—and the wheels of government ground to a halt for more than two days while he lay dying on a sofa in the speaker's office.

After his death on Wednesday, Feb. 23, a congressional committee arranged to move his body by funeral train and steamboat. Flags along the route flew at half-staff when the train left Washington via the Baltimore & Ohio on March 7. Businesses closed and people lined the track with heads bowed as the train passed with its "black-draped car" [40] decorated with heavy cord and tassels. The remains arrived at Baltimore & Ohio's Mount Clare Depot at noon and were displayed in the rotunda of Baltimore's Exchange. The next day, the body was escorted by the Independent Blues to the Philadelphia, Wilmington & Baltimore station at High Street and Canton Avenue (now Fleet Street) where a special train awaited to forward it to Philadelphia.

The route from Philadelphia to Boston is uncertain, but most likely included the Philadelphia & Trenton to Trenton, N.J.; Camden & Amboy to New Brunswick; the New Jersey Railroad and Transportation Co. to Jersey City; steamers to New York City and New Haven, Conn.; the Hartford & New Haven to Springfield, Mass.; the Western Railroad to Worcester; and the Boston & Worcester.

In Boston, a huge crowd met the train and Adams' coffin was placed on a carriage pulled by six black horses trimmed in crepe. The body lay in state for several days in Faneuil Hall, then was taken on the Old Colony line to the new railroad station at Quincy, Mass., for burial in the family tomb.

Zachary Taylor

Zachary Taylor's remains were kept in Washington for several months after his July 9, 1850, death. His funeral train finally departed

Washington on Oct. 25 via B&O. His elegant Baltimore-built funeral coach was pulled along Pratt and Howard streets to Bolton Station on the Northern Central for the trip to Harrisburg, enroute to Pittsburgh and Kentucky.

The journey included a trip across the successive planes of the Portage line; going along for the ride was Old Whitey, the white horse Taylor rode in the Mexican War.

Abraham Lincoln

The marksmanship of John Wilkes Booth at Washington's Ford Theater on Good Friday, April 14, 1865, just days after Lee surrendered to Grant and ended the Civil War, started the final chapter of Abraham Lincoln's connection to the railroads—his funeral train. The nation's jubilation at the impending peace had been cruelly turned to mourning as the nine-car train was assembled in Washington for the roundabout journey back to Springfield, Ill.

The route virtually retraced Lincoln's 1861 itinerary as far as Cleveland except that the previously forbidden Northern Central was used from Baltimore to Harrisburg, thence the Pennsylvania Railroad to Philadelphia. From Cleveland, the dismal entourage traveled the Cleveland, Columbus & Cincinnati to Columbus; Columbus & Indianapolis and Indiana Central to Indianapolis; Lafayette and Indianapolis to Lafayette, Ind.; Louisville, New Albany & Chicago to Michigan City, Ind.; Michigan Central and Illinois Central to Chicago; and Chicago & Alton to Springfield. The trip took from April 21, six days after he died, to May 3. The archives are vague in spots and sometimes contradictory, but the following attempts to piece together Lincoln's long journey home.

Lincoln's body was placed in the East Room of the White House on the 15th, the day he died, where a funeral was conducted on the 19th, then lay in state in the rotunda of the U.S. Capitol until 6 a.m. on the 21st. A procession escorted the casket three blocks to the B&O station at New Jersey Avenue and C Street N.W. The large contingent included Ulysses Grant, the first lieutenant general since George Washington; and the new president, Democrat Andrew Johnson. Mrs. Lincoln was ill and so she and son Tad didn't make the trip. Only those holding tickets for the funeral train were allowed in the depot, except passengers taking the regular 7:30 a.m. train for Baltimore.

No bands, bugles or drums sounded a single note. Behind the station, the special stood ready, steam up. The engine was No. 238, a Thatcher Perkins 4-4-0 built by B&O's Mount Clare Shop force earlier that year. Sister engine 239 was spotted ahead of the funeral train, ready to leave 10 minutes in advance as a pilot. Both locomotives were trimmed in black, brass work shrouded, with the Stars and Stripes bound in sable. Behind the 238 were six passenger cars and a baggage car, all new, similarly festooned. Then came Lincoln's funeral car, followed by a special PW&B coach intended for the family and a military honor guard. The coach normally hauled railroad officials, being nicknamed the "officers' car,"[337] but the president and Mrs. Lincoln had traveled in it several times courtesy of PW&B President Samuel Felton.

Even more magnificent was the funeral car just ahead.

The 42-foot, 6-inch-long hardwood coach, 8 feet 6 inches high and wide, was the first built for the president's use—by the United States government in the U.S. Military Railroad's car shops in Alexandria, Va., six miles from Washington, from December 1863 to May 1864. The USMRR was composed of parts of the Manassas Gap; Alexandria, Louden & Hampshire; and Orange & Alexandria lines, all confiscated by the government for the war's duration. Myron Hawley Lamson, a B&O mechanic, served as assistant foreman on the job.

The car was equipped with a modern heating system and sumptuous fittings of all kinds. It contained three rooms from front to back: a lounge/wash room, Lincoln's quarters, and a conference room—largest of the three. Interior walls were padded with rich, corded crimson silk upholstery halfway to the ceiling. The upper deck, between the transoms, contained panels upon which were painted coats of arms of the 35 states then forming the Union. The woodwork above the doors and windows was painted zinc white with decorations in gold and the national colors. Below the windows was woodwork of natural wood, oak and walnut; curtains were of light green silk. The conference room was furnished with a 7½-foot-long sofa and reclining chairs upholstered in red plush. The sofa could be fashioned into upper and lower berths, a forerunner of Pullman innovations. Smaller sofas and chairs filled the other rooms.

The car featured open platforms and a raised roof with rounded ends. Four trucks were placed underneath to provide a smooth ride, equipped with broad-tread wheels to enable the car to ride on nearly all gauges, but because of the car's weight and the way the trucks were mounted, it rode quite poorly and often jumped the era's stub switches. Axle ends were covered with protectors in the shape of American eagles. The exterior bore large 5- by 2-foot oval metal medallions displaying the U.S. coat of arms. Above them, painted between the windows in small gold letters, were the words "United States."

Lincoln didn't use the car while alive because of charges that it was too pretentious. But one of Lamson's men, James T. Barkley, recalled that there was a time when Lincoln hadn't reached a decision to stay away from it. "Lincoln would visit us two or three times a month during construction," Barkley said. "Sitting on a sawhorse, he would suggest changes." [389a1]

After making one trial trip on the O&A to Warrenton Jct., Va., it sat unused until the assassination. One source stated that Lincoln was finally convinced to go along on another trial trip—on Saturday, April 15, the day he died.

Lamson supervised alterations to the car to carry the remains of Lincoln back to Springfield. The work included installation of a catafalque in the conference room of the car and removal of furniture and railings.

The silver-trimmed coffin was loaded onto the train as engineer Thomas Beckett and fireman C.A. Miller waited on the 238. At 7:50, the family's minister, Phineas D. Gurley, pastor of the New York Avenue Presbyterian Church, paused at the step of the hearse car and offered a prayer. As he spoke, engineer William Galloway eased pilot engine 239 away, and at 8 a.m., Beckett opened his throttle. Lincoln's body was on its way home.

More than 250 persons were authorized to ride the train, including an all-services military honor guard, senators and congressmen, four governors, a special delegation from Illinois and the press. Some went the whole distance, others came and went.

In charge of the funeral car were John McNaughton of the U.S. Military Railroad's mechanical department in Alexandria; Tom Pendel, White House doorkeeper; and Harry Smith, a plainclothes White House policeman. The latter two had intimate knowledge of the president's associates and government officials, making them invaluable in handling visitors. Two other skilled aides were along: Frank T. Sands, undertaker; and Dr. Charles P. Brown, embalmer. They were to see that the casket and corpse stayed in proper condition.

Seven people who had accompanied Lincoln from Springfield in 1861 were aboard. History says son Robert was the only member of the immediate family up to it, and he was hollow-eyed and drawn. He had come just before departure and had taken a seat alongside two friends, presidential secretaries John G. Nicolay and John Hay. (Inexplicably, Robert wrote a letter in 1905 in which even he denied being on the train.) [432] The secretaries, along with Judge David Davis, would ride only to Baltimore, returning to Washington to effect the presidential transition. The body of Robert's and Tad's brother, Willie, who had died in 1862, was on board, having been exhumed from a Georgetown cemetery for relocation in the family plot in Illinois. The boy's

remains rode in the funeral car at the foot of his famous father's bier. The other faithful were Ward Lamon, the only one of the seven who had been with Lincoln over every mile of his inbound trip, even on his secret detour, and Gen. David Hunter.

The sound of the muffled engine bell and cracks of exhaust from the balloon stack caught the attention of an outbound regiment of the 8th U.S. Colored Artillery enjoying a hearty breakfast in a building behind the depot called "Soldier's Rest." [337] The battle-worn veterans jumped into formation at trackside, saluting as the martyred emancipator went by, not a dry eye among them. Regiments surrounding the station snapped to attention and stood at present arms. The massed spectators pressed for a better look at the distinguished guests on the rear platform, including President Johnson. All had removed their hats until the mortuary caravan rolled out of sight.

A vast uniformed assembly from camps around the city met the train upon its arrival at Baltimore's Camden Station at 10 a.m. At the station's entrance stood an impressive catafalque built for the occasion, headed by four matched jet-black horses somberly adorned. The body was taken to the rotunda of the Merchants Exchange, where it remained on display for several hours.

A U.S. Military Railroad engine hauls out the Lincoln funeral car at the line's Alexandria, Va., shop.

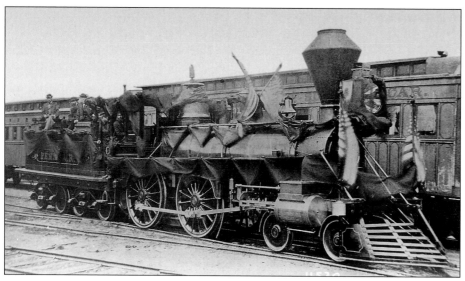

Engineer John E. Miller and friends pose with PRR engine 331 in Harrisburg, Pa., as they wait to haul Lincoln's funeral train from there to Philadelphia on April 22, 1865.

Willie's coffin stayed in the hearse car, under guard, throughout the trip.

(Incidentally, the train's arrival in Baltimore was re-enacted on NBC's *Wide, Wide World* broadcast of Sunday, Feb. 12, 1956. Starring in the shot were B&O's famous *William Mason* steam locomotive and sailors dressed as Union soldiers. The 175th Infantry Regiment of the Maryland National Guard had been asked first to provide a detachment, but Col. Roger Whiteford refused to let his men wear "Yankee uniforms." Forty-eight-star American flags were only partially furled, hoping only 35 stars would show. The three-minute live segment was never seen by those who participated in it.)[23]

While the president's remains were being viewed, the Washington escort was driven to Eutaw House and was served a buffet luncheon courtesy of the city. Later, Lincoln's body was taken to the Northern Central's Bolton Station in the northern section of the city for a 3 p.m. departure.

A pilot engine and one coach, in the charge of Capt. George B. Kaufman, left at 2:50. The car was occupied by Simon Cameron, a director of the Northern Central and a secretary of war under Lincoln, other NC directors and Harrisburg friends. Cameron had been unable to secure accommodation for his large group on the funeral train and provided his own transportation over his own railroad.

Now the funeral train consisted of a baggage car, seven first-class coaches, the funeral car and escort car, the latter two transferred by horse from Camden Station.

The NC conductor was William Henry Harrison Gould, who had remembered well the morning of April 15. "I walked over to the Calvert Street Railway Station (downtown) … about 7 a.m. When I reached the rear entrance … I noticed that all traffic on the road was at a standstill. I asked the gateman, Samuel Goldstein, who evidently was a little excited, why no trains were running."

"Don' you hear the news?" Goldstein exclaimed to Gould in an irrational burst of venom. "Lincoln was kilt last night. And Stanton is kilt, and everybody was kilt, and you done it—git out of here!"[274]

Gould, first scared of and then angry at Goldstein, roamed around the station, noticing that guards had taken it over. Passengers were allowed in, but couldn't leave. Trains didn't resume operation until afternoon. He went home and hung out his flag.

On the morning of the 21st, Gould was first in line on the extra board for a conductor's job and got the word at 12:30 he would take Lincoln's train north. "I was in the funeral car at various times in my line of duty," Gould recalled. "A part of the time the face lid was removed from the coffin, and I had several opportunities of seeing the face of the martyred president. His face was calm and

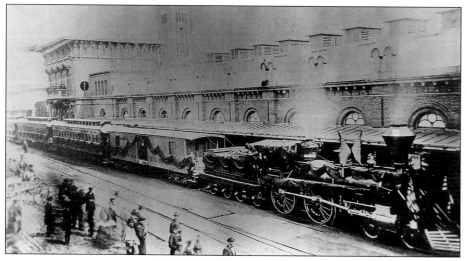

PRR engine 331 has coupled onto Lincoln's funeral train as the cortege prepares to leave Harrisburg, Pa., April 22, 1865.

peaceful. He looked as if he were asleep in pleasant dreams. The body was dressed in black, with white shirt and black tie. I was informed that the suit he had on was the suit he wore at his first inauguration. "None of the train crew were in uniform—in fact, in those days no uniform was worn by passenger train crews. I wore a black suit of clothes and black hat. I wore a plate marked 'conductor.' "[274]

Gould said about 75 men—no women—were on board beside the crew, all of whom wore a special badge that served as their ticket. They moved back and forth through the train, distinguished, sad and solemn. None of the soldiers were in uniform. All the conversation was on Lincoln's greatness and untimely demise.

The only two stops between Baltimore and Harrisburg that cloudy and warm day were at Parkton, Md., and York, Pa., both for water.

"When the train stopped at York, a delegation of six ladies were allowed to enter the funeral car and lay a large wreath on the coffin," Gould said. "It was the most solemn trip I ever took on a train. … There was a fine drizzle of rain; it seemed to me that nature was weeping because of Lincoln's death."[274]

In Harrisburg at 8 p.m., the rain became a downpour. A civic and military display was canceled and the body was taken directly to the hall of the House of Representatives until 10 Saturday morning. The train departed eastward on the PRR at 11, behind PRR engine 331 piloted by John E. Miller.

Miller recalled that schoolchildren had strewn so many flowers over the track that, when crushed, they rendered it so slippery he almost stalled more than once.

Arrival at the PW&B station on Broad Street in Philadelphia was at 4 p.m., whereupon a long procession escorted the casket to Independence Hall. It was guarded by six soldiers, the longest surviving of which was W. Henry Gilbert, who was later honored by President Franklin D. Roosevelt.

Miller recalled that the sidewalks in front of the old hall were littered with hoop-skirts and bustles crushed in the congestion. Here, as at all other stops enroute to Springfield, thousands came out to meet the spectacle. Trainloads of mourners from all points around met the cortege amid lanterns, bonfires, flags and floral arrangements. Stations were draped in black, artillery boomed, bands played, schools were closed. Crowds wept, waved, even fainted as the train passed.

In Philadelphia, a rumor flew about that a keg of powder had been found underneath the plumed vehicle placed at 6th and Chestnut streets to serve as a bier. The rumor was false, but it nearly caused a riot. What was found was a soldier's discarded canteen mug, and it was under the undertaker's carriage, not Lincoln's hearse. Coffee grounds stuck in the bottom were mistaken for powder grains. The assassination was still very much on people's minds.

At 1:17 a.m., the historic assembly room was cleared to permit the undertaker and embalmer to freshen up the body; shuffling feet by the thousands had covered everything with a layer of fine lint. Dr. Brown deftly restored the familiar features to normal appearance, using a fine camel's hair brush and a bit of cosmetic.

On Monday the 24th, the train left from C&A's Kensington Station in Philadelphia at a few minutes after 4 a.m., with Elias Toy as conductor. The coming daylight delineated the train as it now was made up—six bright yellow passenger cars, a yellow baggage car, the deep chocolate-colored hearse carriage and crimson official car.

An unnamed crewman left the following recollection: "I was waiting … for (the train) to start, as it was my duty to accompany it to Newark. I had and have little desire to look upon faces from which the light of life has departed; but suddenly it came upon

Guards attend to their duties as the Lincoln funeral train, appropriately festooned, prepares to leave Harrisburg, Pa., April 22, 1865.

PRR engine 331 pauses at West Philadelphia with Lincoln's funeral train April 22, 1865.

me that I had never seen the great president, and must not let go by this opportunity to behold at least the deserted temple of a lofty soul. To my grief I found it was too late; the police had drawn their line across the path in front of Independence Hall. But my earnest desire prevailed, and I was the last to pass in the window and behold, in a sudden dazzle of lights and flowers, the still features of that face we all now know so well.

"Then I went my way into the night and walked alone northward to the distant station. Soon I heard behind me the wailing music of the funeral dirge. The procession approached—the funeral train moved out beneath the stars. Never shall I forget the groups of weeping men and women at the little towns through which we slowly passed, and the stricken faces of the thousands who, in the cities, stood like mourners at the funeral of a beloved father. Thus, as came the dawn and the full day, through grieving states was borne the

body of the beloved chieftain, while the luminous spirit and example of Lincoln the Leader of the People went forth into all the earth along the pathway of eternal fame."[241]

Upon arrival at Jersey City, the body was ferried—some say on the *New York* and some the *Jersey City*—to New York's Debrosses Street ferry station at 10 a.m., where funeral guns boomed and a procession escorted it to the rotunda of City Hall.

At one point during the crosstown move, a woman leaned out of a tenement window and exclaimed, "Well, is that all that's left of Ould Abe?" A voice from the crowd retorted, "It's more than you'll ever be!" The woman was nonplussed by her sudden celebrity. "Oh, I've nothing against him," she replied. "I never knew him or cared for him, but he died like a saint."[412]

The train left the Hudson River Railroad's Thirtieth Street Station—where the 7th Regiment was lined up as an honor guard—at 4 p.m. the fol-

lowing afternoon, Tuesday the 25th. Only the hearse car and escort car were floated across the Hudson and were added to a seven-car consist for resumption of the westward journey. Ironically, the train was pulled by HR locomotive *Union*, which hauled the president-elect's special four years before, and the *Constitution*, which pulled the inaugural pilot train.

HR's instructions were standard fare for such movements. It had right over everything in both directions, and opposing trains had to go into sidings at least 10 minutes before the special was due. The pilot train was to operate 10 minutes ahead of the special with identical rights. Opposing trains stayed put until the special had passed. It was told to slow down through all towns and villages. The departure of that afternoon's train 10 from Thirtieth Street Station was delayed because of the special.

By now, towns had had more time to prepare their demonstrations and crowds swelled into the thousands.

They had read news accounts of earlier stops and wanted to improve and outdo what had gone before. Elaborate floral archways began to appear over or alongside the tracks. Tarrytown, N.Y., repainted the side of a building to represent the American flag. Scores of volunteers served elaborate fare at meal stops.

The train arrived at East Albany at 10:55 p.m., where the casket was moved by ferry to the state capitol in Albany. The funeral and honor guard cars were uncoupled from the train and moved to the New York Central depot in Albany via Troy and the Hudson bridge, the same detour Lincoln had used in 1861.

The train continued west at 4 p.m. Wednesday the 26th behind one of the largest engines on the NYC, the *Dean Richmond*. Engineer George W. Wrightson decorated his steamer with flags and black bunting, then wired a framed picture of Lincoln to the smokebox and draped flags around it. He lashed its bell so it couldn't move and fastened a wire to the clapper. "In this way I tolled the bell all through the cities and many newspapers commented on it," he recalled. "I counted eight and then pulled the wire, then eight and pulled

again. We traveled very slowly and there were great crowds all along the way. There were guards at all cross roads and there was great fear expressed that the train might be ditched."[452]

At each switch, Wrightson peered cautiously from his cab. Each one had been spiked to prevent tampering until the train had passed, even though the cortege had been given right of way over all other traffic.

"When we reached the depot at Syracuse, the train was greeted by the most impressive demonstration I have ever seen," Wrightson recalled. "The train shed was covered with the national colors and black festoons. An immense, silent throng had waited hours to glimpse the cortege."[452]

At the sight of Lincoln's portrait, the crowds drew back. Some waved small flags. Others wept openly. Once the train was by, they stepped to the track and watched it fade into the distance.

Dawn broke at 5 a.m., and Batavia, N.Y., presented former President Millard Fillmore. He and other western New York notables boarded here as an escort to Buffalo. Engines and crews were changed during the 10-minute stop. The out-

bound engine and crew also pulled the inaugural train four years before. Arrival in Buffalo was at 7, and breakfast was taken at Bloomer's Dining Saloon. The casket was taken to St. James Hall until the journey continued at 10:10 that night.

"The intensity of feeling seemed, if possible, to grow deeper as the president's remains went farther westward, where the people more especially claimed him as their own," noted Brevet Brig. Gen. Edward D. Townsend, head of the honor guard.[337]

In Westfield, N.Y., five women boarded the train as its engine took on wood and water. They laid a floral wreath on the casket inscribed "Ours the Cross; Thine the Crown." There was no sign of Grace Bedell, the young miss who had written to Lincoln several years before advising him to grow whiskers.

At 3 a.m. the train made an unscheduled stop in Erie, Pa., where citizens, not expecting a ceremony, improvised a torchlight parade.

From Erie, the Cleveland, Painesville & Ashtabula's *William Case* pulled Lincoln's train, again the same one used on that stretch in 1861. John Benjamine was engineer. The *Idaho*, with J.W. McGuire in charge, served as pilot engine.

Upon arrival in Cleveland at 7 a.m. Friday, April 28, the casket was taken to a temporary structure in a park on Superior Street, where thousands stood in the rain for hours to pay their respects. The body was returned to the station for a midnight departure.

A Cleveland & Pittsburgh yard engine, the *Dispatch*, operated by Bill Simmons, pulled the train backward to the Euclid Street Station, where the Cleveland, Columbus & Cincinnati's *Nashville* took over, operated by George West. It was preceded by the pilot engine *Louisville* with E. Van Camp at the throttle.

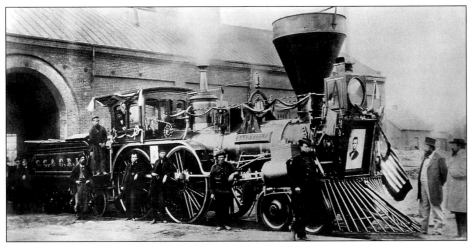

CHARLES G. CHANEY COLLECTION/SMITHSONIAN INSTITUTION

Cleveland, Columbus & Cincinnati Railroad's engine Nashville *prepares to leave the Cleveland roundhouse and forward Lincoln's funeral train to Columbus on an overnight run April 28-29, 1865.*

The Lincoln funeral train pauses on a siding in Chicago May 1, 1865, where it will soon continue to Springfield, Ill., for the martyred president's burial.

The nation's mourning was so intense that even the yard engine was decorated, according to Martin Fetter: "I was a lad then, not more than 15. When I reported for work … I was surprised to find engine No. 40, the *Dispatch*, standing on a siding with a large crowd around her. I was gaping at the crowd when the boss came over and said: 'That engine's going to pull President Lincoln's funeral train … and I'd like you to help trim her.'

"Grabbing some waste, I started by shining up the brass around the cab. For a time I worked alone. Then the engineer, Bill Simmons, and the fireman, Joe Denslow, came over with the boss's daughter, Lavina Hamm. They had white and black bunting and a large portrait of Lincoln in a gilt frame. I assisted Bill in putting up the picture right out in front of the engine, then we fastened several yards of bunting around it. Joe and Lavina draped the sides. Before they got through, I climbed on top and muffed the bell.

"All in all, it was a good job. Between the folds of bunting you could see the blue enameled sides, and there was a gold stripe showing above. After that, I hurried up to the square where Abe Lincoln had been lying in state. I wanted to get a last look at him. But I was too late. They'd taken him away."[241]

Once Columbus was attained at 7:30 a.m. the 29th, the body was taken to the state Capitol rotunda until its 8 p.m. departure. Traveling via Piqua and Bradford, Ohio, and Richmond, Ind., the train arrived at Indianapolis at 7 a.m., Sunday the 30th. James Gourley was engineer. Mourners saw the body in the statehouse there, then the grim procession left town at midnight.

The three railroads bearing the train from Indianapolis to Chicago issued joint instructions. A schedule was printed for the pilot train, with orders that the funeral train follow by 10 minutes. The cortege was limited to 5 miles an hour by stations, and the bell was to be rung through all towns. Every telegraph office was to be open and report the train's advance, and the pilot train was not to pass any such office, "coming to a full stop if necessary,"[337] before determining that the funeral train had left the last office. A "safety signal" was to be displayed by a man on the ground at each switch, bridge and curve: a white light by night and a draped white flag by day. The pilot engine was to carry two red lights by night and a draped American flag by day to indicate a following train, and crews were told to take along enough red lights, flags and extra men to give proper notice to the funeral train of anything that would cause delay. Finally, each road was to operate on its own standard time, and "all engines and trains of every description will be kept out of the way."[337]

On board during this stretch was Lt. Col. Elijah W. Halford, retired U.S. paymaster, who later served as secretary to President Benjamin Harrison. At the time of the Lincoln train, he was a reporter for the Indianapolis Journal whose "late night dispatches" made good reading. Excerpts follow:

Zionsville, Ind., 12:40 a.m. "Large assemblage of people with lighted lamps and torches … and upon learning in which car was the president's remains, they flocked about it with the greatest anxiety, eagerly endeavoring to get a look at

The Nashville *has been moved to Cleveland's Euclid Street Station, where it will couple to Lincoln's funeral train for the overnight run to Columbus.*

the remains."

Whitestown, Ind., 1:07 a.m. "Around a large bonfire are congregated about one hundred people. The men remained with uncovered heads. ...

Lebanon, Ind., 1:30 a.m. "...Both town and county were gathered together to honor the dead. Lamps, torches and bonfires send their brilliant light ... suspended from wires and transparent lamps, behind which are dropped flags dressed in mourning. A beautiful arch of evergreens and roses was erected, under which the cars passed ... more fairy-like than real."

Lafayette, Ind., 3:35 a.m. "Private residences are brilliantly illuminated, contrasting strangely with the black drapery which shades the windows and doors. ... A band of music discoursed appropriate airs."[200]

Transferring to the Louisville, New Albany & Chicago at Lafayette, the locomotive *Persian* took over, under the able hands of engineer A.

This pass permitted members of the Lincoln party to board the special train carrying him to his inauguration in Washington, D.C.

Rupert and conductor Harry Nuishan Esq. A Mr. Rhodes was in charge of the pilot engine *Rocket*.

Halford continued:

Reynolds, Ind., 5:05 a.m. "A great many farmers and their families have come—some of them 20 miles—to pay their respects to the dead."

Francisville, Ind., 5:45 a.m. "The ... people ... stand on tip-toe to get a look at the coffin."

Lucerne, Ind., 6:25 a.m. "The usual signs of bereavement are seen. The people (are) wearing mourning badges ..."

LaCroix, Ind., 7:50 a.m. "Quite a nice demonstration was made ... by ... (those) who viewed the cortege in the most sacred manner."[200]

When 11-year-old Martin T. Krueger heard the firing of a cannon in Michigan City that morning, he thought Confederates were shelling the town. He and several companions were on their way to Waterford to plant potatoes for "Old Man Perry,"[241] but they hurriedly hid their molasses sandwiches under a bridge and headed for the business district.

The immigrant German learned

CHARLES G. CHANEY COLLECTION/SMITHSONIAN INSTITUTION

Chicago & Alton engine 58 brings Lincoln's body home to Springfield, Ill., on the morning of May 3, 1865.

that Lincoln's train had arrived at 8:25, and was spotted under a large and beautiful temporary structure trimmed in black and white and ornamented with evergreens and flowers. Krueger couldn't understand much English then, but he was able to comprehend that children could not view the body unless accompanied by their parents. And a detail of soldiers enforced the regulation.

The train had to wait about an hour for a special sent from Chicago to meet it. Once the crowd grew, the resourceful young Krueger managed to see the body by hiding himself behind the hoop skirt of a woman guards presumed to be his mother. Not understanding English, he failed to heed the guards' admonition to keep moving and stopped for a "good look"[241] at the dead president. A guard grabbed him by the collar and the seat of his pants and tossed him over the observation platform into a patch of sand burrs. Undaunted, Krueger posed for a photograph with a crowd under the funeral arches.

From Michigan City, Michigan Central Railroad engine *Ranger*—operated by engineer Edward Wilcox—and pilot engine *Frank Valkenberg* took charge for the lap into Chicago. Those on board thanked the ladies of Michigan City for a white fish breakfast served with the best linen and silver in the New Albany & Chicago freight depot. Perhaps that breakfast explains why several of the notables from Washington were left behind, but with the help of an "express engine,"[241] they overtook the train at Porter Station.

Reported Halford: "We are now in the care of ... R.A. Rice Esq., general superintendent, and C. Knowlton Esq., assistant superintendent ... they are unremitting in their care and attention."[241]

Chicago's Park Place, on the lake front, was attained at 11 a.m. Monday.

Temporary platforms were installed to handle the funeral party, which accompanied the casket to the courthouse on Clark Street. The public was permitted to view the remains until 8 p.m. Tuesday, after which they were moved to the Chicago & Alton depot on Canal Street for a 9:30 p.m. departure.

Said to have carried the presidential party on the last leg of its sad journey was the car *Pioneer*, George M. Pullman's 13th production and the "first sleeper built in the modern manner."[18] Tradition has it that Mrs. Lincoln had inspected the car during a visit to Illinois earlier that year and was enchanted with it. She didn't forget its beauty, and when the funeral train was being planned, the widow is said to have requested that the *Pioneer* be coupled to it in Chicago for her use on the rest of the journey. A request of the presidential widow is not to be denied, so the story goes, so the Chicago & Alton made arrangements to use the car at considerable trouble and expense since its width necessitated the widening of clearances along station platforms and on bridges. Some scholars today, however, believe the story to be a fabrication, since no mention of it appeared in the press until two "recollections" of Pullman officials were published in 1888—meaning it may have been an advertising myth hatched up by George M. Pullman himself—and since Mrs. Lincoln wasn't even on the train.[237]

Chicago & Alton No. 40, the pilot engine, with Henry Russell on the righthand seatbox, departed at 9:20, followed 10 minutes later by engine 58, with James Colting at the throttle. Arrival in Springfield was at 9 a.m., an hour late, on Wednesday, May 3. The train had covered 1,662 miles in 12 days. More than 1.5 million people were estimated to have seen it.

"The city is so crowded," one

newspaperman complained, "that it is impossible to procure lodging in a bar room or on a pool table."[452]

Trains from every point on the compass arrived to add more people to the lines filing past the bier, which had been placed in the hall of the House of Representatives in the statehouse.

"The soldiers on guard in the capitol and around the grounds kept hurrying the crowd along," one young Illinois infantryman recalled. "They had to, you see, for there were always thousands of more waiting outside."[452]

The next day the body was taken to the public vault in Oak Ridge Cemetery for temporary interment. As a chorus sang "Peace, Troubled Soul," the casket was closed for good. It would later be moved to its final resting place in a magnificent tomb and monument built with state funds.

The funeral car stayed in the Chicago & Alton yard in Springfield for some time, finally being returned to Alexandria. Even while the train was enroute, the government had placed ads for its sale in several newspapers. The "funeral trappings" were removed once the car was back in Alexandria and divided up as relics. "I got one of the large tassels and some of each of the other decorations," said Assistant Master Car Builder Sidney D. King, "and put them in a case made of the same materials as the trimming of the car."[364]

The funeral car was given one more government assignment—in June, it carried the remains of Mrs. William Seward, wife of Lincoln's secretary of state, to Albany, N.Y., for burial. It was shunted around the country and largely forgotten until it was destroyed in 1911 [see Page 377].

Ulysses S. Grant

Death caught up with Ulysses Grant at 8:08 a.m. on Thursday, July 23, 1885, at his mountain hideaway at Mount McGregor, N.Y.

Within a half hour, a waiting engine at the mountain depot was on its way down to Saratoga Springs to bring back a local undertaker named Holmes. The mortician returned on the train, bringing an ice coffin in which to place the emaciated body. Holmes and Stephen J. Merritt, a New York funeral director, did the embalming, which took two days. The coffin, constructed so that the body lay on a false bottom under which a supply of ice retarded deterioration, also had sides that could be let down to facilitate embalming. Once that was done, the ice was no longer needed, but the body was kept in the coffin until the permanent casket arrived. There was a proposal to return the body by riverboat from Albany, but Grant's family felt that his life was resolutely bound with the railroads and would have none of it.

Plans were completed for the move—all the way by rail—long before the general succumbed to his cancer. One detail hadn't been tied down—where the body would be buried. Several cities fought over the honor, and the remains stayed locked up in the cottage of Joseph W. Drexel, the New York City tycoon who had persuaded developer W.J. Arkell to use Grant's presence to ensure the development of his Mount McGregor resort, for nearly two weeks until the issue was resolved. Washington argued that they should be interred in the nation's capital, but New York City won out since it was his home for years after the war.

During the interim, mourners came to the mountaintop by the trainload and seemed to be interested in nothing else of Arkell's little empire than Drexel's cottage with its moribund occupant. They plucked sprigs of fern or blossoming wild flowers near the path the general had used when walking or riding in his carriage, placing them carefully in a book or paper as a priceless keepsake.

Meanwhile, plans for the funeral trains continued.

"The body will be placed on what is known as an 'observance'," D.H. Fonda of the narrow-gauge Saratoga, Mount McGregor & Lake George line explained to reporters. "That is a car 35 feet long, with standard posts at the corners and sides which support a roof over all. The car is enclosed on all sides to a height of 3 feet. Every part of the car will be draped in mourning. Next will come a car called *Eastern Outlook*, to be used by the family. Others will follow."[184]

The funeral car's lengthwise seats were removed from the rear to make room for the coffin. Seats were left in the front for an honor guard. The family preferred a quiet service at Mount McGregor as opposed to a military service in New York, but Major Gen. Winfield S. Hancock, who was placed in charge of arrangements, brought up trainloads of soldiers with 10-pounder guns and ammunition. They prepared to fire salutes not only when the funeral train departed, but also when Hancock arrived from his current assignment at Governor's Island.

Another contingent was left at Saratoga to fire a salute when the train passed that point.

Delaware & Hudson engine 210 waits to forward Ulysses Grant's body from Saratoga Springs to Albany, N.Y., on a train provided by the New York Central & Hudson River line Aug. 4, 1885.

Delaware & Hudson engine 210, draped with 250 yards of black cashmere, prepares to depart Saratoga Springs, N.Y., with President Grant's remains Aug. 4, 1885.

The specially built coffin was carried up the mountain on July 29. It was of polished oak, lined with copper, covered with dark purple velvet, and had full-length solid silver handles and a gold nameplate engraved "U.S. Grant." Once it was removed from its heavy oak case, the general's body was transferred to it from the ice coffin. The body was dressed in a suit of black broadcloth with a Prince Albert coat. There was a white linen standing collar and a black silk scarf was tied in a plain bow at the throat. Patent leather slippers over white stockings covered the feet. There were gold studs in the shirt front and plain gold buttons in the cuffs. A heavy piece of plate glass forming the inner top of the coffin was sealed airtight by 60 screws and a flag draped over all. Grant's uniform and sword had already gone to the Smithsonian Institution, and although the lack thereof caused some complaints, the family never requested their return.

No detail was too lavish. The nation considered Grant a hero who brought the Civil War to an end and saved the Union. When battles were raging almost at the walls of Washington, it was his bold advance that saved the capital. Even Southerners appreciated his fairness. When Gen. Robert E. Lee surrendered, Grant told the boys in gray to keep their horses—they would need them for plowing. The South never forgot that.

Some discoloration was noticed at one point under the glass, and embalmers hastened to apply a bleaching lotion to the body's face to quiet the critics.

Souvenir hunters became such a problem that the funeral car had to be taken down the mountain to Saratoga and placed under lock and key. Despite being guarded, relic hunters had seriously damaged its ornaments and even cut out a large piece of the car itself. At the Balmoral Hotel, where ladies were making mourning rosettes with which to trim the car, "every speck of black cloth which was trimmed off from these rosettes was eagerly picked up by the visitors and carried off."[296] The relic hunters "would cut the cottage all to pieces inside of a week," one article said, "and not leave a stick or stone of it standing if the property should be left unprotected."[296]

On Monday, Aug. 3, Gen. Hancock and his staff arrived on the 10 a.m. train. One of the batteries was ready to fire a salute, but Hancock had the good sense to stop it. After a perfunctory procession through the cottage's parlor to view the body and on up to the hotel, the party returned to Saratoga for the night and the cottage was once again opened to the public.

People began arriving early on Tuesday, Aug. 4, the day of the funeral—by farm wagon, buggy, stage, carriage and on trains as fast as the little engine could wag the overloaded cars up the mountain and go back for more. The salutes began at dawn and continued every 30 minutes. The public was admitted to the cottage at 9:30, and the service started promptly at 10.

Thirteen Grand Army of the Republic veterans reverently carried the coffin down to the train. Troops with reversed arms led the way, with bugles sounding a dirge. The honor guard lifted the catafalque into the converted observation car, the first of six cars on the train. Shortly after the 1 p.m. salute, Engineer Martin shut off all steam from the cylinders and his train eased down the grade of its own weight. Sweeping around curve after curve to right and left, the train passed slowly down the mountain. Once enroute, Hancock ordered the coffin opened and the honor guard members "were accorded the privilege of taking their last look at the remains of the illustrious dead."[296]

A second train left the mountaintop at 3 p.m. with the ladies—all of them, that is, except Grant's wife, Julia. She decided to stay put.

In the valley, the Saratoga, Mount McGregor & Lake George's track met the Delaware & Hudson Railroad and, at Saratoga Springs, its narrow-gauge engine puffed up

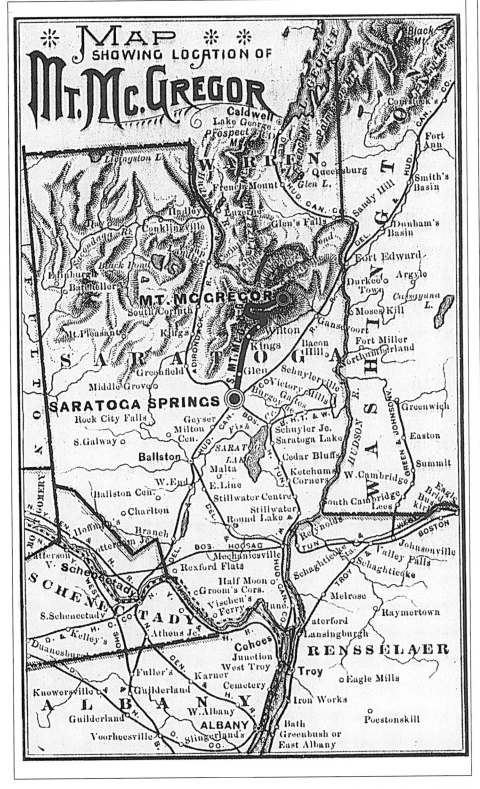

NEW YORK PUBLIC LIBRARY

Map from an 1884 promotional piece titled "Mount McGregor, the Popular Summer Sanitarium, Forty Minutes from Saratoga Springs," shows the narrow-gauge Saratoga, Mount McGregor & Lake George Railroad, which provided for Ulysses S. Grant his last train ride in life and his first in death.

alongside the New York Central & Hudson River's black-draped standard-gauge nine-car special operated by engineer Willis G. Fisher.

The NYC&HR train was draped from the pilot to its markers. The engine's boiler rails had festoons of crepe, the sides of the cab were covered, and the sides of the tender were completely sheathed with black cloth radiating from rosettes. All the cars had draperies, and their exteriors were covered except for the windows.

Once the body was transferred to the private car *Woodlawn*, owned by NYC&HR President Cornelius Vanderbilt II, the standard-gauge train departed. The pause had only been a few minutes—and after the 2:10 p.m. departure, the town protested the fact that an extended stay was not planned there. It reached Albany at 3:40. When Voorhies, the local railroad superintendent, climbed out of the cab, he remarked to one of the officials: "During this trip you have heard no sound of bell or whistle." Nor did either sound on the whole trip.[184]

After lying in state in the state Capitol in Albany, the body was returned to its funeral car at noon Wednesday, Aug. 5, for the trip to New York City. Respectful crowds were out all the way. As the black train rumbled across the Hudson River bridge just south of Albany, it was between two dense lines of people. Hundreds of persons nearest the tracks laid coins on the rails to have them flattened beneath the wheels.

Near Poughkeepsie the travelers passed a work train, and the track gang stood with heads uncovered. At Cornwall they were met by a crowded steamboat from New York.

A few minutes above West Point, they ran into a thunderstorm and Grant's son had to move to the other side of the car. They could see dark clouds directly over the military post. Now a cannon on the hill began booming a salute. At 3:27, the train rolled slowly past the little station. Cadets stood at present arms along the track. A band played a subdued version of "Sweet Spirit, Hear My Prayer." As the train moved on, the music mingled with thunder muttering over the river and the boom of the salute. There were more flattened coins, more priceless mementos.

In New York, the general's body lay in state three nights and two days until it was placed in a temporary tomb on Riverside Drive on Aug. 8. Among those attending the funeral were ex-presidents Hayes and Arthur and President Cleveland.

On April 27, 1897, President McKinley dedicated the permanent tomb. A wreath on the body's chest, its oak leaves having been gathered by Mrs. Grant, her daughter, and the president's doctor's two daughters at Mount McGregor and assembled and varnished by Grant's male nurse, Henry McQueeney, was found still intact even after those 12 intervening years.

James A. Garfield

The attack on James Garfield in Washington's Baltimore & Potomac passenger station proved to be fatal at 10:30 p.m. Monday, Sept. 19, 1881, despite his long summer of rest and recuperation in Washington and at Long Branch, N.J. A funeral train—with the new president, Chester A. Arthur, and a past president, Ulysses S. Grant, aboard— brought Garfield's body back from Long Branch to Washington on Wednesday, Sept. 21.

On the way back, Mrs. Garfield kept pushing back the curtains in her window to see the mourners gathered at every crossing.

Her husband's body lay in state under the Capitol's rotunda. Services were held there, with Arthur and former presidents Grant and Hayes in attendance.

The five-eighths of a mile of track installed overnight to get Garfield to his cottage 15 days before was just as promptly removed. A spike taken from the siding was kept by E.T.M. Carr, Long Branch's general agent. Its side was inscribed to read "James A. Garfield, Francklyn Cottage, Elberon, Sept. 6-21, 1881; Central R.R. of N.J."[262]

From the Capitol, Garfield's coffin was borne by members of his Vermont Avenue Disciples Church to the funeral train for the sad return to Cleveland via Baltimore and Harrisburg on the B&P and Pennsylvania railroads. Departure was at 5:16 p.m. Friday, Sept. 23. Multitudes lined the route most of the night, including Civil War veterans and workmen holding pine torches aloft, and flowers were strewn along the right of way.

The cortege arrived at Altoona, Pa., at 1:35 a.m. Saturday, meeting a crowd that had been assembling for nearly three hours. "The train was in charge of Conductor George Long and was drawn by engine No. 91, Mr. Sol Hofmaster, engineer," the local newspaper reported. "The train consisted of six coaches all heavily draped with the emblems of mourning. The second contained the casket, which was mounted on a raised platform so that it was in plain view to the crowd through the windows of the car. The casket was covered with cloth, and had six massive silver handles on the sides. A wreath of immortelles was laid on the lid, and another was suspended over the casket from the roof of the car. At the head of the coffin was a profuse floral display of natural flowers. A sentry sat at the head and one at the foot of the remains. The other cars contained Mrs. Garfield and family and the intimate friends. The large crowd which got inside of the fence climbed on the cars and peered into the windows, but in other respects was orderly."[9b]

After an engine trade, the procession got under way again after 10 minutes with conductor J.G. Mullin

THOMAS W. DIXON JR. COLLECTION

Baltimore & Potomac engine 318 prepares to leave the B&P station in Washington for Cleveland with the body of slain President James A. Garfield Sept. 23, 1881.

and engines 178 and 426, engineers Michael Dailey and Paul Sharp.

The article also noted a second train of 10 cars carrying members of Congress and other dignitaries.

Among those decorating the locomotive that would haul the train out of Wellsville, Ohio, was Martin Fetter, who had helped decorate the little engine *Dispatch* for Lincoln's funeral train.

After arrival in Cleveland and services there, Garfield's body was taken in a four-mile procession to Lakeview Cemetery in that city.

For his evil deed, Garfield's assassin, Charles Guiteau, was tried, sentenced to death, and hanged on June 30, 1882.

Today, riders on the ex-Denver & Rio Grande Western segment called the Cumbres and Toltec Scenic Railroad see a 7-foot granite memorial to Garfield as they pass through the Toltec Gorge 9,637 feet above sea level not far from Chama, N.M. The monument was erected by members of the National Association of General Passenger and Ticket Agents, who were holding their annual convention in Denver and happened to be at that exact spot on an excursion trip when the nation paused to honor its fallen president.

The B&P, incidentally, had a gold star mosaicked into the depot floor at the spot where Garfield fell, but it attracted so many curiosity seekers and blocked traffic through the station to such an extent that it was soon removed and placed in the Smithsonian Institution.

The depot itself was razed after the opening of the new Washington Union Station in 1907.

Chester A. Arthur

The New York Central & Hudson River provided a funeral train for the family and bearers of Chester Arthur's body on Monday, Nov. 22, 1886, four days after his death in New York City from complications of Bright's disease. After the funeral in the Church of the Heavenly Rest, the train bore the private party back to Albany for the formal attentions of the governor and legislature and a graveside rite and burial in Rural Cemetery.

Muffled drums rumbled as Arthur's body was loaded aboard the five-car train at New York's Grand Central Station. It was placed on the *Woodlawn*, the private car of NYC&HR President Cornelius Vanderbilt II that carried Ulysses Grant's body from Saratoga Springs, N.Y., to New York City the year before.

The cortege pulled out at 10:10 a.m., with President Grover Cleveland standing on the station platform with his top hat over his heart.

Once the soldiers who had escorted his body to the station marched away, the crowd dispersed.

The train was supposed to take four hours to reach Albany, switch to the Delaware & Hudson and continue three miles to the cemetery, arriving a little before 3 p.m. But the trip to Albany took only three hours and 12 minutes, including a water stop at Poughkeepsie, and arrived in the state capital at 1:20 p.m., 55 minutes early. D&H engine 210, the same locomotive that brought Grant's funeral train in from Saratoga Springs, was coupled on and the last leg of the trip started at 1:26.

When the cemetery was reached at 1:40, about 200 people already on hand were surprised to see it arrive so early. It halted on a crossing at the cemetery entrance to allow passengers to disembark, then the 210 and the *Woodlawn* were cut off and eased up the track to a point closer to the gravesite. While the passengers made their way on foot, the flowers were unloaded and placed on funeral director Marshall W. Tebbutt's flower wagon for a short run up a hill to the grave. Then the locomotive and catafalque car backed down to the crossing, where Tebbutt's funeral coach stood waiting to take the casket to the grave. The burial was all over and the mourners were returning to the train when they met a large contingent of last-minute arrivals who missed the whole episode. The train soon departed, leaving Albany at 4:45 and arriving in New York City at 7:15 p.m.

Meriting a word is the funeral train of Jefferson Davis, who, after all, was president of a part of this country during the Civil War.

Davis died in Biloxi, Miss., in 1889. After being buried temporarily in New Orleans, his body was returned to Richmond, Va., in 1893 for reburial.

The four-day journey began May 28.

It traveled on the Louisville & Nashville from New Orleans to Montgomery, Ala.; the Western Railway of Alabama to West Point, Ga.; the Atlanta & West Point to Atlanta and the Richmond & Danville to Richmond, including a side trip from Goldsboro to Raleigh, N.C., and return.

The fallen leader was accorded all the accolades and honors worthy of a chief of state at several major stops along the way.

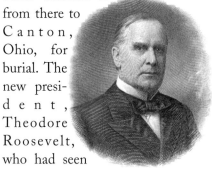

The PRR provided two funeral trains for William McKinley in 1901. One took his body from Buffalo back to Washington, the other wheeled it from there to Canton, Ohio, for burial. The new president, Theodore Roosevelt, who had seen Lincoln's funeral procession in New York in 1865, rode all the way.

McKinley's services began on Sunday, Sept. 15, with a funeral in the home where he had stayed in Buffalo. Then the body lay in state in City Hall until 10:30 that night. The six-car funeral train departed for Washington at 8:47 a.m. Monday, 10 minutes after the departure of a light engine as pilot.

McKinley's casket had been placed on a raised bier in Pullman 8-section lounge/observation car *Pacific* and covered with an American flag in full view of the thousands who gathered at trackside; the train was festooned with black crepe. McKinley's widow was aroused from her daze at Harrisburg when she heard a choral society sing her husband's favorite hymn, "Nearer My God to Thee," and wept for the first time since leaving Buffalo. While enroute, Roosevelt and his inherited Cabinet transacted business that couldn't wait.

Upon arrival in Washington at 8:38 p.m. Monday, McKinley's body spent its last night in the White House in the flower-banked East Room. Then it was taken to the Capitol for a service on Tuesday.

The second funeral train—similarly decorated—departed Washington Tuesday evening in three sections

ARTHUR DUBIN COLLECTION

The resting place for William McKinley's coffin is ready to accept its solemn cargo on Pullman 8-section/lounge/observation car Pacific *in Buffalo Sept. 16, 1901.*

BROWN LIBRARY

The McKinley funeral train pauses at Williamsport, Pa., enroute from Buffalo to Washington on Sept. 17, 1901.

This 8-year-old wooden Pullman product, 8-section/lounge/observation car Pacific, *waits in Buffalo to carry the remains of William McKinley back to Washington, then Canton, Ohio.*

amid heavy rain that seemed to suit the occasion. The first departed at 8 p.m. with eight carloads of politicians and press; the second, the funeral train proper, left at 8:10 and carried seven cars; the third, carrying Army and Navy officers, departed at 8:20 p.m.

In every town, the cortege passed flag-draped poles and houses clad in mourning. Silent and bareheaded crowds lined the route and stood in homage at every crossing. The route followed the Ohio River for miles and steamboats saluted the deceased with long, mournful whistle blasts. In Pittsburgh, a bold youngster climbed the outside of a high church steeple to get a good view.

The procession arrived in Canton, Ohio, at noon Wednesday for a third service and burial. When McKinley's body was being carried out of his home in Canton at 3:30 p.m., the nation bowed in respect for five minutes.

Warren G. Harding

Warren Harding's death in San Francisco on Thursday, Aug. 2, 1923, transformed his cross-country touring train into a funeral cortege that returned his body to Washington, then home to Marion, Ohio, for burial. Its locomotives were draped less ostentatiously than those on earlier such missions.

Embalmers fitted the body in a cutaway morning coat and black trousers and placed it in state in the big drawing room of the Palace Hotel's presidential suite on Friday morning. A hearse carried it to the Southern Pacific train at 7 p.m. The 12-car special, pulled by a Pacific-type locomotive, left Third Street at 7:15, 15 minutes late. It remained intact across the continent, with the exception of locomotives and dining cars. Draped in black, it departed in silence, at first moving inch by inch, barely creeping from the train sheds while a sorrowing throng watched. To avoid the ferry crossing of San Francisco Bay, it detoured down the peninsula via the Dunbarton cutoff and east and north via Stockton to the route of the *Overland Limited*.

All SP crews were handpicked according to their records of safety and efficiency. A pilot train consisting of a coach and business car ran 20 minutes ahead of the special to Ogden, Utah. Stops were made at Newark, Calif., to add a helper engine and at Altamont to remove it.

341

CHARLES G. CHANEY COLLECTION/SMITHSONIAN INSTITUTION

Southern Pacific engine 2400 is ready to leave San Francisco Aug. 3, 1923, with the remains of President Warren G. Harding.

CHARLES G. CHANEY COLLECTION/SMITHSONIAN INSTITUTION

The Superb's *brass railing is subdued with black crepe as Warren Harding's funeral train pauses in Chicago Aug. 6, 1923.*

Roseville, Calif., was reached at 11:40 p.m., and a 10-minute stop was made to change engines and crews and water the train. Two Mikado 2-8-2 type engines were used from Roseville to take the train over the Sierras to Truckee, past the 7,018-foot summit. The helper was removed at

C&NW locomotive 1654 brings Warren Harding's funeral train into Chicago Aug. 6, 1923.

Truckee, and a Pacific 4-6-2 type replaced the other "Mike" at Sparks, Nev., to finish the SP run into Ogden.

"I shall never forget that journey," Secret Service agent Edmund Starling wrote in his memoirs. "The nation was grief-stricken. Every town and city through which we passed was in mourning. People stood by the side of the tracks singing hymns while we went slowly through. Masons in full dress uniforms, with helmets and plumage, were waiting at each stopping place on the long, 3,000-mile journey. Sometimes it was the middle of the night when we crept slowly into a station, the bell of our locomotive clanging dolefully. From either side of us out of the misty night would come the flicker of white garments, then the low rolling tones of thousands of men softly singing "Lead Kindly Light" or "Nearer My God to Thee." Across the breadth of the continent there seemed to be no sound but the beating of our bell and the voices, rising up and washing over our train like a tide."[363]

Crowds began increasing at Reno at 6 a.m. Saturday. Bells tolled and an official delegation presented floral tributes. Later in the day, Harding's secretary, George B. Christian, had to refuse further offerings of flowers because there was no space left on board for them.

The 840-mile trip to Ogden was completed at 8:59 p.m. Saturday, six minutes early, making an elapsed time via SP of 25 hours and 44 minutes, which was 21 minutes faster than the *Overland Limited's* time on a route 58 miles longer, including regular stops. It left that point via Union Pacific on time at 9:15.

The train's locomotive slipped a driving wheel tire at Chappell, Neb., but through the quick action of its engineer an accident was averted. After a slight delay, the locomotive of the *Pacific Limited*, which was waiting at that station for the special to pass, was drafted into the special service. The mishap consumed an hour, and shortly thereafter a storm slowed progress more. Grand Island, Neb., was reached an hour and a half late, but 45 minutes had been made up by the time the train met a throng of 40,000 at Omaha at 3 a.m. Monday.

Another 10 minutes had been made up once the train arrived at Cedar Rapids, Iowa, on the Chicago & North Western. But once Mrs.

B&O P-6a Pacific 5233 is decorated and ready to pull President Harding's funeral party from Garrett, Ind., to Willard, Ohio, Aug. 6, 1923.

Harding saw the large crowd there, she asked that the train wade through any crowd slowly so everyone could see the casket. Officers lost all hope of running on time.

C&NW's precautionary steps received praise in the trade press for being "a little more complete"[310] than the other roads involved. In addition to the pilot train of locomotive, baggage car and business car, extra locomotives were fired up and fanned out to be held at Boone and Clinton just in case. Stations as well as locomotives were decorated. In addition to the usual spiked switches, crossings were closed 10 minutes after the pilot train passed and not reopened until the funeral train went by.

The crowds kept growing. Stores were closed and entire populations turned out. Reporters remarked that more people came out to see this presidential funeral train than any other, perhaps as many as 3 million. People lined the track literally all across Illinois. In Chicago, 300,000 were on hand for the 5:50 p.m. Monday arrival. Hot journal bearing boxes on two of the cars had complicated things further; it took more than three hours to cross the city and departure was at 9:30 p.m., six hours behind.

Efforts were made to make up time on the overnight run via B&O through Indiana and Ohio, but massive crowds foiled that plan. The train passed tiny Newton Falls, Ohio, at 8:42 a.m. Tuesday, Aug. 7, where

President Warren Harding's funeral train passes through Panther Hollow at Oakland, Pa., carrying Harding's remains past Carnegie Institute's Machinery Hall on Aug. 7, 1923.

Guards protect access to the platform of the private car Superb *as Warren Harding's funeral train pauses for an engine trade at B&O's Glenwood shops in Pittsburgh Aug. 7, 1923.*

B&O P-5 Pacific 5217 stands suitably decorated with its crew at Cumberland, Md., Aug. 7, 1923, ready to replace P-1d Pacific 5052 and forward President Harding's funeral train to Washington.

thousands had slept or rested in the station, on baggage carts, in autos and on the lawn all night. Hundreds of persons had placed coins on the track and scrambled for them as mementos after the cars had flattened them. The situation grew worse in western Pennsylvania, and as a result, arrival in Washington was at 10:22 p.m., Tuesday, almost nine hours late.

For hours, thousands had been jammed in the station concourse, packed against the iron fence shutting off the train platform. The train backed in so the funeral car would be near the exit. Mrs. Harding was the first off, leaning on Christian's arm. President Coolidge and a small group of high officials were waiting. There was no sound but the throbbing of the air pump on the B&O's weary Pacific. A band in the concourse began playing "Nearer My God to Thee" as the

A solemn engineer in Cumberland, Md., pauses from his duties momentarily for the camera as he prepares his engine to take Warren Harding's funeral train to Washington Aug. 7, 1923.

casket was gently lifted down from the special door cut in the side of the private car *Superb.* On the great flag spread over it, a single wreath was laid.

The military guard assumed position. Uniformed men raised their burden and began walking slowly through the station. Outside, a squadron of cavalry and a battery of field artillery stood at attention. The casket was placed on a caisson and a low-voiced command brought sabres flashing to salute. The cavalcade swung into column formation and the march to the White House began. After lying in state in the Capitol rotunda prior to a funeral service there, the grim procession started Wednesday evening to Marion, Ohio, for burial, on the last leg of its 4,000-mile trip. The train was routed PRR to Mansfield, Ohio, thence Erie to Marion. Conditions were unchanged. Crowds filled station plazas and country road crossings all the way. At Riderwood, Md., on PRR's Northern Central line from Baltimore to Harrisburg, florist O.R. Thomas had covered the track with flowers for a distance of 150 yards. "All through the

Pallbearers unload Warren Harding's casket from a window of the Superb *upon arrival in Marion, Ohio, Aug. 9, 1923.*

After Warren Harding's funeral train returned to Washington, still to be covered was the long road home to Marion, Ohio. Here, PRR engine 3750 prepares to leave Washington on the second lap of this sorrowful journey on Aug. 8, 1923.

RICHARD ANDRÉ/C&O HISTORICAL SOCIETY COLLECTION

Having discharged its casket and funeral party, Erie locomotive 2933 backs Warren Harding's funeral train to the North Grand Avenue crossing in Marion, Ohio, near the Studebaker-Wolff Rubber Co. plant. Guards still line the parallel Erie and NYC main lines.

night, time after time, the locomotive slowed down and we heard people singing," the Secret Service's Starling recalled.[363]

Doing the honors on the Erie were heavy class K-5 Pacific locomotives 2928 and 2933, suitably draped in black. Engineer J.H. Cronenwett, on the 2933, was a classmate of Harding's in grade school. He brought his school chum home to central Ohio at noon Thursday, several hours behind schedule.

Franklin D. Roosevelt

At 1:15 p.m. on Thursday, April 12, 1945, Franklin Roosevelt lost consciousness in his leather armchair at the Little White House in Warm Springs, Ga., and at 3:35 p.m., he died, the victim of a massive cerebral hemorrhage.

Roosevelt's staff hurled itself into a flurry of arrangements. Press representatives were summoned, and they dashed for telephones. The world was told about the president's death 22 minutes after it occurred and only moments after his wife, Eleanor, had been summoned back to the White House after a speaking en-gagement.

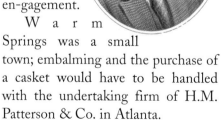

Warm Springs was a small town; embalming and the purchase of a casket would have to be handled with the undertaking firm of H.M. Patterson & Co. in Atlanta.

It didn't take long for a crowd to start gathering at the Warm Springs depot. "An hour after the news first broke, the newspapers and radio sta-

tions got folks there" and they began stringing long black cables, Southern Railway Station Agent C.A. Pless recalled. "One broadcasting station set up south of my depot against the road, one in front between the office and the tracks, one in the colored waiting room, two in the shed between the colored waiting room and the baggage room. The crowd kept building and milling. All of a sudden, the woods were full of folks, hundreds of them. It looked like people just fell out of the sky."[19]

The radio had said Mrs. Roosevelt was coming to Warm Springs, and the crowd hoped to catch a glimpse of her. They talked in whispers as they filled the lobby of the Warm Springs Hotel. Under a portrait of Roosevelt, reporters slumped on a sofa. They fidgeted and fumed, looking at their watches, exchanging recollections, impatient

346

to be admitted to the grounds of the Warm Springs Foundation. One of them heard an excited woman in a phone booth shout to a distant friend, "Yes, I was just driving through town. Boy, what a thrill this is!"[19]

The writers' reverie was broken when Warm Springs Mayor Frank Allcorn held up his hands for attention.

"The president and his party," he said, "were to have attended a barbecue at 4 o'clock, and they came and told us he died. We had all the food prepared. You may come and eat it if you're hungry, or it will only go to waste."

At first, nobody moved. Then Allcorn said, "It's on the house."[19]

Planning was initiated for a funeral train that would return the body to Washington for the funeral, then go to Hyde Park for the burial. Presidential aide Bill Hassett called the Southern Railway to order the train to be at Warm Springs no later than 7 the next morning. The word

Above: *A color guard stands watch over the casket of Franklin Roosevelt in the lounge of the* Conneaut *as the POTUS funeral train leaves Warm Springs, Ga., April 13, 1945.*

spread fast up and down the system.

It would take 10 engine crews and four train crews to haul the double-headed funeral train along the 721.5-mile route from Warm Springs to Washington. Other locomotives would have to be in readiness along the way. It would be a long couple of days for the railroad. Telephones in dispatchers' offices and crew callers' offices began ringing incessantly. Crews had to be called; dining car and Pullman men had to be pulled off their regular runs and other fellows located to take their places.

Engineer Claude E. Blackmon, who pulled the president's specials most of the time on the Greenville

The Conneaut's *lounge window has been removed and the ramp is ready. A hearse pulls up at the Warm Springs, Ga., station so military men can transfer the casket of Franklin D. Roosevelt from the vehicle to the train April 13, 1945.*

The Roosevelt funeral train, pulled by Southern PS-2 4-6-2 type locomotives 1262 and 1337, arrives at Terminal Station, Atlanta, April 13, 1945.

Division, was near his radio when the first bulletins were flashed. Soon, the caller at Atlanta's Inman Yard was on the phone.

"Claude," said the voice, "Supt. Cheney just called from Greenville and wants you to handle the president's funeral train. I don't know when it will run, maybe tonight or maybe tomorrow. Stick around the phone, buddy!"[262]

Blackmon got the call the next day.

"I've pulled the president many times," he said, "and it was always a pleasure and an honor, but the last trip was the hardest run I've ever made. We all felt like a member of the family was dead."[262]

Every effort was made by officers of each branch of railway service to secure the men for this trip who com-

posed the president's regular crews. L.P. Wesley, Pullman's assistant district superintendent in Atlanta, was at his desk when company service inspector Dave Gahagan phoned from Warm Springs with the news. Five minutes later, Wesley had the company's Washington office on the line, calling for Pullman Conductor W.A. Brooks and the six porters belonging to the train.

It was 30 minutes before train No. 37, the *Crescent Limited*, was due to leave Washington, the only connection that would put the men into Atlanta for the special. Brooks was on his regular run, but all six porters were in the city. The time was short, but it turned out that No. 37 left the nation's capital an hour late and all six made the train. They reached Atlanta a few minutes ahead of the special from Warm Springs. Brooks was reached on his train by wire and returned to Washington. Several hours behind his porters, he joined the funeral train at Greenville, S.C.

Thursday's dinner hour found Atlanta's roundhouse crews readying 4-6-2 Pacific-type locomotives 1262 and 1337 for the deadhead move to Warm Springs. Road foremen Tim Haulbrook and A.C. McLeod watched as General Roundhouse Foreman Ferman White superintend-

Southern Railway PS-4 Pacifics 1409 and 1394 pull Franklin Roosevelt's funeral train through Richland, S.C., April 13, 1945.

ed the inspections. Engineers H.E. Allgood and O.B. Wolford and firemen H.L. Decker and A.A. Washington were called for 6 p.m. and reported to Terminal Station. Six extra porters were selected from the huge Atlanta roster to ride down to Warm Springs and back to Atlanta, where they would be relieved by the regular men. The train was backed onto track 10, its regular spot on the west side of the station, to await the nod from Warm Springs to start down the road.

For three hours, crews and management sat on the ties talking about their lost friend and experiences with his train. Several passenger runs entered and left the station, apparently without anyone on board knowing that the equipment on track 10 was the fallen chief executive's funeral conveyance.

At 9:45 p.m., Supt. W.F. Cooper, Trainmaster A.W. St. Clair and Conductor Emmit Whittle came down the track 10 stairway. Whittle clutched a set of orders; they were about to be on their way.

At 9:53, Allgood and Wolford opened their throttles and the train eased under the Mitchell Street Viaduct and exited Terminal Station. Once reaching Williamson, 53.3 miles south of Atlanta and 30.7 miles from Warm Springs, the Pacifics were turned to be headed north the next day. With a pilot engine pulling from the rear, the 1262 and the 1337—headed the wrong way—pushed their train the rest of the way.

At 1:25 a.m. on Friday the 13th of April, 1945, the flanged cortege stole into the station with whispered chugs. Country farmers sat on a curb, hugging their knees and watching. They made no noise; they seldom spoke.

Sharp observers noted that the consist had been changed. For one thing, added capacity was needed, so the yard forces in Atlanta spliced an

Military personnel keep back the crowd as Franklin Roosevelt's funeral train arrives in Greenville, S.C., April 13, 1945.

extra sleeper into the mix, making 11 cars. Secondly, the casket was too big to fit through the *Ferdinand Magellan's* rear door, and the car's sealed windows could not be removed. So, ironically, Roosevelt's body could not be returned for its burial in the car that had become the symbol of his travel. This honor was thus transferred to the *Conneaut*, the Secret Service car, which had an observation parlor and removable windows. For this run, it would be on the rear of the train behind the *Magellan*.

Floodlights were turned on; the grim task of loading the presidential party's automobiles and personal belongings commenced. While the crowd watched, workmen entered the *Conneaut* and stripped the observation parlor of everything except a circular mirror on the forward wall.

Two miles away, in the cottage, embalmers had been delayed. They had arrived at 10:45 p.m., but were prohibited from working on the body

until after Mrs. Roosevelt arrived at 11:25. She; Dr. Ross McIntire, FDR's doctor; and Press Secretary Steve Early had flown by Army plane into Lawson Field at Fort Benning, where a car had picked them up.

First, Eleanor had long talks with FDR's personal secretary, Grace Tully, and the presidential cousins, Daisy Suckley and Polly Delano. Who told her that the president's girlfriend, Lucy Rutherfurd, had been with him when he collapsed isn't known, but bets are on Aunt Polly, the family gossip. The first lady thought the romance had ended in 1918; she had no clue that it had continued all these years, and now she learned about it at the worst possible time. She shook visibly, then composed herself and went into the bedroom where valet Arthur Prettyman and Filipino houseboy Irineo Esperancilla had carried the stricken chief. Five minutes later she emerged, solemn and dry-eyed.

Finally the embalmers got the

Franklin Roosevelt's funeral train stands at Greenville, S.C., while the Southern Railway changes its engines April 13, 1945.

nod at 12:35 a.m. The president had been dead nine hours; arteries were so plugged that the formaldehyde pump stopped twice. Injections with a syringe, over many parts of the body, had to suffice. It was a long night for the embalmers, too.

"While our assistants were proceeding with the preparation," recalled Atlanta mortician Fred Patterson, "it was found that the funeral train was to leave the next morning at 10 o'clock (war time) and … no provision had been made for a casket bier or anything on which to place the casket. I asked one of the Secret Service men if the Marine Corps who guarded the president had a carpenter. After some time, he awoke Hoke Shipp [the foundation's executive housekeeper] who discussed the making of two pedestals. It was finally decided, however, to make a bier in the form of a very strong table 2 inches longer than the casket and 2 inches wider, with a molding around the top to prevent the casket from slipping."[19]

Shipp awoke his staff carpenter, A.G. Moody, and brought him to a pile of pine timber cut on the grounds that he had been saving for a special occasion. He put Moody to work building the 20-inch-high bier while he went to the Marine detachment barracks. Since the 84- by 26-inch, 760-pound coffin was bronze, he decided to drape the bier with two greenish brown Marine blankets.

The supply sergeant asked Shipp when the blankets would be returned. Shipp warned they probably wouldn't be. The sergeant knew of no regulation governing the issuance of blankets for a presidential funeral and objected. Shipp said he would ask the commanding officer.

"You can't do that," the sergeant protested. "He's asleep."

"I'll wake him," Shipp threatened. Now the sergeant had a graver crisis, and relented.[19]

At the foundation's Georgia Hall, White House travel officer Dewey Long and Secret Service chief Mike Reilly worked out the funeral train's schedule. R.K. McClain, Southern's assistant vice president over the operating department, sent out orders from Washington to divisional chiefs; officers up and down the line were being awakened to study them. McClain had spent his lunch hour the day before studying FDR's scheduled April 18 return to Washington. When he heard about the death, he had invalidated the first plan and started on a second. When an order came to

travel slowly, he started a third. Briefly, it advised: "Lv. Warm Springs, Ga., 11 a.m.; arrive Williamson, Ga., 12:01 (take on water); arrive Atlanta, Ga., 2 p.m. (change engines and crews); Gainesville, Ga., 3:40 p.m. (water); Greenville, S.C., 6:50 p.m. (change engines and crews); Hayne, S.C., 7:55 p.m. (coal and water); Salisbury, N.C., 11:10 p.m. (change engines and crews); Danville, Va., 1:50 a.m. April 14 (ice and water); Monroe, Va., 4:15 a.m. (change engines and crews and water); Applegate, Va., 5:40 a.m. (Let No. 30 pass); Charlottesville, Va., 6:20 a.m. (use telephone); Weyburn, Va., 6:55 a.m. (coal and water); Bealton, Va., 8:15 a.m. (Let No. 48 pass); arrive Washington Union Station 10 a.m."[42]

Heavy Pacifics, the resplendent iron horses that had hauled Roosevelt south for years in their brilliant green livery with silver-rimmed drivers, would haul the president's body on its last journey north of Atlanta.

At 2:30 a.m., Hassett went to Carver Cottage to end up lying awake all night. Marines constructed a ramp that would be used to load Roosevelt's body onto the train as crews removed one of the *Conneaut's* windows on the hotel side. McIntire, Early and Lt. Cmdr. Howard Bruenn, FDR's cardiologist, went to bed on the train. They tumbled all night long as they heard the whining of trucks grinding down the long Pine Mountain grade in low gear, carrying soldiers from Fort Benning and baggage from the compound into the village. The baggage trucks were guided up the right of way to the baggage cars, with men shouting in the night.

The hammering, banging, shouting and throbbing of the locomotives' air pumps kept villagers awake all night. Finally, preparations were finished about 4 a.m., and the tired railroad crew began to think about finding something to eat.

"We hadn't had a bite since supper in Atlanta," Road Foreman Haulbrook recalled. "It was about daylight when the Warm Springs Hotel manager sent word for us to come to the hotel. 'Boys,' he said, 'the barbecue we prepared for the president yesterday is still in the kitchen. I know you fellows are tired and hungry, so come in and help yourselves. I'll have the cook warm it up for you.'"[262]

By 10, presidential aides were back at the Little White House. The casket was lying open in the living room near the president's bedroom door. A glass covered the body, which was outfitted in a double-breasted blue business suit flecked with gray, a soft white shirt, black socks, and a dark blue-and-white four-in-hand tie the president wore at his 1941 inauguration. The lower part of the body was covered with the president's boat cloak.

Mortician Patterson's dignity began to fray when he asked that his

Above: *Roosevelt's coffin has been removed from the* Conneaut *and loaded onto a horse-drawn caisson at Washington Union Station for the slow, mournful march to the White House April 14, 1945.*

351

aide, Haden Snoderly, be given room on the train with his embalming equipment.

"You see," he explained quietly, "the family has two funeral directors waiting, according to what I hear. One is Gawler in Washington; the other is Mrs. Ralph Worden in Hyde Park. The remains are going to require additional embalming, and Snoderly will offer his assistance without interfering with the others."[42]

His request was passed upward from Lt. Cmdr. Bruenn and Hassett to the man who enjoyed taking charge—Dr. McIntire. "Sorry, no room," he snapped. Patterson assured the admiral that Snoderly wouldn't require much room. "No room on the train," the admiral shot back, and Patterson stormed out.[42]

Soon it was time to go, but there were hitches. The caisson had not arrived. Pallbearers weren't in evidence. The flag to be draped over the casket had disappeared. Patterson's Sayers and Scoville Cadillac hearse was pressed into duty as the funeral vehicle; the pallbearers showed up in the nick of time, and a flag was lowered from a pole on the grounds and hastily dusted off. The procession started at 10:25, with about 2,000 soldiers leading the way along the red clay road down the mountainside.

Behind the hearse was Mrs. Roosevelt's closed car, where the first lady sat stiffly with a fur cape around her neck and the Roosevelts' dog Fala curled at her feet. With her were cousins Daisy and Polly and secretary Grace Tully. In the car behind them were Hassett, Early, McIntire and Bruenn; other cars followed. Lucy Rutherfurd had been ushered off the property moments after the president's collapse.

The procession moved between two lines of helmeted paratroopers standing at parade rest. Now and then, tears slid down a boy's face. One

soldier swayed slightly as the hearse rolled by, then caved in and rolled off the shoulder of the road into a ditch.

Mrs. Roosevelt preserved the president's tradition of going by Georgia Hall to wave at the patients as they left. Many were on crutches, some in wheelchairs, a few in rolling beds. But they were all there. As the cortege entered the driveway, it stopped. Coast Guard Chief Petty Officer Graham Jackson, who had driven down Thursday to take part in a minstrel show that night, was playing "Going Home" and "Nearer My God to Thee" on his accordion. Tears flooded his pained face.

Then the drums resumed their dreadful beat and the cortege moved on. Thirty-six minutes after it left the Little White House, it arrived at the station. Flowers sent by the president's local friends had been placed all around the *Conneaut*. Ten military pallbearers and three undertakers— those in front crouching and grabbing the rounded bottom and those in back holding it on their shoulders—lifted the casket up the trainside ramp and through the car's empty window slot. Ten more servicemen inside grabbed hold and placed it on the bier. Shipp and Moody had done their work well—a few inches of the flag-draped coffin were visible to those outside.

A guard of four servicemen— Army, Navy, Marine and Coast Guard—posted itself at each corner of the coffin and stood like stone statues. The window was reinstalled and screwed in tightly as Mrs. Roosevelt boarded the *Magellan* without looking back and reporters standing on the stone ballast scribbled their final notes. Conductor Whittle stood halfway up the track, trying to see both ends of the train.

Patterson searched inside the *Conneaut's* bare parlor for a place to hide the sealing gun and embalming chemicals—they would be needed by

Gawler in Washington. He shoved them under the bier, where the Marine blankets would hide them. A Secret Service man made him explain what he was up to.

Early approached the superintendent.

"Mr. Cooper," he said, "the people down here were the president's very good friends and neighbors, and it is the request of Mrs. Roosevelt that you instruct your enginemen, wherever they see groups of people along the railroad or at the crossings, to slow down sufficiently for them to have a last view of the casket. We have elevated it across the car that this vision might be had."[262]

The train had taken 22½ hours to come down, across a territory that could easily be traversed in 12. But Roosevelt liked to ride the rails slowly. This last northbound trip would be no exception. Arrival in Washington a full 24 hours later would be soon enough.

Hardly anyone noticed the moment when the train started at 11:13 a.m. The curving track sloped toward Atlanta on a 1 percent grade; the engineer simply released his brake and allowed it to coast away as smoothly as glass through a profusion of hillside sassafras and weeds.

It was Friday—Friday the 13th— and everybody knew the president never started a trip on a Friday.

Minutes after the train disappeared around the first bend, the loading ramp vanished. Souvenir hunters tore it to pieces.

Early gave the press association reporters—Merriman Smith of United Press, Harold Oliver of The Associated Press and International News Service's Robert Nixon—copies of the Jefferson Day speech Roosevelt was to have delivered that night. A Democratic National Committee ghostwriter had put this ending in the president's mouth: "The only limit to our realization of tomorrow will be our doubt of today."[19] Roosevelt liked that, but he had crossed out "doubt" and written "doubts." Then he added a sentence, his last words to the American people: "Let us move forward with strong and active faith."[42]

At Williamson, the train moved out of western Georgia's hills onto the mainline, continuing into furrowed farm country. Sweaty farmers behind plows stopped their mules in midfield to gawk. Children hurried to fence rails. Sheriffs' cars and soldiers holding their carbines at present arms stood like sentinels at each crossing.

"It was a personal matter with each of the half-million or more people who would wait along the right of way to say goodbye to a man they knew, but had never met," wrote author Jim Bishop. "Someone who, they were certain, had protected them and whom they could not protect. It was admiration, respect, love and curiosity. Above all, it was a feeling of having known this man—his big winning smile, his reassuring voice, his sly asides, most of all the intimacy of his repeated phrase, 'You and I know …' "[42]

The reporters, too drained from their all-night coverage to feel tired, plunged mechanically back to work and pounded out stories about the undelivered speech. They would be dispatched from the train at Atlanta. One reporter said they could get enough material for their night stories between Warm Springs and Greenville; after that, they could go to bed. They had fanned out in Warm Springs, talking to all the locals they could, so they could saturate the wires with local color "sidebars."

In the *Magellan's* lounge, Eleanor applied her mind to duty rather than grief. Late in the morning she sent for Miss Tully and they worked out a thank-you note for the thousands of sympathy notes that had been wired to Warm Springs and were now piling up in Washington. One, from a little boy in Chicago, said, "I was sorry I couldn't come to the funeral."[19] It was accompanied by a bouquet picked from his back yard. The card they devised had a thin black border and read: "Mrs. Roosevelt and her family thank you very much for your condolences and appreciate your kind thought."[19]

Eleanor asked Miss Tully to record any instructions or wishes the president might have expressed about personal gifts. She told her the Boss had promised the portrait of John Paul Jones that hung behind his White House desk to Dorothy Brady, whose maiden name was Jones. The painting had been unearthed years before by FDR's friend Louie Howe in a secondhand shop. He paid $25 for it, finding out later who it portrayed and discovering that it was one of the few portraits for which the Naval hero had sat in person. Each name Miss Tully wrote down, with a corresponding gift, brought back a similar flood of memories.

At one point, Eleanor asked Miss Tully hesitatingly, "Did Franklin ever give you any instructions about his burial?"[19]

Miss Tully recalled that the question was hard for the first lady to utter. "Her eyes welled and her voice broke. It was only momentary. It was the only time during the whole ordeal that I ever saw her almost lose her control."[19]

Miss Tully was unable to provide much information. About a year before, the Boss had expressed the desire to be buried at sea, an idea she said Americans wouldn't appreciate. Later he asked her about a memo he

New York Central Hudson type locomotive 5283 pulls the Roosevelt funeral train through Cold Spring, N.Y., April 15, 1945, enroute to Hyde Park for the presidential burial service.

thought he had dictated to her about his burial arrangements, but she never found it and he said he'd dictate another. He never did, but the original memo—written by the president himself in pencil—was found in his bedroom safe at the White House the day after his body was buried.

Eleanor was certain written instructions existed. "He was too historically minded to do otherwise," she told Miss Tully. "I would be unconcerned about such things and he would get angry. He would say, 'It's important how things will appear in history.' This is something he inherited from his mother. She was very concerned with history. That's why she always collected every snitch of everything and kept them as family mementos."[19]

She knew her husband would not want his body to lie in state. "We have talked often," she told Miss Tully, "when there had been a funeral at the Capitol in which a man had lain in state and the crowds had gone by the open coffin, of how much we disliked the practice; and we had made up our minds that we would never allow it."[19]

Two hours or so after departure, Hassett sought out Mrs. Roosevelt.

"I could say little," he recalled. "She [was] very gracious; expressed gratitude and appreciation of all the arrangements I had helped to make… [she was] very generous in her words and calm and composed. [I] assured her I was standing by if I could be of service. [I] returned to my own compartment in the [Conneaut]. [I was] by myself most of the time as the train coursed through the April countryside. Everywhere grief and reverence."[166]

Eleanor spent most of the ride to Washington by herself. "At a time like that, you don't really feel your own feelings," she wrote. "When you're in a position of being caught in a pageant, you become part of a world outside yourself and you act almost like an automaton. You recede as a person. You build a facade for everyone to see and you live separately inside the facade. Something comes to protect you."[19]

The pain must have been crushing for her—to lose her husband and find out at the same time he had been in love with another woman for at least 27 years. But she masked her boiling emotions and at one point asked Mrs. Brady and Miss Tully to sit with her.

Aunt Polly came too—unbidden. The secretaries braced themselves for the question, "Who was with Franklin when he died?" They didn't know how they would answer, because they didn't know if she knew. If she didn't, they didn't want to be the ones to tell her. If she did, their evasiveness could nail them to blatant lies. Eleanor spared them the question; she already knew the answer.

All along the line, schools dismissed classes and children marched to the right of way.

"I never saw the like," Haulbrook remarked. "The stations were jammed with folks; at every crossing, where two soldiers stood at attention as we passed, were crowds that craned their necks to see over the ones in front."[262] Immense clusters of people stood awed and hushed as the train threaded its way between the factories, squalid garages and rundown residential sections of Atlanta. Men and women were perched on the roofs of warehouses and tenements for a better view. Near Terminal Station, traffic was jammed for blocks. As the train passed under the Mitchell Street Viaduct and paused on track 9 at 1:32 p.m., a streetcar passing overhead stopped. Passengers stood up to watch. Thousands lined the bridges, streets and banks above the tracks.

"We faithfully carried out our last orders," Haulbrook said, "and were 15 minutes late when we pulled into Atlanta station, the only time during the 50-odd trips he made over this road as president that it was late. Never to my knowledge was there even a hotbox to slow it down."[262]

On the platform were 2,000 white-gloved soldiers from Camp Sibert, Ala., bearing bayoneted rifles at present arms, lined up as an honor guard. While the cars were iced and the light Pacifics replaced with heavy Pacifics 1409 and 1394, more than 20,000 persons passed through the gates down to the tracks and marched by the train. Prettyman walked Fala along the platform. The Scottie's tail wagged vigorously as flash bulbs went off.

The few dozen reporters and dignitaries allowed close to the train gathered around the Conneaut. Early stepped from the car and Mayor William B. Hartsfield handed him a basket of white gladiolus and red roses. The two men stepped inside and placed them at the body's head. They were the only flowers in the car. Hartsfield removed one rose from the spray, returned to the platform and handed it to Mrs. Charles F. Palmer, wife of a New Deal housing official.

Hartsfield and Early entered the Magellan and the mayor told Mrs. Roosevelt: "There are no words to express our feelings of sorrow today.

"I understand," she answered.[19]

The cortege departed at 2:10 p.m. Blackmon was at the throttle of the 1409; his fireman was Omer Ayers. L.B. Griffith and R.H. Pope trailed them on the 1394.

Through the afternoon, small planes circled the train. The press association trio sat in the diner, too tense to sleep and too tired to talk. As they neared Gainesville, Ga., Merriman Smith pointed to a cotton field they were passing. In the middle of the field, a portly black woman had fallen to her knees and was flailing her arms in the air. Other women fell to

The Roosevelt funeral train stands at Hyde Park, N.Y. Most mourners have gone up the hill to the Roosevelt estate for the president's burial service.

the ground, clasping their hands together. They were sharecroppers at a spring planting, assuming a posture of total supplication. Smith thought of Roosevelt's D-Day prayer of the previous year: "Some will never return. Embrace these, Father, and receive them, Thy heroic servants, into Thy kingdom."[266]

The afternoon sun dipped behind Persimmon Mountain as the train clickety-clacked tediously across a bridge below Lake Keowee. At the edge of darkness, many passengers were having dinner as the train chugged through a new crowd at Greenville, S.C. Once again, there were new engines and a new crew. But there was one difference—relieving engineer O.L. Cocksey and fireman G.M. Cox fastened an American flag across the front of their engine, the 1401, as O.B. Cocksey and "Box" Childers oiled around the second new engine, the 1385. The flag was the

only decoration the train carried throughout its entire journey. It had been borrowed for its solemn duty from Southern's Greenville shop at the order of roundhouse foreman "Dot" Schultz. The 1401 reposes today in the Smithsonian Institution in Washington, a lasting memorial not only to the age of steam but to the Roosevelt era as well.

Twice that evening, Roosevelt's maid, Lizzie McDuffie, walked through the train to the *Magellan*, offering to help since the first lady had not brought along her maid. Each time, Eleanor thanked her and said she needed nothing.

At Hayne, S.C., a great and unusual fatigue came over Mrs. Roosevelt. She ate dinner and asked that the president's bed be prepared. Polly and Daisy offered to sit with her, but she preferred to be alone. Her rest was fleeting. She couldn't sleep, so she leaned on an elbow, peering out into

the night. She watched farmers' families at crossings, hands over hearts. She later wrote:

"I lay in my berth all night with the window shade up, looking out at the countryside he had loved and watching the faces of the people at stations, and even at the crossroads, who came to pay their last tribute all through the night.

"The only recollection I clearly have is thinking about (Millard Lampell's) *The Lonesome Train*, the musical poem about Lincoln's death." ("A lonesome train on a lonesome track / Seven coaches painted black / A slow train, a quiet train / Carrying Lincoln home again ...") "I had always liked it so well—and now this was so much like it.[228]

"I was truly surprised by the people along the way; not only at the stops, but at every crossing. I didn't expect that because I hadn't thought a thing about it. I never realized the full

With the Conneaut *in its uncustomary position behind the* Ferdinand Magellan, *Franklin Roosevelt's funeral train leaves Cold Spring, N.Y., behind as it plies its way toward Hyde Park for the burial service on April 15, 1945.*

scope of the devotion to him until after he died—until that night and after."[19]

At 10:45 p.m., the party arrived in Charlotte, N.C. Surrounding the station for five blocks, people huddled in the dark. As the train stopped, a Boy Scout troop sang "Onward, Christian Soldiers."

"It started ragged at first, but then it spread and swelled," Merriman Smith recalled. "Soon eight or ten thousand voices were singing like an organ. Those people were scared to death. They weren't singing for a departed soul. They were singing for themselves, to hold themselves up, as though they were asking, 'What are we going to do now?' "[19]

"When the hymn ended, Negroes knelt down and began to sing spirituals," added AP's Harold Oliver. "A lot of whites joined them. The Negroes were separated to one side, by themselves. Most of them never got to vote for FDR, but they came out late at night to pray for him."[19]

Now, in the darkness, with shades drawn, the train cut through the moonlit countryside. The cars were all black except one—the *Conneaut.* Its shades were up, its parlor dimly lit to reveal the visible fragment of the flag and the four stone-still sentries.

At Salisbury, N.C., the 1400 and the 1367 replaced the 1401 and 1385. Engineers were S.A. Shuping and O.L. Pierce; firemen were V.G. Faison and R.H. Eller.

Toward midnight, Lizzie McDuffie went to bed.

"I don't think I slept hardly any that night," she remarked. "I turned off my lights and lifted my shade. I thought about everything in the world, about all the trips we'd made to Warm Springs, to California with the grandchildren and different places like that. Lying in my berth, and knowing the president's body was lying in the back, I couldn't get away from thinking of conditions of things when Mr. Roosevelt became president. I lay there and thought about the bread lines I saw on the very day I was leaving my home in Atlanta to go to Washington to work for him. I thought about a man who was a friend of ours, who was an insurance collector who was very prosperous. He had lost his position because people didn't have any money to pay their life insurance. I thought of him so much because three years later I remember going home and meeting him on the street all dressed up nice. He had gotten his job back collecting insurance and his children had started back to school. It was just another picture than what it was when I left.

"And I lay there and thought of the terrible blunder I made when the King and Queen of England came to Washington [in 1939]. There was a man named Charles Thompson that worked at the White House and he wanted their autograph. One day I overheard him tell somebody, 'Take this picture upstairs and see if you can't get Lizzie McDuffie to get them to autograph it. Lizzie'll do anything you ask her for.' Well, I heard that and spoke up. I said, 'I'll ask. They can't do anything except say "yes" or "no".' And I asked one of those English people to try to get it for me. Later Mrs. Roosevelt said to me, 'Why, Mrs. McDuffie'—most of the time that's what she called me— "why, you shouldn't have asked any member of the queen's staff. You should have carried it to Mrs. [Edith] Helm or Miss Thompson.' She wasn't angry, though. Mrs. Roosevelt never got angry. She'd just say, 'There's one thing about it, Lizzie. If you benefit by the mistake you have made, then everything will be all right.' She is the most considerate person that was ever born, Mrs. Roosevelt is."[19]

Hassett made a few notes in his diary before going to bed.

"FDR made his last journey from Warm Springs this morning—the strangeness and unreality of all that has happened in so brief a time. President Truman has already taken over and is, I suppose, at the desk in the Executive Office where the late Boss sat for more than 12 years. The deeper lesson of it is that no matter how unexpected the change, the succession is quiet and orderly and the processes of government continue."[19]

Somewhere in the night, the panting steam locomotives stopped at a water tank sandwiched between two cliffs of farmland. As the fireman of the lead locomotive stood on the tender and swung the penstock around with a long iron hook, he didn't see the face of a black man disappear from the top of one of the cliffs. Soon he had come back with other faces, sleepy ones. A deep voice began singing the sad sweet notes of "Hand Me Down My Walkin' Cane"—a wish that Roosevelt would have identified with during most of his life. Other voices, some shrill, picked up the words. Dark faces appeared on the other cliff, then ran back to their shacks awakening the very young and the very old. They picked up the song, too, but couldn't hear for the rushing of torrents of water and didn't keep together with the other choir. The fireman wondered why. The train inched forward until the second locomotive was in position. The pipe returned, gushing clear, cold water into the hot, grimy tender. The mourners offered another chorus, singing until the pipe was slammed away a second time and a roar of sound and skyward showers of sparks announced that the train was leaving. Those who would work the fields tomorrow had paid their respects tonight.

The passengers spent the night fitfully; the train moved through town after town, the crowds waiting unfailingly. At Monroe, Va., the last engine trade took place. The 1366 and the 1406 were coupled on for the last leg to Washington, with engineers C.R. Yowell and T.S. Hunter and firemen H.D. Ansboro and S.C. Curtin.

At 6:20 a.m., the train reached Charlottesville, Va., and at 8:15, Yowell and Hunter eased their steeds onto the long siding at Bealton, Va. They were just 45 miles out of Washington, but had to pull off to let No. 48, the northbound *Southerner*, fly by. Yowell's mind was on business. This time, he would take the president directly into Union Station and back into a team track, looking for a signal from Trainmaster J.W. Shelton so he could spot the *Conneaut's* window directly beside another hastily built wooden ramp.

No. 48 roared past while passengers on the standing train finished eating breakfast and packing. The special was back on the mainline at 8:27, chugging slowly toward Manassas. The sun was up now as the cortege passed wooded dells and small streams racing toward the Rappahannock. Dogwoods dropped petals like a little flower girl at a wedding; neatly terraced farms sported bursting barns and faded Bull Durham signs.

Hassett got up and brought Mrs. Roosevelt a message that had come overnight from Edith Helm, the White House's social secretary. She wanted to know what hymns to select for the White House funeral. Eleanor chose the Navy hymn, "Eternal Father, Strong to Save," and "Faith of Our Fathers."

She added that she wanted the service to incorporate the words from her husband's first inaugural address that she felt meant more to him than any of his others: "The only thing we have to fear is fear itself."[19] She told Hassett she wanted those words inscribed on her husband's tombstone, but this wasn't done since among Roosevelt's papers was a memo stipulating that the stone be marked only with the names of the president and Mrs. Roosevelt and their birth and death dates.

The train lumbered across the Long Bridge spanning the Potomac, its wheels creating a roaring sound as it rumbled through the Virginia Avenue Tunnel under the U.S. Capitol. At 9:40, it stopped at K Tower and backed into the easternmost of two team tracks next to the mail and express warehouse along the eastern side of Union Station beyond track 30. Yowell moved his train at a walk; Flagman R.P. Iseman waved his free arm slowly in a circle from the *Conneaut's* bottom step. The platform, Iseman saw, was full of fashionable people. The entire Supreme Court and Cabinet, the Roosevelt family, President Truman, 15 appointed congressmen and 15 appointed senators were there. At 9:50, the rear coupler nosed close to the track's bumper post and Iseman held his arm straight out; Yowell stopped.

Iseman shoved a Secret Service agent aside and jumped off to make sure the window that would be removed was opposite the ramp. It was. He stood on tiptoes and signaled another stop signal. The train sighed as the locomotives uncoupled and the air hoses parted.

First to enter the *Conneaut* were Roosevelt's daughter, Anna; his son Elliott; and Elliott's wife, actress Faye Emerson (the other sons, Franklin Jr., James and John, were in the service in the Pacific and either couldn't come home or made it too late). Then Franklin Jr.'s wife, Ethel; and John's wife, Anne, followed. Then President Truman led the assembled officials in, followed by Major Harry Hooker, an attorney and old family friend; Malvina Thompson, Eleanor's secretary; and Edith Helm. None of them went at first toward the *Magellan*, where Eleanor waited in the lounge.

All of them could be seen from the platform, looking down at the casket. One or two wept. Valet Arthur Prettyman led family members into the *Magellan.* Behind them came Truman; Jimmy Byrnes, recently resigned director of the Office of War Mobilization; and former Vice President Henry Wallace, now Commerce secretary. The new president proved his political acumen by inviting them along: "They both thought they ought to be sitting where I was. A lot of people in the country thought so, and so I thought asking them was the proper thing to do."[255]

Eleanor, ever gracious, had an especially warm handshake for Wallace. She radiated an aura of sympathy for those trying to comfort her. Some of them sobbed, while the widow added to her small smile and ladylike phrases a few timid pats on selected shoulders. She was embarrassed at the ordeal.

Military pallbearers from Fort Myer, in white gloves and braided shoulder cords, unloaded the coffin the same way it had come on board—through the window opening—this time onto a horse-drawn caisson. At 9:58, the procession started toward the White House, moving onto crowd-lined Delaware Avenue and turning west at Constitution Avenue. The funeral would be in the East Room of the White House at 4 p.m.

Folks milling around Union Station asked Porter Fred Fair for souvenirs from the presidential car. "I had never really thought about [getting souvenirs] until then, but before I left I got these," he said, holding up a drinking glass, a bar of soap and a half-used box of wooden matches with the blue and white Pullman Company emblem. "This was his drinking glass," he pointed proudly. "It is just like he left it. It's still got his fingerprints on it."[67]

Three trains waited at Union Station when the cortege returned at 9:30 p.m. for the trip to Hyde Park. The second, a 13-car special added to haul members of Congress, the Supreme Court, diplomats and additional mourners, was lined up on track 20. The third was for an escort of 454 Marine officers and men. The presidential train had been lengthened to 17 cars; some had been removed, several more had taken their places.

The POTUS train quartered the Truman and Roosevelt families, Cabinet members and their spouses and the heads of most of the major federal agencies. Secret Service precautions were extraordinary—never had such an assemblage of government leaders traveled on a single train.

The B&O stationed protect steam engines at Washington, the PRR stationed several protect wreck trains between there and New York, and the NYC positioned emergency equipment along its Hudson River line. All freight trains were ordered to reduce speed to 30 miles an hour two hours before the funeral train passed and grind to a halt altogether an hour in advance. Passenger trains traveling in the same direction as Roosevelt's train could not pass it without specific authority, and those going the opposite way had to pass at no more than 20 miles an hour. Yard operations adjacent to main tracks were suspended during the passing, and hostlers were prohibited from firing up steam engines lest safety valves pop with their startling loud whoosh. Baggage trucks were removed from station platforms everywhere along the way.

Dewey Long had to allocate space to 196 people on the funeral train and 78 others on the congressional train. Because there were so many high-ranking government officials to be catered to, the task was a protocol nightmare.

Grace Tully arrived just as the casket was being hoisted up to the window slot.

"I usually boarded on the rear end of the train when the Boss was alive,"

The exhaust behind the Roosevelt funeral train indicates that NYC Hudson 5244 has arrived, ready to couple on and pull the train backward to Poughkeepsie for servicing during the president's burial service.

she said, "and did so that night out of habit only to find that I had intruded on President Truman, his wife and daughter, and Jimmy Byrnes."[415]

Byrnes, who was talking, looked up and stopped.

"I remember how surprised I was to see him," Miss Tully said, "and at first I didn't realize I was bursting in on the president of the United States. Though I had seen Mr. Roosevelt's coffin, my mind had not yet accepted the fact that he was dead. Suddenly I came out of my daze and apologized for what I had done, and went on through the car toward my own compartment."[415]

Records show that GG-1 electrics 4909 and 4911 just back from a "super inspection" and cleaning at Wilmington, Del., PRR shops, were chosen to pull the funeral and con-gressional trains, although they don't mention which locomotive pulled which train. In any event, Roosevelt's was the first POTUS funeral train to have electric power, and indications are that it required two of the mighty engines. At precisely 10 p.m., the crew started "doubling" the train—the locomotives pulled the front 10 cars from No. 2 team track, and backed in No. 1 team track to get the rear seven. They stalled three times while trying to lug the cortege out of town; the third yank broke a coupler between two cars, delaying the scheduled 10:20 p.m. departure.

While the funeral train was struggling to leave, the congressional train departed without incident at 10:42, 27 minutes late. Along with its distin-guished passenger list, it also carried two baggage cars containing 15 truck-loads of flowers that had shown up to be taken to the cemetery despite the family's request that there be none.

The funeral train finally cleared New York Avenue at 11:03, 39 minutes late.

In a car carrying 13 reporters and five radio men, the heavy mood of the day began to lift and the newsmen began to joke. William C. Murphy Jr. of the *Philadelphia Inquirer* grew impatient with the delay and wise-cracked to his fellows: "The Republicans have always known it would be hard to get Roosevelt out of Washington."[42]

Murphy was asked by one of his colleagues why he didn't get off the train and go home while he had the chance. The *Inquirer*, he was remind-ed, would be fed more wire material than it could possibly use.

"No sir," Murphy replied. "You guys will be coming back as soon as the old man is buried, but not me. I'm going to sit by his grave for three days and see if he really rises."[19]

Near midnight, the train rumbled quietly into PRR's Baltimore depot. Margaret Truman got out of bed and carefully lifted her shade to look out upon glowing flares illuminating what she described as "row on row on row of impassive, solemn faces."[19]

She got the feeling that it was an intrusion to be looking unseen at the naked grief of others. She lowered the shade and the train stole on through the dark city.

Her father's mind also was on the people outside. "Every place we stopped there'd be a crowd just as if—well, you'd think the world had come to an end," he sighed. "And I thought so, too."[255]

"Sleep was practically impossible," Margaret wrote. "When I did sleep, I had nightmares about trying to open a window and escape from a small suffocating room."[100]

Hassett said goodnight to Mrs. Roosevelt. "On going to bed," he wrote, "found I was to share a compartment [G, Car 5, in the sleeper *Glen Brook*] with Leighton McCarthy [who had been associated with Roosevelt at Warm Springs]. Always the courtly gentleman, Leighton; I finally had to order him to take the lower and myself climbed into the upper berth."[166]

In Car 3, the *Roald Amundsen*, Truman was having an intense discussion with Byrnes, sizing him up as a future secretary of state. Byrnes had been at Yalta, and had an exact knowledge of the agreements reached there.

Despite the banter in the press car, the mood permeating the train was one of grief. More liquor than food was consumed.

In Car 6, the *Wordsworth*, where most of the Cabinet was, Postmaster General Frank Walker and Commerce Secretary Henry Wallace each sat gloomily by himself. Some drank heavily. Others watched. Treasury Secretary Henry Morgenthau commented privately to one of his colleagues that Secretary of State Ed Stettinius looked "nervous as a witch."[42] Morgenthau informed the gathering that when he had seen Roosevelt the night before he died, the Boss's hand shook more than usual as he poured a cocktail before dinner. But otherwise he looked well and his mind clicked rapidly and accurately as Morgenthau submitted a few matters for clearance.

The mask of politeness was in tatters. Secretary of the Interior Harold L. Ickes, with a pinched face and tart tongue, was the most talkative in the car, free with unflattering comments about the new president—some in his hearing. He bickered with his red-haired wife, saying over and over, "You don't understand the time we're living in."[19] Mrs. Ickes left the car and sat up until 1:30 with her old friend Miss Tully.

Harry Hopkins, a close Roosevelt confidant who had been commerce secretary during the chief's second term, was telling anyone who would listen that Truman's name had definitely not been "pulled out of a hat"[19] five months ago, that Roosevelt had been watching his performance for some time and had put him on the ticket because he enjoyed prestige in

the Senate, where peace treaties would have to be ratified, had led his Senate committee well and was popular. In truth, at this point few people recognized the short, bespectacled Missourian. By the time this great debate was settled, or maybe just tabled because of weariness, the train was nearing Philadelphia.

The train drew onto Penn Station's track 12 in New York at 4:36 a.m. Sunday. POTUS trains always used tracks 11 and 12 because they led directly to and from the Hudson River tunnels and required no change of track. Amid a heavily guarded platform, the locomotives were changed and at 5 a.m. the cortege eased away. It was pulled backward into Mott Haven Yard in the Bronx, via the New Haven branch from New Rochelle, and paused there from 6:20 to 6:40 a.m.

One source said the congressional train ran around it here so all the mourners could be in place when it arrived at Hyde Park, but Southern and PRR archives agree that the congressional train departed Washington first and ran ahead of the funeral train all the way. The latter was originally scheduled to leave Washington at 10 p.m. and the congressional train at 10:05, but these plans were changed perhaps because of the need to double the funeral train before departure.

Secret Service men, patrolmen, detectives and military police formed a circle around the funeral train while it sat in Mott Haven Yard, keeping spectators away. Soldiers manned submachine guns atop a viaduct at 156th Street. Military police patrolled the streets between Park and Sheridan avenues and from 156th to 161st

On Saturday, April 14, 1945, as preparations were being made for a Franklin Roosevelt memorial service in the Erie Railroad shops at Hornell, N.Y., Supt. George Seitz brought in photos of the two Erie locomotives, 2928 and 2933, that had hauled President Harding's funeral train into Marion, Ohio, on Aug. 9, 1923. By some quirk of fate, both locomotives were being repaired at that moment in the Hornell shops.

streets.

Truman, in his bedroom, was holding a dawn conference with Ickes. Wallace sat alone in one of the diners with hot cereal and coffee. A gang of car washers worked the train. One laborer sloshed a bucket of water against the window. Wallace ducked, then smiled.

Grudgingly, the train headed for Hyde Park—along the edge of the Hudson, through Spuyten Duyvil, rumbling loudly on the Harlem River bridge with the sheer green of the Palisades on the other shore. At Harmon, NYC 4-6-4 No. 5283 and NYC buffer coach 1310 eased against the train, swelling it to 18 cars for the last leg of the trip.

Hassett went back to ask if he could be of service to Mrs. Roosevelt. He excused himself as the Secret Service OK'd his passage through the *Roald Amundsen*, Truman's car. He noted in his diary: "Haven't met the president or any of his staff as yet."[166] The line between the Truman and Roosevelt people was growing sharper—intentionally. The outs were in, and they remembered that the Roosevelt crowd paid scant attention to the vice president except to relay messages from the Boss.

Hassett found Mrs. Roosevelt sitting at a window staring at passing rails. She emerged from her reverie to offer her cheery "good morning"[42] and to say she needed nothing. Hassett thought the scenery across the Hudson was breathtaking, but Eleanor didn't seem to notice it. She returned to watching the silvery rails slide by.

In the gray Sunday morning farther north, the procession neared the tiny town of Garrison, opposite West Point. A man writing for the *New Yorker's* "Talk of the Town" positioned himself near the track. Another man and his small son arrived.

"You've got to remember every-thing you see today," the father said. The boy shivered. "It's awfully cold."[19]

Two or three dozen automobiles collected, including Model A Fords and a 1942 Cadillac. Their occupants seemed more excited than sad as they stood by the station, and the writer thought that proper: "Franklin Roosevelt would have preferred to have left his world with more of a bang than a whimper."[452]

As they waited, they gossiped. "I couldn't tell old Mrs. Beldon on Friday. The shock would have been too much for her."

"I wish … he'd managed to hang on until Germany was licked."

"I wish the people would all stand in one place on the platform. It would make a bigger tribute."[239]

A Garrison boy in a red-and-blue-striped Mackinaw blanket dashed to the watchman's shack and back, shouting: "Be here in three min-utes."[19]

Three minutes went by. No train. A group of bearded Capuchin brothers, wearing sandals and brown cassocks with white cords, arrived. They had walked a mile from their monastery at Glenclyffe.

A woman in the crowd said: "It'll be just terrible if I don't see him." A man assured her, "They'll slow up when they see us."

A plume of white smoke appeared over the trees. The first train passed, and 15 minutes later the 5283 curved into view. Some men removed their hats, as others had for Lincoln, Grant and Arthur. The panting Hudson pounded by, then car after car. The youth with the Mackinaw shouted, and for an instant they all had a clear view of the flag-draped coffin as the *Conneaut*, with its military guard, rumbled past and was gone up the track.

"I saw him!" a little girl cried. "I saw him real plain!"

Her mother, embarrassed, said:

"You couldn't have seen him. He was sleeping under the American flag."

"I saw him," the girl insisted.[19]

The boy and his father, among the first to come, now started to leave.

"I saw everything," the boy said.

"That's good," the father answered. "Now make sure you remember."[19]

On board, Roosevelt's daughter, Anna, and Col. John Boettiger, her second husband, breakfasted early. She was cheerful, making her way through the train greeting passengers and trying to keep the conversation away from her father's death. She had also sought the Truman people and had exchanged greetings.

Several miles to the north, Captain Francis Resta, leader of the Army Band of the United States Military Academy at West Point, labored over a difficult decision as the band bus grunted across the Mid-Hudson Bridge toward Poughkeepsie. He had to act fast; Hyde Park was only six miles up the river.

Resta lumbered down the aisle to the seat of First Sergeant Mervin Chamberlain. Glancing toward a young bugler in the rear, he told Chamberlain, "We can't take a chance on him. Look, he's chewing his fingers off, he's so jumpy. I say let Fisher do it. He's cool, sure of himself. Go tell him."

Chamberlain moved toward first chair solo cornetist Master Sergeant Newell E. Fisher. He spoke a few words, Fisher nodded, and Chamberlain returned to his seat. Fisher pondered his new assignment—to play taps at his commander in chief's burial. The opportunity had seemed so remote just 2½ days ago when his young son had said, "The man in the light house is dead," and his daughter had corrected the boy: "Junior's got it wrong. It said the man in the WHITE House is dead."[19]

His first sad duty as president concluded, Harry S. Truman boards the Roosevelt funeral train at Hyde Park, N.Y., for the return to Washington April 15, 1945.

The bus stopped near a private siding at the edge of the Roosevelt estate to await the train. The track was one of several built in the area to hold private cars of the wealthy who lived along the banks of the Hudson in Dutchess and Putnam Counties.

Mahopac, Cold Spring, Hopewell Jct., Wappinger's Falls, Poughkeepsie, Arlington, Pleasant Valley—names that had been so familiar to FDR—passed in succession. The funeral party was getting closer to its destination.

At 8:08 a.m., seven minutes early,

the congressional train arrived at Hyde Park. It quickly disgorged its clientele and was on its way. Near Poughkeepsie, engineer C.J. Potter was handed a message as fireman T.J. Doyle watched. It confirmed that the congressional train was out of the way—good news, for they had only a few miles to go.

The funeral train eased onto the siding at the Roosevelt estate just below Hyde Park and stopped for unloading at 8:40, having "some difficulty in getting it exact,"[165] according to NYC passenger representative

Herbert H. Harwood Sr. The last part of the train was still on the main line; stepboxes were positioned on the ballast so those passengers could disembark, then someone decided to pull the train up at 9:20 to unload them more safely. The family got off at 9:50 and the coffin was once again lifted through the *Conneaut's* window slot.

The mighty blast of a cannon rocked the earth. Fifteen seconds later, the violence exploded again. Then again and again, at 15-second intervals, 21 times in all. The sound carried across the Hudson and back again, like old thunder. Birds fled as a sexton grabbed the bell rope at Roosevelt's home church, St. James Episcopal, in the village. The deep bronze pealing reverberated through the town and into the skies. Those already in the rose garden heard a faint hum and glanced skyward. From a grove of leafy trees came several thundering bombers, soaring over Crum Elbow as silent mourners squinted into the sunlight. The pallbearers slid the coffin into a hearse that carried it a short distance to the foot of a great bluff below the family homestead.

There, it was laid on a caisson led by six brown horses. Behind the caisson followed a seventh brown horse; its head and most of its body was hooded, stirrups turned backward, a sword and an upside-down boot hanging from the left one—the symbol of a fallen warrior.

Led by the West Point band in dark blue tunics and light blue trousers with white stripes, the caisson began its climb up the winding, thickly wooded dirt "river road" Roosevelt's father had had graded in 1870.

At the top of this hill, FDR was born on Jan. 30, 1882; now, 63 years later, in his mother's rose garden, his body would be laid to rest.

Henrietta Nesbitt, FDR's White House housekeeper, alighting from the Pullman *Glen Gordon*, noticed crews unloading flowers from the baggage cars that had been set off nearby. The burial was still an hour and 20 minutes away; some remained on board for a while.

Automobiles began a shuttle service, taking mourners up to the cliff where young Franklin used to lie on his belly in his rich, sheltered childhood and watch NYC trains and river steamers—likely the setting that kindled in him a lifetime love of trains and travel.

Hassett rode up the hill canopied with old elms and edged with wild violets. It was another fair day, the river dimpled by a westerly breeze. Riding with him were Mrs. Nesbitt and Edwin Pauley, the Democrats' treasurer.

The train returned to Poughkeepsie to be cleaned and resupplied, pulled backward by NYC Hudson 5244 and an idler coach pointed south. Dewey Long had allotted only an hour and a half to do the job and return to Hyde Park, but he made it. The burial accomplished, the train—scheduled to leave Hyde Park at 11:30—managed to get away 20 minutes late, according to PRR records. "The car in which Mrs. Roosevelt and the family rode [now] was last on the train," Hassett noted. "The president, Mrs. Truman, Miss Truman, and the aides in the next-to-the-last car."[166] The congressional train left at 12:18 p.m., 28 minutes late.

As the funeral train proceeded down the Hudson shore, presidential press aide Jonathan Daniels checked on his father, Josephus.

"I found him alone in his compartment looking out of the window at the river moving by," he wrote. "I knew he was seeing an even longer stream. It was more than strange that he … who had been born before Lincoln's funeral, should be riding on the speeding train headed … southward from the great funeral at Hyde Park. He had seemed old—and a little old-fashioned—beside Franklin Roosevelt when [as secretary of the Navy under Woodrow Wilson] he had brought Roosevelt to Washington as assistant secretary of the Navy, and almost as a boy. Now Roosevelt was dead and [Josephus] was very tired."[103]

Daniels noted a change of atmosphere:

"The train which had come up slowly and proudly in the morning altered its pace and character as it rolled down the valley from Hyde Park. A kind of wake, which dignity and official grief had restrained before, began in the compartments of those most hurt. There were signs of a new decisiveness among those who in death and change were most hopeful. Outside, some small crowds of the curious watched in Beacon and Peekskill, where so many had watched in the morning. The train moved, scarcely slowing, through the towns."[103]

At Mott Haven, where the special rested from 1:50 to 2:50 p.m., its consist was changed for the final time. Pullman *Sunbeam*, a 2-compartment, 1-drawing room, buffet/lounge/observation car, was substituted for 12-section, drawing room sleeper *Crusader Rose*.

Hassett checked on Eleanor again.

"She (was) very calm and composed, gracious and thoughtful, as through all the long ordeal from Warm Springs last Thursday to the rose garden (at Hyde Park) this morning. Merely asked me to notify the White House to prepare dinner for nine tonight."[166]

"Night came on as it moved again through the darkness and the lights of Jersey," Daniels continued. "There were no more stops, and some of the passengers were sure that for them and for much more this was the end of the ride."[103]

Sometime that evening as the train rumbled down the busy PRR mainline, Dewey Long was able to lie down. He didn't sleep, he said, until he got home in Silver Spring, Md., that night, but it was something to have a little rest.

He had not been to bed since the morning of the 12th, more than three days.

The train arrived back at Washington at 8:35 p.m., 40 minutes late. Pullman Special Agent/Inspector P.C. Darcey noted a successful run:

"minor repairs enroute."[149]

Dwight D. Eisenhower

U.S. railroading was praised around the world for its handling of Dwight D. Eisenhower's cortege in 1969. Once Eisenhower, 78, died of heart disease in Washington's Walter Reed Army Medical Center on Friday, March 28, a plan went into effect that had been in development virtually since he left office eight years before. The Chesapeake & Ohio/Baltimore & Ohio, Norfolk & Western and Union Pacific pulled off a 2,804-mile, 85-hour movement called "MAIN (Military Authorization Identification Number) 200" that trundled from Washington, D.C., to Abilene, Kan., March 31-April 2 with appro-priate grace and solemnity.

Ike was a military man most of his life; the 10-car special was arranged by the Army and was a closely held military secret. The Eisenhower family "was horrified by the circus atmosphere" that had sur-rounded the Robert Kennedy train of a year before, a family friend explained, and feared a repeat of the tragic deaths associated with it [See Page 292]. The Eisenhower move-ment would be simply a funeral pro-cession, a family matter.

The body, dressed in Ike's military uniform and the Eisenhower jacket he made famous, was moved Saturday from a mortuary to Washington's National Cathedral, where a small family service was held and some pub-lic viewing was permitted. On Sunday, it was transferred to the Rotunda of the U.S. Capitol, where 60,000 mourners filed through as it lay in state. The body was returned to the cathedral on Monday for a 30-minute service attended by mourning world leaders. Afterward, the proces-sion to Union Station—and Kansas—began in the chilly springtime dusk.

To the strains of "Army Blue," the West Point hymn, and a 21-gun salute, nine military pallbearers car-ried Eisenhower's GI-issue gunmetal steel coffin across a hushed Union Station concourse to a simple, humble baggage car, the C&O 314. Eisenhower had insisted his remains be hauled as any other serviceman's would. Widow Mamie Eisenhower, at age 72 bowed and frail, had arrived 10 minutes earlier and inspected the car personally.

The flag-draped casket was placed on its catafalque after being carried inside the 314 through the rearmost door on the fireman's side. An American flag and the presidential standard stood beside the bier on the engineer's side. The dozen enlisted men belonging to the honor guard and their commander would see to it that five of them continuously guard-ed the coffin until it reached Abilene.

AT&SF business car *Santa Fe*, assigned to Santa Fe President John S. Reed, was requested for Mrs. Eisenhower because the couple had used it many times. They had ridden it frequently on golf outings to Palm Springs, Calif., including the ride a year before, after which he was strick-en with his final illness. Now, like a riderless horse, the car would leave town without Ike, carrying his widow and family. Oxygen was placed on board in case it was needed by Mrs. Eisenhower, who had a rheumatic heart condition.

The *Santa Fe*'s crew included Wallace Blackburn of Chicago, a chef, and Larry Wright of Topeka and Warren Nobles of Chicago, stewards. The trio had made several trips with the first family. The car had a well-equipped kitchen, crew quarters, a din-ing room seating eight to 10 with a television on one wall, four double bed-rooms, and an observation-end sitting

Posing for a company photographer is the crew of the pilot train that will precede Dwight Eisenhower's funeral train westward from Washington. From left are engi-neer H.F. Tulloh, fireman R.L Davis, conductor R.O. Meeks and flagman C.D. Richardson.

A catafalque, draped in black and bordered by the U.S. and presidential standards, awaits the body of Dwight D. Eisenhower in C&O baggage car 314 at Washington Union Station March 31, 1969.

About 700 people stand attentively despite the early hour and cold temperature as the Eisenhower funeral train rolls through Charleston, W.Va., April 1, 1969.

room with desk and radio-telephone.

The *Santa Fe*'s boarding list included Mrs. Eisenhower in room A, Ambassador-designate to Belgium and Mrs. John Eisenhower (son and daughter-in-law) in B, Col. and Mrs. G. Gordon Moore (Mamie's sister) in C and Dr. Milton Eisenhower, who later served on C&O/B&O's board of directors, in D. This brother, however, nine years younger than Ike, missed the trip. He began feeling dizzy before the funeral and checked himself into Walter Reed for tests.

With everyone on board, two Washington Terminal RS1 yard engines nosed against the rear of the eight-car cut in track 17 and, at 6:50 p.m., March 31, 1969, pulled it north and shoved it into track 25, coupling it to the rider coach and C&O E8 diesels 4028 and 4016 and B&O E9 1457. Then, a third switcher went in on track 17 for the *Santa Fe* and placed it on the rear of the rest of the train. At 7:09, MAIN 200 eased into the darkness of the Virginia Avenue Tunnel, and Ike's body was on its way home.

As the gleaming blue, yellow, and gray streamliner traced the historic path through northern Virginia under a full moon, spectators crowded to trackside in city and country alike, jamming station platforms and grade crossings, standing for hours, and slowing the train from 50 miles an hour to 5 or 10. The numbers grew as word of the train's progress was spread by the news media and lower-echelon railroaders; the railroad hierarchy maintained its silence. Respectful but chilled bystanders sang hymns, waved flags and raised sparklers through this last night of March. As those who had held candles to mark the passage of earlier funeral trains, many of these mourners dimmed their automobile headlights. Signs read, "Ike, We Miss You," and "Mamie, We're With You," or similar condolences.

Once the journey had started, there were the usual unforeseen bugs to be worked out, such as some changes in room assignments. But the first real problem on the train involved alcoholic beverages. Ordered not to stock them, the C&O/B&O felt there would nevertheless be a demand for them and had stashed away a small amount on board.

As it turned out, that supply was imbibed quickly and a clamor arose for more. A military man approached a railroad officer, arguing that it had been a mistake to prohibit alcohol and asked what could be done. The train was in Virginia, which had a state monopoly on liquor sales. And it was night—meaning all the liquor stores were closed. State police were sent searching for a store that could be reopened, when someone remembered that the railroad's own commissary at Charlottesville, although shut down, still contained ample stocks. Access to a store was, in fact, arranged, but it was the railroad's supply that was used and the state police were called off.

Meanwhile, nighttime did nothing to dissuade the crowds.

At Manassas, 1,000 people gathered; at Culpeper, about 250 and a VFW color guard were on hand; and at Orange, another 300, some of whom waited 90 minutes. At Charlottesville, some 2,000-plus were at the depot, 50 of them singing the "Battle Hymn of the Republic." A thousand more greeted the special at Waynesboro after it climbed Afton Mountain. At Staunton, there were 1,500. At Clifton Forge, a throng of 1,100 started gathering at 10 p.m, keeping the YMCA restaurant next to the depot busy serving coffee and hot tea until Passenger Extra 4028 West arrived for a crew change and departed at 12:27 a.m., April 1.

Automobiles were lined up all

AT&SF office car Santa Fe *slips away from the Huntington, W.Va., station as Dwight Eisenhower's funeral train continues westward on the C&O April 1, 1969.*

through the downtown area of White Sulphur Springs, W.Va. A crowd of more than 1,500 shivered in a 10-degree chill, including a retired Army colonel in full dress uniform. *The Greenbrier*, the C&O's resort hotel where Ike had spent many relaxing moments in world affairs and golfing, wanted to give the general his final salute. Honor guard members, in return, saluted the colors from a Dutch door of the 11-bedroom sleeper *Homestead*.

Crowd counts at Hinton and Prince, W.Va., were 500 each, including children in pajamas, coats and blankets; at Montgomery, 1,000; at the state capital, Charleston, 600 to 700, with the National Guard and Gov. Arch Moore's honor guard in frontier costumes of white buckskin, presenting arms. At St. Albans, about 450 were out.

At Huntington, perhaps 1,500 people were kept away from the station platform and jammed the parking plaza; one man had driven 200 miles down from Akron, Ohio. The temperature in this Ohio River valley city was 25 degrees; nevertheless, spectators were adorned in blankets,

pajamas and hair curlers. The local ministerial association offered a 30-minute religious service before the train arrived, with singing and flag-waving schoolchildren. The Jaycees provided free coffee.

An American Legion honor guard and World War I veterans in uniform were on hand. All this, starting at 5 a.m.

Officials on the train were impressed. In the first response of the journey, Col. Clements Riley of the U.S. Department of the Army got off the train briefly and thanked them.

An extra locomotive, coach and sleeper were standing nearby if needed, but were not dispatched.

The crowds continued as the new day arrived: Kenova, 50; Ashland, Ky., 2,000 and a color guard; Russell, 200; South Portsmouth, 700; Newport, 100.

At Cincinnati, the train, minus its diesels, was looped on the coach yard balloon track north of the Union Terminal so it could head west on the B&O. It was also run through the washer, despite the cold drizzle, but as in Washington, the baggage car was hand-scrubbed. Now, by intention,

the third of three passenger diesels coupled in a C&O-C&O-B&O configuration would head the train on its home road.

Meanwhile, a memorial service to have been led by Ohio Gov. James Rhodes inside Cincinnati Union Terminal was canceled at the Eisenhower family's request. Instead, Ike's older brother, Edgar, having seen the crowds at Kentucky towns while at breakfast aboard C&O business car 15, emerged during the 88-minute Queen City stop to thank everybody.

"We are especially grateful to the many schoolchildren who have turned out across the country to pay their respects," Edgar told a crowd in the waiting room. "This has been a tremendous strain on Mrs. Eisenhower, but she seems to be bearing up well."[389am] Perhaps concern for the widow was one reason that Dr. D.J. Foglia, a medical doctor working for the railroad on retainer, rode the train from Cincinnati to St. Louis.

Mamie had expressed concern because she had seen people saluting her car instead of the 314. So someone, either Edgar or Mamie, asked that bunting and American flags be rounded up—and somehow they were—for the baggage car. Mrs. Gordon Moore, Mamie's sister, stepped off the train and supervised their placement. Railroaders had trouble making them stay in place, and officers cast a wary eye on them the rest of the way to Abilene.

One of the flags became so tattered that it had to be replaced at St. Louis. Then, while the train raced along the UP near Manhattan, Kan., some bunting tore off one side of the 314. Since Mrs. Eisenhower had instructed that any dislodged decorations were to be retrieved lest they become someone's souvenir and destroy the occasion's dignity and privacy, the special made a momentary stop and the materials were collected.

The train tried to proceed through Indiana and Illinois at 50 mph, but it fell further behind schedule wading through masses of humanity at restricted speed in towns large and small. The scenes often were touching: children standing along a retaining wall on Cincinnati's west side, at attention in the pouring rain, American flag in one hand and saluting with the other; an old man on a hillside holding up a large, framed portrait of Eisenhower; hundreds of schoolchildren each clinging to a small flag, lined up along a farmer's fence; a snappy salute from an aged Indiana farmer standing alone in his field, wearing his Eisenhower jacket and Army hat; masses crowding every station and highway crossing with almost religious awe, waving flags, presenting salutes, holding hands over hearts.

At Aurora, Ind., 750 people, including 30 high-school boys holding flags, lined the entire length of the depot platform. At Seymour, 6,000 were in attendance, for by now it was afternoon and school was out. In Washington, Ind., a railroad town of 11,000 population, 10,000 to 15,000 came to see the train. Gov. Edgar D. Whitcomb handed a bouquet of red geraniums and white lilies to a military officer for Mrs. Eisenhower. Edgar Eisenhower again stepped off the train and termed the turnout "a great tribute."[389am]

At St. Louis Union Station, a brass band played and 650 spectators watched as Mamie, son John, and grandson David came out on the *Santa Fe's* rear platform for the first time. Mrs. Eisenhower said several times, "I'm most grateful for all the expressions of love." David took her hand, and added, "I feel the same way."[389am] Brother-in-law Edgar, in the depot, remarked that "I want to pay my deepest and sincerest respects to all the thoughtful persons who have lined the tracks and have come to the station."[386f]

Now in the charge of three Norfolk & Western passenger diesels, MAIN 200 departed St. Louis and proceeded westward into the night toward its prairie destination. On board, people settled down to enjoy the ride, trade Eisenhower stories, or catch a few winks. Only once did a railroad man have to stop a military officer who, having had too much to drink, tried to enter the family section of the train in his skivvies.

Out of Kansas City in the wee hours of Wednesday behind shiny Armour yellow passenger diesels of the Union Pacific, the train arrived at Abilene, 158 miles west of Kansas City, at 6:56 a.m.

Adherence to the schedule had varied from seven minutes early at Kenova, W.Va., and Russell, Ky., to 94 minutes late at Carrollton, Mo., where N&W's Kansas City line intersects Santa Fe's route for 29 miles of joint operation (putting MAIN 200's rear car on home rails for a time). Initial Washington departure had been 39 minutes behind schedule, and final arrival at Abilene 11 minutes late—not bad for a secret train that everybody knew about.

In the shadows of the Sunflower Hotel and the grain elevators lining the UP tracks, the train now became the centerpiece of more pomp and ritual, this time managed by the Fifth Army.

"Operation Kansas," Ike's burial plan, filled 100 pages. Officers had actually constructed a model of the town, rehearsing their moves over and over, leaving nothing to chance.

First, baggage car 314 was switched so that it would fall behind C&O diner 1921 to spot it adjacent to the family cars for the unloading ceremony. It was positioned near the front of the train originally to ensure no one would go inside except the

honor guard and family.

In an operation that otherwise was virtually flawless, one last-minute glitch threatened to unravel everything, and on nationwide television at that. Everyone had overlooked the fact that the casket would have to be unloaded from the engineer's, or north side, opposite where it went in. This revelation caused great consternation and anxiety in rearranging flags and removing drapery framework in a precious few minutes, but it was done.

Another minor snafu: The long trip had worn out the honor guard, and their uniforms were in disarray. As a result, another honor guard was used in the procession and burial. Understandably, the travelers were disappointed.

According to plan, at 9:57 a.m., President Richard M. Nixon's limousine pulled up at trackside (he had flown out) and the 314's door opened precisely at 10. The coffin was eased out into a hearse as the Fifth Army Band played "Hail to the Chief," "Ruffles and Flourishes" and "God of Our Fathers." The family disembarked and entered vehicles, signaling the start of a 12-block ride along Buckeye Street (Kansas highway 15) to the Eisenhower Center as 20,000 people watched in person and millions on TV.

Abilene, a quiet town of 7,337 people at the northern end of the Chisholm Trail, had its flags out, and photos of Eisenhower graced several store windows. Businesses—draped in black streamers and wreaths—were closed on this April 2, 1969.

Nixon eulogized his former boss on the steps of the Eisenhower Library, and burial followed inside a chapel called the Place of Meditation, beside the Eisenhowers' 3-year-old son who had died of scarlet fever in 1921. The entire event took place within sight of Ike's boyhood home in what

Above: *At least one mourner waves a flag and a military officer salutes as Eisenhower's funeral train passes the Newport, Ky., station April 1, 1969.*

Right: *Guards have kept the crowd at a respectable distance while Eisenhower's funeral train eases past the platform at Newport, Ky., April 1, 1969.*

Left: *The Eisenhower funeral train crosses the Ohio River and eases past the Cincinnati skyline on its way to Abilene, Kan., April 1, 1969.*

B&O conductor A.F. Hoskins, left, and head brakeman A.C. Peak consult a St. Louis Division timetable at Cincinnati Union Terminal before taking Dwight Eisenhower's funeral train westward.

Above: *Fulfilling Mamie Eisenhower's request, C&O/B&O officials attach bunting and flags to C&O baggage car 314, which is carrying the remains of her husband, Dwight D. Eisenhower, at Cincinnati Union terminal April 1, 1969. The man holding the upper right corner of the flag is David A. Watts Jr., director of passenger services; behind him is William F. Howes Jr., his assistant.*

Right: *The Eisenhower funeral train passes mourners at North Vernon, Ind., April 1, 1969.*

was a cornfield when he was a lad.

Nixon recalled how blustery it was that day.

"I remember that the wind was blowing strongly and threatened to blow the flag off the casket," he wrote to the author. "[Former] President Johnson and I stood up and held the flag on the casket for a few moments as the eulogy continued."[283]

Once the casket was removed from car 314, the world spotlight shifted from the train. The UP crew switched the 314 back to its original position behind the rider coach, C&O 1637, and proceeded westward to Solomon, eight miles, to turn the equipment on a wye track and be prepared for whatever came next.

The turning maneuver involved heading up the Beloit branch at Solomon, which doubled as the east leg of the wye at that point, and having a local engine—UP GP9's 326 and 272—couple to the rear of the train and pull it backward through the west leg and on to Salina, 15 more miles, for a crew change and refueling. Speculation had the family returning to Harrisburg, Pa., closest stop to the Eisenhower farm at Gettysburg, on three cars, with the remainder of the equipment deadheading back to Washington. So because railroad officers thought nothing would happen until at least midafternoon, the funeral train's six sleeping-car porters, the six-man crew of C&O diner 1921, and the attendant on 5-bedroom lounge *Dana*, all of whom had been on duty almost constantly since leaving Washington, were sent to bed. The next meal would be dinner for a skeleton crew since most of the passengers, even many of the railroaders, had detrained at Abilene.

At Solomon came the first hint that duty would beckon soon, however. A local radio broadcast being monitored on the train said Mrs. Eisenhower would go to the home of

C&O/B&O/WILLIAM F. HOWES JR. COLLECTION
With bunting still in place on the funeral car, Dwight Eisenhower's funeral train proceeds around a gentle curve west of North Vernon, Ind., April 1, 1969.

a family member, then return to the railroad station.

Well, railroad officers mumbled, if that's the case, there had better be a train there. Now some urgency gripped the turning operation—on a wye with one leg that looked as if it hadn't been used often. The radius was tight, the move slow and tense. But once completed, the Union Pacific showed its running style in grand fashion. The train ran "like the devil," one officer recalled, and returned to Abilene at about 1 p.m., just as Mrs. Eisenhower's convoy drove up.

No one knew what would happen until about 2 p.m., when Mamie notified the military she would return to Washington instead of Gettysburg. Sid Cox, civilian traffic manager for the Military District of Washington, informed the railroad that the family wanted to leave at 3 p.m., arrive in Washington at 8 a.m. the second morning, make no lengthy stops enroute and not run fast.

William F. Howes Jr., C&O/

C&O/B&O/WILLIAM F. HOWES JR. COLLECTION
Dwight Eisenhower's oldest brother, Edgar, right, chats with B&O flagman James H. Hargis on the rear platform of C&O business car 15 during a stop at Washington, Ind. Hargis, nicknamed "the colonel," served on Ike's staff in Europe.

B&O's assistant director of passenger services, scurried to a telephone booth and called Everett L. "Tommy" Thompson, C&O/B&O manager passenger operations, in Baltimore. "I'll call you back in 20 minutes," Howes told Tommy. "I have to have a schedule to give to the UP, N&W and our operating men."[189]

Thompson had completed the schedule by the time Howes called back and he hurriedly copied the information on a porter's call card.

Again, opposing trains were to be at a standstill. Lost time was to be recovered slowly on this "very slow schedule."[424] Standards for the return were not POTUS, but demanding nonetheless.

On top of the hasty departure, the family wanted to eat in the diner. Mrs. Eisenhower said she was tired of eating in the *Santa Fe*. A shocked Ken Cox, C&O/B&O superintendent of passenger food service, explained that the fire in the Prestolog stove had been banked and all he had was sandwiches and soup.

370

Mamie Eisenhower and her grandson, David, thank the folks at St. Louis for showing their respects to the aggrieved. Mamie's sister, Mrs. G. Gordon Moore, stands in the doorway of AT&SF private car Santa Fe.

"That's great," the former first lady answered, much to Cox's relief. "That's exactly what I want. I've been eating big meals back in the *Santa Fe*. I just want something simple."[189]

Cox immediately mobilized the 1921's crew. The hasty, unplanned luncheon turned out to be the only meal Mrs. Eisenhower took in the diner. Some family members were served ham-and-cheese sandwiches. Mamie said it was a "pleasant change."[189]

Everything was ready for departure. All went well throughout the afternoon, evening and night back on the UP and N&W across eastern Kansas and Missouri, and onto the B&O and across Illinois … until the next morning, Thursday, April 3, in Indiana.

Railroad officers and Secret Service agents were chattering in the lounge of the *Dana* as the train rolled past the plowed Hoosier State cornfields. Suddenly, an agitated and haggard Julie Nixon Eisenhower barged out of bedroom C and announced that she was sick. She asked that the train be stopped.

The Secret Service agents were willing, but railroaders talked them into proceeding until the next town, lest Julie need a phone and facilities for medical help. The next village, still 10 miles short of Seymour, Ind., was Brownstown (population 2,750), where the train was halted at the grade crossing of a road that intersected the railroad, ran through the town's Ewing subdivision and ended on U.S. 50 at the other end of town.

Julie, who only wanted to get her feet on solid ground, alighted from the train with several agents. Her husband was still asleep. As fidgeting officers watched, Julie and the agents disappeared into the Twin Town Drug Store, then came out, only to walk farther from the train, onto U.S. 50 and out of sight.

By this time, Mrs. Eisenhower had come forward, inquiring with great excitement, "What in the world is going on?" She became upset that she had insisted David and Julie accompany her on the return trip because "this all has been too much for her."[189]

After another 20 or 30 minutes, a car drove up to the train, and Julie got out; the car was driven by James Butt, the Brownstown pharmacist.

It seems that Julie had descended upon the unsuspecting merchant, animatedly wanting to know where his pay phone was. There was no pay phone, Butt had stammered. Then Julie demanded to use his personal phone, telling him she wanted to call the White House. She wanted to ask her daddy to dispatch an Air Force jet to the airport in Cincinnati to pick her up and take her home.

"Sure," Butt snapped, growing suspicious of the harried young woman and her bodyguards. "If you want to use the phone, go up to the Hillcrest Motel on Route 50 and use their pay phone," he told Julie.[189]

A colonel who had also jumped off the train entered the drug store on the heels of the departing sojourners and found out what had happened. Incensed, he showed some identification and convinced pharmacist Butt that Julie was for real, and the pair hurriedly took off in Butt's car to catch her. Once the phone call was made, everybody returned to the train.

The railroad now had two problems. One was the military. Railroaders were ordered not to divulge what had happened in Brownstown. Even though they had lost 42 minutes, they were to arrive in Cincinnati on time so as not to arouse anybody's suspicions.

And, they couldn't run too fast,

With hearse ready, the Eisenhower funeral train rolls into Abilene, Kan., April 2, 1969, for another presidential burial service.

either. Fortunately, there was enough slack built into the schedule to hide the stop.

The other problem was Julie. Everybody decided her difficulty was claustrophobia—she had been cooped up on the train for nearly four days now. Admittedly, the bedrooms were cramped when both berths were down. Edgar Eisenhower agreed to move out of bedroom D, taking the room in the *Santa Fe* intended for Milton Eisenhower. That allowed officials to fold back the partition between C and D, giving Julie and David a suite. And the Secret Service gave them the run of the train. No longer would Julie have to take her meals with the family in the *Santa Fe* and be restricted to the rear three cars. Now they could eat in the diner with the railroaders and military.

Julie got quite a kick out of it. In fact, by the time the train arrived in Cincinnati two hours later, she was feeling fine and sent the Air Force plane back to Washington without her.

By Thursday evening, a less formal atmosphere prevailed on the train. Everybody loosened up, even seeking mementos of the trip. The railroad quickly ran out of menus, and although it was agreed that more would be printed after the trip, that did little to appease the immediate clamor.

People had been seen all along the right of way retrieving flattened coins from the rails. Why not an Eisenhower-flattened coin instead of an Eisenhower menu? Those who rode the train credit Mrs. Eisenhower with the idea.

So at Ashland, Ky., after dark, two stops were actually made. While the public gawked from one side of the train, officers slipped off the other with a bag of coins contributed by eager staff people, and radioed the engineer to pull ahead a few feet. Instant souvenirs!

It turned out the family members wanted the mementos also, so the same maneuver was executed again in Huntington while Mrs. Eisenhower and John popped out of the *Santa Fe* to thank 500 onlookers for condolences.

The schedule turned out to be quite accurate. Only the UP cheated and ran fast. The return movement arrived in Kansas City 50 minutes early and departed 87 minutes early. N&W got into St. Louis early, and it was out on the B&O on time. After that, the operation didn't vary at principal points more than six minutes, and backed against the upper-level post on Washington Union Station's track 13 Friday morning one minute early. Still, no information was being released, on Army orders. Railroad public relations and operating officers were urging the military to relent, though, because they were getting so many inquiries.

A difficult mission had concluded, and the railroads' planning and execution had been virtually flawless. A lot of people liked that.

"I want to tell you of my appreciation for your great assistance to me and my party during our sad journey to Abilene and return," Mrs. Eisenhower wrote C&O/B&O President and Chief Executive Officer Gregory S. Devine in a letter dated April 25, 1969.

"While I realize that the burden on your facilities was almost intolerable, I found that every arrangement was efficiently and carefully handled to assure my comfort and convenience.

"May I add that the presence of your outstanding operating personnel and their familiar faces helped tremendously to lift our spirits at a very difficult time.

"John and the other members of my family join in sending you our special gratitude."[424]

Maj. Gen. Charles S. O'Malley Jr., commander of the Military District, said much the same in his letter of May 13:

"Because of the worldwide news coverage and the great national interest concerned with the burial of such an important individual, it was absolutely essential that all funeral

Former President Eisenhower's body is taken out of C&O baggage car 314 for the last leg of the journey to its burial site in Abilene, Kan., April 2, 1969.

details and ceremonies be conducted with dignity, preciseness, and utmost professionalism," he penned. "I was gratified to observe the outstanding manner in which your company responded to this critical event and the splendid manner in which you carried out your essential mission."[424]

C&O/B&O officers, representing all four railroads, met with Army personnel April 18 and 25 to discuss payment for MAIN 200. The railroads billed the Army for $85,384, but several items were disallowed and a final payment of $76,197 was mutually agreed upon. Of this total, $56,182 went to C&O/B&O, $11,305 to N&W and $13,210 to UP. Of C&O/B&O's portion, $1,755 went to AT&SF for operation of the *Santa Fe*. Expenses included:

Train and engine crews	$8,699
Locomotive expenses	7,512
Car expenses	5,327
Joint terminals:	
(WUT-CUT-TRRA-KCT)	12,925
Food services	6,098
Sleeping-car porters	2,979
Pullman Company	9,239
Maintenance-of-way forces	21,663
Business car *Santa Fe*	1,755
TOTAL	$76,197

"In seeking payment for handling the Eisenhower funeral train, we proceeded on the theory that none of the railroads involved desired to make a profit," C&O/B&O wrote to the other roads, "but we believe that it was fair and appropriate that each of us should be reimbursed for direct expenses incurred."[424]

With settlement on a ticket basis rejected as insufficient for a movement of such magnitude, expense estimates had been furnished by N&W and UP to C&O/B&O, which prepared a cost statement and added 15 percent for contingencies such as delays to regular traffic, extra crew costs, preparation time and managerial time.

The Pullman Company furnished estimates to the railroads, which C&O/B&O doubled "as a reasonable allowance for the separation payment and wind-up expenses which Pullman will allocate on the basis of 1969 units of expense."[424] But C&O/B&O also noted that cars were made available without per diem or mileage charges.

The terms "separation" and "wind-up" related to Pullman's exit from the sleeping-car business.

Intended for Jan. 1, 1969, all railroads weren't prepared to begin maintaining the cars by then, so the Pullman lease and Pullman pool were still in operation. The Eisenhower cars were staffed by C&O/B&O porters who formerly worked for Pullman. In fact, it was fortunate that the equipment pool was still in existence, because that's where some of the cars used on the Eisenhower train came from, and they probably would have been scrapped had they been removed from the lease to Pullman and returned to C&O/B&O.

Incidentally, the Eisenhower train and the 100-car General Motors movement to and from *The Greenbrier* resort the next month were Pullman's last major special movements.

Army news releases, finally mentioning the Eisenhower train, said the whole funeral cost $259,734.

But dollars and cents can't tell the whole story.

Aside from the steam locomotive and the passenger train, few aspects of the railroad industry capture the public imagination as does the aura surrounding a POTUS movement. Since the days of John Quincy Adams, crowds have been lured to trackside whenever a chief executive—or his remains—have passed through. Nowadays, presidents pass over at 35,000 feet, where no one can see or become part of the event. Once again, the railroad is a step removed from public awareness and pride, and Americans have lost another sliver of their heritage.

Perhaps MAIN 200 was our last good look at that era and its aura. In that case, our photographs, faded clippings—yes, even our flattened coins—will have to suffice to remind us of what once was.

The Victorian elegance of the 1883 private car Edgemere *greeted Theodore Roosevelt and his Cabinet when they reboarded the McKinley funeral train in Washington Sept. 17, 1901, for the trip to Canton, Ohio.*

The Cars They Rode

10

Starting with the Baltimore & Ohio's "middle carriage" on Andrew Jackson's train in 1833 and the "distinct car"[436] of William Henry Harrison's inaugural trip in 1841, railroads moved the nation's presidents on special cars for more than 150 years.

When President Tyler went to Boston in 1843 to dedicate the Bunker Hill Monument, the Camden & Amboy provided coach No. 19 for his use just after a complete rebuilding. It had six-wheel trucks, a variety of seats including several styles of reclining chairs and a privy on one platform. After the trip, the car was renamed for Tyler. Once beyond the C&A, it's possible the president continued his journey on an actual private car. The New York & Harlaem built one for its chief executive, Samuel R. Brooks, in 1841 or '42.

It may be that Abraham Lincoln, on his trip to Gettysburg in 1863, rode one of the B&O's office cars as described in the travel account of a young English gentlewoman named Isabelle Stuart Trotter, who toured America in 1858. The car she described had an observation/sitting room at one end and a central stateroom, with an aisle leading to the pantry/crew quarters:

"Though [B&O President] Mr. [John W.] Garrett talked of the directors' car, we presumed it was only a common carriage such as we had been accustomed to, but appropriated for their use; instead we found a beautiful car, 40 feet long by 8 feet wide. ... Outside: painted maroon, highly varnished with Canada balsam; the panels picked out with dark blue. Inside: painted pure white, also varnished. Ceiling the same, divided into small narrow panels, with excellent ventilators at each end. Round the car there were 22 windows ... and three brilliant lamps in the sitting room and hall, and one in the bedroom; these were lighted when passing through the tunnels. There were three hooks in the wall serving for hat pegs, and at the same time to support two flags for signals. A large map of the mountain pass from Cumberland to Wheeling hung over the sofa opposite the table. The table was covered with green baize stretched tightly over it. On the table were placed a large blotting-book, ink, and pens, three or four daily newspapers which were changed each day, the yearly report of the railway, a peculiar timetable book, containing rules for the guidance of the station men, times of freight and passenger trains meeting and passing each other, &c. Papa has these. The sofas are cov-

LIBRARY OF CONGRESS

Abraham Lincoln's presidential car—which turned out to be his funeral car—at Alexandria, Va.

ered with a pretty green Brussels carpet (small pattern) quilted like a mattress with green buttons, chairs covered with corded woolen stuff, not a speck or spot of ink or smut on anything. A neat carpet, not a speck or spot on it, a sheet of tin under and all around the stove. Pantry cupboard containing knives and forks, spoons and mugs. Bedroom berths much higher and wider than in a ship. Red-colored cotton quilts, with a shawl pattern, two pillows to each bed, pillowcases of brilliant whiteness, sofa bed larger and longer than a German bed. White Venetian blinds occupied the places usually filled by the door panels and window shutters. Green Brussels carpet like the cover of the sofa; three chairs to match. The windows in the sitting room had grey holland curtains running on wires with very neat little narrow strips of leather, and a black button to fasten them, and a button and well made buttonhole below to keep them from blowing about when the window is open. Looking glass in neat gilt frame, hung over a semicircular console in the bedroom, another near the wash-handstand, where a towel also hangs. Two drawers for clothes, &c. under berths. Tablecloth for meals, light

drab varnished cloth, imitating leather, very clean and pretty, china plates, and two metal plates in case of breakages. Luncheon consisted of excellent cold corned beef, tongue, bread and butter, Bass's ale, beer, whiskey, champagne, all Mr. [Henry] Tyson's [B&O master of machinery]. We supplied cold fowls, bread and claret. The door at the end opens on a sort of platform or balcony, surrounded by a strong high iron railing, with the rails wide enough apart to admit a man to climb up between them into the car, which the workmen always do to speak to Mr. Tyson. Usual step entrance at the other end. The platform can hold three arm chairs easily, and we three sat there yesterday evening, talking and admiring the view."[436]

Cars that carried presidents were not always cared for properly after serving their country.

The Lincoln funeral car, which cost $10,000 to build, was purchased for $6,840 from the government in 1866, the year after it bore the 16th president's body back to Illinois. The purchaser was Sidney Dillon, president of the Union Pacific Railroad—which Lincoln had authorized in 1862 as a major part of the nation's

first western railroad who bought it for use as a private car and pay car.

The car was used on the great Pacific railway excursion of October 1866, celebrating the UP's attainment of the 100th meridian at milepost 247 near Gothenburg, Neb., reached in 182 working days. Among the passengers were UP Vice President Thomas C. Durant, Rutherford B. Hayes, George M. Pullman and Robert Todd Lincoln. The car rode next to the rear car, occupied by Durant and his personal party.

Later it was used as an emigrant car, then it was sold to the Colorado Central. It was returned to UP ownership when that road bought the Colorado Central in 1879, and remained on that division as a dining car—and still later as a construction gang's camp car. By 1886, it was stationed on the Marysville, Kan., branch, "a relic of faded gentility,"[436] fitted with bunks for section hands and numbered 04. In the early 1890s, it was stored in North Platte, Neb., its windows boarded over and its exterior weatherbeaten. An observer in 1893 saw it on a siding in Omaha after it had arrived from North Platte. On top was painted "Colorado Central Railroad" and under the windows was

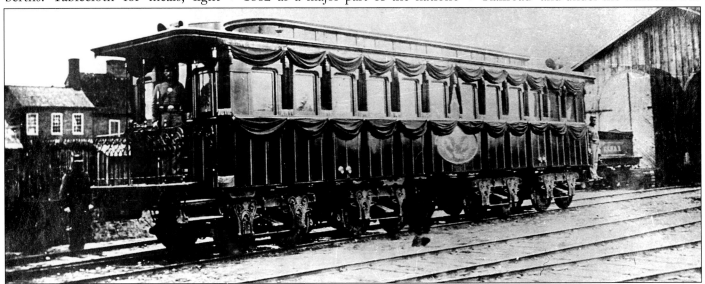

Lincoln's funeral car in a later view—April 20, 1865—properly decorated for the funeral movement.

painted "work train." It was so worn with age and abuse that almost no one recognized it as Lincoln's car.

It had been placed in a shed in Omaha and surrounded by guards with an eye toward restoration and display at that year's Columbian Exposition in Chicago, but the necessary $5,000 couldn't be found. It was refurbished, however, for Omaha's Trans-Mississippi Exhibition in 1898, where souvenir hunters picked at its rotten flanks. It was dilapidated now, bullet holes scarring the wood. A showman named Franklyn B. Snow bought "the most sacred relic in the United States"[436] in 1903 and arranged to display it at the World's Fair in St. Louis in 1904. After that notoriety, it was forgotten again.

In 1905, it was seen—neglected and ignored—on a Chicago & Alton siding at Joliet, Ill. Its mechanics' liens were paid off and the car was bought by real estate tycoon and Soo Line Railroad President Thomas Lowry that year to attract investors to his Columbia Heights, Minn., real estate development in a Minneapolis suburb.

Lowry tried to give the car to several historical organizations but found no takers. Finally, the Minneapolis Park Board took it and erected a temporary shelter. Then a grass fire spread over ten blocks of the development on March 15, 1911, igniting the relic and burning it into a mass of charred wood and iron. People picked up ashes from the blaze as souvenirs. All that was left was a piece of one window frame, which was made into a tie clasp for a coach at the University of Minnesota in Minneapolis.

Surviving in the Union Pacific Museum in Omaha are the car's original furnishings, including a walnut desk, reclining chair, a part of the silver service, a mirror, four oil paintings rescued by George Pullman himself, and two davenports—including the extra long one for Lincoln's use.

Several U.S. presidents used the *Maryland,* built for B&O President Garrett at Baltimore's Mount Clare shops in 1872. Hayes, Harrison, Cleveland and McKinley used it so often, in fact, it is said they began to think of it as their own. The *National Car Builder* magazine of February 1873 furnished a description:

"... When not in use it is kept in a special house at the Camden Station. ... The car ... is 51 feet long by 10 wide outside the body, runs on six-wheel trucks with strong check-chains attached, and with Dinsmore springs on the equalizers. Iron body-transoms are used. ... The outside of the car is painted a light yellow, with nothing in the way of external ornamentation to attract special attention or indicate the quality of the interior fitting-up, which is in the best Pullman-coach style. The car is designed to run always in the rear of a train, so as to afford a view of the track from the end windows. A glance at the arrangement of the interior indicates at once that the vehicle is designed for but one principal occupant with his traveling suite. There are four distinct compartments, a porter's room, stateroom, a sleeping and toilet room with side passage and closets, and the parlor or drawing room. The porter's room occupies about 10 feet of the forward end of the car, with a closet for tablewear on one side of the door, and a Baker & Smith heater on the other. Next to this is the stateroom with an upper sleeping berth on each side, and seats for eight persons underneath, and which can be transformed into two lower berths. Next is the central compartment, occupying a space of about 17 feet in length, and

One would never know from its appearance in its declining years, but the sleeper Pioneer *was rumored to have created some stirs on two occasions when Mrs. Abraham Lincoln and Ulysses S. Grant demanded that station platforms be removed and clearances altered to give the car's wide body room to pass by. Both stories, however, are thought to be fabrications.*

Built in 1872 as the office car Maryland *for B&O President John W. Garrett, this wooden car hauled several U.S. presidents. Sold to the Quebec Central Railway and renamed* Sherbrooke, *it enjoyed a remarkable second life, lasting until 1959.*

containing the principal sleeping and toilet room, and corridor, with a door and two windows in the partition between. There are also included in this division a water closet and linen locker, communicating with the sleeping room. This room is sumptuously furnished. Across one end is a curtained lounge. The bedstead is an elaborate piece of cabinet work in French walnut, surrounded with heavy double damask crimson and green curtains. The window curtains are of the same description, and hung, like the others, on silver-plated rods. Two large mirrors occupy the spaces between the windows. The remaining portion of the car, comprising a space of about 15 feet and extending to the rear end, constitutes the drawing room, which is entered by a door from the side passage above mentioned. Its furniture consists of a large and elegant sofa lounge, an oblong black walnut center table with marble top, two easy chairs of the Pompadour style and two others of a different pattern. This apartment has five windows on each side and three in the end, these last affording a fine view of the track. The spaces between the side windows are occupied with mirrors, and the curtains are of the same kind as those in the sleeping room. The floors have Brussels carpets. The interior finish-

ing throughout is in solid black walnut, with elaborate raised paneling of French walnut 'burl,' with semicircular tops. The general effect is somewhat somber, but is relieved by light gilt mouldings above the windows. The artificial lighting is done by four of Williams, Page & Co.'s improved plated lamps. Carroll ventilators are used, and all the windows have double sashes. In the central passageway is a washstand with a reservoir underneath holding a barrel of water, which is raised by a small force-pump. The inside door windows are beautiful specimens of embossed glass."[436]

The *Maryland* ended up in the hands of A.V. Kayser & Company, a Philadelphia broker, where in May 1908 it was purchased by the Quebec Central Railway and renamed *Sherbrooke*. It was assigned to that railroad's general manager and carried all manner of Canadian notables. As late as June 1949, one of its original blankets—stamped *Maryland* in a flowery 19th-century scroll—was still in use. After a distinguished 87-year career, the *Sherbrooke* was dismantled in August 1959 at the Angus Shops of QC parent Canadian Pacific in Montreal.

B&O office car 100, built by the Pullman Company in 1929, originally carried the *Maryland* name and is said

to be the car U.S. presidents used most of the time while traveling on the B&O. The last known whistlestop use of the car was by Arizona Sen. Barry Goldwater in his 1964 campaign against President Lyndon Johnson. It is now owned by Jeff Millerick of Santa Rosa, Calif.

Cleveland was reported to have used occasionally a narrow-gauge coach on fishing trips in northwestern Pennsylvania. Built in 1880 by Billmeyer and Small of York, Pa., for the Bradford, Bordell & Kinzua Railroad, it was sold in 1907 by BB&K successor Big Level & Kinzua to the East Broad Top Railroad, where it became coach No. 20. This car still carries excursion passengers over the four-mile EBT at Rockhill Furnace, Pa.

One of the most notable private cars of the period used by presidents was George M. Pullman's own, the *P.P.C.* Named for the Pullman Palace Car Co., the letters were interwoven into an elaborate monogram on the car's sides. It was outshopped at the company's Detroit shops in June 1877. The car was intended as a rental car, and was used as such for at least 15 years—being advertised at a rental fee of $85 a day.

But it fast became Pullman's pet.

Mounted on 12 wheels, its carbody housed an observation room nearly 8 feet long that contained chairs and a double sofa. Passing into the corridor, a visitor next came to a private suite, consisting of a 7-foot room with an extension sofa bed and adjoining a toilet with wardrobe and lockers. Next came a large central parlor/dining room with an 8-foot table separating a double sofa on one end from a reed organ on the other. Beyond was the kitchen-pantry area, which included two open sections and another toilet equipped with a small bathtub. Both end platforms were reduced in size to allow an enlarged interior, making the most of the car's 53-foot length.

The satinwood interior was finished in the Eastlake style, and the side walls were pierced with triple-window sets laid out with a broad center pane that was flanked by narrow sidelights. Fifteen expert wood carvers fashioned exquisite geometric turnings, panels and mouldings from the best cabinet woods available.

The ceilings were painted to represent such scenes as the "bullrushes" with young Moses omitted; another of fuchsias and hummingbirds.[436] The lamps and other metal fittings were gold-plated; and the car also boasted a small bathtub. Construction cost estimates vary from $25,000 to $50,000.

Presidents Grant through McKinley used the *P.P.C.* courtesy of Pullman, although Grant used it after he left office. The company dispatched it to San Francisco to meet the old warrior when he returned from an around-the-world trip in 1879, and carried him across the continent.

It 1887 the *P.P.C.* received electric lights. Five years later, it was lengthened to nearly 67 feet and the exterior remodeled with the addition of a

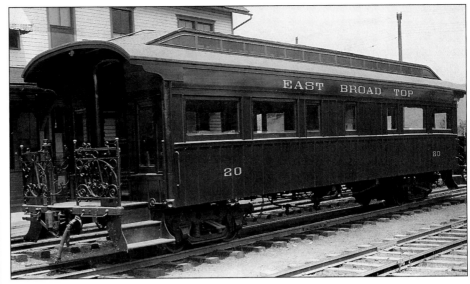

THOMAS W. DIXON JR. COLLECTION

The narrow-gauge Bradford, Bordell & Kinzua Railroad parlor car 20 said to have been used by Grover Cleveland on fishing trips in Pennsylvania ended up as the president's office car on the East Broad Top Railroad.

THOMAS W. DIXON JR. COLLECTION

How much of the interior of 1880 East Broad Top Railroad parlor car 20 was there in Grover Cleveland's day is anyone's guess, but late in life the car certainly looks spiffy.

more modern clerestory roof. Mrs. Pullman used the car extensively after her husband's death in 1897, renaming it *Monitor*—his telegraphic code name. It was placed in storage at the Pullman shop in Calumet, Ill., when she died in 1920 and was broken up the next year.

Two of the four cars on Benjamin Harrison's inaugural train of 1889 were fancy indeed. PRR baggage/smoker 692 boasted a bar, buffet and barbershop—the latter feature advertised as a new development for crack streamliners a half-century later. An engine that supplied power for the train's electric lights was placed in the baggage compartment. PRR private car 120, built in 1871 for Pennsy President Thomas Scott and named in Harrison's time the *George B. Roberts,* was 63 feet long and had an elaborate wood-burning fireplace in the 14-foot main lounge, framed by a mantle that reached to the top of the car. The mantle was bracketed by large bookcases and cabinets which the Pennsy said were for "display of bric-a-brac."[436] It was outfitted with painted Gothic windows, red body and two brown trucks each equipped with 12 green wheels. The lounge was carpeted with the finest of Wilton, a luxurious woven style, and was furnished with reclining chairs handsomely carved and upholstered in brocaded wine plush. Its sleeping apartment was furnished in oak and contained a bed, stationary washstand and closets. The dining room was done in walnut and the kitchen in hardwood. Electric call bells were placed throughout the car, as were ornate brass, oxidized silver and nick-

el trimmings and it is thought to be the first private car carrying a bathtub. The railroad hailed its car as "the most complete private car ever built."[436] It was particularly proud of the potted plants and blooming flowers that lined the windows. Newspapers across the land saluted the train as "a veritable palace on wheels."[436] Correspondents sent thousands of words about the rolling wonder, not only to papers in this country but to publications abroad. A subsequent all-steel PRR presidential car built in 1928 [see page 391] used the same number.

The five-car Pullman-built train Harrison used on his 1891 trip to the West Coast was ornate throughout. It included:

- Baggage/smoking/library car *Aztlan,* built in 1887. The baggage section contained a dynamo to power the train's electric lights and all kinds of supplies including President Harrison's "liquid"[267] stocks, Secretary of Agriculture Jeremiah Rusk's garden seeds and Postmaster General John Wanamaker's Sunday School leaflets. A swinging door led to the smoking/library section of the car, which was upholstered in olive plush. Bookcases on either side of the car contained 200 standard works and beneath each case was a desk with liberal supplies of writing materials. The compartment also

contained a wall clock, two electric screw fans and a barber shop.

- Diner *Coronado,* built in 1889. Seats and seat backs were done in pearl-gray straw, harmonizing with the car's silver lamps and silvery metal work and contrasting with its oak woodwork and green plush curtains. A newspaper article said the kitchen was "presided over by an experienced Afro-American cook, which fact is noted cheerfully by the people of his race as a slap at the French 'chef'."[267] Pantries and refrigerators were laden to capacity with all manner of bottled goods.

- Twelve-section, 1-drawing room, 1-compartment sleeper *New Zealand,* built in 1889. The plush in open sections of the president's car was a dull blue and the curtains were seal brown; three newspaper representatives were quartered there. The en suite drawing room and compartment, occupied by President and Mrs. Harrison, were models of artistic taste. All the woodwork was enameled in white and decorated with floral patterns in gilt moldings, while the seats and sofas were covered with a rich shade of terra cotta blush.

- Six-drawing room sleeper *Ideal,* built in 1890. Each drawing room featured coloring and design distinctively its own. Salmon, saffron,

The private car Philadelphia *was practically new when President Wilson and his first wife, Ellen, used it to travel to* The Greenbrier *resort at White Sulphur Springs, W.Va., in the spring of 1914.*

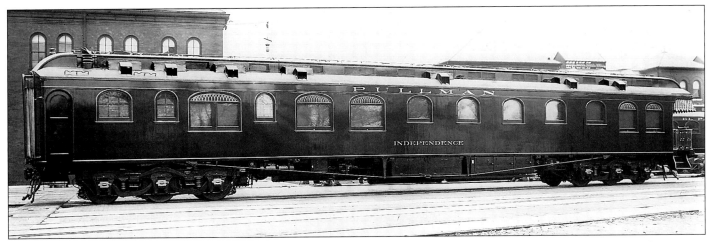

President Wilson rode the wooden private car Independence, *twice in 1916, 10 years after it was built. Pullman archives reveal that Wilson also rode the* Colonial, Columbia, Constitution, Federal, Ideal, Mayflower, National, Republic *and* Superb *that year, making a total of 25 trips.*

light green, crushed strawberry, olive and electric blue were the hues employed. Some of the wood was mahogany and natural, much of it delicately tinted. Occasionally, a berth panel was adorned with gold mottling and a floral border within the glittering molding.

• Eight-section lounge observation *Vacuna,* built in 1889. The open sections in the forward end were upholstered in blue and metal-fitted in brass. Separated from them by a buffet was the observation compartment, with 16 plush-cushioned willow chairs. The windows were large and made of the finest plate glass. Also in the *Vacuna* was a popular assortment of literature and writing desks beneath the bookcases. Electric fans were provided here, too. The rear platform, protected by a brass-topped bronze railing, was spacious enough to seat seven or eight people who wanted to enjoy the open air.

The entire train could be illuminated with oil, but every lamp inside and out was equipped with electric power. "In each berth," a newspaper said, "incandescent lamps can immediately be fitted should the occupant desire to read in bed."[267]

McKinley is known to have traveled in the *Olympia,* a private car built by Pullman in 1899, and the *Yale,* a 12-section, 1-drawing room buffet sleeper built by Pullman in February 1901. His body was returned from Buffalo to Washington and Canton, Ohio, in Pullman's 8-section lounge observation car *Pacific.*

By 1897, several railroad men were upset that the president didn't have a private car of his own. In February, the editor of *Railroad Car Journal* formed a committee of master car builders to design a joined pair of eight-wheel cars and a drive was launched to have the supply industry donate the necessary materials. The supply trade showed little enthusiasm for the project and the Master Car Builders Association refused to endorse the plan. The project was

tabled.

Robert D. Heinl, writing for *Leslie's Illustrated Weekly* of June 1, 1911, suggested that a three-car special train be constructed for the president's use. "The people ... have a right to see more of the president. ..." Heinl wrote. "Especially in latter years, (they) have yielded to the expressed wish of the people that they travel, but it has been at the expense of a tremendous amount of physical discomfort and even personal risk."[174]

Heinl was critical of presidential travel in his day.

"Along with his immediate party," he wrote, "he is packed into a single private car and buffeted about in a manner neither befitting his dignity as head of the nation nor in proportion to a man's physical endurance. Visitors by the tens of thousands attempt to

President Wilson used the 4-year-old private car National *when he transported the body of his first wife, Ellen, to its burial in Rome, Ga., Aug. 10-11, 1914.*

Wilson also rode the Advance, *above, a steel private car built by Pullman in March 1911—once in 1914 and once in 1915. Records show it didn't carry a president again until Coolidge boarded twice in 1924.*

swarm aboard the car. There is the inevitable reception committee which meets him enroute and at the station ahead, besides hundreds of others who have a perfect right to be present. And all hands congregate in a frightful scramble —where? In a small compartment, about a quarter as large as the average man's sitting-room, in which the air, because of the crush, is invariably foul. It is the president's dining room, workshop and all. Besides having to weather the confusion and discomfort of a constantly changing assemblage, he has no appropriate place to attend to urgent matters or the preparation of speeches. He has not the slightest privacy. Besides the voices and train noises, there is the incessant banging of typewriters and enough other nerve-wracking distractions to drive a steel-nerved individual to an asylum. Topping it off are the fumes wafted in from the cooking end of the car, which do not add to the pleasure, especially on days when the chef is preparing odoriferous delicacies for a presidential repast."[174]

Heinl proposed that a special train would be safer than coupling cars to the rear of regular runs, and suggested that it be financed from the president's annual $25,000 travel allowance. He revealed that Charles D. Norton, President Taft's presidential secretary, had drawn up a secret set of plans for a collision-proof, up-to-date, steel-vestibuled train that he submitted to Congress, but no action was taken.

The *Denali,* the car Warren Harding used in Alaska in 1923, was nearly lost in a warehouse fire during the summer of 1966. Coupled to an ore car and boxcar, it escaped with only blistered paint when firemen snagged it with a cable and pulled it to safety with a commandeered coal truck. The car is on display today in Fairbanks.

The *Superb,* the car that carried Harding and his pioneer loudspeaker system across the continent on that trip and was pressed into service as his funeral car, was built by Pullman in 1911. It became the *Los Angeles* in 1925, but the original name was reinstated a year later. It became Charleston & Western Carolina business car 101 when Pullman divested in 1947. When the Atlantic Coast Line absorbed the C&WC in 1959, it became that road's office car 301. In the middle '70s, successor Seaboard

This Pullman-built office car started life in 1905 as Great Northern compartment/observation car 760 for use on the Oriental Limited. *But its greater claim to fame was as the Alaska Railroad office car* Denali, *for as such it carried Mr. and Mrs. Warren G. Harding on their 1923 tour of Alaska just days before the president's death.*

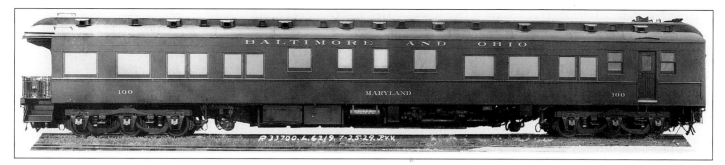

Business car 100, built by Pullman for B&O in 1929 and christened as the second Maryland *on that road, was said to have hauled several U.S. presidents—including Herbert Hoover—and was last used in presidential whistlestop service by Barry Goldwater in 1964.*

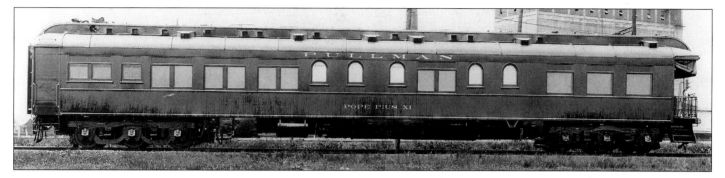

This excellent broadside is significant because it shows the private car Superb, *which took President Harding across the country in 1923 and then brought back his body. You might have trouble discerning that, however, since in this photo the car is called* Pope Pius XI. *In June 1926, it and six other cars were temporarily repainted cardinal red trimmed in gold and referred to as* The Cardinals' Train. *The cars carried a trainload of Roman Catholic cardinals, clergymen and laity from around the world from New York to the XXVIII International Eucharistic Conference in Chicago, the first such conference held in the United States. A month later, the cars' original livery and names were restored.*

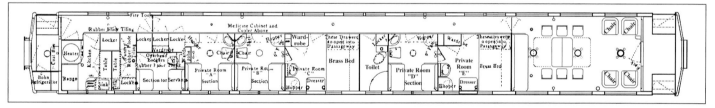

Floor plan of the Superb *shows the car's unusual arrangement of lounge and dining room combined at the rear.*

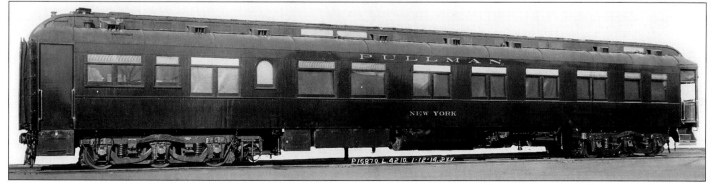

Another car that hosted President Wilson was the New York, *a steel Pullman product of January 1914. He rode it five times in 1915 and twice in 1916, but records reveal no other rides by Wilson or any other president in this car.*

Coast Line gave it to the Southeastern Railway Museum in Duluth, Ga., which is operated by the Atlanta chapter of the National Railway Historical Society Inc. Its only mate was the *Ideal,* a steel car also, used by Harding. Their unusual floor plan included a combined observation and dining area at the rear and a long row of staterooms for the occupants and their servants.

Most noted as carriages of presidents are seven private cars built by Pullman in 1927 and 1929 for general rentals. Six were named for explorers—the *Marco Polo, Henry Stanley, David Livingstone, Robert Peary, Roald Amundsen* and *Ferdinand Magellan,* and one carried the designation *Pioneer.*

Of those seven, the most famous was the *Ferdinand Magellan*—outshopped in August 1929 and eventually customized for the exclusive use of the president of the United States.

Until the onset of World War II, 20th-century presidents traveled on standard private Pullmans. They didn't ride on specific cars, but during Franklin Roosevelt's term, the *Roald Amundsen* was most frequently assigned to him. After Pearl Harbor, Secret Service chief Mike Reilly and presidential Secretary Steve Early decided their boss should have a car modified to offer maximum protection. Roosevelt approved the idea only when told it would benefit other presidents as well. The Pullman Company selected the *Magellan* for this historic new mission because it was due into Pullman's Calumet, Ill., shops shortly for inspection and repairs. Records show the president had used it only once during its unaltered state, in 1939.

"Let's make it a little more comfortable,"[149] Roosevelt told Reilly. So at Calumet, the number of staterooms was reduced from five to four to allow enlarging the dining and observation rooms. Steel armor plating ³/₈-inch thick was riveted to the car's sides, floor, roof and ends, making it bulletproof and bombproof. Three-inch bulletproof glass that would stop .50-caliber machine gun fire replaced conventional safety glass in the windows. Escape hatches were installed in the observation lounge's ceiling and on the side of the car near its center above the shower. Special trucks, wheels and roller bearings were installed to support the additional weight. Cars of this nature usually weighed about 80 tons, but this one now weighed 285,000 pounds, a whopping 142.5 tons.

Painted Pullman green, the *Magellan* was 83 ½ feet long, 14 ½ feet high and 10 feet wide. Inside, on either side of the front entrance aisle, were refrigerators, an ice hatch and storage compartments—one for ammunition. Next was the galley, pantry and servants' quarters—which included a small upper and lower berth, lavatory, shower and closet. Overhead were hot and cold water storage tanks, air-conditioning equipment, blowers and fans.

The dining—or conference—room was the car's largest. It was furnished with a 38- by 72-inch solid mahogany table, which seated eight in matching chairs upholstered in green and gold striped satin damask. Wall candelabras and chandeliers were gold-plated and the four china cabinets and 11 buffet drawers were felt-lined. The walls were paneled in limed oak and the ceiling was ivory, etched in antique gold. Carpeting was blue-gray. From the dining room rearward, along a limed oak corridor, were four staterooms—D, C, B and A. Guest rooms D and A were identical, each with an upper and lower berth, toilet, closet, vanity table, chair and medicine cabinet above the wash basin. Both were carpeted in dark green, with light green walls and brass electrical features and hardware.

Rooms C and B formed the presidential suite, with a connecting bathroom in between. Room C, for the president, was painted blue-green with matching deep-pile carpet and satin-chrome fixtures. The lower bed was permanent, slightly larger than a conventional berth. A standard upper berth pulled down from above. Room B, for the first lady, was decorated in peach and beige, with satin-chrome hardware. It was equipped with a full-sized permanent bed, vanity table, closet, wash basin and cabinet. The connecting room had a bathtub and shower, toilet, wash basin and cabinet, with chrome fixtures and a black-and-white-check linoleum floor. Railings were installed throughout to help President Roosevelt swing himself about and travel through the car.

The 12-foot observation lounge had soft cream woodwork and green carpeting. Its walls were padded and tufted in a light brown material resembling leather. Furnishings included two barrel chairs and a sofa upholstered in medium blue and four armchairs in brown. Eight windows and 16 ceiling fixtures provided illumination.

Each room on the *Magellan* had a telephone. When standing, these phones were connected to standard lines via a trainside outlet provided by the telephone company; when moving, they were connected to a communications network first in B&O car 1401, then the *General Albert J. Myer.*

The open-end brass-railed platform behind the lounge was equipped with five microphone connections and, on the roof, permanent loudspeakers. Small boxes on either side of the platform contained outlets for additional speakers and telephones. Between the lounge and platform was a 1,500-pound door that looked like the entrance to a bank vault and couldn't be opened from the outside.

When he first saw it, Harry Truman quipped that he hoped the Secret Service never forgot the combination. While flagmen always had permission to occupy the car to perform their duties, they always entered it from the front after passing through the Secret Service's lounge car.

The *Magellan* took on the appearance of a monstrous caterpillar. Its roof was redone as an ungainly turtle-back casement, and the undercarriage became a maze of boxes, pumps and mechanical gear. Sixteen lockers housed batteries and other electrical and telephone equipment, a standby compressor for the plumbing system and 6,000 pounds of ice for the air conditioning. Cooling was achieved by a water pump that forced ice water through cold copper tubing up to a ceiling evaporator, where blowers forced cool air out through ceiling ventilators arranged through the full length of the car. Steam heat kept the interior comfortable in the winter and provided the staterooms and galley with plenty of hot water. The swollen giant's weight made it the heaviest passenger car to operate in this country; one engineer said that it "drags like a brickbat on the tail of a kite."[262] The *Magellan* was presented to Roosevelt on Dec. 18, 1942.

For security reasons, no number or name appeared on its sides; a presidential seal was affixed to the rear platform railing and only the name *Pullman* graced the letterboards to avert suspicion that it was something special. From a distance it looked like any other private car.

At first, Roosevelt boarded the *Magellan* as he did other cars by means of a 300-pound ramp built for him by order of Central Railroad of New Jersey General Manager R.W. Brown. Ordered on Jan. 27, 1933, the ramp was completed Feb. 28, in time for Roosevelt to use it on March 2 when he boarded a CNJ train at Jersey

The Magellan's *lounge.*

The Magellan's *dining room—where Truman determined he would win the 1948 election.*

Pullman private car Ferdinand Magellan *is stripped at Pullman's Wilmington, Del., shop for 1942 rebuild.*

Floor plan of the Ferdinand Magellan *and sister cars before the* Magellan's *rebuild. A photo of the* Magellan *before its rebuild appears on the contents page of this book.*

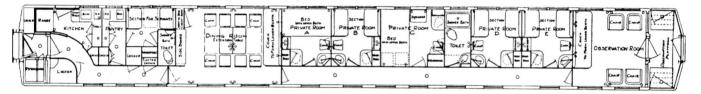

Above: *Floor plan of the* Magellan *after its rebuild.*

Right: *The* Magellan *as restored and displayed by the Gold Coast Railroad Museum in Miami, Fla.*

Left: *Rear view of the* Magellan, *with presidential seal, ready to go in Washington.*

Below: *The* Magellan *after Hurricane Andrew dropped an aluminum shed on it in 1992, causing only minor damage.*

Above, left: Left rear platform elevator of the Ferdinand Magellan, *installed for Franklin Roosevelt, seen from outside car, in raised position. Above, right: Left rear platform elevator, seen from outside car, in lowered position. Below: Left rear platform elevator, seen from rear platform, in raised position.*

City, N.J., enroute to his inauguration. Once the president was on board, his ramp was stored in the baggage car. He was most sensitive about public information concerning his disability and never allowed newsmen to take photographs of him on the ramp or while he was being assisted in any way—although some were taken anyway [see Page 145].

At White House travel officer Dewey Long's suggestion, the rear steps on both sides of the *Magellan* were removed and replaced by electric elevators—eliminating the need for the cumbersome ramp. They were equipped with sensors to bring them to a precise stop at the top or bottom of the platform and were designed to look as much as possible like standard equipment. The work was done by the Naval Gun Factory at Washington's

Navy Yard; they were removed after Roosevelt's death.

When the president started using it, the *Magellan's* ownership was transferred from Pullman to the Association of American Railroads, which in turn leased it to the government. In 1946, it was sold to the government for $1 (some sources say $10)—the only Pullman car ever owned by the federal government—and carried the simple designation *U.S. Car No. 1*. The AAR's rebuild cost has never been revealed.

Roosevelt used the rebuilt car almost exclusively, piling up 50,000 miles on board, but Truman used it more than that because it was available to him for a longer period of time—the '48 campaign alone covered 29,432 miles.

Eisenhower used the car only three times, referring to it as "that old ark."[413] The last time anyone at the White House rode it in Ike's day was when Mamie took it to Groton, Conn., on Jan. 21, 1954, to christen

the nuclear submarine *Nautilus.*

On Aug. 24, 1945, the *Magellan* was moved to Pullman's Wilmington, Del., shops for removal of FDR's elevators and other special appliances. Several PRR officers used that as an occasion to suggest to Pullman that a lightweight car of "modern" design be built for the president, eliminating the need of hauling around the ultraheavy *Magellan.* A draft suggested the old fortress be scrapped, but the final version composed the next day recommended that it be restored to normal weight and remodeled for use as a sleeper. The suggestion was ignored.

Franklin Snow of the Wardman Park Hotel in Washington suggested in a letter to the White House on Sept. 15, 1948, that the *Magellan's* name be changed to *America, George Washington* or *Mayflower,* or something else that would have a bearing "upon our own country and historical associations." Truman's assistant press secretary, Eben A. Ayers, replied two days later that consideration would be

delayed until after Truman's West Coast campaign trip. The idea was forgotten.[413]

After Mamie's 1954 trip, the *Magellan* stood idle for four years at the Army's transportation depot and maintenance shop at Fort Holabird, Md. The White House declared it surplus government property in April 1958 and Army records of its travels were destroyed six months later. Radio, telephone and public address systems were removed and sold, and the car was offered to the Smithsonian Institution. Incredibly, the Smithsonian took no action.

The surplus property declaration set in motion a complex set of negotiations to determine the car's future. On June 9, the utilization and sales division of the Federal Supply Service of the General Services Administration wrote to the director of field administration of the Department of Health, Education and Welfare, announcing that the Army wished to dispose of the *Magellan* as "there is no

The government leased B&O combination passenger/baggage car 1401 between 1942 and 1952 to serve as a communications car, keeping the president of the United States in touch with the White House and the world wherever he happened to be on the nation's railroads.

This Army hospital car was converted to a presidential communications car in 1952 to replace leased B&O combine 1401. The new communications carriage was named General Albert J. Myer *in honor of the Army's first chief signal officer.*

Christened Seaboard Air Line No. 1 in 1924, this car was CSXT's office car Baltimore *when it transported President and Mrs. George Bush through six states during the fall of 1992.*

further federal need for this railway car, and it is available for donation through your agency."[429] A week later, HEW dispatched a memo to its regional directors to see if any of the state agencies handling surplus property wanted it.

Somehow the Brotherhood of Locomotive Engineers learned in early January 1958 that the *Magellan* would soon be retired. Its *Locomotive Engineer* of Jan. 17 stated that *U.S. No. 1* was scheduled to be dismantled and had been offered to the Baltimore & Ohio Museum in Baltimore.[429]

Robert L. Beekman, a co-founder of the newly organized Gold Coast Railroad Museum in Florida, who was also a member of the BofLE, saw the article and wrote to the brotherhood's president asking how the car might be acquired. He also contacted the University of Miami, with which Gold Coast was associated at the time. In June, when the car's availability was announced, the university applied for it.

On Aug. 11, Dr. James M. Goddard, the school's executive vice president, wrote to the Florida Development Commission asking that it attempt to obtain the *Magellan* and add it to the steam locomotive, coach and caboose already operating on its South Campus. It was done, and HEW eventually asked its regional property director in Charlottesville, Va., to allocate the car to the Atlanta Region, which in turn allocated it to the Florida commission, which gave it to the university "for educational purposes." An "acquisition cost" reflecting the car's value exclusive of its historical worth—was set at $2,500, which the GSA later increased to $80,277.53.[429]

The *Magellan* left Fort Holabird on Jan. 12, 1959, arriving at Washington's Union Station at 8:35 p.m. on B&O train 17, the *Cleveland Night Express*. At 12:05 a.m. on the 13th, it departed for the South on RF&P/SAL's *Palmland*, near the locomotive and unoccupied. It arrived in Miami a few hours late, around noon on the 14th, and was hauled seven miles back to Seaboard's Hialeah Yard. The next morning, it was coupled to a local freight for the 15-mile trip over SAL's Homestead Branch to the university's South Campus.

The *Magellan* was displayed on campus until November 1966, when Gold Coast moved its operation 50 miles north to Fort Lauderdale on a steam special consisting of all of Gold Coast's rolling stock. With the move, Gold Coast disassociated itself from the school and title to the car passed to the museum.

Gold Coast's holdings were subsequently moved again. Several of the treasures, including the *Magellan*, were placed on display under a large aluminum and steel shed at 12400 S.W. 152nd St. in Miami. The shed collapsed—slightly damaging the *Magellan*—when Hurricane Andrew roared across southern Florida early on the morning of Monday, Aug. 24, 1992.

Until Ronald Reagan's trip in 1984, the car was rarely moved. It was listed in the National Register of Historic Places in 1978 and Gold Coast received permission in 1979 to restore its presidential seal. During each of his five whistlestops, Reagan referred to the car's "historical significance" and after the trip he thanked Gold Coast for its use.

In August 1990, the *Magellan* was deadheaded to Ogdensburg, N.Y., to commemorate the 50th anniversary of Franklin Roosevelt's signing of a U.S.-Canadian bilateral defense agreement. It moved on CSX to Park Jct. in Philadelphia; Conrail to Norwood, N.Y.; and the St. Lawrence Railroad to Ogdensburg. Roosevelt actually rode the *Roald Amundsen* on the 1940 trip, but it—in Scottsdale, Ariz., in an unrestored condition—couldn't travel.

Pennsylvania Railroad's second No. 120, built in PRR's Altoona, Pa., shops in 1928, was named *Pennsylvania*. It was used by John F. Kennedy and, it is said, by Presidents Franklin Roosevelt, Truman and Eisenhower. It was sold to New York City attorney George Pins in 1971 and is now owned by Philadelphia engineer/businessman Bennett Levin. The car was used on a five-car train carrying members of the national press on Conrail from New York City's Grand Central Station to Hyde Park, N.Y., to publicize the American Broadcasting Company's two-part "ABC Theater" television special "Eleanor and Franklin" before it aired Jan. 11-12, 1976.

The *Baltimore*, CSX business car 317, was used by George Bush on all of his 1992 whistlestop trains. Originally called *Baltimore No. 1*, the Pullman product was placed in service on the Seaboard Air Line Railroad June 2, 1924—the year of Bush's birth. First to use the car was SAL President Davies Warfield of Baltimore, an uncle of the Dutchess of Windsor. It was subsequently called *Carolinian No. 1* and *Virginia No. 1* before being renamed *Alabama* in 1971. It received its present name in 1986 and was used extensively by Richard D. Sanborn, president and chief executive officer of CSX Transportation's Distribution Services unit at the time, who opted for rail travel over air whenever possible. In fact, when Sanborn was transferred from Jacksonville, Fla., to Baltimore, he lived on the car while his home was being built.

Another presidential rail trip is being hatched up in the Franklin Roosevelt era. White House travel officer Dewey Long, right, and his aide, Edwin "Jiggs" Fauver, center, confer with Western Union representative Carroll S. Linkins at Washington (D.C.) Union Station. They are in front of Pennsylvania Railroad coach 1733, which was named for the telegraph chief.

Appendix

Sample Train Consists

Typical consists are listed for the trains of some presidents and candidates and one first lady. Motive power is listed if known; car ownership is shown for all but originating railroads.

Ulysses S. Grant:

• D&H, Saratoga Springs, N.Y., Aug. 4, 1885 (funeral): locomotive 210; baggage car; four coaches; Wagner drawing-room cars *Catskill*, *Highlander* and *Excelsior*; and catafalque car *Woodlawn* (remains) (owned by NYC&HR President Cornelius Vanderbilt II).

Rutherford B. Hayes:

• CB&Q, Chicago-Omaha, Sept. 2-3, 1880: locomotive 169 (engineer J.B. Cooley); baggage car; "special" car No. 50; C&NW diner *St. Charles*; directors' car 99 (for Gen. William T. Sherman); and UP directors' car (Hayes).

• UP, Cheyenne-Ogden, Sept. 4-5, 1880: baggage car; C&NW dining car *St. Charles*; CB&Q director's car 99 (Secretary of War Alexander Ramsey and Gen. William T. Sherman); a Pullman sleeper (Gen. A. McD. McCook, Col. Barr and presidential sons Birchard and Rutherford Hayes); and UP director's car (Hayes).

• SP, Casa Grande, Ariz., Oct. 25, 1880: locomotive 39; baggage car; two sleepers; a diner; and Central Pacific director's car (Hayes).

Chester A. Arthur:

• NYC&HR, New York, N.Y., Nov. 22, 1886 (funeral): catafalque car *Woodlawn* (remains); private car (pallbearers); drawing room car (family); and two coaches (all owned by NYC&HR President Cornelius Vanderbilt).

Benjamin Harrison:

• PRR, Indianapolis, Feb. 25, 1889: baggage/ smoker 692; Pullman 12-section, drawing room/buffet sleeper *Maywood* (press); Pullman private car *Iolanthe* (relatives and friends); and private car 120 (Harrison).

• Richmond & Danville, Washington, D.C., April 13, 1891: Pullman baggage/smoker/library *Aztlan*; Pullman diner *Coronado*; Pullman 12-section, drawing room sleeper *New Zealand* (Harrison) and 6-drawing room sleeper *Ideal*; and Pullman 8-section/lounge/observation car *Vacuna*.

Grover Cleveland:

• PRR, Altoona, Pa., April 28, 1893 (enroute to Columbian World's Fair in Chicago): ex-Woodruff baggage/buffet/library *Raleigh*; Pullman diner *Magdelin*; Pullman 12-section, 2-drawing room sleeper *Charmion*; Pullman 6-drawing room sleeper *Superb* (Cabinet members); and Pullman private car *Wildwood* (Cleveland).

William McKinley:

• PRR, Washington, D.C., Oct. 4, 1899: Pullman baggage/buffet/smoker/barber *Atlantic*; Pullman 12-section drawing room sleeper *Exton*; Pullman diner *Gilsey*; Pullman 7-compartment, 2-drawing room sleepers *Chili* and *Omena* (Cabinet); and Pullman private car *Campania* (McKinley).

• PRR, Buffalo, N.Y., Sept. 16, 1901 (funeral): Pilot: locomotive 134.

POTUS: locomotives 408 and 27; ex-Woodruff baggage/buffet/library *Raleigh* (press); ex-Wagner 12-section/1-drawing room/buffet sleeper *Belgrade*, (press); Pullman 12-section, 1-drawing room sleeper *Naples* (senators); Pullman 7-compartment, 2-drawing room sleeper *Hungary* (President Roosevelt and cabinet); Pullman private car *Olympia* (Mrs. McKinley); and Pullman 8-section lounge/observation *Pacific* (remains).

• PRR, Washington, D.C., Sept. 17, 1901 (funeral): baggage/passenger car; Pullman diner *Waldorf*; Pullman 12-section, 1-drawing room sleepers *Belgravia* and *Naples*; Pullman private car *Edgemere* (T. Roosevelt and Cabinet); Pullman private car *Olympia* (Mrs. McKinley); and Pullman 8-section lounge/observation *Pacific* (remains).

William Howard Taft:

• Denver & Rio Grande, Salida, Colo., Sept. 23, 1909: engine 168; coach; business cars P, B and N (all narrow gauge).

Warren G. Harding:

• Alaska R.R., Seward, Alaska, July 13, 1923: baggage car; business car B-1; a smoker; 14-section sleeper *Fairbanks*; 10-section sleeper *Talkeetna*; 10-section sleeper *Anchorage*; compartment-observation car *Kenai*; diner *McKinley Park*; private car *Denali*; and a flatcar.

Herbert Hoover:

• C&O (by trackage rights), Washington, D.C., June 14, 1931: club/baggage car; Imperial salon coach; standard diner; Pullman 12-

section drawing room sleeper; Pullman 10-compartment sleeper (press); 6-compartment 3-drawing room sleeper (aides and Secret Service); club diner (family); and Pullman private car *Henry Stanley* (Hoover).

Franklin D. Roosevelt:

- CNJ, Jersey City, N.J., April 21, 1933: B&O class P-7 Pacific 5308; Pullman baggage/buffet/ smoker/ barber *Eagle Point*; B&O diner 1059; Pullman parlor cars *Myrtle* and *Honora*; and Pullman 3-compartment, 2-drawing room lounge observation *Central Grove* (Roosevelt).
- Southern, Washington, D.C., Nov. 15, 1934: Pullman 12-section 1-drawing room sleeper *Knickerbocker* (*Fishers* returning); Pullman club car *William Moultrie*; Pullman 8-section 1-drawing room 2-compartment sleeper *Stonewall Jackson*; Pullman 6-compartment 3-drawing room sleeper *Glen Dochart* (returning only); Pullman 10-compartment sleeper *Greensburg*; B&O diner 1036 (*Martha Washington*) (Southern 3168 returning); Pullman 6-compartment 3-drawing room sleeper *Glen Stream*; and Pullman private car *Robert Peary* (Roosevelt).
- PRR, Washington, D.C., Feb. 23, 1935: GG-1 class locomotive 4800; baggage 4894; Pullman 8-section, 1-drawing room, 2-compartment sleeper *Royal Oak*; Pullman parlor/lounge *Rotary Club*; Pullman 10-compartment sleeper *Greensburg*; diner 8005; Pullman 6-compartment, 3-drawing room sleeper *Madison Square*; and Pullman private car *Robert Peary* (Roosevelt).
- UP, Council Bluffs, Iowa, Sept. 26, 1935: Pilot train: baggage cars 1830 and 1895; coach 1214; business cars 117 and 103. POTUS train: B&O 70-foot baggage car; dormitory club

2750; Pullman 10-section, 2-compartment, 1-drawing room sleeper (crew); Pullman 6-compartment, 3-drawing room sleeper *Glen Ayr* (cameramen); LA-class lounge 1554; Pullman 6-compartment, 3-drawing room sleeper *Glen Sutton* (press); diner 387; Pullman 6-compartment, 3-drawing room sleeper *Glen Dower* (press and guests); Pullman 6-compartment, 3-drawing room sleeper *Glen Arden* (staff); and Pullman private car *Robert Peary* (Roosevelt).
- RF&P, Washington, D.C., Jan. 9, 1943: Pullman baggage/buffet/ smoker/barber *Eagle Gorge*; Pullman 10-section, 2-compartment, drawing room sleeper *Lake Vineyard*; B&O 1401 (communications); Pullman 8-compartment/ lounge *Conneaut* (Secret Service); and Pullman private car *Ferdinand Magellan* (Roosevelt).
- PRR, Washington, D.C. (14th Street Yard), April 13, 1943: RF&P 4-8-4 610; B&O baggage car 664; B&O combine 1401 (communications); Pullman 8-section, restaurant/lounge/observation sleeper *Circumnavigators Club* (crew); Pullman 6-compartment, 3-drawing room sleepers *Glen Cliff*, *Penn Square* and *Glen Doll*; B&O diner 1059; Pullman 8-compartment/ lounge *Conneaut* (Secret Service); and Pullman private car *Ferdinand Magellan* (Roosevelt).
- B&O, Alexandria Jct. (Washington, D.C.), Oct. 26, 1944: passenger diesel 59; automobile/baggage car 748; Pullman baggage/buffet/ smoker/barber *Old Colony*; combine 1401 (communications); Pullman 10-section, 1-drawing room, 2-compartment sleeper *Fort Travis*; Pullman 6-compartment, 3-drawing room sleepers *Glen Aray*, *Cervantes* and *Monument Square*; diner 1070; Pullman 6-compartment, 3-drawing room sleeper

Times Square; Pullman 1-compartment, 1-drawing room buffet/ observation/ lounge sleeper *Andrew W. Mellon*; Pullman 6-compartment, 3-drawing room sleeper *Glen Doll*; Pullman *Conneaut* (now 7-compartment/buffet/ lounge); and Pullman private car *Ferdinand Magellan* (Roosevelt).
- Southern, Washington, D.C., March 29, 1945: B&O baggage car 748 (for a bulletproof Packard and two Secret Service automobiles); baggage car 549; Pullman 12-section, 1-drawing room sleeper *Imperator* (crew); B&O combine 1401 (communications); Pullman 8-section sleeper/lounge *Hillcrest Club*; Pullman 6-compartment, 3-bedroom sleepers *Glen Doll* and *Wordsworth*; diner 3155; Pullman 7-compartment/buffet/lounge *Conneaut* (Secret Service); and Pullman private car *Ferdinand Magellan* (Roosevelt).
- Southern, Warm Springs, Ga., April 13, 1945 (funeral): light Pacifics 1262 and 1337; B&O auto baggage 748; baggage 549; Pullman 12-section, 1-drawing room sleeper *Imperator*; B&O combine 1401 (communications); Pullman 8-section, 5-bedroom sleeper *Clover Pasture*; Pullman 8-section diner/ lounge *Hillcrest Club*; Pullman 6-compartment, 3-drawing room sleepers *Glen Doll* and *Wordsworth*; diner 3155; Pullman private car *Ferdinand Magellan* (U.S. No. 1) (Mrs. Roosevelt); and Pullman 7-compartment/buffet/lounge *Conneaut* (remains).
- PRR, Washington, D.C., April 14, 1945 (funeral): Pullman 12-section, 1-drawing room sleeper *Crusader Rose*; B&O combine 1401 (communications); Pullman 6-compartment, 3-drawing room sleeper *Glen Willow*; Pullman 7-compartment, 2-drawing room sleepers *Glengyle* and *Treonta*; Pullman 6-compart-

ment, 3-drawing room sleeper *Glen Gordon*; diner 4478; Pullman 6-compartment, 3-drawing room sleepers *Glen Doll, Glen Lodge, Glen Canyon, Wordsworth, Glen Brook* and *Howe*; diner 4497; Pullman private car *Roald Amundsen* (Truman); Pullman private car *Ferdinand Magellan* (U.S. No. 1) (Mrs. Roosevelt); and Pullman 7-compartment buffet/ lounge *Conneaut* (remains).

Wendell Wilkie:

- PRR, New Castle, Pa., Oct. 3, 1940: K-4s Pacifics 3766 and 3773; Pullman 12-section, drawing room sleeper *Banavie*; B&O baggage car 635; Pullman 14-section sleeper *Starlight*; Pullman 10-section, drawing room, 2-compartment sleeper *Colorado*; Pullman 6-compartment, 3-drawing room sleepers *Romney* and *Glen Craig*; Pullman 7-compartment, 2-drawing room sleeper *President Washington*; diner 7995; Pullman 6-compartment lounge *Wayneport*; Pullman 7-compartment, 2-drawing room sleeper *President Harrison*; Pullman 6-compartment, 3-drawing room sleeper *Glen Manor*; diner 7997; Pullman 6-compartment, 3-drawing room sleeper *Glen Dee*; Pullman lounge *Hornell*; Pullman 8-compartment lounge *Waterview*; and Pullman private car *Pioneer* (Willkie).

Thomas E. Dewey:

- GN, Castle Rock, Wash., Sept. 19, 1944: 4-8-2 2501; PRR baggage/ darkroom car 5779; dormitory car 1003; Pullman 10-section, 1-drawing room, 2-compartment sleeper *Lake Onota*; Pullman 6-compartment, 3-drawing room sleepers *Franklin Square, Glen Lodge, Glen Aray* and *Glen Garry*; diner 1034 (*Montana*); Pullman 6-compartment, 3-drawing room sleeper *Glen Willow*; Pullman 2-compartment, 1-drawing room, buffet sun room

lounge *Sun-Gold*; Pullman 30-chair lounge *Gwladys*; Pullman 6-compartment, 3-drawing room sleeper *Glen Manor*; and Pullman private car *David Livingston* (Dewey).

Harry S. Truman:

- B&O, Washington, D.C, March 3, 1946: Diesel 78; combine 1401 (communications); Pullman 12-section, 1-drawing room sleeper *Merlin* (dining car crew); Pullman 8-section lounge sleeper; four Pullman 6-compartment, 3-drawing room sleepers; diner 1064; another Pullman 6-compartment, 3-drawing room sleeper; and private car *Ferdinand Magellan* (U.S. No. 1) (Truman).
- PRR, Washington, D.C, June 3, 1948: B&O baggage car 748 (automobiles); B&O combine 1401 (communications); Pullman 12-section 1-drawing room sleeper *St. Ives* and Pullman 6-compartment 3-drawing room sleepers *Wordsworth, Glen Valley* and *Glen Roy* (rail officers, White House overflow and short-haul passengers); two diners; Pullman 6-compartment, 3-drawing room sleepers *Monument Square* and *Raphael* (press); Pullman 1-drawing room 1-compartment/ lounge *Andrew W. Mellon* (press working/lounge); Pullman 6-compartment, 3-drawing room sleepers *Glen Muick* and *Lochard* (press); Pullman 6-compartment, 3-drawing room sleeper *Glen Eyre* (staff); Pullman 1-compartment, 1-drawing room, lounge/buffet/ sun room *Costilla* (White House staff); Pullman 2-single bedroom, 2-double bedroom, 2-compartment, 1-drawing room lounge /sleeper *Minnesota Club* (Secret Service); and private car *Ferdinand Magellan* (Truman).
- PRR, Washington, D.C., Sept. 17, 1948: GG1 locomotive; B&O combine 1401 (communications);

Pullman 16-section tourist sleeper 4062 (dining car crews); Pullman 6-compartment 3-drawing room sleepers *Wordsworth, Brahms, Logan Square, Raphael* and *Washington Square*; two diners; Pullman 6-compartment, 3-drawing room sleepers *Monument Square* and *Cole*; coach 4291 (working press); baggage-dormitory lounge 6704; Pullman 6-compartment, 3-drawing room sleeper *Glen Aray*; Pullman 1-drawing room, 1-compartment lounge *Costilla* (White House staff); Pullman 6-compartment-buffet/ lounge *Waldameer* (Secret Service); and private car *Ferdinand Magellan* (Truman).

Dwight D. Eisenhower:

- CB&Q, Denver, Colo., July 3, 1952: 82-seat rider coach (to Omaha); C&NW baggage car 8761 (from Omaha); C&NW lounge 7331 (from Omaha); Pullman 12-section 1-drawing room sleeper *Oakdale* (from Omaha); Pullman 6-compartment 3-drawing room sleeper *Glen Main* (from Omaha); Pullman 6-compartment 3-drawing room sleepers *Glen Dee* and *Glen Garry*; club/lounge *Lincoln Club* (to Omaha); a 48-seat diner (to Omaha); C&NW diners 6961 (*Mission Delores*) and 6960 (*Presidio*) (from Omaha); Pullman 6-compartment 3-drawing room sleepers *Glen Fee, Glen Adelaide, Veronese* and *Defoe*; Pullman 7-compartment 2-drawing room sleeper *President Harrison*; and business car *Blackhawk* (Eisenhower).
- B&O, Washington, D.C., Nov. 1, 1956: passenger diesels 30 and 30A; coach 3593 (crew); three Pullman 6-compartment, 3-drawing room sleepers; diner 1035; a Pullman 1-drawing room, 1-single bedroom buffet/ lounge car; USAX *General Albert J. Myer* (87325) (communications); another Pullman 6-compart-

ment, 3-drawing room sleeper; and office car 100.

- B&O, Washington, D.C., Oct. 31, 1958: two coaches; a diner; USAX *General Albert J. Myer* (87325) (communications); and office car 902.
- C&O (by trackage rights), Washington, D.C., March 31, 1969 (funeral): Pilot from Washington: passenger diesels 4026 and B&O 1456; baggage car 305; 10-roomette, 6-bedroom sleeper *City of Beckley* (2640); and coach 1646. Pilot from St. Louis: N&W passenger diesels 3808 and 3815; N&W baggage car 112; N&W coach 511; and N&W business car 200. Pilot from Kansas City: UP passenger diesels 958 and 928; and UP coaches 5425 and 5523. POTUS: C&O passenger diesels 4028, 4016 and B&O 1457 (N&W passenger diesels 3488, 508 and 511 from St. Louis and UP passenger diesels 926, 907 and 967 from Kansas City); coach 1637 (crews); baggage car 314 (remains); 11-bedroom sleeper *Homestead* (2800) (honor guard and other military); 10-roomette, 6-bedroom sleepers *City of Newport News* (2606) (military and railroad officers) and *City of Charleston* (2641) (railroad personnel); business car 15 (railroad and military officers); diner 1921; 11-bedroom sleeper *Mount Vernon* (2803) and B&O 5-bedroom lounge *Dana* (7502) (family and friends); and AT&SF private car *Santa Fe* (Mrs. Eisenhower).

Adlai Stevenson:

- DL&W, Hoboken, N.J., Oct. 3, 1956: dormitory car 202 (ex-Pullman 12-section 1-drawing room sleeper); Pullman 6-compartment, 3-drawing room sleepers *Glen Douglas*, *Glen Rosa* and *Glen Nevis*; Pullman 12-roomette, 1-single room, 4-double bedroom sleeper

Oak Mills; Pullman 14-single room sleeper *Night Side*; 36-seat diner 463; Pullman 6-compartment, 3-drawing room sleepers *Glen Almond* and *Schubert*; Pullman 12-roomette, 1-single room, 4-double bedroom sleeper *Oak Pass*; Pullman 1-drawing room,/1-single room,/lounge sleeper *Maine*; Pullman 3-compartment/1-drawing room/ lounge sleeper *Dixie Springs*; and office car 98.

- NYC, Chicago, Ill., Oct. 17, 1956: baggage car; dormitory car; Pullman 6-compartment, 3-drawing room sleepers *Glen Pond*, *Glen Alice*, *Glen Athol*, *Glen Alta* and *Glen Ashdale*; 13-double bedroom sleepers *Schuyler Mansion* and *Apthorpe House*; Pullman 1-drawing room/1-single room/ lounge sleeper *Maine*; Pullman 3-compartment/1-drawing room lounge sleeper *Palm Valley*; and private car 3. (This train also carried an NYC diner, but its nomenclature and position is unknown.)

Richard M. Nixon:

- NYC, Saginaw, Mich., Oct. 22, 1956: baggage car; Southern 12-section, 1-drawing room/dormitory sleeper *McCants*; Pullman 14-single room sleeper *Night Line*; Pullman 13-double bedroom sleepers *Lorain County*, *Wayne County* and *Erie County*; GTW 40-seat diner 1346; Pullman 8-section/lounge sleeper *Highland Country Club* and Pullman 6-double bedroom lounge sleeper *Virginia Beach* (press); Pullman 6-compartment, 3-drawing room sleeper *Glen Dee*; Pullman 2-compartment, 1-drawing room/ lounge sleeper *Sunrise* (guests); Boston & Maine 6-compartment, 3-drawing room sleeper *Gounod*; and PRR business car 100 (Nixon).
- DL&W, New York, N.Y., Oct. 31, 1956: a PRR baggage car; a PRR heavyweight crew dormitory car; Pullman 4-double bedroom, 4-

compartment, 2-drawing room sleepers *Imperial Lea*, *Imperial Crest*, *Imperial Lawn* and *Imperial Terrace*; Pullman 12-duplex single room, 5-double bedroom sleeper *Martin Brook*; Pullman 3-double bedroom, 1-drawing room/lounge sleeper *Colonial Mansions*; Pullman 6-double bedroom lounge sleeper *Cypress Falls*; PRR 48-seat diner; PRR parlor/buffet/ lounge (receptions); Pullman 12-duplex single room, 5-double bedroom sleeper *Magic Brook*; and PRR business car 100 (Nixon).

- PRR, Washington, D.C., Oct. 24, 1960: baggage car 5601; 21-roomette crew sleeper *Peter Shoenberger*; 12-duplex single room, 5-double bedroom sleepers *James Hay Reed*, *Mirror Brook* and *Morning Brook*; 12-duplex single room, 4-double bedroom sleepers *Center Creek* and *Crane Creek*; 3-double bedroom, 1-drawing room lounge sleepers *Colonial Flags* and *Colonial Crafts*; diner 4524 (press); diner 4523; coach/lounge 1123 (reception); 12-duplex single room, 5-double bedroom sleeper *Magic Brook* (staff); 12-duplex single room, 4-double bedroom sleeper *Coldwater Creek* (staff); and Wabash business car 400 (Nixon).
- PRR, Cincinnati, Ohio, Oct. 22, 1968: dormitory coach; coach (press); C&O tavern/lounge 1903; two coaches, a sleeper/lounge and two stripped diners (press); a twin-unit diner; tavern/lounge (reception); a 10-roomette, 6-double bedroom sleeper and two 7-drawing room parlor cars (staff); and C&O business car 15 (Nixon).
- PC, Washington, D.C., Jan. 24, 1970: Pilot: coaches 869, 807 and 866; and Metroclub 885. POTUS: snack-bar coaches 852 and 850 (press); Metroclub 884 (Secret Service and communications); and Metroclub 883 (Nixon).

John F. Kennedy:

- SP, Portland, Ore., Sept. 7, 1960 (shows only Pullman-operated SP cars): 4-double bedroom, 4-compartment, 2-drawing room sleeper 9100; 22-roomette sleepers 9303 and 9300; 10-roomette, 6-bedroom sleepers 9039, 9030, 9031 and 9037; 10-roomette 5-bedroom sleeper 9209; and private car 99 (Kennedy).
- NYC, Ann Arbor, Mich., Oct. 14, 1960: a baggage car; two lounge sleepers; two diners; three 10-roomette, 6-bedroom sleepers; and business car 10 (Kennedy).
- PRR, Washington, D.C., Dec. 2, 1961: GG-1 electric 4883; USAX *General Albert J. Myer* (87325) and 89511 (communications); 4-double bedroom, 4-compartment, 2-drawing room sleepers *Imperial Park*, *Imperial Point* and *Imperial View* (staff and press); 6-double bedroom buffet lounge sleeper *Spruce Falls* (staff); diner 4525; dining room 4626; kitchen/ lounge 4627; parlors 7142 and 7132 (*Paul Revere* and *Henry Knox*) (guests); 6-double bedroom buffet lounge *Elm Falls* (staff and Secret Service); and private car *Philadelphia* (120) (Kennedy).

Lady Bird Johnson:

- RF&P, Washington, D.C., Oct. 6, 1964: USAX *General Albert J. Myer* (87325) and 89511 (communications); PRR 10-roomette, 5-double bedroom sleeper *Cascade Heights* (crew); PRR 12-duplex single room, 5-double bedroom sleepers *Morrow Brook*, *James Hay Reed* and *Memory Brook*; PRR 12-duplex single room, 4-double bedroom sleepers *Chartiers Creek* and *Joseph Horne*; a twin-unit diner (ownership and nomenclature unknown); PRR 6-double bedroom/lounge sleeper *Locust Falls*; PRR 12 duplex single room/4-double bedroom sleepers *Cabin Creek* and *Cross Creek*; PRR

6-double bedroom/lounge sleeper *Juniper Falls*; L&N tavern/lounge 3052 and ACL lounge *Winter Haven* (press); PRR 6-double bedroom lounge sleeper *Sassafras Falls*; Southern office car 14 and PRR parlor/observation car *Queen Mary* (7125) (Mrs. Johnson).

Barry Goldwater:

- B&O, Washington, D.C., Sept. 28, 1964: passenger diesels 1454-2414-1438; baggage/dorm/buffet/lounge car 1239 and 10-section, 2-compartment, 1-drawing room sleeper *Loch Lomond* (crew); 10-roomette, 6-double bedroom sleeper *Tuscarawas*; UP 4-compartment, 4-double bedroom, 2-drawing room sleepers *Imperial Palm*, *Imperial Letter* and *Imperial Rock*; PRR 6-double bedroom/lounge sleeper *Beech Falls*; IC 4-compartment, 4-double bedroom, 2-drawing room sleepers *Chicagoland* and *St. Louisian*; 38-seat diner 1091 (*Pittsburgh*); UP 4-4-2 sleeper *Imperial Robe*; PRR 12-duplex single room, 5-double bedroom sleeper *Maiden Brook*; 10-roomette, 6-double bedroom sleeper *Guyandotte*; 5-double bedroom/lounge *Metcalf*; tavern/ lounge 3302; 10-6 sleeper *Auglaise* (press); CRI&P 4-4-2 sleeper *Golden Desert*; and office car 100 (Goldwater).

Robert F. Kennedy:

- UP, Cheyenne, Wyo., April 27, 1968: two passenger diesels headed by the 932; coach 5551; diner 4803; lounge 6205; coach 5544; diner 4801; lounge 6201; and business car *Arden* (101) (Kennedy).
- PC, New York, N.Y., June 8, 1968 (funeral): Pilot: GG1 4932; and three sleepers. Funeral train: GG1's 4901 and 4903; baggage car 7607; streamlined coaches 1524, 1535, 1484, 1531, 1581 and 1528; standard 48-seat diner 4484; streamlined coaches 1501, 1483, 1503 and

1530; twin-unit diner 4609-4608; streamlined coaches 1541, 1591, 1512 and 1522; streamlined parlor 7146 (*Matthias W. Baldwin*); ex-NYC business car 30; and business car *Pennsylvania* (120) (remains). Protection power: GG1's 4900 and 4910.

George McGovern:

- UP, Omaha, Neb., May 6, 1972: passenger diesels 939 and 907; coach 5474 (crew and staff); Auto-Liner dome-lounge *Linoma* and Auto-Liner 5407 (guests); Auto-Liner 501, (*Big Eight*); and Auto-Liner 500 (*Omaha Club*) (press); and Auto-Liner open-platform sleeper-lounge 100 (McGovern).

Gerald R. Ford:

- GTW, Flint, Mich., May 15, 1976: road switcher 1776 and Amtrak passenger diesels 203 and 214; two Amcafe coaches; two Amcoaches; two Amclubs; and Amtrak private car 10000 (Ford).
- GM&O, Joliet, Ill., Oct. 16, 1976: two Amtrak passenger engines; three Amdinettes; one Amcafe; one Amclub; two 84-seat Amcoaches; and Amtrak private car 10000 (Ford).

Jimmy Carter:

- Conrail, New York, N.Y., Sept. 20, 1976: two Amtrak E60 electrics headed by 966 (two P-30 units, headed by the 718, from Harrisburg); Amtrak baggage car; five Amcoaches; two Amcafes; three Amdinettes; one Amclub; and Auto-Liner Corp. private car 101 (Carter).

Ronald Reagan:

- Chessie System (B&O), Dayton, Ohio, Oct. 12, 1984: Pilot: class GP40-2 road switchers 4440 and 4441; cabooses 904092, 904145 and 904017. POTUS: GP40-2 4444;

Amtrak diesels 276 and 275; Amfleet II cafe-lounge 28104; Amfleet II coaches 25061, 25028, 25101, and 25090; Amtrak baggage car 1231 (communications); Amfleet II cafe-lounge 28001; Amcoach 25007; Amtrak baggage car 1163 (communications); Amfleet II cafe-lounge 28006; SBD private car *Virginia*; C&O private car 7; and the *Ferdinand Magellan* (Reagan). Chase: GP40-2's 4442 and 4443; cabooses 904061, 904062 and 904065.

Michael S. Dukakis:

• Conrail, Pittsburgh, Pa., April 24, 1988: two Amtrak diesels; three Amfleet I coaches; one Amdinette; and Amtrak private car A10000 (Dukakis).

• NS, Belleville, Ill., Aug. 19, 1988: two Amtrak diesels; an Amtrak baggage car; an Amtrak 10-roomette, 6-double bedroom sleeper (Amtrak employees and Secret Service); an Amtrak diner; an Amdinette; an Amfleet II coach; an Amtrak Heritage-fleet dome coach; an Amfleet II coach; an Amdinette; and Amtrak private car A10000 (Dukakis).

• SP, Bakersfield, Calif., Oct. 30, 1988: Pilot: Amtrak diesel 285; Amtrak coach 34041. Candidate: Amtrak diesels 244 and 247; Amtrak sleeper 32002; Amtrak coach 34032; Amtrak lounge 33009; Amtrak baggage/coach 31004; Amtrak diner 38017; Amtrak baggage/coach 31016; Amtrak transition dorm 39909; and private car *Sunset* (150) (Dukakis).

Dan Quayle:

• NS, Charlotte, N.C., Aug. 25, 1992: class GP49 diesel 4604; Jerome Bollick's sleeper/dome *Southern Vista*; and North Carolina State Transportation Museum's private car *Doris* (Quayle).

George Bush:

• Conrail, Columbus, Ohio, Sept. 26, 1992: Pilot: CSX B36-7 diesels 5866 and 5935; AEE diner *Bay Point*; and CSX track observation car 318. POTUS: CSX CW40-8 locomotives 1992 and 7810; CSX baggage car 362 (equipment); CSX business car *Washington* (crew); CSX power car/4-bedroom sleeper *Kentucky* and UP 8-bedroom sleeper *Omaha* (crew); UP diner *City of Los Angeles* (press editing/filing); UP coaches *Texas Eagle* and *City of Salina*, CSX lounge *Tennessee*, and UP coaches *Sunshine Special* and *Portland Rose* (press); UP dome coach *Challenger* (White House Press Office); UP power car 207; UP dome lounge *Walter Dean* (guests and VIPs); UP diner *Overland* (White House Communications Agency); CSX conference car *Indiana* (WHCA and Secret Service); CSX diner *Greenbrier* and AEE diner *Zurich* (White House senior staff); UP business car *Selma* (back-up control) and CSX office car *Baltimore* (Bush). Chase: CSX CW40-8 diesels 7811 and 7809; ex-RF&P baggage car 28; CSX private car *West Virginia*. Backups: CSX cabooses 16632, 16624 and 904051.

• NS, Atlanta, Ga., Oct. 20, 1992: Pilot: diesels 7084 and 4630; NGRX coach 1503. POTUS: CSX CW40-8 1992; GP60 diesel 7140; UP 207 (power car); UP sleeper *Cabarton* (crew); STLC diner *Cuivre River* (press file/edit); NGRX 1512 (press kitchen); NGRX 1511 (press diner); UP coaches *City of Salina*, *Texas Eagle*, *Portland Rose* and *Sunshine Special* (press); UP diner *City of Los Angeles* (White House Press Office); CSX conference car *Indiana* and UP diner *Overland* (WHCA); UP dome coach *Challenger* (VIPs);

AEE diner *Chicago* and UP dome/lounge *Walter Dean* (White House senior staff); New Georgia Railroad office car 300 (control); UP office car *Selma* (backup control); and CSX office car *Baltimore* (Bush). Chase: diesels 7058 and 4611; AEE sleeper *Paris*.

• WC, Burlington, Wis., Oct. 31, 1992: pilot GP40 diesels 3006 and 3007; lounge *Sierra Hotel*; private car *Prairie Rose*. POTUS: CSX CW40-8 1992 (7812); GP40 diesel 3000; UP sleeper *Cabarton* (crew); UP power car 207; STLC diner *Cuivre River* (press file/edit); C&NW diner 450 (*Cedar River*) (press); C&NW full-length dome/lounge 421 (*Powder River*) (press); UP coaches *City of Salina*, *Texas Eagle*, *Portland Rose* and *Sunshine Special* (press); UP diner *City of Los Angeles* (White House Press Office); CSX conference car *Indiana* and UP diner *Overland* (WHCA); UP dome coach *Challenger* (VIPs); UP diner *City of Portland* and UP dome/lounge *Walter Dean* (White House senior staff); New Georgia Railroad office car 300 (control); UP office car *Selma* (Secret Service); and CSX business car *Baltimore* (Bush). Chase: GP40 diesels 3012 and 3023.

Bill Clinton:

• MARC, Washington, D.C., April 5, 1993: GP39 diesels 71 and 72; coach 150 (press); coaches 163 and 166 (for regular commuters); coach 154 (White House staff); and Amtrak private car *Beech Grove* (10001, Clinton).

Elizabeth Dole:

• New England Southern, Tilton N.H., Dec. 8, 1995: GP18 diesel 503; Southwind Rail Travel Ltd. coaches *Chickadee* (ex-B&M) and *Southwind* (ex-L&N); business car *Granite State*.

Bibliography and Acknowledgements

Notes in the text refer the reader to the bibliographical references below. Photo credits appear with their photographs.

1. Abels, Jules; *In The Time of Silent Cal*; New York: G.P. Putnam's Sons; 1969.
2. *Abilene* (Kans.) *Reflector-Chronicle*: Eisenhower Memorial Edition; Abilene, Kan.: Reflector-Chronicle Publishing Corp.; undated.
3. "Abraham Lincoln was a Railroad Man"; *The Railway Clerk*; Cincinnati, Ohio: The Brotherhood of Railway and Steamship Clerks, Freight Handlers, Express and Station Employees; Oct. 1, 1961.
4. Adams, Larry; Boone, Iowa; clippings.
5. Adams, Walter M.; North Little Rock, Ark.; recollections.
6. Alaska Railroad; *1923 Annual Report*; Anchorage, Alaska: U.S. Department of the Interior; 1924.
7. Alsop, Joseph; *FDR: A Centenary Remembrance*; Thorndike, Maine: Thorndike Press; 1982.
8. *Altoona Mirror*; Altoona, Pa.: Altoona Mirror Division, Thompson Newspapers Group:
   8a. Feb. 26, 1889.
   8b. Sept. 27, 1920.
9. *Altoona Tribune*; Altoona, Pa.:
   9a. Sept. 22, 1866.
   9b. Sept. 29, 1881.
   9c. Oct. 23, 1952.
10. Alvarez, Eugene; *Travel on Southern Antebellum Railroads*; University, Ala.: The University of Alabama Press; 1974.
11. Ambrose, Stephen E.; *Eisenhower—Volume I: Soldier, General of the Army, President-elect, 1890-1952*; New York: Simon & Schuster (Touchstone); 1983.
12. Ambrose, Stephen E.; *Eisenhower—Volume II: The President*; New York: Simon & Schuster (Touchstone); 1984.
13. Amtrak; Washington, D.C.; corporate files.
14. *Amtrak News*; Washington, D.C.: National Railroad Passenger Corp.:
   14a. June 1, 1976.
   14b. Oct. 1, 1976.
   14c. Nov. 1, 1976.
15. Anderson, David D.; *William Jennings Bryan*; Boston: Twayne Publishers, a division of G.K. Hall & Co.; 1981.
16. Angier, Jerry; Cape Elizabeth, Maine; recollections.
17. "A Periscope Preview"; *Newsweek* magazine; New York: Newsweek Inc.; Oct. 11, 1948.
18. "A Query about President Lincoln's Funeral Train"; *The Pullman News*; Chicago: The Pullman Co.; February 1930.
19. Asbell, Bernard; *When FDR Died*; New York: Holt, Rinehart & Winston; 1961.
20. Atwater, Susan Eisenhower; Washington, D.C.; interview.
21. Aurand, The Rev. Charles W.; Huntington, W.Va.; many, many patient hours of research.
22. Ayers, Eben A.; Truman Library papers.
23. *Baltimore Sunday Sun*; Nov. 9, 1980.
24. Baer, Christopher T.; *Canals and Railroads of the Mid-Atlantic States, 1800-1860*; Greenville, Wilmington, Del.: The Regional Economic History Research Center, Eleutherian Mills-Hagley Foundation Inc.; 1981.
25. Baker, John; Richmond, Va.; recollections.
26. Ballard, Charles L.; Poestenkill, N.Y.: Mohawk & Hudson chapter, National Railway Historical Society Inc.; recollections.
27. Baltimore & Ohio Railroad Historical Society Inc.; Baltimore, Md.; files from the office of Operating Vice President Charles W. Van Horn.
28. Barclay, R.O.; New Albany, Ind.; recollections.
29. Barger, Ralph L.; *A Century of Pullman Cars, Volume I: Alphabetical List*; Sykesville, Md.: Greenberg Publishing Co. Inc.; 1988; archives and research.
30. Barnard, Harry; *Rutherford B. Hayes and His America*; Indianapolis: Bobbs-Merrill Co.; 1954.
31. Bartels, Michael; Lincoln, Neb.; clippings, archives and recollections.
32. Beach, John; Massillon, Ohio; clippings and recollections.
33. *Beacon Journal*; Akron, Ohio: The Beacon-Journal Publishing Co.; Oct. 13, 1984.
34. Bell, H.C.F.; *Woodrow Wilson and the People*; Garden City, N.Y.: Doubleday, Doran & Co. Inc.; 1945.
35. Bell, J. Snowden; *The Early Motive Power of the Baltimore and Ohio Railroad*; New York: Angus Sinclair Co.; 1912; Felton, Calif.: Glenwood Publishers; 1975.
36. Beebe, Lucius, and Clegg, Charles; *Hear the Train Blow: A Pictorial Epic of America in the Railroad Age*; New York: E.P. Dutton & Co. Inc.; 1952.
37. Beebe, Lucius, and Clegg, Charles; *Mansions on Rails*; Burbank, Calif.: Howell-North Books, a subsidiary of Darwin Publications; 1959.
38. Beebe, Lucius, and Clegg, Charles; *Narrow Gauge in the Rockies*; Burbank, Calif.: Howell-North Books, a subsidiary of Darwin Publications; 1958.
39. Beebe, Lucius, and Clegg, Charles; *Rio Grande, Mainline of the Rockies*; Burbank, Calif.: Howell-North Books, a subsidiary of Darwin Publications; 1962.
40. Bemis, Samuel Flagg; *John Quincy Adams and the Union*; New York: Alfred A. Knopf Inc.; 1970.
41. Berry, W.W.; "The President Cleveland Special"; *Milwaukee Road Magazine*; Chicago: Chicago, Milwaukee, St. Paul & Pacific Railroad; undated.
42. Bishop, Jim; *FDR's Last Year: April 1944-April 1945*; New York: William Morrow & Co.; 1974.
43. Boller, Paul F. Jr.; *Presidential Anecdotes*; New York and London: Oxford University Press; 1981.
44. Boller, Paul F. Jr.; *Presidential Campaigns*; New York and London: Oxford University Press; 1984.
45. Boller, Paul F. Jr.; *Presidential Wives*; New York and London: Oxford University Press; 1988.
46. Boller, Paul F. Jr.; Fort Worth, Texas; letter to author.
47. Boyd, Jim, editor; Carstens Publications Inc. (*Railfan and Railroad* magazine, successor to *Railroad Magazine*); Newton,

N.J.; files.

48. Breck, Sam; Ann Arbor, Mich.; recollections.

49. Bredehoeft, Mrs. Charles; Fork, Md.; transportation notices.

50. Bredehoeft, Wayne; Fork, Md.; recollections, transportation notices.

51. *Brierchat*; White Sulphur Springs, W.Va.: The Greenbrier; April 1956.

52. Briggs, Peter A.; Briggs Business Communications; St. Paul, Minn.; archives and letter to author.

53. Brinkley, David; *Washington Goes to War*; New York: Alfred A. Knopf Inc.; 1988.

54. Brookshire, Curtis; Laurel, Md.; clippings, editing.

55. *Brotherhood of Locomotive Firemen and Enginemen's Magazine*; Washington, D.C.: The Brotherhood of Locomotive Firemen and Enginemen; April 1958.

56. Brovald, Ken C.; *Alaska's Wilderness Rails: From the Taiga to the Tundra*; Missoula, Mont.: Pictorial Histories Publishing Co.; 1982.

57. Bryan, William Jennings and Mary Baird; *The Memoirs of William Jennings Bryan*; Philadelphia, Chicago and Washington: The United Publishers of America; 1925.

58. *Bureau of Engraving and Printing—100 Years*; Washington, D.C.: U.S. Department of the Treasury; 1964.

59. *Burlington Northern News*; Fort Worth, Texas: Burlington Northern Railroad; summer 1990.

60. Burner, David; *Herbert Hoover: A Public Life*; New York: Alfred A. Knopf Inc.; 1979.

61. Burns, Richard Dean; *Harry S. Truman: A Bibliography of His Times and Presidency*; Wilmington, Del.: Scholarly Resources Inc.; 1984.

62. Bush, George; campaign statements Sept. 26-27, 1992.

63. "Campaign Trains That Rolled Over the B&O"; *Baltimore & Ohio Magazine*; Baltimore, Md.: The Baltimore & Ohio Railroad Co.; December 1948.

64. "C&EI Operates Presidential Train First Time In Its 103 Years of Service"; *Chicago & Eastern Illinois Railroad Employees Magazine*; Chicago, Ill.: The Chicago & Eastern Illinois Railroad; November-December 1952.

65. Cafky, Morris; *Colorado Midland*; Denver, Colo: The Rocky Mountain Railroad Club; 1965.

66. Cafky, Morris; Canon City, Col.; letter to author.

67. Campbell, Crispen Y.; "Porter served presidents on the move"; Minneapolis: *Minneapolis Tribune*; June 26, 1983.

68. Campbell, G. Murray; "The Lincoln Inaugural and Funeral Trains"; Boston: The Railway & Locomotive Historical Society Inc.; *Bulletin No. 93*, October 1955.

69. "Carload Andy"; "The Grover Cleveland Wedding Train"; The Switch Lamp; *Railroad Magazine*; New York: Popular Publications Inc.; June, year not shown.

70. *Canton Daily Repository*; Canton, Ohio; Sept. 2, 1880.

71. Carman, Harry J., Syrett, Harold C., and Wishy, Bernard W.; *A History of the American People, Vol. II*; New York: Alfred A. Knopf Inc.; 1961.

72. Carpenter, John; Murphysboro, Ill.; recollections.

73. Carpenter, Liz; *Ruffles and Flourishes: The warm and tender story of a simple girl who found adventure in the White House*; Garden City, N.Y.: Doubleday & Co. Inc.; 1970.

74. Carroll, John W.; White Marsh, Md.; personal letter, clips.

75. Carter, Jimmy, Library; Atlanta, Ga.; documents.

76. Casey, Phil; "Headwaiter Reid, 70, Recalls Life With Presidents, Favors Truman"; Washington, D.C.: *The Washington Post & Times Herald*; July 5, 1959.

77. Casto, James E.; Huntington, W.Va.; recollections.

78. Chapple, Joe Mitchell; "Discovering Alaska with President Harding"; *McClure's Magazine*; New York: McClure Publishing Co.; October 1923.

79. Chesapeake & Ohio Historical Society; Clifton Forge, Va.; clippings and newsletters.

80. *Chicago Evening Journal*; Chicago, Ill.; Sept. 2, 1880.

81. Chitwood, Oliver Perry; *John Tyler: Champion of the Old South*; New York: D. Appleton-Century Co.; 1939.

82. Clark, Robert; Washington, D.C.; interview.

83. Cleaves, Freeman; *Old Tippacanoe: William Henry Harrison and His Time*; New York: Charles Scribner's Sons; 1939.

84. Clifford, Clark M.; Washington, D.C.; interview.

85. Clifford, Clark M.; *Counsel to the President*; New York: Random House; 1991.

86. *Columbus Evening Dispatch*; Columbus, Ohio; March 6, 1946.

87. Combs, Samuel Duff; *Harding Car Restoration Project, Phase I*; Fairbanks, Alaska; 1988.

88. Conte, Robert S.; *The History of The Greenbrier: America's Resort*; Charleston, W.Va.: Pictorial Histories Publishing Co.; 1989; research.

89. Coolidge, Calvin; *The Autobiography of Calvin Coolidge*; New York: Cosmopolitan Book Corp.; 1929.

90. Cordic, Regis; "Pete and Harry"; *Trains* magazine; Waukesha, Wis.: Kalmbach Publishing Co.; December 1985.

91. Cornell, Frank W.; Lewiston, N.Y.; clippings.

92. Corns, John B.; Owings Mills, Md.; recollections.

93. Cudany, Brian J.; *Rails Under the Mighty Hudson*; Brattleboro, Vt.: The Stephen Greene Press; 1975.

94. Cupper, Dan; Harrisburg, Pa.; clippings.

95. *Daily Arizona Citizen*; Tucson, Ariz.; Oct. 25-26, 1880.

96. *Daily Nebraska State Journal*; Falls City, Neb.: Journal Publishing Co.; May 14, 1891.

97. "Daily Newspaper Office on a Train"; *Railway Review*; Chicago, Ill.: Railway Review Inc.; Sept. 18, 1920.

98. *Daily Nonpariel*; Council Bluffs, Iowa: Sept. 3, 1880.

99. *Daily Press*; Jeffersonville, Ind.; Oct. 21, 1964.

100. Daniel, Margaret Truman; *Harry S. Truman*; New York: William Morrow & Co.; 1972.

101. Daniel, Margaret Truman; *Bess W. Truman*; New York: Macmillan Publishing Co.; 1986.

102. Daniel, Margaret Truman; letter to author.

103. Daniels, Jonathan; *The End of Innocence*; Philadelphia, Pa.: J.B. Lippincott Co.; 1954.

104. Daniels, Josephus; *The Life of Woodrow Wilson, 1856-1924*; New York: Holt, Rinehart & Winston; 1924.

105. Davis, Burke; *The Southern Railway: Road of the Innovators*; Chapel Hill, N.C.: The University of North Carolina Press; 1985.

106. Davison, Kenneth E.; *The Presidency of Rutherford B. Hayes*; Westport, Conn.: Greenwood Press; 1972.

107. Dawson, Donald; Washington, D.C.; interview.

108. "Denali"; *The Moose Gooser*; Anchorage, Alaska: Alaska-Yukon chapter, National Railway Historical Society Inc.; July 1967.

109. *Detroit News*; Sept. 27, 1992.

110. Dewey, Frank; Jacksonville, Fla.; interview.

111. Dixon, Thomas W. Jr.; *Chesapeake & Ohio Allegheny Subdivision*; Alderson, W.Va.: The Chesapeake & Ohio Historical Society Inc.; 1985.

112. Dixon, Thomas W. Jr.; "Presidential Specials and Campaign Trains on the C&O"; undated article.

113. Dixon, Thomas W. Jr.; Lynchburg, Va.; clippings.

114. Dolinger, Milton B.; Cleveland; interview.

115. Donovan, Robert J.; *Conflict and Crisis: The Presidency of Harry S. Truman, 1945-1948*; New York: W.W. Norton & Co.; 1977.

116. Donovan, Robert J.; *Tumultuous Years: The Presidency of Harry S. Truman, 1949-1953*; New York: W.W. Norton & Co.; 1982.

117. Donovan, Robert J.; Falls Church, Va.; interview.

118. Dubin, Arthur D.; *Some Classic Trains*; Waukesha, Wis.: Kalmbach Publishing Co.; 1964.

119. Dubin, Arthur D.; *More Classic Trains*; Waukesha, Wis.: Kalmbach Publishing Co.; 1974.

120. Dudley, Hugh J.; North Alabama Railroad Museum Inc., Huntsville, Ala.; research.

121. Duke, Paul; "Dukakis Revealed: Thomas 'Elusive' Dewey"; *The New York Times*; New York: The New York Times Co.; Sept. 9, 1988.

122. Duncan, Owen L.; Huntington, W.Va.; interview.

123. Edson, William D.; Railroad Names: *A Directory of Common Carrier Railroads Operating in the United States 1826-1989*; Potomac, Md.: William D. Edson; 1989; research.

124. Eisenhower, Dwight D.; *Mandate for Change: The White House Years - a Personal Account, 1953-1956*; New York: Doubleday & Co. Inc.; 1963.

125. Eisenhower, Dwight D., Library; Abilene, Kan.; documents.

126. Eisenhower Election Committee; *Procedure for Rear-Platform Appearances*; Sept. 30, 1952.

127. "Eisenhower Special Handled Without a Hitch"; *Louisville & Nashville Employees Magazine*; Louisville, Ky.: The Louisville & Nashville Railway; November 1952.

128. Elmore, Thomas; Huntington, W.Va.; newspaper clipping.

129. Elsey, George M.; Washington, D.C.; documents, interview.

130. Falkner, Leonard; *The President Who Wouldn't Retire*; New York: Coward-McCann Inc.; 1967.

131. Faulkner, Harold U.; *From Versailles to the New Deal: A Chronicle of the Harding-Coolidge-Hoover Era*; New Haven, Conn.: Yale University Press; Toronto: Glasgow, Brook & Co.; London: Geoffrey Cumberlege Oxford University Press; 1950.

132. Ferrell, D. Jack; Moundsville, W.Va.; recollections, letters to the author.

133. Ferrell, Robert H.; Off the Record: *The Private Papers of Harry S. Truman*; New York: Harper & Row Publishers Inc.; 1980.

134. "First in War, First in Peace and Often in Boone"; *Boone News-Republican*; Boone, Iowa; Sept. 13, 1965.

135. Fitch, Edwin M.; *The Alaska Railroad*; New York, Washington and London: Frederick A. Praeger; 1967.

136. "Fire in Fairbanks Threatens Harding's Railroad Car"; *The Seattle Times*; Seattle, Wash: Seattle Times Co.; Sept. 4, 1966.

137. Fitzmaurice, Walter; "President Truman's Campaign Special"; *Trains* magazine; Waukesha, Wis.: Kalmbach Publishing Co.; March 1949.

138. Folliard, Edward T.; "Restive 'Ferdinand' Gets Exercise"; *The Washington Post*; Washington, D.C.: The Washington Post Co.; June 15, 1947.

139. Ford, Gerald R., Library; Ann Arbor, Mich.; documents.

140. Ford, Gerald R., Rancho Mirage, Calif.; letter to author.

141. Foster, Maj. Gen. Hugh F., USA rtd; Furlong, Pa.; documents, interview.

142. *Fremont News-Messenger*; Fremont, Ohio: The Gannett Satellite Information Network Inc.; Aug. 27, 1880.

143. Frick, Henry; Fort Worth, Texas.; documents.

144. Furman, Bess; White House Profile: *A social history of the White House, its occupants and its festivities*; New York and Indianapolis: The Bobbs-Merrill Co. Inc.; 1951.

145. Gardner, Harvey; Scituate, Mass.; Southern Pacific train orders handed to 1948 Truman special.

146. Garrison, Webb; *A Treasury of White House Tales*; Nashville, Tenn.: Rutledge Hill Press; 1989.

147. Garvey, James J.; "Rutherford B. Hayes: The Grand Western Tour of 1880"; unpublished college history paper supplied by the Rutherford B. Hayes Library, Fremont, Ohio.

148. George, Alexander (Associated Press); "Campaign Travel is Pretty Soft—But Bryan and Others Roughed It"; *Louisville Courier-Journal*; Louisville, Ky.: The Courier-Journal Co.; Sept. 19, 1948.

149. Gold Coast Railroad Museum; Miami, Fla.; documents.

150. Goodheart, David; "Pursuing the POTUS"; *Railfan & Railroad* magazine; Newton, N.J.: Carstens Publications Inc.; March 1993.

151. Gonga, Gary Joseph; "Hayes and Unity"; unpublished A.B. thesis for St. Meinrad Seminary, St. Meinrad, Ind.; May 1965.

152. Gordon, Gordon; "Campaign Trains"; *Railroad Magazine*; New York: Popular Publications Inc.; February 1953.

153. Graff, Robert D.; Ginna, Robert Emmett; Butterfield, Roger; *FDR*; New York: Harper & Row Publishers Inc.; 1963.

154. Grannon, Marjorie Wilson; Englewood, Fla.; interview.

155. Grant, Charles; Evergreen, Colo.; interview.

156. Grant, Gen. Ulysses S.; letters to Julia Dent Grant, July 17 and 21, 1868.

157. Grant, Mrs. Ulysses S.; *The Personal Memoirs of Julia Dent Grant*; New York: G.P. Putnam's Sons; 1975.

158. Grant, Maj. Gen. Ulysses S. III; *Ulysses S. Grant, Warrior and Statesman*; New York: William Morrow & Co.; 1969.

159. Hall, R.J., and Wuchert, R.P.; *Memories of the New Haven*; Wallingford, Conn.: Cedar Hill Productions; 1983.

160. Haller, Dorothy; "White House on Wheels"; *Tracks* magazine; Cleveland: Chesapeake & Ohio Railway; January 1948.

161. Hamilton, Kent F.; "The Lincoln Funeral Car"; courtesy Louis A. Warren Lincoln Library and Museum, Fort Wayne, Ind.

162. Harris, Richard W.; Norfolk Southern Corp. Public Relations Dept., Atlanta, Ga.; archives.

163. *Harrisburg Telegraph*; Harrisburg, Pa.; Sept. 4, 1919.

164. Harwood, Herbert H. Jr.; *Impossible Challenge*; Baltimore, Md.: Barnard, Roberts & Co.; 1979.

165. Harwood, Herbert H. Jr.; Baltimore, Md.; archives, letters to author.

166. Hassett, William D.; *Off the Record with FDR*; New Brunswick, N.J.: Rutgers University Press; 1958.

167. Hatch, Alden; Edith Bolling Wilson: *First Lady Extraordinary*; New York: Dodd, Mead & Co.; 1961.

168. Havens, Jack; Huntington, W.Va.; interview.

169. Hayes, Rutherford Birchard, Library; Fremont, Ohio; archives, Hayes scrapbooks and correspondence.

170. Headley, Hon. J.T.; *The Life and Travels of General Grant*; Philadelphia: Hubbard Bros.; 1879.

171. Hechler, Ken; *Working with Truman*; New York: G.P. Putnam's Sons; 1982.

172. Hechler, Ken; Huntington, W.Va.; interviews, archives.

173. "He Guarded the Great and Near-Great: Captain Ernie Chapman Retires after 47 Years of Adventurous Railroading"; *Baltimore & Ohio Magazine*; Baltimore, Md.: The Baltimore & Ohio Railroad Co.; November 1957.

174. Heinl, Robert D.; "The President's Special Train: Plans Which Have Been Discussed Regarding a Safe and Appropriate Manner for the Chief Executive of the Nation to Travel"; *Leslie's Illustrated Weekly*; New York: Frank Leslie; June 1, 1911.

175. Heldenfels, R.D.; "Truman Sailed To Potsdam From Newport News Pier"; *Daily Press*; Newport News, Va.: The Daily Press Inc.; July 7, 1975.

176. Helm, Edith Benham; *The Captains and the Kings*; New York: G.P. Putnam's Sons; 1954.

177. Henebry, Ray; "HSC Student Rides Kennedy Special"; Scottsbluff, Neb.: Hiram Scott College student newspaper.

178. Henry, Robert Self; *Trains*; Indianapolis: The Bobbs-Merrill Co.; 1957.

179. Henson, Fred C.; "Rails for the Chief"; *The Railway Conductor* magazine; Cedar Rapids, Iowa: Order of Railway Conductors and Brakemen; January 1950.

180. Hesseltine, William B.; *U.S. Grant, Politician*; New York: Dodd, Mead & Co.; 1935.

181. Hensley, Tim; "Did L&N engineer help Truman win '48 election with remark from Dewey?"; *CSX News*; Jacksonville, Fla.: CSX Transportation; October 1988.

182. Highsmith, Carol M., and Landphair, Ted; *Union Station: A Decorative History of Washington's Grand Terminal*; Washington, D.C.: Chelsea Publishing Inc.; 1988.

183. Holbrook, Stewart H.; *The Story of American Railroads*; New York: Bonanza Books, a division of Crown Publishers Inc.; 1947.

184. Holden, Jim; "General Grant's Last Ride"; *Railroad Stories* magazine; New York: Popular Publications Inc.; September 1935.

185. Hoover, Irwin Hood "Ike"; *Forty-two Years in the White House*; Westport, Conn.: Greenwood Press; 1962 (originally New York: Houghton Mifflin Co.; 1934).

186. Hoover, Herbert, Library; West Branch, Iowa; archives.

187. Hoover, Herbert Clark; *The Memoirs of Herbert Hoover*; New York: The Macmillan Publishing Co.; 1952.

188. Howe, George Frederick; *Chester A. Arthur: A Quarter-Century of Machine Politics*; New York: Frederick Ungar Publishing Co.; 1934.

189. Howes, William F. Jr.; Jacksonville, Fla.; many, many hours of research, archives, interview.

190. Hoyt, Edwin P.; *Franklin Pierce: The Fourteenth President of the United States*; New York: Abelard-Schuman; 1972.

191. Hoyt, Edwin P.; *James Buchanan*; Chicago: Reilly & Lee Co.; 1966.

192. Hubbard, Freeman H.; "Political Stand-in"; *Tracks* magazine; Cleveland: The Chesapeake & Ohio Railway; October 1950.

193. Hubbard, Freeman H.; *Railroad Avenue*; New York and London: McGraw-Hill Book Co. Inc.; 1945.

194. Hubbard, Freeman H.; "Seven Cars Painted Black"; *Railroad Magazine*; New York: Popular Publications Inc.; December 1962.

195. Huddleston, Eugene; notes for newsletter story; Alderson, W.Va.: The Chesapeake & Ohio Historical Society; undated.

196. Humphreys, Paul; Huntington, W.Va.; interview.

197. Hungerford, Edward; *The Story of the Baltimore and Ohio Railroad, 1827-1927, Volumes 1 and 2*; New York: G.P. Putnam's Sons; 1928.

198. "Ike Coming to Boone!"; Boone, Iowa: *Boone News-Republican*; June 22, 1980.

199. "Ike visits the N&W"; *Norfolk & Western Magazine*; Roanoke, Va.: The Norfolk & Western Railway; October 1952.

200. Indianapolis Journal; May 2, 1865.

201. Jackson, Andrew; letter to Andrew Jackson Jr., June 6, 1833; Library of Congress.

202. Jacobs, Harry A.; *The Juniata Canal and Old Portage Railroad*; Hollidaysburg, Pa.: Blair County Historical Society; undated.

203. Jacobs, Warren; "Lincoln on the New Haven and The Boston & Albany Railroads"; Boston: The Railway and Locomotive Historical Society Inc.; *Bulletin No. 33*, February 1934.

204. Jacobs, Warren; "The Old Hudson River Railroad Depot and Abraham Lincoln in New York"; Boston: The Railway & Locomotive Historical Society Inc.; *Bulletin No. 55*; May 1941.

205. Jakobsson, Ejler; "Whistle Stop," *Railroad Magazine*; New York: Popular Publications Inc.; August 1956.

206. James, Bessie Rowland and Marquis; *The Courageous Heart: A Life of Andrew Jackson for Young Readers*; New York: Bobbs-Merrill Co.; 1934.

207. Jenkins, Roy; *Truman*; New York: Harper & Row Publishers Inc.; 1986.

208. Johnson, Lady Bird; *A White House Diary*; New York, Chicago and San Francisco: Holt, Rinehart and Winston; 1970.

209. Johnson, Lyndon Baines, Library; Austin, Texas; documents.

210. Johnston, A.W. Jr.; Pawley's Island, S.C.; interview.

211. Johnston, Angus James II; *Virginia Railroads in the Civil War*; Chapel Hill, N.C.: The University of North Carolina Press; 1961.

212. Johnston, Hank; *Railroads of the Yosemite Valley*; Glendale, Calif.: Trans-Anglo Books, a division of Interurban Press; 1963.

213. Jones, Bartow; Point Pleasant, W.Va.; interview.

214. Keckley, Elizabeth; *Behind the Scenes. Or, Thirty Years a Slave, and Four Years in the White House*; New York: Oxford University Press; 1988.

215. Kelly, Frank K.; *The Fight for the White House: The Story of 1912*; New York: Thomas Y. Crowell Co.; 1961.

216. Kelly, S.J.; "Running the Locomotive of Lincoln's Train"; *Cleveland Plain Dealer*; Cleveland: Plain Dealer Publishing Co.; Aug. 12, 1936.

217. Kelly, Theodore; Jacksonville, Fla.; interview.

218. Kennedy, John F., Library; Boston; documents.

219. Kirkpatrick, Joel; "Your railcar, sir"; *Focus* magazine; Roanoke, Va.: Norfolk Southern Corp.; first quarter 1991.

220. Klein, Philip Shriver; *President James Buchanan: A Biography*; University Park, Pa.: The Pennsylvania State University Press; 1962.

221. Kuhn, Ferdinand; *The Story of the Secret Service*; New York: Scholastic Book Services, a division of Scholastic Magazines Inc.; New York: Random House; 1957.

222. Kunhardt, Dorothy Meserve and Phillip B. Jr.; *Twenty Days*; New York: Castle Books; 1965.

223. Kureth, Raymond; "Linking Lincoln with the B&O Line," *Baltimore & Ohio Magazine*; Baltimore, Md.: The Baltimore &

Ohio Railroad Co.; February 1935.

224. La Cossitt, Henry; "He Takes the President on Tour," *The Saturday Evening Post*; Indianapolis, Ind.: The Saturday Evening Post Society; June 16, 1951.

225. Lamb, Blaine; California State Railroad Museum; Sacramento, Calif.; recollections.

226. Lane, Wheaton J.; *Commodore Vanderbilt: An Epic of the Steam Age*; New York: Alfred A. Knopf Inc.; 1942.

227. Larson, Bethene Wookey; "Franklin D. Roosevelt's Visit to Sidney (Neb.) During the Drouth of 1936"; *Nebraska History* magazine, Lincoln, Neb: Nebraska State Historical Society; spring 1984.

228. Lash, Joseph P.; *Eleanor and Franklin: The Story of Their Relationship Based on Eleanor Roosevelt's Private Papers*; New York: New American Library; 1971.

229. Leech, Margaret, and Brown, Harry J.; *The Garfield Orbit*; New York: Harper & Row Publishers Inc.; 1978.

230. Levin, Bennett; Philadelphia; information on ex-PRR business car 120.

231. Lewis, Lloyd D.; Jacksonville, Fla.; clippings, research, many, many hours of editing.

232. Leyendecker, Liston Edgington; *Palace Car Prince: A Biography of George Mortimer Pullman*; Niwot, Colo: The University Press of Colorado; 1992.

233. Lillegard, Dee; *Encyclopedia of Presidents: John Tyler*; Chicago: Children's Press; 1987.

234. Little, Herb; Charleston, W.Va.; letter to author.

235. Locomotive Engineer; Cleveland: Brotherhood of Locomotive Engineers; Feb. 4, 1966.

236. Long, Barbara (Mrs. Dewey); Silver Spring, Md.: interview, letters to author.

237. Long, Charles; Leatherhead, Surrey, England; information on Lincoln funeral train.

238. "Long Time No See"; *GM&O News*; Mobile, Ala.: The Gulf, Mobile & Ohio Railroad; Aug. 15, 1953.

239. Lorant, Stefan; *The Glorious Burden: The American Presidency*; New York: Harper & Row Publishers Inc.; 1968.

240. "Loud Speaking Device on President Harding's Car"; *The Pullman News*; Chicago, Ill.: The Pullman Co.; August 1923.

241. Louis A. Warren Lincoln Library and Museum; Fort Wayne, Ind.; clippings.

242. Lucas, Walter Arndt; *The History of the New York, Susquehanna & Western Railroad*; New York: Railroadians of America; 1939, 1980.

243. Lyons, Stephen; Montreal, Quebec, Canada; Canadian Pacific archives.

244. MacCorkle, William Alexander; *The Recollections of Fifty Years*; New York, London: G.P. Putnam's Sons, 1928.

245. Maguire, Jack; "Odd Lots: Presidential Specials"; *Railway Progress* magazine; Washington, D.C.: Federation for Railway Progress; May 1956.

246. Manchester, William; *The Glory and the Dream: A Narrative History of America, 1932-1972, Volume One*; Boston: Little, Brown & Co.; 1974.

247. Manners, William; *TR and Will: A Friendship that Split the Republican Party*; New York: Harcourt, Brace & World Inc.; 1969.

248. McDowell, Miss Aubin Aydelotte; *White Sulphur Springs as Known in History and Tradition*; Louisville, Ky.; undated.

249. McFeely, William S.; *Grant: A Biography*; New York: W.W. Norton & Co.; 1981.

250. McGrory, Mary; "Whistlestop: A Campaign Idyl"; *Washington Star*; Oct. 21, 1956.

251. McGrain, John W.; "The Presidents in Baltimore County"; *History Trails*; Baltimore, Md.: Baltimore County Historical Society; summer, fall and winter 1987.

252. McMorris, Robert; "Centennial Stirs Memories of Ike"; Omaha, Neb.: *Omaha World-Herald*; Oct. 17, 1990.

253. McMurtry, R. Gerald; "Lincoln's Inaugural Train: The Memorable Journey of the President-Elect to Washington in 1861"; *Locomotive Engineers Journal*; Cleveland: The Brotherhood of Locomotive Engineers; February 1933.

254. Miers, Earl Schenck, editor; *Lincoln Day-by-Day: A Chronology; Volumes II and III*; Washington, D.C.: Lincoln Sesquicentennial Commission; 1960.

255. Miller, Merle, *Plain Speaking*; New York: G.P. Putnam's Sons; 1974.

256. Miller, Richard Lawrence; *Truman: The Rise to Power*; New York: McGraw-Hill Book Co. Inc.; 1986 edition.

257. Millerick, Jeff; Santa Rosa, Calif.; information about B&O office car 100.

258. Milne, Chris; Cambridge, Mass.; recollections.

259. Mishke, Jim; Albuquerque, N.M.; archives.

260. Moaney, Delores; Washington, D.C.; interview.

261. Moffat, Dr. Charles; *Ken Hechler: Maverick Public Servant*; Charleston, W.Va.: Mountain State Press (University of Charleston); 1987.

262. Monroe, Herbert G.; "President's Special"; *Railroad Magazine*; New York: Popular Publications Inc.; November 1945.

263. Moran, Philip R., editor; *Calvin Coolidge, 1872-1933: Chronology-Documents-Bibliographical Aids*; Dobbs Ferry, N.Y.: Oceana Publications Inc.; 1970.

264. Morgan, David P.; "White Flags for a Late president"; *Trains* magazine; Milwaukee: Kalmbach Publishing Co.; July 1962.

265. Morgan, H. Wayne; *William McKinley and His America*; Syracuse, N.Y.; Syracuse University Press; 1969.

266. Morgan, Ted; *FDR: A Biography*; New York: Simon and Schuster; 1985.

267. Morning World Herald (of Omaha, Neb.); May 14, 1891.

268. Morris, Roger; "Playing Poker, Making History"; *The New York Times*; New York; The New York Times Co.; May 19, 1991.

269. Morris, Roger; Richard Milhous Nixon: The Rise of an American Politician; New York: Henry Holt & Co. Inc.; 1989.

270. Morrow, Esther; Vienna, W.Va.; interview.

271. Morton, Jack, and Petrie, Ross; "The 'Ferdinand Magellan': United States No. 1"; *NMRA Bulletin*; Chattanooga, Tenn.: The National Model Railroad Association Inc.; June 1967.

272. Mrozek, David J.; Ann Arbor, Mich.; recollections.

273. Myers, Elisabeth P.; *Rutherford B. Hayes*; Chicago: Reilly & Lee; 1969.

274. *National Tribune*; May 27, 1915; Fort Wayne, Ind.: Louis A. Warren Lincoln Library and Museum.

275. *Nemaha County Herald*; Auburn, Neb.; May 6, 1943.

276. Nesbitt, Henrietta; *White House Diary*; Garden City, N.Y.: Doubleday & Co. Inc.; 1948.

277. Nevins, Allan; *Grover Cleveland: A Study in Courage*; New York: Dodd, Mead & Co.; 1958.

278. Nevins, Allan; Polk: *The Diary of a President*; New York: Longmans, Green & Co.; 1952.

279. Newman, Larry G.; "The First Attempt to Kill Lincoln"; undated clipping supplied by Carstens Publications Inc.; Newton, N.J.

280. *Newsweek* magazine; New York, N.Y.: Newsweek Inc.; March 18, 1946.

281. Niven, John; Martin Van Buren: *The Romantic Age of American Politics*; New York: Oxford University Press; 1983.

282. Nixon, Robert G.; oral history interview at Truman Library.

283. Nixon, Richard Milhous; Saddle River, N.J.; letter to author.

284. Noall, William F.; "Fred Fair: Presidential Pullman Porter"; *Focus* magazine; Roanoke, Va.: Norfolk Southern Corp.; summer 1985.

285. Nowak, Edwin S.; Rochester, N.Y.; information.

286. "Odds and Ends of Railroading," *Railway Age* magazine; New York: Simmons-Boardman Publishing Corp.; July 1930.

287. Olcott, Charles S.; *American Statesmen: William McKinley, Volumes I and II*; Boston: Houghton Mifflin Co.; 1967.

288. Orlando Sentinel; Nov. 12, 1972.

289. Page, Elwin L.; *Abraham Lincoln in New Hampshire*; Boston: Houghton Mifflin Co.; 1929.

290. "People of the Week"; *U.S. News & World Report*; New York: U.S. News & World Report Inc.; Dec. 11, 1953.

291. Phelan, Mary Kay; *Mr. Lincoln's Inaugural Journey*; New York: Thomas Y. Crowell Co.; 1972.

292. Phillips, Cabell; *The Truman Presidency: The History of a Triumphant Succession*; New York: Macmillan Publishing Co.; 1966.

293. Phillips, Don; "Fastest President on Wheels"; *Trains* magazine; Milwaukee, Wis.: Kalmbach Publishing Co.; April 1970.

294. Phillips, Don; "Richard M. Nixon: Trackside and on-train experiences that led to the White House"; *Trains* magazine; Milwaukee, Wis.: Kalmbach Publishing Co.; November 1971.

295. Pins, George; Brooklyn, N.Y.; information on PRR private car 120.

296. Pitkin, Thomas H.; *The Captain Departs: Ulysses S. Grant's Last Campaign*; Carbondale, Ill.: Southern Illinois University Press; 1973.

297. Plemons, Pat; Memphis, Tenn.; documents.

298. "President Truman's 1948 Campaign Speaking Appearances," Truman library.

299. Pofahl, Eugene; Huntington, W.Va.; research.

300. "POTUS and Two Other Specials Pay Us a Visit"; *Louisville & Nashville Employees Magazine*; Louisville, Ky.: Louisville & Nashville Railroad; November 1948.

301. "POTUS: The Heartland Special"; *Trains* magazine; Milwaukee: Kalmbach Publishing Co.; January 1985.

302. "President and Prince Were His Guests"; *The Pullman News*; Chicago: The Pullman Co.; February 1926.

303. "President Harding's Funeral Train"; *The Railway Gazette*; New York: Simmons-Boardman Publishing Corp.; Aug. 31, 1923.

304. "President Roosevelt Thanks B&O Crew for a Fine Run"; *Baltimore & Ohio Magazine*; Baltimore, Md.: The Baltimore & Ohio Railroad Co.; September 1934.

305. "Presidential Special"; *Tracks* magazine; Cleveland: The Chesapeake & Ohio Railway; May 1956.

306. Prial, Frank J.; "Reagan Takes a Page From Truman's Campaign"; New York: *The New York Times*; Oct. 12, 1984.

307. Price, Buck; Miami Shores, Fla.; letter to author.

308. Price, Dennis R.; Carlsbad, Calif.; archives.

309. *Railroad Magazine*; New York: Popular Publications Inc.; February 1952.

310. *Railway Age* magazine; New York: Simmons-Boardman Publishing Corp.; Aug. 18, 1923.

311. *Railway Review*; Sept. 18, 1920.

312. Raleigh, Walter; "The President Takes a Railway Trip"; *Transportation* magazine, publication data not shown; August 1930.

313. Rathke, Bob; Buffalo Grove, Ill.; research.

314. Rayback, Robert J.; *Millard Fillmore: Biography of a President*; Buffalo, N.Y.: Henry Stewart Inc., for the Buffalo Historical Society; 1959.

315. Rayburn, Richard, executive vice president operations; "POTUS CONFIDENTIAL: Instructions for Handling of Special Train at the Disposal of the President of the United States of America"; Baltimore, Md.: Chessie System Railroads; Oct. 5, 1984.

316. Reagan, Ronald W.; Los Angeles, Calif.; letter to author.

317. Reid, Jimmy, and Cosgrove, Mike; Southeastern Railway Museum, Duluth, Ga.; research.

318. Remini, Robert V.; *Andrew Jackson and the Course of American Democracy*, Vol III; New York: Harper & Row Publishers Inc.; 1984.

319. Remlap, L.T.; *The Life of General U.S. Grant*; Hillsdale, Mich.: W.E. Allen & Co.; 1885.

320. Reston, James B.; quoted in *Headlight*; New York: The New York Central System; November 1956.

321. Rigdon, William M., U.S. Navy ship's clerk; Franklin Roosevelt trip logs, Washington, D.C.: U.S. Government; 1942 and 1943.

322. Rivers, John; College Park, Ga.; research.

323. Roadcap, Bob; Richmond, Va.; research.

324. Robertson, Archie; "Murder Most Foul"; *American Heritage* magazine; New York: American Heritage Publishing Co. Inc.; August 1964.

325. Robertson, Nan; "First Lady To Go Whistle-Stopping"; *The New York Times*; New York: The New York Times Co.; Sept. 13, 1964.

326. *Rocky Mountain News*; Denver, Colo.: Denver Publishing Co.; April 14, 1959.

327. Roosevelt, Franklin D., Library; Hyde Park, N.Y.; documents.

328. Roosevelt, Theodore; *The Autobiography of Theodore Roosevelt*; New York: Octagon Books, a division of Farrar, Straus and Giroux Inc.; 1975.

329. Ross, Irwin; *The Loneliest Campaign: The Truman Victory of 1948*; New York: New American Library; 1968.

330. Rovere, Richard H.; "Letter from a Campaign Train"; *The New Yorker* magazine; New York: The New Yorker Magazine Inc.; Oct. 9, 1948.

331. Rowland, Ross E. Jr.; Lebanon, N.J.; papers, correspondence relating to proposal to operate campaign train for H. Ross Perot; 1992.

332. Rozum, Fred; Scottsdale (Ariz.) Railroad and Mechanical Society; clips.

333. *Salisbury Post*:
   333a. Aug. 24, 1992.
   333b. Aug. 27, 1992.

334. Sandburg, Carl; *Abraham Lincoln, The War Years; Volume Two*; New York: Harcourt, Brace & Co.; 1939.

335. Scott, John; Huntington, W.Va.; interview.

336. Seacrest, James C.; "Not in the Timetable"; *Nebraskaland* magazine; Lincoln, Neb.: The Nebraska Games and Parks Commission; August 1981.

337. Searcher, Victor; *The Farewell to Lincoln*; Nashville, Tenn.: Abingdon Press; 1965.

338. Segal, Edward; "The Whistle-Stop Campaigns"; *Washington Journalism Review*; Washington, D.C.: College of Journalism of The University of Maryland; July/August 1988.

339. Seidel, David; Columbus, Neb.; Union Pacific archives, research, clippings.

340. Sell, J.J., Wheeling Division superintendent; The Baltimore & Ohio Railroad Co., instructions governing Eisenhower campaign special and other company correspondence, telegrams and instructions in the author's collection; September 1952.

341. "Senator Goldwater 'Whistle Stops' on the B&O"; *B&O News*; Baltimore, Md.: The Baltimore & Ohio Railroad Co.; Oct. 13, 1964.

342. "Served Four Presidents"; *Trains* magazine; Waukesha, Wis.: Kalmbach Publishing Co.; November 1949.

343. Shanley, Bernard; diary of 1952 campaign trip; Eisenhower Library.

344. Sheehan, Michael T., editor; "Seventy-Fifth Anniversary of the Wilson Wedding"; *Woodrow Wilson House News, Volume II, Issue 4*; Washington D.C.: Woodrow Wilson House Museum; Winter 1990.

345. Shenkman, Richard, and Reiger, Kurt; *One-Night Stands With American History: Odd, Amusing, and Little-Known Incidents*; New York: William Morrow & Co. (Quill); 1982.

346. Shepherd, Jack; *Cannibals of the Heart: A Personal Biography of Louisa Catherine and John Quincy Adams*; New York: McGraw-Hill Book Co.; 1980.

347. Shippen, W.H.; "Man Who Serves Up Trains For Presidents To Be Honored"; Washington, D.C.: *Washington Evening Star*; Jan. 8, 1953.

348. Sievers, Harry J.; *Benjamin Harrison, Hoosier Statesman*; New York: University Publishers Inc.; 1959.

349. Sievers, Harry J., editor; *William McKinley, 1843-1901, Chronology-Documents-Bibliographical Aids*; Dobbs Ferry, N.Y.: Oceana Publications Inc.; 1970.

350. Simon, Elbert; Binghamton, N.Y.; train consists.

351. Sinclair, Andrew; *The Available Man: The Life Behind the Masks of Warren Gamaliel Harding*; New York: Macmillan Publishing Co.; 1965.

352. Skala, Mary Jane; "Heartland Special: Chessie carries President Reagan on triumphant whistlestop tour"; *Chessie News*; Jacksonville, Fla: Chessie System Railroads; October/November 1984.

353. Small, Collie; "The Campaign Trains Roll Again"; *Collier's* magazine; New York: The Crowell-Collier Publishing Co.; Oct. 2, 1948.

354. Smith, Charles M., New York Central System Historical Society Inc., Strafford-Wayne, Pa.; letters to author.

355. Smith, Gene; *When the Cheering Stopped: The Last Years of Woodrow Wilson*; New York: William Morrow & Co.; 1964.

356. Smith, Ira R.T.; *Dear Mr. President: The Story of Fifty Years in the White House Mail Room*; New York: Julian Messner Inc.; 1949.

357. Smith, Jesse; Ona, W.Va.; Bush scrapbook.

358. Smith, Merriman; *A President is Many Men*; New York and London: Harper & Brothers; 1948.

359. Smith, Sidney; "When the President Rides"; *Railroad Man's Magazine*; New York: Frank Munsey Co.; May 1931.

360. Southern Railway; Washington, D.C.; memo concerning POTUS train handling; June 18, 1941.

361. "Special Train Not Swank; Necessity, Says Coolidge"; *Railroad Age* magazine; New York: Simmons-Boardman Publishing Corp.; July 1929.

362. Starbuck, G.F.; "How the Lincoln Funeral Car Was Built," *B&M Magazine*; Boston, Mass.: Boston & Maine Corp.; undated.

363. Starling, Col. Emund W.; *Starling of the White House*; Chicago: People's Book Club; distributed by Simon & Schuster; New York; 1946.

364. Starr, John W. Jr.; *Lincoln and the Railroads*; New York: Dodd, Mead & Co.; 1927.

365. Staufer, Al; *B&O Power*, Carrollton, Ohio: Standard Printing and Publishing Co.; 1964.

366. Stearns, Henry P.; "The Watertown & Waterbury Railroad"; *The Shoreliner*; Volume II, Issue 2; Grafton, Mass: New Haven Railroad Historical-Technical Association; 1980.

367. Steinberg, Alfred; *Woodrow Wilson*; New York: G.P. Putnam's Sons; 1969.

368. Steinheimer, Richard; *Electric Way Across the Mountains*; Tiburon, Calif.: Carbarn Press; 1980.

369. Stevenson, Wade J.; Othello, Wash.; interview.

370. Stover, John F.; *History of the Baltimore and Ohio Railroad*; West Lafayette, Ind.: Perdue University Press; 1987.

371. Stowe, David H.; Bethesda, Md.; interview.

372. Strates, E. James; Orlando, Fla.; research.

373. Sullivan, Mark; *Our Times: 1900-1925, Volume III: Pre-war America, and Volume IV, The Twenties*; New York: Charles Scribner's Sons; 1940.

374. Tanner, Virginia; "GPA Dan Moorman Recalls Journeys with President Roosevelt"; *Baltimore & Ohio Magazine*; Baltimore, Md.: The Baltimore & Ohio Railroad Co.; May 1945.

375. Tanner, Virginia; "Journeys with President Roosevelt," *Baltimore & Ohio Magazine*; Baltimore, Md: The Baltimore & Ohio Railroad Co.; May 1945.

376. Tanner, Virginia; "Riding 'Special' on the Batimore & Ohio with President Roosevelt"; *Baltimore & Ohio Magazine*; Baltimore, Md.: The Baltimore & Ohio Railroad Co.; October 1938.

377. Tanner, Virginia; "We Take the President and Mr. Churchill on Historic Journey"; *Baltimore & Ohio Magazine*; Baltimore, Md.: The Baltimore & Ohio Railroad Co.; April 1946.

378. Taylor, Tim; *The Book of Presidents*; New York: Arno Press; 1972.

379. terHorst, J.F., and Albertazzie, Col. Ralph; *The Flying White House*; New York: Coward, McCann & Geoghegan Inc.; 1979.

380. "The B&O ... Route of the Presidents"; The Baltimore & Ohio Railroad public relations department; Baltimore, Md.; undated brochure.

381. "The Campaign Train ... It Appears Slated for a Comeback in National Election This Fall"; *Baltimore & Ohio Magazine*; Baltimore, Md.: The Baltimore & Ohio Railroad Co.; June 1960.

382. "The Departure of an Ex-President"; *Baltimore & Ohio Magazine*; Baltimore, Md.: The Baltimore & Ohio Railroad Co.; March 1953.

383. "The Gold Coast Railroad's Famous U.S. Presidential Pullman 'Ferdinand Magellan' "; Miami, Fla.: Gold Coast Railroad

Museum; undated.

384. "The Great Upset of '48" (Public Broadcasting System television special first aired Nov. 3, 1988); Washington, D.C.: WETA (Washington Educational Telecommunications Association) Magazine.

385. *The Herald-Advertiser*; Huntington, W.Va.: July 11, 1971.

386. *The Herald-Dispatch*; Huntington, W.Va.:
    386a. Sept. 30, 1920.
    386b. March 5, 1946.
    386c. March 6, 1946.
    386d. Dec. 8, 1952.
    386e. Nov. 14, 1953.
    386f. April 2, 1969.
    386g. Sept. 27, 1992.

387. *The Huntington Advertiser*; Huntington, W.Va.:
    387a. April 4, 1912.
    387b. April 5, 1912.
    387c. June 21, 1923.
    387d. June 23, 1923.
    387e. March 4, 1946.
    387f. Sept. 25, 1952.
    387g. Oct. 23, 1952.
    387h. March 27, 1956.
    387i. Aug. 4, 1969.
    387j. Dec. 11, 1973.

388. *The Mixed Train*; Omaha, Neb.: The Camerail Club; June 1972.

389. *The New York Times*; New York: The New York Times Co.:
    389a. Jan. 7, 1853.
    389b. Sept. 14, 1866.
    389c. Sept. 15, 1866.
    389d. Aug. 8, 1868.
    389e. Aug. 2, 1868.
    389f. April 6, 1883.
    389g. April 7, 1883.
    389h. April 21, 1883.
    389i. April 23, 1883.
    389j. July 31, 1883.
    389k. April 24, 1891.
    389l. April 25, 1891.
    389m. Sept. 20, 1911.
    389n. April 11, 1914.
    389o. Oct. 15, 1914.
    389p. Sept. 5, 1919.
    389q. June 21, 1923.
    389r. July 16, 1923.
    389s. Dec. 6, 1924.
    389t. June 10, 1925.
    389u. March 5, 1946.
    389w. July 2, 1952.
    389x. Sept. 23, 1952.
    389y. Sept. 27, 1952.
    389z. Oct. 2, 1952.
    389aa. Oct. 4, 1952.
    389ab. Oct. 12, 1952.
    389ac. May 8, 1953.
    389ad. Nov. 14, 1953.
    389ae. Nov. 16, 1953.
    389af. Sept. 13, 1964.
    389ag. Oct. 3, 1964.
    389ah. Oct. 4, 1964.
    389ai. May 16, 1976.
    389aj. Oct. 12, 1984.
    389ak. Oct. 13, 1984.
    389al Feb. 13, 1930.
    389am April 2, 1969.

390. *The Parkersburg News*; Parkersburg, W.Va.: The Ogden Newspapers Inc.; March 5, 1946.

391. "The President Rides Our Rails"; *Missouri Pacific Magazine*; St. Louis: The Missouri Pacific Railroad Co.; August 1952.

392. "The President Travels B&O"; *Baltimore & Ohio Magazine*; Baltimore, Md.: The Baltimore & Ohio Railroad Co.; December 1958.

393. "The Savannah, nee Marco Polo: FDR's earlier private car"; *Focus* magazine; Roanoke, Va.: The Norfolk Southern Corp; summer 1985.

394. "The Train From Yesterday"; *Info* magazine; Omaha, Neb.: The Union Pacific Railroad; November-December 1990.

395. *The Washington (Evening) Star*; Washington, D.C.; Dec. 13, 1973.

396. *The Wheeling Intelligencer*; Wheeling, W.Va.: The Ogden Newspapers Inc.; Sept. 25, 1952.

397. *The Wheeling News-Register*; Wheeling, W.Va.: The Ogden Newspapers Inc.; Oct. 11, 1984.

398. "The Whistle-Stop: An American Political Tradition"; Association of American Railroads News Service; Washington, D.C.; September 1964.

399. Thomas, Lately; *The First President Johnson: The Three Lives of the Seventeenth President of the United States of America*; New York: William Morrow & Co.; 1968.

400. Thompson, Everett L. "Tommy": trip logs, now owned by the Baltimore & Ohio Railroad Historical Society, Baltimore, Md.

401. Thompson, Terrance; "Riding the Rails to Victory"; Kansas City, Mo.: *The Kansas City Star*; May 6, 1984.

402. Thomson, Charles A.H., and Shattuck, Frances M.; *The 1956 Presidential Campaign*; Washington, D.C.: The Brookings Institution; 1956.

403. Thomson, David S.; *HST: A Pictorial Biography: The Story of Harry S. Truman, 33rd President of the United States*; New York: Grosset & Dunlap; 1973.

404. Tilp, Peter; *The Pennsy Color Book*; Upper Darby, Pa.: The Pennsylvania Railroad Technical and Historical Society; 1988; expertise and archives.

405. *Time* magazine; New York: The Time Inc. Magazine Co., a division of Time-Warner Magazines; Oct. 6, 1952.

406. *Toledo Blade*; Oct. 12, 1984.

407. "Transportation for Candidates"; *Traffic World* magazine; Washington, D.C.: Journal of Commerce; March 4, 1944.

408. Tribbett, A.E.; McMechen, W.Va.; interview.

409. Tribble, Edwin, editor; *A President in Love: The Courtship Letters of Woodrow Wilson and Edith Bolling Galt*; Boston: Houghton Mifflin Co.; 1981.

410. Trostel, Scott D.; Fletcher, Ohio; recollections.

411. Trout, Robert; "Trainman Without Portfolio"; *Atlantic Coast Line Railroad News*; Jacksonville, Fla.: The Atlantic Coast Line Railroad Co.; September-October 1964.

412. Trudeau, Noah Andre; "Last Days of the Civil War"; *Civil War Times Illustrated*; Harrisburg, Pa.: Cowles Magazines; August 1990.

413. Truman, Harry S., Library; Independence, Mo.; archives.

414. Truschel, Rita; "Lincoln and Railroads"; Niagara Falls, N.Y.: *Niagara Gazette*; Feb. 12, 1981.

415. Tully, Grace; *F.D.R., My Boss*; Chicago: People's Book Club; New York: Charles Scribner's Sons, distributor; 1949.

416. "Two Presidents Arrive at Baldwin Depot"; *Baldwin Midland Champion*; Baldwin City, Kan.: The Midland Railway; undated.

417. Underhill, Robert; *Truman Persuasions*; Ames, Iowa: Iowa State University Press; 1981.

418. *Valparaiso Visitor*, Valparaiso, Neb.; May 6, 1943.

419. Van Beck, Todd W.; "Chester A. Arthur: An Underrated President"; *American Funeral Director* magazine; Cincinnati, Ohio; October 1988; research.

420. Van Hook, Donald W.; Charlottesville, Va.; title of the book.

421. Wallace, Harold Lew; "The Campaign of 1948"; Ph.D. dissertation; Bloomington, Ind.: Indiana University; 1970.

422. Ward, Jim; Hinton, W.Va.; interview.

423. Watson, Don, and Brown, Steve; *Texas & Pacific Railway*; Erin, Ontario, Canada: The Boston Mills Press; 1978.

424. Watts, David A. Jr.; Pueblo, Colo.; interview, C&O/B&O files.

425. Wayner, Robert J.; *Pullman and Private Car Pictorial*; New York: Wayner Publications; 1972.

426. Wayner, Robert J.; *Railroad Work Equipment and Special Service Cars*; New York: Wayner Publications; 1987.

427. Wayner, Robert J.; *The Complete Roster of Heavyweight Pullman Cars*; New York: Wayner Publications; 1985.

428. Wayner, Robert J.; *The Pullman Scrapbook*; New York: Wayner Publications; 1971.

429. Wayner, Robert J.; New York; archives.

430. Weaner, Karl H.; Weaner, Zimmerman; Defiance, Ohio; letter to author.

431. Weisinger, Ralph; *The Ross Perot For President Campaign Train Project Book*; Lebanon, N.J.: Steam Locomotive Corp. of America; 1992.

432. Wesolowski, Wayne; Lisle, Ill.; information on Lincoln funeral train.

433. Westing, Frederick; *Penn Station*; Seattle, Wash.: Superior Publishing Co.; 1978.

434. "Whistle-Stop Campaigning"; *Illinois Central magazine*; Chicago: Illinois Central Railroad; November 1964.

435. "Where the people are"; *Railway Age* magazine; New York: Simmons-Boardman Publishing Corp.; Oct. 26, 1964.

436. White, John H. Jr.; *The American Railway Passenger Car*; Baltimore, Md.: The Johns Hopkins University Press; 1978.

437. White, John H. Jr.; *The American Railroad Freight Car: From the Wood-Car to the Coming of Steel*; Baltimore, Md.: The Johns Hopkins University Press; 1993.

438. White, Roger B.; "A Presidential Train Wreck"; *Maryland* magazine; Baltimore, Md.: Network Publications; summer 1990.

439. Whittier, John Greenleaf; *Poetical Works*; Boston: Houghton, Mifflin & Co.; and James R. Osgood & Co.; 1881.

440. "Willkie Special to Tour 18 States"; *Railway Age* magazine; New York,: Simmons-Boardman Publishing Corp.; September 1940.

441. Williams, Charles Richard; *Diary and Letters of Rutherford Birchard Hayes, Nineteenth President of the United States, Vol. III*; Columbus, Ohio: The Ohio State Archaeological and Historical Society; 1924.

442. Williams, John D.; Fairbanks, Alaska; Fairbanks Historical Preservation Foundation; documents.

443. Williams, T. Harry, editor; *Hayes: The Diary of a President, 1875-1881*; David McKay Co. Inc.; 1964.

444. Wilmington, C.F.; "With Willkie: Railway Express Serves Republican Presidential Campaign Train on Nationwide Itinerary"; *The Express Messenger*; New York: Railway Express Agency Inc.; December 1940.

445. Wilson, Charles Morrow; "Lamplight Inauguration"; *American Heritage* magazine; New York: American Heritage Publishing Co. Inc.; December 1963.

446. Wilson, Charles Morrow; *The Commoner: William Jennings Bryan*; Garden City, N.Y.: Doubleday & Co. Inc.; 1970.

447. Wilson, Edith Bolling; *My Memoir*; Indianapolis, New York: The Bobbs-Merrill Co.; 1938.

448. Wilson, William H.; *Railroads in the Clouds: The Alaska Railroad in the Age of Steam, 1914-1945*; Boulder, Colo.: Pruett Publishing Co.; 1977.

449. Wisconsin Central Ltd.; "POTUS Train General Plan"; Stevens Point, Wis.; Oct. 30, 1992.

450. Withers, Bob; "Ike's Trains: Campaigning on the B&O," and "Ike's Trains: When Ike Went to the Greenbrier"; *Trains* magazine; Waukesha, Wis.: Kalmbach Publishing Co.; February 1990.

451. Withers, Bob; "Ike's Trains: Final Journey to Abilene"; *Trains* magazine; Waukesha, Wis.: Kalmbach Publishing Co.; March 1990.

452. Withers, Bob; Huntington, W.Va.; Associated Press and Gannett News Service dispatches, observations on Bush campaign train, CNN videotape on Bush train, Baltimore & Ohio Railroad Co. archives, undated clips.

453. Withers, Sue Ann; Huntington, W.Va.; editing, and many patient months of understanding and support.

454. Wollenhaupt, Gary; "President revives whistle-stop tour"; *CSX Today*; Jacksonville, Fla.: CSX Transportation Inc.; September/October 1992.

455. Wood, W. Don; *The Unique New York and Long Branch*; Earlton, N.Y.: Audio Visual Designs; 1985; research.

456. "Woodrow Wilson's Fairy Cross: A Virginia talisman plays a part in a presidential campaign"; *Virginia Cavalcade* magazine; Richmond, Va.: Virginia State Library and Archives; Winter 1958.

457. Woodward, W.E.; *Meet General Grant*; The Literary Guild of America (Horace Liveright Inc.); 1928.

458. Worth, Fred L.; *The Presidential Quiz Book*; New York: Bell Publishing Co., distributed by Crown Publishers Inc.; 1988.

459. "You Ought to Know"; *Railway Age* magazine; New York: Simmons-Boardman Publishing Corp.; July 4, 1960.

Special Notes

- A videotape of George Bush's 1992 campaign train is available from Goodheart Productions, P. O. Box 47131, Chicago, Ill. 60647.

- The author thanks his talented newspaper colleagues John Gillispie and Kelly Bragg, who proofread and edited the text.

Index

Aardmore, Okla. 211
Abilene, Kan....................... v, *237*, 244, 364, 366, 367, *368*, 370, 372, *373*
Dwight D. Eisenhower Center 367
Dwight D. Eisenhower Library ...v, vi, 244, 367
Dwight D. Eisenhower Place of Meditation 367
Sunflower Hotel 367
Acheson, Dean 187, 272
Acker, Marge 252
Acker, Robert L. *220*
Ackers, Bob 133
Adams, J.B. 319
Adams, Daniel L. 279
Adams Express Co. 48
Adams, John ix
Adams, John Quincy .... v, 1, 325, 373
Adams, Louisa (Mrs John Quincy) 1
Adams, Rachel (Mrs. Sherman) 248
Adams, Sherman 247, 248, 253, 255, 261
Adderly, Charles 186
Adirondack (train) 323
Admiral (train) 292
Advance (private car) *382*
Agg, Mrs. T.R. 201
Agnew, L.G. 169
Aiken, S.C. 176
Aikin, Md. 170
Air Force One (plane) 291, 294, 297, 309, 320
Akerson, George 121, 125
Akron, Ohio 19, 43, 65, 125, 221, 278, 356
Rubber Bowl 221
Akron Jct., Ohio 235
Alabama [see *Baltimore* (private car)]
Alaskan Engineering Commission 111
Alaska Railroad 108, 111, *113-116*, *382*, 393
Alban, Clifford 291
Albany, N.Y. 1, 21, 32, 37, 40, *133*, 163, *188*, 218, 224, 331, 334, 335, 337
Delavan House 21
Rural Cemetery 339
Albany, Ore. 195
Albion, Ind. 305
Alderson, W.Va. *64*, 91
Alexandria Jct., Md. 170, 276, 394
Alexandria, Louden & Hampshire R.R. 326
Alexandria, Va. 53, 97, 213, 276, *286*, *287*, 326, 327, 334, *375*
RO Tower 276
Allamuchy, N.J. 176, *177*
Tranquility (home) 176
Allcorn, Frank 174, 347
Allegan, Mich. 263
Allegheny City, Pa. 19
Allegheny, N.Y. 6
Allegheny Portage R.R. 124, 325, 326
Allen, Ben F. 101
Allen, Mrs. James 288
Allen, Owen 243
Allentown, Pa. 263
Allgood, H.E. .... ix, 348, 349
Alliance, Neb. *75*
Alliance, Ohio 19, 65, *68*
Sourbeck's Hotel 19
Altamont, Calif. 341
Altamont, W.Va. 218
Alto, Ga. 156
Alton, Ill. 297
Alton, Railroad *128*
Altoona Mirror, ...58
Altoona, Pa. 34, 48, 58, 107, 124, 270, 297, 309, 338, 391, 393
Logan House 35
Altoona, Wis. 222
Amarillo, Texas 159
Ambrose, Stephen E. 242
American Association of Private Car Owners 300
American Bankers Association 123, 125
American Broadcasting Co. 308, 391
American European Express 312, 398
American Federation of Labor 242
American Freedom Train 200
American League 323
American Legion 120, 366
American Red Cross 98, 99, *105*
American Society of Newspaper Editors 189
American Telephone & Telegraph 108, 300, 302
Amtrak 294-297, *299*, 301, *304*, 309, 322, 323, 397, 398
Anacostia Jct., Md. 153, 170, 176, 276
Anchorage (sleeper) 393
Anchorage, Alaska 111, 113
Anderson, Deck 69
Anderson, Howard 176
Anderson, Ind. 268-270
Andover, Mass. 6
Andrew Jackson (locomotive) *2*
Andrew W. Mellon (sleeper) 394, 395
Andy Johnson (steamboat) 33
Annapolis, Md. 74
Ann Arbor, Mich. 33, 281, *282*, 397
Ansboro, H.D. 357
Apple Grove, W.Va. 246
Applegate, Va. 351
Appleton, Wis. 261
Apthorpe House (sleeper) 396
Aquia Creek. Va. 3, 4
Arbuthnot, Roy 237
Arcola (sleeper) 48
Arden (office car) 292, 397
Arkell, W.J. 39, 40, 335
Arlington, N.Y. 362
Arlington, Ohio 318
Arlington, Va. 171
Arlington Cantonment 153
Arlington National Cemetery 171, 183, 292
Arthur, Chester A. 51-54, 338, 339, 361, 393
Arthur, Nell 54
Arvey, Jack 200, 201
Asbell, Bernard 173
Ashland, Ky. 107, 213, *216*, 366, 372
Ashtabula, Ohio 19, 32
Associated Press 138, 146, 167, 169, 173, 239, 246, 254, 259, *352*, 356
Association of American Railroads ...... v, 139, 153 291, 389
Atchison, Topeka & Santa Fe Rwy. 6 42, 46, 61, *77*, 101, 102, 105, 109, *123*, 197, *198*, 208, 283, 364, *366*, 367, *371*, 373, 396
Athens, Ohio 289
Atlanta & West Point R.R. 339
Atlanta, Ga. .... ix, 44, *56*, 60, 81, *132*, 133, 134, 156, 173, 174, 321, 339, 346, 348-354, 356, 384, 391, 398
Armour Yard 321
Inman Yard 348
North Avenue Yard .... ix, 133
Patterson, H.M. & Co. 346
Terminal Station .... ix, *348*, 349, 354
Atlantic & Great Western Rwy. 42
Atlantic (baggage/buffet/smoker/barber car) 393
Atlantic (locomotive) 1, *2*, 74
Atlantic Charter 151
Atlantic Clipper (plane) 155
Atlantic Coast Line R.R. 155, 156, 259, 277, 286, 382, 397
Atlantic Conference 151
Atlantic Express(train) 58
Atlantic, Mass. 263
Atterbury, William W. 132
Attlee, Clement 181
Atwater, Susan Eisenhower vi
Auburn, Neb. 161
Auglaise (sleeper) 397
Augusta, Ga. 277
Augusta, Ga., National Golf Club 277
Aurora, Ind. 367
Aurora, Ill. 44
Austin, Linus 49
Austin, Texas 262
Auto-Liner Corp. 294, 397
Avery, Idaho 110, 111
Avila, Manuel Camacho 157, 158, *167*
A.V. Kayser & Co. 378
Ayers, Eben A. 389
Ayers, Omer 354
Ayersville, Ga. 156
Aztlan (baggage/smoker/library car) 380, 393
Baa Hozhnilne (train) 289
Babcock, Orville 35
Bacall, Lauren 207
Bachelder, Toi 154, 173
Bacon, John Mosby 41
Baden, W.Va. 246
Badger, S.D. 68
Baffa, John 301
Baker, James 303
Baker, John 301
Baker, Joseph B. 7
Baker, Ore. 232, 235
Baker, Russell 290
Bakersfield, Calif. 249, 281, 309, 398
Bald Knob, Ark. 157
Baldwin, Kan. 87
Baldwin Locomotive Works ... 56, *58*, 146, 159, 197
Baltimore [also *Alabama, Baltimore No. 1, Carolinian No. 1* and *Virginia No. 1*] (private car) .... ii, *vii*, 310, *311*, 312, 316, 319-323, *390*, 391, 398
Baltimore & Ohio Magazine 146, 181, 281
Baltimore & Ohio R.R. .... ii, v, vi, ix, 1, 2, 4, 5, 7, *11*, 22-25, 31, 35, 37, 41, 42, 54, *68*, 69, 74, 78, 82, 91, 92, 107, 108, *117*, 118, 119, 122, 125, *127*, *128*, 131-133, 135, 136, 140, 141, *142*, 146, 147, 149, 153, 155, 156, 162, *164*, 166, 170, 171, 176, 178, 179, 181, *182*, *183*, 184, 186, 187, 188, *192*, *195*, 197, 199, 200, *203*, *205*, *209*, 215, *216*, 218, 221, 223, 224, 226, 227, 230, 235, 243, *245*, 247, 255, 257, 258, 263, 264, *269*, 270, *272*, 273-279, 281, 289, 291, 300, 302, 305, 323, 325, 326, 328, 343, 344, 358, 364,-366, *369*, 370-373, 375-378, 384, 389, 390, 391, 394-397
Baltimore & Ohio Railroad Historical Society vi
Baltimore & Potomac R.R. 41-43, 47-53, 58, 61, *68*, 73, 338, 339
Baltimore & Susquehanna R.R. 325
Baltimore, Md. .... vi, 1-5, 7, 18, 21-28, 31, *34* 37, 41, 42, 47, 48, 91, 99, 107, 186, *192*, 200, 218, 247, 258, 279, 300, 309, 325-329, 338, 345, 360, 370, 377, 391
Baltimore & Ohio Museum 24, 391
Barnum's City Hotel 3, 5, 7
Bolton Station (B&S/NC) 7, 24-26, 28, 326, 328
Calvert Street Station (B&S/NC) ...7, 22, *34*, 328
Camden Station (B&O) 7, 22-25, 28, 323, 327, 328, 377
City Hotel 325
Eutaw House 328
Fifth Regiment Armory 279
Merchants Exchange 325, 327

Mount Clare Depot (B&O) 325
Mount Clare Shop (B&O) *23*, 326, 377
Mount Royal Station (B&O) 279
North Street Depot (B&S) 325
Orioles Park 323
Outer Depot 1
Pennsylvania Station (PRR, PC, Conrail)
.... 192, 300, 360
President Street Station (PW&B) 23, 325
Three Tuns Inn 1
Union Depot 41, 48
Wilson Street Tunnel 41
Baltimore No. 1 [See *Baltimore* (private car)]
Baltimore Orioles 323
Banavie (sleeper) 148, 395
B&O Special (train) 230
Bankhart, Iola 264
Bannon, Barney 58
Barclay, R.O. 162
Barkley, Alben 164, 200
Barkley, James T. 327
Barnes, John S. 28
Baroni, Geno 300
Barron, Jim 302, 306
Barrows, Roberta 153
Barstow, Calif. 197
Bartee, T.H. 319
Bartlett's Familiar Quotations (book) 272
Bassett, Jim 250
Bassett, Va. 258
Batavia, N.Y. 331
Batchelder, E.W. 57
Batesville, Ark. 264
Bath, N.Y. 218
Baton Rouge, La. 5
Battle Creek, Mich. 33, 278, 295
Bay City, Mich. *252*, 260
Bay Point (diner) 398
Bayard, Ohio 19
Beacon, N.Y. 363
Beall, Robert 2, 3
Bealton, Va. 351, 357
Beaucoup, Ill. 218, 221, 243
Beckett, Thomas 327
Bedell, Grace 20, 331
Bedford, Va. 258
Beech Falls (sleeper) 397
Beech Grove (private car) 323, 398
Belfield, Va. 53
Belgrade (sleeper) 393
Belgravia (sleeper) 393
Belington, W.Va. 278
Bell, Alexander Graham 51
Bell, Jack 169, 246
Bellaire, Ohio 92, 255
Bellefontaine, Ohio 92, 255
Bellefonte Central R.R. 274
Belleville, Ill. 309, 398
Belleville, W.Va. 247
Bellows Falls, Vt. 117
Bells, Texas 208, 210
Beloit, Wis. 127, 263
Belpre, Ohio 92
Beltz, Harry *178*, 270
Bement, Ill. 16
Bengston, J.R. 319
Benicia, Calif. 45
Benjamine, John 331
Benwood Jct., W.Va. *245*, 246, 247, 255,
257, 258, *269*
Berkeley, Calif. 189, *191*, 196
University of California at Berkley 189
Berle, Milton 253
Berlin, Conn. 263
Berlin, East Germany 215
Berney, Lois 153
Berry, Albert 64, 65
Berry, W.W. 57
Bethesda (Md.) Naval Hospital 168
Bethlehem, Pa. 218
Beverly, Mass 84
Bewley, Tom 240

Biaggi, Mario 300
Biffle, Leslie 222
Big Eight (coach) 397
Big Four Rwy. [see Cleveland, Cincinnati,
Chicago & St. Louis Rwy.]
Big Level & Kinzua R.R. 378
Big Timber, Mont. 261
Biloxi, Miss. 339
Billings, Mont. 74, 101, 106
Billmeyer & Small Co. 378
Binghamton, N.Y. 6, 263
Birch Island Station, Ontario 163
Birke, William 245
Birmingham, Ala. 60, 81, 82, 322
Bishop, Jim 173, 353
Bishop, Richard M. 41
Bismarck, Mo. 309
Bismarck, N.D. 101
Black Hawk, Colo. 36
Black Rock, Utah 45
Blackburn, Luke P. 54
Blackburn, Wallace 364
Blackhawk [see also *Robert Peary* (private car)]
.... 237, 395
Blackmon, Claude E. 347, 348, 354
Blaine, James G. 49, 50, 51, 55
Blair, Francis P. Jr. 24, 25
Blair, W.W. 24
Blanchester, Ohio 289
Bliss, D. Willard 51
Bloomingburg, Ohio 186
Bloomington, Ill. 67, 74, 260, 297
Blue Ridge (train) 294
Blythe, Samuel 116
Boettiger, Anna Roosevelt [see Roosevelt, Anna]
Boettiger, John 361
Bogart, Humphrey 207
Boggs, Hale 286-288
Boise (or Boise City), Idaho 61, *231*, 270
Bolivar, Mo. *192*, *195*
Bolivar, Simon *192*, *195*
Bollick, Jerome 309, 398
Bolling Field Army Air Corps Base, Md. 153
Bone, Scott C. 112
Bones, Helen 96
Bonham, Texas 210, 211
Boone, Iowa 237, 243
Booth, John Wilkes 21, 29, 326
Borah, Bill (horse) *79*
Borah, Jake *79*
Borah, William 101
Bosley, Wyo. 232
Boston & Albany R.R. 84, 171, 224
Boston & Maine Rwy. 6, 263, 323, 396, 398
Boston & Worcester R.R. 325
Boston, Mass. 4, 84, 91, 92, 98, 120, 140,
171, *172*, 224, 262, 275, 278, 325, 275
Back Bay Station 262
Beacon Park 171
Boston Arena 92
Faneuil Hall 325
South Station 262
Symphony Hall 92
Boston Red Sox 96
Boulder City, Nev. 141
Boulder Dam 141, 142
Bound Brook, N.J. 132
Bowling Green, Ky. 106
Bowling Green, Ohio 318-320
Bradford, Bordell & Kinzua Rwy. 378, *379*
Bradford, Ohio 332
Brady, Dorothy Jones 151, 152, 157, 158, 163,
165, 173, 353, 354
Brahms (sleeper) 395
Brandon, W.W. 82
Branham, C.F. 244, 246
Brantford, N.D. 234
Brawley, Mrs. Bill 285
Bray, Bill 235
Brayford, F.W. 101
Breckenridge, Minn. 234
Bredehoeft, C.C. 170, 197

Bredehoeft, Wayne 197
Brennan, Bernard 239, 240
Briceburg, Calif. 147
Bridge, Gardner 138, 169
Bridgeport, Conn. *172*
Bridgeport, Ohio 92
Bridgeport, W.Va. 226
Brighton Park, Ill. 118, 119, 322
Brimfield, Ohio 44
Briggs, Peter A. 322
Bristol, Va./Tenn. 60, 71, 121
Broad Pass, Alaska 11, 112
Brockton (sleeper) 48
Brockton, Mass. 270
Broken Bow, Neb. 232, 235
Broker's Train (train) 38
Brookline, Mass. 171
Chestnut Hill 171
Brooklyn Jct., W.Va. 246
Brooks, Arthur 99, 104
Brooks, Don 300
Brooks Locomotive Works 86
Brooks, Ned 221
Brooks, Samuel R. 375
Brooks, Walter A. 134, 174, 181, 348
Brotherhood of Locomotive Engineers 186,
262, 391
Brotherhood of Sleeping Car Porters 135
Brown, Charles P. 327, 329
Brown, Charlie 253, 254
Brown, Frank E. 291
Brown, John 25, 55
Brown, Joe 49
Brown, Joseph 41
Brown, R.W. 385
Brown, William 134
Brown, Wilson 163
Browne, E.W. 319
Brownell, Herbert 215, 252, 253
Brownfield, Texas 160
Browning, Orville H. 16
Browns, Ill. 263
Brownstown, Ind. 371
Hillcrest Motel 371
Twin Town Drug Store 371
Brownsville, Texas 159
Bruenn, Howard 168, 173, 175, 351, 352
Brule, Wis. *119*
Brunswick, Md. 235, 294
Bryan, Mrs. William Jennings (Mamie) 63, 68
Bryan, William Jennings 63-69, 73, 74, 83, *84*, 92
Bryne, Brendan 300
Buchanan, James 6, 7
Buffalo & State Line R.R. 20, 32
Buffalo, N.Y. 20, 21, 32, 69, 71, 73, *190*, 218,
224, 263, 331, 340, *341*, 381, 393
American House 21
Bloomer's Dining Saloon 331
Exchange Street Station 21
St. James Hall 331
Temple of Music 73
Buffalo, Rochester & Pittsburgh Rwy. 6
Bull, Steve 294
Bulloch, Minnie 174
Bunell, Colo. 160
Buran, A.C. 191
Burgoon, Isadore H. 41
Burkhardt, Ed 322
Burlington & Missouri River R.R. 61
Burlington, Ill. 44
Burlington, Iowa *229*, 230
Burlington Northern R.R. 294
Burlington, Wis. 321, 398
Burnside, A.E. 25
Bush, Barbara (Mrs. George) ..... ii, 311, 312, *314,
315*, 316-322, *390*, 391, 398
Bush, Dorothy 297
Bush, George .... ii, vi, vii, 301, 309-313,
314-315, 316-322, *390*, 391, 398
Bush, Marvin 321
Butt, James 371
Butte, Mont. 110, 194, 234

Byrnes, James 371
Cabarton (sleeper) 398
Cabin Creek (sleeper) 397
Cadiz Jct., Ohio 18
  Parks House 18
Cafky, Morris 146, 147
Cain, Harry 253
Calabasas, Calif.:
  Lockheed Corp. 274
Caldwell, Ohio 89, 92
Calexico, Calif. 166
Callahan Station, Fla. 53
Callicoon, N.Y. 6
Calloway, E.C. 74
Calumet, Ill. 379, 384
  Pullman Shops 379, 384
Calverton (lounge car) 242, 244, *246*
Cambridge, Mass.:
  Harvard Univesity 105
Cambridge, Ohio 92
Camden & Amboy Rail Road
  & Transportation Co. 1, 3, 5, 22, 31, 325, 329, 375
Cameron, J.D. 26
Cameron, Simon 328
Cameron, W.Va. 258
Campania (private car) 66, *67*, 393
Campbell, Mary 153
Camp Carson, Colo. 159
Camp Forest, Tenn. 157
Camp Gruber, Okla. 157
Camp Joseph T. Robinson, Ark. 157
  Branch Immaterial Replacement
  Training Center 157
Camp Sibert, Ala. 354
Campbell, George 244
Camp Meade, Pa. *66*
Camp Silbert, Ala. 354
Canadian Pacific Rwy. 163, 275, 378
Cannon, Joseph G. 13
Canon City, Colo. 205
Canton, Ohio 43, 44, 65, 66, 71, 263, 340, 341, *374*, 381
Cantwell, Alaska 112
Capa, S.D. 120
Cape Girardeau, Mo. 263
Capitol Limited (train) *117*, 118, 140, 197
Carbondale, Ill. 281
Cardinal (train) 302
Cardinals Train (train) *383*
Carey, Idaho 193
Carlinville, Ill. 10, 37, 297
Carlson, Frank 242
Carmi, Ill. 243
Carolinian No. 1 [see *Baltimore* (private car)]
Carpenter, Les 287
Carpenter, Liz (Mrs. Les) 285-289
Carr, Albert Z. 218
Carr, E.T.M. 52, 338
Carroll, Charles 135
Carroll, John Lee 41
Carroll, William E. 135
Carrollton, Mo. 367
Carter, Jimmy 297, *298*, *299*, 300, 397
Carter, Rosalynn (Mrs. Jimmy) 297, 299, 300
Casablanca, Morocco 154, 155
Casa Grande, Ariz. 45, 46, 393
Cascade Bridge, N.Y. 6
Cascade Heights (sleeper) 397
Casper, Wyo. *231*, 232, 235
Castle Rock Survivors Association 169
Castle Rock, Wash. 169, 191, 219, 395
Catskill (sleeper) 393
Cedar City, Utah 110
  Zion Park 110
Cedar Falls, Iowa 263
Cedar Rapids, Iowa 343
Cedar River (diner) 398
Center Creek (sleeper) 396
Central City, Colo. 36
Central Grove (sleeper) 394
Central Ohio R.R. 18
Central Pacific R.R. 45, 393
Central R.R. of New Jersey 38, 51, 52, *69*, 132, 218, 338, 385, 394
Centralia, Ill. 263, 281
Cervantes (sleeper) 394
Chadron, Neb. *75*
Challenger (coach) 398
Challenger (space shuttle) 306
Chama, N.M. 339
Chamberlain, Mervin 361
Chamblin, Walter Jr. 125
Champaign, Ill. 10, 11, 260
Chandler, William E. 52, 53
Chandler, Zachariah 38
Chapel Hill, N.C. 5
  University of North Carolina 4, 5
Chapman, A.H. 14
Chapman, Ernest 107, 118, *127*, *164*, *183*, 188, 200, *216*, 221, *227*
Chapman, Kan. 160
Chapman, Oscar L. 189, 198-200
Chappell, Neb. 343
Charleston & Savannah Rwy. 53
Charleston & Western Carolina Rwy. 157, 382
Charleston, Ill. 12, 14
Charleston, S.C., ... 286, 287
Charleston, W.Va. 69, 91, 126, 213, 246, *365*, 366
  Municipal Auditorium 213
Charlestown, Mass. 3
  Bunker Hill Monument 3
Charlotte, N.C. 258, 286, 287, 309, 356, 398
Charlottsville, Va. 276, 277, 351, 357, 365, 391
Charmion (sleeper) 393
Chartiers Creek (sleeper) 393
Chase, William 48
Chattahoochie, Fla. 286
Chattanooga, Tenn. 25, 60, 71
Chautauqua 68, 69
Cheney, Wash. 233
Cherokee, Calif. 45
Chesapeake & Ohio Rwy. .... v, 53, 56, 69, 91, 96, 97, 107, 125, 148, 171, 198, 199, 212, 213, *215*, 244, 245, 263, *274*, 275-277, 281, 291, *293*, 294, 302, 322, 364-367, *369*, 370, 372, 373, 393, 393, 396
Chessie System Railroads 294, 300-308, 397, 398
Chessie 29 (private car) *274*, 276, 277
Cheyenne, Wyo. 45, 102, 110, 160, 292, 397
Cheyenne Jct., Wyo. 232, 393
Chiang, Madame Kai-shek 156
Chickadee (coach) 398
Chicago (diner) 398
Chicago & Alton R.R. 11, 33, 37, 42, 99, 105, 325, *333*, 334, 377
Chicago & Eastern Illinois Rwy. 74, 263, 271
Chicago & North Western Rwy. 37, 54, 71, 95, 101, 120, *123*, 140, 149, 190, 222, 223, 234, 260, 261, 263, 322, 343, 393, 395, 398
Chicago & Rock Island R.R. 6
Chicago, Burlington & Quincy R.R. 42, 44, 59, 61, 67, *75*, *84*, 120, *130*, 141, 159, 161, 230, *231*, 232, 237, 240, 242, 393, 395
Chicago Commercial Club 117
Chicago Cubs 140
Chicago Evening Journal 44
Chicago Great Western R.R. 100
Chicago, Ill. 10, 11, 31, 33, 35, 37, 41, 42, 44, 54, 63, 67, 69, 71, 91-93, 95, *104*, 117-119, 121, *122*, 140, 149, 156, 164, 166, 167, 170, *185*, 187, 190, 191, 200, 222-224, *226*, *228*, 230, 234, 235, 237, 239, 241, 257, 260, 262, 263, 278, 296, 297, 299, 314, 320, 322, 326, 332, 334, *342*, 343, 353, 364, 377, *383*, 393, 396
  Blackstone Hotel 166, 224
  Board of Trade 272
  Dearborn Station 170
  Chicago Colliseum 93
  Chicago Stadium 224
  Fifty-first Street Coach Yard 154
  Grand Central Station *117*, 235
  International Amphitheater 237
  Grand Pacific Hotel 44
  Mercy Hospital 95
  North Western Station 95, 241
  Park Place 334
  Soldier Field 322
  Union Station *104*, 241
Chicagoland (sleeper) 397
Chicago, Milwaukee & St. Paul Rwy. .... ii, 54, 57, 97, 104, 110, 111
Chicago-Pittsburgh-Washington-
  Baltimore Express (train) 118
Chicago Press & Tribune 10
Chicago, Rock Island & Pacific Rwy. 63, 100, *124*, *125*, 164, 165, 200, 211, 242, 260, 263, 397
Chicago, St. Paul, Minneapolis & Omaha Rwy. 222, 223
Chicago Tribune .... ii, 33, 194, 225, 226, 288, 297
Chico, Calif. 45, 231
Chickaloon, Alaska 111
Childers, "Box" 355
Childers, John 302
Childress, Tenn. 121
Chili (sleeper) 393
Chillicothe, Ohio 41, 279, 289
Chippewa Falls, Wis. 321, 322
Chittendon, R.C. ii
Chotiner, Murray 250-252, 255, 264
Christian, George B. 342, 344
Christian Science Monitor 137, 146
Christopher, Dave 300
Churchill, Winston .... vii, 151, 153, 154, 171, 179, *180*, 181-187
Cicero, Ill. 241
Cincinnati Exposition 41
Cincinnati, Hamilton & Dayton R.R. 41, 42
Cincinnati, Ohio 17, 34, 35, 41, 64, 91, 150, 162, 163, 221, 223, 243, 252, 253, 257, 271, 272, 281, 291, 294, 302, 313, 325, 366, 367, *368*, 371, 372, 396
  Burnet House 17
  Cincinnati Union Terminal 272, 366, *369*, 373
  Grand Hotel 41
Cincinnatian (train) 223
Cinnebar, Mont. 54
Circumnavigators Club (sleeper) 394
Citation (horse) 212, 214
City of Beckley (sleeper) 396
City of Charleston (sleeper) 396
City of Los Angeles (diner) 398
City of Newport News (sleeper) 396
City of Portland (diner) 398
City of Portland (train) 232, 233
City of Salina (coach) 398
City Point, Va. *26*, *27*, 28, 29
Civiletti, Benjamin 300
Civilian Conservation Corps. 172
Claffey, Elizabeth 187
Clark, Harlan T. 186
Clark, Bob 253, 254
Clark, Tom 210
Clarksburg, W.Va. 91, 171, 218, 266
Claremont, N.J. 132, 148, 150
Claremore, Okla. 157
Clay, Lucius 252
Clement, Percivial Wood 17
Cleveland & Erie R.R. *324*
Cleveland & Pittsburgh R.R. 18, 19, 331
Cleveland & Toledo R.R. 33
Cleveland, Cincinnati, Chicago & St. Louis ....
  (Big Four) Rwy. 108
Cleveland, Columbus & Cincinnati R.R. 326, 331
Cleveland, Frances Folsum 54-57
Cleveland, Grover 6, 54-57, 230, 338, 339, 377, *379*
Cleveland Night Express (train) 391
Cleveland, Ohio 19, 21, 32, 33, 43, 48, 49, 123, 124, 224, 243, 253-255, 257, 260, 263, 277, 278, *324*, 326, 331, *332*, 338, 339, 377, 393
  Carter Hotel 254, 255
  Cleveland Public Auditorium 254
  Euclid Street Station 19, 331, *332*
  Kennard Hotel 32
  Lakeview Cemetery 339

Linndale Station 260
Weddell House 19
Western Reserve University 49
Cleveland, Painesville & Ashtabula R.R. ... 19, 21, 32, *324*, 331
Cleveland Plain Dealer 101
Clifford, Clark M. 179, 181, 184-186, 189, 195-197, 199-210, 207, 210, 211, 213-215, 218, 221, 222, 223, 225
Clifton Forge, Va. 276, 277, 365
Clinton, Bill ...... v, vi, 313, 317, 318, 321-323, 398
Clinton, Chelsea 323
Clinton, Hillary Rodham (Mrs. Bill) ... 313, 318, 323
Clinton, Iowa 343
Clinton, Ill. 10
Close, Gilbert 98
Clover Pasture (sleeper) 394
Cloverport, Ky. 162
Coates, Wilma (or "Wilmer") 193
Cochocton, N.Y. 6
Cochocton, Ohio 18
Cochrane, Henry Clay 25, 26
Cocksey, O.L. 355
Coeur d'Alene, Idaho 101
Coffin, Tristram 184
Cold Spring, N.Y. *353*, *356*, 362
Coldwater Creek (sleeper) 396
Cole (sleeper) 395
Cole, Albert 61
Cole, Vicki Lynn
[See also Gray, Vicki Lynn Cole] 291
Collins, C.J. 141
Collinson, John T. 302
Colonial (private car) *89*, 92, *381*
Colonial Crafts (sleeper) 396
Colonial Flags (sleeper) 396
Colonial Mansions (sleeper) 396
Colorado (sleeper) 395
Colorado & Southern Rwy. *62*, 160, 232
Colorado Central R.R. 376
Colorado Eagle (train) 278
Colorado Midland Rwy. 74, 78, *79*
Colorado Springs & Cripple Creek District Rwy. 74
Colorado Springs, Colo. .... v, 61, 78, *79*, 80, 159, 204, 267, 277, 278
Colting, James 334
Colton, Calif. 208
Columbia Broadcasting System 140, 184, 286, 295, 323
Columbia Heights, Minn. 377
Columbia, Pa. 325
Columbia, S.C. 260, 287
Columbian (train) 230
Columbian Exposition 377
Columbine II (plane) 274
Columbus & Indianapolis Central R.R. 326
Columbus & Xenia R.R. 18
Columbus, Neb. *137*, *139*, 294
Columbus, Ohio 18, *30*, 34, 40-42, 98, 99, *100*, *103*, 107, 149, 181, 183, 186, 187, 197, 243, 263, 279, 281, 291, 310-312, 326, *331*, 332, 398
Buckeye Steel 312
Deshler-Warwick Hotel 312
Ohio State University 99
Mound Street Yard 312
Parsons Yard 311
Scioto Tower 313
Comet (locomotive) 19
Comstock Lode 45
Concord, N.H. 6, 323
Congdon, H.P. 222
Congress of Industrial Organizations 198
Congressional Record 227
Conkling, Roscoe 37, 50
Conneaut (sleeper) .... ix, 156, *347*, 349, 351, 352, 354, 356-358, 361, 362, 394, 395
Conneaut, Ohio 19, 21
Connellsville, Pa. 118, 119
Connelly, Matthew J. 189, 218, 225, 235
Conners, Chuck 297
Conover, N.C. 309
Consolidated Rail Corp. (Conrail) 295, 297, 299, 309, 311-313, 317, 319, 321, 391, 397, 398
Constitution (engine) 21, 320
Constitution (private car) *381*
Cook, Matthew Scott 41
Cooley, J.B. 393
Coolidge, Calvin .... vii, 78, 107, 117-120, *123*, 344, *382*
Coolidge, Mrs. Calvin (Grace) 117-120
Coolidge, Prudence Prim (dog) 120
Coolidge, Rob Roy (dog) 120
Cooper, Henry A. 193
Cooper, W. F. 349, 352
Copper River & Northwestern Rwy. 113
Coraopolis, Pa. 200
Cordic, P.R. "Pete" 199, 200
Cordic, Regis 199
Cordova, Alaska 113
Cornelia, Ga. 321
Cornell, Douglas 146
Corning, N.Y. 6
Cornpone Special (train) 281
Cornwall, N.Y. 153, 237
Coronado (diner) 60, 380, 393
Corpus Christi, Texas 158, 159
Corpus Christi Naval Air Training Center 159
Corriher, Fred 309, 310
Corry, Pa. 263
Cortelyou, George *68*, 73
Costilla (lounge car) 395
Cotter, Ark. 264
Bull Shoals Dam 264
Coughlin, Jerry 57
Coulee City, Wash. 233
Council Bluffs, Iowa 141, 142, 394
Cowan, C. Vernon 291
Cox, G.M. 355
Cox, Jacob D. 37
Cox, James 107, 108
Cox, Ken 370, 371
Cox, Sid 370
Cox, Tricia Nixon [see Nixon, Tricia]
Craft, Charles ix
Crane Creek (sleeper) 396
Crawford, W.S. 291
Creamer, William 22
Credit Union National Association 234
Crescent Limited (train) 133, 348
Crestline, Ohio 190, 194, 200, 265
Creston, Iowa 230
Crewe, Va. 258
Cronenwett, J.H. 346
Cronkite, Walter 295
Cross Creek (sleeper) 397
Crown Point, Ind. 290
Crusader Rose (sleeper) 363, 394
CSX News 218
CSX Transportation Inc. ..... ii, 218, 303, 310-313, 316-323, 391, 398
Cuivre River (diner) 322, 398
Culkin, Francis D. 227
Culpeper, Va. 281, *292*, 365
Cumberland, Md. 4, 5, 64, 91, 184, 199, 235, *344*, *345*, 375
Cumbres & Toltec Scenic R.R. 339
Cuppinger, M. 52
Curry, Alaska *114*
Curry Hotel *114*
Curtin, S.C. 357
Curtis, Sumner 110
Custer, George 31, 34
Cutler, Robert 242
Cuyahoga Falls, Ohio 19
Cypress Falls (sleeper) 396
Czolgosz, Leon 73
Dailey, Pat 54, 56
Daily Arizona Citizen 45, 46
Daily, Michael 339
Dale, Billy .... vi, 300
Dallas, George M. 4
Dallas, Texas 93, 208, 210, 211, 262
Rebel Stadium 210
Daley, Richard J. 299
Dana (sleeper/observation car) 370, 371, 396
Daniel, Margaret Truman, [see Truman, Margaret]
Daniels, Jonathan 173, 189, 363
Daniels, Josephus 363
Danville, Ill. 16, 271
Danville, Va. 351
Darby, Ohio 311
Darcey. P.C. "Pat" 133, 363
Darcey, J.M. 134
Darcey, Marian (Mrs. P.C.) 133
Dasch, R.E. 184
Davenport, Iowa 242
David Livingston (private car) 384, 395
Davis, Calif. 196
Davis, David 16, 21, 325
Davis, Henry Gassaway 55
Davis, Jefferson 21, 29, 46, 339
Davis, Jess 156
Dawson, Donald S. 200, 209, 210, 221, 226, 227, 273
Dawson, Thomas S. 110
Dayton Daily News 302
Dayton, N.Y. 6
Dayton, Ohio 108, 221, *293*, 300-302, 307, 397
Dayton Union Terminal *301*, 302
Wright Patterson Air Force Base 301, 304, 306
Dean Richmond (locomotive) 331
Dearborn, Mich. 122
Greenfield Village 122
Decatur, Ala. *70*
Decatur, Ill. 10, 15, 16, 61, 185
Decker, H.L. .... ix, 349
Deer Lodge, Mont. 140
Deer Park, Md. 41, 55, 56
Defiance, Ohio 274
Defiance College 274
FC Tower 275
Defoe (sleeper) 395
De Graves, Edward 166
DeHaven, J.R. 240
De Kalb, Ill. 190, 191
Delano, Laura "Aunt Polly" *154*, 156, 173, 349, 352, 354, 355
Delano, Sister (dog) 156
Delaplaine, P.H. 64
Delaware & Hudson R.R. *188*, 275, *335*, 336, 339, 393
Delaware, Lackawanna & Western R.R. 73, 78, 78, 218, 278, 396
Del Monte, Calif. 61, 71, 72
Valencia Street Station 71
De Mille, Cecil 208
Deming, N.M. 208
Denali (private car) 111, *116*, 382, 393
Denis, Miss Olive W. 125
Denison, Texas 210, 262
Dennison, Ohio 40, 58, 92, 99
Dennison, William 18
Denny, Caleb S. 58
Denslow, Joe 332
Dent, Frederick Tracy 35, 36
Denver & Rio Grande R.R. 61, 74, *80*, 85, 393
Denver & Rio Grande Westerm R.R. 146, 147, 204, 239, 267, 339
Denver, Colo. .... v, 36, 37, 47, 61, 85, 86, 102, 109, 110, *121*, 159-161, 197, 203-205, 237, 239, 339, 395
Brown Palace Hotel 102
Fitzsimmons General Hospital 160
Lowry Field 160
Matropole Hotel 61
Northwestern Auto Co. 204
Remington Arms Ordnance Plant 160
Windsor Hotel 85
Deposit, N.Y. 6
Derby, Ohio 186
Des Moines, Iowa 100, 126, 201, 202, 250
Fort Des Moines Hotel 100
Des Moines Register 250
Deshler, Ohio 29, 300, 306, *308*
Detroit, Mich. 32, 33, 42, 122, 126, 198,

199, 262, 263, 278, 281, 295, 296, 320, 378
   Cadillac Square 198
   General Motors .... *x*, 266, 319, 373
Detroit, Toledo & Ironton R.R. 291
Detroit United Rwy. 87
Devens, Charles 41
Devine, Gregory S. 372
Dewey, Frances (Mrs. Thomas E.) 169, 215, 219
Dewey, Thomas E. .. ii, 138, 163, 164, 169, 175,179,
   189, 191, 199, 201, 207, 208, 210-212, 214, 215,
   218, 219, 221, 223-226, 235, 243, 253, 254, 395
Dexter, Iowa 201, 202, 214
Diaz, Porfirio 85-87
Dictionary of American History 228
Dillon, Sidney 54, 376
Dimmick, Mary Scott 61
Dinner Key, Fla. 155
Diplomat (train) 218, 278
Disalle, Mike 270
Disney, Walt 24
Dispatch (locomotive) 331, 332, 339
Dixie Clipper (plane) 155
Dixie Springs (sleeper) 396
Dixon, George 235, 242
Dodge City, Kan. 42, 46, 197
Dole, Elizabeth (Mrs Robert J.) 323, 398
Dole, Robert J. 323
Dolinger, Milton B. 308
Doolittle, James R. 31
Donaldson, Sam 308
Donnelly, Phil M. 186
Donovan, Robert J. 196, 199
Doris (private car) 309, 398
Doswell, Va. 171
Doud, Mrs. John 260, 274, 277
Douglas, John Hancock 39
Douglas, Paul H. 230
Douglas, Stephen 9, 11-13, 18, 31, 33
Douglas, William O. 164
Doyle, T.J. 362
Drain, Erma 162
Draney, John 73, 78
Drescher, George 181, 182
Dresden, Ohio 18
Drexel, Joseph W. 39, 40, 335
Dreylinger, John vi
Drifton, Fla. 286
Drown, Jack 250
DuBarry, J.N. 25
Dudley, Harvard 265
Dukakis, Michael S. 309, 398
Duke, James B. 309
Dulles, John Foster 266
Duluth, Ga. 384
   Southeastern Railroad Museum 384
Duluth, Minn. 222, 223, 261
Duncan, Mrs. P.O. 244
Duncansville, Pa. 124
Dundas, Ohio 263
Dunkirk, N.Y. .... *x*, 5, 6
   Loder House 6
Dunham, W.M. 244
Dunlop, Va. 156
Durand, Mich. 295
Durant, Thomas C. 376
Dwight, Mrs. Martha Campbell 244, 245
Eagle Point
   (baggage/buffet/smoker/barber car) 394
Early, Stephen T. 151, 157, 158, 349,
   351, 352, 354, 384
East Albany, N.Y. 21, 331
East Broad Top R.R. 378, *379*
East Grafton, W.Va. 218
East St. Louis, Ill. 56, 140, 197, 218
East Switch, Mont. 234
East Tennessee, Virginia & Georgia R.R. 60
Eastern Outlook (coach) 335
Eastwick, Pa. 170
Eau Claire, Wis. 222
Eckles, Jim 74
Edgemere (private car) *374*, 393
Effingham, Ill. 56

Pacific House 57
Ege, George Frederick 60
Eisenhower, Barbara (Mrs. John) 241
Eisesnhower, David 367, 371, 372
Eisenhower, Dwight D. .... v, vi, vii, ix,
   178, 188, 192, *236*, 237, *238*, 239-264, 266, 267,
   270, 272-279, 295, 364-367, *368*, *369*, 370, 373,
   389, 391, 395, 396
Eisenhower, Edgar 366, 367, *370*, 372
Eisenhower, John 365, 367, 372
Eisenhower, Julie Nixon [see also Nixon, Julie]
   .... 371, 372
Eisenhower, Mamie [Mrs Dwight D.].... *236*, 237,
   242-247, 251, 255, 256, 258, 260-262, 273, 275,
   277, 278, 295, 364-367, *369*, 370-372, 389
Eisenhower, Milton 274, 276, 365, 372
Eisenhower Special (menu) 242
Eisenhower Special (train bulletin notice) 245
Elberon, N.J. 49, 52, 73, 338
   Francklyn Cottage (home) 338
Elcina, Ore. 232
Elizabeth (wife of King George VI) 147, 357
Elizabeth, N.J. 292
Elizabethton, Tenn 121
Elkhart, Ind. 264
Elkins, Stephen B. 55
Elkins, W.Va. 278
Elko, Nev. 127, 129
Elko Nev. 127, 129
Ellender, Allen J. 288
Eller, R.H. 356
Ellicott's Mills, Md. 1, *2*
Ellsworth, Elmer 16, 19
Elm Falls (sleeper) 397
Elmira, N.Y. 6
   Brainard's Hotel 6
Empire Builder (train) 234
El Paso, Texas 71, 85, 87, 165, 208
El Portal, Calif. 116, 147
El Reno, Okla. 165
Elsey, George 169, 170, 199, 207,
   210, 215, 218, 223, 227
Elyria, Ohio 33, 278
Emory Station, Utah 45
Empire Builder (train) 234
Emporia, Kan. 42
Emporia, N.C. 156
Enfield, N.C. 156
Engineering Society vi
Engler, John 320
Engler, Michelle (Mrs. John) 320
Englewood, Ill. 164, 242
Erie (steamer) 5
Erie & North East R.R. 20
Erie County (sleeper) 396
Erie Lackawanna R.R. 291
Erie, Pa. 20, 21, 263, 324, 331
Erie R.R. 223, 263, 281, 345, 346, 360
Ertegun, Mehmet Munir 183
Escalone, Mexico 87
Esperancilla, Irineo 349
Etter, Minn. 57
Eugene, Ore. 116, 194, 195, 253, 292
Evans, Bob 93
Evans, Mrs. Tom 188
Evansville, Ind. 161, 162, 243, 292
   Republic Avaition Corp. 161
Everett, Edward 25, 27, 28
Everhart, Robert 48
Excelsior (sleeper) 393
Exeter, N.H. 12
   Phillips Exeter Academy 12
Exton (sleeper) 393
Eyler, Lucius "Sackhead" 300, 305
Fair, Fred D. 134, 165, 168, 174, 188, 214, 358
Fairbank, Ariz. 166
Fairbanks (sleeper) 393
Fairbanks, Alaska 112, 382
   Nordale Hotel 112
Fairmont, W.Va. 258
Faison, V.G. 356
Falcon, Idaho *111*

Falls City, Neb. 242
Farmington, Ill. 12, 14
Farragut, David G. 31, 34, 35
Farragut, Mrs. David G. 32
Fast Flying Virginian
   (or *F.F.V. Limited*) (train) 91, 96, 97
Fast Mail (train) 234
Fauver, Edwin "Jiggs" *392*
Fayette Station, W.Va. 91
FDR's Last Year (book) 173
Federal (private car) *381*
Federal (train) 275
Federal Bureau of Investigation 301, 302
Federal Council of the Churches of Christ 181
Felknor, Rhea 194, 195
Felton, Samuel M. 22, 24, 326
Ferdinand Magellan
   (also U.S. Car No. 1) (private car) .... ii, *iii*, ix,
   119, 131, 139, 163-157, 159-161, 164-167,
   168, 169, 171, 173, 174, 176, *177*, 181-184, 186-
   189, 191, 193, 194, 197, 200, 201, 203, 204, 211,
   212, *213*, 214, 222, 223, 225, 227, 230, *231*, 233,
   264, 268, 272-275, 300-302, *303*, 305, 306, 309,
   310, 349, 352-355, *356*, 358, 384, 384, 384, 385,
   386, *387*, 388, 389, 391, 394, 395, 398
Ferraro, Geraldine 301
Ferrell, D.J. "Jack" 244, 246, 247, 255, 281
Fetter, Martin 332, 339
Field, Eugene 272
Fillmore, Millard .... *x*, 5, 21, 331
Findlay, Ohio 318
Fish, Hamilton 38
Fisher, E.A. 291
Fisher, Newell E. 361
Fisher, Willis G. 337
Fishers (sleeper) 394
Fishkill, N.Y. 21
Fitchburg, Mass. 263
Fitzmaurice, Walter 189, 190, 191, 200,
   205, 213, 222, 318
Fleeson, Doris 287
Fletcher, Ohio 301
Flint, Mich. 199, 278, 295, 297, 312, 320, 397
   Bishop International Airport 320
Flomaton, Ala. 288
Floral Park, N.Y. 80
Florence, Colo. 146
Florida Development Commission 391
Florida East Coast Rwy. 155
Flour Bluff, Texas 159
Flour Bluff Jct., Texas 159, *167*
Foglia, D.J. 366
Folliard, Edward T. 207, 267
Fonda, D.H. 335
Ford, Betty (Mrs. Gerald R.) 295, 297
Ford, Gerald R. 295-197, 397
Ford, Henry 122
Forest Grove, Ore. 45
Forrestal, James 153
Forsyth, Mont. 74
Fort Benning, Ga. 157, 349, 351
   Lawson Field 349
Fort Crook, Neb. 161
Fort George G. Meade, Md. 155
Fort Holabird, Md. 389, 391
Fort Knox, Ky. 162
Fort Lauderdale, Fla. 391
Fort Leavenworth, Kan. 42
Fort Lewis, Wash. *162*, 164
Fort Myer, Va. 358
Fort Ogelthorpe, Ga. 157
   Third WAAC Training Center 157
Fort Omaha, Neb. 66
Fortress Monroe, Va. 53
Fort Riley, Kan. 160
Fort Scott, Kan. 41
Fort Stedman, Va. 28
Fort Travis (sleeper) 394
Fort Washakie, Wyo. 54
Fort Wayne, Ind. 170, 190, *240*, 263
Fort Worth, Texas 157, 159, 208, 210, 262
   Ben Brook siding 159

Dutch Branch Training Center 159
Fox, George 173
Fralick, E.H. 15
Francis, Warren 169
Francisville, Ind. 333
Frank Valkenburg (engine) 334
Frankfort, Ky. 212
Frankfort, Ind. 263, 293
Franklin Square (sleeper) 242, 244, 395
Franklinton, N.C. 5
Frazeyburg, Ohio 18
Frederick, Md. 2, *20*, 24, 183
   Dorsey's City Hotel 2
Freedom, Pa. 18
Freeburn, Henry 47, 48
Freehold, N.J. 52
Freeport, Ill. 10, 263
Fremont, Neb. *76*, *292*, 294
Fremont, Ohio 41–43, 47–49
   Spiegal Grove (home) 47, 49
French, Thomas 110
Fresno, Calif. 207, 250, 292
Frietchie, Barbara 183
Fry, James B. 25
Fulbright, J. William 264
Fulton, Mo. 179, *180–182*, 183
   Westminster College 179, 186
Gage, Lyman J. 66
Gahagan, David 134, 348
Gainesville, Ga. 351, 354
Gainesville, Texas 208
Galena, Ill. 35, 37
Galesburg, Ill. 44, 59, 230
   Knox College 230
Gallipolis (Ferry), W.Va. 246
Gallitzin, Pa. 35, 124
Galloway, William 327
Galva, Ill. 44
Galveston, Texas 61
Galvin, William 264
Gamble, Robert J. *85*
Gap, Pa. 7
Garden City, N.Y. 80
Gardiner, Mont. 110
Gardner, Jim 310
Garfield, Hal 50, 51
Garfield, Jim 50, 51
Garfield, James A. 42, 43, 46, 47, 49–52,
   55, 73, 78, 338, 339
Garfield, Lucretia (Mrs. James A.) 49, 51, 338
Garner, Ettie (Mrs John Nance) *148*
Garner, John Nance "Cactus Jack" 140, 148,
   166, 208–210
Garrett, Ind. 343
Garrett, John W. 25, 26, 41, 54, 375, 377, *378*
Garrison, N.Y. 361
Gary, Ind. 96, 190, 194, *203*, *205*, *206*
Gaston, N.C. 4
Gastonia, N.C. 321
Gates, Bill 288
Gearheart, Bertram W. 207
Gehrig, Lou 140
General (locomotive) 24
General Albert J. Myer (communications car)
   .... 136, 276, 384, *390*, 395–397
Geneva, N.Y. 263
Genoa, N.D. 234
George B. Roberts (also PRR 120 [1st])
   (private car) 380
George Washington (ocean liner) 98
George Washington (train) *148*
Georgetown, Colo. 36
Georgia Tech 221
Gerow, Leonard T. 258
Gettysburg, Pa. 8, 23, 24, 25, 27, 370, 375
   Little Round Top 27
   National Soldiers' Cemetery 25
Gilbert, Howard 294
Gilbert, W. Henry 329
Gillette, Frederick H. 109
Gilmore Jct., Neb. 160, 161
Gilsey (diner) 393

Girard, Pa. 20
Girdwood, Alaska. *114*
Glasgow, Mont. 234
Glen Adelaide (sleeper) 395
Glen Alice (sleeper) 396
Glen Almond (sleeper) 396
Glen Alta (sleeper) 396
Glen Aray (sleeper) 394, 395
Glen Arden (sleeper) 394
Glen Ashdale (sleeper) 396
Glen Athol (sleeper) 396
Glen Ayr (sleeper) 394
Glen Brook (sleeper) 360, 395
Glen Canyon (sleeper) 395
Glen Cliff (sleeper) 394
Glenclyffe, N.Y. 361
Glen Craig (sleeper) 395
Glen Dee (sleeper) 395, 396
Glen Doll (sleeper) 394, 395
Glen Dochart (sleeper) 394
Glen Douglas (sleeper) 396
Glen Dower (sleeper) 394
Glen Eyre (sleeper) 395
Glen Fee (sleeper) 395
Glen Garry (sleeper) 395
Glen Gordon (sleeper) 363, 395
Glengyle (sleeper) 394
Glen Lodge (sleeper) 395
Glen Main (sleeper) 395
Glen Manor (sleeper) 395
Glen Muick (sleeper) 395
Glen Nevis (sleeper) 396
Glen Pond (sleeper) 396
Glen Rosa (sleeper) 396
Glen Roy (sleeper) 395
Glen Stream (sleeper) 394
Glen Sutton (sleeper) 394
Glen Valley (sleeper) 395
Glen Willow (sleeper) 394, 395
Glenwood Springs, Colo. *61*, 80
Glenwood, W.Va. 246
Goddard, James M. 391
Gold Creek, Mont. 54
Golden City, Colo. 36
Golden Desert (sleeper) 397
Goldsboro, N.C. 53, 339
Goldstein, Samuel 328
Goldwater, Barry 285, 287, 289,
   290, 310, 378, 383, 397
Gollaher, Austin 19
Gomez Palacio, Mexico 86
Goodheart, David 314, 316, 318–320
Goodrich, James P. 99
Goodson, Kenneth P. 291
"GOP" (train) 237, 240
Gordon, John B. 28
Gore, Albert Jr. 321, 323
Goshen, N.Y. 5
Gossett, Jack 156
Gothenburg, Neb. 376
Gould, Jay 37
Gould, William Henry Harrison 328, 329
Gounod (sleeper) 396
Gourley, James 332
Grafton, W.Va. 69, 107, 162, 218, 223,
   255, 257, 258, 266, 289
Graham, Billy v
Graham, Wallace 184, 189, 200, 202
Grand Army of the Republic 40, 61, 336
Grand Blanc, Mich. .... *vii*, 310, 312, 320
Grand Island, Neb. 160, 193, 194, 232, 294, 343
Grand Junction, Colo. 239
Grand Rapids, Mich. 197, 281, 295
Grand Soldiers & Sailors Reunion of 1880 43
Grand Trunk Western Rwy. 199, 260,
   262, 281, 295–297
Granite, Colo. 78
Granite City, Ill. 272
Granite State (business car) 398
Grant, Ellen "Nellie" 36, 38, 39
Grant, Frederick Dent 39, 40
Grant, Harry L. 74

Grant, Jesse Root 36
Grant, Julia Dent 35–39, 336, 338
Grant, Orville 37
Grant, Ulysses S. 25, *26*, 28, 29, 31–40,
   54, 55, 326, 335, 336–339, 361, *377*, 379, 393
Grant, Ulysses S. "Buck" Jr. 35, 36
Grants Pass, Ore. 252
Grantville, Kan. 36
Graves, Peter 297
Gray, Vicki Lynn Cole,
   [see also Cole, Vicki Lynn] 306
Grays Ferry, Pa. 170
Grayson, Cary 98–106
Great Northern Rwy. 110, 169, 195, 223, 234,
   261, 263, *382*, 395
Great Western R.R. 12, 14
Greeley, Horace 20, 21
Green, A.C. 160
Green Bay, Wis. 260, 261
Green Island, N.Y. 21
Green River, Wyo. 54
Greenbrier (diner) 318, 319, 398
Greenfield, Mass. 263
Greensburg (sleeper) 394
Greentown, Ohio 44
Greenville, S.C. 156, 321, 348, *349*,
   350, 351, 353, 355
Greenway, Jack 93
Griffith, James 176
Griffith, L.B. 354
Grinnell, Iowa 201
   Grinnell College 201
Groton, Conn. 275, 389
Grover Cleveland Wedding Train (train) 56
Guernsey, Wyo. 232
Guilford Tranportation Indstries 323
Guiteau, Charles 50, 51, 339
Gulf Coast Lines 159
Gulf, Mobile & Ohio R.R. 260, 297, 397
Gunnison, Colo. 85
   Gunnison Tunnel 85
Gurley, Phineas D. 327
Guyandotte (sleeper) 397
Guyandotte, W.Va. 246
Gwladys (lounge car) 395
Hackmeister, Louise "Hackie" 150–153, 173
Hagerty, James 214, 250, 251, 258
Halford, Elijah W. 58, 332–334
Hallanan, Walter 247
Halleck, Charles 254
Hamilton, Ohio 221
Hamlin, Hannibal 22
Hamm, Lavina 332
Hamm, R.P. 41
Hamtramck, Mich. 199
Hancock, Winfield Scott 335, 336
Hand, Victor 314, 316, 318, 320
Hanks, Dennis 14
Hanna, Mark 65
Hanna, Wyo. 232
Hannegan, Robert 163, 164, 166, 187
Hannibal & St. Joseph R.R. 36, 42
Hannibal, Mo. 42, 46
Hanover Branch R.R. 25
Hanover Jct., Pa. *8*, 25–27
Harber, W. Elmer 211
Harden, Leroy 111
Hardester, Dave 103
Harding, Florence (Mrs. Warren G.) 107, 108,
   110–113, *114*, 116, 334, 344, *382*
Harding, Warren G. .... vii, 107–113, *114*, *115*,
   116, 134, 188, 205, 341, *342–345*, 346, 360, 382,
   383, 384, 393
Hargis, James H. *370*
Harmon, N.Y. 361
Harpers Ferry, W.Va. (or Va.) *11*, 24, 55, 183, 218
Harrill, Nathan 321
Harriman, W. Averell 193
Harris, Bob 245
Harris, G.S. 294
Harrisburg, Pa. 22, 24, 27, *30*, 35, 40, 41, 84,
   218, 263, 290, 309, 326, 328

Jones House ... 22
Harrison, Benjamin ... 57-61, *64*, 65, 131, 332, 377, 380, 393
Harrison, Carrie (Mrs. Benjamin) ... 58, 59, 61, 380
Harrison, Russell B. ... 60, 61
Harrison, William Henry ... 2-4, 17, 57, 325, 375
Hartford & New Haven R.R. ... 325
Hartford, Conn. ... 224, 262
Hartford, W.Va. ... 247
Hartsfield, William B. ... 354
Harwood, Herbert H. Sr. ... 150, 171, 176, 362
Haslemere (sleeping car) ... 59
Hassett, William D. ... 151-154, 169-176, 347, 351, 352, 354, 357, 360, 361, 363
Hastings, Minn. ... 57
Hastings, Neb. ... 61
Hart, Bill ... 302, 304, 305, 307
Hartz, Bill ... 246
Haulbrook, Tim ... 248, 354
Havens, Jack ... 244
Havre de Grace, Md. ... 23
Havre, Mont. ... 234
Hawesville, Ky. ... 212
Hawkes, William H. ... 51
Hay, John ... 25, 71, 327
Hayden, Ind. ... 187
Hayes, Birchard Austin ... 41, 42, 55, 393
Hayes, Fanny ... 43
Hayes, Lucy (Mrs. Rutherford B.) ... 40-49
Hayes, Rutherford B. ... vii, *30*, 40-49, 65, 66, 338, 376, 377, 393
Hayes, Rutherford Platt ... 393
Hayes, Scott Russell ... 43
Hayes, Webb Cook ... *49*, 66
Hayne, S.C. ... 351, 355
Hazzard, George W. ... 16, 21
Heard, Bruce ... 309
Heartland Special (train) ... 300, 302, *303*, 305, 306
Hechler, Ken ... *v*, 227, 228, 230, 233, 235, 265-272, 278
Heinl, Robert D. ... 381, 382
Helena, Mont. ... 110, 234
Helm, Edith Bonham ... 357, 358
Helper, Utah ... 267
Henderson, Ky. ... 212, 243
Henderson, N.C. ... 5
Henry Knox (parlor car) ... 397
Henry Stanley (private car) ... 125, 179, 384, 394
Hensley, Tim ... 218, 219, 221
Herald-Dispatch ... v, vii, 245
Herron, Mrs. John ... 45
Hertzberg, Henrik ... 300
Hickman, Jack ... 78
Hicks, Charlie ... 174
High Point, N.C. ... 309, 310
Highland Country Club (sleeper) ... 396
Highland, N.Y. ... 132, 151, 152, 154, 170
Highlander (sleeper) ... 393
Hightown, N.J. ... 1
Hillcrest Club (sleeper) ... 394
Hillings, Patrick ... 237, 241, 250
Hilton, Frank ... 59
Hinkle, Ore. ... 233
Hinkley Locomotive Works ... 15
Hinman, Wilbur ... 83
Hinton, W.Va. ... 91, 366
Hitchcock, Albert ... 191
Hitchcock, Ethan A. ... *68*
Hobart, Garret Augustus ... *69*
Hoboken, N.J. ... 73, 98, 278, 396
Hodges, J.A. ... 181
Hoffman, David ... 308
Hofmaster, Sol ... 338
Holidaysburg, Pa. ... 325
Holland, Mich. ... 224, 296
Holly, Mich. ... 316, 320
  Holly Hotel ... 320
Holt, Rush ... *246*
Homestead (sleeper) ... 366, 396
Honest Abe (train) ... 297
Honolulu, Hawaii ... 151, 251
  Pearl Harbor ... 151
Honora (parlor car) ... 394
Hooker, Harry ... *152*, 358
Hooley, James L. ... 310
Hoover, Herbert ... 109, 111, *114*, 121-129, 135, 139, 140, 219, 285, *383*, 393
Hoover, Irwin Hood "Ike" ... 97, 98
Hoover, Lou (Mrs. Herbert) ... 122, 125, 126
Hopewell Jct., N.Y. ... 362
Hopkins, Harry ... 142, 144, 148, 151, 153, 155, 163, 360
Hopkinsville, Ky. ... 104
Hornell (lounge car) ... 395
Hornell (or Hornellsville), N.Y. ... 6, 360
Horseshoe Curve, Pa. ... 124, 270
Hoskins, A.F. ... *369*
Hot Springs, Va. ... 83, 97
  The Homestead ... 83, 97
Householder, Charles ... 133
Houston, Texas ... 71, 262
Hovey, Alvin P. ... 58
Howard, O.O. ... 24
Howe (sleeper) ... 395
Howe, Louis ... 353
Howes, William F. Jr. ... *369*, 370
Huddleston, Eugene ... 213
Hudson, N.Y. ... 21
Hudson, Ohio ... 19
Hudson River R.R. ... 21, 330
Hughes, Charles Evans ... *97*
Hughes, Emmitt ... 261
Hughes, Harry ... 300
Hull, Cordell ... *141*, 265
Hull, Frances (Mrs. Cordele) ... 265
Humboldt, Nev. ... 127
Humphreys, Paul ... 245
Humphreys, Robert ... 250, 252-255, 257
Hungary (sleeper) ... 393
Hungerford, Edward ... 181
Hungry Horse, Mont. ... 266, 270
Hunt, Clyde ... 140
Hunt, Ward ... 37
Hunter, David ... 327
Hunter, T.S. ... 357
Huntington Advertiser ... 294
Huntington, Collis P. ... v
Huntington, D.H. ... 45
Huntington, Ore. ... 232
Huntington, W.Va. ... v, vi, 63, 64, 69, 91, 107, 150, 213, 244-247, *248*, 277, 294, 302, 310, 311, 320, 366, 372
  Huntington East High School ... v
Huntsville, Ala., ...71
Hurricane Andrew ... 310, 387, 391
Hutchinson, Kan. ... 109
Hyattsville, Md. ... 92, 276
Hyde Park, N.Y. ... *viii*, ix, 132, 134, 140, 147, 148, 150-155, 163, 164, 169-173, 175, 176, 347, 351, *353*, *355*, *356*, 358, 360-363, 391
  Crum Elbow ... 132, 153
  Springwood (home) ... 132, 152, 170
  St. James Episcopal Church ... 363
Ickes, Harold L. ... 140, 360, 361
Ickes, Jane (Mrs. Harold L.) ... 360
Idaho (locomotive) ... 331
Idahoan (train) ... 232
Idaho Falls, Idaho ... 110, 193
Ideal (private car) ... 107, *381*, 394
Ideal (sleeper) ... 380,393
Idler (private car) ... 65
Idler, "Baldie" ... 56
Illinois Central R.R. ... 6, 9, 10, 12, 13, 56, 67, 71, 170, 260, 263, 279, 281, 326, 397
Illinois Publishers Association ... 297
Imperator (sleeper) ... 394
Imperial Crest (sleeper) ... 396
Imperial Lawn (sleeper) ... 396
Imperial Lee (sleeper) ... 396
Imperial Letter (sleeper) ... 397
Imperial Palm (sleeper) ... 397
Imperial Park (sleeper) ... 397
Imperial Point (sleeper) ... 397
Imperial Robe (sleeper) ... 397
Imperial Rock (sleeper) ... 397
Imperial Terrace (sleeper) ... 396
Imperial View (sleeper) ... 397
Independence (plane) ... 274
Independence (private car) ... *381*
Independence, Mo. ... ii, 100, 179, 188, 192, 203 224, 225, 273
  Truman, Harry S., Library ... vi
Indiana (conference car) ... 310, 322, 398
Indiana Central Rwy. ... 326
Indianapolis & Cincinnati R.R. ... 17
Indianapolis, Decatur & Springfield R.R. ... 42
Indianapolis, Decatur & Western Rwy. ... 61
Indianapolis, Ind. ... 16, 17, 34, 42, 56-58, 61, 99, 121, *128*, 149, 223, 326, 332, 393
  Bates House ... 16
  Butler University ... *128*
  Indianapolis Colliseum ... 99
  Union Station ... 16, 17, 56-58
Indianapolis Journal ... 332
Indianapolis, Peru & Chicago Rwy. ... 42
Ingalls, M.E. ... 63
Inter-California Rwy. ... 166
International Eucharistic Conference (XXVIII) .. 393
International-Great Northern R.R. ... 159
International Ladies' Garment Workers' Union ... 219
International Livestock Exposition ... 117
International News Service ... 173, 193, 195, 211, *236*, 253, 254, 352
Interstate Commerce Commission ... 138
Iolanthe (private car) ... 393
Iron Curtain (or "Sinews of Peace" speech) ... *180*, *181*, 184, 265
Ironton, Ohio ... 150, 244
Irvington, Ky. ... 162, 212
Irwin, Mabel ... 174
Iseman, R.P. ... 238
Jackson, Andrew ... 1, 2, 74, 179, 375
Jackson, Andrew Jr. ... 2
Jackson, Graham ... 352
Jackson, Thomas J. "Stonewall" ... 183
Jackson, Mich. ... 260
Jackson, W.Va. ... 218
Jacksonville, Fla. ... 53, 66, 67, 156, 391
  Yukon Air Corps Base ... 156
Jaeckle, Edward ... 215
James Hay Reed (sleeper) ... 396, 397
Jamesburg, N.J. ... 52
Jamestown, N.Y. ... 263
Jamison, John ... 43
Janeway, E.J. ... 73
Jasper, Ala. ... 60
Jefferson Barracks, Mo. ... 161
Jefferson City, Mo. ... 161, *183*, 186, 187, 252
Jefferson, Thomas ... ix, 38
Jeffersonville, Madison & Indianapolis R.R. ... 34
Jersey City (ferry) ... 339
Jersey City, N.J. ... 22, 37, *69*, 140, 150, 325, 330, 385, 388, 394
Jessel, George ... 207
Jester, Beauford ... 210
Jewett, Mrs. T.L. ... 18
Jervis, Richard ... 96, 97, 118, 124, 129
Joe Smith Express (train) ... 278
John P. Jackson (boat) ... 22
John Hancock (packet boat) ... 325
Johnson, Andrew ... 31-35, 326, 327
Johnson, Claudia "Lady Bird" (Mrs. Lyndon B.) ... 281, 285-289, 397
Johnson City, Tenn. ... 121
Johnson City, Texas:
  LBJ Ranch ... 289
Johnson, John ... 57
Johnson, Louis ... 171, 200
Johnson, Luci ... 285, 287, 288
Johnson, Lynda Byrd ... 285, 287
Johnson, Lyndon B. ... 210, 281, *284*, 285, 286, 288-290, 370, 378
Johnson, Victor ... 230
Johnston, A.W. ... 294
Johnstown, Pa. ... 34, 325
Joliet, Ill. ... 297, 377, 397

Jones, Bartow ... 247
Jones, Freeman ... 258
Jones, George W. ... 41
Jones, John Paul ... 253
Jones, W.S. ... 134
Jorgensen, Frank ... 237, 239-241
Joseph Horne (sleeper) ... 397
Juarez, Mexico ... 85, 87
Judd, Norman ... 22
Judd, Ollie ... 50
Junction City, Kan. ... 203
Juniper Falls (sleeper) ... 397
Jurkoski, Frank ... *236*
Justus, Ohio ... 263
Kalama, Wash. ... 45
Kalamazoo, Mich. ... 278, 281, 295
Kamela, Ore. ... 45
Kanawha & Michigan Rwy. ... 69
Kannapolis, N.C. ... 321
Kansas City, Memphis & Birmingham R.R. ... 60
Kansas City, Mo. ... 41, 46, 100, 161, 196, 203 205, *237*, 242, 251, 295, 367, 372, 396
  Kansas City Terminal Rwy. ... 373
Kansas City, Topeka & Western R.R. ... 46
Kansas Pacific Rwy. ... 35, 37
Karr, Harry A. ... 120, 121, 125, 131, 189, 205, 206
Kaufman, Aloys S. ... 186
Kaufman, George B. ... 328
Kaufman, Ron ... 321, 322
Kearney, Patrick ... 51
Keifer, J. Warren ... 41
Kelker, Colo. ... 159, 160
Kelly, Edward ... 164
Kelly, Louis S. ... 242, 246, 247
Kelly, Theodore ... 318, 319
Kenai (sleeper) ... 393
Kennedy, John F. ... *280*, 281, *282*, 283, 292, 391, 397
Kennedy, Robert F. ... 292, 364, 397
Kenney, H.P. ... 22
Kenova, W.Va. ... 107, 243, 244, *245*, 246, 247, 255, 257, 366, 367
Kensington, Md. ... 163
Kentucky (power car) ... 311, 398
Kerr, Robert S. ... 210, 211
Key Biscayne, Fla. ... 294
Keyser, W.Va. ... 91, 162, 184, *192*, 218, 266
Kilburn, Bill ... 300
Kileyville, Ohio ... 314
Kinderhook (home) ... 2
Kinerian, Eileen ... 272
King, Sidney D. ... 334
Kissimmee City, Fla. ... 53
Kitchens, Neal ... 174
Klein, Herb ... 281
Klippel, E.A. ... 141
Kohler, Walter J. ... 261
Kokomo, Ind. ... 223, 263
Knickerbocker (sleeper) ... 394
Knipp, Don ... 306
Knowland, Joseph ... 237
Knowland, William ... 239, 251
Knowles, Christy ... 305
Knowlton, C. ... 334
Knox, Frank ... 151
Knoxville, Tenn. ... 25, 60
Kouts Tower, Ind. ... 223
Krueger, Martin T. ... 333, 334
La Croix, Ind. ... 333
La Crosse, Ind. ... 223
La Crosse, Wis. ... 57
Lady Bird Special (train) ... 285-288
Lafayette & Indianapolis R.R. ... 16, 326
Lafayette, Ind. ... 16, 263, 326, 327
Lafond, C.H. ... 246
LaGrande, Ore. ... 233
Lake Chautauqua, N.Y. ... 68
Lake City, Minn. ... 57
Lake Erie & Western R.R. ... 41, 42
Lake Onota (sleeper) ... 395
Lake Shore & Michigan Southern Rwy. ... 42, 43, 48, 49
Lake Shore R.R. ... 21
Lamon, Ward Hill ... 9, 16, 18, 21-25, 327
Lampell, Millard ... 355
Lamson, Myron Hawley ... 326, 327
Lancaster, Isaiah ... 42
Lancaster, Pa. ... 6, 7
  Wheatland (home) ... 7
Landrieu, Moon ... 300
Lane, Neb. ... 160, 161
Lansing, Mich. ... 198, 260, 278, 281, 295
Lantry, Josh ... 57
Lapeer, Mich. ... 260
La Porte, Ind. ... *241*
Laredo, Texas ... 158, 159
Laramie, Wyo. ... 36, 194
Larned, Kan. ... 42
Larson, Siegrid ... 99, 102, 103
Las Vegas, Nev. ... 142, 144
Lathrop, Carl ... 86, 87
Lausche, Frank J. ... 190, 221
Lawrenceburg, Ind. ... 17
Lawrence, David ... 106
Lawrence, George ... 16
Lawrence Jct., Pa. ... 149
Lawrence, Kan. ... 36, 42
Leadville, Colo. ... 61
League of Nations ... vi, 98, 99, 102, 106, 108
Leahy, William D. ... 163
Leavenworth, Kan. ... 35, 36, 42
Lebanon, Ind. ... 16, 333
Lebanon, N.J. ... 322
Lee, Robert E. ... 326, 336
Left Behind Club ... 248
Legare, Hugh S. ... 4
Legg, Elton ... 191
Lehigh & Hudson River Rwy. ... 176
Lehigh Valley R.R. ... 132, 263
Lenroot, Irvine L. ... *118*
Leslie's Illustrated Weekly ... 381
Leviero, Anthony ... 265
Levin, Bennett ... 391
Lewis, Drew ... 310
Lewis, Lloyd D. ... 306
Lexington, Ky. ... 212
Lexington, N.C. ... 309, 310
Liberty Limited (train) ... 125
Library of Congress ... vi, 228
Life magazine ... 286
Light's Golden Jubilee ... 122
Lima, Ohio ... 41, 170, 281, 291, 300, 305, 306
Limeville, Ky.:
  NJ Cabin ... 311
Lincoln, Abraham ... vi, vii, 6, 8, 9-29, 31-33, 40, 42, 73, 163, 260, 324, 326-332, 334, 339, 340, 355, 361, 363, 375-377
Lincoln and the Railroads (book) ... vi
Lincoln Club (club car) ... 395
Lincoln, Edward ... 15
Lincoln, Ill. ... 297
Lincoln, Mary Todd ... vii, 11, 15, 17, 19, 21, 22 24, 28, 326, 334, *377*
Lincoln, Neb. ... 61, 63, 230
  Baird Tower ... 230
Lincoln, Robert Todd ... vii, 11, 15, 17, 19, 21, 22, 73, 327, 376
Lincoln, Sarah Bush ... 12, 14
Lincoln, Thomas "Tad" ... 15, 17, 19, 22, 29, 326, 327
Lincoln, William Wallace "Willie" ... 15, 17, 19, 22, 327, 328
Linkins, Carroll S. ... *392*
Linoma (lounge car) ... 397
Linwood, N.C. ... 321
Little Current, Ontario ... 163
Little, Herb ... 246
Little Miami R.R. ... 18, 34
Little Rock & Memphis R.R. ... 60
Little Rock, Ark. ... 60, 61, 157, 264
Little Silver, N.J. ... 38
Livingston, Mont. ... 54, 261
  St. Andrew Episcopal Church ... 261
Livonia, Mich. ... 320
  Marriott Hotel ... 320
  St. Andrews Episcopal Church ... 320
L.H. Tupper (engine) ... 21
Lloyd, David D. ... 264, 265, 268
L.M. Wiley (locomotive) ... 15
Loch Lomond (sleeper) ... 397
Lochard (sleeper) ... 395
Lockwood, Paul ... 214
Locomotive Engineer magazine ... 391
Locust Falls (sleeper) ... 397
Loder, Benjamin ... 5
Lodge, Henry Cabot Jr. ... 275
Lodge, Henry Cabot Sr. ... 104
Logan Square (sleeper) ... 395
Logansport, Ind. ... 218, 263, 292
London, England ... 151, 181, 184
London, Ohio ... 18
Long Beach, Calif. ... 262
Long Branch, N.J. ... 37, 39, 49, 51, 338
Long, Dewey ... vi, 131, 133, 150, 151, 154, 155, 158, 159, 161, 163, 165, 171, 173, 188, 194, 207, 214, 225, 226, 230, 273, 351, 358, 363, 388, 392
Long, George ... 338
Long Island City, N.Y. ... 80
Long Island R.R. ... 80, 92, 275
Longview, Texas ... 108
Longworth, Alice Roosevelt ... 74, 215
Look Ahead Neighbor Special (train) ... 242, 250, 251, 260
Lorain County (sleeper) ... 396
Lord Chesterfield ... 60, 61
Lordsburg, N.M. ... 208
Los Angeles (see *Superb*) (private car)
Los Angeles, Calif. ... 45, *60*, 61, 71, 101, 102, 105, 141, 142, 194, 196, 207, 208, 249, 250, 253, 254, 262
  Ambassador Hotel ... 196
  Central Station ... 142
  El Capitan Theater ... 254
  Gilmore Stadium ... 207
  Greater Los Angeles Press Club ... 196
  Hollywood Bowl ... 207, 211
  Mission Yard ... 249
  University of Southern California ... 45
Los Angeles Daily News ... 249
Los Angeles Times ... 169
Louis, Joe ... 210
Louis, John L. ... 210
Louisiana, Mo. ... 42
Louisville (locomotive) ... 331
Louisville & Nashville Employees Magazine ... 212
Louisville & Nashville R.R. ... 81, 96, 106, 162, 211, 218, 243, 286, 339, 397, 398
Louisville, Ky. ... 34, 35, 52, 53, 122, 162, 212
  Seventh Street Station ... 122
Louisville, New Albany & Chicago Rwy. ... 326, 333
Lowry, Robert ... 325
Lowry, Thomas ... 377
Lubin, Isador ... 170
Lucas, Henry W. ... 133, 134, 154
Lucern, Ind. ... 333
Lund, Utah ... 110
Lupura, Walter E. ... 174
Lynchburg, Va. ... vi, 60, 71, 258
MacCorkle, William Alexander ... 69
MacLeish, Archibald ... 173
Madera, Calif. ... 45, 250
Madison, James ... ix
Madison, Wis. ... 234
  University of Wisconsin ... 234
Madison Square (sleeper) ... 394
Magdelin (diner) ... 393
Magic Brook (sleeper) ... 394
Magnuson, Warren G. ... 194
Mahopac, N.Y. ... 362
Maiden Brook (sleeper) ... 397
MAIN 18345 (train) ... 160
MAIN 200 (train) ... 364, 365, 367, 373
Maine (sleeper) ... 396
Maitland, Fla. ... 53
Maloney, Martin ... 52
Manassas Gap R.R. ... 326

Manassas, Va. 357, 365
Manhattan, Kan. 160, 366
Manhattan Limited (train) *122*
Manhattan Project 179
Mankato, Minn. 223
Mansfield, Dan. 52
Mansfield, Mike 233
Mansfield, Ohio 170, 345
Marco Polo (private car) *142*, 145, 146, 160, 384
Margolis, Joe 297, 289
Marietta, Ohio 92, *277*, 289
Marietta, Okla. 210
Marion, Ohio 107, 281, 291, 341, 360
 Studebaker-Wolff Rubber Co. *346*
Marion, Ill. 263, 345
Mariposa, Calif. 147
 Big Trees Grove 147
Marshall, George 200, 218, 261, 267
Marshall, Paul 291
Marshall, Texas 108
Marshall, Thomas 13
Martha Washington (diner) 394
Martin, Elbert 94
Martin, Larry 190
Martin Brook (sleeper) 396
Martinsburg, Pa. 274
 Blair County Airport 274
Martinsburg, W.Va. 91, 108, 218, 266
Martinsville, Va. 258
Maryland [1st] [see also *Sherbrooke*] (business car)
 .... 41, 54, 377, 378
Maryland [2nd] (also B&O 100)(business car)
 .... 378, *383*
Maryland Area Rail Commuter 323, 398
Marysville, Calif. 251
Marysville Journal-Tribune 317
Marysville, Kan. 160, 376
Marysville, Ohio *312, 313, 315*, 317
 McCullough's Hardware 317
Mason City, W.Va. 107, 247
Mason, Lynn 185
Mason, Wayne 313
Mason, Wilbur Nesbitt 90
Massillon, Ohio 65, *298*
Massoth, Clifford 281
Master Car Builders Association 381
Matanuska, Alaska 111
Mathias, Charles 300
Matthias W. Baldwin (parlor car) 397
Mattoon, Ill. 12, 13, 225
Maxwell Field, Ala. 157
May, John 120
Maybrook, N.Y. 176
Mayflower (private car) 85, *93*, 95, 98-100, 103-106, *381*
Mays, J.W. 134
Maywood (sleeper) 393
McAbee, Howard O. 146, 187
McAdoo, Eleanor Wilson 105
McAlester, Okla. 211
McCall, Harrison 237
McCann, J.E. 34
McCann, Kevin 275
McCants (sleeper) 396
McCarthy, Henry 163
McCarthy, Joseph 261, 267
McCarthy, Leighton 173, 360
McClain, C.C. *317*, 319, 320
McClain, R.K. 351
McClanahan (sleeper) 242
McClellan, George B. 9, 24, 183
McCluer, Frank 179, 186
McCook, A. McD. 393
McCormac, Keith 249, 250
McCrea, John 154
McCullough, John 19
McDuffie, Irvin 144
McDuffie, Lizzie 355-357
McElfresh, Walter J. 244
McElroy, Jim 255
McGee, John 39
McGovern, George 294, 397

McGrath, J. Howard 198
McGrory, Mary 278
McGuire, J.W. 331
McIntire, Ross 155, 163, 173, 349, 351, 352
McIntyre, Marvin 140, 142, 144, 146
McKee, J.R. 61
McKee, "Kid" 58
McKee, Mary Scott Harrison 61
McKeever, Bernard 48
McKeithen, John J. 288
McKinley, Abner 66
McKinley, Ida (Mrs. William) 65, 66, *67*, 69, *70*, 71, *72*, 73, 340
McKinley, Nancy Allison 65, 66
McKinley Park (diner) 393
McKinley, William .... vi, 43, 63-66, *67, 68*, 69, 70, 71, *72*, 73, 74, *75*, 78, 81, 94, 134. 271, 338, 340, *374*, 377, 379, 381, 393
McLean, John Forbes 300
McLeod, A.C. 348
McNaughton, John 327
McNutt, Earl 327
McQueen Locomotive Co. 57
McQueeney, Henry 338
Meacham, Ore. 110
Mead, Ed 309
Meade, George G. 25, 28, 31
Medford, Ore. 251
Mellon, Thomas *364*
Memory Brook (sleeper) 397
Memphis, Tenn. 60, 71, 105, 263
Menlo Park, Calif. 45
Menoken, Kan. 160
Mentor, Ohio 46
Merced, Calif. 87, 116, 147, 202, 250
Mercer, Lucy Page [see Rutherfurd, Lucy Page Mercer]
Merlin (sleeper) 187, 395
Merrick, N.Y. 80
Merritt, Stephen J. 335
Mesta, Pearl 211
Metcalf (sleeper) 397
Meteor (boat) 45
Metroliner (train) 291, 294, 297, *299*, 300, 396
Mewshaw, Frank 264
Mexico City, Mexico 87
Miami, Fla. 155, 156, 294, 300, 305, 310, *386*, 391
 Gold Coast R.R. (museum) 300, 302, 310, *386*, 391
 Hialeah Yard 391
 Military Jct. 155
 University of Miami 391
 South Campus 391
Michigan Central R.R. 33, 326, 334
Michigan City, Ind. 33, 326, 333, 334
Michigan Southern & Northern Indiana R.R. 33
Midas, Calif. 102
Middlebury, Ohio 43
Middletown, N.Y. 5
Midland City, Ohio 186
Midway, Ky. 212
Milburn, John C. 73
Miles, Eddie 302
Milford, Mich. 320
Miller, C.A. 327
Miller, Charles E. 52
Miller, John E. *328*, 329
Millerick, Jeff 378
Millwood, W.Va. 107, 247
Milwaukee Sentinel 321
Milwaukee, Wis. 93-95, 223, 260, 261, 265
 Emergency Hospital 94, 95
 Hotel Gilpatrick 93, 94
Minneapolis, Minn. 57, 234, 377
 Minneapolis Park Board 377
 Vine Street Depot 57
Minneapolis, St. Paul & Sault
 Ste. Marie (Soo Line) Rwy. 222, 377
Minnesota Club (sleeper) 395
Minot, Charles 5
Minot, N.D. 234
Mirror Brook (sleeper) 396

Mission Delores (diner) 395
Mission San Gabriel, Calif. 45
Missoula, Mont. 194, 233, 234, 255, 256, 263
Missouri, Kansas & Texas Rwy. 41, 42
Missouri-Kansas-Texas R.R. 208, 210, 211, 262
Missouri Pacific R.R. 145, 146, 157, 159-161, 186, 187, 197, 199, 225, 242
Mitchell, Laura Platt 41
Mitchell, Mark *259*
Mitchell, R.S. 106
Mitchell, Samuel 134, 135, 204
Mitchell S.D. *83*
 Mitchell Corn Palace *83*
Mobile, Ala. 288
Mondale, Walter 297, *298*, 299, 304, 305
Monitor (see also *P.P.C.*) (private car)
Monmouth, Ill. 44
Monmouth Jct., N.J. 52
Monmouth Park, N.J. 38
Monroe, James (President) ix
Monroe, James (Ohio state senator) 18
Monroe, Va. 351, 357
Monroe, Winnie 43
Montana (diner) 395
Montauk, N.Y. 80
Monterey, Calif. 45
Monterrey, Mexico 158
 Military Field 158
Montgomery, Ala. 21, 81, 82, 339
 Union Station 81
Montgomery, W.Va. 92, 213, 366
Montreal, Quebec 378
 Angus Shops (CP/QC) 378
Monument Square (sleeper) 394, 395
Moody, A.G. 350, 352
Moon, Roy 300
Moore, Arch 366
Moore, C.H. 10
Moore, Edward H. 211
Moore, Mabel F.D. "Mike" (Mrs. G. Gordon)
 .... 365, 366, 371
Moorhead, Minn. 263
Moorman, Daniel L. .... ix, 131-133, 140, 146, 148, 153, 166, 181, 182, 223
Morgan, David P. v
Morganthau, Elinor (Mrs. Henry) 133
Morganthau, Henry 133, *141*, 360
Morning Brook (sleeper) 396
Morrow Brook (sleeper) 13
Morning Express (train) 13
Morrow, Esther 389
Morten, W.R. 187
Mosby, Esther 60
Moscow, Soviet Union 215
Mott, Edward H. 6
Moundsville, W.Va. 247, 255
Mount Holly, Vt. 117
Mount McGregor, N.Y. 39, 40, 335, 336, *337*, 338
 Hotel Balmoral 39, 336
Mount Sidney, Va. 277
Mount Sterling, Ky. *212, 213, 215-217*
Mount Sterling, Ohio 186
Mount Vernon (sleeper) 396
Mount Vernon, Ill. 212, 219, 263
Mountain Spur, Mont. 234
Mountain State Forest Festival 278
Muleshoe Bend, Pa. 124
Mullin, J.G. 338
Munster, N.D. 234
Murphey, William M. 264, 279
Murphy, Charles S. 189, 190, 193-195, 199, 211, 225, 235, 264, 268, 269
Murphy, John B. 95
Murphy, Joseph 96-98
Murphy, William C. Jr. 359
Muskegon, Mich. 263, 281
Myrtle (sleeper) 394
Naperville, Ill. 44
Napier, Randy 300
Naples (sleeper) 393
Narrowsburg, N.Y. 6
Nashua, N.H. 323

Nashua, Mont. 234
Nashville (locomotive) 331, *332*
Nashville, Chattanooga & St. Louis Rwy. ... 60, 67
Nashville, Tenn. 32, 67, 331
   Tea Room 67
"Nathan, Edgar" (phantom roommate) 247
National (private car) 96, 381
National Association of General
   Passenger & Ticket Agents 339
National Broadcasting Co. 291, 328
National Car Builder magazine 377
National Docks R.R. 132
National Limited (train) 162, *272*, 273, 277, 278
National Park Service 300
National Plowing Contest 201
National Press Club 169
National Railway Historical Society Inc. 384
National Railways of Mexico 86, 157
National Register of Historic Places 391
Nauden, Emory A. 291
Neely, Matthew M. 213
Neenah, Wis. 261
Neosho Falls, Kan. 41, 42
Nesbitt, Henrietta 154, 363
Nessen, Ron 297
Neustadt, Richard E. 268
New Albany & Chicago R.R. 334
New Albany, Ind. 122, 162
Newark, Calif. 341
Newark, N.J. 297, 329
Newark, Ohio 18, *30*, 40, 41
New Bedford, Mass. 262
New Brunswick, N.J. 22, 325
New Castle, Colo. *78*, 79
New Castle, Pa. 148, 149, 199, 263, 395
Newcomer, Ohio 18, 92
New England Express (train) 323
New England Southern R.R. 323, 398
New Georgia R.R. 322, 398
New Haven, Conn. 325
New Haven, W.Va. 247
New Jersey R.R. & Transportation Co. *17*, 22, 325
New London, Conn. 105, 151
New Market, Ohio 34
New Orleans, La. 32, 71, 262, 285, 286, 288, 339
   Jung Hotel 288
   New Orleans Union Passenger Terminal 288
Newport, Ark. 264, 267
Newport, Ky. 64, 65, 366, *367*
Newport News, Va. 171
   Norfolk Navy Yard 171
New Rochelle, N.Y. 132, 275, 360
Newsweek magazine 189, 190, 221
Newton Falls, Ohio 230, 343
Newton, Kan. 109
Newton, Mass. 171
New York (ferry) 330
New York & Erie R.R. .... x, 5
New York & Harlaem R.R. 375
New York & Long Branch R.R. 38, 52
New York Central R.R. .... *viii*, 6, 21, 32, 132
   150, 171, 176, 218, 225, 242, 243, *244*, 253, 257,
   258, 260, 262-264, 269, 275, 278, 281, *282*, 331,
   353, 358, *359*, 361-363, 396, 397
New York Central & Hudson River R.R.
   .... 37, 39, 84, *335*, 336, 339, 393
New York, Chicago & St. Louis
   (Nickel Plate) R.R. 223, 263
New York City, N.Y. .... *vi*, 4-6, 14, 21,
   22, 31, 37-39, 54, 58, 73, 92, 95, 96, 108, 125,
   131, 132, 147, 148, 150, 196, 215, 224, 225, *238*,
   242, 253, 259, 262-264, 272-275, 278, 291, 292,
   297, 323, 330, 335, 337-340, 358, 360, *383*, 391,
   393, 396, 397
   Brooklyn 54, 80
      Flatbush Avenue 80
   Manhattan.........................5, 32, 249
      Astor Hotel (or House) 5, 22, 274
      Battery Park 5, 32, 147
      Castle Garden 4
      Church of the Heavenly Rest 339
      City Hall 339

Cortlandt Street Ferry 22
Debrosses Street ferry station 330
General Electric Co. 266, 267, 310
Gilsey House 54
Grand Central Station 39, 262, 339, 391
Irving Hotel 5
Madison Square Garden 95, 225, 278
Pennsylvania Station 92, 140, *238*, 274
   275, 278, *323*, 363
Thirtieth Street Station 22, 330
Waldorf-Astoria Hotel 274
Queens 275
The Bronx 132, 275, 360
Mott Haven Yard 132, 150, 360, 363
One Hundred Thirty-eighth
   Street Station 275
New York Connecting R.R. 132, 275
New York Herald 15, 25
New York Herald-Tribune 196, 251, 252, 254
New York, New Haven & Hartford R.R. 74,
   132, 176, *220*, 224, 262, 263, 275, 360
New York Post 248-250
New York Staats-Zeitung 12
New York Sun 106
New York Times .... *vi*, 21, 96, 100, 199,
   218, 264, 265, 278, 289, 290
New York World 39, 92
New York World's Fair 147
New Yorker Magazine 200, 205, 214, 361
New Zealand (sleeper) 60, 380, 393
Niagara Falls, N.Y. 73, 147, 163
Nicholson, Henry *268*
Nickel Plate Road
   [see New York, Chicago & St. Louis]
Nicolay, John G. 15, 25, 327
Night Line (sleeper) 396
Night Side (sleeper) 396
Niles, Mich. 278, 295, 296
Niles, Ohio 65
Nixon, "Checkers" (dog) 254, 258, 262
Nixon, Harry 244, 255
Nixon, Julie
   [see also Eisenhower, Julie Nixon] 252, 254
Nixon, Pat (Mrs. Richard M.) 252, 254,
   .... 255, 257, *279*, 291
Nixon, Richard M. 237, 239-241, 248-258,
   262-264, *277*, 278, 279, 281, 283, 291, *293*, 294,
   306, 367, 370, 371, 396
Nixon, Robert G. 173, 193, 195, 211, 214, 352
Nixon, Trisha 252, 254
Nixon Special (train) 249
Nobles, Warren 364
Noll, Austin 297
Norby, Marian 214
Norfolk & Western Magazine 258
Norfolk & Western Rwy. *58*, 60, 71, 107,
   121, 150, 243, 255, 258, 263, 279, 286, 292, 364,
   367, 370-373
Norfolk, Ark. 264, *266*
   Norfolk Dam 264
Norfolk Southern Corp. 309, 320, 398
Norfolk, Va. 286
North Bend, Ohio 17
North Eastern R.R. 53
North La Crosse, Wis. 57
North Little Rock, Ark. 264
North Missouri R.R. 36
North Nenana, Alaska 112, *113*, 115
North Petersburg, Va. 156
North Philadelphia, Pa. 123
North Platt, Neb. 161, 193, 294, 376
North Powder, Ore. 232, 233
North Vernon, Ind. 187, *369*, *370*
   Whitcomb Yard 187
Northern Central Rwy. 7, 22, 24-26, *34*, 35,
   41, 47, 326, 328, 345
Northern Pacific Rwy. 45, 54, 61, 74, *87*,
   101, 110, 195, 233, 261, 263
Northfield, Minn. *84*
Northumberland, Pa. 278
Norton, Charles D. 83, 84, 87, 382
Norwood, N.Y. 391

Novi, Mich. 320
Noyes, Charles Rutherford 45
Noyes, David M. 218
Noyes, Horatio 45
Nugent, Luci (Mrs Pat) [see Johnson, Luci]
Nuishan, Harry 333
NYC Jct., N.Y. 218
Oakdale (sleeper) 395
Oakland, Calif. 45, 61, *77*, 207, 261
   Sixteenth Street Station 261
Oakley, Mich. 264
Oakley, Ohio 162, 289
Oak Mills (sleeper) 396
Oak Pass (sleeper) 396
O'Brien, Bill 37
O'Brien, Bill 37
O'Brien, Hugh 297
Oceanic (private car) 92
Oceanport, N.J. 38
O'Connor, Basil 173
O'Connor, Moira 290
Odair, Wash. 233
Odenton, Md. 47
Odin, Ill. 10
Ogden, Utah 45, 71, 102, 110,
   141, 206, 341, 342, 393
Ogdensburg, N.Y. 391
Ohio & Mississippi R.R. 17
Ohio & Pennsylvania R.R. 18, 19
Ohio River R.R. 69
Oil City, Pa. 263
Oklahoma City, Okla. 208, 211
   Oklahoma State Fairgrounds 211
Old Colony R.R. 325, 394
Oliver, Harold 173, 352, 356
Oliver, John 48
Olney, Ill. 263
Olympia (private car) 69, 71, 381, 393
Olympia, Wash. 45
Olympian (train) *97*
Omaha (sleeper) 398
Omaha Club (club car) 397
Omaha, Neb. 36, 54, 57, 61, 66, 67, 71,
   96, 100, 120, 141, 142, 160, 161, 192, 193, 230,
   237, 242, 243, 250, 251, 292, 294, 343, 376, 377,
   393, 395, 397
   Ak-Sar-Ben Coliseum 193
   Glenn L. Martin Co. 60
   Union Pacific Museum 377
O'Malley, Charles S. 372, 373
O'Meara, John 51
Omena (sleeper) 393
O'Neal, Chester 109
"Operation Kansas" (Eisenhower burial plan) ... 367
Orange & Alexandria R.R. 326, 327
Orange, Va. 126, 213, 365
Orangeburg, S.C. 287
Oregon & California R.R. 45
Oregon City, Ore. 45
Oregon Short Line R.R. 102
Oriental Limited (train) 382
Orlando, Fla. 53
Ormandy, Eugene 291
Oshkosh, Wis. 321
Ospring, "Dutch" Andy 57
Ottawa, Ohio 300, *305*, 306, *307*
Ottawa, Quebec *188*, *190*, 275
   Union Station 275
Ottumwa, Iowa 230, 263
Oulahan, Richard V. 61
Overland (diner) 310, 321, 398
Overland Limited (train) 222, 341, 342
Owensboro, Ky. 212, 243
Oxford, Ohio *128*
Oyster Bay, N.Y. 80, 92
Pabst, George H. Jr. 124
Pacific (lounge/observation car) 340, 381, 393
Pacific Limited (train) 343
Pacific Rwy. of Missouri 35
Packenham, Mary 288
Paden City, W.Va. 247
Page Brook, Va. 60

Page, John E. 60
Painesville, Ohio 19
Palm Springs, Calif. 364
Palm Valley (sleeper) 396
Palmer, John M. 10
Palmer Lake, Colo. 160
Palmer, Mass. 91
Palmer, Mrs. Charles F. 354
Palmland (train) 391
Palo Alto, Calif. 61, 121, *123*, 126, 129
Pan American Airways 155
Pan-American Exposition 69, 73
Paramount Publix Corp. 125
Paris (sleeper) 398
Paris, France 98, 106, 107, 218
Parkersburg, W.Va. 41, 69, 91, 107, *127*, *195*, 218, 244, *245*, 246, 247, *248*, 255, 263, 265, 266, *268*, 281, 289
Parkton, Md. 329
Parr, Clem 244
Parsons, Wilton B. "Jerry" 261
Pasadena, Calif. 45
Pasco, Wash. 101
Patrick Station, Va. 29
Patterson Creek, W.Va. 64, 184, 218, 235
Patterson, David T. 31
Patterson, Fred 350-352
Patterson, Martha Johnson 31
Paul Revere (parlor car) 397
Pauley, Edwin 363
Payne-Aldrich Tariff Act 85
Payne, Henry C. 74
Payne, A.C. *369*
Pearson, Drew 226
Peekskill, N.Y. 21, 363
Pelican (train) 276
Pelley, John 153
Pendel, Tom 327
Pendergast, Tom 193
Pendleton, Ore. 233
Penn Central 291, 292, 294, 396, 397
Pennoyer, Sylvester 61
Pennsylvania (PRR 120 [2nd]) (business car) *280*, *282*, 391, 397
Pennsylvania Central R.R. 34
Pennsylvania R.R. 5, 7, 22, *30*, 40, 42, 44, 48, 52, 54, 56, 58, 59, 61, 66, 71, 80, 83, *89*, *91*, 92, 99, 105, 107, 120, 121, *122*, 123-126, *127*, 131, 132, 140, 147-149, 153, 155, 156, 170, 176, 188, 189, 190, 197, 200, 204, 205, 218, 223, 223, 225, 235, *238*, *240*, 242, *256*, 259, 262, 263, 272, 274-276, *277*, 278, *280*, 281, *282*, 285, *287*, 299, 326, *328*, 329, *330*, 338, 340, 345, 358-360, 363, 380, 389, 391, *392*, 393-397
Peoria & Eastern Rwy. 260
Peoria, Ill. 59, *128*, 260, 261
  Rock Island Station 260
Pere Marquette Rwy. 198
Perkins, George C. 45
Perkins, Thatcher 326
Perlman, Al *282*
Perot, H. Ross 322
Perrysburg, Ohio 300, 306, 307
  Maumee High School 307
  Perrysburg High School 307
Perryville, Md. 291
Persia (steamer) 97
Persian (locomotive) 333
Peru, Ind. 292
Peter Shoenberger (sleeper) 396
Petersburg Rwy. 4, 53
Petersburg, Va. 4, 5, 28, 29, 258, 259, 286
Pettit, John 13
Philadelphia (private car) 96, *380*
Philadelphia & Trenton R.R. 2, 22, 325
Philadelphia Athletics 123
Philadelphia Inquirer 359
Philadelphia, Pa. 1, 3, 5, 6, 22-24, 31, 42, *55*, 96, 124, 132, 170, 194, 215, 218, 242, 262, 278, *280*, 283, 291, 294, 300, 309, 323, 325, 326, *328*, 329, 360, 378, 391
  Broad Street Station 42
  Continental Hotel 22, 31
  Convention Hall 215, 278
  Independence Hall 22, 323, 329, 330
  Kensington Station 22, 329
  Merchants Exchange 6
  Merchants Hotel 6
  Park Jct., Pa. 391
  Shibe Park 123
  Special Train Yard 283
  Thirtieth Street Station (PRR, PC, Conrail, Amtrak) 291
Philadelphia Phillies 96
Philadelphia Public Ledger 101
Philadelphia Railway World 59
Philadelphia Symphony Orchestra 291
Philadelphia, Wilmington & Baltimore R.R. 2, 3, 22-24, 31, 37, *55*, 325, 326, 329
Phillipos, Wendell 33
Phillipsburg, Pa. 176
Phleger, C.R. 271
Phleger, T.F. 271
Phoenix, Ariz. 262
Pierce, Benjamin 6
Pierce, Franklin 6
Pierce, Jane (Mrs. Franklin) 6
Pierce, O.L. 356
Piermont, N.Y. .... *x*, 5
Pinkerton, Allen 22-24
Pins, George 391
Pioneer (sleeping car) 145, 334, 377
Pioneer (private car) 384, 395
Pioneer Limited (train) *104*
Piqua, Ohio 301, 304, 305, 332
Pitcairn, Alexander 58
Pitcairn, Jack 58
Pittman, Key 142, 144
Pittsburgh (diner) 397
Pittsburgh & Lake Erie R.R. 199
Pittsburgh, Columbus & Cincinnati R.R. 134
Pittsburgh, Fort Wayne & Chicago R.R. 44
Pittsburgh, Pa. 19, 34, 35, 58, 64, 91, 106, 107, *178*, 187, 199, 200, 230, 257, 262-264, *269*, 270, 278, 281, 290, 297, *298*, 309, 325, 326, 341, *344*, 398
  Glenwood Shops *344*
  Monongahela House 19
  P&LE Station 199
Pittsburgh Post 59
Platt, Thomas 50
Plattsmouth, Neb. 259
Pleasant Valley, N.Y. 362
Pledge, Charlie 74
Pless, C.A. 174, 346
Plymouth, Mich. 312, *317*, 319, 320
Plymouth, Vt. 117
Pocatello, Idaho 61, 110, 193, 196
Point of Rocks, Md. 163, 235
Point of Rocks, N.J. *17*
Point Pleasant, W.Va. 69, *82*, 246, 247, 255
Polen, Bob 186
Polk, James K. 4
Polk, Sarah Childress (Mrs. James K.) 4
Polo, Mo. 201, 203
Pomona, Calif. 249
Pontiac, Ill. 297
Pontiac, Mich. 199, 262
Pony Express (train) 160
Pope, R.H. 354
Port Columbus, Ohio 187
Port Everglades, Fla. 187
Port Jervis, N.Y. 5
Porter Station, Ind. 334
Portland, Ore. 45, 61, 101, 111, 140, 169, 195, 253, 263, 281, 292, 397
  Benson Hotel 253
  Grand High School 253
Portland Rose (coach) 398
Portland Rose (train) 232
Portland Special (train) 45
Portsmouth & Lancaster R.R. 6
Portsmouth, Ohio 255
Potsdam Conference 179, 181, 195
Potter, C.J. 362
Poughkeepsie, N.Y. .... *viii*, 21, 22, 132, 150, 152, 176, 337, 339, *359*, 361, 362, 363
  Nelson House 150, 152
Powder River (lounge) 398
Powell, Jody 300
P.P.C. (see also *Monitor*) (private car) 378, 379
Prairie Rose (private car) 398
President Grant (sleeping car) 118
President Harrison (sleeper) 395
President Washington (sleeper) 395
Presidential Special (train) 295
Presidential Special Unlimited (train) 309
Presidio (diner) 395
Presque Island, Maine 194
Prettyman, Arthur 134, 161, 173, 174, 349, 354, 358
Prince, W.Va. 366
Princeton, Ill. 44
Princeton, N.J. 4, 123
  Princeton University 95
Privette, Coy 310
Probert, L.C. 125
Providence, R.I. 4, *201*, *220*
Provo, Utah 206
Pueblo, Colo. 74, 102, 103, 146
  Memorial Stadium 102
Pugh, Charles Edmund 43
Pullman (or Pullman Palace Car) Company vi, ix, 108, 121, 133, 134, 136, 138, 139, 146, 155, 156, 168, 169, 174, 179, 181, 187, 204, 205, 222, 237, 242, 276, 326, 334, 340, *341*, 347, 348, 358, 363, 373, 377-382, *383*, 384, 385, *386*, 389, 391, 393-397
Pullman, George M. 139, 334, 376-379
Pullman, Mrs. George M. 379
Pullman News 61, 108
Purcell, Okla. *198*
Quayle, Dan 309, 310, 320, 398
Quebec Central Rwy. 378
Queen Mary (parlor/observation car) 285, *287*, 288
Quincy, Ill. 9, 16
Quincy, Mass. 325
Racine, Wis. 43
Radio Coporation of America 242
Rafshoon, Jerry 300
Railroad Car Journal 381
Railway Express Agency 149
Railway Gazette 80
Raleigh (baggage/buffet/library car) 393
Raleigh & Gaston Rwy. 4
Raleigh, N.C. 5, 286, 321, 339
Ramsey, Alexander 42, 45, 46, 393
Randall, Alexander 31
Ranger (locomotive) 334
Rankin, Mrs. W.B. 105
Rankin, W.B. 105
Raphael (sleeper) 395
Rather, Mary 286, 288
Ravenna, Ohio 19, 230
Ravenswood, W.Va. 247
Rawlins, John 32, 37
Rawlins, Wyo. 232
Rayburn, Sam 210
Reading Rwy. 132, 170, 218, 263
Reagan, Ronald 207, 297, 300-308, 310, 391, 397
Red Bank, N.J. 147
Red Bluff, Calif. 251
Redding, Calif. 45, 251
Redding, Jack 211
Red Hill, Va. 81
Redlands, Calif. *77*
Red Wing, Minn. 57
Reed, John S. 364
Reese, Jack 86, 87
Reid, Billy 108, 188, 277
Reilly, Michael 131, 158, 161, 163, 173, 174, 351, 384
Reith, George 255
Relay (or Relay House), Md. 1, 4, 5, 25
Remagan, Germany 172
Reno, Nev. 102, 250, 342

Renovo, Pa. 218
Rensselaer & Saratoga R.R. 21, 37
Republic (private car) *381*
Resta, Francis 361
Reston, James 218, 278
Reynolds, Ind. 333
Rhinebeck, N.Y. 21, 151
Rhodes, James 366
Rice, R.A. 334
Rice, Thomas 277
Richardson, C.D. *364*
Richardson, Robert *271*
Richey, Lawrence 124, 125
Richland, S.C. *348*
Richmond & Danville R.R. *56*, 60, 339, 393
Richmond & Petersburg R.R. 4, 53
Richmond, Fredericksburg & Potomac R.R. 3, 4, 52, 97, 155, 156, 171, 213, 259, 277, 285, 286, 310, 391, 394, 397
Richmond, Ind. 99, 221, 332
Richmond, Va. 3-5, 29, 53, 259, 286, 339.
Rider, Jacob 47, 48
Riderwood, Md. 345
Ridgeway, Ohio 312
Rigdon, William M. 156-163
Riley, Clements 366
Riverdale, Md. 170
River Queen (boat) 28, 32
Riverside, Mass. 171
Rixey, P.M. 71, 73
Roald Amundsen (also NYC 17) (private car) 148, 151, *152*, 153, *154*, *162*, 242, 360, 361, 384, 391, 395
Roanoke, Va. 60, 258
Robb, Lynda Bird Johnson (Mrs. Charles) [see Johnson, Lynda Bird]
Robert Peary [see also *Blackhawk* (private car)] *137*, 141, 144, 237, 384, 394
Robinson, Amos 318
Robinson, Bill 254
Robstown, Texas 159
Rochester, N.Y. 21
General Railway Signal Corp. 191
Rochester, Pa. 18, 19
Rock, James L. 182
Rock Island, Ill. 201, 242
Rocket (locomotive) 333
Rocket (private car) *80*
Rockhill Furnace, Pa. 378
Rockwell, Almon F. "Jarvis" 51
Rocky Ford, Colo. 103
Rodman, Hugh 109, 112
Rogers, Ken 300
Rogers, William P. 250, 252, 253
Romagna, Jack 192
Rome, Ga. 96, 381
Romney (sleeper) 395
Romulus Sanders (locomotive) *4*
Roosevelt, Alice [see Longworth, Alice Roosevelt]
Roosevelt, Anna (Mrs. John Boettiger [2nd]) 133, 173, 358
Roosevelt, Anne (Mrs. John) 358
Roosevelt, Betsy Cushing (Mrs. James) 140
Roosevelt, Edith (Mrs. Theodore) 81
Roosevelt, Eleanor (Mrs. Franklin D.) *131*, 133, *134*, *136*, *137*, *139*, 140, *141*, 144, 146, 147, 153, 154, 157, 159, *167*, 171, 176, 183, 346, 349, 352-355, 357, 358, 360, 361, 363, 384, 394, 395
"Rover" 133
Roosevelt, Elliott 159, 358
Roosevelt, Ethel (Mrs. Franklin D. Jr.) 358
Roosevelt, Faye Emerson (Mrs. Elliott [2nd]) 358
Roosevelt, Franklin D. ii, vii, *viii*, ix, 81, 107, 126, *128*, 129, *130*, 131-135, *136*, *137*, 138-142, *143*, 144-148, 150-176, *177*, 179, 183, 188, 189,, 208, 254, 261, 265, 273, 329, 346, 347, *348*, 349-363, 384, 385, 388, 389, 391, *392*, 394, 395
Roosevelt, Franklin D., Jr. 358
Roosevelt, James 140, *141*, *145*, 167, 168, 358
Roosevelt, Murray, The Outlaw of Falahill (Fala) (dog) 132, 135, 148, *150*, 157, 160, 161, 168, 254, 352, 354
"The Informer" 161
Roosevelt, Ruth (Mrs. Elliott [1st]) 157
Roosevelt, Theodore ii, vii, *62*, 74, *75-77*, 78, *79*, 80-83, *89*, 91-95, 210, 340, *374*, 393
Roper, Daniel C. 141
Roseburg, Ore. 45, 116, 251, 253
Rosenman, Samuel 148, 170, 233
Roseville, Calif. 206, 342
Roslyn, N.Y. 80
Ross, Charles 112, 184-187, 189, 193, 196, 204, 212, 218, 225
Ross, Thomas 15, 16
Ross, Lillian 219
Rotary Club (parlor car) 394
Rouses Point, N.Y. 275
Rovere, Richard H. 200, 205, 214
Rowe, James H. Jr. 189
Rowland, Ross E. Jr. 322
Roxie the Railroad Dog (dog) 80
Roy, John 47, 48
Royal Canadian Mounted Police 275
Royal Gorge (train) 373
Royal Oak (sleeper) 394
Royal Oak, Mich. 87, 262
Rubenstein, David 300
Rucker, Erle 291
Ruge, David 303
Ruiz Cortines, Adolfo 275
Rupert, A. 333
Rusch, D.T. 184
Rushville, Ind. 149
Rusk, Jeremiah M. 61, 380
Russell, Donald 387
Russell, Henry 334
Russell, Ky. 311, 366, 367
Ruth, George Herman "Babe" 140
Rutherfurd, Lucy Page Mercer 176, *177*, 349, 352
Rutherfurd, Winthrop 176
Rutland, Vt. 117
Ryan, Charles B. 63-65
Sabin, Dan 302, 308
Sable, Colo. 160
Sacramento, Calif. 45, 61, *72*, 101, 196, 207, 237, 250, 251, 261, *270*, 292
Sacred Cow (plane) 156, 187
Saddam Hussein 318
Saginaw, Mich. 260, 281, 312, 320, 396
St. Albans, W.Va. 266
St. Charles (diner) 393
St. Clair, A.W. 349
St. Clairsville, Ohio 92
St. Ives (sleeper) 395
St. Joseph & Council Bluffs R.R. 36
St. Joseph, Mo. 36, 37, 100, 251, *271*
St. Laurent, Louis S. 275
St. Lawrence R.R. 391
St. Louis, Alton & Terre Haute R.R. 34
St. Louis Car Co. 322, 398
St. Louis Cardinals 123
St. Louis, Iron Mountain & Southern 61
St. Louis, Mo. ii, 33-37, 41, 46, 56, 65, 65, 91, 99, 104, 106, 108, 120, 179, *181*, 184, 186, 187, 197, 211, 212, 224-226, 242, 253, 263, 272, 273, 278, 297, 309, 366, 367, *369*, *371*, 372, 377, 396
Kiel Auditorium 225, 272
Southern Hotel 33
Statler Hotel 99
Terminal Railroad Assoc. of St. Louis 106, 373
Union Station ii, 106, 179, 181, 184, 225, 263, 267
St. Louis-San Francisco (Frisco) Rwy. 157, 211, 263
St. Louis, Vandalia & Terre Haute R.R. *54*, 56
St. Louisan (sleeper) 397
St. Marys, W.Va. 247
St. Paul, Minn. 46, 54, 57, 101, *118*, 119, 127, 223, 242, 263
Salem, Ore. 253
Salida, Colo. 85, 393
Salina, Kan. 160, 370
Salineville, Ohio 19
Salisbury, N.C. *236*, 258, 309, 321, 351, 356
Knollwood Elementary School 321
Salisbury Post 309, 310
Salt Lake City, Utah 45, 61, 102, 141, 196, 204
Mormon Tabernacle 102
Sam Hill (locomotive) 19
Sampson, Jim 300
Samuel Wiggins (locomotive) 17
San Antonio, Texas 71, 159, 208, 210, 262, 309
San Bernardino, Calif. 197
San Diego & Arizona Eastern Rwy. 166
San Diego, Calif. 101, 164-166, *168*, 208
Sanborn, Richard D. 391
Sanchez Crossing, Mexico 158
Sand Spring, Kan. 160
Sanders, Everett *118*
Sands, Frank T. 327
Sandusky, Ohio 224
Sandy Hook, N.J. 147
Sanford, Fla. 53
San Francisco, Calif. ix, 45, 61, 69, 71, *72*, 101, 108, 116, 169, 173, 196, 207, 262, 341, *342*, 379
Grand Palace (or Palace) Hotel 45, 61, 116, 341
Valencia Street Station 71
San Jose, Calif. 45
San Marscal, New Mexico 46
Santa Barbara, Calif. *72*
Santa Fe (private car) 364, 365, *366*, 367, 370-373, 396
Santa Fe, N.M. 46
Santa Rosa, Calif. 378
Sappington, Mont 110, *111*
Saratoga, Mount McGregor & Lake George R.R. 39, 335, 336, *337*
Saratoga Springs, N.Y. 37, 39, 40, 335, 336, 337, 339, 393
Sassafras Falls (sleeper) 285, 397
Saturday Evening Post vi, 116
Savannah, Florida & Western Rwy. 53
Savannah, Ga. 53, 287
Sawyer, Dr. Charles E. 109, 116
Sayre, Jessie Wilson 105
Scheidler, Bob 300
Schenectady Locomotive Works 78, *79*
Schenectady, N.Y. 21
Schenck, Robert C. 26
Schrank, John 94
Schubert (sleeper) 396
Schultz, "Dot" 355
Schumach, Murray 289
Schuyler Mansion (sleeper) 396
Scott, Henry T. 71
Scott, John Jr. 302-304, 306, 307
Scott, Thomas A. 22, 40, 43, 380
Scottsdale, Ariz. 391
Scottsville, Va. 81
Scranton, Pa. 278
Scripps-Howard (newspaper chain) 228
Seaboard Air Line Rwy. 286, *390*, 391
Seaboard Coast Line R.R. 382, 384
Seaboard Express (train) 107
Seaboard System Railroads 302, 398
Seaton, Fred 247, 258
Seattle, Wash. 61, 92, 101, 113, 116, 164, 169, 194, 195, 261
Boeing Co. Inc. 309
New Washington Hotel 101
Sedalia, Mo. 42
Seibold, Louis 92
Seitz, George 360
Sell, J.J. 244, 246, 255
Selma (private car) 310, 313, 398
Selma, N.C. 286
Sembly, James 301
Severn, Md. 47, 48
Seward, Alaska 111, 112, 393
Seward, William H. 14, 24, 25, 31, 35
Seward, Mrs. William H. 334
Sexton, George D. 66
Seymour, Horatio 37
Seymour, Ind. 367, 371
Shakespeare Ranch, N.M. 46
Shamokin, Pa. 47

Shanley, Bernard 247, 248, 250, 258
Sharp, Paul 339
Shelbyville, Ky. 212
Shelton, J.W. 357
Shepard, Alan 297
Shepperd, John Ben 285
Sherbrooke [see also *Maryland* [1st] (private car)]
.... 378
Sheridan, Phillip H. 35-37
Sherman, James 84, 85, *88*
Sherman, Rachel 45, 46
Sherman, Texas 210
Sherman, William T. 25, 35-37, 41, 42, 44-46,
   55, 393
Shields, James P. 262
Shipley, W.V. 108
Shipman, Va. 133
Shipp, Hoke 350-352
Shive, Bill 321
Shoemaker, Samuel 48
Shore, Dinah 196
Short, Joseph 265
Shoup, Jack 147
Shuping, S.A. 356
Shurtz, Carl 9
Sidney, Ohio 263, 300, 301, *304*, 305, 306
Sierra Hotel (lounge car) 398
Silver Spring, Md. 151, 152, 156, 218,
   235, 247, 264, 363
Simmons, William (locomotive engineer)
.... 331, 332
Simmons, William D. (White House employee)
.... 145, 193
Simpson, Barney 42
Simpson, Howard E. 132
Simpson, Matthew 132
"Sinews of Peace" (speech) [see Iron Curtain]
Sioux City, Iowa 149, 263
Sioux Falls, S.D. 68, 100
Sirica, John 300
Sistersville, W.Va. 247
Slaybaugh, Walter G. 161
Sloan, Samuel 22
Sly, John Q. 98
Small, Robert T. 101
Smeltzer, George 291
Smith, Alan B. 125
Smith, Alfred E. 121
Smith, B.F. 10
Smith, Charles 71
Smith, Harry 327
Smith, I.P. 244
Smith, Ira R.T. 83, 84
Smith, Merriman 151, 166, 173, 174, *177*,
   182, 195, 196, 294, 352, 354-356
Smith, Robert 61
Smith, T.C. 186
Smith, William H. 41
Smith, William Prescott 25
Smithburg, W.Va. 226
Smithers, Edward W. "Doc" .... vi, 66, 83, 131
Snead, Sam 276
Snoderly, Haden 351
Snow, Franklin 389
Snow, Franklyn B. 377
Sollace, Mrs. Harriet Little Platt 41
Solomon, Kan. 370
Soo Line
   [see Minneapolis, St. Paul & Sault Ste. Marie R.R.]
South Amboy, N.J. 5
South Bend, Ind. 224, 242
Southern Exposition 53
Southern Pacific Rwy. *36*, 45, 46, *60*, 61, 71,
   72, *77*, 101, 102, 116, 127, 142, 147, 165, 166,
   195, 206, 208, 249, 261-263, 281, 292, 309, 341,
   342, 393, 397, 398
Southern Rwy. .... ix, *70*, 71, 81, 121, 132-134,
   156, 174, 213, 258, 263, 276, 281, 285, 286, 291,
   346, 347, *350*, 351, 355, 360, 394, 396, 397
Southern Vista (sleeper) 398
Southerner (train) 357
South Florida R.R. 53

South Minneapolis, Minn. 57
South Portsmouth, Ky. 366
Southwind (coach) 398
Southwind Rail Travel Ltd. 398
Sowers, Jack 225
Spaman, Guy 158
Sparkman, John 254
Sparks, Nev. 342
Spartanburg, Pa. *256*
Spartanburg, S.C. 321
   Waffle House 321
Spencer, N.C. 309
   North Carolina Transportation Museum
.... 309, 398
   North Carolina Transportation History Corp.
.... 309
Spingarn, Stephen J. 211
Spokane, Wash. 101, 110, 194, 233, 235, 261
Spokesman-Review 194
Spotswood, N.J. 1
Springfield, Ill. .... vi, 10, 12-15, *29*, 33, 40,
   42, 61, 260, 297, 326, 327, 329, *332*, *333*, 334
   Chenery House 15
   Oak Ridge Cemetery 334
Springfield, Mass. 91, 224, 262, 263, 325
Springfield, Mo. 93
Sproul, Robert Gordon 189
Spruce Falls (sleeper) 397
Stager, Anson 18
Stalin, Josef 171, 184, 195, 196, 215
Stanton, Edwin M. 328
Staunton, Va. 365
Starlight (sleeper) 395
Starling, Col. Edmund W. 81, 82, 96-98,
   101, 102, 104, 106, 120, 126, 127, 131, 142, 144,
   147, 342, 346
Starrucca Viaduct, N.Y. 6
Stassen, Harold 248, 258
State College, Pa. 274
   Pennsylvania State College 274
State Line, Ill. 10, 16, 18
   State Line Hotel 16
Steam Locomotive Corp. of America 322
Stearns, Frank 118, 119
Stearns, George 23
Stearns, Mrs. Frank 118
Steelman, John R. 235
Stender, Bob 302, 307, 308
Stephens, Tom 258
Stettinius, Ed 360
Steubenville & Indiana R.R. 18
Steubenville, Ohio 18, 34, 40, 89, 92, 263
   Pennsylvania Station 92
Stevens, Glenn L. 260
Stevens Point, Wis. 321, 322
Stevens, Ruth 174
Stevens, Thaddeus 33, 34
Stevenson, Adlai (presidential candidate)........ *178*,
   247, 253, 254, *259*, 260, 261, 264, 266, 272-274,
   278, 396
Stevenson, Adlai (vice president)........... 230
Stewart, J.S. 264
Stockton, Calif. 250, 309, 341
Stonewall Jackson (sleeper) 394
Stowe, David 266, 268, 270, 272
Strand, A.E. 74
Strauss, Robert 297
Strohl, B.L. 295
Strong, George Templeton 31
Strout, Richard L. 124, 137, 138, 146
Suckley, Margaret 148, 152, 157,
   173, 349, 352, 355
Suffolk, Va. 286
Sullivan, Katherine 306
Summerfield, Arthur 248, 250, 253-255
Sumner, Charles 33
Sumner, Edwin V. 16, 21, 29
Sun Valley, Idaho 193
Sunbeam (lounge car) 363
Sunbeam (private car) 95
Sun-Gold (lounge car) 242, 395
Sunlight (lounge car) 242, 245

Sunrise (sleeper) 396
Sunset (private car) 309, 398
Sunshine Special (coach) 298
Superb (private car) 108, *342*, *344*,
   345, *381*, 382, 383
Superb (sleeper) 393
Superior, Wis. *123*, 222, 263
   Cedar Island Lodge *123*
Sussex, Wis. 321
Suresnes, France 102
Swann, Walter 258
Swem, Charles 98, 101
Susquehanna, N.Y. 6
Symm, A.W. 261
Syracuse, N.Y. 21, 85, 331
Syria (sleeper) 48
Tacoma, Wash. 45, 61, 101, 108, 111
Taft, Charles 83
Taft, Horace 85
Taft, Nellie (Mrs. William Howard) 83, 85, *86*
Taft, Robert A. 90, 194, 197, 237, 239, 240,
   241, 244, 253, 261, 271
Taft, William Howard 83-85, *86*, 87, *88*, *89*,
   90-93, 95, 273, 382, 393
Taggert, Henry 142, 144
Talkeetna (sleeper) 393
Tallahassee, Fla. 288
Tames, George 199
Tanner, Virginia 146, 181
Tanque San Diego, Mexico 158
Tarrytown, N.Y. 331
Taunton, Mass. 262
Taylor, James 294
Taylor, Ohio 149
Taylor, Old Whitey (horse) 326
Taylor, Pa. 218
Taylor, Zachary 5, 325, 326
Teapot Dome Scandal 109, *112*, 116
Tebbutt, Marshall W. 339
Tehama, Calif. 61
Tennessee (lounge car) 312, 398
Terra Alta, W.Va. 223
Terre Haute & Alton R.R. 12, 13
Terre Haute & Indianapolis R.R. 34, *54*, 56
Terre Haute, Ind. 56
   Union Station 56
Terrell, Scurry 93-95
Texarkana, Texas 61
Texas & Pacific Rwy. 40, 61, 108, 208, 210, 261
Texas Eagle (coach) 398
Texas Mexican Rwy. 159
Texas Rangers 323
The Flying Dutchman (locomotive) 24
The Spirit of America! (train) 310, 311, 321, 322
The Whistle Stop (newsletter) 290
Thomas, O.R. 345
Thomasville, Ga. 286
Thomasville, N.C. 321
Thompson, Charles (reporter).............. 96
Thompson, Charles (White House employee) .. 357
Thompson, Everett L. "Tommy" 156-162,
   206, 218, 222-224, 226, 230, 232-235, 246, 247,
   258, 264, 370
Thompson, Frank 59
Thompson, Malvina "Tommy" 146, 157, 357, 358
Thorntown, Ind. 16
Three Forks, Mont. *87*
Thurmond, Strom 223
Thurmond, W.Va. 91
Thurmont, Md. 183
   Camp David (or Shangri-La) 183, 294
Tilden, Samuel J. 40
Tilton, N.H. 323, 398
Times Square (sleeper) 187, 394
Tindale, Carl 221, 243
Tindale, Cecil 243
Tindale, Lee H. 218, 219, 221
Tipp City, Ohio 304
Tippin' Club 258
Tipton, Ind. 42
Tirey, Bob 300
TLC Publishing Inc. vi

Toledo & Wabash Rwy. 16
Toledo, Ohio 33, 46, 199, 278, 281, 291, 300, 312, 313, 319, 320
   Stanley Yard 312, 319
   Toledo Municipal Airport 275
   Toledo Terminal R.R. 275
Tolono, Ill. 10, 13, 16, 260, 281
Topeka, Kan. 41, 42, 46, 364
Tourtellotte, John E. 41
Tower, Rich 295-297
Townsend, Edward D. 331
Townshend, Smith 51
Toy, Elias 329
Tracks magazine 277
Tracy, Benjamin F. 59
Traffic World magazine 163
Train For a Change (train) 297
Trains magazine .... v-vii, 189, 318
Trans-Mississippi Exposition 66, 377
Travell, Janet 286, 287
Trenton, Mo. 203
Trenton, N.J. 2, 22, 292, 297, 325
   Trenton House 22
Treonta (sleeper) 394
Tribbett, A.E. 281
Trinidad, Colo. 159
Trostel, Scott 301, 304-306
Trotter, Isabel Stewart 375
Trout, Robert 140
Trowbridge, Roland E. 43
Troy, Mont. 266
Troy, N.Y. 21, 275, 331
Troy, Ohio 271, *302*, 303, 304
Troy Union R.R. 21
Truckee, Calif. 102, 206, 342
Truman, Anderson Shippe 212
Truman, Bess (Mrs. Harry S.) 188, 192, 197, 202-204, 207-209, *212*, 213, 222-227, 230, 235, 272, 359, 363
Truman, Harry S. .... ii, v-vii, ix, 112, 135, 164, 166, 169, 171, *178*, 179, *180*, 181-215, *216*, *217*, 218, 219, *220*, 221-227, *228*, *229*, 230, *231*, 232-235, 260, 261, 264-273, 285, 295, 299, 300, 305, 310, 318, 320, 322, 357-361, *362*, 363, 385, 389, 391, 395
Truman, Margaret .... v, 179, 184, 187, 188, 192, 197, 200, 202-204, 207-213, 222-227, 230, 235, 270, 273, 318, 359, 360, 363
Truman, Mary Jane 202, 221
Truman Special (train) 197
Tubby, Roger *272*
Tuck, Dick 283, 290
Tulare, Calif. 250
Tumulty, Joseph 98, 99, 102, 104-106
Tucson, Ariz. 45, 46
Tucumcari, N.M. 165
Tullahoma, Tenn. 157
Tully, Grace 131-133, 148, 151, 153-155, 157-159, 161, 163-166, 170, 172, 173
Tulsa, Okla. 157, 169, 211, 349, 352-354, 358-360
   Douglas Aircraft Co. 157, 274
Tuohy, Walter J. *276*, 277
Turner, Booth 291
Turner, Roy 198, 199, 211
Tuscarawas (sleeper) 397
Tuskegee Ala.:
   Tuskegee Institute 81
Tyler, Bob 4
Tyler, E.B. 41
Tyler, John 2-4, 54, 212, 375
Tyree, Frank 82
Tyson, Henry 376
Uhrichsville, Ohio 18, 92
Underwood, Iowa 100
Underwood, W.J. 57
Union (locomotive) 21, 230
Unglaub, John M. 48, 49
Union League Club 194
Union Pacific Corp. 310
Union Pacific R.R. .... vi, 35, 36, 45, 54, 61, 71, 102, 110, 141, 142, 160, 161, 193, 203, 232, 237, 292, 294, 309, 310, 312, 322, 342, 364, 366, 367, 370-373, 376, 377, 393, 394, 397, 398

Los Angeles & Salt Lake Line 110
Uniontown, Ohio 43
Uniontown, Pa. 5
United Airlines 246
United Cos. of New Jersey 37
United Features Syndicate 287
United Nations 173, 207, 230, 275
United Nations Conference
   (or World Security Conference) .... ix, 173
United Press 151, 173, *177*, 182, 195, 196, 249, 352
United Press International 294
U.s. Army Signal Corps 265, 268
U.S. Bureau of Engraving & Printing
   .... 153-155, 170, 172
U.S. Bureau of Reclamation 85, 193
U.S. Department of Commerce 265
U.S. Department of Health, Education and Welfare
   .... 389, 391
U.S. Department of Housing and
   Urban Development 300
U.S. Department of State 265
U.S. Department of Transportation:
   U.S. D.O.T. Library vi
U.S. General Services Administration 389, 391
   Federal Supply Service 389
U.S. Military R.R. 26, *28*, 326, 327
U.S. Office of War Mobilization 358
U.S. Public Works Administration 140
U.S.S. Akron (airship) 125
U.S.S. Henderson (cruiser) 111, 116
U.S.S. Houston (cruiser) 142
U.S.S. Michigan (battleship) 6
U.S.S. Missouri (battleship) 183
U.S.S. Monaghan (destroyer) *145*
U.S.S. Nautilus (submarine) 275, 389
U.S.S. Ohio (battleship) 69
U.S.S. Potomac (cruiser) 155
U.S.S. Quincy (cruiser) 171
U.S.S. United States (ship) 34
U.S.S. Warrenton (destroyer) 147
Urbana, Ohio 99
Usher, John P. 25
Utica, N.Y. 21, 37, 84, *88*, 263
Uvalde, Texas *148*, *166*, 208
Vacuna (sleeper) 60, 381, 393
Vaccaro, Tony 235
Valdosta, Ga. 286
Valentine, Texas 208
Valley Forge, Pa. *127*
Valley, Neb. 160, 161
Valley Rwy. 43
Valparaiso, Neb. 160, 161
Van Buren, Martin 2
Van Camp, E. 331
Van Horn, Charles R. 188, 279
Van Horn, Charles W. 187
Vancouver, British Columbia 113
Vandalia, Ill. 57
Vandalia, Ohio 304
Vanderbilt, Cornelius, "Commodore" 1, 152
Vanderbilt, Cornelius, II 337, 339, 393
Vanderbilt, Frederick 152
Vanderbilt, Mrs. Frederick 152
Vanderbilt, William H. 39, 40
Vaughan, Harry 179, *180*, 182, 184, 185, 187, 193
Veronese (sleeper) 395
Victorio .... .46
Victory Special (Dewey's train) 214, 221
Victory Special (Truman's train) 225
Villard, Henry 12, 15, 54
Vincennes, Ind. 187, 271
Vinson, Fred 215
Vinson, Mrs. Fred 273
Virginia (private car) 302, 398
Virginia Beach (sleeper) 396
Virginia City, Nev. 45
Virginia Dawn (private car) 302
Virginia No. 1 [see *Baltimore* (private car)]
Voinovich, George 316
Voinovich, Janet (Mrs. George) 316
Wabash, St. Louis & Pacific R.R. 46
Wabash R.R. 61, 260, 263, 271, 275, 281, 292, 396

Wabash Rwy. 41
Waco, Texas 210
Waldameer (sleeper) 222, 395
Waldorf (diner) 393
Waldrop, W.D. *240*
Waldzak, Jimmy *252*, 260
Walker, Frank 360
Walker, Turnley 174
Wallace, George 288
Wallace, Henry A. 148, 164, 215, 358, 360, 361
Wallace, Henry C. 109
Wallace, Lew 58
Walla Walla, Wash. 45
Walmsley, J.W. ii
Walnut Ridge, Ark. 309
Walter Dean (lounge car) 398
Wanamaker, John 61, 380
Wapakoneta, Ohio 263
Wappinger's Falls, N.Y. 362
Warfield, Davies 391
Waring, Fred 262
Warren, Earl 212, 237, 239-241, 248
Warm Springs, Ga. .... ix, 132, *136*, 147, 148, 148, 154, 157, 172-175, 346, 349, 351, 353, 356, 357, 360, 363, 394
   Carver Cottage 351
   Georgia Hall 351, 352
   Little White House 132, 157, 174, 175, 346, 351, 352
   Warm Springs Foundation 157, 173, 346, 351
   Warm Springs Hotel 174, 346, 351
Warrensburg, Mo. 197
Warrenton Jct., Va. 327
Warrenton, N.C. 4
Warwick, Ohio 235
Washburne, Elihu B. 24
Washington (former C&O 7) (private car)
   .... 302, 303, 306, 307, 310, 398
Washington, A.A. .... ix, 349
Washington, Booker T. 81
Washington, George ... ix, 15, 34, 55, 58, 290, 326
Washington City (locomotive) 18
Washington, D.C. .... ii, vi, ix, 1-5, 7, 9, 13-16, 18, 22, 24, 25, 28, 29, 31, 35, 37, 38, 40-43, 47-54, 58, 59, 60, 65, 66, *68*, 69, 71, 74, *75*, *76*, 78, 80, 83, *91*, 92, 96, 98, 102, 104-106, 108, 110, 117-123, 125, *126*, 127, 131, 132, 134, 135, *136*, 140-142, 146-148, 150, 152, 153, 156, 162-164, 166, 169, 170, 172-174, 176, *180*, 181, 187-189, *192*, 196, 199, 200, 207, 211, 213, 218, 221, 223, 225-228, 230, 235, 242, 247, 250, 252-254, 258, 259, 264, 265, 268, 272, 274-279, *280*, 281, *282*, 283, 285, 287, 289, 291, 292, 294, 297, 300, 302, 304, 307, 309, 314, 318, 319, 322, 325-328, 363-367, 370, 372, *374*, 381, *387*, 388, 389, 391, 393-398
   B&O Station 3, 24, *68*, 325
   B&P Station 49-53, 58, *68*, 73, 338, 339
   Beltway Station 300
   Catholic University 152
   Executive Mansion [see also White House]
   .... 3, 5, 15, 25, 27, 31, 35, 38, 54, 57, 325
   Ford's Theater 73, 326
   F Tower 235
   Gadsby's Hotel 2
   Georgetown 272, 327
   Gridiron Club 221
   Hausler's 151
   Jefferson Memorial 156
   K Tower 358
   National Burial Grounds 325
   National Cathedral 364
   Navy Yard 388
      Naval Gun Factory 388
   New York Avenue Presbyterian Church 327
   Old Executive Office Building vi
   Riggs House 50
   Soldiers Rest 327
   Smithsonian Institution 335, 339, 355, 389
   Statler Hotel 221
   Vermont Avenue Disciples Church 338
   Virginia Avenue Tunnel 358, 365

Virginia Tower 276
Walter Reed Army Medical Center 364, 365
Wardman Park Hotel 389
Washington Terminal 181, 365, 373
Washington Union Station ii, *68*, 83, 90, 96, 98, *105*, 106, 125, *126*, 140, 146, 147, 151, 156, 163, 170, 187, 189, 197, 200, 213, 224, 227, 235, 273, 275, 277, 283, 285, 291, 300, 339, 344, 351, 357, 358, 364, *365*, 372, *392*
   Presidents Entrance 98, *105*
White House (see also Executive Mansion).....v, vi, 19, 37, 40, 45, 50-52, 66, 73, 83, 90, 92, 96-99, 102, 105, 106, 119, *123*, 124, 125, 131, 133-136, 141, 142, 147, 150, 151, 153-157, 163, 164, 169, 170, 171, 176, 179, 181, 187-190, 193, 197, 200, 204, 206, 208, 211, 224-228, 230, 235, 245, 265, 272-275, 283, 285, 287, 294, 300, 302, 305, 307, 317, 320, 321, 323, 326, 327, 340, 345, 346, 351, 353, 354, 357, 358, 361, 363, 371, 388, 389, *392*, 395, 398
White House Communications Agency ... 320, 398
White House Press Office 317, 398
White House Travel (or Transportation) Office
.... vi, 90, 300, 317, 320
   Willard Hotel 22, 24
   Woodrow Wilson House vi
Washington, Ind. 273, 367, *370*
Washington Post 207, 251, 267, 308, 318
Washington Square (sleeper) 395
Washington Star 278, 294
Wasilla, Alaska 111
Waterford, Ind. 333
Waterford Jct., N.Y. 21
Watertown, S.D. 68
Waterview (lounge car) 395
Watson, Edwin M. "Pa" 152, 163, 171
Watson, Mrs. Edwin M. 171
Watt, Bob 300
Watts, David A. Jr. .... v, 295-297, 300, *369*
Waycross, Ga. 310
Wayne County (sleeper) 396
Wayne, G.W. ii
Wayner, Robert vi
Wayneport (sleeper) 395
Waynesboro, Va. 365
Webster, Daniel .... *x*, 2, 3, 5
Webster, Fletcher 2
Webster, Mo. 35
Webster, N.P. 124
Wedemeyer, Albert C. 265
Weehawken, N.J. 132
Welch, Ronald 262
Welles, Gideon 28, 31
Wells, Coy 300
Wells, E.A. 169
Wellsville, Ohio 18, 19, 339
Wendover, Wyo. 232
Wesley, L.P. 134, 348
West Branch, Iowa *124, 125*
West End, Pa. 200
West, George 331
West Philadelphia, Pa. 22, *330*
West Point, Ga. 339
West Point, N.Y. 32, 39, 337, 361, 363, 364
West Port Royal, S.C. 156,157
   Parris Island Marine Corps Base 156
West Virginia (private car) 398
Western Associated Press 41
Western Electric 108
Western Express (train) 66

Western Maryland Rwy. 278
Western Oregon R.R. 45
Western Pacific R.R. 45, 128, 237
Western R.R. 325
Western Rwy. of Alabama 339
Western Union 18, 136, 184, 196, 253, 258, 285
Westfield, N.Y. 20, 32, 331
Westminster, Md. 25
Westport, Mo. 196
Weyburn, Va. 351
Weyman, Stan 286
Wheatley, Mont. 234
Wheeler, Burton K. 140
Wheeling, W.Va. (or Va.) .... 5, 69, 107, 187, ... 244-246, 248, 254-258, 263, 269, 281, 375
   Hempfield yard 255
   Island Stadium 256
   McLure Hotel 256
   Stifel Field 256
   WR Tower 255
Wheeling & Lake Erie Rwy. 263
When FDR Died (book) 173
Whitakers, N.C. 156
Whitcomb, Edgar D. 367
White, Ferman .... ix, 348
White, Horace 10
White, Roy B. 181, 187
White, Sarah 51
White Sulphur Springs, W.Va. .... *52*, 53, *86*, ... 96, 274, 275-277, 365, 366, *380*
   The Greenbrier .... 53, *86*, 96, 97, 275, ... 277, 366, 373, *380*
   White Sulphur High School 277
Whiteford, Roger 328
Whitehall, Mont. 261
Whitesboro, Texas 208, 210
Whiteside, Kan. 160
Whitestown, Ind. 333
Whitney, Henry C. 12
Whitney, Walter C. 15, 16
Whittier, John Greenleaf 183
Whittle, Emmit 349, 352
Wilbur, Wash. 233
Wilcox, Edward 334
Wildwood (private car) 393
Wilkes-Barre, Pa. 263
Willard, Ohio 119, 221, 275, 343
William Case (locomotive) 331
William Mason (also B&O 25) (locomotive)
.... 23, 24, 328
William Moultrie (club car) 394
William Pennington (locomotive)................ 22
Williams, G. Mennen 197
Williamsburg, Va. 2
Williamson, Ga. .... ix, 349, 351, 353
Williamson, Platt 15
Williamstown, Pa. *340*
Williamstown, Mass. 49
   Williams College 49
Willkie, Mrs. Fred 150
Willkie, Mrs. Wendell L. 149
Willkie, Phillip 230
Willkie, Wendell L. 148-150, 163, 289, 395
Willmar, Minn. 263
Willow, Alaska 111
Willow Run, Mich. 157
   Ford Motor Co. 157
Wills, David 28
Wilmington & Manchester Rwy. 53
Wilmington & Weldon Rwy. 53
Wilmington, C.F. 149

Wilmington, Del. 2, 3, 37, 38, 108, 170, 262, 291, 359, *386*, 389
Wilmington, N.C. 53
Wilson, Bob 273
Wilson, James *68*, 71
Wilson, J.J.S. 15
Wilson, Edith Bolling Galt (Mrs. Woodrow [2nd]) 96-106
Wilson, Ellen Louise Axson (Mrs. Woodrow [1st]) 96, *380, 381*
Wilson, Frank J. 161
Wilson, Woodrow .... vii, 54, 84, 91, *93, 94*, 95-107, 134, 160, 363, *380-382*
Winegar, Alice 173
Winona, Minn. 57, 85
Winston-Salem, N.C. *236*, 258
Winter Haven (lounge car) 397
Winton Place, Ohio 162
Wisconsin Central Ltd. 321, 322, 398
Wise, Henry A. 25
Wise, John S. 38
Witchita, Kan. 103-106
Withers, Bob .... v-vii
Withers, Sue Ann vi
Witzler, LeAnn 307
Wixom, Mich. 320
Wolford, O.B. .... ix, 349
Women's Christian Temperance Union 45
Wood, Enoch 125
Woodlawn (private car) 337, 339, 393
Woodlawn Jct., N.Y. 132, 275
Woodruff Sleeping & Parlor Coach Co. 393
Woods, Rose Mary 252
Worcester, Mass. 92, 262, 325
Worden, Mrs. Ralph 352
Wordsworth (sleeper) 360, 394, 395
Work, Hubert 109, 111, 129
Worthington, Minn. 149
Wright, Gary .... vi, 317
Wright, Larry 364
Wright, "Sleepy" 81, 82
Wrightson, George W. 331
Wrightsville, York & Gettysburg R.R. 325
Wyeville, Wis. 222
Xenia, Ohio 118
Yale (sleeper) 381
Yalta, Soviet Union 171, 172, 360
Yellowstone National Park 53, 54, 110
Yermo, Calif. 141
Yokum, S.H. 109
Yorba Linda, Calif. 282
York & Maryland Line R.R. 325
York, Pa. 263, 329, 378
Yosemite National Park 45, 87, 116
Yosemite Valley Rwy. 87, 116, 147
Young America (locomotive) 7
Young, Brigham 204
Young, J. Weimar 48
Young, Maria 91
Young, Robert R. 213
Young, Solomon 196, 204
Youngstown, Ohio 41, 278
Yowell, C.R. 357
Ypsilanti, Mich. 33
Yuma, Ariz. 46
Zane, Dick 296
Zanesville, Ohio 41, 263
Zionsville, Ind. 332
Zurich (diner) 398